DICTIONARY
OF AMERICAN
UNDERWORLD
LINGO

HYMAN E. GOLDIN
Editor in Chief

FRANK O'LEARY
General Editor

MORRIS LIPSIUS
Assistant Editor

THE CITADEL PRESS/NEW YORK

BOARD OF UNDERWORLD ADVISERS

Bad Bill—operated in every section of the country in a variety of criminal pursuits. He has been in the following prisons and jails: Leavenworth Disciplinary Barracks; Texas State Penitentiary; Sacramento, Cal., County Jail; Utah State Prison; Indianapolis, Ind., County Jail; Grand Rapids, Mich., County Jail; Allegheny County Penitentiary, Pittsburgh, Pa.; Governor's Island Disciplinary Barracks, N. Y.; Raymond Street Jail, Brooklyn, N. Y.; Hartford, Conn., County Jail; Cleveland, O., County Jail; Columbus State Penitentiary, Columbus, O.; Sing Sing State Prison, Ossining, N. Y., and other N. Y. State prisons.

Big Department—operated as extortionist, impersonating police officer, and as a jewel thief among the elite of New York City. He has served prison terms in Clinton Prison, Dannemora, N. Y.; Sing Sing State Prison, Ossining, N. Y., and other N. Y. State prisons.

Bubbles—operated as robber, forger, and burglar in the New England, Middle Atlantic, South Atlantic, and Gulf States. Served terms in Massachusetts State Prison; Sing Sing State Prison, Ossining, N. Y., and other N. Y. State prisons.

Butch—operated as bank robber, strike breaker, election fraud boss, automobile-theft gang boss, pinball and slot-machine operator, and strong-arm terrorist. His career covered the Middle Atlantic, Central, Mountain, and Gulf States. Prison terms in eight county jails and three N. Y. State prisons and in other institutions he does not wish named mark his career.

Chink—operated as purse-snatcher, safe-robber and armed holdup man in twenty-nine states. He admits six prison terms but wishes to name only Western State Penitentiary, and Allegheny County Penitentiary, Pa.; Michigan State Prison; Sing Sing State Prison, Ossining, N. Y., and other N. Y. State prisons.

Chop Chop—operated as strong-arm terrorist, burglar, and robber, especially in Pennsylvania and New York. He refuses to disclose any other areas of activity. He has served terms in Pennsylvania and N. Y. State prisons, but refuses to name specific prisons.

Dippo—operated exclusively as a pickpocket; arrested on forty-two occasions in the Middle Atlantic States, New England area, and several

Central States. This record covers twenty-five years since his first arrest at fourteen years of age.

Duke—operated as a pickpocket, confidence swindler, robber, carnival thief, and strong-arm man. His operations have covered thirty-six states. Besides serving terms in N. Y. State prisons, he was imprisoned in five scattered county jails and four state penitentiaries which he refuses to name.

Hal the Rebel—specialized in various types of criminal activity in the Southern and Gulf States. He has served terms in Florida State Prison and in several county jails in that area, and in N. Y. State prisons.

Iggy—operated as robber, carnival thief, and confidence swindler in the Middle Atlantic, South Atlantic, and New England States. His knowledge of the illegal narcotics ring operations, especially in the traffic in, use, and effects of marijuana, has been indispensable. He has served terms in various state prisons.

Jo Jo—operated as robber and burglar in the Pacific and Middle Atlantic States. Served terms in San Quentin, California, Sing Sing State Prison, Ossining, N. Y., and other N. Y. State prisons.

Red Mack—operated as a burglar and robber in the East Central States and the Middle Atlantic group. He has served terms in the Ohio State Penitentiary, Sing Sing State Prison, Ossining, N. Y., and other N. Y. State prisons.

Slim—operated as a counterfeiter and forger for twelve years, serving several Federal and State prison terms in areas that he will not permit us to name.

Stubs—nationwide larcenist, forger, and swindler with numerous arrests and only one conviction. Refuses to permit us to print further details.

The Colonel—operated as confidence swindler and forger in thirty-six states scattered over the nation. He requests that no further details be made public.

The two inmate compilers wish to express their special gratitude to Christopher DeSimeone for his invaluable services. His devoted friendship was a constant source of encouragement to them. He performed endless chores for them not expecting any remuneration. Without his help, the task of collecting material for this work would have been much more difficult if not impossible.

COMPILERS' NOTE

ONLY half the names of our advisory staff are listed above along with those portions of their criminal records which they permitted us to print. The others were insistent upon concealing not only their identity but their records as well. Each has his own reasons for such secrecy, reasons which we have been forced to respect.

To all these men we owe a tremendous debt of gratitude.

EXPLANATORY NOTES

Abbreviations—The abbreviations used here are those generally observed. In many instances where likelihood of error is remote, no abbreviations have been used to indicate parts of speech.

Cross references—Cross references are indicated by the use of boldface. Since the DICTIONARY is divided into two parts, the reader will do well to remember that cross references in one section refer only to terms within that section.

Sections—The English-Underworld Section serves as an index to the Underworld-English portion of the DICTIONARY. While it has been made as complete as possible, fine shades of distinction among synonyms may be found by turning to the underworld term in the Underworld-English Section.

INTRODUCTION

THE *Dictionary of American Underworld Lingo* is the product of many years of painstaking research. Every word of the manuscript was written within the walls of one of the country's major prisons—an institution situated at what might justly be called the penal crossroads of America. Its unique position enabled the compilers to carry on their work among representatives of the underworld population of every state in the nation, and the prestige which they enjoyed among their fellow inmates gave them an unprecedented opportunity for producing a more authoritative and comprehensive work than had ever been attempted before. Occupancy of positions of trust within the prison, close association with the prison chaplain (who collaborated in the preparation of the volume), and experience in the underworld, inside and outside of prison, extending over a quarter of a century—these were additional factors which counted heavily in the compilation of a dictionary which so eminent an authority as H. L. Mencken has called "the best thing of its kind I have ever seen."

Every trade and profession has its distinctive vocabulary. Doctors, insurance brokers, seamen, and short-order cooks all have a jargon of their own, designed to fit their special interests. But the language of the criminal world has always been distinguished from the argots of the various legitimate callings by its unusual richness and variety. This has many causes. For one thing, criminals practice dozens of specialized techniques, many of which have all the complexity of fully developed trades, and their own peculiar idioms. Again, the underworld holds to moral standards which are at variance with those acknowledged by the greater portion of society, and, accordingly, its citizens are impelled to invent expressions for a range of ideas and attitudes which goes beyond the narrow technical concerns of a typical occupational specialty. Moreover, the fact that the criminal does not enjoy the security conferred by accepted attitudes which are universally recognized in our society has a further twofold effect upon his language. First, much of it constitutes an implicit criticism of traditional mores, particularly with respect to those aspects of the social code which most concern the criminal population—the legal system, standards of group loyalty, and standards of sexual morality. Then, as might be expected of a radically unconforming segment of society,. a segment that lives by its wits, and under the constant threat of serious legal sanctions, its speech has unusual directness, pungency, and vigor.

For these reasons, the jargon of criminals has long been of interest to students of language and sociology. But the general public, too, has commonly taken a lively, if less active, interest in the argot of the underworld—witness the vast number of stories, novels, and motion pictures in which criminal slang, or a reasonable facsimile, is introduced in order to enhance a tale of cops and robbers, or add flavor to an account of life outside the law.

The attraction which the language of criminals has exercised over the minds of scholars and laymen alike is attested to by the long and honorable history of dictionaries of underworld slang. At least one ancestor of the present work can be traced back to the fifteenth century. In modern times, however, in spite of the fact that much devoted scholarship has been expended upon the subject, its students have worked for the most part under the crippling handicap of having no real contact with the life of the underworld, and therefore have had little opportunity to acquire a substantial fund of information about its activities, or the insight to interpret aright what was already known. Long before actual work upon the *Dictionary of American Underworld Lingo* had been initiated, the compilers were acutely aware of the pressing need for a thorough, authoritative work of this kind. The attention of scholars and the amateur interest of the general public were not the only factors which spoke for the desirability of such a project. Law-enforcement agencies of the nation, fully aware of the need for authentic information in this field, stood to benefit immeasurably by a study of criminal argot presented in a manner which underscores its psychological and sociological implications.

The three directors of the work of compilation, two long-term convicts and a prison chaplain, possessed first-hand knowledge of the criminal population whose language they wished to record and interpret. Assisted by a board of more than a score of expert advisers whose qualifications were born of years of criminal activity and years of imprisonment alike, the editors had good hopes of producing a work of unexampled authenticity and comprehensiveness. The result of their labors is a vocabulary of the language of crime, and an encyclopaedia of criminal practice and technique. It is an authoritative word-picture of the thoughts and habits of an entire class of human beings—and perhaps something more: the picture of a whole society seen through its back door, in its criminal rendezvous, its brothels, its prisons and reformatories, its unreclaimed lower depths.

For students of psychology, sociology, penology, and related subjects, the *Dictionary of American Underworld Lingo* is a social document of immediate significance, representing field research on the part of men steeped in the life of the underworld. In its pages, a little-known phase of American culture paints its own portrait. Here are reported at first hand the typical attitudes of the criminal class, its philosophy of life, reflected in every aspect of social relations and private morality. Especially revealing is the insight afforded into the sexual mores of men living under the pressure of social ostracism.

Students of language will find this volume a fascinating case-book of the dynamics of linguistic change and development. It demonstrates the persistence of terms which have figured in thieves' cant for hundreds of years, and highlights the evolution of new ones adapted to the purposes of criminal society in an industrial age.

Besides its usefulness as a source-book containing a rich fund of precise data dealing with underworld life, the *Dictionary of American Underworld Lingo* provides writers with the genuine speech of the criminal element. The Underworld-English, English-Underworld arrangement of the material facilitates finding the authentic slang equivalent for common English expressions. And, a feature which writers are in a special position to appreciate, a profusion of model sentences illustrates actual criminal usage and captures the living accents of a speech that is always graphic, realistic, and forceful.

For the general reader, this book provides the key to the mind of the underworld, the entrée to the confraternity of professional criminals living in the no-man's-land outside the law. The underworld organizations which flourish in the nation's prisons in spite of the penal authorities, the tricks of the thousand and one rackets which victimize the American people, the details of criminal techniques in specialties ranging from safe-cracking to organizing prison-breaks—all are described here in the words of the men who know them from personal experience.

Criminal slang is the language of grifters, pickpockets, cracksmen, hijackers, confidence men, strong-arm men, forgers, counterfeiters, arsonists, sneak thieves, burglars, bank robbers, dope-peddlers, swindlers, kidnappers, white slavers, and of the practitioners of innumerable other underworld specialties. Encountering this language for the first time, the respectable reader is likely to be puzzled. Individual words, though exhibiting a strong family resemblance to American English, may yet seem strange and foreign not only in sound but in rhythm. But many of these terms have in the past found their way into the language of respectability, and many more will undoubtedly do so in the future. The *Dictionary of American Underworld Lingo* contains some 5,000 constant elements which constitute the basic vocabulary of the language of the American underworld. Many of these terms have a number of separate and distinct meanings, and accordingly appear with multiple definitions. All the terms included are, generally speaking, in nationwide usage. Local terms, for the most part, have been included only in the measure that they appear to be destined for early incorporation into the national argot.

The problem of selection is complicated by the fact that every underworld hangout, every racket, each of the nation's 26 Federal penal institutions, 125 state prisons, reformatories, and penitentiaries, 3,450 county jails and workhouses, and each of its 100,000 local police lock-ups has cant terms peculiar to itself and incomprehensible to outsiders. These are cherished like inner-family nicknames, not to be shared until, in the course of time, they trickle out into the public domain. If they strike that particular note of serviceability and color which lengthens the life-span of elements of language, they will move rapidly into the current idiom of the underworld. Worthy candidates for such a distinction will soon find their way into the mainstream of criminal argot, the broad, basic "lingo"—shared in common, and understood by all underworld sophisticates—which is presented in this work.

For comprehensiveness, authenticity, and detail, the *Dictionary of American Underworld Lingo* is without a rival. The fact is that even among the members of the underworld, there are few who would undertake to define, in isolation, more than a handful of the terms included in this volume, although any alert and experienced criminal would immediately understand these expressions when used in their natural context. For this reason, the editors have tried to include several underworld terms in each of the illustrative sentences, a feature that should aid the reader greatly in acquiring the "feel" of this unfamiliar idiom.

The reader will also find it helpful to remember that the "lingo" is not used indiscriminately, upon all occasions. Primarily, it serves one of two purposes: to conceal one's intentions from a potential victim, or to impress an audience with one's own criminal sophistication. The first-mentioned use is naturally the most important; it is the stock in trade of carnival swindlers, for example, whose success is largely dependent upon their ability to exchange verbal signals unintelligible to their intended prey. In its second function, criminal slang is an agreeable ornament of the social life of the underworld. Where criminal concerns alone are in question, the "lingo" is the most convenient, and hence the most common, form of speech. As conversation becomes more general, however, as in discussions of sports or politics, the language shifts to the common argots employed by all Americans for such purposes. Consequently, one must not expect to hear Stalin spoken of as the "muscle-ghee" (strong-arm crook) of Europe, "putting the arm on" (using force or the threat of force upon) other powers, and "glomming (seizing) all the "mahoska" (loot) he can get his "dukes" (hands) on. The citizen of the underworld would express all this in much the same fashion as his favorite radio commentator.

Finally, it must be emphasized that the *Dictionary of American Underworld Lingo* is not the work of professional scholars, whose knowledge of criminal life is almost wholly academic, gleaned of necessity from the record of traditional linguistic studies. This volume was written in the only way possible, by men who have served a long apprenticeship "on the turf," and followed additional courses in the nation's prisons, the professional finishing schools of the underworld. Accordingly, the refinements of formal lexicography have not been attempted here. The problems of word-derivation, for instance, require for their solution a background of technical philology which does not figure among the equipment of the editors and their advisors. Rather, so far as linguistic preparation is concerned, these men are interested amateurs. They are, however, highly qualified in their own specialties, and their aim has been to produce a work which might serve as a source-book for students, writers, and law-enforcement agencies, and as a survey of a little-known portion of contemporary society for the information and amusement of the general reader.

UNDERWORLD-
ENGLISH
SECTION

A

Abbey. One who impersonates a clergyman as a means of swindling the devout.

Abbey, on the. Engaged in or by means of the abbey.

Abbey, the. The act of impersonating a clergyman or religious worker as a means of swindling the devout.

Accident. The act of being murdered or assaulted after a threat or warning. "Mister, a lotta ghees (men) that don't pay off have accidents happen to them."

Ace. 1. A good fellow. 2. A dollar. 3. A one-year jail or prison term.

Ace in. To gain entrance into or association with. "That combination is making a nice buck pushing junk (selling narcotics). I gotta ace in there."

Ace it. To prove oneself trustworthy in an emergency; as, for example, under police grilling. "Mike the Burglar is one ghee (fellow) you can count on to ace it when there's a rumble (interference) on a caper (robbery)."

Aces. Excellent; perfect; trustworthy.

Ace through. See **Ace it.**

Aces with, to be, or **to be in.** To be thoroughly liked and trusted.

Act, n. A pretense, as in feigning loyalty, insanity, illness, and the like.

Act, v. To deceive through pretense; to put on an act.

Action. Criminal activity. "Shape up (be present) tonight, Joe, there's action —a Brooklyn score (robbery)."

Actor. A faker; a swindler.

Adjy. An agitator.

Adjy, v. (P) To agitate; to incite to riot; to foment trouble between others. "These crumbs (schemers) adjy new micks (newcomers) to kick over (riot), but they duck the swindle (avoid the trouble) before the blow-off (upheaval) comes."

Ad-man. An impostor, posing as an advertising solicitor, who sells worthless advertising space by misrepresentation or by implied threats. "This ghee (fellow) is a good ad-man. We'll give him a send-in (send him in) to rehash (swindle again) them joints we shook (swindled) already." [Note: The first extortion is the Shake; every successive extortion is a Bite or a Rehash. Victims, angered by successive extortions, sometimes refuse to make any further payments. In such cases a new solicitor is often needed.] See **Limb-joint. Tapman. Tap, the.**

A. G. The Attorney General, or his office.

Agent. The operator of a wheel or game, usually at a carnival or amusement park. "Office (tip off) the agent the tip is red (crowd is prosperous and eager to spend)."

Ague. (Obs.) Loss of courage in a crisis.

Aigey. A share.

Air, v. To get rid of. "Air that stiff (fool, casual criminal, outsider)."

Airedale. One who is fawningly loyal, as a dog to a master. "I ain't playin' the fall guy (one who takes sole blame) on this rap (charge). What do I look like, an airedale?"

Alibi ghee. 1. A defense witness who is used to substantiate the defendant's alibi. 2. One who is never without an alibi or an excuse.

Al-joe. See **Alzo.**

Alky. Illegally distilled alcohol.

All. (P) The whole of a prison sentence, with no time off for good behavior. "The Board told Jack to bring (serve) it all."

All caught up. 1. Marked for death; finished. 2. Having the status of a habitual criminal; that is, subject to life imprisonment upon subsequent conviction. 3. Exhausted or petered out, as a specific racket or criminal activity, or an area exploited to the point of exhaustion. 4. (P) Exposed; unable to dissemble further. "You're all caught up, Lou. No more contracts (favors). I'm hip (aware) you were peddling all the swag (stolen food, etc.) I got you." [Note: Peddling is a high misdemeanor in prisons in the Northeast.]

All copper. 1. A policeman who cannot be bribed or intimidated. 2. A brazen informer with the ideology of a policeman.

Alley. See **Arch.**

Alley rat. A petty thief who robs his victims in alleys and hallways.

All muzzler. One who is entirely without principle according to underworld standards.

All of it. 1. See **All.** 2. A life sentence to prison.

All-right ghee. An excellent fellow.

All screw. (P) Exceedingly harsh or severe, as a prison guard in carrying out prison rules. "That new hack (guard) is all screw, but he ain't two-faced like other hacks that cut up jackpots (talk pleasantly) with you and then later pinch (report) you for mopery (petty infractions)."

All sewed up. Protected against interference by police or rival gangs; having a jury or high official committed in one's favor through bribery or other means; assured of success in any venture planned.

All washed up. See **Washed up.**

Altar. Toilet flush-bowl; a bucket or any similar substitute.

Alvin. (West) Farmer; hick. "Yeah, some alvin beefed on (complained about) us to the town clown (constable)."

Alzo (frequently followed by the preposition "in"). 1. A setup, often including bribery, under which a gang may operate in a specific area with immunity; the area itself. "We got the alzo in here. Ain't another cannon-mob (pickpocket gang) can hustle (steal in) this tip (crowd)." 2. Arrangements necessary for the domination of a racket, or for the operation of an illegal establishment in a specific area. "Guinea Mike's got every nautch-joint (brothel) in town tied up with the alzo in." 3. The advantage gained over rivals through bribery or political connections. "No bangin' (shooting) needed. We got the alzo on Lefty's mob. The bulls (police) will have them all vagged (committed to jail for vagrancy) in a week." 4. A lucrative area for theft. "Wait'll we hit them two-stemmers (big towns) around Seattle. We'll glom onto (steal) plenty in them alzos."

Amscray. Flee; get away quickly; keep moving.

Anchor, n. 1. A safety catch on tie-pins designed to thwart pickpockets; any similar device for securing valuables to the person or clothing. 2. A reprieve or stay of execution of sentence in the case of a condemned man. 3. (P) A short-circuiting wire, one end of which is connected to the radio earphones and the other to the metal washbasin, thus diverting the current from other listeners. "I'd like to get the fink (rat) with that anchor on the line."

Anchor, v. 1. To fasten; to fix. 2. To grant a condemned man a stay of execution. 3. To remain in one place, as on guard; to settle down; to wait. "Cover that out (means of escape). Anchor there and throw slugs (shoot) if anyone tries to crash out (burst out and give alarm)."

Anchor and prop. A tiepin and safety clasp designed to thwart pickpockets. "We put the nippers (cutters) on the mark's (victim's) anchor and prop, and he didn't even know he was beat (robbed)." [Note: While an aid pokes an opened newspaper in the face of the victim, the actual thief cuts the tie off above the point where the tiepin is fastened.]

Angel. 1. A prospective victim for thieves or swindlers; esp. one who pays **protection** money; an habitual victim of extortion. **2.** (P) A friend whose assignment gives him access to food stores or other desirables which he is then able to steal. "My mess-hall angel just lost out (lost his job)."

Angel cake and wine. (P) A diet of bread and water prescribed as a form of punishment.

Angle. To maneuver adroitly.

Angles, the. The subtleties of crime and a criminal career; the conventions, means of evasion and deceit, and in general, the whole bag of tricks at the command of an experienced convict or criminal.

Ankle. To walk. "We ankled down the stem (avenue) right into a snatch (arrest) for vag (vagrancy)."

Anklets. (P) Leg-irons.

Ant-paste. (P) Chocolate pudding.

Apple. A big shot; a personage of real or pretended distinction in the underworld. "Mike's got to be an apple in the alky (alcohol) racket now."

Apple-knocker. Farmer; hick. "Them carny grifters (carnival thieves) beat (robbed) that old apple-knocker out of twenty skins (dollars)."

Apple pie. (Irish-American parlance, New York City and vicinity) A passive pederast.

Approach, n. The technique of accosting a prospective victim, or of entering upon the scene of a projected crime. "Tail (follow) the copper (policeman) till he rings in (telephones his precinct house); then we'll make the approach to the lay (place to be robbed)."

Approach, v. To accost a prospective victim. "Approach this hoosier (rustic) slow. We can't afford to blow (bungle) this touch (job)."

April fool copper. A private detective; a small town, shabbily uniformed policeman.

Apron. Bartender.

Apsay. A very stupid or unsophisticated person.

Arch. A dark alley (used figuratively, as to pay off under the arch; to fight one's way out of a debt.) "The tipster (purveyor of information to thieves) gets his cut (share) under the arch on this score (robbery)."

Arm, the. n. **1.** A crushing headlock which robs the victim of consciousness before the commission of a crude crime, such as robbery or rape; the **mugg. 2.** Force; the threat of force. **3.** Without payment, as on the arm. "C'mon, we'll go out and free load (get without payment) some scat (whiskey). I can put it on the arm in these joints."

Arm. v. To lock one's arm around a victim's head and crush it; to **mugg.** "You arm the mark (victim) and I'll snatch (seize) the turkey (bag containing the valuables)."

Arm-cramper. (P) A hard, quick blow on the arm muscle.

Arm-man. Any criminal or ruffian who uses a crushing headlock on his victims; usually, a robber or rapist; a strong-arm criminal; a **mugger.**

Around. Sophisticated. (Used figuratively, as to have been around; to be experienced in the ways of the underworld.) "Yeah, Clipper, I'm wrapping up (giving up) hustling (stealing). I been around, seen all the angles. It's loused up (spoiled) with depression bums (casual crooks)."

Around the horn, to ride one. To move an arrested criminal suspect from one police station to another in order to prevent him from seeing his attorney. Thus, the suspect is barred from securing a writ of habeas corpus until the police have finished questioning him.

Artillery. 1. Firearms of any kind;

pistols. 2. A hypodermic needle, or any substitute such as a safetypin, eyedropper and teaspoon for crude hypodermic injections of narcotics.

As'ole. A chump; fool; dolt; worthless fellow.

Aspirin-hound. One addicted to excessive use of aspirin. [Note: Addicts either take it internally or roll the powdered tablet in cigarettes.]

Attempt to gog. (Literally, "attempt to look.") Used figuratively, as highway mopery and attempt to gog (a distortion of "highway robbery and attempt to kill.") Mind your own business. [Note: This is a stock answer to the inquisitive person who asks, "What are you in for."] See **Stabbing a horse and stealing his blanket.**

Aunt. The eldest of a group of male oral copulators living together in a **camp.** "Them fags (degenerates) learned the boosting grift (shoplifting profession) from their aunt."

Auntie. The proprietor of a house of prostitution; an **aunt.**

Away. In prison.

Awlay! Law! The police are coming! Keep moving!

Axe, n. (P) A knife, razor, or similar edged weapon.

Axe. v. To make an entry by force for purposes of wrecking, robbing, or extortion.

Axeman. (P) 1. A prison barber. 2. One who uses a knife when fighting.

B

Backboard. The strip of wood against which dice must be rolled in shooting craps to insure against cheating. See **Pad roll. v.; Gaff,** v.

Back-gate commute. (P) Death in prison. "To take a back-gate commute" —To commit suicide. "To get a back-gate commute"—To die.

Back-gate parole. (P) See **Back-gate commute.**

Backs. Crude counterfeit paper money with only one face printed, usually used for swindling rather than for general passing.

Back up. (P) The death chamber in the death house. "Them kids in the C.C.'s (condemned cells) take the trip back up tomorrow night unless they get a commute (commutation of sentence to life inprisonment)."

Bad-eye, n. A menacing glance; an angry or threatening stare. "Take a powder (get out of here), crumb (phony). You ain't puttin' the bull on (intimidating) me with that bad-eye crap."

Bad-eye, v. To subject a person to the bad-eye.

Badge-man. (P) A prisoner who serves as an informer for the authorities. "That muzzler (contemptible fellow) ain't kidding me. He's an undercover badge-man."

Badger. One who specializes in **the badger.**

Badger, the. A form of extortion through blackmail in which victims are framed by the criminal in conjunction with a woman posing as his wife or sister. [Note: Victims are enticed into compromising positions. The blackmailer then appears on the scene, claiming that the girl is his wife or sister. Extortion follows.]

Bad man. 1. A dangerous person even when measured by the standards of the underworld. 2. An informer; a treacherous person.

Bag, n. A dissolute, slovenly, or lewd woman; a slut. "That bag was sharp stuff (clever and attractive) till the junk (drugs) hooked (got the best of) her."

Bag, v. 1. To arrest. 2. (P) To lock up because of a violation of prison rules. 3. (Eastern prison usage) To place under observation as a psychopath. "That bug doctor (psychiatrist) is gonna bag you yet. If you're conked up okay (sane), I'm glad I'm a wack (psychopath)."

Bag onto, v. 1. To lay hands upon; to seize; to steal. 2. To be alert; to listen. "Bag onto that ghee's spiel (talk). There's a hipster (smart underworld frequenter)."

Bag your head or **lip.** (P) Shut up; hold your tongue.

Bail out. 1. (P) To secure the release of a fellow prisoner from his cell when he has been left there through the guard's oversight. 2. To get one out of an annoying situation, as when a bore is talking dully and incessantly to him.

Bait, n. Dupe; decoy; cover-up. "Plant (station) that punk (kid) to lay zex (act as lookout), and no one will rumble (notice) us with him for bait."

Bait, v. To lead on; to decoy; to lead into a trap.

Baker, the. The electric chair; the executioner. "Yeah, Joe's a dead pigeon (as good as dead); it's the baker sure."

Balky, n. A bully; a stubborn or obstinate person; one who is habitually flippant. "I'm gonna flatten (knock down) that balky if he keeps playin' the dozens on me (calling me names reflecting on my ancestry)."

Balky, a. Bellicose; flippant; stubborn.

Ball-breaker. 1. A bitter disappointment; the cause of a bitter disappointment. 2. A strict disciplinarian; a slave-driver; one who plagues others with requests for favors. "No more contracts (favors) for that ghee (fellow). He's a bitch of a (very persistent) ball-breaker."

Ball lump. (Hobo) A sandwich, or other cold food handout, wrapped in paper.

Ballplayer. 1. One who betrays his accomplices when bribed, as by leniency or legal immunity. 2. One who seeks the least risky assignment in a criminal undertaking. 3. Anyone capable of being influenced through bribery or similar means. "The D. A. (District Attorney) was a ballplayer so the beef (complaint) was squared (quashed)."

Balls! A common expression of disgust.

Balls. Testicles; hence, a symbol of manliness; courage; nerve. "It takes balls to heel (assault) a screw (guard) in that stir (prison)." [Note: A severe beating, loss of time credits, solitary confinement, and bread-and-water diet are customary penalties for assaulting an officer.]

Balls, to have by the. To have in a helpless position. "Them coppers (policemen) made a meet (appointment) with me to square a rap (quash a charge) for two G's. I had 'em right by the balls if I wanted to put the finger on (tip off the D. A. about) them."

Bally, n. (Carnival) The **spiel** or sales-talk made by a barker to the crowd.

Bally, v. (Carnival) To ballyhoo; to talk to a crowd; to serve as a barker at an amusement park. "When Joe ballies the tip (crowd) the grifters (thieves) sure go to town."

Baloney. 1. A woman of loose morals. 2. An automobile tire.

Bamboo. An opium pipe.

Band. (South) A woman. "They just snatched a chiv-man (a knife-fighter) and lagged him (put him in prison) for carving his initials on his band."

Bandbox. 1. Any prison or jail from which it is easy to escape. 2. The county workhouse. "Every ghee on the grift (stealing) that hits that bandbox beats (escapes from) the joint."

Bandhouse. (Illinois area) A city penitentiary; a county jail. "I pulled sleeping time (a short term) in that bandhouse, but it's a crumb-joint (full of informers, pimps, bums, degenerates, and the like)."

Bandhouse clip. (Illinois area) A prison haircut in which the head is completely shaven.

Bang, n. 1. Thrill; "kick." 2. Injection of a drug. 3. Sexual intercourse.

Bang, v. 1. To shoot. 2. To have sexual intercourse. 3. To inoculate with a drug.

Bang a reefer. To smoke a cigarette of marijuana. "I got the leaps (nervous reaction) after that trick (crime). I'm gonna hit the camp (flat) and bang a few reefers."

Banged to rights. Caught red-handed. "The bulls (police) had me banged to rights, heeled (armed) and swagged up (laden with stolen goods). For three C's (three hundred dollars) I got an S.S. (suspended sentence) and a floater (order to leave town)."

Banger. A hypodermic needle; an addict of hypodermic drug injections. "I ain't hustlin' (stealing) with dudes (fellows) that use a banger. They're poison." [Note: Police force addicts to implicate accomplices by withholding drugs.]

Bang in the head or **noggin.** To shoot to kill.

Bang it out. To oppose by force the

invasion of a territory by a rival gang; to "shoot it out" with one's enemy, a victim, or the police. "I ain't standing a pinch (submitting quietly to arrest). If there's a rumble (interruption) stick and bang it out."

Bang-job. An assault or killing with firearms. "The dicks (police) are tryin' to pin the rap on (convict) Cheesecake for that bang-job on Chuck Collins."

Bang-man. 1. A professional killer. 2. (Rare) A safe-blower. 3. **A bangster.**

Bang out. 1. To shoot one's way out; to typewrite; to write. 2. To shoot and kill.

Bangster. A drug addict who takes injections by hypodermic needle.

Bang-up, a. Skillful; expert. "Chips is gonna fill (join our ranks) on that jug heist (bank robbery). He's a bang-up wheelman (driver)."

Bank. The backer, or backers, of a gambling house or policy-numbers game; a croupier.

Banker. An operator of a policy-numbers game.

Banker's bit. (P New York State). An indeterminate sentence of five to ten years, the usual term imposed upon bankers who abscond or defalcate.

Banner. (Western and Central U.S. prisons) A sign placed on cell door to denote that the occupant has been locked in for violation of rules pending a hearing. See also **Carry the banner.**

Bar. A heavy crowbar, usually with a tapering or clawed end for use by burglars.

Bargain, v. To dicker for an opportunity to plead guilty to an offense less serious than that named in the indictment. "I'll bargain with the D. A., but I ain't gonna cop out (plead guilty) without I get a break (unless I'm given consideration)."

Bargain day. A term used by district attorneys visiting prisoners under indictment in the **bull pen,** indicating that the prosecution will accept pleas of guilty to lesser crimes than those named in the indictments. Such pleas are often accepted when it is necessary to clear up overcrowded calendars.

Barker. 1. (South and West) A pistol; a revolver. 2. (Pl.) Shoes; feet.

Barlow. A woman of loose morals; a harlot. "Butch is on the up-and-up (more or less within the law), shylocking (lending money usuriously) a little and doubled with (living with) some barlow."

Barnacle. 1. Whore; a loose woman; a slattern. 2. (New York City localism) A cheap furnished room or flat.

Bar out. To refuse admittance; to deny membership or association.

Bar out of a joint. See **Bar out.**

Barrel, in the. 1. (P) Locked up for violation of prison rules involving serious penalty. 2. (P) Confined to the segregation block or a punishment cell on a diet of bread and water. 3. Heavily in debt. 4. Arrested, facing certain conviction. "Kippy was bagged (caught) dead-bang (red-handed). He's in the barrel."

Barrel, over the. (Southern prisons) In a position of readiness for the barrel punishment. 2. Helpless; out of funds.

Barrel, the (Southern prisons) A whipping across the buttocks, covered with a towel, with a thonged leather strap while the victim is laid across a barrel. The punishment is usually dealt out before the assembled prisoners.

Barrel house. Any crude plant in which liquor is illegally distilled and sold; a cheap saloon.

Barrel-house bum. One who habitually loiters around illegal plants, cheap bars or saloons, waiting for free-drink handouts.

Barrel punishment. (Southern prisons) A punishment meted out to convicts, in which the victim is placed over a barrel and lashed.

Bar-spreader. 1. A screw-jack or heavy bar which burglars use to force an entry. 2. (P) A screw-jack or bar used to spread cell bars in an attempted jail-break.

Baseman. A thief who seeks the least risky asignment in a criminal undertaking. Compare **Outfielder; distance ghee.**

Bash in. To smash, as one's skull, with a bludgeon; to burst into by force, as a vault or home.

Bastille, the. A State or Federal prison.

Bat. 1. A prostitute or loose woman. 2. (P) A prison guard's club or cane, often with ferruled tip ostensibly to tap out orders to a company of marching convicts. [Note: Two taps signify, forward march; one tap—halt! A series of frantic taps—help! Several sharp taps—stop talking! get in line! button your jackets! "Line up, button up, shut up," is the daily prison chant.] "That screw's (guard's) got me blowin' my top (going crazy) bangin' that bat. What, does he get off the nut (derive sexual pleasure) like that?"

Bat, to go to. 1. To go to the limit for a friend or associate. 2. To stand trial. "I'm chasing that cop-a-plea mouthpiece (lawyer who induces clients to plead guilty) and gonna go to bat."

Bat-carrier. (Rare) A stool pigeon for the police; a labor provocateur.

Batch. (P) A quantity of home brew. "The P.K. (Principal Keeper) caught Mike with a batch of potato water (a fermentation of potato peelings, yeast, and sugar)."

Batter. To panhandle.

Batter, on the. Operating as a panhandler; by panhandling technique.

Batty, a. Insane; mentally deficient; crazy.

Bazoo, n. Mouth. "That big bazoo will get you a chiv (knife) in your ribs yet."

B-backs. A kind of playing cards, backed with diamond-shaped patterns which run flush with the borders. A slight trimming of the edges makes key cards easily identifiable in cheating.

Beach, on the. (Elmira Reformatory, N. Y.) Confined to **the beach.**

Beach, the. (Elmira Reformatory) A punishment wing in which prisoners are placed on bread and water rations. "Ten lousy days on the beach and the crumb (weakling) is beefing (complaining)."

Beachcomber. (Rare through obsolescence) A hanger-on, or sycophant, among thieves; one who hesitates to steal but runs errands, minds weapons, and does other odd jobs for criminals, living on the crumbs from their tables. Compare **Lob.**

Beagles. (P) Sausages.

Beak. (Central and Mid-Atlantic States; rare) A Criminal Courts judge.

Bean. (Irish-American, especially in New York State) The hymen. "To cop a bean"—To have sexual intercourse with a virgin.

Beast. A prostitute or lewd woman; a very homely or slatternly woman.

Beat, n. 1. The area in which criminals operate, especially when enjoying eminent domain there, either through police protection or by the right of might. 2. A successfully accomplished theft. 3. An escape from prison or custody. "Phil the Fire-bug made a nice beat out of the bughouse (insane asylum)."

Beat, v. 1. To escape; to run away. 2. To win a discharge or acquittal. 3. To rob. "They beat the sucker for a nice pocket-touch (proceeds of his pockets)."

Beat, a. See **Beat up, to look.**

Beat a joint. To rob a place; to escape from any place of confinement. "Three new micks (new arrivals) clipped (assaulted) a screw (guard) and beat the joint."

Beat a mark. To rob a victim; to rob a place.

Beat a rap. See **Beat a stretch.**

Beat a stir. To escape from a prison.

Beat a stretch. To avoid a prison sentence by a narrow margin, winning acquittal or a suspension of sentence.

Beat a sucker. See **Beat a mark.**

Beat looking. See **Beat up, to look.**

Beat one for his socks. To rob a victim of everything he possesses.

Beat the bishop. (P) To masturbate. [Note: The expression takes its meaning from the shape of a bishop's miter.]

Beat the chair. (P) To escape electrocution, as by being adjudged insane, or through any other means such as gubernatorial commutation of sentence, jury verdict, prison break, or even suicide. "Harry the Horse got a dead-bang fall (an arrest red-handed) for a knock-off (killing) but he copped a plea (pleaded guilty to a lesser offense) and beat the chair."

Beat the dummy or pup. (P) To masturbate.

Beat the pups. (South) To make a successful escape from bloodhounds. "The ketchup-dogs (bloodhounds) were hot on Gyp's pratt (in close pursuit) but the ghee beat the pups."

Beat up, to look. Having the appearance of having lived a life of great suffering, bitter disappointment, or dissoluteness; prematurely old; worn out. "You're getting loused up (devoid of good reputation) runnin' around with that gunsel (pederast). He's a beat up looking punk (degenerate) anyhow."

Beef, n. 1. (P) A formal report in writing submitted by a prison officer concerning the misconduct of a convict. 2. A confession of guilt implicating others. 3. Gossip; small talk. 4. A protest; a complaint; a call for police assistance; a preferment of criminal charges. "There's a tough beef in all the joints (newspapers) about that score (robbery). The big shot figures we may have to kick back (return) the swag (loot)."

Beef, v. 1. To protest; to register a formal complaint; to call for police assistance; to prefer criminal charges. 2. (P) To submit a formal written report of a convict's misconduct. 3. To implicate accomplices through a confession of guilt; to inform upon. 4. To gossip.

Beef department. Complaints, in general; the act of complaining or whining; one who habitually whines or complains. "Blow (flee), Ed, the play is ranked (criminal plan is thwarted). That sucker will be on the beef department any minute."

Beefer. A talkative person; a chronic whiner.

Beef murder. 1. To make a full confession implicating many accomplices as a bid for leniency or legal immunity. 2. To complain loudly to the authorities, or to the newspapers, in a demand for drastic action. "There ain't no wail louder than the wail of a sucker, except the squawk (complaint) of a racket ghee (thief) who's beat (robbed). He beefs murder."

Beer flat. An apartment in which liquor is sold and consumed, often used as a place of gambling or prostitution.

Beetle. 1. An extremely unattractive woman. 2. A slow race horse. "Imagine a geezer on the make (a thief) throwing his iron (money) on the beetles!"

Belch. To inform the police; to turn State's evidence. "Chill (ignore) that flea (informer). He belched on his partners."

Belcher. 1. The mouth. 2. An informer; one who turns State's evidence. "The D. A. has a swag of (large number of) belchers stashed away (in protective custody) hollering murder (informing freely)."

Belly robber (P) The civilian cook employed in a prison. 2. (P) The warden of a prison who makes it a policy to economize on food.

Belly the wall. To stand facing the wall. A command which usually accompanies the familiar "Hands up!" during a robbery.

Belly up. 1. To belly the wall. 2. To crowd close to a stall at a carnival or amusement park. When the customers have sufficiently "bellied up," the stage is set for pickpockets and swindlers.

Belt out. 1. To arrest; to convict; to commit to prison. 2. To knock unconscious.

Bench nibs. (Very rare) A judge.

Bend. (Near South, close to Atlantic coast) To steal, especially automobiles.

Bend, the. The bend made in the corner of a playing card in the "three-card Monte" swindle. The victim thinks one of the swindlers is in league with him, bending winning cards, but the bend is later transferred to a losing card while the victim's attention is momentarily drawn away.

Bend a bar over. To assault with a bludgeon.

Bend one's ear. To bore with excessive dull talk. "That wig (judge) bent Joe's ear for an hour, and then settled (imprisoned) him for a sawbuck (ten years)."

Bend over. (P) To serve as a passive pederast. "I'll bend you over," connotes the utmost in contemptuous threats.

Bender. 1. A drunken orgy; a narcotic debauch. 2. (P) A passive pederast.

Benny. An overcoat. "That bum is no heist-man (hold-up man). He got his bit (sentence) for boosting (lifting) a benny."

Bent. Stolen.

Bent one. Any stolen article, especially an automobile.

Bent rubber. Stolen automobile tires; tires sold in evasion of wartime rationing regulations.

Berry. (Central and Mid-Western States) A clothesline.

Berry, to pick a. (Literally, among hobos; ironically elsewhere) To steal clothes from a clothesline. (A sarcastic answer to inquisitive people. "I'm arrested for picking a berry," signifying "Mind your own business.")

Bet on the muscle. (P) To make wagers in prison, having no money to pay if one loses. The loser faces the risk of having to fight, of being knifed, or of having to ask for protective custody.

Better him than me. (N. Y. State prisons) A hackneyed cynical remark almost certain to follow an announcement of the death or misfortune of anyone outside the convict's sphere of immediate interest. The prison equivalent of "So what?"

Bezark. (Mildly contemptuous) A woman.

B.I. A Buick automobile.

Bible. (Rare) To swear.

Big apple. A big shot; one who has, or creates the illusion of having, influence, money, etc. "There ain't no big apples in this stir (prison). You pull a tough bit (serve a harsh term) here."

Big Ben. The prison whistle or siren, used to signal escape, fire, or riot. "Big Ben's gonna bust loose. Some new ghee just took a powder (fled) from the farm."

Big bit. 1. A long prison term. 2. A more than proportionate share of loot. "I got a sweet penman (clever forger) to scratch our paper (to write our checks), but he wants the big bit on every score (forgery)."

Big corner. See **Big end.**

Big crush. A wholesale prison escape.

Big cut. See **Big end.**

Big day. (P) (West) Visiting day. "My old partner's coming in big day and plant (place conveniently) a couple of briars (hacksaw blades) for me."

Big department, the. Any U. S. Government law enforcement agency. [Note: This term, originally used by the Department of Justice and Treasury Department agents during Prohibition, was adopted by extortionists impersonating Federal agents. When accosted by local police, the extortionist's gruff, "It's okay, we're from the big department," was more convincing than the most perfectly counterfeited credentials.]

Big end, the. A more than equal share of loot, frequently demanded by leaders of a gang. "Okay, Sapper, I'll fill (join you) on this trick (robbery), but no big ends. I want a full cut (share)."

Big-eye, n. A look of wonderment, covetousness, fear, etc.

Big-eye, v. To look at with covetousness, wonderment, fear, etc. "Man, you ought to see that sucker (victim) big-eye that smoke-wagon (big gun). They ought to put wheels under a rod (gun) like that."

Big-eyes. (Chiefly rural) A plain-clothesman or detective.

Big ghee or **biggie.** See **Big apple.**

Biggie. Exaggerated; pretentious. "This ghee is sure getting biggie ideas in his noggin (head)."

Big hello. (P) An excessively friendly greeting, usually with an ulterior motive.

Big house, the. (West) A state prison or penitentiary.

Big keister. (Literally) big buttocks; (figuratively) luck. "What a big keister you've got making parole the first time up."

Big noise. (P) (Very rare) A prison warden. [Note: No general term for prison wardens exists. "Big shot," "Skipper," "The Man" are heard often. Usually each warden is labelled with some designation peculiarly fitting to his personality or policy—more often than not, uncomplimentary. "Promising Jack," "Big-hearted Al," "Belly-robbing Charley," "Shortcon Bill" are actual examples from scattered corners of the nation.]

Big number. (P) (Slightly derisive) A convict who affects airs on the basis of a white-collar job, possession of sums of money sent steadily by friends or relatives, the knack of being a prison success, etc.

Big piece. See **Big end.**

Big shot. 1. One who has or creates the illusion of having great influence or wealth or importance. 2. (Rare) A prison warden. 3. A gang leader.

Big store. A rendezvous of extortionists, especially impersonators of Federal agents. "I'll see you at the big store. Flash has the new tins (badges) and creeds (credentials) ready." [Note: Procedure is the same as that of Federal agents. Fake officers enter illicit establishments, exhibit pocket commission, badges, and forged search warrants. Proprietors invariably offer a bribe with a minimum of encouragement.]

Big top. (Rare) The main cell-block of a prison.

Big winey. See **Winey.**

Bill. A one-hundred-dollar note. "That load (automobile) stood me six bills (six hundred dollars).

Bill-poster. A writer and passer of forged checks.

Bim or **bimbo.** A woman.

Bimmy. A prostitute or dissolute woman; a drunkard.

Bindle. 1. (Hobo) A bundle of bedding and belongings. 2. (P) (Occasional variant) A bundle, especially of food or clothing, from home or friends. 3. A small packet of powdered drugs. ("A bindle of H"—heroin; "A bindle of M" —morphine; "A bindle of C"—cocaine.)

Bindle-boy. A young tramp who carries bindle for an older road-agent, panhandles for him, and often serves pederastically.

Bindle-bum. See **Bindle-stiff.**

Bindle-stiff. 1. A hobo who carries a bindle. 2. (P) One who has nothing; a pauper. "That bindle-stiff ain't got a pretzel (has nothing)."

Bing. (P) 1. The punishment cells; cooler or segregation block. 2. A local jail. 3. An addict's dose of narcotics.

Bingle. 1. Narcotics. 2. A purveyor of narcotics to addicts.

Bird. 1. A fellow, especially a suspicious-looking stranger. 2. The common "razzberry." "Some dude just hit the cooler (punishment cells) for giving the warden the bird."

Bird-cage. A revolving dice-shaker used to insure against swindling in the roll of dice. The management's percentage renders crude dishonesty unnecessary. [Note: Hitting a **backboard** with the dice is required where bird-cages are not available.]

Bird with the long neck. See **Play the bird with the long neck.**

Biscuit. 1. The rump; the buttocks. 2. The head. "To hit in the biscuit"—to kill. 3. A woman. 4. (Rare) A safe or vault. 5. A pistol or revolver. "Dump (get rid of) that biscuit; some fence (dealer in stolen goods) was knocked off (murdered) with it."

Biscuit, on one's. See **Pratt, on one's.**

Bit. 1. A prison term. 2. Portion or share of proceeds from any criminal activity. ("Gapper's bit"—small share to a minor accessory. "Big bit"—a major share of loot. "Tipster's bit"—share to purveyor of criminal information.) 3. (P) A heavy time penalty for violation of prison rules.

Bit-borrower, n. One who defrauds others by borrowing a little at a time with no intention of repaying.

Bitch. 1. ("Bitch of a ———") An extraordinary specimen or example.

("A bitch of a place"—a miserable place. "A bitch of a ghee"—a notorious fellow.) 2. A slut; a trollop. 3. An excellent or unfortunate turn of events. "That load (stupid fellow) made us blow (lose) a five-G touch (a five-thousand-dollar theft). Ain't that a bitch!)"

Bitch-of-a-criminal. (Humorous) An habitual criminal with three or more serious convictions. "Yeah, Jake, you're a bitch-of-a-criminal, all right; you done five bits for everything from mopery on the high seas to spitting on the sidewalk (from one kind of stupidity to another)."

Bitch's curse, the. The imprecation of a prostitute. [Note: It is believed superstitiously by many that those who rob a prostitute or a degenerate will meet with very bad luck.]

Bite, n. The act of extorting, soliciting, or borrowing. "The bulls (police) put the bite on his joint (establishment) regular."

Bite, v. To beg; to borrow with little intention of repaying; to extort. "I gotta bite my fence (dealer in stolen goods) for fall dough (expenses to fight an arrest) for the mouthpiece (lawyer)."

Bite, on the. 1. Begging or borrowing small sums with no intention of repayment. 2. Engaged in petty extortion of sums from proprietors of shady establishments without rendering oneself liable to legal qualification as an extortionist or blackmailer.

Bite to death. To extort, blackmail, solicit, or borrow to the limit of a victim's capacity to pay. "You got them nautch-joints (brothels) bitten to death. Better give 'em a chance to get some fresh (money)."

Black gold souper. A cheap watch.

Blackjack. To beat with a blackjack.

Black Maria, the. Enclosed van for conveying prisoners to and from jails.

Blackstone. (Rare) A judge. "That blackstone must have figured you was a cat hitting you with triple life (three consecutive life terms)."

Black top. A tent used for gambling by carnival employees. "A couple of strange weeds (strangers) just heisted (held up) the black top."

Blade. 1. (P) A hacksaw blade. 2. A knife, razor, or any edged weapon. "Heel up (arm yourself) with a blade before that ghee cops a sneak (assaults unexpectedly) on you."

Blaht. See **Blot.**

Blank. 1. A zero; a loser. 2 (Carnival) A worthless prospect for a swindle, having no money or being too shrewd. 3. A dolt; a worthless fellow. "Skid (get rid of) that blank. I ain't stepping out (stealing) with any stiff (fool) like him."

Blanket. (P) Cigarette paper.

Blanket-presser. A very lazy fellow who lies frequently on a made bed.

Blanket-stiff. (Hobo) See **Bindle-stiff.**

Blast, n. 1. A complaint to police; a newspaper anti-crime crusade. 2. A confidence man's planned campaign of talk and action. "To put the blast on"—to lie convincingly to.

Blast, v. 1. To shoot. 2. To give a final sales talk in a projected swindle. 3. To smoke marijuana. "Get out the old gage (marijuana) and let's blast."

Blast the roach. To draw deeply on a marijuana cigarette.

Bleaso! Flee! Get out of here quickly! Keep moving!

Bleed. To blackmail; to extort money from.

Blind, n. 1. A standing frame enclosing an imitation safe-front which is placed in front of a real safe to screen safe-robbers' operations and to deceive police or passersby. 2. Any deceptive exterior concealing an illegal establishment or criminal activity.

Blind, v. To beat, stab, or assault viciously in any manner, other than by shooting. More specifically, to poke the stiffened middle and index fingers into a victim's eyes as a prelude to beating him. "I'm gonna blind that muzzler (unprincipled fellow) if he don't knock off (stop) adjying (slandering) against me."

Blind, a. Without previous investigation; without information or plan—implying recklessness in criminal actions. "We hit that joint (establishment) blind on the heist (hold-up) and scored (profited) for seven yards (seven hundred dollars)."

Blind baggage. The baggage car behind the engine.

Blind fence. One who unwittingly buys stolen goods.

Blind pig. See **Pig,** meaning 2.

Blind steer. An unplanned robbery, impulsively executed. "Them young punks will get a million boffos (years in prison) stepping out on them blind steers."

Blister. A woman of loose morals; a harlot.

Block. A genuine gold-cased watch as differentiated from thin-plated watches.

Blocks. (P) The vari-shaped blocks used by psychologists in giving form tests. ("To be hit with the blocks"—to be so tested.)

Blood dough. Money earned by contemptible means. [Note: Kidnap ransom, money gained from the sale of narcotics or through prostitution is held in contempt by many criminals. The forger, for example, views with scorn hold-up men and their earnings.]

Bloomer. Any criminal venture that nets profit in negligible amount—usually, the result of misinformation; an empty safe; a penniless victim. "A blank yesterday; another stiff (profitless undertaking) today. That makes us draw a pair of bloomers. We might as well get ourselves a dinner pail (go to work)."

Blot out. (Rare) To kill.

Blot, the. (Pronounced blät) The underworld.

Blotto. A member of the underworld. "Sure, Legs was blotto; got his lump (large sum of money) and wrapped up (quit criminal activities)."

Blouser. A woman of ill repute; a prostitute.

Blow, n. 1. (Rare) A revolver. 2. (P) An escape. 3. A pursuit by the police; an interruption of a criminal act. "We got a blow on that Jersey heist (holdup) but lammed (escaped) before the law got there."

Blow, v. 1. To move on; to flee; to escape from the scene of a crime or from prison; to jump bail, parole, or probation. 2. To blast with explosives, as a safe. 3. To lose; to bungle. "Don't blow that piece (revolver); it cost me a double-sawbuck (twenty dollars)."

Blow a parole. (P) To lose a chance for parole by committing a serious violation of prison rules.

Blow-card. 1. A worthless playing card drawn in a game which ruins a potentially winning hand. 2. Any thing or event that spoils what had appeared to be a promising situation. "The touch (theft) was a pushover till the rumble (interruption) came. That gapper (passerby) spotting us was the blow-card."

Blow coke. To sniff cocaine.

Blowed-in-the-glass-stiff, n. (Very rare) A very inept or slow-witted person; a penniless victim of a crime. [Note: This term formerly denoted a very dependable and likeable fellow.]

Blow-in, n. A newcomer; a person from out-of-town.

Blow-off, n. The climax. "The blow-off was when the rapper (complainant) couldn't make (identify) me."

Blow off, v. 1. To bring to a conclu-

sion, as a crime. 2. To pursue; to interrupt criminals in the commission of a crime. "The pete (safe) was ready to go (open) when we got blowed off and had to take a powder (flee)."

Blow one's roof or **top.** 1. To smoke marijuana. 2. To go almost berserk with rage, fear, joy, etc. 3. (P) To become insane. "Anyone'd like to blow his top after a treyer (three years) in that stir (prison)."

Blow one up. (Leavenworth Federal Prison) To smoke a cigarette, especially by stealth when smoking is forbidden. "Let's have your jack (tobacco) and wrappers (cigarette papers). I want to blow one up."

Blow parole. To break parole by fleeing jurisdiction and becoming a fugitive. "I'm going out on the turf (general field of crime) as soon as I hit the pavement (am released), so I might as well blow parole right away."

Blow snow. To sniff cocaine.

Blow stir. (P) To escape from prison.

Blow the gaff. To inform on associates; to expose a plot; to incriminate others through either stupidity or malice. "Listen, crumb, if you blow the gaff on this racket, you're a dead pigeon (you will be slain)."

Blow the whistle. 1. (P) To sound the escape siren. 2. To complain or to inform the police. "What moxie (nerve) that fink (informer) has! He blows the whistle right in front of your kisser (face)."

Blow-up, n. (Chiefly in the West) Information based upon rumor. "Flatten out (hide). Maybe it's only a blow-up but I hear the finger is on us (we've been betrayed to the police)."

Blow wise. (A variant of New York and New England "get wise") To wake up to what is going on; to become suddenly alert. [Note: Imperatively used in warning.]

Blow your nose. (N. Y. State prisons) Shut up; stop complaining.

Blubber. (P) Pinching of the cheek between thumb and forefinger. "This blubber business is a wolf's (active pederast's) handshake in prison."

Blue. (Carnival; antonym of **red**) Poor paying; not prosperous—applied to a carnival crowd of spectators.

Blue room. 1. The back room in a police station where suspects are examined by proper or, frequently, by **third degree** methods. 2. (P) The solitary confinement chamber in which excessively harsh punishments are inflicted. "The screws (guards) kicked The Lunger's brains out in the Blue Room 'cause he wouldn't stand for buckwheats (discrimination) in the shop."

Blue sky racket. The promotion of stocks or bonds in a company capitalized illegally. [Note: Named after the "blue sky law," framed to curb what its originators termed the "capitalization of the blue sky."]

Blunderbuss. A sawed-off shotgun.

Board, the. (P) The Parole or Pardon Board.

Boast, the. (P) The promise to live up to parole terms. ("To make the boast"—to be granted parole.)

Boat, n. (P) A transfer of convicts from one prison to another. "I'm dropping in a tab (note) to make an Auburn boat."

Boat, v. (P) 1. To transfer a convict to another prison. 2. To get rid of. "Boat that fleabag (nobody). No one rumbles (talks to) him but punks (passive pederasts)."

Boat race. A fixed horse race.

Body-snatch. A kidnapping.

Boff. 1. To punch; to hit with a blow. 2. To pass a heavy prison sentence upon. "That ain't no sentence they boffed you with; that's a paragraph."

Boffo. 1. A dollar. 2. (P) One year. "Old John is in stir (prison) fifteen boffos and the Board hits him with three months for investigation. That's a real lousing around."

Boiler. 1.(P)A small contraband electric stove, usually built into a pocket-size tobacco can and concealed in a book with the center of the pages cut out. 2. A still. 3. An automobile, usually stolen. "We'll use a legit (legitimate) boiler with hot (stolen) plates on the trick (robbery)."

Bollix. To bungle.

Bone-factory. A hospital.

Bone-orchard. (P) A cemetery, especially the prison graveyard. "A twenty-year bit (sentence) and nine years short time (unexpired previous sentence); I'll finish this bit in the bone-orchard."

Bones. Dice.

Bonnet. The head. ("To hit in the bonnet"—to shoot to death, not necessarily in the head.)

Booby. 1. A jail, usually small and rural. 2. See **Booby-pinch**.

Booby-hatch. 1. A county jail or station house. 2. An insane asylum. "Between the barnacles (women) and the lush (alcoholic drinks) you'll wind up in the booby-hatch yet."

Booby-pinch or booby-rap. 1. A petty charge; an arrest brought on by one's own stupidity. 2. (P) A report for a trivial rule violation or for something at which only fools are caught.

Boodle. 1. A concealed roll of money. 2. Stolen property. 3. (P) A package from home. 4. Counterfeit currency. "I'll lug (carry) the boodle and you push (pass) one piece at a time. That way a ghee without a record (criminal record) can beat the rap (win acquittal) if he's dropped (arrested)."

Boodle-belt. A money belt.

Book. To arrest formally. "Joe got a pick-up (arrest on suspicion) but he ain't booked for nothing yet. Buzz (contact) his lip (lawyer)."

Book, the. 1. The full penalty of the law imposed by the Court or the order of the Parole Board. 2. One who books bets on the horses or the dice; a croupier. 3. Life imprisonment or an equivalent sentence. "That chump got hit with the book for mopery (a petty charge)."

Bookful. See Book, the, 1 and 3.

Bookie. A professional taker of bets, especially on the horse races. "My partner is making a nice clean buck (involving no risk or pangs of conscience) shaking down (extorting from) bookies."

Bookie-joint. An establishment that accepts bets on the horse races.

Boomer. A swiftly growing community, hence good prospect for thieves and carnival grifters.

Boost, n. 1. A successful shoplifting operation. 2. A successful pocket-picking operation. 3. Any successful theft of articles near to hand; (loosely) an automobile theft. 4. The act of kneeing a person in the buttocks.

Boost, v. 1. To pick pockets. 2. To steal anything ready to hand; to steal automobiles. 3. To strike anyone in the buttocks with the flexed knee. 4. To shoplift. "The nautch-joints (brothels) are doing so tough, all the hustlers (prostitutes) are out on the boost."

Boost, on the. 1. Engaged in or by means of shoplifting. 2. Engaged in or by means of pocket-picking.

Boost, the. The shoplifting profession.

Booster. 1. A professional shoplifter. 2. A pickpocket. "I'm coming home from a touch (theft), lushed to the nuts (drunk) and loaded with swag (stolen goods). Some booster must have beat (robbed) me because I wind up home without a pretzel (penniless)."

Boosting-Ben. A shoplifter's coat, often tailored to provide ample space for thief's hooks and stolen goods.

Boosting grift, the. See Boost, the.

Boot, n. 1. A thrill. 2. The so-called "Oregon boot": a heavy iron manacle that fits over the foot and ankle, making escape virtually impossible. It is used on road-gang convicts in some States; often a boot is affixed to each foot, in addition to handcuffs on the wrists, in transfer of convicts. The men are forced to work while wearing this instrument as punishment in several State institutions in scattered areas. 3. (Pl.) The feet. ("To put the boots to" —to kick.)

Boot, v. 1. To assault by kicking. 2. To bungle; to lose; to fail. "You must be an awful load (dolt) to boot a soft touch (easy theft) like that."

Boot around. 1. To beat, especially by kicking or inflicting blows with the flexed knees. 2. To bungle; to lose. "We had a nice thing pushing the mooch (selling narcotics) till you booted it around."

Boot the gong around. To smoke an opium pipe; to smoke marijuana.

Boss. (P) A term used by inmates to address any prison official.

Bottom deal, n. The card cheat's technique of dealing previously arranged cards from the bottom of the deck.

Bottom-deal, v. To employ the bottom deal.

Bottoms. See Tops.

Bounce. 1. To go; to hurry. 2. To cash, as a bad check or counterfeit money. 3. To become enraged. "Watch that D. A. bounce when I spring my alibi; it's a whip (extraordinary)!"

Bounce bum paper. See Bounce sour paper.

Bouncer. A bad check.

Bounce sour paper. To cash fraudulent checks or other forged instruments.

Bowler. An opium smoker. "Habit bowlers with plenty of dough don't crack up like other junkeys (narcotic addicts)."

Box. 1. A safe or vault. 2. (P) Any slotted box, such as that made available by the warden, principal keeper, or the parole board, in which inmates place notes requesting interviews, informing against fellow convicts or officers, and the like. 3. (P) The prison segregation block for housing recalcitrants or inmates under protection. "Whitey just hit the box for flipping (knocking down) that screw (guard) that was giving him buckwheats (unpopular assignments) in the shop."

Box-car numbers. Any large number; a long prison sentence.

Boxcars. A stroke of misfortune. See **Throw boxcars.**

Box-man or -worker. A safe-cracker.

Boy. A passive pederast. [Note: There is a peculiar overtone in the way this word is spoken when used in this sense that suggests its connotation even to the most ingenuous.]

Boy scout. A petty thief whose criminal acts are juvenile or childishly ineffectual; a fool.

Boy-scout dough. Small, petty sums.

Boys, the. The members of the underworld. ("One of the boys"—an underworld citizen in good standing.)

Brace. To solicit. "Step over and brace the tipster (tip-off man) for some work (criminal activity)."

Bracelets. Handcuffs. "Lucky Lou just slipped the bracelets going to court and took it on the lam (escaped)." [Note: A little grease or the manipulation of the mechanism permits escape from many old-style handcuffs. Picking the lock is simple, but the custodian must be unusually careless.]

Braid. (P) A ranking prison official; prison officials as a group. "Zex (on the alert). The Warden and a swag of (lot of) braid is on the prowl (walking around)."

Brake. (P) A lever-controlled bar running the length of a tier of cells, holding them closed even when individual cells are unlocked.

Brand, n. The act or result of **branding.**

Brand, v. 1. To mark, as with a knife cut on the face. 2. To brand as a traitor, degenerate, informer, etc., by spreading the information throughout the underworld. 3. See **Louse up.**

Brass or brass hat. (P) See **Braid.**

Brass up. (Very rare) To apportion loot according to agreement or previous understanding.

Brat. A youthful passive pederast or oral sodomist.

Break. 1. An escape. 2. A confession of guilt under questioning. 3. Any concession or stroke of good fortune, as a suspension of sentence, parole grant, successful escape, etc. 4. The word or deed that openly marks the beginning of a criminal action. "Make the break when I come into the joint (establishment). Don't flash your rod (exhibit your gun) until I reach (commence to draw my gun)."

Break a year. (P) To commence serving the last year of one's prison sentence. "Once I break the year, Dizzy, this bit (sentence) is in the old bageroo (practically over)."

Break one's balls. To annoy, harass, plague, as with requests for loans and favors, with foolish questions and bids for sympathy. "This ghee is always breaking my balls with contracts (requests for favors)."

Break one's hump. 1. To work excessively; to compel another to overwork. 2. See **Break one's balls.**

Break one's license. To arrest and convict a thief who has operated for a long period with phenomenal luck or bought immunity. "You had a nice run, Scoop. About due for the bulls (police) to break your license, ain't you?"

Break out. To produce from one's pocket or other place of concealment. "C'mon, break out with the swag (loot) and gimme my split (share)."

Breaks, the 1. The good and bad turns of fortune in life; the "ups and downs." 2. The subway, railroad, or other transit station; any similar place where crowds move and assemble, a rich hunting ground for pickpockets. "Me and Slick hit the breaks in Penn Station for some sweet scores (lucrative thefts)."

Break the book. To win all the operating money of a gambling establishment, a booker of bets, or the like.

Break-up, n. Melted-down scrap silver or gold, especially from stolen jewelry broken up to prevent identification. "The rocks (diamonds) were phonies (artificial) in that slum (jewelry). We got more dough for the break-up than for that crap (worthless junk)."

Break up, v. 1. To remove stones from stolen jewelry and melt down the metal mountings. 2. (P) To run amok and wreck cell furnishings. "That new fish (newly-arrived inmate) with the big bit (long sentence) blew his top (cracked up mentally) and broke up last night."

Break up the bit. (P) To seek transfer to another prison or assignment to another job to break the monotony of a prison term. "I'm looking to make a boat (secure a transfer) to some other can (prison) when I get over the hump (complete half of my sentence) so I can break up the bit."

Bree. (Carnival) A girl.

Breeze. To make a getaway; to walk away. "Breeze, Joe, the joint (place) is red hot (under close police surveillance)."

Breezer. An open automobile.

Briars. Hacksaw blades. "Plant (conceal) briars in the soles of your shoes in case you get a drop (arrest)."

Bricks, on the. See **Pavement, on the.**

Bricks, the, n. The free world outside prison. "That ghee found a home (fits admirably) in stir (prison). He'll be out trying to get himself a new bit (another sentence) as soon as he hits the bricks."

Bridewell, the (Illinois and environs) The city or county penitentiary; the Chicago institution of that name.

Brig. 1. (Rare) Any prison, jail, or place of confinement. 2. (Rare) (P) The punishment cells.

Bring. (P) To serve time in prison. "Those parole ghees (men) told me to bring another treyer (three years)."

Bring heat. See **Draw heat.**

Britch. (Pickpocket lingo) A side trousers pocket. "Fan (search) the port (left-hand) britch."

Britch-kick. See **Britch.**

Britch-score. A theft from the side pocket of trousers.

Broad. A girl or woman.

Broad a ghee hustles with. A man's feminine criminal partner.

Broad-mob. A gang of swindlers working the **three-card monte** swindle.

Broadsman. A professional card cheat.

Broads with ears. Playing cards with the edges of certain key-cards slightly turned up or down in crude swindling operations.

Broad-tosser. A dealer in **three-card monte** swindle.

Brodie. 1. An arrest. 2. A feigned faint or fit to win hospitalization or narcotics. 3. A long chance; a gamble. "Take a brodie on this trick (theft). If the score (theft) clicks we're in (nicely situated)."

Broke from stir. To be released; to be paroled.

Brown, n. 1. (Prohibition era trade term) Whiskey. [Note: "Brown plaid" was in occasional use to distinguish

Scotch from rye.] 2. The buttocks; the anus.

Brown, Mr. (or "one of the Brown family") A passive pederast.

Brownie. A heavy machine gun.

Buck, n. 1. (P) A prison chaplain. 2. A dollar; a tidy sum. ("A nice [or good] buck"—a good income.) ("A clean buck"—a crooked dollar earned with a minimum of force, misery to others, or risk to oneself.) ("A legit buck"—a more or less honest dollar.)

Buck, v. (Western and Central States) To refuse all work or a specific assignment. "You zibs (fools) can buck if you want to. I can tool by (shirk through) easy enough."

Buck a combination. See **Buck a combo.**

Buck a combo. To work a racket in defiance of a preexistent group monopoly. "Every ghee that bucks that combo winds up in the river (dead)."

Bucket. 1. (P) The portable toilet in unmodernized prison cell-blocks. 2. (P) The buttocks; the rump. "That muzzler (low fellow) don't do no tough bit (painful prison term). And he didn't get that bucket just from sitting on it (he's probably a passive pederast)."

Bucket brigade. A company of convicts marching to and from their cells bearing their slop-buckets.

Bucks, to be in the. To be well supplied with money.

Buckwheat. (P) To abuse; to overwork; to discriminate against. "Them crumby (dirty-natured) hacks (guards) are buckwheating me to death."

Buckwheats. (P) Abuse; overwork; undesirable assignments; discrimination. "How come you're dishing out buckwheats to me? What am I, a creep (person of no principle) or something?"

Bug, n. 1. An insane or highly neurotic person; a mental defective. 2. (P) Any self-inflicted wound, sore, irritation, etc., to shirk work or secure drugs. 3. A burglary alarm. "There ain't no bug on this joint and the lay (place) ain't kipped (protected by watchmen). Let's charge out (go to work)."

Bug, v. 1. To commit to an insane asylum. 2. To wire for burglary protection. "That keister (safe) is bugged like the U. S. Mint, but we'll throw a jumper (current diverter) on it and go to work."

Buggy. An automobile.

Buggy-bandit. An automobile thief.

Bug-house. An institution for the criminally insane or for mentally defective delinquents.

Bug-house square. (Hobo) A Chicago rendezvous of bums, hobos and soapbox orators; any similar rendezvous in any city.

Bug-juice. (P) Ammonia or tear-gas discharge. "Some ghee with a .bum clock (bad heart) near kicked off (died) when the screws (guards) threw that bug-juice at him."

Bug on, to have a. (P) To be in an ugly mood. "We're pulling (serving) the bit (sentence), ain't we? We got a license (right) to get a bug on. The shop screw (guard) bugs up (becomes irritable) 'cause his old lady louses him around (quarrels with him), then he comes in and buckwheats (abuses) us."

Bugster. A night watchman. "Tail (follow) the bugster on his rounds and put the slug on (overpower and bind) him when he's through."

Bug-test. A psychiatric or psychometric test, regarded suspiciously by criminals as an attempt to find them insane.

Bug up. (P) To be in an ugly mood; to arouse one's anger. "Don't bug our shop screw (guard) up or we'll get honey (abuse) all day."

Build-up, n. The work preparatory to a confidence swindle; the act of building up. See **Build up, v.**

Build up, v. To inspire confidence in anyone, especially in a prospective victim of a swindle. "Build me up with this mark (victim) and I'll take his shoes off (leave him penniless)."

Bull. 1. A detective; less commonly, a uniformed policeman. 2. (P) Any kind of meat on the prison menu. 3. (California prisons) A prison guard. 4. A cock-and-bull story; an impressive lie. 5. Bull Durham tobacco.

Bull-buster. (Chiefly West and Central areas) A thief who frequently resists arrest; a drunk who enjoys fighting the police.

Bull-chain. (Southern prisons) A long, heavy chain run through individual leg-shackles at night to prevent escape. "The Johnny (guard) found the bull-chain chopped (cut) and four cons gone over the hill (escaped)."

Bull-dyker. A lesbian.

Bull fighter. See **Bull-buster,** n.

Bull pen. 1. A dormitory or enclosure where men sleep en masse. 2. A barred and locked cell-like enclosure in which prisoners await appearance in court. "I caught the D. A. making his bargain day (day on which lighter sentences are offered for guilty pleas) rounds of the bull pen and copped out (pleaded guilty) for a sixer (six-month sentence) in the pen (penitentiary)."

Bull ring camp. A house of male prostitution (a rare institution where virile males are provided for male and female degenerates.)

Bull's-eye. (Nearly obsolete) A shielded flashlight that casts a thin pencil of light, used by burglars. See **Glim.**

Bum, n. 1. (Connecticut and a few scattered prisons) A prison guard. 2. A woman without self-respect. 3. A fellow; a person; any outsider, not of the gang, hence a suspect.

Bum, v. To beg; to borrow with no intention of repaying.

Bum, a. Having serious flaws; relatively worthless. ("A bum deal"—a raw deal.) ("A bum fall" or "A bum pinch" or "A bum collar"—a charge of which one is innocent.)

Bum, on the. 1. Homeless and without means of support; living by panhandling. 2. Bad; ill; out of order.

Bum beef. See **Bum rap.**

Bum clock. 1. A defective heart. 2. (Very rare) A heart lacking in courage.

Bum finger. 1. A false accusation, especially an identification by a victim of a crime that one really did not commit. 2. (P) An unjust accusation of rule violation.

Bump, v. See **Bump off.**

Bumper (or **Pussy-bumper**). A moral eccentric in sex relations with women; a male oral copulator whose degeneracy extends only to women.

Bump-off, n. A murder.

Bump off, v. To murder.

Bum rap. 1. (P) A charge of which one is innocent; any false accusation. "I ain't putting the chill on (snubbing) you, Mike. That's a bum rap. You ain't barred out (refused admittance) of this joint no time."

Bum steer, n. A false tip; a misleading piece of information, especially when given to thieves by a tipster. "One more bum steer from that fingerman (tipster) and I'm throwing slugs (shooting him)."

Bum steer, v. To mislead by means of a **bum steer.**

Bunco. A swindle at cards, pool, or any similar game. "Imagine that dude (fellow), hip to (familiar with) all the angles and blowing his roll (losing his money) on a pool bunco."

Bunco-steerer. One who lures prospective victims to crooked card games, pool halls, etc. "Old Jim wrapped up (quit) the heavy (safecracking); he's a bunco-steerer now for a Boston joint."

Bundle. 1. A large sum of money; the cash returns of a theft. 2. A long prison term. "Jake's got a real big bundle to pack away (serve) on this one."

Bundle-hipe, n. The short-change racket involving paper money.

Bundle-hipe, v. To clutch folded banknotes between the fingers so as to count both ends of a bill as separate bills, thrust the wad quickly upon a bewildered short-change victim, and leave.

Burn, n. A deliberate concealment of a portion of loot in order to cheat accomplices of their full share.

Burn, v. 1. To glare at. 2. To die by electrocution. 3. To burglarize safes and vaults with an oxy-acetylene torch. 4. To infect with veneral disease. 5. To cheat accomplices by withholding a portion of loot. "That louse burned his partners for their end (share) of the touch (loot) and lammed (fled)."

Burn down. To shoot dead. "Connecticut Red had plenty of guts (courage). He came out throwing slugs (shooting), and the dicks (police) burned him down. But he took one with him."

Burner. 1. A thief who withholds loot to cheat accomplices. 2. A safe-cracker who uses an oxy-acetylene torch. "Soup (nitroglycerine) won't dent that crib (safe); get Joe, the burner."

Burnese. A catarrhal powder high in cocaine content, used by many drug addicts.

Burn-job. A safe-cracking in which an oxy-acetylene torch is used.

Burn the midnight oil. To smoke the opium pipe.

Burn up. 1. To become enraged; to provoke violent anger. 2. To exhaust an area so that crime ceases to be profitable there. 3. To glare at fiercely or with open suspicion. "Don't round

(turn) now. Some ghee that looks like law (a policeman) is burning us up."

Burn up the pavement. To take sudden flight. "Barney Bullets was burning up the pavement with the bulls (police) hot on his tail (in close pursuit) when the slug (bullet) winged him."

Bury. 1. To sentence to a long prison term. 2. (P) To commit to the segregation quarters for an indefinite stay. 3. To conceal; to hide. 4. To betray; to testify against in court.

Bush-parole. (P) An escape by a convict working outside the prison walls.

Bushwhack. To assault suddenly from ambush, especially in "lover's lane" holdups or purse-snatchings.

Bushwhack, on the. Engaged in or by means of **bushwhacking.**

Bushwacker. One who **bushwhacks.**

Business, the. 1. A thorough job; the limit; a killing or assault. 2. The maximum, as of a prison sentence. 3. A pistol, revolver, knife, or any deadly weapon. 4. A passive pederast; a morally loose woman. 5. The act of sexual intercourse.

Business-copper. A policeman open to bribery. "Lucky that a business-copper collared (arrested) me on the rap (charge), or I couldn't have squared (quashed) the beef (complaint)."

Businessman. Any complainant, witness, policeman or other similarly interested person who will accept a bribe. "He's a right copper (policeman who can be bribed), Joe—a businessman."

Busters. Crooked dice. "The book (proprietor) is too hep (smart) to ring in busters in that joint. You'd get your head handed to you (killed)."

Bust in. 1. To force entry, as in a burglary; to enter premises at pistol point. 2. To walk in brazenly where one is uninvited; to break in rudely upon a conversation.

Butcher. 1.(P) A prison doctor or dentist. 2. Any crude or inept operator, as a barber, card player, etc. 3. A killer of some notoriety.

Butt. (Central and Western states) A fractional part of a month or week which still remains to be served in prison. "Man, I'm going whacky (crazy) finishing up this butt."

Butterfly man. (Rare) One who issues or cashes bad checks.

Button, n. The badge of a policeman or other agent of the law; a stolen or counterfeit badge used by an extortionist; a **tin.** "Hit (confront) that stiff (gullible victim) with a button, and he'll go on a shake (pay extortion money)."

Button, v. To lock or otherwise protect against burglary, as a safe or vault. "They sure got that peter (safe) buttoned tight, but we'll take it with one shot (explosive charge)."

Button, on the. In great haste; at great speed. "I just seen Willie coming down the drag (street). I didn't rumble (hail) him 'cause he was on the button and I didn't want to rank him (give away the scheme) if he was making a play (engaged in a criminal venture)."

Buttons. Anything of petty value, especially stolen goods; a paltry sum of money. "I ain't hustling (stealing) for buttons, Rubberlip. If the score (theft) ain't worth a few G's (thousands) for my end (share), get someone else to fill **(fill in)."**

Butts. See **Aigey.**

Butzo. Watch out! Be on the alert! Run!

Buy. To bribe. ("Can be bought"— ready to accept a bribe or bow to equivalent inducement or pressure.) ("Can be bought but won't stay bought"— ready to accept a bribe but not to be trusted to carry out the bargain.)

Buyer. One who criminally receives stolen goods.

Buy new shoes. To jump bail, parole, probation, etc.

Buzz, n. The act of buzzing; the purse-snatching racket among women shoppers in the market.

Buzz, v. 1. To approach; to solicit; to question. 2. To take into one's confidence; to talk secretly to. 3. To telephone to or contact by other such means. 4. To betray slyly; to put the **zingers** in on. 5. To snatch, especially a woman's purse from a baby carriage; to operate as a **moll-buzzer.** "Me and the kid are hitting the market to buzz the molls (women shoppers)."

Buzzard. A petty crook; a leech who lives off gratuities doled out by successful thieves and racketeers.

Buzzer. 1. A thief who snatches purses from baby carriages; a **moll-buzzer.** 2. One who habitually talks sotto voce when soliciting, seeking information, etc. 3. (Carnival) A confidence man who lures victims to crooked games. "There's a buzzer who knows how to work a tip (select prospects among a crowd)."

Buzz-man. (P) An informer.

C

C. 1. Cocaine. 2. A hundred dollars. "Beetlehead's partner burned (cheated) him for a C-and-a-half on that last score (theft) they made."

Cabaret. 1. (P) To listen to a radio program of night-club bands, until the central set is turned off. 2. (P) To lie awake indulging in erotic fantasy and masturbation. "You better knock off (stop) reading that hot stuff (pornography) and going cabareting or you'll wind up bugged (committed to insane asylum)."

Cabbage. (P) Paper money. "That hack (officer) will bring swag (contraband) in as long as you got the cabbage."

Cab-joint. A restaurant that charges exorbitantly; a brothel or other illegal establishment whose patronage depends upon taxicab-driver **steerers.**

Cackle-factory. A hospital for the criminally insane or for mentally defective delinquents. "Get bugged (committed) and hit the cackle-factory. You do a good bit(easy term) there except for the workouts (beatings)."

Cadet. A pimp, especially a scout who procures new girls in the white slave traffic. "You never see them two-bit (cheap) cadets hitting the can (going to prison) with a load (long term) of boffos (years."

Cadillac. A one-ounce package of any of the white powdered drugs. "Hello, Sniffy, get me a cadillac of C (cocaine) from the pusher (narcotic seller)."

Cake and wine. (P) The bread and water ration in punishment cells.

Calaboose. 1. A station house or local jail. 2. A prison or penitentiary. 3. (P) A punishment cell.

Call girl. A visiting prostitute procured by telephone. "Some hip (smart) dude (fellow) ought to line them call girls up in a union. There's a whole swag (lot) of them in the racket."

Calling card. Fingerprints. "Mitt up (wear gloves) on this caper (robbery) unless you want to leave your calling card for the dicks (police)."

Call the turn. 1. To make an accurate guess, estimate, or prediction. 2. To pick a suspect out of the police **line-up** and formally identify him as guilty of a crime. "The mark (victim) pegged (recognized) me right off the pop. One gander (look) and he called the turn."

Camisole. (P) A strait jacket.

Camp. 1. A house of prostitution. 2. An apartment used for riotous parties. 3. (Loosely) A flat used by thieves to hide loot, conceal fugitives, etc.; a drop. 4. The joint residence of a group of epicenes. "The wagon (police-patrol) backs up to that camp every week for a load of nances (sodomists)."

Can, n. 1. A prison; a jail; a station house. 2. The buttocks. 3. An ounce of morphine. 4. A safe or vault.

Can, v. To cease; to desist from. "Can that cowboying (reckless thievery) or you'll be buried (imprisoned for a long term)."

Can, on one's. See **Pratt, on one's.**

Canary. 1. (Rare) A convict. 2. An informer. "The D. A. has a cage full of canaries in the county jail singing (informing) for him."

C-and-M. A mixture of cocaine and morphine. "Them junkeys (drug addicts) hooked on (habituated to) c-and-m would rat (inform) on their mothers for the whizz-bang (potent drug mixture)."

Candy. 1. Anything very desirable and easily secured, as loot; a choice area in which to ply one's racket; a pretty girl. 2. Youths attractive to degenerates. "Do you see all the candy hitting that joint? It must be a fag camp (degenerates' apartment)."

Canetta. See **Can.** (**Big canetta.** See **Big keister.**)

Canetta, on one's. See **pratt, on one's.**

Canister. 1. A pistol or revolver. 2. A jail, a safe, or a container of any kind made of metal. 3. The buttocks.

Can-maker. One who makes bombs for terrorists.

Canned goods. (Central and Western prisons) A virgin; a sexually innocent man or woman. "No boys (passive pederasts) for me, Joe. They're strictly canned goods that ain't putting out (practicing pederasty) when you see them with me."

Canned heat. Alcohol from a sterno cooking device.

Cannon. A pickpocket. "Whizzo is one cannon who is tops at kissing the dog (facing the victim as he is robbed)."

Cannon, the. The pickpocket trade.

Cannonball. 1. A small round safe frequently found inside a vault or a larger safe. 2. (P) A letter smuggled out of prison to avoid censorship; a kite.

Cannonball Peter. 1. See **Cannonball,** (1). 2. A cylindrical safe with laminated tool-proof doors, effectively resistant to all burglary technique except oxy-acetylene burning. "What a lousy racket! You do a week-ender (week-end burglary) taking a big cannonball peter and wind up with record books, an old souper (watch), a gat (pistol) and peanuts (small sum of money) for your end."

Cannon-mob. A gang of pickpockets. "Doing a single-o (working independently) won't get you nothing in that town. A big ginzola (Italian) cannon-mob has the alzo (police or political protection)."

Cannon-squad. A special police squad detailed to guard against pickpockets.

Canojerod. Any article or thing that one does not want to designate by name. "Stash (hide) that canojerod for me."

Can-opener. 1. A sectional curved bar, with a point to be inserted into a drilled or chiseled hole in a safe, to rip the steel plating. In principle it is similar to a common household can-opener. 2. A safecracker who works with a can-opener.

Can-shooter. A safeblower.

Cap. To serve as a fast-talking aide to a confidence man, driving home with emphasis and timely remarks the come-on scheme. "The Colonel readied-up (prepared) the sucker, and I walked in to cap him for as sweet a five-G (five-thousand-dollar) touch (theft) as the con (confidence game) ever brought."

Caper. 1. A trick, easy of accomplishment. 2. A professional theft or fraud. "I was knocked out (arrested) on a caper in Boston, laying paper (passing bad checks)."

Capper. 1. A confidence man's aide whose duty it is to **cap.** 2. One who directs or lures customers to a gambling den, house of prostitution, or other illegal resort. "Sadie's nautcheries (brothels) got the hack-drivers and coppers in town on the payroll as cappers."

Carat, eighteen (or **twenty-two carat**). A unit of measure or degree, comparable to the measure of weight in gold. "So, you eighteen-carat loads (fools) think you're grifters (quick-witted thieves), eh?"

Carbolic dip. (P) The convict's first bath in prison.

Carny, n. (Carnival) A carnival; a carnival worker; the carnival world.

Carny, a. Pertaining to, or characteristic of, a carnival or the carnival world. "As soon as this dude cracked (spoke) in the lingo, I pegged (recognized) him as carny."

Carny grifter. A professional pick-pocket, a small-time confidence man, or any other crafty thief who operates at carnivals.

Carry. (P) To bear, as the burden of a long prison term. "What are you carrying on this bit (sentence), Box-car?"

Carry iron. See **Lug iron.**

Carry the banner or stick. To stay up all night, having no money to pay for lodging. "You ain't got to carry the banner, Joker, not since Smith and Wesson made all men equal, but you gotta do the bit (prison term) when you take a fall (get arrested)."

Carton. (P) The ten-package carton of cigarettes serving as a standard unit of value in prison in lieu of contraband cash.

Carve initials in one. To cut or slash a person with a knife, razor, or similar edged weapon. "That kid rates a medal instead of a new bit (new sentence he will receive) for carving his initials in that wolf (active pederast). If he squawked (complained) to the officials, they'd slough him (lock him up) in segregation for protection for the rest of his bit (term)."

Case, n. 1. A card-dealing box, often with a false bottom for swindling; a holdout box. 2. (Ironical) No chance whatsoever. "Spring (be released) on a rap (charge) like yours? What a case you got!"

Case, v. 1. To watch and study the movements of an intended victim, as when planning a holdup. 2. To survey the premises selected to be robbed.

Case, a. Last; only remaining; last of its kind.. "That's my case pack of butts; kick back (return them)."

Case dough. All of, or part of, the last of one's money; bare expenses. "We scored (completed thefts) three times last week and you're on case dough already. That's the crap. I ain't stepping out on the heist (sticking up places) every night."

Case note. A dollar bill; one's last dollar. "I give up my case note for that box of slugs (bullets). Now we gotta make a score (theft)."

Case out. See **Case, v.**

Caser. 1. A dollar. 2. (Rare) One who investigates the scene of a projected crime. "The caser says this trick (robbery) is candy (easy) three-handed (for three robbers)."

Catch rope. To be hanged.

Catch slugs. To be shot. "That fink (informer) buried (gave testimony against) Joe. He's gotta catch slugs."

Cat-house. A house of prostitution.

Cat-life. (P) (Rare) More than one life sentence imposed upon a prisoner, to run consecutively. "They oughta give them cat-life cons a catnip ration and bug (commit to an insane asylum) their judges."

Catsup hounds. (P) Bloodhounds. "Jake lammed (escaped) with the cat-sup hounds hot on his tail (in close pursuit)."

Caught flat-footed. 1. Arrested on a dead-banger with no chance to flee or resist. 2. Arrested when without **fall dough;** caught with damning evidence on one's person.

Caught in a snowstorm. Under the influence of narcotics, more specifically of heroin, morphine, or cocaine.

Caught up. See **All caught up.**

Cave. (Rare) A prison cell. "I gotta hit the cave. The man (warden) took me off the count-out (roster of trusties remaining out of cells late) on that pinch (report)."

C. C. 's. (P) The cells of those condemned to death; the death house. "Two new mickeys (new arrivals) hit the c.c.'s today for that knock-off (murder) in Brownsville."

Cecil. Morphine.

Cell, v. (P) To reside; to lock in a

certain cell. "You cell in the north wing, eh? I used to lock (live) there."

Center-fielder. A thief who avoids risky assignments; an over-cautious thief. "You center-fielders sure bug me up (anger me); maybe you want to stay home and still get a cut (share of loot)?"

Chain-gang Charley. (South) The foreman of a convict chain gang.

Chain-man. (Obsolete) Specialist in stealing watches and chains worn in vests.

Chair, the. The electric chair; a sentence of death by electrocution. "You better cop that plea (plead guilty to a lesser offense) or it's the chair sure."

Chalk-in, n. (P) A formal report or lock-up for violation of prison rules. "That new hack (guard) makes you blow your top (suffer a nervous attack) the way he bangs that club, but he don't give you no chalk-in for mopery raps (trivial offenses)."

Chalk in, v. To report or lock up for violation of prison rules. "That new screw (guard) chalked in twelve dudes (men) the first day he was on in the weave shop."

Chalk out. (P) To strike the name of a deceased inmate from the records. "That old ghee was chalked out last night; yeah, the rope (suicide by hanging)."

Character. An outstanding storyteller, comedian, or poseur; a rare or fantastic individual. "Get a load of that character; ain't he a whip (an extraordinary fellow)!"

Charge. An addict's dose of narcotics.

Charged up. Under the influence of narcotics or alcohol; emotionally disturbed. "Don't rumble (notice) Whitey; he's all charged up today."

Charge out. To start out fully equipped on any criminal enterprise; to go to work criminally. "Don't forget, everyone hit the scatter (meeting place) after the score (robbery). Un-load (get rid of loot and weapons) first and get there clean. All right, let's charge out now."

Charity stuff. A promiscuous woman. "She's a funny dame. She done three bits (prison sentences) for boosting (shoplifting) but she won't hustle (practice prostitution); strictly charity stuff."

Chase. To order an undesirable person to keep his distance.

Chatterbox. 1. A typewriter. 2. A machine gun.

Chatterer. A machine gun. "That gunsel (passive pederast) wound up with good people (underworld aristocrats) 'cause he handled a chatterer in the war."

Cheaters. Spectacles; eyeglasses.

Cheat them. 1. (P) To have one's prison term shortened by parole, commutation, pardon, court action, or death.

Check out. (P) To leave prison by any means: death, escape, parole, discharge, court order, or transfer to another prison. "I'm checking out of this joint (place) if I can make a boat (transfer to another prison)."

Cheese-eater. (N. Y. State prisons) An informer. "All them cheese-eaters get fat. Only right ghees (good fellows) get chivved (knifed) or knocked dead (killed)."

Cheese it! Look out! Danger! Police!

Chef, n. An expert in the proper burning of the pill in an opium pipe.

Chef, v. To serve as a **chef.**

Chef left and right. To have the gift of ambidexterity in tending the opium pipe.

Cherry, n. The hymen. ("To cop a cherry"—to seduce a virgin.) ("To break one's cherry on a heist"—to engage in one's first holdup.)

Cherry, a. Virginal, unspoiled; (by figurative extension) having no criminal record or no previous experience in a given kind of crime. ("To be cherry on the cannon"—to be without experience in picking pockets.)

Chestnut-stabber. An Italian.

Chicken. A catamite, especially one used as a decoy by extortionists to blackmail susceptible men.

Chicken feed. Small change.

Chicky or **Chiggers.** Beware! Look out! Police!

Chill, n. 1. A feeling of sudden apprehension; temporary or permanent loss of nerve. 2. The act of knocking unconscious or killing. 3. A hostile or cold greeting; a deliberate avoidance of another's greeting. 4. (Very rare) An arrest; a conviction; a commitment to prison. 5. A renunciation because of fear; a lack of interest in (a given matter). "Them peters (safes) don't pay. I got a chill on the heavy (safe-cracking), Lou."

Chill, v. 1. To lose one's nerve. 2. To refuse to identify a suspect because of fear. 3. To lose interest in a person or thing. 4. To knock unconscious or to kill. 5. To avoid, or to greet with studied hostility, coldness, or reserve. 6. (Very rare) To arrest, convict, or commit to prison. 7. To cause another to be frightened or devoid of self-confidence. "That creep (low fellow) is all softened up for you to flatten (knock out). I chilled him good."

Chill the beef or **the rap.** To terrorize witnesses or complainants by force or threats into withdrawing from a case. "If the rapper (complainant) can't be squared (induced to drop the prosecution), we'll chill the beef."

Chill off. To become discouraged or fearful and then withdraw. "I don't like the trick (piece of criminal work). As soon as I cased (surveyed) the joint (place), I chilled off."

Chink. (Rare) Money.

Chip, n. (The near South) A cash register. "The joker (fellow) behind the chip was hip to (familiar with) the note-laying racket (short-change game), and he beefed (called for police)."

Chip cop. To use a sticky substance in the palm of the hand, or any similar deception, to steal chips in a gambling house.

Chippie. A promiscuous woman. "That chippie put the horns on (was unfaithful to) every ghee (man) she doubled with."

Chippy, v. To trifle with the use of narcotics. "You can't chippy with that whizz-bang (cocaine and morphine mixture) and not get hooked (addicted to narcotics)."

Chippy around. 1. See **Chippy.** 2. To be sexually promiscuous. "Knock off (stop) chippying around with them blisters (cheap women). We blew (lost) three scores (thefts) account of that."

Chips. Money. ("In the chips"—prosperous.) "We'll be back in the chips—or in the clink (prison)."

Chirp, n. The sound involved in chirping, either in its homosexual significance or as a pickpocket's signal. "Some dude (fellow) gave Slug the chirp (suggesting his homosexual attractiveness), and he's out with a chiv (knife) tryin' to find the creep (low fellow)."

Chirp, v. 1. To make an exaggerated kissing sound which may be humorous or insulting. 2. To signal by a chirping sound to one's pickpocket accomplices that the victim's wallet has been taken, and that it is time to slip away.

Chisel. To take every petty and unfair advantage in one's relations with others.

Chiseler. One who consistently **chisels.**

Chiv, n. A stiletto, knife, razor, or other edged weapon.

Chiv, v. To use a **chiv** in fights. "Being a dukester (fist-fighter) ain't no good in the can (prison). You just get yourself chivved by some punk kid out for a rep (reputation as a tough)."

Chiv-man. One who habitually carries or wields a **chiv.**

Choke. To extinguish or dim a light. "Choke that glim (flashlight). This joint ain't supposed to be kipped (protected by watchman or alarm), but I heard something."

Chop, n. 1. A share or portion of loot; the house percentage in gambling; the percentage going to a syndicate as a sort of "license fee" to operate criminally in a given area. 2. A cut inflicted with a **chiv.** 3. (P) A prison haircut.

Chop, v. 1. To cut a person with a **chiv.** 2. To hacksaw, as prison bars, in an escape attempt. 3. To stop by force, as a victim screaming an alarm. 4. To quit; to cease. "Chop the cracks (pointed remarks). Half the ghees (people) in the joint are riding the earie (listening)."

Chop a bar. (P) To hacksaw or file a door or window bar as a means of escape. [Note: Hacksaw blades are often hand-made by notching teeth in a steel clockspring.]

Chop a bit. (P) To reduce a prison sentence by court action, commutation, or resentence.

Chop down. 1. To knife, bludgeon, or knock down with a blow of the fist. 2. To shoot.

Chop it up. To talk; to exchange underworld yarns. "These creeps (undesirables) are always chopping it up about big scores (robberies), and they ain't got a pretzel (cent)."

Chopper. 1. (P) A hacksaw blade. 2. (P) A knife or razor. 3. A machine gun.

Chop up jackpots. See **Chop it up.**

Chuck, n. Food.

Chuck, v. To eat.

Chuck a dummy. To feign an injury or faint, either in an accident insurance racket, or in prison to shirk work or to obtain drugs.

Chuck horrors. A drug addict's aversion to food, especially when breaking a narcotic addiction habit.

Chump. 1. An underworld novice. 2. A working person; a **mark; a sucker.**

Chunk. 1. A relatively large sum of money. 2. (P) A long prison term. "Jake Stutter goes up for his chunk today. He figures to get hit with the works (the maximum penalty)."

Church-rat. A contemptible thief who robs church poorboxes or the purses of the devout.

Chutes. (Among pickpockets) The subway.

Cipher. (Hobo) A panhandler who can beg only contemptibly paltry sums.

Circulation, in. Free; not in prison. ("Back in circulation"—recently discharged or paroled; released from prison punishment cells.) ("Out of circulation"—in jail or prison; in the prison solitary or segregation cells.)

Circus. A group performance of diversified degeneracy staged for a private audience.

C-joint. An establishment where cocaine is sold to addicts.

Clam. 1. A paper dollar. 2. The mouth. "Shut your clam; there's a wrong ghee (informer) next to you."

Clam up. See **Dummy up.**

Clap. Gonorrhea.

Clatter. A police patrol wagon. "You dudes keep hitting that camp (prostitutes' apartment), and the clatter will back up there for you."

Claw. The skilled pickpocket in a gang.

Clean, v. To rob of everything of value; to leave penniless. "A hustler (thief) is a sucker to leave these hoosiers clean in the match game (confidence swindle). Leave 'em a couple of skins (dollars), and they don't beef (complain) so loud."

Clean, a. 1. Innocent of weapons, stolen goods, or incriminating evidence. 2. (P) Free of contraband, stolen prison stores, or weapons. 3. Completely without funds; empty. "When we crashed the joint (forced our way into the place), it was clean. We didn't score for (make a theft of) a meg (cent)."

Clean buck. Money acquired criminally but without the use of force. [Note: Some criminals exclude dealing in narcotics, prostitution, etc., from the clean buck category.] "Sam the schmecker (narcotic user) is grabbing a nice clean buck on the short-con (small confidence game)."

Cleaners, to take to the. To rob or swindle of all one's money. "Them hustlers (professional gamblers) rung in busters (crooked dice) and took me to the cleaners."

Clean one. A stolen automobile, altered to avoid ready identification. "There's more dudes riding around in them clean ones than in legit buggies (honestly acquired automobiles)."

Clean up the calendar. 1. To plead guilty to a number of charges, including those of which one is innocent, in a bargain with police. This "solution" of open cases for the police brings from them a promise of leniency in court. 2. For the police to coerce a "confession" "solving" all open cases on the docket of the same nature. 3. To charge a suspect with all of the unsolved crimes similar in type to the one for which the suspect has been arrested. "Yeah, them coppers hit me with a swag (lot) of raps (charges) to clean up the calendar. They duked in (induced) suckers (complainants) I never seen before to finger (identify) me."

Clearing house. 1. A crooked brokerage house that markets unregistered stolen bonds or certificates as well as counterfeited securities. 2. An establishment in which good checks drawn to another's order are cashed. "Smash (cash) that stiff (check) at the clearing house."

Clemo. Executive clemency.

Clincher. (P) A cigarette clenched between fingertips and extinguished to be smoked again. "I knew that phony big shot when he smoked clinchers (was penniless)."

Clink. 1. A county jail or a prison. 2. (P) A punishment cell; the **cooler;** the **bing.** "Joe Tarpy hit the clink for a lot of cabbage (money) they knocked him off (caught him) with on a fan (search)."

Clink-cuckoo. See **Stir-bugs.**

Clinker. (South) The leg-chain by which chain-gang convicts are fettered. "Some ghee (fellow) in Georgia chopped the clinker with a John Sperl (file), went over the hill (fled), and took the ketchup-hounds (bloodhounds) with him for pets."

Clinkeroo. A clink, verbally underscored for emphasis. "Yeah, Blinker, that Holland County jug (jail) is a real clinkeroo. You know you're doing a bit (serving time) in that crumb-joint (miserable place)."

Clinkers. Shackles, especially for fettering the ankles.

Clip. 1. To rob; to swindle. 2. To kill. 3. To assault with a bludgeon, knife, or other weapon. "We'll clip the big ghee (leader) of the mob, and the other creeps (minor gangsters) will take a powder (flee), but quick."

Clip a butt. To extinguish a partially smoked cigarette and save it for later smoking.

Clip-joint. An establishment where patrons are robbed or outrageously and illegally overcharged. "Zip is scoring for (making) a nice buck (good money) as a muscle-man (bouncer) for a clip-joint in Harlem."

Clipper. See **Clincher.**

Clip-stand. (Carnival) A crookedly operated concession.

Clock, n. 1. The heart. 2. Courage; nerve. "What a clock you got to buck that combo (compete with that gang)."

Clock, v. To watch the movements of a prospective victim of crime, especially a watchman on his rounds.

Clocker. A watchman who punches a time clock on his rounds.

Clout, n. A theft, especially from markets or shops; the act of shoplifting.

Clout, v. To steal, especially from markets and shops; to shoplift.

Clout, on the. Engaged in, or by means of, the **clout.**

Clout a heap. To steal an automobile.

Clouter. A thief, especially one who eschews force.

Clown. A constable or small town police officer. "Nervo and his mob snatched (kidnapped) the town clown and cowboyed (recklessly invaded) into the jug (bank)."

Cluck. 1. A counterfeit coin. 2. A stupid or inept person.

Clunk. An ordinary person; a "guy."

C-Note. A one-hundred-dollar bill; one hundred dollars.

C. O. Dick. (Central and Western U. S.) A Central Office detective; a headquarters man.

Coffee-and. Any light meal: coffee and cake. Hence, anything picayune, petty or cheap. ("Coffee-and dough"—unimportant money.) ("Coffee-and touch"—a petty theft.)

Coffee-and grifter or **hustler.** 1. A petty thief or racketeer. 2. A cheap prostitute.

Coffee-and pimp. One who lives off the earnings of cheap prostitutes. "A bunch of them street-corner coffee-and pimps took a drop (were arrested) on that short-arm heist (rape charge)."

Coffee-grinder. A machine gun.

Coffin. 1. A safe. 2. A cell.

Coffin-varnish. (Prohibition era) Any beverage with a denatured alcohol base.

Coke. Cocaine.

Coked up. Under the influence of cocaine or a mixture of cocaine and morphine.

Cokey, n. A drug addict; a user of cocaine.

Cold. 1. Cut-and-dried; ready for easy execution. 2. Unconscious. 3. Characterized by little police activity or law enforcement. "The rap (charge) is cold now. Your mouthpiece (lawyer) made a deal to turn yourself in, cop a plea (plead guilty to a lesser offense) and get an S.S. (suspended sentence)."

Cold-cock. To knock unconscious with a weapon, a blow of the fist or an arm-grip around the neck. "I got a bum rap (unjust charge) for cold-cocking some ghee with the mugg (arm-lock) and rolling (robbing) him."

Cold-deck, n. A deck of playing cards, stacked or otherwise prepared for cheating; the act of robbing by **cold-decking.** "We gave the mark (victim) the old cold-deck for five C's (five hundred dollars)."

Cold-deck, v. 1. To cheat by using stacked, marked, or otherwise prepared decks of cards. 2. To cheat or swindle in any manner similar to card-cheating.

Cold-duke, n. A hostile reception; a snub.

Cold-duke, v. To snub; to receive with open or veiled hostility. "Yeah, Shorty, I left the can (prison) full of working stiff (honest worker) ideas but all these joints (places) where I look for work sure cold-duke me."

Cold lay. A person or place to be robbed with no difficulty or a minimum of risk. "This score (robbery) is a real cold lay. I can't figure why no one beat (robbed) the joint before."

Cold slough. A home or apartment from which occupants are absent.

Cold-slough prowl or **worker.** A burglary of a **cold slough.**

Cold turkey. Cleanly and suddenly; to the point, without preliminary explanations. "I told the creep (undesirable) cold turkey to cop a mope (get away)."

Collar, n. An arrest; a seizure in the act of committing a crime; (P) a report for rule violation.

Collar, v. To catch in the act of a

crime; to arrest; (P) to report for rule violation. "Watch your step and don't get collared for mopery (a trivial offense) now that we're red hot (badly wanted by the police)."

Collat. Collateral; anything of value, easily convertible into cash; any valuable loot other than cash. "There ain't much color (cash) in this touch (theft), but about five G's (thousands) collat."

College. A State prison or penitentiary. "Yeah, they sent Mike back to college to learn a few capers (crooked tricks) he missed in the ref (reformatory)."

Color. Money; cash. "You got to show plenty color in that joint (gambling house)."

Combination. 1. A criminal gang or syndicate. 2. The combination dial of a safe or vault; the pin, sleeve and tumbler-box as a mechanical locking unit. "Knock that combo off the keister (safe) and punch the guts out (smash the mechanism inside)."

Combo. See **Combination.**

Combo shot. A blast of picric used in cracking a safe or vault.

Come-along. See **"V."**

Come clean. 1. To confess or inform the police. 2. To produce all of the loot for equal division, withholding none.

Come-off. A happening; an event; an outcome. "What was the come-off that turned the heat on (drew police attention)?"

Come off a trick. To return from any profitable thievery.

Come-on. 1. A gullible prospect for swindling. 2. Any device by which a victim is led into a swindle; swindle-bait.

Come-on ghee. A swindler.

Come out swinging. (P) A shouted cell-to-cell invitation to fight when the cell-doors open, usually said in jest. "Come out swinging in the morning and I don't mean your hips."

Come through. 1. To be loyal, refus-

ing to inform on accomplices; to send money to associates in prison. 2. To confess; to implicate others. 3. To pay, as tribute, "protection" sums; to produce concealed loot upon the demand of suspicious associates. "A couple of guinea footballs (bombs) ought to get these joints (establishments) in line and make 'em come through."

Coming down hill. (P) Serving the second half of a prison term.

Commute, n. (P) A conditional pardon by the governor or pardon board; a commutation, or shortening, of sentence.

Commute, v. (P) To issue a **commute.** "This Governor don't commute nobody but stoolies (informers)."

Comptroller. The divisional head of a policy-number syndicate.

Con. 1. The confidence game; the swindling racket. 2. A convict. 3. A plausible lie; a hypocritical remark. "Save that con. If it's a bite (loan you want) spring your duke (say so). I ain't got it anyhow."

Con, on the. Engaged in, or by means of any **con-game.**

Con along (or **Con**). To practice the con.

Con-broad. A woman swindler, or aide to swindlers.

Conducer. (Carnival) A carnival man who stands among the spectators and controls the crooked gaming wheel by a thin wire. [The operator spins the wheel and leaves the stand to convince the spectators of his honesty.] "That conducer has lots of grift sense (sixth sense of a thief). He feeds out a lot of come-on (inducement) prizes, and the suckers love it."

Coney Island. The police-station chamber in which subjects are questioned or given the **third degree.** "The bulls (police) took him down to Coney Island, kicked in his cruller (beat him severely) and made him come through (confess)."

Con-game. Any of the smoother swindles, ranging from the panhandler's long-winded appeal to the high-pressure technique of the suavest promoter; the **con.**

Conk, n. The head. "I'll bend a bar over that flea's conk if he messes with me"; by extension, intelligence, sanity. "If you're conked up okay (sane), I'm a wack (psychopath)."

Conk, v. To strike on the head with a weapon or bludgeon.

Conk-crusher. 1. A bludgeon. 2. One habitually armed with a bludgeon for criminal use.

Conk on the cruller. To beat on the head with a bludgeon.

Con-line. A smoothly persuasive line of talk.

Con-man or **-merchant.** A confidence man; a swindler; any smooth talker; a liar. "Imagine a lug (stupid fellow) like him a con-man!"

Connection. 1. A politician or other person of influence through whom the law may be circumvented, favors procured, etc. 2. (P) A person through whom contraband or stolen stores may be obtained, favors procured, rules circumvented, etc. ("Meat connection"— one who sells or gives stolen meat; "Junk connection"—a trafficker in narcotics; "Kite connection"—a trafficker in uncensored letters.)

Connection can. A prison, jail, or other place of detention in which political pressure or bribery can procure favors. "I'm going down to see the pollies (politicians) at the club to get Shorty on a boat (transfer) to the State Farm. That's a connection can, and he'll pull a soft bit (serve an easy term) there."

Connection ghee. See **Connection.**

Connection joint. See **Connection can.**

Connection town. A city or town in which venal authorities sell various criminal immunities and protection from outside police interference. [Many gangs operate from these towns, preying on surrounding communities and scurrying back to cover.] "I hit down to Jennifer when I was on the lam (a fugitive); that's the best connection town in the country."

Conner. See **Con-man.**

Conny. (Variant of **Con-man;** sometimes used as a form of address among small confidence operators.) One who leads victims to gambling houses, **clip-joints,** etc. "What's doing, conny? Anything moving on the turf (in the underworld)?"

Con P. K. (Convict Principal Keeper) (P) The most notorious informer in a prison, hence often the most influential. "The con P. K. I don't mind 'cause we know him. These lousy undercover finks (informers) are murder (awful)."

Con racket. See **Con-game.**

Consent job. An automobile theft inspired by the owner in order to collect the insurance.

Con's man. (P) A prison official whose policy it is to decide in convicts' favor in situations in which inconvenience to either the convicts or the guards is unavoidable; a lenient official.

Contact or **Contact ghee.** 1. The go-between who maintains contact between kidnappers and extortion victim. 2. **Connection.**

Contract. (P) A favor; a verbal promise of a favor. "Buzz (ask) Artie to get that kite out (send uncensored letter) for you. I'm lousy with (overburdened with) contracts."

Con turnkey. (P) A convict trusty who locks and unlocks cell-doors under supervision.

Convincer, n. 1. Any word, act, or line of talk that breaks down the skepticism of a swindle victim. 2. A pistol, knife, blackjack, or anything that convinces the victim of his personal jeopardy. "Duck (hide) the convincer till I give you the office (signal) to put it on him (point it)."

Cook, n. One who tends the opium pipe for smokers; a **chef.**

Cook, v. 1. To redistill denatured alcohol. 2. To tend the opium pipe for smokers; to **chef.**

Cookie. Cocaine.

Cook soup. To dissolve a stick of dy- namite in hot water to extract crude nitroglycerine, or **picric,** for safe-blow- ing. "Old Jim cooked the soup but wouldn't lug (carry) it to the touch (burglary). A funny ghee (fellow), but a good pete-man (safe-cracker)."

Cool. 1. Characterized by diminished police activity or public clamor for re- form; characterized by a lessening of legal pressure, as when criminal charges become "old" or no longer of immediate interest to the prosecution. 2. Having lost the element of timeliness, as a crim- inal coup long postponed. "That lay (robbery) is cool now. I chilled (lost interest) on the trick (theft), but case it out (look it over) anyhow."

Cooler. 1. (P) The punishment cells. 2. A slow horse listed as a favorite in a fixed race. "What nice suckers! There's a lot of iron (money) riding on that cooler."

Coolers. Loaded dice or marked cards. "Mickey's mob rung in (introduced by stealth) coolers and broke the book (won all of the money behind the game)."

Cool off (or **Cool**). To lose interest; to diminish in intensity, as police or prosecution interest in a criminal mat- ter.

Cool out. To placate; to pacify.

Coop. 1. A police station or local jail. 2. (P) A punishment cell; any cell.

Coozey. (Collectively) Loose women; prostitutes; passive pederasts, or oral sodomists.

Cop, n. A policeman.

Cop, v. 1. To seize; to grab; to steal. "They hit Lucky Lou with the book

(sentenced to life) for copping a boiler (automobile). He was a four-time loser (convicted of three previous felonies)."

Cop a breeze. To slip quietly away; to escape from custody or an area where one is sought by police. (Im- perative) Get out of here! "We turned the trick (committed the crime) and copped a breeze just before the rumble (interference) brought the squad cars."

Cop a doodle. To serve as a male oral degenerate.

Cop a drag. To smoke a cigarette.

Cop a figary. To move along; to es- cape. (Imperative) Get out of here!

Cop a gander. To glance furtively. "Cop a gander when the mark (intend- ed victim) stashes (hides) the dough."

Cop a heel. 1. To beat another to a theft. 2. To escape from prison or from the scene of a crime. 3. To sneak stealthily away. 4. (Imperative) Move on! Get out of here! 5. To **heel.** 6. To assault without warning. "Four of the Greek's mob with rods (guns) and saps (blackjacks) copped a heel on me and Luke."

Cop a joint. See **Cop a doodle.**

Cop all kinds of pleas. To beg ab- jectly for mercy. "This flea (cowardly fellow) was trying to make a rep (tough reputation) guerilling (ter- rorizing) new mickeys (newcomers). Two punk kids glommed (seized) him, put chivs (knives) to him, and he copped all kinds of pleas."

Cop a mope. 1. (Imperative) Get out of here! Look out! 2. To walk away; to leave. 3. (P) To escape from prison, especially from outside the walls. 4. To flee. "Zex (look out)! Bulls (Police)! Cop a mope!"

Cop a plea. 1. To bargain for and ac- cept a plea of guilty to a lesser crime than that charged in the indictment. 2. To withdraw from an aggressive stand taken; to apologize; to ask mercy. "That crumb (coward) went around shooting his mouth off (talking) about me. When I carved my initials in (cut) him, you shoulda heard him cop a plea."

Cop-a-plea mouthpiece. An unscrupulous criminal lawyer who collects his retainer fee and, if no further sums are forthcoming, advises client to plead guilty whatever the merits of his case.

Cop a sneak. 1. To assault stealthily. 2. (P) To sneak away from one's work assignment. 3. To steal something when one is at a psychological disadvantage; to steal impulsively, without a plan of action or escape. 4. To walk away; to leave.

Cop a Sunday. (Carnival) To strike suddenly with one's best or "Sunday" punch. "The sucker (theft victim) didn't even blink when I copped a Sunday on him."

Cop out. See **Cop a plea.**

Copper. 1. A policeman; a **cop.** 2. (Many prisons) Time off for good behavior; **good time.** 3. An informer; a despicable person. "Screw (get out of here), bum, I don't want no coppers around me."

Copper-hearted. Untrustworthy; cowardly; having the character or ideology of a police agent. "That lousy, copperhearted wheelman (chauffeur) on the score (robbery) turned us all in and took the stand (testified for the State)."

Cork the air. To sniff or blow cocaine up the nostrils.

Corner-turner. (Rare; scattered areas) A fugitive.

Cornfield clemency. (P) (Corn-belt States) An escape, especially from outside prison walls.

Corn-hole. To employ a catamite.

Correspondence-school dick. An amateur sleuth; a prying bystander interfering with criminal operations. "We'll have to put the slug on (knock out) that correspondence-school dick burning us up (watching us), or we can't take (rob) the joint (establishment) tonight."

Corset. A vest, more or less bulletproofed.

Count. (P) The regular check-up of prisoners, occurring several times daily. "I got to hit the shop for the count or they'll think I made a beat (escaped)."

Count me in. Formal acceptance of a bid to take part in any criminal action.

Count me out. Formal refusal of a bid to take part in any criminal action.

Count-out. (P) The privilege that goes with some prison jobs of remaining out of one's cell after other prisoners have been locked in for the night. "A couple of count-out ghees (men) chopped a bar and blew (fled) the joint (place)."

Count out. (P) To have the **count-out** privilege.

Country. See **Take (one) out in the country.**

Count ties. (Hobo) To walk the tracks.

County, the. A county jail or workhouse; often a prison farm or poor farm in rural areas.

Course note. (Carnival) Paper money, except one- and two-dollar bills. "What a boodle (large amount of money) that mark (victim) had! All course notes too!"

Cover. 1. A hideaway; protection. 2. Body-shielding by pickpocket's aide, usually with outspread newspaper, hanging on a subway strap so as to obscure view, etc. "Give me plenty cover when I put the duke down (reach into the victim's pocket)."

Cover-car. An automobile driven as a shield behind the escape-car used by criminals; a car used to pick up criminals when the escape-car is abandoned.

Cover the duke. To aid a pickpocket by shielding his operations from view. "Port britch (left side trousers pocket), Joe; cover the duke."

Cover up. 1. To conceal, especially something of which one is ashamed, or an act which might prove incriminating. 2. To mask the features in whole or in part. "Cover up on this caper (robbery). We can't have our muggs (faces) made (examined for future identification)."

Cowboy, n. A thief who operates in Wild West tradition; a reckless thief; a thief who flourishes weapons or assaults victims unnecessarily. "Them lousy cowboys, only punk kids breaking their cherry (operating for the first time) on the heist (holdup), burned up (overworked) this town."

Cowboy, v. To operate in the manner of a **cowboy.**

Cow-simple. Adolescently girl-crazy.

C-pusher. A peddler of cocaine. "Them C-pushers take a fall (get arrested) and pull a nice soft g-bit (serve an easy sentence in Federal prison)."

Crab. 1. To interfere with or jeopardize another's plan or action; to **rank.** 2. To bungle or defeat one's own criminal ends. "I picked the wrong dame to stall (act as decoy) for us, shaking (extorting money from) that rabbit-snatcher (abortionist), and the trick was crabbed."

Crab a play. See **Crab.**

Crabs. 1. (P) Affliction with crab-like body-lice, especially in hypogastric areas. 2. Anything so valueless as to be irritating; nothing; **pretzels.** "The heavy (safe-cracking) ain't no good no more. It's a ball-breaker (discouraging thing) knocking off (robbing) keisters (safes) and getting crabs for your end (share)."

Crack, n. 1. Any pointed verbal thrust of a sarcastic or insulting nature. 2. A phrase, pregnant with private meaning, woven into apparently innocent conversation between confidence men in the presence of their intended dupe; any similar phrase directed toward the dupe to impress, frighten, or otherwise sway him. 3. A remark, especially an unguarded utterance. "Nix (lay off)

the cracks. There's a hip ghee (wide-awake citizen) at your pratt (behind you)."

Crack, v. 1. To talk freely. 2. To dynamite or rip a safe open. 3. To make an opening remark that forces one to proceed with the crime or to take flight. 4. To talk. 5. To say anything suggesting more than the actual words denote. "I think this dude (fellow) pulled a bit (served a prison term) with me. Crack in the lingo (jargon) and see if he springs (makes any sign of recognition)."

Crack a crib. 1. To break into a safe. 2. To break into a building, apartment, or room for the purpose of robbery.

Crack business. To make verbal overtures as a prelude to striking a bargain with venal authorities.

Cracker box. 1. A small county jail from which escape is easy. 2. A safe or strongbox easily cracked by any safe-cracker.

Crack one's jaw. (Penn. and environs; mid-West; near South) To talk boastfully; to bluster. "You better skid (get rid of) that partner of yours. He's cracking his jaw about every trick you turn (theft you commit)."

Crack out. (P) To escape feloniously from a jail, reformatory, or prison. "Three new mickeys (newcomers) clipped (assaulted) a screw (guard) and cracked out. That's the wire (rumor) I got."

Cramper. (P) A quick, gouging blow on the arm or leg muscle.

Crap. 1. Anything valueless, or nearly valueless. 2. Lies. 3. Any contemptible word or action. "I don't chill (become frightened) from that bad-eye (baleful look) crap. That crumb must think I'm a soft touch (easy mark)."

Crap merchant. A liar; a persuasive talker who lies for profit.

Crapper. A toilet. ("In the crapper" —lost; hopeless; profitless.) "We wound up in the crapper on that touch (robbery), and the steerer (tipster) figured we'd score for (make) a G (thousand dollars) a head (apiece)."

Crapper-dick. A detective who hunts rest-room perverts; an extortionist who victimizes rest-room perverts. "There's a good buck (large sum) in posing as a crapper-dick and shaking down (extorting money from) fags (perverts)."

Crash. 1. To enter premises fraudulently or by force; to break into premises. 2. To enter uninvited, especially to rob or make plans for robbery. "Crash that slum-peddlers' (jewelry salesmen's) racket (party) and get the lay (survey the place). With their broads (women) there, it oughta be a nice heist (holdup)."

Crasher. A house or flat burglar.

Crash in. See **Crash.**

Crash out. (P) 1. To force an exit. 2. To escape prison from inside the walls. "Stop crying (complaining); either hang up (commit suicide) or crash out."

Crate. An automobile, especially a stolen automobile. "Stash (hide) that crate till the heat is off (the police lose interest)."

Crater. See **Pull a crater.**

Crawl. To act cravenly; to plead abjectly; to humble oneself. "I'm hustling (stealing) in this part of town even if that combo (syndicate) has a license (bought immunity). I ain't crawling for nobody."

Crawler. (South) A railroad train.

Crawl out. To slip out of any predicament without regard for principle or self-respect in so doing; to exhibit cowardice; to fail in one's commitments.

Creed. Bogus credentials, especially copies of Federal agents' pocket commissions. "On the shake (extortion) you should never give the suckers a flash of the tin (badge) unless you got to. Spring with (produce) the creed if they get snorky (belligerent or skeptical)."

Creep. 1. Any despicable person; a robber of drunkards; a prostitute working in a **creep-joint;** an informer; a pervert. 2. A petty thief, especially a **door-matter,** one who steals clothing from clotheslines, etc. 3. (P) A contemptible guard or convict.

Creep-joint. 1. A brothel where patrons' clothes are ransacked of valuables through a hinged or sliding panel in the clothes closet. 2. A floating craps, card, or roulette game. 3. A **flop-house;** a prison abounding in **creeps.** "I never pulled a bit (served a term) in a worse creep-joint than this can (prison)."

Crib. 1. A vault, safe, or strong-box. 2. A house of prostitution; one of a row of shuttered or curtained booths in brazenly open prostitution districts. 3. (Rare) One's living quarters; an apartment. 4. (Scattered South, Central and mid-Western U. S.) A petty thief. "That crib spent half his life in lag (prison)."

Crib-man. A safecracker.

Crime school. (P) A reformatory or any juvenile protectory. "Joe Socks hit the big house (state prison) two months after he sprung from (was released from) crime school."

Crimp, n. 1. (Western and Central U. S. prisons) A formal report for rule violation. 2. (Western and Central U. S. prisons) A prison guard; an informer. 3. (Western and Central U. S. prisons) An arrest; a conviction; a prison sentence; a denial of parole application. 4. A failure in criminal operation; deliberate or accidental interference with another's criminal plan of action. 5. A bend in part of a deck of playing cards, terminating a crooked shuffle, to cause a cut at the point desired.

Crimp, v. 1. (Western and Central U. S. prisons) To report a convict for rule violation; to inform on a fellow convict. 2. (Western and Central U. S. prisons) To arrest; to convict; to sentence to prison; to deny parole application. 3. To fail in a criminal plan or cause the failure of another's plan. 4. To end a crooked shuffle of playing cards by bending the deck to the point at which the cut is desired. If the player cutting the cards thwarts the plan, one of the swindlers exposes a card deliberately, thus causing a new deal.

Crimpers. See **Zingers.**

Crip. (N. Y. Catholic Protectory) A crippled person.

Croak. 1. To die. 2. To kill a person. "Imagine that crumb (contemptible fellow). He croaked eleven ghees (persons) and now he's ratting (informing) to save his keister (literally, buttocks; figuratively, life)."

Croaker. A physician or surgeon. "We heisted (held up) the croaker and made him cut the slug (bullet) out of Spider's leg."

Crooked. Legally executed by hanging.

Crooked letter. (P) A letter smuggled out of prison in avoidance of censorship.

Cross, the. A betrayal; a double-cross; an act of treachery. "I gave that flea (contemptible fellow) his first in in (introduction to) the racket and now that I'm in a jackpot (trouble), he puts the cross on me."

Cross-fire, n. The bewildering medley of talk and action with which confidence swindlers rob a victim. "The hoosier (victim) wouldn't go till we threw the cross-fire on so heavy he didn't know what the score was (what was going on)."

Cross-fire, v. To subject to the **cross-fire.**

Cross the road. To leave town, especially as a fugitive from justice.

Cross up. See **Cross.**

Cruise, n. (West and Pacific Coast) A male oral sodomist who makes street pickups. "That cruise we robbed looked like a bum but he went for four C's

(four hundred dollars) on the shake (extortion)."

Cruise, v. (West and Pacific Coast) To walk the streets seeking to rob **cruises.** "Let's cruise West Lake Park for a score."

Cruller. The head.

Crum or **Crumb.** Any vulgar or contemptible person; a wretch; a dirty person; a body-louse; a hobo's roll of bedding and belongings.

Crumb a deal. To bungle a plan. "I knew that jerk would crumb the deal. He sprung (produced) the business (gun) before we took our spots (positions)."

Crumb-joint. 1. An establishment that is **wrong** according to underworld standards, such as one catering to informers, policemen, perverts, etc., and hostile to thieves and gangsters. 2. A dirty lodging house, jail or other establishment. 3. (P) Any prison in which privileges are few, enjoyed chiefly by informers and perverts, where the underworld caste system goes wholly unrecognized. "I gotta make a boat (secure a transfer) out of this crumbjoint to a connection can (prison where money and influence count). A ghee that's got a buck (has money) or a rep (underworld reputation) can't get a flop (recognition) from these screws (prison guards)."

Crumb up. To boil or otherwise disinfect, as verminous clothing; **louse up.**

Crummy, n. 1. A hobo's roll of bedding, utensils, etc. 2. A local lock-up, police station, or workhouse. "Thirty days in that crummy is worse than a treyer (three years) in the big house (state prison)."

Crummy, a. 1. Dirty; infested with lice. 2. Disloyal; unprincipled; despicable. 3. Ridden with contemptible people. 4. Characterized by a lack of wealth or profitable criminal opportunities; infested with police. "This is a crummy town to grift (steal). You can't hit the stem (main street) without getting a pickup (arrest on suspicion)."

Crush out. See **Crash out.**

Cubes. Morphine tablets. "You crumbs (good-for-nothings) can have that kind of dough shoving (selling) cubes to punks (kids). I'd sooner rot in stir (prison) for heist (hold-up operations)."

Cuff, n. 1. Postponement of payment. ("To put on the cuff"—to charge.) 2. A verbal promise to pay. 3. The act of swindling an installment house. 3. (Pl.) Handcuffs or manacles. ("To go out in cuffs"—to leave prison in custody on a pending warrant.)

Cuff, v. 1. To defer payment, usually with no intention of paying; to take on credit by force or intimidation. 2. To give a verbal promise to pay. 3. To swindle, especially installment houses. 4. To handcuff. "Me and Jimmy-run-'em-dizzy snatched the slum-poke (jeweler's wallet) and cuffed the dude (fellow) to a tree."

Curtains. A tragic end; a final crushing of hope; the end. "Jiggers (look out), Flip, the street is lousy with law (policemen) and the out (means of escape) is blocked. Looks like curtains."

C-user. A cocaine addict. "Watch that ghee (fellow). Them c-users are plenty wrong (not to be trusted)."

Cush. (Obsolete, except in rural South) Money, especially a bribe, loot, or other "easy" money.

Cushions. (Chiefly Hobo) Seats in passenger cars, in contrast to perches on freight and baggage cars. ("To ride the cushions"—to pay one's fare; to live in comparative luxury.)

Cut, n. A share. "Get up my cut of the take (receipts), or your joint (establishment) folds (closes)."

Cut, v. 1. To adulterate, as a drug or whiskey. 2. To assault with a knife or other edged weapon. 3. To assess every

player whose turn it is to roll the dice in craps.

Cut a new kisser for one. To cut or slash the face with a knife or other edged weapon. "I'm cutting that fink (informer) a new kisser when I duke him in (lead him) to the right spot."

Cut cake. To practice any of the various short-change swindles.

Cut-deck. Adulterated morphine or heroin mixed with powdered milk.

Cut in. 1. To use force or the implied threat of force. 2. To include in a crime or racket because of one's connections or underworld prestige. "We got too many ends (shares) comin' out of the take (receipts) now, but we gotta cut Louie in. He's got wires (connections)."

Cut it up. See **Cut up touches.**

Cutor. Twenty-five cents; a quarter. "A million-dollar front (appearance), and the crumb (louse) ain't got a cutor."

Cut out. 1. (P) To leave prison, by parole or discharge. 2. To leave; to depart. 3. To declare oneself out, as of a crime or racket. "I'm cuttin' out of this caper (theft). I'm all caught up (risking too big a penalty)."

Cutter. (South; scattered Western areas) The prosecuting attorney. "That cutter can make a bum rap (false charge) stick, Sam; better cop a plea (plead guilty to lesser offense)."

Cutting-match. A fight with knives, razors or similar weapons; an assault with a **chiv.**

Cut to the breaks. (Far West area) Characterized by a minimum of talk and action; cut down to bare essentials; simple. "Me and a dick (detective) that got broke (discharged) for a shake (extortion) were working with the button (police badge) on the cruises (extorting from oral male sodomists). The play was cut to the breaks and we scored (robbed) a dozen a day."

Cut up a touch. 1. To converse; to tell stories, especially of underworld exploits. 2. To divide the loot from a specific crime. "A swag (lot) of dudes (fellows) were looking for a piece (share), but Tuttie and me cut up the touch alone."

Cut up jackies or **jackpots. See Cut up touches.**

Cut up touches. To exchange tales of one's criminal exploits; to talk; to gossip. "Them stiffs (bums) mooch (beg) coffee-and dough (snack money) and sit around cutting up touches about other people's scores (thefts)."

Cycle. See Cannonball Peter.

D

D. A. 1. The District Attorney or his office; any prosecuting attorney. 2. A drug addict.

Daddy (one's). (P) The active pederast in unnatural sexual relations. (Often used humorously) "You smoke my tobacco, hit me with your work and duke me in (lead me into) your swindles (difficulties). What am I, your daddy or something?"

Daisy-chain. See **Circus.**

Damper. 1. A cash register; a money-drawer. 2. (Rare) A jail or prison. 3. A bank. "Case (survey) that damper. It looks like a pushover for a heist (holdup)."

Damper-mob. A gang of thieves preying on banks or on victims selected by spotters stationed in banks.

Damper-pad. 1. A bankbook. 2. A checkbook. "That scratch-mob (forgery gang) must have beat (robbed) me for my damper-pad. I'll phone the jug (bank)."

Dance. 1. To move quickly on orders of armed robbers. 2. To be executed by hanging. 3. To spend the last twenty-four hours in the pre-execution cells, usually pacing nervously to and fro.

Dance Hall, the. (P) The wing in which condemned men spend their last few hours. [Note: Erroneously used synonymously with "death-house."]

Dance hall pimp. A loafer who frequents cheap dance halls and lives wholly or partly on the earnings of taxi-dancers.

Dancing. (P) Nervous with anticipation, having served all but a few days of one's prison term. "Three days and a get-up (day of release)! Man, I'm dancing now!"

Dangler. 1. Any piece of jewelry that dangles free, as a watch-fob, earring, pendant, etc. 2. A freight train.

Dan-O'Leary, on the. (Irish-American) In flight; on the heel-and-toe. "We were making the in (entrance) to that slum-joint (jewelry store) when some crumb (busybody) rumbled (noticed) us and started beefing (calling for police). We took it on the Dan-O'Leary fast."

Dark-cell. (P) In some prisons, a small, ill-ventilated, lightless cell used for punishment and psychopathic observation. "Fritz broke up (wrecked his cell) last night. They got him in the dark-cell waiting for the bug doctor (psychiatrist) to gander (look) him over. If he ain't nuts, that joint will shove him over the line (drive him insane)."

Daub. A color compound, usually kept under the thumbnail, to mark playing cards for cheating during the game.

Dauber. One who paints stolen cars to efface identity.

Daub of the brush. 1. The act of sexual intercourse. 2. (P) The active pederastic act.

D. D. a. Deaf and dumb; loyal to the underworld code.

D. D., v. (Rare) Shut up; don't admit anything; stop talking.

Dead-bang. Red-handed; in the act.

Dead-banger. An arrest in the act, or with ample evidence to convict. "Rubberhead Gordon got a dead-banger on a heist (holdup) down in Philly."

Dead-bang fall or **rap.** See **Dead-banger.**

Dead-bang to rights. See **Dead-bang.**

Dead cert (dead certain). A race-track gambler's term for a horse certain to win, i.e., a "favorite."

Deadhead. 1. (Hobo) An empty train. 2. A useless fellow.

Deadlock, n. (P) A report or lock-up for rule violation.

Deadlock, v. (P) To lock in a cell for punishment.

Dead pigeon. Anyone facing certain punishment, defeat, etc.; one in a hopeless position.

Dead ringer. Anyone bearing a startling resemblance to another; a perfect duplicate.

Dead spit. (abbreviation of "dead spitting image") See **Dead ringer.**

Deal, n. A severe beating; a **third degree** ordeal. 2. A criminal act or plan. 3. Any injustice, fancied or real. "The rapper (complainant) couldn't make (recognize) me, but the beef (charge) stuck. I sure got a deal."

Deal, v. To give one a **deal.**

Death-house . . . (coupled with surname). A common appellation for a district attorney with a long record of convictions resulting in capital punishment; a defense attorney whose cases often result in a sentence of capital punishment. "Death-House Morrisey lost another one. He must be getting a cut (share of the fee) from the ghee that throws the switch (electrocutioner)."

Deck, 1. A measure of any drug, ranging from 10 grains to one ounce, such as morphine, heroin, or cocaine. 2. (Hobo) The top of a freight or passenger train. ("To ride the deck.") 3. The table. "Keep your dukes (hands) on the deck while I'm tossing the broads (dealing in three-card monte). If this sucker hips up (discovers he's being cheated), put the slug on (hit) him and we'll take a powder (flee)."

Deck-hand. A domestic servant, especially a cook or scullery maid.

Declare in. See **Cut in.**

Declare oneself. To state one's rights emphatically, implying readiness to back them up with force.

Declare out. To declare oneself or another out of a crime, racket, gang, etc.

Degenerate. (Eastern carnival) A fool; **sucker;** that is, any customer or prospective swindle victim. "Mooch (walk) down in the tip (crowd) and get that degenerate's line (cash)."

Demier. ("deemer" or "dimer") A dime; ten cents. "We went for (spent) a C (hundred dollars) readying up (preparing) that mark (prospective victim) and didn't clip (rob) him for a demier."

Den. 1. (P) A cell. 2. An opium parlor. "Rocky's up in the den kicking the gong around (smoking opium)."

Dep. 1. (P) The deputy warden; principal keeper. 2. (Sing Sing Prison) A deputy sergeant-at-arms in the now emasculated Mutual Welfare League, self-governing inmate body. These inmates now serve as glorified monitors or assistant guards inside the walls. They are held in contempt by their fellow prisoners.

Depression bum. (P) A professional's term of contempt for an amateur criminal; anyone who has turned to crime under the pressure of economic reverses.

Dep's box. (P) A locked, slotted box in a prison cell-hall into which inmates slip requests for interviews or job assignments, as well as notes informing against fellow-inmates and guards. "Hey, Gabby, take a gander (look) at this tab (note) before I slap it in the Dep's box. You'll spread it all over the joint. So if anyone gets buried (locked up), they'll know I ain't the fink (informer) that put the finger on 'em."

Dep's man. (P) A convict assigned to his job, especially as a trusty, by the deputy warden; an informer who makes a habit of squealing only to the deputy warden. [Note: Wardens, principal keepers, and minor officials usually have their own personal informers. They are useful in internal administrative politics as well as in the running of the prison.]

Derrick. A shoplifter; a **booster.**

Deuce. 1. Two dollars. 2. A two-year prison term. "Bits (prison terms) was tough in the old days, but you got a deuce then where you get hit with a sawbuck (ten years) now."

Deuce of clubs. See **Play the deuce of clubs.**

Devil-dodger. A clergyman.

Dice-hustler. One who operates floating craps games as a means of swindling victims.

Dicer. A hat.

Dick. 1. The penis. 2. ("Yard dick") A railroad policeman. 3. A detective; (loosely) any policeman. "I didn't know I was putting the prowl on (burglarizing) a dick's flat till I found the tin (badge) and biscuit (revolver)."

Diddler. 1. One who impairs the morals of minors; a sex degenerate. 2. A masturbator.

Die. (Rare) To leave the underworld.

Difference. A pistol, revolver, or any weapon used in crimes of violence. "Don't spring (exhibit) the difference on this score (theft) until everyone's at his spot (post)."

Dig, n. An unskilled pickpocket.

Dig, v. 1. To stab or slash. 2. To pick pockets crudely.

Dig a hole. (P) To find a way of escape. (A frequent half-humorous retort when a convict complains that he is serving a long term.) "What! You brought (came to prison with) a double-sawbuck (twenty years)! Dig that hole."

Dig deep! Ominous warning to pay blackmail, extortion sums, or a gambling debt; or to hand over a portion of the loot believed withheld. "Come on! Dig deep! I don't go for that burning (withholding loot) crap (nonsense)."

Digger. A crude pickpocket; a **dig.**

Dig up on. To re-investigate the criminal record of anyone to revive a long-pending charge, or discover a concealed past to justify increased punishment. "I'm trying to get vagged (commited for vagrancy) for a few (short term) so they won't dig up on me."

Dillinger. Any brazen act of banditry or prison escape by combined bluff and force, in the manner of the once notorious John Dillinger. ("To pull a Dillinger"—to operate recklessly.)

Dimmer. An electric light; a flashlight. "Choke (put out) that dimmer, Slim, this window's on the stem (facing the street)."

Dinah. Dynamite; **soup.** "That's a tough keister (safe), but good old dinah will take it."

Dincher. A cigarette butt, usually one that has been smoked more than once, a **clincher;** a **snipe.**

Ding, n. See **Ding-dong.**

Ding, v. 1. To beg on busy thoroughfares. 2. To make a pretense of begging in order to distract a victim's attention while an accomplice commits a sneak-thievery. "Ding that mark (fool) while I snatch (seize) the turkey (bag)."

Dingaling. (Pacific Coast prisons) A convict softened mentally by imprisonment.

Dingbat. 1. A fool; a worthless fellow. 2. (Among mendicants) An effective house-to-house beggar of food, scorned by money-beggars.

Ding-dong. (Hobo) A panhandler.

Ding-donger. A hard-striving and successful thief or mendicant.

Dinger. 1. An old-fashioned burglary alarm bell, once used outside banks, shops, etc. 2. (Rare) Cash register. 3. A bell or bell-like sound. 4. A panhandler, or a thief's aid who pretends to beg. 5. See **Wing-ding,** n.

Dinghe. 1. A Negro, especially one of light-colored skin. 2. (South; Middle Atlantic States except New York) Any ill-lighted pool hall, back-room, etc. which is used as a thieves' rendezvous. "The bulls (police) crashed (raided) the dinghe on Vine Street and gave 'em a frisk (search). They're gonna vag (commit for vagrancy) Tex and the mob."

Dinner burglar. See **Shacker.**

Dinner burglary. See **Shack, on the.**

Dinner-pailer. A workingman.

Dip, n. (Obsolete) A pickpocket.

Dip, on the. (Obsolete) Engaged in, or by means of, pocket-picking.

Dipsy. (In many county jails) One sentenced to a workhouse term as differentiated from those awaiting serious charges.

Dirk. A knife or any similar weapon. "Funny how ghees (fellows) that ain't afraid of a roscoe (gun) chill (are frightened) when they see a dirk."

Dish out. 1. (P) To pour out too lavishly, especially undesirable things, as abuse, lies, work, etc. 2. To impose, as punishment, in a prison or criminal court.

Distance ghee. A thief who likes "safe" assignments, as far from the center of action as possible. "I don't want no part of that distance ghee. He wants to lay zex (stand lookout) in Chi (Chicago) when we're on a score (theft) in the big town (New York)."

Ditch. 1. To leave in the lurch; especially, to flee and abandon accomplices at a critical moment. [This is the most common sin of omission of "lookouts" and drivers of automobiles for criminals.] 2. To get rid of; to dispose of anyone or anything that endangers one's security or proves annoying.

Ditch the leather. To get rid of an emptied wallet picked from a victim's pocket. "Ditch the leather quick. The mark (victim) is fanning himself (feeling for his wallet)."

Dive. To place one's hand in a victim's pocket. 'Put his back up (jostle him into position), Sam, and I'll dive."

Diver. One who robs drunkards.

Divvy, n. (Juvenile and obsolete) A share, especially of loot.

Divvy, v. (Juvenile and obsolete) To divide, especially loot.

Do a bit. To serve a prison or jail sentence. "After I do this bit I'm beating it out of this State. They hit you with too much time (impose too severe sentences) for mopery raps (trivial charges)."

Do a bit on one leg. (P) To serve a light and easy prison term.

Do a bit with one's shoes on. See **Do a bit on one leg.**

Do a chunk. To serve a prison sentence, especially a long term.

Do a crouch. To remain in concealment. "The bulls (police) are hot on your pratt (in close pursuit). Do a crouch, Joe."

Do a hitch, a jolt or a piece. See **Do a bit.**

Do a solo. To confess a crime, implicating one's accomplices. "That fink (informer) did a solo in a knock-off (murder) rap and burned his partners (sent them to death in the electric chair)."

Do a stretch. See **Do a bit.**

Dobey. (Carnival) Anything very remarkable. "Take a gander (look) at that gimmick (crooked device) on that wheel (gaming wheel). Ain't that a dobey!"

Do business. 1. To inform on underworld associates, or give a cash bribe in exchange for leniency. 2. To bargain, when arrested, offering to save the State the expense of a trial if permitted to plead guilty to a lesser offence. "Tell my mouthpiece (lawyer) I'll do business with the D. A. But I ain't copping out (pleading guilty) unless it's a low plea (greatly reduced charge)."

Doctor. To tamper with; to inject ether or alcohol into beer; to cut whiskey or drugs; to alter checks, bonds, currency denominations, etc. fraudulently; to mark playing cards; to load dice; to alter the appearance of anything for the purpose of fraud.

Dodge. A racket; any shady means of livelihood.

Dodger. A handbill for a wanted criminal.

Dog, n. 1. A cowardly or unprincipled person. 2. (P) An extremely harsh or brutal prison official. 3. A disloyal woman; a homely woman. 4. A venereal disease, especially syphilis. "Getting a bite of the old dog (syphilis) started that kid on the heist (holdup). He had to pay croakers (doctors) that wouldn't beef (report) to his people."

Dog, v. To follow; to pursue; to trail. "What's this, a tail? That crate's (automobile's) been dogging us for ten minutes."

Dog-house. A private garage used as a temporary hiding-place for stolen cars. "Stash (conceal) the crate (car) in the dog-house before we have the coppers on our pratts (on our trails)."

Dog it. To exhibit cowardice; to inform under police pressure; to retreat. "Every collar (arrest) that flea ever got he dogged it and spilled his guts (informed to the police)."

Doing handy. Doing all right; working the "angles" of prison or of underworld life successfully. "I should have been born a fink (informer). They're all doing handy in the can (prison) and on the street (outside of prison)."

Do it all. 1. (P) To serve the maximum term, with no **good time** off for good behavior. 2. To serve a life sentence.

Do-little. A thief who poses as a repairer of fountain pens which he never returns.

Doll. A pretty girl.

Dolly sisters. Two uniformed policemen in P. D. car. "The dolly sisters tried to pull us over for a fan (search for weapons), but we copped a mope (escaped)."

Dommo. (P) A prison dormitory.

Doniker. (Carnival) Toilet. ("Wind up in the doniker"—finish anything in utter ruin or failure.)

Doodley, n. (Carnival) Nothing. "A million-dollar cross-fire (high-pressure talk) wasted on that mark, and we wind up with doodley for our end (reward)."

Door-matter. A very petty thief, as one who would steal a door mat. "Oh, you phony door-matters are always cutting up G-note touches (boasting of thousand-dollar gains) and you ain't never seen a double-sawbuck (twenty dollars)."

Door-shaker. A watchman or policeman who tries the doors of locked shops, etc.

Dope. 1. Information. 2. A fool. 3. Narcotics.

Do penance. 1. (Rare) To serve a prison term. 2. (P) To serve time in the punishment cells; or, additional time for rule violation.

D. O. R. (Abbreviation of "discharged on own recognizance") An agreement on record to keep the peace or to appear in court when summoned. "That ghee has some good wires (connections). He got knocked off (arrested) for a shake (extortion) and scored for a D. O. R."

Dose. A venereal infection.

Dose up. To infect with a venereal disease.

Do sleeping time. (P) To serve a very short sentence.

Do soft time. (P) To serve a prison term under very easy conditions.

Doss. Sleep; a bed; a bedroom.

Doss-house. A lodginghouse; a local jail where vagrants may sleep overnight.

Do the rosary. (P) To serve a life term.

Do time. To serve a prison sentence.

Do tough time. (P) To serve a prison term under severe conditions.

Double. A duplicate key, usually

made from an impression taken of tumblers by coating a blank key with paraffin and gently turning it; **screw.** "Get a double made of that screw (key), and we'll prowl (burglarize) the joint."

Double-bank, n. The act of double-banking.

Double-bank, v. To double-cross; to assault an unsuspecting victim. "As soon as I belted (hit) this mug (fellow), three strange weeds (strangers) double-banked me and kicked my lemon (head) in."

Double-barreled. Skilled in degeneracy, especially applied to loose women.

Double-insider. (Pickpocket usage) A pocket inside the vest or shirt.

Double-life. (P) Two life sentences to run consecutively, often imposed to insure against parole. "The judge bugged up (became angry) because I wouldn't cop a plea (plead guilty) to a bum rap (false charge) and he hit me with double-life."

Double-O. 1. A thorough and careful examination. 2. (New York Catholic Protectory) A very close haircut.

Double-saw. 1. Twenty dollars. 2. A prison sentence of twenty years. "Pretty Mouth's mouthpiece (lawyer) wants him to cop out (plead guilty) and settle for a double-saw, but he's going to bat (to stand trial)."

Double-sawbuck or **-sawski.** See **Double-saw.**

Double-talk. An admixture of pig-latin, underworld jargon, and other lingo by which carnival pickpockets, confidence men, and other nefarious operators talk in a patter unintelligible to others. "That j.c.l. (Johnny-come-lately) don't savvy (understand) the double-talk. The fuzz (police) are gonna collar (arrest) him."

Double-willie. (Carnival) Two chances for the price of one at a carnival game, offered as an inducement. "It's time to heat up the tip (stir up the crowd); spring with double-willie."

Double with. 1. To join in criminal partnership with. 2. To live with, with or without the benefit of marriage.

Douche-bag. A term of utmost contempt for a woman.

Dough. Money.

Doughnut. An automobile tire.

Douse. To put out, as a light. "Douse the glim, Turk."

Downtown. (In most of our metropolitan centers) Police Headquarters; Court of General Sessions; Supreme Court. "The rapper (complainant) pegged (identified) me in Magistrate's Court so I was held over for downtown."

Dozens. See **Play the dozens.**

Draft, n. (P) A transfer of inmates from one prison to another.

Draft, v. (P) To include an inmate in a **draft.**

Drag. 1. A street, avenue or road. 2. A dance, a party, or other affair featuring **fags** serving as "hostesses." 3. (Hobo) A slow freight train. 4. A man in feminine attire; feminine attire worn by a **fag.**

Drag, cop a. To smoke a cigarette.

Dragnet. A police roundup of known criminals.

Draw, n. A reasonable sentence; a suspension of sentence. "We had to get up two G's (two thousand dollars) to pull a wire (employ influence) but a draw was worth it."

Draw, v. To receive by chance, as an acquittal, a prison sentence, etc. "Me and Jim crashed the joint and drew a blank (nothing of value) for our end (share)."

Draw a bloomer. To select a site or victim for robbery which brings little or no loot; to make a mistake. "I planted (hid) the swag (loot) of meat with some square (honest-minded fellow) in the shoe shop. I sure drew a bloomer, too; he hollered (reported me) and gave it to the man (officer)."

Draw heat. To attract police attention, as by the use of conspicuous clothes or cars, or by one's crude criminal acts. "Keep them noisy pigs (girls of low character) away from the drop (hide-out). They draw too much heat."

Dream gum. Opium.

Dreams. Opium pellets for opium eating.

Dream wax. See **Dream gum.**

Dreece. Three dollars; a three-year term of imprisonment; any group of three units of time or money.

Driers, to go to the. To be cheated or swindled of one's money. "A couple of mechanics (card-sharps) put the hustle on me with strippers (rim-shaved playing cards), and I sure went to the driers."

Driers, to take to the. To cheat or swindle of one's money by any fraudulent device, as in a crooked gambling game.

Drifter. An occasional thief; an out-of-town thief, unwelcome among local thieves with the **alzo;** an honest hobo who drifts from place to place. "Them drifters got this town red hot (alerted for criminals) clipping (robbing) the wrong people (influential citizens)."

Drill. 1. To wound or kill with firearms. 2. (South; scattered areas) To sentence to jail or prison. "I hear Moe Moonshine was drilled to a handful (five years)."

Drink. Any body of water, especially the ocean.

Drop, n. 1. An arrest. 2. Cache, usually temporary, for stolen goods or for the concealment of fugitives. "Stash (hide) the markers (counterfeit license plates) and boodle (loot) at the drop."

Drop, v. 1. To arrest; to be arrested. 2. To lose, as a criminal court case, an appeal, a game, a sum of money, etc. 3. To bring a person down with a blow, a bullet, etc. 4. To intercept, as a ran-

som note, a letter smuggled out of prison, a threatening letter, etc. 5. (P) To be reported for violation of rules. "Pebbles was dropped planting (hiding) some cabbage (contraband money) he got on a visit. The screws (guards) gave him a strip frisk (nude search)."

Drop a kite or **tab.** (P) 1. To intercept a letter about to be smuggled out of prison; or, pornographic pictures or books; or, homosexual "love notes." etc. 2. To write a note to the authorities, very often informing on a fellow prisoner or on a guard. "Drop this tab in the Dep's Box, will you? I feel funny putting it in with all those fleas (gossips) gapping (looking on), thinking I'm burying (informing upon) someone."

Drop-car. An automobile, usually stolen, to be used for a getaway before changing to the **pickup car.**

Drop-off or **Drop-joint.** 1. A temporary hide-out for stolen goods or **lamesters.** 2. The establishment of a buyer of stolen goods.

Dropper. A professional assassin.

Droppers. Knickerbockers; knee-breeches worn low on the waist-line, secured below the knees. [Note: Anyone wearing his trousers secured above the knees is a **wrong-ghee.**] "That punk (passive pederast) is gonna get flipped (knocked down) posing in them droppers (pretending to be **right**)."

Drop the chuck on. (East, except N. Y. and N. J.) To testify against, or otherwise aid the police in convicting, an associate.

Drop the duke. See **Put the duke down.**

Drop the net on. (P) (Usually in grim humor) To commit to an institution for criminally insane or mentally defective delinquents; to place in an observation cell. "The screws (guards) dropped the net on some new mickey (newcomer) this morning. He came out naked with his belt and a pair of cheaters (eyeglasses) on, lugging his bucket (slop pail)."

Drum. (Chiefly California prisons) A cell.

Dry, n. (Middle Atlantic States, except N. Y.) Bread-and-water diet in punishment cells. "Kansas City Red's in the hole (solitary confinement) on dry for digging (slashing) that rat (informer)."

Dry, v. To take all or most of one's money in gambling, or by swindling, etc. "That lush (fool) went for the come-on (bait) and we dried him for four bills (four hundred dollars)."

Dry, a. Without money, usually as a result of gambling or of having been swindled.

Dry combo. (Hobo) A piece of cake and a sandwich, as a handout in door-to-door begging.

Dry rub. (P) Body contact, in wrestling or "horseplay," patently homosexual.

Ducat. 1. (Carnival) Any ticket or check. 2. A dollar. 3. (In some prisons) A slip granting parole. 4. A warrant for one's arrest especially one pending against a prisoner serving a prison sentence on a previous charge. 5. A doctor's certificate asserting that the bearer is physically incapacitated. Bogus certificates are often used by panhandlers.

Duck. 1. To dodge or to avoid. 2. To flee precipitously; to slip away in secret. 3. (Imperative) Danger! Look out! Beware! 4. To conceal; to put out of sight. "Duck that gat (gun)! There's a gapper (bystander) rumbling (watching)."

Ducker, n. A Dodge automobile.

Duck-soup. Very easy, as a prison term, a robbery, etc.; very gullible, as a victim of crime, an inept gambler, etc.

Dude. A person; a fellow.

Due out. Scheduled for discharge or parole from place of confinement. "The

partner only got a treyer (three years). He's due out next month."

Duff, on the. In flight; in the act of moving farther away from any source of danger.

Duffy silencer. (Irish-American) A lead pipe, a baseball bat, or any similar blunt weapon. "The dude (fellow) pulled a chiv (knife), and they knocked his lemon (head) in with a duffy silencer."

Duke, n. 1. The hand. 2. (Pl.) The clenched fists. 3. A hand, in a game of cards. "I rung in (introduced) the strippers (playing cards shaved down for cheating) and gave everyone a duzey (wonder) of a duke with the sucker blowing his top (frantic) to hipe (up) the ante (stakes)."

Duke, v. To hand, usually surreptitiously. "Duke me the swag (loot), and I'll screw (leave)."

Dukee. 1. (Hobo) A handout of cold food, usually a sandwich, piece of pie, etc. 2. (California State prisons) A sandwich and a slice of pie.

Duke-in, n. An introduction; a come-on.

Duke in, v. 1. To introduce. 2. To ensnare in a swindle; to induce. "Duke the mark (victim) in easy, he's half hip (suspicious)."

Duke out. To get rid of; to declare out; to ease out. "Duke that ghee (fellow) out of the joint. I don't like the way he rides the earie (listens)."

Duker. A handshaker; a come-on man for a confidence swindle mob; a skilled lurer of swindle victims.

Duke's. (P) (Duke's Mixture tobacco) Tobacco for making cigarettes. [Note: In areas where "Bull Durham" is more popular, "Bull" is the equivalent term; "jack" is used in scattered areas.]

Dukester. A fist-fighter.

Dumb-gat. A pistol or revolver with silencer attached.

Dummy. 1. The penis. 2. (P) Bread.

Dummy up! Shut up! Don't talk! Feign innocence! "Dummy up, Pete! This ghee (fellow) ain't kosher (trustworthy)."

Dump, n. 1. An ideal site for leaving murder victims, stripped stolen cars, etc. 2. A railroad or subway station, or any place where crowds leave a common carrier, as pickpockets' field of operations. 3. A house or building, especially a run-down structure. 4. A buyer of stolen goods. 5. (P) Inmates' term of contempt for any penal establishment. 6. Any low-grade establishment; a **joint.**

Dump, v. 1. To dispose of, especially a murder victim; (by implication) to murder. 2. To inform or to testify against. 3. To withhold a portion of loot to defraud associates. 4. To assault; to knock down. 5. To rid oneself of, as incriminating evidence, an undesirable person, etc. 6. To abandon in a crisis. "Jack's partner dumped him, copped out (pleaded guilty) after the deal was to go to bat (stand trial) together."

Dumper. One who informs upon associates; one who withholds portions of loot, with intent to defraud associates; one who leaves accomplices without warning or means of escape when interrupted in crime; a traitor. "That kid brother of mine turned out to be a dumper. He spilled his guts (informed) on Icecart and he got me loused up (under suspicion) with some good people (underworld's best citizens)."

Dust, n. 1. Marijuana. 2. (P) Fine tobacco for hand-rolled cigarettes 3. Cocaine. "That broad (girl) is the best booster (shoplifter) on the turf (in the field). Too bad she blows (sniffs) dust."

Dust, v. 1. To take all or most of one's money. 2. To move on; to leave. 3. To become a fugitive from justice; to run away. "Three lifers dusted that can (prison) yesterday."

Duster. 1. ("a tear duster") A handkerchief. 2. A light sheet-metal door just inside the outer door of many safes. 3. A fugitive from justice; one who jumps bail, parole, or probation. 4. A chicken thief. 5. An expert at getting rid of undesirable persons. "This camp (flat) is loused up (full of undesirables); you're the duster, Tom, give 'em the skids."

Dust-off, n. A not very severe beating, especially in **third-degree** methods. "We gave that flea (petty informer) a dust-off that will keep him in line."

Dust off, v. 1. To administer a **dust-off** to. 2. To discourage or get rid of (undesirables), either by diplomacy or force.)

Dust out. To flee; to become a fugitive from justice. "You better dust out, Lou. I hear the bulls (police) have got a reader (wanted poster) out on you."

Duzey. (Carnival) Anything unusual. "This town is sure red (prosperous)! It's a duzey!"

Dyke. A lesbian.

Dynamite, n. Heroin; cocaine; also, a combination of cocaine and morphine.

Dynamite, a. Dangerous.

Dynamiter. 1. A cocaine addict. 2. A salesman of spurious stock, relatively crude in tactics. 3. (Prohibition era) A liquor salesman whose "buy-or-else" suggestions were consistently effective.

E

Eagle. A criminal who operates only on his own; a **lone wolf;** the act or practice of stealing on one's own, without accomplices. "Playing the eagle is smart stuff. No partners to burn (cheat) or bury (inform against) you"

Ear, on one. (P) Easily and untroubled, generally descriptive of a manner of serving a brief prison term. "I broke the year (started service of the last year) today. That eleven (months) and a wop (fraction of a year) I can pull (serve) on one ear."

Earie. 1. An eavesdropper. 2. The act of eavesdropping. "Zex (look out)! That dude (fellow) on the earie is working too hard (purposefully intent)."

Ears. (P) The stinging blow of snapped forefingers on eartips. [Frequently a forfeit in prison games.]

Easy. Gullible; susceptible; slow-witted; stupid.

Eat one's heart out. (P) To suffer; usually used in the imperative to silence a chronic complainer. "Beefing (complaining) again, bum? Eat your heart out, you sucker."

Edge. Exhilaration just short of drunkenness or narcotic stupor. 2. Advantage through fraud; a percentage, plus proceeds taken fraudulently, as in fixed horse-races, craps, card-games, etc.

Edgework. 1. Dice with rounded edges, easily manipulated in cheating. 2. Any curves, indentations, etc., along the rims of playing cards, easily felt and "read" by skilled cheats.

Eel. A slippery and unprincipled fellow.

Eight-wheeler. A thief who operates on railway freight cars.

El. (N. Y. State) The reformatory at Elmira, New York. "That bit (term) in the El hipped up (instructed) that kid to the wolves (active pederasts)."

Elbows. (Chiefly Central and Western U. S.) Plainclothes policemen, especially pickpocket-squad detectives working in crowds.

Electric cure. Capital punishment by electrocution.

Elephant ears. Any eavesdropper, especially a plainclothesman. "Dummy up (keep quiet), Ziggy, old elephant ears is flapping them (listening to you)."

Elevate. Hands up! [Note: The mark of swaggering amateurs. "Get 'em up" is more common.]

End. A share; a portion. "When the swaggie (buyer of loot) gets his, we'll wind up with peanuts (little) for our end."

Engine, the. The opium pipe and paraphernalia.

Eppis. (Yiddish-American) Something of inconsequential value; practically nothing. "You suckers go out tumuling (in strong-arm work) and packing a heater (carrying a gun), so you get eppis for your end (share) and maybe a long bit (sentence)."

Equalizer. A gun. "The parole dude (commissioner) asks me where I scored for (stole) the equalizer. He says, 'Don't tell me you found it in a garbage can. That story, I heard. Funny thing, I was just gonna spring with (offer) that gag (lie)."

Erie. Var. See **Earie.**

—Eroo. (P) A noun suffix indicating the superlative. "Bitcheroo"—extraordinarily remarkable person or thing; "Chumperoo"—a fool whose folly exceeds that of ordinary **chumps;** "Wackeroo"—an exceedingly stupid **whack.** [Note: Euphony alone limits the free addition of this suffix to all such nouns;

it is occasionally added to a proper noun to emphasize the warmth of a greeting, as, "Pateroo, old boy! What's hot on the turf (in the underworld)?"]

Ex-con. An ex-convict.

Ex-vic. (Very rare) An ex-convict. [Note: A variant of "ex-con" in the scattered areas in which a convict is termed a **vic.**]

Eye-wash. Tear gas.

F

Fade. 1. To cover the roller's bet in a craps game. 2. To move away casually. "Bulls (police), Ed, fade!"

Fade-out, n. An unobtrusive withdrawal from the scene ("to do a fade-out").

Fade out, v. To slip away unobtrusively.

Fading dice. Crooked dice which make it impossible for the roller to throw a winning number.

Fag. A passive homosexual, oral or pederastic.

Faggot. See **Fag.**

Faggoty. Of, like, or pertaining to **fags,** i. e., effeminate. "Who'd figure the faggoty sucker (victim) we picked to clip (rob) would turn out to be law (a policeman). I put the duke down (reached into his pocket) and felt the tin (badge), and I near blew my top (went insane with consternation)."

Fagin. An instructor of youth in crime.

Fag-joint. The residence or meeting place of **fags.**

Fairy. See **Fag.**

Faker. A confidence swindler.

Fall, n. An arrest; a sentence to prison; the specific charge against a suspect.

Fall, v. To be arrested; to be committed to prison. "You gotta fall some time, Bill. You ain't got no business hustling (stealing) if you don't figure on a bit (prison term)."

Fall dough. Money for legal fees, bail, etc. "All you smart guys wind up with no fall dough when you take a drop (arrest)."

Fall from. To be arrested at . . . (place name). "Where did that new fish (prison newcomer) fall from, Polack Town (Buffalo) ?"

Fall guy. 1. Any person, guilty or innocent, who takes full blame to shield others. 2. A fool; a bungling criminal; a stupid tool of crafty criminals. "These stirs (prisons) are full of fall guys and squares (accidental criminals). All the hip (smart) ghees (fellows) hit the counties (county jails) or the street (win acquittals or bribe their way out)."

False alarm. Any insincere or disloyal person. "That false alarm gave me a phony steer (wrong information) on a trick (robbery), and I nearly got a bit (sentence) for mopery (sheer stupidity)."

Family pimp. A loafer who lives with his parents and exists on what he "chisels" from them and others.

Fan, n. The act of **fanning.**

Fan, v. 1. To feel victim's pocket for money-bulge in pocket-picking. 2. To feel for one's purse, the involuntary reaction of a jostled person that tips pickpockets off to location of money. 3. To shoot a revolver rapid-fire fashion. The trigger is pressed and the hammer "fanned" with the heel of the left hand, or the thumb of the right hand. 4. To search for weapons, contraband, etc., by passing the hands over the outside of the clothing. "Unload if you're heeled (armed). They're fanning for chivs (knives)."

Farm. 1. (P) The prison farm. 2. See **Hot car farm.**

Faro bank. (Carnival) The process of letting swindle victims win at a crooked game often enough to keep interest high. "The sucker (victim) is chilling (losing interest); give him the faro bank and duke him back in (reawaken his interest)."

Fart around. To loaf; to waste motions and take unnecessary chances in committing crimes; to indulge in horseplay, or the like.

Fast burners. (P) Cigarettes that have been used as a medium of value for so long that they are no longer smokable, having become stale.

Fast one. 1. Any neat, swiftly executed piece of trickery. 2. A frame-up; any shady or biased court proceedings. "The D. A. gave me a fast one, rushed me to bat (trial) and duked in (had appointed) some stumble-bum of a State lawyer (court-appointed counsel)."

Father Time. (Rare) A criminal courts judge, especially one noted for imposing severe prison sentences. "I gotta go up and get my package (sentence) from old Father Time tomorrow, and there ain't no short-con (persuasive pleading) scoring with (influencing) him."

Fat lip. A bruised mouth resulting from a blow of the fist. ["To get a fat lip"—to receive a beating with the fists.]

Fed, n. Any United States Government agent or official. "The D. A. is dropping the State rap (charge) and he's turning me over to the feds."

Fed, a. Pertaining to United States Government jurisdiction.

Fed rap. A criminal charge in the jurisdiction of the United States Federal Courts.

Feeler. 1. (Rare) One who scouts for persons or places to be robbed by others. 2. Any indefinite word or act used to elicit information, or to sound out a prospective victim of crime. "Give that bull (policeman) that snared (caught) us a feeler. I think he'll do business (take a bribe)."

Feel out. To attempt to elicit information from. "I got a swag (loot) of stamps on a pete-job (safe-burglary). Feel out that cigar store ghee (man). Maybe I can unload (dispose of) them on him."

Fence, n. A buyer of stolen goods.

Fence, v. 1. To sell stolen goods to a professional receiver. 2. To buy stolen goods.

Fence blind. To sell stolen goods to an innocent buyer. "Stash (conceal) that swag (loot) till the heat's off and it'll fence blind for a nice buck (good price)."

Fence-jumper. 1. A renegade gangster who leaves one gang for a rival combination. 2. A part-time thief who works for a living between crimes. "Watch fence-jumpers like that creep. Most of them turn (become informers)."

Few, a. A very short sentence; as days, in a workhouse; months, in a county penitentiary; two or three years in a prison. "I hear that Russian Joe got a few (years) in a Maine stir (prison)."

Fib. (Pickpocket usage) The small watch-pocket in trousers.

Fib score. A theft from the small watch-pocket in trousers.

Fiddle. See **Violin.**

Fiddle-sticks. (Hobo) A railroad brakeman carrying a stick to prod oil-soaked waste in boxes housing axle hubs.

Field, play the. See **Play the field.**

Fiero. A pyromaniac.

Figary. n. A quiet retreat; a walk; an escape. ("To cop a figary"—to get away.) "I'm chilled (worried) on this caper (robbery), Jack; let's grab a figary."

Figure to go. To be apt to yield, as to a robbery, extortion, or other criminal pressure. "This mark (victim) figures to go for the boodle (money) without a beef (complaint)."

Fill. To agree to join a gang of which one is not a regular member in a specific criminal action. "I ran down the roads (tested the traffic lanes) and the out (means of escape) is tough. We gotta get a good wheelman (driver) to fill."

Fill a blanket. (P) To supply enough tobacco to roll a cigarette.

Fillin's. (mid-West and scattered areas) Tobacco for rolling cigarettes.

Fin. 1. Five dollars; a five-dollar bill. 2. The human hand. 3. Five years in prison. "That's one rough stir (prison). I pulled (served) a fin there."

Find a home. (Ironically) To be more comfortable in prison than in "free society." "You don't wanta make the board (obtain a parole), bum, you found a home."

Find an out. See **Out.**

Find in a hallway. To discover the body of a slain man. "You punks heisted (held up) some good people (underworld elite) in that joint of mine. Kick back (return the loot) and don't hold out a meg (cent) or you'll be found in a hallway."

Fin-flipper. A chronic handshaker; a "yes-man."

Finger, n. 1. (Comparatively rare) A plainclothesman disguised as a member of the underworld. 2. A stool-pigeon, especially an underworld member, who buys police immunity in exchange for valuable information; an informer. 3. One who points out victims to a hired killer, thief, or terrorist; the act of pointing out the intended victim. 4. The act of pointing out, naming, or revealing the whereabouts of one wanted by the police; formal identification of a suspect in the police line-up or court. "If it wasn't for a finger, I'd never fall (be arrested) on this rap (charge)."

Finger, v. 1. To point out, name, or reveal the whereabouts of one wanted by the police; to make formal identification of a suspect in a police line-up or in court. "The rapper (complainant) made (recognized) me and fingered me, so I grabbed a plea (pleaded guilty to a lesser offense)." 2. To point out a victim to a hired killer, a terrorist, thieves, etc. "That's the geepo (rat) that fingered Dutch when he got hit in the noggin (shot to death). He'll catch slugs (be murdered) himself yet."

Finger cold turkey. To inform brazenly on an accomplice, an underworld associate, or fellow convict. "The finks (informers) ain't undercover these days; they finger you cold turkey."

Fingerman. One who serves as a **finger**; one who points out victims to hired murderers, terrorists, or other criminals.

Finger-mob. Any gang of thieves enjoying police protection by bribery or by supplying valuable information; thieves having the **alzo** or **fix in**.

Finger's end. The **tipster's** share, usually ten per cent.

Finif. (Yiddish-American) See **Fin.**

Finish up. (P) To serve maximum sentence by order of Parole Board. "That Board (Parole Board) stinks. This ghee (fellow) got a dozen pinches (reports for rule violations) in the can (prison), and he springs (is released). I got none and them muzzlers make me finish up."

Fink, n. 1. A guard hired to protect strikebreakers; a scab or strikebreaker; a labor spy. 2. (Carnival) One who comes not to spend but to find cause for complaint to police. 3. (Mid-West prisons) A prison guard. 4. A stool pigeon; an informer. "You can't get around and promote anything (get stolen food and contraband) in this can (prison). The dump is crummy with finks."

Fink, v. 1. To inform; to confess and implicate others. 2. (P) To inform to prison authorities on fellow convicts. 3. (Carnival) To look for a reason to complain to the police, though one is not patronizing the games, as a non-spending busybody. 4. To protect strikebreakers; to work as a strikebreaker or as a labor spy.

Fink caper. 1. A petty theft. 2. A mean deed.

Firebug. A pyromaniac.

Fireman. (P) A convict who incites enmity among his fellow inmates; an agitator. [Note: Often a good-natured raillery.]

Fire-proofer. (mid-West and near-South) A confidence man who uses religious articles, or impersonates a clergyman, in order to swindle the devout.

Fire-proof peter. A seemingly strong safe which is merely fireproofed but can easily be broken by safe-crackers. "Don't let that fire-proof peter chill (awe) you. That's candy (easy to crack.")

Fireworks. Shooting; a gun-fight between rival gangs, or between police and thieves.

First baseman. Same as **Baseman.**

First-time loser. A first offender; one who has not previously been convicted of a felony.

Fish. 1. A dollar. 2. See **New fish, Relief,** and **Fish, one's.**

Fish-backs. Marked playing cards, especially those with a fish design on the backs which is easily marked.

Fish, one's. (Elmira Reformatory, N. Y., and scattered juvenile institutions) That convict whose number is exactly one thousand higher than one's own. [Note: When one's fish is dressed into prison, it is traditional for one to send him some small token of welcome, as a bar of chocolate or a package of cigarettes. The idea is that the sender is ready for release at just about the time of the arrival of his fish. One's fish symbolically prepares to take up the burden when the other is ready to put it down.] See synonym: **Relief, one's.**

Five-and-fifty-five (Italian-American) A single blow followed by rapid cuffs with the knuckles of the right hand, delivered backhand fashion, fist unclenched, hand semi-limp. This is a gesture of profound contempt, especially when done before onlookers. "The old zool (Italian) started to play the dozens (use abusive language) on me, so I gave him the five-and-fifty-five and spit in his eye."

Five spot, or Spotter. See **Fin.**

Fix, n. 1. An agreement, secured through bribery, chicanery, intimidation, whereby a criminal indictment is quashed, or the severity of a sentence or of a charge lessened. "The fix is in. Don't take no plea (plead guilty to a lesser offense). The worst you'll score for (get) is a draw (suspended sentence)." 2. Any arrangement by which laws, rules, or regulations are circumvented; or by which penalties are evaded; the **alzo.** "Mickey Mouse from uptown and his mob got a license (police permission) to hustle (steal) on the cannon (picking pockets) here. The fix is in solid."

Fix, v. To arrange a **fix.** "The copper won't take (accept a bribe), and the rapper (complainant) won't chill (be intimidated). If we can't fix this beef (complaint), someone's gotta be the fall guy (assume the guilt). It's murder!"

Fixer. Any political hanger-on, lawyer, bail bondsman, etc., who makes a business of **fixing** criminal cases.

Fix the fuzz with some soft. To pay a bribe to the police.

Flag, n. (Rare) An alias.

Flag, v. 1. To warn; to give a signal of any kind. 2. (Rare; scattered areas) To release from custody. 3. (Rare; among hobos) To allow an apparently good prospect for theft or panhandling to pass by unaccosted, frequently on a mere hunch. 4. To hail; to stop; to attract or divert attention. "Flag that crumb (rat) and stall him till I ease the swag (loot) out."

Flag down. To halt.

Flame-chair. (South; rare) An electric chair.

Flap. A loose woman.

Flash, n. 1. Anything designed to attract attention, as a window display, expensive jewelry. 2. Anything used to impress an intended victim. 3. A glance, as at credentials. 4. (Carnival) The stock of prizes exhibited at concession stands to lure the customer, who will receive a **larry** if he wins. 5. A flashlight. 6. A suit of clothes; an outfit. "Yeah, Alibi Al cut out (left) stir (prison) with a flash that looked like he rolled (robbed) a stiff (dead body) for it."

Flash, v. To bring into view with a ·flourish, or with calçulated deliberation, as a revolver, bogus credentials, a roll of banknotes, etc. "Don't flash your biscuits (guns) till I crack (give the word)."

Flash-dough. A roll of banknotes, often a wad of paper with a large note wrapped outside, used in confidence swindles to impress the victim.

Flash the button or tin. To exhibit a badge, genuine or counterfeit, of any law enforcement agent, especially in extortion rackets.

Flatback. (Deep South) A shotgun.

Flat bit. (P) A determinate prison sentence.

Flatfoot. A policeman; a detective; a **bull;** a **dick.**

Flat-joint. (Carnival) A gambling concession. "Kick the gimmick (crooked device for controlling the gaming wheel) off till the fuzz (police) take a powder and blow (leave) the flat-joint."

Flats. 1. Crooked dice. 2. (P) The ground floor of any cell-block.

Flatten. To knock down or out with a blow of the fist.

Flatten out. (mid-West and Central U.S.) To lie low until police activity subsides.

Flatty. See **Flatfoot.**

Flat-worker. A small-time burglar who robs flats and apartments when occupants are absent.

Flea. A petty informer; an unprincipled weakling.

Fleabag. 1. Any prison or jail where conditions are bad, rules severe, guards brutal, inmate informers and perverts given the best assignments. 2. A petty informer; an unprincipled weakling. 3. A dirty rooming house, hotel, jail, or prison. "You struck a home in this fleabag, crumb."

Flea-bitten. Treacherously disloyal.

Fleeper. A petty informer; an underworld "nobody"; a weakling. "What do you talk to them fleepers for? Chill (snub) them, or they'll louse you all up (ruin your reputation)."

Flier. Any risky, unplanned act; a desperate gamble; going to trial against overwhelming odds. "Taking a flier might get you hit with the book (the maximum term.) Chase that State mouthpiece (court-appointed lawyer) and grab a plea (plead guilty to a lesser offense)."

Flinch-bird. (Hobo; far-West) A male oral sodomist who seeks youths around missions and revival meetings.

Flip, v. To knock down by punching.

Flip, a. Flippant; belligerent; stubborn. "That creep always gets flip with dudes (fellows) that made the Board (were granted parole). He knows they can't stand to get in no swindles (get in trouble and endanger revocation of parole)."

Flipper. The hand or the arm.

Flit. (New England prisons) Weak prison coffee.

Float. To roam about aimlessly as a **floater.**

Floater. 1. A tramp or any petty thief who moves constantly from city to city; a vagabond. 2. An order to leave town within 24 or 48 hours or be sentenced for vagrancy. "We got a pick-up (arrest on suspicion) in a two-stemmer (big town) in Kansas. They couldn't pin a rap on us (place a formal criminal complaint) so they handed us a floater."

Flogger. An overcoat.

Flogger-stiff. An overcoat thief; (often extended contemptuously) any petty thief.

Floor-dick. A department store detective.

Floosie. 1. A loose woman. 2. A prostitute. "Some floosie that Flounderfoot Joe dusted off (spurned) fingered him (pointed him out to the police) on this rap (charge)." See **Flossie.**

Flop, n. 1. A sleep or rest; a cheap lodging place. "I didn't have scratch (money) enough for a flop so I got a mopery collar (foolish arrest) for carrying the banner (vagrancy)." 2. A sign of recognition, as when one is surprised in the commission of a crime; attention; a **rumble**; a nod; a concession. "We ditched (got rid of) the patsies (guns) and walked right out of the joint we had been heisting (holding up) past the bulls (police) without a flop." 3. (P) The last night of a prison sentence. "Two (days) and a flop and I hit the street (go free). Roll around! (Time, please pass!)" 4. An arrest. "Tony the Junker took a flop on a dead-banger (red-handed)." 5. A term of contempt, usually applied by skilful pickpockets to those who rob drunkards. "That stumble-bum (inept fellow) ain't no cannon (pickpocket). Even a flop wouldn't hustle with (steal with) that stiff."

Flop, v. 1. To go to bed. 2. To arrest; to be arrested. 3. To rob drunkards. 4. (Scattered prisons) To be denied parole. 5. To recognize; to discover a criminal in the act of committing a crime and to raise a hue and cry. "Some ghee (man) flopped us coming out of the joint with the swag (loot) and set up a murder beef (a terrific outcry)."

Flop game. Any variation of the confidence game in which the victim places his money into a box, purse, or other receptacle, and gets in return a similar receptacle stuffed with scraps of paper or stage money.

Flop-house. A cheap lodging house.

Flop-joint. Any cheap hotel or lodging house; also, a local jail where vagabonds sleep overnight.

Flopper. 1. In the accident insurance racket, one who is adept at hurling himself before automobiles, feigning serious injury, throwing limbs out of joint, etc. "The flopper had the bracelets (handcuffs) on his trick wrist, so he slipped the cuffs and screwed (escaped) on the cops." 2. A thief who combines physical strength with skill at picking pockets, usually robbing his victims while exchanging witty stories as a means of getting close enough to operate. He will use physical force, if necessary, but no weapons, and he scorns thieves who rob only helpless persons.

Flossie or **Floosie.** (far-West) A woman who sells the implied promise of her favors and fails to deliver.

Fluker. (Hobo; far-West) See **Mission stiff.**

Flunk. An inner steel compartment in a safe, protected by a small, light door or **duster.**

Flush. See **Flushed.**

Flushed. Having more money than usual. "You heist-ghees (holdup men) are all the same. You can't see stepping out (robbing) when you're flushed."

Fluter. See **Fag.**

Fly, n. A second-story man; a burglar who is an expert at climbing.

Fly, v. (P) To send through illegitimate channels, avoiding censorship; to smuggle. "Spanny took a fall (was reported) when they knocked off (intercepted) a kite (smuggled letter) he tried to fly out."

Fly a kite. (P) To smuggle a letter out of prison, evading censorship.

Fly horse. A citizen who is on the lookout for criminals.

Fog, n. Confusion aroused in a victim's mind by crooked concession **shills,** confidence men; etc. "Spring (start) now, the cross-fire (bewildering talk) has the sucker (victim) in a fog."

Fog. v. (South) To shoot.

Fold, n. The trick of short-changing a person by folding paper currency and counting both ends of each bill as if they were separate bills. The money is held so that the ends protrude between the fingers at the back of the hand. ["To give a sucker the fold"—to swindle a victim in the above manner.]

Fold, v. 1. To abandon, as a racket, a specific criminal enterprise, a residence, any area that has become unsafe, etc. 2. (P) To sever relations with; to quit a work assignment, accepting penalty, or to secure transfer from it; to give up, as gambling, any risky activity, any bad habit, etc.

Fold a joint. To close an establishment.

Fold up. See **Fold,** v.

Fold-up or **Fold-up joint.** A temporary setup for a swindle, as an office, hotel suite, etc. "You'd never figure a sweet layout like that for a fold-up joint to push (market) hot bonds (stolen or counterfeit securities)."

Foolish powder. Heroin.

Football. A bomb, especially the type suitable for hurling toward an objective in terrorizing business or in strike-breaking.

Foot-pad. (Obsolescent) A robber who stealthily overtakes his victim, holding him up or knocking him unconscious, then robbing him.

Forty. Okay; excellent; trustworthy.

Forty-eight. 1. An arrest on suspicion by which police may hold a suspect for 48 hours' investigation without placing him under formal arrest on a specific charge. The forty-eight can be renewed by technically "releasing" and "re-arresting" suspects. "The coppers held me for three forty-eight's and kicked my cruller in (beat me severely)." 2. An order, under the vagrancy laws of many States, to leave the jurisdiction of a court within forty-eight hours or be sentenced to the county jail.

Forty-eighter. See **Forty-eight.**

Forty strong. (Chiefly among Mexicans and Spaniards; in common use on the Pacific Coast) A strong-arm thief who specializes in the use of the **mugg.**

Fourth of July. A gun-fight.

Four-time loser. A fourth offender; i.e., one who has had three previous felony convictions and is therefore liable to a **life sentence.** [Note: In many States, three felony convictions result in life imprisonment.]

Frail. (Chiefly in near-West) Of weak character; untrustworthy. "Who's the strange weed (stranger)? Looks frail, don't he?"

Frame. See **Frame up.**

Frame-up, n. Conviction and subsequent imprisonment on trumped-up charges, or as a result of any improper —even if legal—procedure. "Every right fall (just arrest) I ever got, I been beefing (crying) frame-up. Now I really got a bum rap (unjust arrest) and nobody gives my sucker's holler (cries of innocence) a rumble (bit of attention)."

Frame up, v. To subject to a **frame-up.** "The coppers had me on a right rap (just charge) all right, but they had to frame me up to make it stick."

Freebie. (Carnival) 1. Anything given free of charge. 2. A habitual borrower or beggar.

Free hole, n. (New York and New Jersey prisons) A dolt; a fool.

Free-hole, a. Stupid; easily taken advantage of.

Free-load. To sponge on others; to

cadge drinks, food, etc., on the strength of one's bad reputation, or by impersonating an officer.

Free-loader. One who **free-loads.**

Freeze. To stop what one is doing instantly, especially in the presence of danger; to become suddenly motionless. "The dick (detective) is right at my pratt (behind me), and I got the sucker's okus (wallet) in my duke (hand) when I hear the zex (whispered warning). I freeze on the spot and I can't blow (flee)."

Freeze on to. To cling tightly to, as a stolen article; to stay close to, as to a prospective victim; to pursue relentlessly. "The bulls (police) picked up my tail (started to follow me) last month, and they're freezing on to it wherever I move."

Freight. A sum paid in bribery. "Squaring (quashing) that pinch (charge) put us on the nut (in debt). But you gotta pay the freight or else."

Fresh. A new supply of money. "We're stepping out and hustle (steal) some fresh today. Gotta get off the nut (out of debt)."

Fresh fish. (P) A newly arrived convict; a group of new inmates arriving together. "A boat (transfer) of fresh fish just got in from Sing Sing. What a crumby (unkempt) looking mob of scratchers (bums)."

Fresh off the street. (P) Newly arrived in prison.

Frill. (Obsolescent) A woman.

Frisk, n. A thorough search of person, effects or premises, usually for stolen goods, weapons, or narcotics; the act of going through a victim's pockets in a robbery.

Frisk, v. To subject to a **frisk.**

Frisker. The member of a gang of thieves, especially burglars or holdup men, designated to search the person of the victim or his premises.

Fritzer. (Scattered States close to Atlantic seaboard) A poor deal; anything of little promise; a "white elephant"; a **stiff.**

Frock. A suit of clothes.

Frog-backs. Paper currency.

Frogskin. A dollar bill.

From Chicago. Okay. [Note: Usually applied to an out-of-towner whose reputation is satisfactory in the underworld.] "Meet Mike the Mooch, boys; he's from Chicago."

From-now-on, n. 1. (P) An indefinite commitment to a segregation or punishment wing, often for the duration of a prison term. 2. (P) A life term or any equivalent prison sentence. "Joe Lemons is buried in stir. He's got from-now-on and some short time (remainder of a previous term) to pull (serve)."

Front, n. 1. One's personal appearance, especially an impressive appearance. "There's a ghee (fellow) with a perfect front for the shake (extortion). Give him a white tin (silver badge) and he'd pass for law (a policeman) anywhere." 2. A business office or other establishment used to cover up illegal or shady activities. 3. An appearance of, and a reputation for, viciousness that inspires terror. "Some dude (fellow) with a few under his belt (several murders to his credit) is the front a shylock (loan shark) setup needs to lineup (control) the rabbits (borrowers)." 4. A suit of clothes; a wardrobe. 5. (P) The Warden's Office; the administration building. 6. Any person who will speak or act for an underworld character when needed; a criminal lawyer.

Front, v. To serve as a **front.** "You front for us, and we'll shake (blackmail) this rabbit-snatcher (abortionist) for a nice buck (plenty of money)."

Front ghee. See **Front,** n.

Front man. See **Front,** n.

Front room. Any large closed automobile; a sedan or limousine.

Fronts. Crudely counterfeited currency, only one side of which is printed —not for passing but for use in swindles where a roll of currency is necessary for a flash. "The sucker watched Sandy tossing the broads (dealing three-card monte) and me clipping him (winning his money). Them fronts Sandy was paying me off in looked good, so the mark (victim) went (entered the game)."

Fruit. Addicted to male oral sodomy or passive pederasty.

Fruit for the monkeys. (Very contemptuous when not uttered in callous bantering) So loose morally as to be the eager passive subject of anyone's advances.

Fruit under the old system, to have been. To be an old hand at perversion, having started under the prison system in which two or more convicts were locked in one cell. [Note: This expression is also part of the callous bantering of prison life.]

Fry. To electrocute; to die in the electric chair. "That's a bad beef (serious complaint). Someone's got to fry."

Frying pan. Any prison or jail located in a hot climate.

Full house. Simultaneous infection with gonorrhea and syphilis, often accompanied by body lice or **crabs.**

Funny paper. Counterfeit money; bad checks or forged instruments of any kind.

Fuzey. (Rare) An alert policeman.

Fuzz. (Carnival) Police; anyone connected with the police. "Six to five (look out)! Fuzz on the march (coming)."

Fuzzy. (Carnival) A policeman.

G

G. A thousand dollars. "If I had two G's I coulda got a sixer (six months) in the pen (city penitentiary) instead of this sawbuck (ten years)."

Gabo. One who talks too much. "That gabo is a bitch (a dangerous fellow). Don't crack (reveal any secrets) to him, or he'll bury you (talk you into prison)."

Gaff, n. 1. (Carnival) A special game or concession crookedly operated. "The l. a. (legal adjuster) says the gaffs can run wide open here. The sheriff took his bit (bribe)." 2. Any device used in the crooked operation of a game of chance. 3. The spin, **pad rolling** or similar controlling of unloaded dice, for the purpose of cheating. "Hit the backboard and take the gaff off when you roll those bones (dice)." 4. The application of pressure, or force, as in police **third degree.** Any lasting difficulty to be suffered, as rough treatment, a prison term, etc. 5. That element that removes chance and reasonably assures a desired outcome; the **fix.** 6. The catch; the trick; the twist or the angle. ["To beat the gaff"—to avoid any obstacle; to outwit the trickery of an opponent; to escape conviction, death in the electric chair, etc.]

Gaff, v. 1. (Carnival) To utilize a **gimmick** or in any way to operate a game crookedly. "You don't need to gaff the wheel with these hoosiers. Kick (release by manipulating the footboard) the gimmick (controlling device) off." 2. To spin, **pad roll,** or otherwise control the roll of unloaded or unshaped dice. 3. To **fix** matters, as by jury tampering, bribing authorities, coercing, wheedling, etc.; to arrange matters to assure a favorable outcome. 4. To arrest; to catch in the act.

Gaff-board. (Carnival) In a wheel-game concession, a sliding board that can be kicked over, releasing the **gimmick** that illegally controls the spin. "Boot that gaff-board, Sam, there's fuzz (police) in the tip (crowd)."

Gaffed deal. A crooked deal, as in card playing. Any situation in which the outcome is prearranged.

Gaff-joint. A crooked gambling establishment; a gaming concession crookedly operated.

Gag. A plot; a concocted story; a trick; a lie. "The bug-doctor (psychiatrist) has the net out (is attempting to commit to an institution for the insane) for the Guzzler. Must be a gag. He goes to bat (trial) for that bang-job (murder) next month."

Gage. 1. An imaginary calibrated scale registering one's emotional level, especially during marijuana smoking. ["To get one's gage up"—to achieve peak marijuana stimulation.] 2. Cheap whiskey. 3. Marijuana. "That mugg is blowing his top (going crazy) hitting (smoking) the gage."

Gaged. Intoxicated.

Gagged-gat. A pistol or revolver equipped with a silencer.

Gal-boy. (Gulf State area prisons) A passive pederast or a male oral sodomist.

Gallagher and Shean. (Obs.) The policeman-sergeant team formerly seen patrolling the streets of big metropolises in police cars.

Gallery, the. The Criminal Identification Bureau, or "Rogue's Gallery," at police headquarters.

Gams. Legs. "This glom (fool) was dropped (arrested) dead bang (red-handed) gandering (looking) at a pair of nifty gams when he was supposed to be laying zex (acting as lookout)."

Gander, n. A surreptitious look; a

hurried glance. "Take a gander, Swat, ain't that law (a policeman) piking us off (watching us)?"

Gander, v. To take a gander at.

Gandy dancer. A cheap crook.

Gang up. See **Double-bank,** v.

Gap. To stand by during the commission of a crime. "While you're clipping (robbing) the joint, I'll gap and stall (delay) any beef (outcry)."

Gaper. A tiny reflector in the palm of the hand or on a ring, used in card cheating. A **kibitzer** wears the device, moves behind the victim of the swindle, and enables his aide in the game to view the victim's cards clearly.

Gapper. 1. One who is present during the commission of a crime, but does not actually participate in it. 2. One who gapes, especially a bystander who might hinder the execution of a crime. 3. A **kibitzer** in a card game; an onlooker.

Gapper's bit. See **Gapper's cut.**

Gapper's cut. A small percentage of loot given to one who has observed but not actively participated in the criminal venture, or to one who has been a minor accessory to it.

Garter. (Very rare) A prison term of uncertain length, with wide difference between minimum and maximum terms.

Gash. 1. The mouth. 2. A prostitute; a passive homosexual; or, all of these as a group. ("Piece of gash" or "hunk of gash.")

Gash-hound. One whose chief avocation is the pursuit of loose women, prostitutes, homosexuals, and the like.

Gassy, n. A talkative person.

Gassy, a. Talkative.

Gat. (Formerly a Gatling machine gun) A gun; a pistol. "Don't put the gat on the dames. They get jumpy and beef murder (scream terribly). Talk to 'em first and then flash (show the gun)."

Gate. 1. To demand a re-throw of the dice in a craps game, a protest against foul rolling by the operator of the game. 2. To get rid of any undesirable person or thing. "Gate that creep (low fellow). He's a needle-knight (drug addict)."

Gay-cat. (Hobo) An inexperienced hand, masquerading as a seasoned hobo; a boy, serving his hoboing apprenticeship, panhandling and stealing for veterans, often serving in a passively homosexual role. "Send that gay-cat out on the stem (street) and make him rustle (get food)."

Gazabo. A man.

Gazers. (Unknown in East) Federal Government agents. "Dump (get rid of) that queer (counterfeit money), the gazers got a tail on (are following) us."

Gazooney. (mid-West prisons) A degenerate, especially a passive pederast; a **punk.**

G-bit. A term in Federal penal institutions.

Geed-up. Intoxicated; under the influence of drugs; (rare) angry.

Geedus. (Pacific coast area) Money.

Geepo. A person, often with the implication that he is an informer, a policeman, or an inquisitive person disposed to report to the authorities.

Geezed up. See **Geed-up.**

Geezer. 1. A person; a guy. 2. A drink of potent liquor.

Geezo (mid-Western prisons) a convict who habitually begs from his fellow inmates.

Gelt. (Yiddish-American) Money.

General. 1. A general alarm for one's arrest; a warrant. "Gus is in Mexico (hiding out of town). They got a general out for him on that snatch (kidnapping)." 2. (P) A complete search of prison premises for stolen stores, contraband, weapons, etc. "Ditch (hide) the chivs (knives). I just got a wire (reliable report) there's gonna be a general."

Georgia scuffle, n. (Carnival) A very crude and often rough handling of swindle victims who are too dull-witted to be subtly prepared for the theft. "Tough going in these tanks (small towns) the way the hoosiers hang on; it's a Georgia scuffle with every mark (victim)."

Georgia scuffle, v. (Carnival) To engage in a **Georgia scuffle.**

German. (Greenpoint, Brooklyn, N.Y. localism) A policeman.

Get. 1. To fulfill a threat of vengeance upon, by vicious assault, murder, or property destruction. 2. To arrest; to shoot or kill in police pursuit. "The bulls (police) got Windy City Si on a heist (holdup) last night. He's sloughed (locked up) in the county (county jail)."

Get a bit chopped. (P) To secure a reduction of sentence. "Some shyster told my brother to kick in (produce) three bills (three hundred dollars) and he'd get my bit chopped."

Get a break. See **Get a valentine.**

Get a fat lip. (Northeastern industrial area, U.S.) To be punched in the mouth; to be beaten with the fists.

Get a floater. To be ordered to leave the jurisdiction of a court in 24 or 48 hours as an alternative to vagrancy sentence.

Get a forty-eighter. See **Forty-eight.**

Get a grindstone and sharpen it. To practice the technique of pickpocketing in order to regain one's lost dexterity by having a confederate pose as a victim.

Get a load of. To make oneself aware of; to listen closely; to watch attentively. "Jiggers (look out), Duke, get on the earie (listen) and get a load of this spiel (conversation). These dudes sound like dicks (detectives)."

Get around. 1. To manage to mix in

the best underworld circles; to make oneself a figure of importance in the underworld. 2. (P) To make something of a career of prison life, managing to secure work assignments which are desirable and obtain contraband and such stolen stores as are available.

Get a tail. To be followed.

Get a ticket. 1. (Many prisons) To receive formal notification that parole has been granted. 2. (P) To be reported for rule violation. 3. To have a warrant for another charge lodged against one while serving a sentence on a previous matter.

Get a valentine. To receive a lesser prison sentence than the term anticipated; to be awarded any favorable decision.

Getaway. A speedy departure from the scene of a crime; an escape. "Too tough a getaway; skip that caper (robbery)."

Getaway boiler. Any automobile, usually stolen, which is used for the execution of a crime and then abandoned.

Getaway car or **load.** See **Getaway boiler.**

Get 'em up. Put your hands up. [Note: "Hands up" is rarely heard outside of fiction. "Get 'em up" is the usual command of armed robbers. "Keep 'em down" or "hands on the table" are frequent variations where the attention of passersby might be attracted by upraised hands. "Reach," "Lift them," and "Elevate" are whimsies of exhibitionist amateurs. "Take it easy, now" or "Be quiet, and no one will be hurt" are effective panic-checks when women or nervous men are victims.]

Get the finger put on. 1. To be arrested on information given to the police, especially by underworld associates. "I wouldn't mind if I got dropped (arrested) on the trick (red-handed) but to clip (steal) the score (loot) and make a clean getaway and then get the finger put on me is what burns me up." 2. To be identified formally by the complainant. 3. (P) To be betrayed to the prison authorities.

Get hep or **hip.** See **Hip up.**

Get hit with. To be sentenced to, as a prison term; to be given, as additional punishment, by a Parole Board. "I hear that new fish (newcomer) in the Power House got hit with a fin (five years) by the Board (Parole Board)."

Get hit with the blocks. (P) To be required by the psychiatrist to duplicate a design with vari-shaped blocks. "I'd like to bet that bug doctor (psychiatrist) couldn't pass the test himself if he got a bit (prison sentence) and got hit with the blocks."

Get hit with the book. 1. To be sentenced to life imprisonment as an habitual criminal; to be sentenced to the maximum penalty provided by law. 2. To be held by a Parole Board for the maximum term.

Get hours. To be ordered out of town, usually within twenty-four hours; to get a **twenty-four,** a **forty-eight,** or a **floater.**

Get hunk. 1. To get satisfaction or revenge. "That fink (informer) tried to get hunk on me for glomming (stealing) his broad (girl) by belching (informing) on me, but he humped (defeated) himself. I beat the rap (was acquitted), and he got a bit (prison term)." 2. To use a passive pederast.

Get it up. An ominous demand for payment of blackmail, **protection** money, gambling debts, portions of loot believed withheld, etc. "What is this, a burn (cheating in division of loot)? Get it all up, Monk."

Get off the gun. To achieve emotional release through drugs or alcoholic drinks; to satisfy one's lust.

Get off the nut. 1. To satisfy sexual desire; to achieve any emotional release. 2. To clear expenses and make a profit. "That touch (proceeds of theft) will get us off the nut nice and set up fall

dough (money for legal fees, bail, etc.)."

Get-on, n. (Pickpocket jargon) Any place where crowds enter cars, trains, elevators, etc. "Times is real tough, Stan; there's more wires (pickpockets) than marks (victims) at them get-ons."

Get one out of hock. 1. To get one out on bail. 2. (P) To effect one's release from punishment cells; (by extension) to get one out of his cell any time, as when the guard inadvertently neglects to leave him out for recreation, church services, etc.

Get one right. 1. To arrest in the act of committing a crime or with incontrovertible proof of guilt. 2. (P) To seize one in a rule violation or with proof of guilt. 3. To trap one in an easily proved violation of underworld code or convention.

Get oneself a banner or a **shingle.** (P) See **Get oneself locked up.**

Get oneself locked up. (P) To commit a deliberate infraction of rules or to ask for protective custody in order to escape the consequences of gambling beyond one's means, informing, etc. "That lousy muzzler (low fellow) blew (lost) half a C (fifty dollars) in a poker game when he didn't have a meg (cent). He better get himself locked up or he'll get chivved (knifed)."

Get oneself sloughed up. (P) See **Get oneself locked up.**

Get one's gage up. To stimulate oneself by smoking marijuana, or, less frequently, by drinking hard liquor.

Get one's load on. To become intoxicated by drink or exhilarated by drugs, especially as a means of fortifying one's courage before the commission of a crime.

Get one's pratt. To arouse one's anger. "Don't it get your pratt when you take (rob) a mark (victim) who has a million-dollar front (appearance) and you get crabs (practically nothing) for your end (proceeds)!"

Get-ons, on the. Engaged in, or by means of, pocket-picking at bus, trolley, or train stops or stations.

Get out the crying towel! (P) Stop complaining! "Get out the crying towel for this bum; he's singing it (complaining) again!"

Get settled for. To be sentenced. "Tennessee Sam got settled for a scratch rap (forgery charge) down East."

Get the book. See **Get hit with the book.**

Get the pen. (In most areas) To be sentenced to State penitentiary. (In New York City and other large cities) To be sentenced to the city or county penitentiary.

Get under the bed! (P) Shut up! "Hey, you in cell A-20, get under the bed! The judge didn't say I had to listen to your crap (meaningless conversation) when he gave me this bit (term)."

Get-up. 1. A holdup; an armed robbery. 2. (P) The morning of one's parole or discharge from prison. "Sunday don't count the way I look at it. So, I got four (days) and a get-up. Roll around!" 3. A disguise; any old or ill-fitting clothes. "Dan just hit the sidewalk (came out of prison). Did you see the crumby-looking State (prison issue) get-up on him? I'm staking him to a front (giving him money for a decent suit of clothes)."

G-heat. The attention of Federal police agencies, as distinguished from that of local police.

Ghee. ("G" pronounced as in "guy") A person; a guy. "I'm playing ball with (stealing with) Slick Stanger. He's a real hip (clever) ghee."

Ghee from downtown. (Applied to detectives in large cities) Headquarters men having gold badges.

Ghee from the West. (mid-West) An out-of-town person, presumably all

right, but to be watched. "Strange weed (stranger) in the garden (vicinity), hey, Jack? A ghee from the West?"

Ghee one hustles with. One's partner in criminal enterprise.

Ghee one knew up above. A former prison mate.

Ghee with the boodle. The member of a gang who has or controls the money.

Ghee with the brass nuts. 1. The boss; the gang leader; the **biggie;** the **big shot.** 2. (P) The prison disciplinarian (the principal keeper, the deputy warden, captain, or sergeant).

Ghost. An attorney, expert in criminal law, who does not himself try criminal cases, but advises other trial lawyers.

Gig. (Carnival) A renewal of pressure; a final effort to swindle a difficult victim. "A tough giver-up (difficult fellow), ain't he? Give him the gig, but heavy."

Giggle academy. A hospital for insane or mentally defective delinquents.

Gilly. See **Gilly-show.**

Gilly-show. (Carnival) A transient show, easily carried from place to place. "Without the gaffs (crooked elements) and the grifters (thieves), the carny (carnival world) would be all gilly-shows."

Gimmick, n. 1. (Carnival) Any of various devices to control a gaming wheel. **Gimmicks** may be operated in the stand by means of a footboard, or controlled from outside the stand by an aide by means of a thin wire. When a wire control is used, the operator gives the wheel a good spin and walks away from it. This has a highly persuasive effect on the crowd. The **tripod, gaff,** or **gimmick** is always so rigged that it can be dismantled in a moment if police investigate. 2. The trick; the catch; the deceptive element, whether concrete or abstract. 3. Any safety attachment on a lock; any gadget that complicates matters and confounds the tamperer. 4. Any device or means by which the element of chance is removed and an outcome prearranged; the **fix**. "The dicks (detectives) won't bother the combo (syndicate of thieves) in this tank (town). The gimmick is in."

Gimmick, v. To trick; to cheat; to use any kind of **gimmick**.

Gimmick up. To rig with a **gimmick;** to **fix;** to prearrange. "It looked like the rap (indictment) was in the sack (certain to be dismissed) for a sure spring (release). But somebody gimmicked it up in the D.A.'s office to bury us (send us to prison for a long term)."

Gin. See **Ginney.**

Ginch. ("A piece of ginch") 1. Prostitutes; loose women; passive pederasts; **fags.** 2. The act of sexual intercourse.

Gingerbread pete. A safe with ornate and impressive exterior but which is capable of being easily cracked.

Ginney. An Italian.

Ginzola. (also **Ginzo**). A **ginney.**

Girl. ("One of the girls") A **fag.**

Give a deal to. 1. To beat severely with superior numbers or force; to subject to the **third degree.** "They mugged him (armlocked his head) and half a dozen ghees double-banked (ganged up on) him and gave him a deal." 2. To **railroad;** to treat unjustly; to **frame up.** "Harry the Hog took a fall (was arrested) in Philly on a phony beef (unjust accusation), and he got a deal— a tenner (ten years) in stir (prison)."

Give a ghee a toss. 1. To recognize; to hail; to acknowledge a greeting, especially with cordiality. 2. To give a suspect a grilling; to question, search, or arrest a criminal suspect. 3. (P) To search a convict's garments or quarters for contraband, stolen goods, etc. [Note: "To fail to give one a toss"—to ignore; to snub.]

Give a joint a play. To patronize an establishment; to direct one's special attention to an establishment, particularly with the purpose of robbing it.

Give a joint a toss. 1. To take notice of, to think of, or to patronize an establishment. 2. To search a place. "The bulls (police) were in last night and gave my joint a toss. They're looking for a pay-off (bribe), I guess."

Give a play. 1. To operate criminally in a given area. "Heist-mobs (holdup gangs) give Miami a heavy play in the winter. Some nice scores (paying thefts) down there." 2. To patronize. "I hear there's a lot of new hustlers (prostitutes) in that nautch-joint (brothel) around the corner. Let's give it a play." 3. To try to gain the confidence of an intended victim. "That copper looks like a businessman (taker of bribes). Give him a play and see if he'll go when you crack (make an offer)."

Give a run. To evade payment of an obligation. "That fink (good-for-nothing) gave me a run for two C's (two hundred dollars)."

Give a thing a flop. See **Give a thing a toss.**

Give a thing a toss. To notice; to think of; to pay attention to. "When the bulls (police) were on our pratt (following us), I never gave it a toss till I heard them pegging slugs (shooting)."

Give one a bit. To inform upon; to place in the position of having to face a certain prison sentence; to sell out, as a lawyer betraying his client.

Give one a cuff. To put off payment of an obligation, often by intimidating the creditor.

Give one a flop. 1. To interrupt, pursue, or attempt to seize a criminal in the commission of a crime or under suspicious circumstances. 2. To recognize; to greet; to take notice of; to give one a **tumble.** "The bulls (police) gave us a flop and frisked (searched) the boiler (car), but our front (appearance) was okay so they told us to cop a sneak (get out of there)."

Give one a hustle. See **Put the hustle on.**

Give one a play. See **Give a play.**

Give one a promote. See **Put the promote on.**

Give one a raust. To give one a **raus.**

Give one a stab. To have sexual relations with.

Give one a steer. To recommend, as a brothel, a gambling house, a place or a person to be robbed; to guide or direct. "This is Trig, boys. He's from Chicago (an out-of-towner who is okay). Give him a steer, Cockeye. He wants to kick the mooch around (smoke the opium pipe) tonight."

Give one the blanket. 1. (P) To throw a blanket over a victim's head and beat him or, less frequently, force him to submit to an act of perversion. 2. To cheat by **padrolling** the dice on a blanket in a craps game.

Give one the business. See **Give one the works.**

Give one the push. (Carnival) To crowd or nudge a potential swindle victim towards a game or stand.

Give one the works. 1. To subject to extreme punishment; to assault; to kill; to apply **third degree;** to sentence to the maximum penalty. 2. To rape; to have sexual intercourse with.

Giver-up. A victim of robbery; one from whom a loan is sought.

Give up. To name accomplices or inform upon underworld associates. "That creep (coward) gave up a lot of good people (fine underworld citizens) so he wouldn't burn (be electrocuted)." 2. To pay.

Give up one's kisser or **mugg.** To go unmasked while engaged in robbery, risking identification. "Get someone else to fill (take my place) on that heist (holdup). You have to give up your kisser to make the in (gain admittance). Count me out."

Giving. Practicing active pederasty, as differentiated from **receiving,** or passive pederasty.

G-joint. (P) A federal penal institution. "I'd sooner hit a G-joint than get loused around (get a raw deal) in these State crumb-joints (dirty, harsh, and contemptible prisons)."

Glad-hander. (P) A handshaker; a back-slapper. "That phony glad-hander is always screwing around (fooling) with the hacks (prison guards) and he winds up in plenty of jackpots (trouble). He'll hip up (get wise) some day."

Glass wagon. (Southern carnival) A hearse. ("To get the glass wagon"— to be slain.)

Glass work. Cheating at cards by means of a **gaper.**

Glaum onto. See **glom onto.**

Glim. 1. A light, especially a burglar's shielded torch. "Nix on that glim; we ain't got a license (police immunity) to clip (steal) around here." 2. The lamp for keeping the opium pipe heated.

Glim-hustler. A peddler of cheap spectacles; a confidence man, posing as an eye specialist, who pretends to see a rare eye disease developing in his victim, writes a prescription on the spot, and contrives to "accept" a fee; often, he follows it through by accepting a sum to arrange for consultations and surgical treatment.

Glimmer. The human eye.

Glimmers. The eyes; eyeglasses.

Glom, n. 1. A worthless dolt; an exceedingly inept person. "That glom screwed up the detail (bungled the plan)." 2. An arrest; a seizure; the act of stealing. "Whiskers (Federal Agents) put the glom on the whole mob, plates (printing plates), queer (counterfeit money), and everything at the hideout."

Glom, v. 1. To grab, as in stealing. "Glom them hoops (rings) as soon as we crash this gullion-joint (jewelry store)." 2. To arrest. "Chet was glommed dead bang (red-handed) for a knock-off (murder)." 3. To seize. "Glom that creep (low fellow) and make him get it up (pay his obligation)." 4. To get a look at; to see. "Did you glom the size of the mahoska (revolver) that dick (detective) had? What a smoke-wagon (shooting-iron)!"

Glom onto. 1. To take illegal possession of. 2. To arrest. 3. (Hobo) To grasp hold of, as a moving train.

Glu. To rob, usually by sneak-thievery. "The ice (diamond jewelry) is in the top drawer. Glu it quick."

G-man. 1. A Federal officer, especially an agent of the F.B.I. or the Secret Service, handling counterfeiting cases. 2. (P) An inmate who secretly acts as an informer against his fellow convicts; a police spy.

G-note. A thousand-dollar bill; a thousand dollars.

Go. 1. (P) To do a thing well or with determination. "There's a ghee (fellow) who can really go with a chiv (fight with a knife)." 2. To die; to escape. "They got the chair (electric chair) all set for those two dudes (fellows) who go tonight." 3. To submit, wittingly or unwittingly, to force, guile, or intimidation; to be tricked, swindled or coerced into surrendering one's money. "How much dough will the joint go for on a muscle shake (extortion by threat of physical violence)?" 4. To yield to the temptation of, such as police promises of leniency in exchange for information, or a specific type of crime or racket. "I can't go for this loft-working (robbing of lofts). It takes too long and them bugs (alarms) worry me." To make a habit of, as to go for narcotics. 5. To yield to force, as a safe, or prison bars to diligently applied hacksaw blades or bar-spreaders. "We'll burn (use an acetylene torch on) that pete (safe) and it's gotta go." 6. To leave prison as a result of parole, discharge, or legal action of the higher courts. "I gotta go when I meet the

Board (Parole Board). I'll have my full max (maximum term) in (served)."

Gob. The mouth.

Go back for seconds. 1. To rob the same victim again; to rehash. 2. (P) To return to prison for a second term, having once been released.

Gobbler. (P) A male oral sodomist.

Go by hand. (Hobo) To walk.

Go cabareting. (P) See **Cabaret.**

Goddamus. (Humorous) A writ of mandamus.

Go down. 1. To commit oral sodomy. 2. To be convicted of a crime; to fail to be granted parole; to be arrested. "We go to bat (stand trial) tomorrow. I still figure we're going down, but we can't get a decent plea (reasonable reduction of charge for pleading guilty) from this D. A."

Go down on a hooker. (P) To leave prison, either during or at the conclusion of one's current term, to face prosecution on a pending warrant. "When I get this sawbuck (ten years) in, I still ain't going nowhere. I gotta go down on a hooker and I figure to wind up with a new bit (sentence)."

Go down the line for. See **Go to bat.**

Gog, on the. Nervous, unstable. "I gotta chill (became worried) with Sam as zex-man (lookout). The dude (fellow) is all right, I guess, but he's on the gog too much."

Go-go in one's eyes, to have. (P) The peculiarly restless eyes of one determined to find a means of escape from prison. "That new mickey (newly arrived inmate) has sure got go-go in his eyes. They'll toot the tooter (blow the escape siren) for him yet."

Go home. (P) To be discharged from prison.

Going-over. A beating, usually administered by more than one assailant; a **third-degree** beating. "That muzzler (low fellow) of a tipster (salesman of criminal information) gave us a bum steer (false information). Let's give him a going-over."

Gold badge man. Any detective or police official who carries a yellow tin; a headquarters man.

Goldbrick, n. One who goldbricks.

Goldbrick, v. To malinger; to use any expedient, as feigning illness, to avoid work or obtain narcotics.

Golfer. A Cadillac automobile.

Gondola. 1. A stolen sedan. 2. (Hobo) A low, open freight-car.

Gonger. An opium pipe.

Gonger, on the. Addicted to smoking the opium pipe.

Gong-kicker. An habitual smoker of opium; (less frequently) one who smokes marijuana.

Goniff. (Yiddish-American) 1. (Carnival) A fool; a chump. 2. A gangster; a thief. "That lousy goniff put the glom on (borrowed and didn't return) my rod (gun)."

Gonsel. See **Gunzel.**

Gooby. (Rare) Prison mess-hall food.

Good buck. 1. A satisfactory income; a clear profit; a **clean buck.** "There's a good buck in shoving junk (selling narcotics), but it's a wrong buck (unethically earned money) and I don't go for it."

Good for a lay. Capable and worthy of being robbed. "There's a nice flash (window display) in that gullion-joint (jewelry store). It ought to be good for a lay."

Good giver-up. One who yields money gracefully to a thief, an extortionist, solicitor, or borrower.

Good head. 1. A respectable girl; a virgin; a girl, not necessarily virtuous, but loyal and discreet in underworld matters. 2. A likeable and trustworthy person; a good fellow.

Good people. (Sing. & pl.) 1. Any loyal member of the underworld; a "respectable" criminal. 2. A person, not of the underworld, who is friendly to or who does business with the underworld. "Hide out in John's joint till the beef (complaint) is chilled (quashed). He's good people."

Goods, the. The real thing; the best of its kind; the thing or person wanted. "That wampole (first-grade marijuana) is the goods, the best of weed (marijuana)."

Good time. (P) The amount of time by which a prison sentence may be reduced as a result of a convict's good conduct or work. [Note: In many States, parole agencies may arbitrarily grant or withhold these credits. The convict views this unfair condition bitterly.] "He lost all his good time getting snatched (reported) for swag (stolen prison stores) and chivving matches (knife fights)."

Goof. A marijuana addict.

Goof-butt. A marijuana cigarette.

Googs. Eyeglasses.

Goon. A hired practitioner of the art of assault and mayhem, retained by unethical strike-bearing agencies, unions and management; a member of a private company police force. "Take a couple of them goons, wreck every truck pulling out, and give the drivers a workout (beating)."

Go on a trick. To engage in a gainful crime.

Goose, n. The act of **goosing.**

Goose, v. To excite a reflex response in anyone by touching the sensitive posterior parts.

Go out. To leave a meeting place for the scene of a crime.

Go out to the country. To drive a victim to any isolated area in order to murder him.

Go over one's head. (P) To continue gambling beyond one's capacity to pay; to bet on the muscle.

Go over the hill. (South and West) To attempt escape from a road- or chaingang. "This ghee (fellow) chopped (cut) the rattler (leg-chain) and went over the hill with the ketchup-dogs (bloodhounds) hot on his tail (in close pursuit)."

Gopher. 1. (West) Any strong safe with an intricate time-locking mechanism, hence to be robbed only by burrowing underground. 2. A burglar who bores through walls, ceilings, or floors to reach his objective. 3. One of a **gopher-mob.**

Gopher-mob. Any gang of burglars who specialize in tunneling toward their objective, especially bank burglars who use this method of circumventing timelocks in vaults of small town banks with inadequate floor and side-wall protection.

Gorilla. See **Guerilla.**

Go South. To secrete a portion of loot on one's person to defraud accomplices of their full share; to **burn;** to **h.o.** "Turn that flea upside down and shake him. He goes South regular."

Gospel ghee. A preacher; a clergyman.

Got a buck. To have money; to be financially well off. "I knew that creep (low fellow) when he was a lush-worker (robber of drunkards). Now he's got a buck he puts the hat on (puts on airs) and don't give me a flop (say, 'Hello')."

Go the route for. See **Go to bat.**

Go through. To search a person or premises for valuables; to search, as police, for weapons, stolen goods, narcotics, etc. "Go through the joint. Cappy says the old dude (fellow) has two G's (two thousand dollars) stashed (hidden)."

Go through the trap. To be hanged in legal execution.

Go to bat. 1. To fight, finance, or otherwise give another one's full support. (Usually followed by the preposition "for.") 2. To stand trial in criminal proceedings.

Go to town. 1. To do any job thoroughly; to prosecute to the full; to act without restraint; to enjoy to the utmost. 2. (P) To seize weapons and assail one's enemies. 3. To practice active pederasty or male oral sodomy; to masturbate.

Got to go. 1. (P) To be entitled to mandatory release, as a convict over whose sentence local parole authorities have no power. "I meet the Board (appear before the Parole Board) next month. I'm declaring myself (telling them just what I think) too, 'cause I got to go. My max (maximum term) is up." 2. To have to die. "That muzzler (informer) is got enough on all of us to bury us (send us to prison for long terms). He's got to go."

Goulash. Misleading information to thieves; a garbled tip.

Go up against. 1. To attempt to rob. "Me and Benny went up against a cannonball peter (sturdy safe) out in Frisco and we busted ten stems (steel drills) without scratching the paint." 2. To have relations with. "I never went up against a partner like Gimpy. He's on the gog (nervous) all the time you're on a touch (theft) with him."

Go wrong. To turn traitor to the underworld or to any accomplice in crime; to become homosexual or otherwise unconventional by underworld standards.

Grab, n. 1. An arrest; a pick-up by police on suspicion. 2. (P) A report or lock-up for violation of prison rules.

Grab, v. 1. To seize, as in the loan shark racket, the property of a victim who cannot meet the usurious interest rates. ("To make a grab.") 2. To derive one's income from a criminal enterprise or activity. 3. To steal; to take by force. 4. To give one a **grab.** (Variant, "to grab off.")

Grab a hot one. 1. To steal an automobile. 2. (P) To practice passive pederasty or male oral sodomy; to **cop a doodle.**

Grab salvation. (Hobo) To pretend conversion to secure food, lodging, etc., at missions and revivals.

Grab scenery. (Hobo) To ride the top, or to lean out through the open door of a freight car.

Grad. An ex-convict. (Usually preceded by the name of prison, as, "A Sing Sing grad," etc.)

G-rag. A cloth for cleaning, cooling, and holding an opium pipe.

Grand. A thousand dollars.

Grandstand play. Any ostentatious show of force, bravado, liberality, etc., made to impress onlookers, as the **five-and-fifty-five.**

Granny. See **G-rag.**

Grapes. Hemorrhoids.

Grapevine. A gossip channel; the source of the **hot wire.** [An overworld term, seldom heard in the underworld. See **Wire, the.**]

Gravel-eye. A glass eye.

Gravy. (Obsolescent) Anything, especially money, obtained with little effort; any gain surpassing expectations. "We all got a nice cut (share) shaking the joint (extorting money from the establishment) and the weekly pay-off is gravy."

Gravy hound. (Central and Western prisons) A convict who complains of stomach ills to enjoy a soft diet in the prison hospital.

Graze. (mid-West and scattered areas) To eat at the general prison mess or **main line.**

Grease. 1. A bribe; protection or tribute money. "Get the grease up, Charlie, it's the only thing to take the sting out of the beefs (criminal charges)." 2. (Carnival) Sums of money which the **suckers** are allowed to win at gaming wheels to stimulate their greed and increase their eagerness to play. 3. Trouble, especially an arrest. ("In the grease"—arrested.) 4. **Picric** and dynamite used in safeblowing; **soup.**

Greaseball. Anyone of Latin type, especially an Italian.

Greasy aces. Specially finished aces which can be felt and palmed by playing-card cheats.

Greek bottom. The crooked dealer's technique of dealing the second card from the bottom of the deck. The use of the bottom card to shield the trick is a refinement of the cruder **bottom deal.**

Green goods. Counterfeit money. "A lot of them schmeckers (drug addicts) pushing (passing) green goods around here like it was legit (legal). Hole up (go into concealment) for a while."

Green goods game, the. Any of various confidence swindles in which the victim pools a sum of money and is finally left with an empty package or purse. There are thousands of variations, chief of which revolves around the **money machine.**

Green ice. Emeralds. "There's a swaggie (buyer of stolen goods) in Detroit that takes gullion (jewelry). Try him on that green ice."

Greybacks. A kind of vermin that infests clothing. "Smarten up, crumb, and read that shirt (delouse your shirt). What are you doing, making pets of them greybacks?"

Greystone college. A prison or penitentiary.

Griddle, n. Any uncomfortably "hot" spot. ("To put on the griddle"—to subject to **third degree;** to slander.)

Griddle, v. To subject to police **third degree** questioning, slander, scandal, etc.

Griffo. Marijuana.

Grift, n. The act of **grifting;** the **grifting** profession.

Grift, v. To work any of the less brazen forms of crime; to live by graft and cunning in criminal operations; to operate as a pickpocket, shoplifter, card-sharp, carnival swindler. "There's too many stiffs (inept fellows) grifting these days and not enough marks (victims) to kife (rob)."

Grift, on the. Engaged in, or by

means of, the **grift.** "I tell you, Grubber, there ain't big scores (large sums of money) on the grift, but there ain't no big bits (long prison terms) either. No spinach on the heavy for me (no more major crime for me)."

Grifter. One who makes his living by grifting; (loosely) a thief.

Grift-sense. (Carnival) A natural or developed talent for **grifting.** "That j.c.l. (newcomer) ain't got no grift-sense. Some hoosier will reef (rob) him for his poke (wallet) yet."

Grind. The confidence man's or panhandler's persuasive and energetic line of talk; **grifting** in an area in which the victims have little money and yield only to great pressure.

Grind, v. To make a living by means of the **grind.**

Growler. 1. (P) The coffee pot or can, especially in prisons where cooking is forbidden and the brewing of coffee is done surreptitiously. 2. (P) The container in which home-made alcoholic brew is brought from the place of concealment to a place where it may be drunk with least risk. 3. A large tin can, bucket, pitcher, etc.

Grub. 1. To engage in petty crime. 2. To beg or chisel.

Grub, on the. Begging or borrowing without any intention of repayment; penniless, hence reduced to cadging. "Yeah, I got chilled (fearful) after that last bit (prison term), but I couldn't stand to be on the grub with all them dudes (fellows) in the neighborhood making nice touches (a lot of money)."

Grubber. One who **grubs.**

Grubbing grift. An unprofitable type of criminal enterprise. "The cannon (picking pockets) is a grubbing grift among them dinner-pailers (working people)."

G-string. (Southern chain-gang) The string or wire by which chain-gang convicts hold up the heavy chain while walking.

Gueril (or **Gorill**). To coerce; to bulldoze; intimidate. "We can gueril all of them joints (establishments) and get put on the payroll steady."

Guerilla (or **Gorilla**). A touch guy, with or without weapons; usually a bodyguard or performer of dirty work for **big shots.** "A little grease (bribery) and a few wires (wire-pulling), and we took the union over with a handful of guerillas."

Guin. See **Guinea.**

Guinea. An Italian.

Guinea football. A crudely made bomb, especially a time-bomb. "I'm blowing my top (going crazy with worry). I told the D.A. that gimme this bit (prison sentence) that I'm gonna get (injure) him. I just read where he got a guinea football by mail. What a case I got to make parole now."

Guinea wrench. (N.Y. Catholic Protectory) A baseball bat used in a fight. "They put chivs (knives) up to the new mick (newcomer) and he cold-cocked (knocked unconscious) three of them with a guinea wrench."

Guinny. A **guinea.**

Guinzola. (also **Guinzo**). An Italian. "Them guinzolas got the alzo (police immunity) in this town. Don't buck that combo (syndicate). They're murder (dangerous)."

Gullion. 1. Jewelry, especially stolen jewelry. "Gullion touches (loot) are pea soup (no good). It's like hustling (stealing) for the fence (buyer of stolen property)." 2. Anything so cheap or so difficult to dispose of as to be not worth stealing. "Glom (grab) the wood (money) and leave the gullion alone." 3. (P) Food; prison fare. "The cons kicked over (rioted) account of the gullion on the main line (regular prison mess)."

Gullion-joint. A jewelry store.

Gullion-poke. A jewelry salesman's gem wallet.

Gumdrop cocktail. A potion of denatured alcohol obtained by straining shellac through cheesecloth to remove gum particles.

Gum-foot. (Obsolescent) A plainclothes policeman or detective.

Gumfoot Gus (or **Gum-shoe Gus**). Anyone who moves about stealthily, especially one suspected of spying on criminals.

Gummio. 1. (N. Y. Catholic Protectory) A boy with whom few associate, because he is either very stupid or **wrong**; a misfit. 2. See **gummy.**

Gummy. A flunkey; a hanger-on, used to run errands and do menial tasks.

Gump. (Hobo) A stolen chicken; a mud-baked hen. [Note: The chicken is baked thus: It is first cleaned internally; then wet clay is packed about the body without plucking it, and the bird is baked in a fire made in a hole in the ground with embers packed all around it. In about an hour, the bird is removed; the hardened mud-pack is cracked with a kick and then lifted off, the feathers adhering to it.]

Gump-glommer. A chicken thief.

Gumshoe-worker, n. (Obsolete) A sneak thief.

Gun, n. 1. The pocket-picking profession. ("On the gun"—engaged in or by means of picking pockets.) 2. Any thief, especially a pickpocket. "Blow (leave town). They're picking up all the guns and hitting them with sixers (six months in the workhouse)." 3. An extra hand taken in for a difficult robbery or burglary. "We could use another gun on this touch (robbery). It ain't a safe caper (undertaking) three-handed (with three men)." 4. A close scrutiny. "Take a good gun around the joint for a bug (burglar-alarm)." 5. The accelerator in an automobile. "Hit the gun, the bulls (police) are right at our keister (behind us)." 6. The penis. ("To

get off the gun"—to have sexual intercourse.)

Gun, v. 1. To be on the alert. 2. To look over carefully; to scrutinize. "Round (turn) easy and gun that dude (fellow) riding the earie (listening so intently)."

Gun, on the. 1. Engaged in, or by means of pocket-picking. 2. On duty at cashier's desk, ticket booth, carnival stand, etc. 3. Peering with criminal intent; observing with the intention of informing authorities. "Who's that creep (inquisitive fellow) on the gun? Take a gander (look)."

Gun for. 1. To go armed in search of a person with intent to assault or kill him. "Mickey's mob is out gunning for Chink." 2. To act as lookout during the commission of a crime; to lay **zex.** "Plant (station) Luke outside to gun for us."

Gun-joint. An establishment patronized by pickpockets.

Gunmaker. See **Gunsmith.**

Gun-mob. A gang of thieves, especially of pickpockets. "That shot (pickpocket) hustled (stole) with the best gun-mobs in the grift (profession)."

Gun-moll. A gun-carrying woman thief, usually the mistress of a thief or gangster. "Some red-headed gun-moll is heisting (holding up) all the little jugs (banks) out West with two punks (youngsters)."

Gunner. 1. (Carnival) One who operates the **gimmick** on a crooked gaming wheel. "The patch (legal adjuster) okayed this tank (said the town will allow gambling wheels). Plant (station) the gunner and go to town (use all the swindling tricks)." 2. The roller in a craps game. "Swing the tops (crooked dice) in when this gunner misses out (misses his point)."

Gunning-over. A close inspection. "Round (turn) easy and give that joint a good gunning-over. Spot (locate) the pete (safe)."

Gun rap. A charge of illegal possession of firearms. "The mouthpiece (lawyer) wants five C's (five hundred dollars) to get my gun rap squashed (quashed)."

Gunsel. See **Gunzel.**

Gunsmith. An experienced pickpocket who trains young **guns,** or pickpockets.

Gunzel. 1. (P) A male oral sodomist, or passive pederast. 2. A brat. 3. (By extension) An informer; a weasel; an unscrupulous person.

Gurdy. (Abbreviation of "hurdy-gurdy") (P) A run-around; a wild goose chase; a raw deal. "My broad (girl) put the finger on (informed on) me and took it on the duff (ran away) with my partner. My mouthpiece (lawyer) clipped me (took my money) and gave me a bit (mismanaged my case and had me sent to prison). What a gurdy I got!"

Gut-robber. See **Belly robber.**

Guts. 1. Nerve; courage. "That ghee (fellow) sure had plenty of guts to step in single-o (alone) and lift (hold up) two heeled (armed) dicks (detectives)." 2. The locking mechanism of a safe. "Those old petes (safes) were soft touches. You just busted the combo (combination dial) off and punched (drove a steel punch into) the guts out."

Gutter hype. A penniless addict of hypodermic injections who uses a safety pin to perforate the skin, heats the solution of heroin or morphine in a teaspoon over a lighted match, and slowly drops the drug through an eyedropper.

Guzzle. To strangle by an armlock, rendering a victim unconscious. "Things is awful hot since them lush-workers (robbers of drunkards) guzzled a few."

Guzzler. One who **guzzles** victims.

H

H. Heroin. "My partner kicked (cured himself of) an H habit (addiction). I told him I won't grift (steal) with no junkeys (drug addicts)."

Habit. Addiction to narcotics. "I gotta skid (get rid of) that barlow (woman) of mine. She's got a C (cocaine) habit."

Habit smoker. A person addicted to opium smoking, as distinguished from a **pleasure smoker.** "A habit smoker is okay if he's got plenty of wood (money). It's no spinach (no good) for hustlers (thieves and prostitutes) that gotta kick (break) a habit (addiction) when they get a bit (prison term)."

Habitual. A person convicted of three or more felonies and therefore subject to a **life** term as an habitual criminal.

Hack, n. 1. A prison guard. "This new mick (newcomer) don't act right (conventionally). He's always buzzing (talking confidentially with) the hacks." 2. A watchman. "They got an old hack in this joint we're gonna clip (rob), but he's a lush (drunkard). Most of the time he's on the nod (half asleep)."

Half a case or **slug.** Fifty cents.

Half in stir. Out on bail; certain of a prison sentence; badly wanted by the police on criminal charges.

Handed. (Always preceded by, and hyphenated with, a numerical adjective, as two-handed, five-handed, etc.) Has reference to the number of people involved in an act.

Handful. (P) A five-year prison term. "That new fish (newcomer) only brought (was sentenced to) a handful, and he sings it (whines) like he had a man-size bit (long sentence)."

Hand it to one. To assault; to shoot.

Hand-job. (P) Masturbation practiced upon another.

Handle. 1. Petty borrowing; an attempt at chiseling. "That jerk is always on the bite (borrowing). He just put the handle on me for a deuce (two dollars)." 2. Real name, as distinguished from an alias.

Handorgan. A sub-machinegun.

Handout. 1. Anything given to a beggar or a hobo, especially cold food. 2. Anything so easily stolen that it might ironically be referred to as a gift. "A cannon's (pickpocket's) heaven is a crowded joint with plenty of 'beware of pickpockets' signs around, and the marks (victims) fanning (patting their pockets) for their pokes (wallets). Yeah, they're handouts."

Hang. 1. To be convicted of a criminal charge. "Abé's a sure pop to hang on that rap (charge)." 2. To inform or testify against an accomplice. "That muzzler (low-life) copped a plea (pleaded guilty) and he's going to hang his partners (in exchange for leniency)." 3. (With "on") To indict and convict. "They hung a bum rap (charge of which he was innocent) on Biff."

Hang a rap on. 1. To convict, especially on a charge of which the accused is innocent. 2. (P) To cause to be convicted in the Warden's Court on the basis of a false or exaggerated report. "The hack (guard) is gonna hang the rap on someone for all that swag (stolen material) leaving the shop."

Hang a shingle on. (P) To report and lock up a convict for rule violation, placing a **shingle** or bad behavior report on his door.

Hanger. (Pool-hall loan word) 1. A woman's purse on a strap, easily severed and stolen. 2. Anything very easy of accomplishment. "Get the rods (revolvers) out. I got a trick (robbery) set up for us that's a hanger." 3. (P) A brief or not too unpleasant prison term. "This bit (sentence) will be a hanger

American Underworld Lingo

if that barnacle (girl) of mine kicks in with a buck (sends me a few dollars) regular."

Hanging D. A. A prosecuting attorney with a high record of convictions, especially in murder cases carrying the death penalty.

Hanging judge. A criminal judge who is in the habit of imposing harsh sentences.

Hangout. Headquarters; rendezvous.

Hang out. To frequent; to patronize regularly, especially an underworld rendezvous.

Hang paper. To pass fraudulent checks.

Hang up. 1. Shut up! 2. To give up or abandon any criminal profession; to quit. "I'm hanging up when I pull (serve) this bit (sentence)." 3. To defer payment with the intention of cheating a creditor. "You ain't hanging me up for my cut (share of the loot)." 4. To commit suicide by hanging. "That dude (fellow) that came on the last boat (transfer of prisoners) is blowing his top (losing his sanity). He'll hang up one of these nights."

Hang your nose on the wall! Face the wall! [Usually snarled as a command during a hold-up when a victim shows too much curiosity.]

Hapas capas. 1. A writ of habeas corpus. "What, a double sawbuck (twenty-year sentence)! They can't do that. Get yourself a hapas capas." 2. An inmate amateur lawyer.

Happy dust. Cocaine. "Pushing (selling) happy dust to broads (woman) is a fink's (rat's) racket. Count me out."

Hard. (Carnival) Small change; coins, as distinguished from paper money. "Lug (get rid of) the springfield (victim). The okus (wallet we stole from him) is dry (empty) and there's nothing but hard in his kick (pocket)."

Hard-covered book. (P) Common prison expression for a book, as distinguished from magazines, periodicals, etc. "Them hard-covered books is what I want. Magazine stories are too short."

Hard-on. A grudge. "Every bull (policeman) in town has a hard-on for an ex-con. I'm blowing (leaving) this tank (town)."

Hard on for, to have a. To have a grudge against. "The hacks got a hard on for Gyp and Swaggie, and they're sure giving them honey (plenty of abuse)."

Hard stuff. Coins; change as distinguished from bills. "Stick the soft (bills) in your kick (pocket) and the hard stuff in the bag; leave the damper (cash register) clean (empty)."

Hardware. 1. Firearms; knives, razors, etc.; weapons in general. 2. Burglar's tools. 3. All hard alcoholic beverages.

Hard way, the. 1. Death by violence, as suicide or being slain while shooting it out with police or rival gangsters. 2. (In throwing dice) Making the dice turn up in a pair of numbers, as two 1's, two 2's, etc. 3. Any course of criminal action punishable by long-term imprisonment or death. "I'll stick to the scratch (forgery); nix on the heist (hold-up), that's the hard way."

Harness. 1. A policeman's uniform. 2. An outer framework of reinforced steel built around a safe, vault, or strong box. "What do these joints want with a keister (safe)? They got a bug (alarm) and a harness on them, and you get crabs (nothing of value) when you kick them open (crack them)."

Harness-cop. A uniformed policeman. "That harness-cop on this beat takes (accepts bribes). You can square (fix) any rap (charge) but rape. He hates a short-arm heister (rapist)."

Hash trap. The mouth.

Hat (a "hunk of hat"). A passive pederast; a **fag**; a loose woman. "Mickey's partner (criminal associate) turned out to be a hunk of hat in the big house (prison)."

Hatch. 1. (P) Punishment cells. 2. (P) (Rare) Any cell. 3. Any place of detention, as a station-house, county jail, prison, institution for the criminally insane, etc.

Hatchet-man. 1. Chinese Tong murder-agent, many of whom still kill their victims with the traditional hatchet, though pistols are now supplanting the old weapons. 2. (P) An agitator; a chronic gossiper and slanderer. "These cans (prisons) are knocked up with (full of) hatchet-men."

Haul. The proceeds of a crime; the loot. "These bums ain't grifters (shrewd thieves). Half of 'em never got no more than a sawbuck (ten dollars) for a haul." 2. The period of a sentence yet to be served. "A fin (five years) ain't wood (isn't negligible). It's a big haul in any man's stir (prison)."

Have a buck. To have a steady income; to have plenty of money.

Have a load on. To be under the influence of narcotics or alcohol.

Hawk, n. (Carnival) A specialist in spotting officers of the law. [It is the hawk's duty to warn the **stick** when there is **fuzz** present, usually by calling out some such phrase as, "Hello, Captain," "Hey, Joe Fuzzy," or the like.] "Kick the gaff off (release the device controlling the gaming wheel). The hawk is giving us the wire (signal that police are on the grounds)."

Haymaker shuffle. The card-cheat's most sensational trick. He arranges the cards as he picks them off the table so as to deal every player an excellent hand. The winning hand is always dealt to a confederate.

Head. 1. (P) Used idiomatically, as "Bag your head"—Shut up! Get out! Scram! "Hold your head"—Keep calm! Take it easy! 2. (P) Any person; a woman. ("A good head"—a regular fellow; "a right head"—a loyal girl.) 3. A woman. "That head of Trigger's

stuck through three bits (prison sentences) and sent him a buck (goodly sums of money). She's an ace (good fellow)."

Head cold. A case of gonorrhea.

Headlight, n. (South) A light-skinned Negress. "That headlight is one smart hustler (thief). She boosted (shoplifted) for years and stayed out of lag (prison)."

Heap. n. An automobile, especially one that is badly battered.

Heart. A combination of courage and underworld loyalty; **moxie; balls.** "Don't worry, them coppers ain't getting Joe the Bug to open up (inform upon his associates). He's got too much heart."

Heat, the. 1. Intensive police activity; police pressure put upon criminals as a result of public resentment against widespread crime, newspaper crusades, political reform campaigns, etc.; extensive police raids and arrests. "We can't grift (steal) in this heat. Blow (leave town) for a while." Used idiomatically, as: "The heat is on"—police activity in a given area is at its peak; the police are on one's trail. "Stash (hide) that collat (negotiable loot). You can't fence (sell) it for peanuts (any appreciable sum) when the heat is still on." "The heat is off"—police activity has subsided; one need no longer be in immediate fear of police. "All right, the heat's off. Put them one-armed bandits (slot-machines) back in the joints and gimmick them up (fix the gears so that our percentage is greatly increased). We gotta get off the nut (raise money for expenses, bribes, etc.) quick." 2. (Sections of South and Central U. S.) A revolver or pistol. "Go get the heat. There's some crimp (informer) we gotta take care of (kill)."

Heater. (West, mid-West and South) A revolver; any firearm capable of being used with one hand.

"Prowling (burglary) with a heater draws (results in) the book (a life sentence); you better ditch it (get rid of it)."

Heat up a tip. (Chiefly Carnival) To rouse the interest of a crowd by ballyhoo, offers of a special prize, or by any other means, often in order to swindle them with crooked gaming wheels or to enable pickpockets to rob them more effectively.

Heavy, n. 1. An armed robber. 2. (Scattered; chiefly Pacific Coast) Armed robbery. 3. A safe-cracker. 4. The safe-cracking profession. "There's no dough (money) on the heavy these days, and these gopher tricks (underground burrowing robbery operations) are too tough."

Heavy, a. Having a considerable sum of money, as a victim about to be robbed. "That joint is heavy enough for a re-hash (a second robbery of the premises)."

Heavy, on the. 1. Operating as a safe-burglar; by means of safe-burglary. 2. (Chiefly Western area) Operating as an armed robber; by means of armed robbery.

Heavy bit. A long prison stretch. "Croaking (killing) a hack (prison guard) is a chair rap (punishable by the electric chair). Those dudes (fellows) are lucky if they can settle for a heavy bit (by pleading guilty to a lesser degree of murder or manslaughter)."

Heavy heeled. Heavily armed; plentifully supplied with money, especially on one's person; having plenty of anything of value.

Heavyman. 1. (Scattered; chiefly Pacific Coast) An armed robber. 2. A safe-cracker, especially a specialist in **ripping.** "All the old-time heavymen would blow their roof (go crazy) working on these timers (time-locked vaults). You can't rip (smash) them, blow (dynamite) them, or burn them (open them with the oxy-acetylene torch)."

Heavy paper. Cash loot of great value. "I ain't hustling (stealing) for that big-bellied fence (buyer of stolen goods). Scores (robberies) with heavy paper and no collat (loot sold to a fence at greatly depreciated values) are my meat (what I want)."

Heavy time. 1. A long prison sentence. 2. Crimes of violence, as safe-blowing, armed robbery, etc. "I'm wrapping up (quitting) the heavy time (with its big penalties) and pushing (selling) schmeck (narcotics—penalties for which are relatively light)."

Hedgehopper. A professional swindler of accident insurance companies who continually moves from town to town in order to escape exposure. "That hedgehopper's got a trick knee (which he can throw out of joint at will) that made him a bundle (lot of money). He's got the courts knocked up (tied up) with bites (litigation growing out of his activities)." [A clever hedgehopper is ever on the alert for open manhole covers, badly lighted hallways, broken stairways, torn hallway carpets, etc., providing the opportunities for him to feign injury.]

Heel, n. 1. A form of sneak thievery wherein a cashier or bank teller is diverted by an aide while the principal steals a sum of money. [The heel is commonly executed in the following manner: The thief offers a large bill to the cashier. While the latter opens the cash register to make change, an aide rushes up and, announcing that he is in a great hurry, asks for a brand of cigars which he knows to be at the bottom of the showcase. As soon as the cashier turns and stoops to get the cigars, the thief seizes several large bills from the open cash register. When deftly executed, the theft is seldom discovered until the thieves have departed. A similar technique made it necessary for bank tellers to cease leaving packages of bills where they could be removed with the aid of a cane slipped through the barred window of the cage.] 2. An informer; a mean or contemptible person.

Heel, v. 1. To use rough tactics; to assault suddenly, especially by stealth and with superior force; to commit an armed assault upon an unarmed victim. 2. To take flight from the scene of a crime, deserting one's accomplices. ("To heel out of a joint"—to flee helterskelter.) 3. To rob by means of the **heel** technique. 4. To leave one's hotel or boarding house without paying one's bill. 5. To run away; to flee; to escape; to take to one's heels. "Let's grab a drag (freight train) and heel town. They got our muggs on the board ('wanted' circulars, with our photographs, distributed)."

Heel a joint. 1. To rob by means of the **heel**. 2. To fish a pair of trousers or a purse through a ground-floor window while occupants sleep. 3. To cheat the landlord by allowing others to sleep in quarters where rent is paid for one or two.

Heeled. 1. Having a dangerous weapon on one's person or within one's reach; armed. 2. Having ample money on hand; **heavy heeled.** 3. (Rare) Intoxicated or under the influence of drugs.

Heeler. 1. A bouncer, especially in shady establishments. 2. An apartment sneak thief. 3. A deserter, or betrayer of one's accomplices when in danger; a thief who who employs the **heel** technique. 4. The act of evading payment of a hotel bill. 5. Any ward politician whose tactics are those of a ruffian. "Them heelers gotta chill (frighten) the coppers on this beef (complaint) if they want muscle men to work for the club (local political club)."

Heel out. To go or leave hurriedly. "Heel out, Tony. See if that's a bull (policeman) gandering (looking at) the camp (apartment)."

Heel up. To arm oneself, especially

with a gun or a knife. "We better heel up with chivs (knives). Them creeps (weasels) looking for a rep (bad reputation) like to cop a sneak (attack one by surprise)."

Heist. 1. A holdup; an armed robbery. 2. A kick, usually in the buttocks, delivered with a flexed knee. ("A heist in the keister"—a boot in the rear with the knee.)

Heist, on the. Engaged in, or by means of, armed robbery.

Heister. See **Heist-man.**

Heist in the pratt. Kick in the buttocks, especially with the knee.

Heist-man. A holdup man; an armed robber. "Most of the right guys (loyal underworlders) are heist-men. Them scratchers (forgers), fire-bugs (arsonists), and short-arm bandits (rapists) turn out to be finks (informers)."

Heist-rap. A holdup charge; a prison sentence for a holdup.

Hello. (P) The standard form of salutation in prison **tabs**, as well as in prisoners' letters home; to give one a **big hello.**

Hep, to be. 1. Experienced in the underworld; sophisticated; having underworld wisdom; alert. 2. Having inside information; aware of; "wise to." "Nix! The sucker (victim) is hep."

Hep-broad. A smart girl in terms of underworld sophistication, especially one useful in criminal enterprise.

Hep-ghee. 1. One who is thoroughly hep. 2. Any civilian or officer who is on the alert to prevent a crime; anyone who is aware that a crime is being committed; a policeman in civilian clothes. "Nix cracking (stop talking so unguardedly), there's a hep-ghee at your pratt (right behind you)."

Hep up. 1. To become familiar with the customs and law of the underworld; to teach such knowledge to another. "Ain't that ghee (fellow) ever going to get hepped up? He done three bits (prison sentences) and he don't know the score (what it is all about) yet." 2. To learn, or to advise another of, any secret, furtive plan, or deed. "Hep Tuttie up that the bulls (police) are on his pratt (trail)." 3. (Imperative) Get wise! Watch your step! Stop that! "C'm'on, hep up! Them gappers (passers-by) are burning us up (looking at us suspiciously)."

Hey, rube! (Carnival) "Help!" A common call for assistance in a brawl on the carnival grounds.

Hicks. Shells, usually walnut shells, used in the **shell game.**

Hide. 1. A wallet or a woman's purse. 2. Loose women; prostitutes; passive pederasts. ("A piece of hide"—sexual intercourse; the passive partner in the act.)

Hide-out, n. 1. (P) A place of concealment on prison grounds where a prisoner might hide before attempting to escape. [Note: A successful plot may result in the guard being withdrawn after eleven days, on the assumption that the prisoner has succeeded in leaving the enclosure.] 2. A criminal's place of concealment. "Stash (conceal) yourself in the hide-out, Nig; the heat is on (the police are clamping down)." 3. One who attempts to escape from prison by concealing himself in a hide-out; the attempt itself. "There is a swag (lot) of food in the hideout. Wait for a rainy day and hole up (conceal yourself there)."

Hide out. v. 1. To hide from the police. 2. (P) To conceal oneself on prison grounds, hoping to escape after dark. "Bob is gonna hide out, and hit the wall (attempt to escape over the wall) some foggy night."

High. Exhilarated; stimulated, as by marijuana, narcotics in general, or by a fortunate turn of events; elated. "Five C's (five hundred dollars) on a pocket-touch! A score (theft) like that'd make any cannon (pickpocket) feel high."

High as a kite. Drunk; elated; under the influence of drugs; **charged up.** "That first baseman (overcautious thief) won't step out till he's as high as a kite."

Highball, n. A signal, especially of okay, summons, or greeting.

Highball, v. To signal; to give the okay; to summon; to greet.

Highway mopery. 1. Any contemptibly petty or stupid offense resulting in arrest. 2. (P) Any foolish infraction of prison rules or any careless act resulting in a report or **lock-up.** "I don't mind a collar (report) for swag (stolen prison stores) or something, but these highway mopery pinches (reports) are murder (intolerable)."

Hijack, n. The act of **hijacking.**

Hijack, v. 1. To hold up and take any truck and its contents. 2. To steal from other thieves or racketeers illegal or stolen goods. "A mob of loftmen (loft-burglars) made the touch (theft) and then Slasher's combo (gang) hijacked them for the works (whole thing)." 3. (P) To use two or three accomplices in a pocket-picking operation, involving rough jostling and diversion of attention, as when a victim leaves a streetcar, train, elevator, etc. "The mark (victim) had a boodle-belt (money belt), and we had to hijack him to make the score (theft)."

Hijacker. One who **hijacks.**

Hill billy. A crude simpleton; a rustic.

Hip. See **Hep.**

Hip, on the. 1. Smoking the opium pipe. 2. (Rare) On the alert; wise in the ways of the underworld.

Hipe, n. 1. The short-change racket, especially involving coins, as distinguished from **laying the note,** involving currency. [A common form of the hipe is that in which a swindler counts the correct change into his own hand in plain view of the victim, then pushes it hurriedly into the victim's hand in such a way as to impel him to pocket it before counting the coins. A coin has been deftly palmed and exchanged for another of lesser value.] 2. Any confidence racket or swindle involving dexterity, cleverness, fast talk, and a small sum of money. 3. The act of raising gambling stakes in swindling a victim who has been inveigled by being permitted to win a few bets.

Hipe, v. 1. To borrow money by pledging property which has already been pledged to others, the value of the property being less than the total indebtedness; to hypothecate. 2. To short change or swindle by means of the **hipe.** 3. To raise gambling stakes in order to swindle a victim who has been permitted to win several "come-on" bets. "I put the bend on (bent the corner of the key card) and the hoosier (victim) beat us for half a yard (fifty dollars). Then we hiped him and he went for (was robbed of) a C and a half (a hundred fifty dollars)." 4. To carry on a confidence racket in which petty sums are involved. 5. To rob or cheat by outwitting, not by force.

Hiper. A short-change swindler or any petty confidence game operator. One who **hipes.**

Hip-ghee. See **Hep-ghee.**

Hippy. (West and East-Central U. S.) Mentally affected or dulled by too many years of imprisonment.

Hipster. See **Hep-ghee.**

Hip to the bug. Aware of the presence of a burglar alarm and prepared to defeat it.

Hip to the kip. Aware of the presence of a night watchman and his routine movements.

Hip to the lay. Having inside information about a specific crime to be committed; well versed in the organization details of a racket; aware of what is going on. "You can crack (talk freely) with the Leaper. He's hip to the lay."

Hip up. See **Hep up.**

Hit, n. The simultaneous holding by many bettors of the winning number in the policy numbers racket. [Note: The pay-off is usually 600 to 1, less 10 per cent runner's bonus, on an actual 1000 to 1 gamble on treasury balance or clearing house figures. The odds are somewhat varied when the race-track pari-mutuel figures are used as the basis of the game.] "Half of them bankers (policy number operators) take a powder (run away) when they get a bad hit."

Hit, v. 1. To indulge in, as to "hit the schmeck" (narcotics), or to "hit the weed" (marijuana). 2. (P) To go to; to be sent to; to arrive at. (Used in such phrases as, to "hit the cell"; "hit the hospital"; "hit the yard"; "hit the cooler," etc.) "Any time you hit the slough (are locked up), buzz (get in touch with) this mouthpiece (lawyer). He's the best fixer in town."

Hit-and-run-play. Any crime which is dependent upon accurate timing, economy of movement, and swift flight. "The broad (girl) we planted (stationed) in the jug (bank) pulled a phony (feigned) faint. The teller rounded (turned around) and I glommed (stole) four C's (four hundred dollars) from his cage and mooched out (walked out) in a hit-and-run-play that was a honey."

Hit a slab. To be slain; to wind up in a local morgue. "The way that dude (fellow) cowboys around (shooting and holding up indiscriminately) he figures to hit a slab any day."

Hit a tea pad. To visit a marijuana den.

Hit a tower. (P) To be punished, as a prison guard, by assignment to lonely guard-turret duty. "My kite (smuggled letter) connection (carrier) got caught and hit a tower."

Hitch. (Rare) A prison term.

Hitch up the reindeer. To procure

narcotics and prepare for indulgence. "Hitch up the reindeer, and we'll go for a sleighride"—get some cocaine or other narcotics and we'll enjoy ourselves.

Hit in the biscuit, bonnet, or cruller. See **Hit in the head.**

Hit in the head. To shoot to kill. [Note: The expression does not necessarily imply a head wound.] (Reflexively: "To hit oneself in the head"—to commit suicide by shooting.)

Hit in the noggin. See **Hit in the head.**

Hit in the squash. (New England area) See **Hit in the head.**

Hit isolation. (P) To be placed in the segregation wing, either as punishment or in protective custody. "The punk (passive pederast) that put the slug on (assaulted) some turk (active pederast) didn't hit isolation. He might get boffed (sentenced to) with a new bit (prison term)."

Hit izo. See **Hit isolation.**

Hit oneself in the bonnet. To commit suicide by shooting, especially when arrest is imminent. "What balls (courage) Lou had! He knew if the bulls (police) grabbed him he'd be buried (get a staggering sentence) so he knocked off (killed) two cops and hit himself in the bonnet."

Hit oneself out. See **Hit oneself in the bonnet.**

Hit one with. 1. To make a show of anything with the intent to coerce or impress, as a pistol, a bogus or genuine officer's badge, etc. "Hit the mark (victim) with the tin (badge) and you can shake him for plenty (extort plenty of his money)." 2. To give something unpleasant, undesirable, or counterfeited, as a forged check, a prison sentence, a bogus bill, etc. "I tried to hit the fence (buyer of stolen goods) with a stiff (forged check) but he's too hip (smart)."

Hit the beach. (Elmira Reformatory,

N. Y.) To be sent to a punishment cell on reduced rations.

Hit the bricks. (P) To be paroled, discharged, acquitted, or otherwise set free. "Hawk's got a flat bit (definite sentence) so he's gotta hit the bricks (parole may not be denied legally)."

Hit the ceiling. 1. To become berserk with fear, anger, joy, etc. 2. To become exhilarated as a result of smoking marijuana. "Jumpin' Joe hits the ceiling after a little of that tea (marijuana) and kicks the lemon off (beats) that bag (woman) of his."

Hit the deck. To fall down; to lie down; to be knocked down. "Old Jim was slow on the heel and toe (running) so he hit the deck and the bull (policeman) thought he pooped (shot) him and stayed hot on my tail (pursuing me). So no one got glommed (caught)."

Hit the flats with. (P) To throw out of the cell onto the ground floor of the cell-block, especially weapons or contraband during a search. "They're going to frisk (search), Sam. Hit the flats with that hot boiler (small contraband cooking stove)."

Hit the flop. To go to bed; to go to one's rooms.

Hit the hump. (Central and Western prisons) To attempt to escape.

Hit the jackpot. 1. To receive a great quantity of anything at one time, whether desired or not. 2. (P) To receive the maximum punishment or sentence.

Hit the kip. See **Hit the flop.**

Hit the main drag (or the main stem). See **Hit the main line.**

Hit the main line. 1. To go on the main street to beg, steal, etc. 2. (P) To go to the prison mess hall for a meal. 3. To inject drugs into the median cephalic vein.

Hit the needle. To take a hypodermic injection of drugs; to be addicted to drug injections.

Hit the pavement. See **Hit the bricks.**

Hit the pipe. To smoke opium. "Going for (being addicted to) the mahoska (narcotics) is pea soup (no good), but hitting the pipe for pleasure (occasionally) is okay if you got a buck (money)."

Hit the population. (P) To be released from segregation, punishment cells, hospital, or other place of seclusion. "That fink (informer) buried (testified against) too many. They ain't gonna let him hit the population (leave segregation)."

Hit the porch. (San Quentin and Folsom Prisons, Calif.) To report before the yard sergeant for rule violation on a kind of porch overlooking the prison yard, whence men are marched before the disciplinarian for hearing and punishment.

Hit the pot. To drink excessively.

Hit the road. 1. To flee a town or area. "I ain't getting vagged (committed for vagrancy) in them cans (jails) around here. Let's hit the road." 2. (Hobo) To leave town or **jungle** camp and travel. [Note: The standard order to a hobo, tramp, or bum to move on is: "Hit the road, bum."]

Hit the sewer. To inject drugs hypodermically into the median cephalic vein.

Hit the sidewalk. See **Hit the bricks.**

Hit the stem. To walk along the street, especially to steal or beg.

Hit the street. See **Hit the bricks.**

Hit the turf. 1. To go to steal; to engage in any criminal venture as a means of making one's livelihood. 2. To go street-walking. 3. (Hobo) To take to the road; to go out on the street or road to beg.

Hit the wall. See **Hit the hump.**

Hit up. To solicit; to ask a favor of or make application to.

Hit with a bit. To sentence to a prison or jail term; to be sentenced. "The mark (victim) made my mugg (recognized my face), and I figured I'm a cinch to get hit with a bit, but he wouldn't rap (press the charge)."

Hit with a lily. (Coarse jocularity rather than narrative) To murder.

Hit with a swag. 1. To palm off stolen goods on an innocent receiver; to **fence blind.** "Popeye Pete duked me in (introduced) to some broad (girl) that wanted ice (diamonds). I hit her with a swag that the fence (buyer of stolen goods) wouldn't give pretzels for (wouldn't give a cent for)." 2. (P) To inveigle another into carrying stolen prison stores, especially by deceiving him as to the contents of package. "That crumb (unprincipled fellow) hit me with a swag that was red hot (badly wanted by the guards) to bring into his cell. I'll knock him on his keister (rump) if he pulls that again."

Hit with buckwheats. (Northeastern industrial area prisons) To subject to abuse or persecution. "There's a screw (guard) that's a right ghee (good fellow). Finks (informers), peddlers (traffickers in stolen prison stores), and punks (passive pederasts) get hit with plenty of buckwheats when he's got the shop (prison factory)."

H-joint. An establishment where heroin is sold to addicts.

H. O. To withhold fraudulently a portion of receipts or loot; to **hold out.** "That louse is gonna get his cruller (head) kicked in h.o.-ing on me."

Hock, in. 1. Out of funds; broke. 2. In pawn.

Hog-box. See **Holdout box.**

H. O. ghee. 1. One who cheats his accomplices by withholding portions of loot. (Literally, a hold-out guy.) "You're blowing your top (getting foolish) working with that h.o. ghee; they're all rats." 2. (P) One who seeks to avoid sharing food, tobacco, etc., with those from whom he takes all he can get.

Hold-back, n. (P) A denial of application for parole.

Hold back, v. To subject to a **hold-back.**

Hold down. To guard or control, as a door, a room, during the commission of a robbery. "Hold down that out (means of escape; exit), Tiger, while we clip (rob) the joint."

Hold heavy. To be well supplied with ready cash.

Holding. (Limited to "what are you holding?" and the response, "I'm holding. . . .) 1. To have money in one's possession. "We gotta get fall dough (legal fees, bail money, etc.) up or Pigeon is buried (certain to go to prison for a long term). What are you holding, Lucky?" 2. (P) To have in one's possession contraband cash, cigarettes, tobacco, or other medium of exchange.

Hold it up. (P) So long! Good-bye! Keep your chin up! [A common expression of leave-taking.]

Hold one's end up. 1. To take care of one's responsibilities; to protect one's own interest. "Them fleepers (underworld nobodies) ain't putting the chill on (frightening) me. I'll hold my end up if they wanta try to muscle in (exploit our territory)." 2. To take the part of another; to protect the interests of another. "You ain't pushing my partner around. I'm holding his end up so get hep (wise) to yourself."

Hold-out, n. One who **holds out.** The act of holding out.

Hold out. v. 1. To cheat one's accomplices by withholding portions of loot. 2. (P) To keep secret; to withhold, as information. 3. To refuse to divulge information under police pressure. 4. (P) To conceal one's tobacco, extra food, etc., in order to avoid sharing it with others. "Every time I put

the bite on you (ask you for something), you ain't holding nothing. What are you doing, holding out, you single-o (selfish) bum?"

Holdout box. A mechanical box in which playing cards are shuffled and dealt through a slot that feeds out losing cards from a concealed compartment at will of crooked operators.

Hold the bag or **sack.** To be left in the lurch; to be deserted by one's associates when in trouble; to be betrayed by one's partners in crime; to be the only member of a gang not to confess and, consequently, stand trial alone when confronted with the testimony of one's accomplices; to be left "holding the bag." "As soon as we got rumbled (interrupted), my partners hit the lam-car (escape car) and blew (fled), leaving me to hold the sack."

Hold your head! (N. Y. State prisons) 1. Good-bye! So long! Keep your chin up! 2. Don't lose your head! Don't lose your temper!

Hole. 1. (P) The punishment cell where inmates are put on bread-and-water diets. "Sam hit the hole for silent insolence (refusing to answer a guard or glaring at him). 2. (P) A possible means of escape. "I got me a telephone number bit (long term). Gotta find a hole." 3. (P) A cell. "Where do you count, in the hole? (Are you checked in outside your cell, in a trusty assignment, or in your cell, with the bulk of the population?)" 4. A fugitive's hideout; a place of concealment of kidnaped victims. 5. The subway (as pickpocket's field of operations).

Hole up. To take cover when wanted by the police; **flatten out.**

Holler. See **Holler copper.**

Holler copper. 1. To complain to the police. "We were putting the shake on (extorting money from) mahoska pushers (narcotic traffickers); it's a nice thing, they can't holler copper." 2. (Loosely) To confess, implicating accomplices. "These bums calling everyone else finks (informers) are the first ones to holler copper when they take a drop (are arrested)." 3. (P) To complain to prison authorities; to inform upon fellow convicts. "Someone beat (robbed) him for three skins (dollars) and he hollered copper. That louses him up with me."

Holler murder. See **Holler copper**

Hollywood stew. (San Quentin and Folsom Prisons, Calif.) Creamed codfish.

Holy Joe. (P) A prison chaplain of Christian denomination. "Holy Joe is on the beef department (complaining) because I ain't hitting services (attending church services)."

Home relief. (P) Money, food, or clothing received from home or friends outside prison. "That whack (idiot) drops (loses) his home relief to them mechanics (card sharps) in the yard and then grubs (begs) everyone else for the makings (tobacco and cigarette papers)."

Homey. (South; rare elsewhere, except among Negroes) A person from one's neighborhood, home town, or State. "Me and my homey just done a sixer (six months) in lag (jail)."

Honey. 1. (New York, New Jersey, and neighboring States, especially in prison) Deliberate discourtesy to, mistreatment of, those whom one dislikes; abuse. "All that muzzler (low fellow) can get from me is honey since he proved he's a single-o (selfish) fleabag (pig)." 2. Anything or any person that excites admiration or pleasure, especially a person easily and profitably victimized. "What a honey that mark (victim) was! He went for the green goods game (switch of good money in a pool for fake money) and didn't know he was beat (robbed) when we rausted (got rid of) him."

Hood. A thief or racketeer. (Rarely) A ruffian who works for a living. "Some little punk working for a bank just took a powder (fled) with two hundred G's ($200,000), and all the hoods are trying to beat the dicks (police) snatching him."

Hoodlum. See **Hood.**

Hoodoo. See **Jinx.**

Hook, n. 1. A pickpocket, usually the skilled operator in a gang. "There's too many hooks working that short (trolley or bus line). We'll hit the hole (subway)." 2. (Often figurative) The hand as an instrument of crime. "Dodo's got his hooks in most of the clipjoints (crooked gambling houses, restaurants, brothels, etc.) in town." 3. An arrest. "Jim Penny took a hook with a scratch-mob (forgery gang) in Providence." 4. (Central and mid-Western States) A straight razor. 5. (Very rare) A prison. 6. A long-nosed person. 7. The nose.

Hook, v. 1. To make a narcotic addict of. "That baloney (girl) is hooked on the schmeck (drugs)." 2. To swindle; to trick; to defraud. "I hooked him with readers (marked cards) and he's gonna stay hooked (I'll give him no chance to win his money back)." 3. To arrest, with conviction almost certain. "Pete's hooked as a two-time loser (second offender)."

Hooker. 1. A prostitute. 2. A warrant for re-arrest pending one's release from prison. "I'm dropping a tab (writing a letter) to the D.A. to try to get this hooker off." 3. A thief, especially a pickpocket.

Hook-joint. 1. A house of prostitution; a **nautch-joint.** 2. Any establishment that pads bills or otherwise swindles its patrons; a **clip-joint.** "What a sucker's holler (outcry) them hoods (thieves) put up when they're beat (robbed) in them hook-joints! Tough givers-up."

Hooko. 1. Any long-nosed person. 2. The nose.

Hooks, the. A professional shoplifter's device, concealed inside the slit armpit of an oversized **boosting-ben**. A neatly made cloth panel inside and outside the slit conceals the hooks on which large quantities of stolen goods may be slung.

Hooks are in, the. 1. All preparations have been made for one's conviction, defeat, or destruction. "The hooks are in to settle (commit to prison) you, Turk. This beef (criminal charge) has gotta stick (must result in conviction)." 2. (P) Plans have been made by the authorities or by one's fellow convicts to subject one to abuse. "They got me pegged (branded) as a screw-hater (hater of officers) and the hooks are in to buckwheat (abuse and discriminate against) me."

Hooks are out, the. The police net is being spread; a police hunt has begun. "Hole up (conceal yourself) tight, Joe, the hooks are out for you on that pete-job (safecracking matter)."

Hook-shop. A house of prostitution.

Hook up with. 1. To join in criminal partnership. 2. To marry, or live with in extra-marital relationship.

Hooligan. A rowdy, or ruffian, not necessarily of the underworld fraternity; (loosely) a **hood;** a thief or racketeer. "We copped a mope (made a getaway) after the come-off (happening) and the law is trying to pin the rap on some hooligans they picked up (arrested), a bunch of working-stiffs (honest workmen)."

Hoop, n. A ring. Usually, an imitation gold ring marked "14 carat" to defraud purchasers. "The fence (buyer of stolen goods) won't touch them hot (stolen) hoops, only the other slum (jewelry)."

Hoosegow. 1. A police station-house or local jail. 2. (P) The lock-up, or punishment wing, in prison.

Hoosier. 1. Any gullible or credulous person; a victim selected by pickpockets or by any organized mob of thieves. 2. A rustic or country dweller as differentiated from a **slicker.**

Hoosiers. (P) Sightseers or students visiting a prison. "Get a load of them hoosiers gandering (gaping at us) like we was monkeys in the zoo."

Hootch. Alcoholic liquor.

Hop. To become a fugitive; to **lam.**

Hop a parole. To violate parole obligations by fleeing the jurisdiction of the parole board. "You're a sucker to hop a parole if you ain't hitting the turf (going back to crime)."

Hop bail. To flee the jurisdiction of a court, automatically forfeiting one's bail bond. "The rap (charge) looked like I'd hit the street (be acquitted). I'd a hopped bail if I knew the D. A. could settle me for mopery (secure a conviction on such a flimsy case)."

Hophead. A drug addict. "A hophead would sell his mother out; don't grift (operate in rackets) with any of them creeps (rats)."

Hopped up. 1. Under the influence of narcotics; exhilarated by drugs. 2. "Hopped up over"—almost berserk with enthusiasm, fear, or other violent emotion.

Hop-scotch. (Carnival) To move constantly from one show to another. "He ain't no j.c.l. (newcomer). That dude (fellow) has got a lot of grift sense (racketeering experience). He's been hop-scotching around for years."

Hop town. To flee a city or town, especially when wanted by police.

Horneo. (N. Y. City Catholic Protectory) An inmate whose conversation and manners betray an abnormal preoccupation with sex.

Horns, the. 1. (Among Italians) The symbol of cuckoldry. "The guy's hep (smart) in the grift (racketeering) but he sure lets that chippie (girl) of his put the horns on him something awful." 2. The sign of a dupe, or of one who is cheated. "That creep (rat) will burn (cheat in division of loot) you plenty. He puts the horns on everyone he hooks up with (associates with in crime)." 3. Hoodoo; a jinx. "I can't score for (steal) a pretzel (thing). Some muzzler (low fellow) has put the horns on me."

Horny. (Juvenile) Preoccupied with sex.

Horseman. (Prohibition era) A collector for venal police and Federal agents of protection money from speakeasy establishments and illegal stills. "Them lousy horsemen got me knocked up (financially exhausted). I'll have to wrap up (close) this joint."

Horse-to-horse. Everything being equal. "Get rodded up (armed). Horse-to-horse we can muscle (force) that mob out of the grift (racket)."

Hose, n. 1. The traditional piece of rubber hose used in police **third degree** methods because it leaves no mark. 2. Sexual intercourse.

Hose, v. 1. To have sexual intercourse with. 2. To subject to unduly severe punishment. "That's an awful way to hose a ghee (fellow), a double sawbuck (twenty-year sentence) for spitting on the sidewalk (committing a petty crime)." 3. To cheat; to swindle. "That muzzler (unprincipled fellow) tried to hose me for a half a C (fifty dollars) of my end (share)."

Hosing. Unduly severe treatment or punishment, as an excessive prison sentence; the act of betraying or cheating one's accomplices; any betrayal of trust. "That swag-buyer (buyer of stolen goods) gave us a hosing on that ice (deal involving stolen diamonds)."

Hospital, the. Prison. [Note: This term is especially useful in explaining the absence of an imprisoned member of the family to children or aged parents.]

Hot. 1. Stolen; illegally produced or obtained; dangerous to handle. ["Hot

ice" or "hot slum"—stolen jewelry; "hot dough"—counterfeit money, or money paid as kidnap ransom, presumably with serial numbers noted by the police.] 2. Wanted by police. "I gotta hole up (go into hiding). I'm red hot." 3. Characterized by intense police activity; under police surveillance. "Cop a mope (go away). The neighborhood's hot." 4. Angry. "It gets you hot to draw a blank (get no money out of a prospective victim) after all that build-up (preliminary effort)." 5. Skilled; keyed up to perform with more than customary skill. 6. Recently stolen, hence, being sought by the police.

Hot, on the. In flight while making a getaway; quickly; **on the lam.** "We made (robbed) the damper (cash register) on the hot and copped a mope (fled)."

Hot as a forty-five. ("Forty-five"— large calibre pistol) 1. Wanted on a serious charge or series of charges. 2. Extremely **hot.**

Hot boiler. 1. A stolen automobile. 2. (P) A contraband stove, usually electric; a canned-heat unit [a can filled with sand and sprinkled with gasoline, or any similar contrivance, used by inmates in prisons in which individual cooking is forbidden].

Hot boiler farm. See **Hot car farm.**

Hot boiler hustler. Anyone engaged in the stolen car racket.

Hot car farm. A place, usually located inconspicuously in the suburbs and having the appearance of a junkyard, where stolen cars are altered to escape police identification. Motor-block numbers are carefully changed.

Hot crate. A stolen automobile.

Hot dough. Counterfeit money; stolen money the registration numbers of which are listed and watched for by the police.

Hot foot. (Very rare) A fugitive, usually a bail-jumper.

Hot heap. A stolen automobile.

Hot in the biscuit. (P) Greatly excited; angry; sexually stimulated; **horny.** "Jim the gun (pickpocket) is all hot in the biscuit since the board (parole board) hit him with (deferred his parole for) a deuce (two years). He figured to spring (be released)."

Hot joint. 1. An occupied residence which is the object of a robbery; a **hot slough.** 2. Any establishment known to be frequented by police or stool pigeons, or which has often been raided by the police. "This is too hot a joint, full of lamesters (fugitives); let's cop a mope (leave here)." 3. A dangerous town for criminal operations; any illegitimate establishment.

Hot load. A stolen automobile. "Get out and put the glom on (steal) a hot load for that score (robbery) tomorrow. Drive it in the plant (hiding place) overnight and switch the markers (equip it with counterfeit license plates)."

Hot one. 1. A stolen automobile, especially one stolen within the past twenty-four hours, hence an object of intense police search. 2. Anything stolen or contraband. "Don't rumble (talk to) me now. I'm carrying hot ones (stolen articles of any kind)." 3. Anything very amusing, curious, or extremely interesting. "Here's a hot one: in some can (prison) out West they snatched (caught) two ghees (fellows) making a beat (attempting to escape), dressed them in panties and brassieres and stood them up where all the other cons could gander (look at) them."

Hot on one's pratt. In close pursuit; on one's trial; at one's back. "Joe put the duke down (reached into the victim's pocket), but the sucker got hep (wise). He started beefing (raising an outcry), and Tom had to conk him (hit him on the head). Then we lammed (fled) with the hoosiers hot on our pratts."

Hot on one's tail. See **Hot on one's pratt.**

Hot paper. 1. Forged checks or instruments; counterfeit or stolen stocks or bonds; marked playing cards. 2. (P) A newspaper, in prisons where newspapers are contraband.

Hot rig. A stolen automobile.

Hot seat. The electric chair; the **hot spot.** "Those two ghees (fellows) are practically in the hot seat. A copper (policeman) and a hack (prison guard) got knocked off (slain) in that beat (attempted escape)."

Hot short. A stolen automobile, especially one that has been stolen within the past twenty-four hours, and is consequently the object of active police search. "That hot short belongs to the D.A. He'll sure be burnt up when he finds out his own boiler (car) was glommed (stolen) and used on a heist (stick-up)."

Hot slough. An occupied dwelling which is the object of burglary.

Hot slough worker. One who burglarizes **hot sloughs.**

Hot spot or **squat.** The electric chair.

Hot stickers. 1. Stolen postage stamps. 2. Counterfeit postage, revenue, or similar stamps.

Hot stove. (P) A contraband stove for cooking; a **hot boiler.** "Some rat (informer) beefed (told) that I had a hot stove but I yentzed (outwitted) the hack (guard) that came for it. I gave him a dummy with a phony broom-wire coil and planted (hid) the good one."

Hot stuff. 1. Stolen, illegal, or contraband goods. 2. (P) Pornographic literature or pictures. 3. Any thing or person remarkably interesting or entertaining. "Well, I'm gonna listen to that old pete-man (safe-cracker) cut up jackpots (tell stories). He's hot stuff."

Hot tomato. A passionate woman; an unusually brazen or tough woman.

Hot trap. A stolen automobile.

Hot wire. A reliable and up-to-the-minute report; direct inside information. "I just got a hot wire from a right copper (policeman friendly to the underworld) that English Ed is opening up (informing) on plenty.'"

Hours, get. See **Get hours.**

House. 1. The operator of any gambling game. 2. A brothel.

House dick. A hotel detective.

House mother. The proprietress of a house of prostitution.

House of all nations. A brothel featuring a variety of races and nationalities.

How's you and me? (N. Y. State prisons) A standard greeting, foreshadowing a request for a favor or a loan. "How's you and me, Joe? Can I put the bite on (borrow from) you for some Duke's (tobacco) till the buy (delivery of store purchases)?"

How thick? (Carnival) Agent's question to shill (worker in the crowd) regarding the extent of a prospective victim's visible money. [The question is woven into a pattern of argot understood only by carnival workers and the answer is indicated by the thumb and forefinger held as far apart as the thickness of the wad of money.]

Howzit? (A corruption of, "How is it?") The customary prison greeting alternating with, "What's hot?" "What's stirrin'?" "What's on the move?"

Hucks. See **Hicks.**

Hudson-pup, n. An old Essex automobile.

Hummer. An arrest on a charge of which one is innocent; a bum rap; a stiff; a phony rap.

Hump, n. 1. (P) The halfway mark in a prison term. "Once I hit over the hump, I'll pull the rest of this bit (sentence) on one ear (very easily)." 2. Loose women and prostitutes as a class; the act of copulation. 3. (P) A passive pederast; pederasty.

Hump, v. 1. To have sexual intercourse with. 2. To cheat; to send to prison unjustly; to abuse or maltreat. "Oh, brother! Did I get humped! My mouthpiece (lawyer) sold me out, my broad got herself a new dude (fellow), and I'm doing forty boffos (years in prison)."

Hump for the monkeys. See **Fruit for the monkeys.**

Hump one to death. To outwit completely, especially one who is a martinet or who seeks to press an advantage. "Two of them floor dicks (department store detectives) are giving me a tail (following me) around the joint and I'm humping them to death boosting (shoplifting) right under their noses."

Humps. Playing cards with "readable" curves and bumps along the edges, not discernible to untrained eyes or fingertips.

Hump under the old system. See **Fruit under the old system.**

Hundred-percenter. 1. A wholly trustworthy fellow. One who is entirely loyal —or disloyal—to the code of the underworld.

Hundred percent screw. (P) An excessively strict prison guard.

Hundred percent wrong. Wholly disloyal, or contemptuous of, underworld conventions.

Hungry. Money-mad, especially for bribes, protection sums.

Hunk of hat. 1. A prostitute or loose woman. 2. A passive pederast; a male oral copulator.

Hunk of quiff, skin, or **snatch.** See **Hunk of hat.**

Hurdy. (P) (Abbreviation of hurdygurdy) A run-around; a wild goose chase; a "song and dance"; a false promise. "The mouthpiece (lawyer) gave my people a real hurdy, promised to spring (bring about the release of) me for five yards (five hundred dollars)."

Hush-hush. A gun with a silencer; a dumb-gat; a sissy rod.

Hustle. 1. To steal professionally, especially in gangs. 2. To practice prostitution for a livelihood. 3. To gamble professionally.

Hustle, on the. Stealing; practicing prostitution; gambling; engaging in any criminal racket.

Hustle, the. 1. Professional thievery, prostitution, gambling, or any similarly illegal means of livelihood. 2. Trickery; guile; a fraud; swindle. ("To give one a hustle"—to attempt to swindle.)

Hustle blind. To steal without previous information concerning the victim or the site of the crime. "These punks out hustling blind bang (shoot) people, get boy-scout dough (small sums) and screw up the works (make things difficult for) on everyone out to make a buck."

Hustler. 1. A professional thief, especially one operating with a gang. 2. A prostitute. 3. A professional crap shooter; any professional gambler.

Hut. (P) (Rare) A cell.

Hymie. (Hobo) Sexual intercourse. "To knock off a hunk of hymie."

Hype. See **Hipe.**

Hype, on the. 1. Engaged in, or by means of, the short-change swindle. 2. Addicted to hypodermic injections of narcotics. 3. In the act of raising the stakes in a card swindle. 4. Engaged in or by means of any form of the **hipe.**

Hype-stick. A hypodermic needle; any crude substitute for a hypodermic needle.

Hypo. 1. A drug addict who injects drugs by means of a hypodermic needle. [Note: In the absence of the needle, the addict will often heat the solution in a teaspoon by holding a match beneath it, prick the skin with a pin and drop the heated liquid into the surface wound from an eyedropper.] 2. A hypochondriac.

I

I. C., on the. On the lookout; looking inquisitively, as a bystander observing criminals prior to or during the commission of a crime.

I. C., the. The act of serving as a lookout or being on the I. C.

Ice. 1. Diamonds 2. (By extension) Gems of any kind; any jewelry set with gems. 3. (P) Anything valuable. "That phony peddler (one who sells stolen prison stores) is handing out ice. He wants a pack of butts for that lousy State mud (coffee)."

Ice, on. 1. In prison. 2. (P) In punishment cells, usually on reduced rations of bread and water.

Ice-box, the. 1. The morgue. 2. (P) The isolation or segregation block.

Ice-house. (Scattered areas U. S.) A jewelry store. "Every gullion mob (gang of jewel thieves) in Chicago is out to reef (rob) that ice-house."

Ice-man. 1. (P) Any official or inmate whose promises are not to be relied upon. 2. One who makes ostentatious gifts of worthless or trivial things. "Can you imagine this? This ice-man is putting on an act giving State stuff (stores issue) out like it was his own." 3. A buyer of stolen diamonds. 4. A jewel thief.

Idea-pot, the. The head; the mind.

Idle, n. The companies or cell-blocks in which the unemployed are grouped.

Idle, a. (P) Having no work assignment, a condition shared by almost all prison populations.

If money. If things turn out well. "I meet the Board (Parole Board) next month, so I'll be back on the turf (out stealing) in a couple of months if money."

Iggy, n. (Carnival) The cold shoulder; the act of ignoring; feigned ignorance. "The patch (legal adjuster) knocked me off (caught me) pulling a sneak (exceeding the limit on stakes at the gaming wheel) and he's giving me the old iggy."

Imbeciles. (Carnival) Those who are gullible enough to be taken in by crooked carnival games.

I.M.M. Impairing the morals of a minor.

In, n. 1. Any relationship with a person or persons in authority which enables one to procure special privileges or to circumvent the law. 2. Entrance by force or guile, especially in the furtherance of a burglary. 3. An introduction; an invitation; entree to circles ordinarily closed to underworld members.

In, a. 1. Included; sharing in; having the status of an accomplice. 2. Having money, connections, and a measure of underworld security, usually as a member of a criminal syndicate. 3. (P) Enjoying better than average prison conditions as the result of political or social connections.

In, adv. In prison.

In action. Actively engaged in criminal or racket activities, as differentiated from remaining under cover or living off past earnings.

In a fog. Bewildered, as a victim confused by the cross-fire of talk and action of confidence swindlers.

Info. Information, especially of a more or less secret nature.

In hock. 1. In pawn. 2. In debt; in need of money.

Inkpot. A drinking establishment, especially as a rendezvous for underworld members.

In line. 1. In conformity with accepted standards or customs. 2. In submission, especially to extortion or "protection" demands. "Them mooch-joints (narcotic selling establishments) in

Brooklyn ain't kicking in (paying extortion). Put the muscle on them ghees (fellows) and get 'em in line."

In-man. 1. (Among burglars) One who specializes in gaining entry into premises to be robbed. 2. Any "inside" accomplice in a crime, as an employee or guest at the place to be robbed.

In Mexico. In parts unknown, as a fugitive from justice. "Swaggie's in Mexico. They got a knock-off (murder) reader (warrant) out on him with a plenty heavy tail (reward offered)."

Inside. 1. Imprisoned. 2. (P) Housed and employed inside prison walls. "They pulled Mike inside. No swindle (he got in no trouble). He come out in his Sunday front (clothes) to go to work and the screw (guard) figured he was looking to cop a mope (attempt to escape)."

Inside job. 1. A crime committed in collusion with an employee or a guest at the place of crime. 2. (P) A work assignment inside prison walls. "I got to get an inside job. I'm blowin' my top (going crazy) watching them broads (girls) and crates (cars) go by."

Inside man. 1. An accomplice who is in the confidence of a victim or victims whom he betrays, usually a trusted employee. 2. Any thief working inside the premises to be robbed, as opposed to outside **wheelman, zex-man,** etc. "That stiff (slow-thinker) ain't no good as a zex-man (lookout). That tough kisser (face) of his draws heat (attracts police attention). He's a good hustler (thief) though as an inside man."

Insider. 1. (Among pickpockets) An inside coat pocket; a vest pocket. The act of picking an inside pocket. "The mark (victim) rumbled (became aware) when we was making (robbing) the insider. We did a tearaway (took flight) when he started beefing murder (crying for help)."

In spades. Doubly; with double emphasis. "That dude (fellow) was sure a fink (informer), in spades. He ratted

(informed) on me, and when I was settled (sent to prison) he sends me them wish-you-were-here cards from summer joints (resorts)."

In the back. (P) 1. In that wing of the prison which is reserved for the condemned. 2. In the segregation or isolation wing.

In the back room. 1. (P) See **In the back.** 2. (Rare) In the electrocution chamber.

In the barrel. In debt beyond capacity to pay; in any desperate or helpless predicament.

In the biscuit. 1. In the head. 2. (P) (Literally) In the buttocks or the anus. (Figuratively) In one's most vulnerable spot. ("To get it in the biscuit"— to be used as a passive pederast or a whore.) "This fall guy (taking full blame) business is the crap. You pull a tough bit (harsh prison term). They don't kick in with a buck (send money for incidentals), and you get it in the biscuit (get a raw deal all around)."

In the cards. According to one's destiny; fated. "I'm too old to go legit (go to work for a living) now. I'll hit the turf (go back to crime) and maybe get a good run (a long interval outside of prison) if it's in the cards."

In the can. 1. In prison; **in; in stir.** 2. See **In the biscuit.**

In the center. 1. See **In the middle.** 2. On the table; aboveboard; in plain view. "Get the dough up in the center. There ain't gonna be no shoving down (cheating in division of loot)."

In the crapper. See **In the biscuit** and **In the doniker.**

In the doniker. (Literally) In the toilet. (Figuratively) In a hopeless predicament; irretrievably lost; ruined. "Looks like I'm gonna wind up in the doniker (imprisoned) if this rapper (complainant) don't pull off (withdraw charges)."

In the drink. See **In the river.**

In the hole. 1. (P) In solitary con-

finement on bread-and-water rations.
2. (P) Heavily in debt.

In the middle. In an untenable position.

In the red. (Carnival) Making money; abounding in gullible people who are easily swindled.

In the river. Murdered; slain and tossed into any body of water. "Them snitch-sheets (yellow journal newspapers) claim the fink (informer) in my rap (case) ended up in the river. I figure he pulled a Crater (disappeared voluntarily)."

In the sack. 1. Murdered by the sack method. 2. See **In the satchel.**

In the satchel. 1. Assured of success; favorably predetermined. "The rapper (complaining witness) pulled off (withdrew charges), the zinger is in (a bribe has been taken), and hitting the bricks (being acquitted) is in the satchel for me." 2. In a desperate predicament, especially as one who faces certain conviction. 3. Under control; amenable, as a result of bribery or intimidation. "I'll be okay now that I got the bulls (police) in the satchel. They'll do business (accept a bribe) if I kick back to the sucker (make restitution)."

In the sewer. See **In the doniker.**

In the stepping dough. Rich; wealthy; affluent. "I was getting in the stepping dough when I took this fall (was arrested). That shyster (lawyer) got it all now, and my broad (girl) is gonna have to hustle (walk the streets) to eat."

Iron. 1. (Carnival) Money. 2. Firearms.

Iron-house, n. (Pennsylvania and near South) 1. A local jail. 2. (Rare) The segregation jail within a prison.

Irons. Handcuffs.

Iron-worker. A safe-cracker.

Iso. (P) See **Izo.**

Isolation. (P) Segregation cellblock. [Note: Convicts are segregated for punishment, protection from violence of other convicts, or for psychopathic observation.]

Ixnay. (Pig-Latin for "nix") Danger! Stop what you are doing or saying.

Izo. (P) The isolation block of punishment cells. See **Isolation.** "Dump (get rid of) that hot boiler (contraband cooking stove). The screws (guards) are frisking and that's an izo rap (offense)."

J

Jabber. A drug addict who takes hypodermic injections; a **hypo**; a **needle-knight.** "Watch that jabber or you'll wind up in a jackpot (trouble). He's poison (not to be trusted)."

Jaboff. An injection of any narcotic.

Jack, n. 1. A blackjack. 2. (Obsolescent) Money. 3. (Various Western and Central prisons) Tobacco for hand-rolled cigarettes.

Jack, v. To beat with a blackjack. "If that flea (good-for-nothing) doesn't stop lousing me up (slandering me), I'm gonna jack his brains out."

Jacket. 1. (P) Any case-history folder in the central record office. "The man (official) says I got two hookers (pending warrants) in my jacket." 2. A strait-jacket.

Jackie up. To involve in serious trouble, especially arrest. "This two-stemmer (big town) we're hitting now is red (full of rich prospects), but don't get jackied up with the fuzz (police)."

Jackies. See **Jackpot.**

Jackpot. 1. Serious trouble; an arrest; a brawl. "Nobody but a wack (fool) gets himself in a jackpot in a tough town to do business (where officials are not venal) when he's a lamester (fugitive)." 2. (Pl.) Highly imaginative boasts of past criminal exploits; autobiographical tales. "Chopping up old jackpots agáin, eh?" 3. A severe or maximum prison sentence. "I sure hit the jackpot. I took a brodie (chance) going to bat (standing trial on the chance of acquittal). Now I got twenty-five boffos (years) and short time (the unexpired portion of a previous sentence)."

Jag. (Carnival) An inept person; a dolt. "An awful lot of jags in the lumber (newcomers) coming from them ragbags (small carnivals)."

Jaggy, n. (Carnival) Anyone seeking pleasure without spending money— hence, an object of contempt. "The lot is loused up with jaggies and stunkeys (hypercritical customers)."

Jaggy, a. Having the characteristics of a jag or a jaggy.

Jail-bait. Young girls, so called because of legal penalties involved in sexual intercourse with them.

Jail time. (P) Period spent in local jails while awaiting trial and sentence. [Note: "Jail time" is usually deducted from the total term served.] "There's a bug (fool) doing forty boffos (years), and he's beefing about a lousy four days' jail time he didn't get credit for."

Jake, a. Okay; safe; trustworthy; ready. "What are you dummying up (keeping your mouth shut) for? You can crack (talk freely). These ghees (fellows) are jake."

Jake, n. Jamaica ginger. "Some big jig (Negro) just got tossed in the can (jail) for getting full of jake and throwing slugs (firing pistol shots) on the main stem (main street)."

Jakey. See **Jake.**

Jam. 1. Trouble; difficulty; legal trap; an arrest. 2. (P) Difficulty with prison authorities or fellow convicts; a report or lock-up. 3. Petty stolen goods, as inexpensive watches, or costume jewelry.

Jam a pete. To jam the complex locking system of a safe when attempting to force it open. This is usually the result of failure to line up the combination tumblers properly before smashing the mechanism.

James. Whimsical personification of **jimmy.**

Jammed up. 1. Arrested; in serious trouble. 2. (P) Locked up for rule violation; in difficulty with fellow convicts; burdened with additional time to serve by Parole Board.

Jamoka. Coffee.

Jane. (Obsolete) a girl.

Jap. (Chiefly among carnival and transient grifters) A Negro.

Jawbone time. (In many Central and mid-Western prisons) See **Jail time.**

Jay. 1. First letter of **jug,** hence, a bank, especially as a prospective object of crime. 2. Variant of **John** or **Square-John.**

J. C. L. (Carnival; abbreviation of "Johnny-come-lately") A tyro; an inexperienced operator. "That J. C. L. made (recognized) the fuzz (policemen) right off. He's got talent."

Jeans at half mast. Caught in the act of passive pederasty; caught redhanded and at a disadvantage in any misdeed.

Jerk, n. A stupid or inept fellow. [Note: Common usage altered the original definition, namely, a chronic masturbator, although this definition is still in current underworld usage.]

Jerk, v. 1. To withdraw or cause to be withdrawn, as a warrant, a criminal charge, a witness, etc. "The mouthpiece (lawyer) wants a yard and a half ($150) to have that hooker (pending warrant) jerked." 2. (P) To effect one's return from prison to court, especially on a writ of habeas corpus or similar procedure, usually to have sentence reduced. "I'm getting jerked back to New York to get my bit (term) chopped."

Jerk-off, n. The act of masturbation; a chronic masturbator.

Jerk off. v. To masturbate.

Jerk off a hooker. To withdraw, or cause to be withdrawn, a warrant pending against a convict currently serving a prison term.

Jerk off a rapper. To effect the withdrawal of a complainant or prosecuting witness from a criminal proceeding.

Jerk off a sticker. See **Jerk off a hooker.**

Jerk town or **jerkwater.** A very small town.

Jerry. A short-barreled or snubnosed 38-calibre revolver, often concealed in the sleeve.

Jesus stiff. 1. A tramp who specializes in living off missions, the clergy, etc. (a term of opprobrium). 2. (P) A convict who seeks to ease his living conditions and increase parole chances by insincere religious display.

Jig or **jigaboo.** A Negro.

Jibboney. An Italian.

Jig-cut. (Near South, close to Atlantic Coast) A deep knife or razor wound.

Jigger. 1. One who stands watch; the act of standing watch; an exclamation of warning. 2. (P) One who watches for officials or inmate informers while accomplices violate rules. 3. (Corn Belt and Northwestern States) An armed robber; a hold-up man.

Jigger-man. A lookout; one who stands watch to warn accomplices of impending danger.

Jiggers! A danger signal to stop what one is doing or make a getaway.

Jig-lover. (P) A term of contempt for any white who is "too" intimate with Negro inmates.

Jim. (Chiefly Central and mid-Western States) To bungle. "That zib (fool) jimmed a cold lay (easy theft) on me."

Jim a deal. (Central and parts of mid-West) To bungle, especially a crime.

Jimmy, n. A bar, usually with a pointed or tapered end, for forcing entry through doors or windows.

Jimmy, v. To force or pry open with a jimmy.

Jinny. (Rural areas, South) Any disreputable barroom, often linked with prostitution.

Jinx. 1. The symbol of bad luck. 2.

Any person or thing superstitiously believed to attract bad luck.

Job. 1. A crime committed professionally. 2. A beating. ("To do a job on"—to beat severely.)

Jocker. An active pederast.

John. 1. (Short form of **Square-John**) One who is ridiculously gullible; a naive working person. "That John has his leather (wallet) in his right britch (trousers pocket) and he's on the nod (half asleep). Spring (get the wallet)." 2. (P) A newcomer to prison who is not of the underworld.

John Law. A policeman; any officer of the peace. "Freeze (stop what you are doing). John Law is on the mooch (walking this way)."

Johnny. (South) A prison guard; a chain-gang guard. "That new kid is going to clip (assault) the Johnny and go over the hill (attempt to escape)."

Johnny Creep. (Southern prison camps) A guard on night duty outside the convicts' barracks or cage-wagon.

Johnny Yegg. (Obsolescent) A yegg, or traveling safe-blower. "Old Johnny Yegg is hooked up with gopher mobs (thieves who tunnel into bank vaults or fur lofts) or he's a dinner-pailer (working man) these days."

John O'Brien. A box-car.

Johnson family, the. (Chiefly South-Central and Southwest) The underworld. ["One of the Johnson family"—of, or friendly to, the underworld; **right.**] [Note: The allusion is to a legendary family of criminals among whom were included venal sheriffs who were the first to establish **protection towns** where outlaws were "protected" from the law.] "Best thing for a fugitive in this part of the country is to head down to Lem's place in the Ozarks. Don't worry. He's one of the Johnson family."

John Sperl. (South; rare) A file, especially as tool for severing a chain-gang **rattler,** or prison bar. "John Sperl is the baby to get us out of this lag (prison), not a mouthpiece."

Joint. 1. Any illicit or dubiously legal establishment. 2. Any premises or place. "What kind of a joint did you crash (burglarize) on this drop (arrest)?" 3. A newspaper, magazine, or any periodical. 4. The penis. 5. (Very rare; Negro) A package of cigarettes.

Joint wise. Familiar with the ways of a specific prison and its officials, hence able to serve a sentence there with a minimum of discomfort.

Joker. (Very mildly contemptuous) A person.

Jolt. A prison sentence.

Jonah. See **Jinx.**

Jook or **jook joint.** (South and Southwest). Hard labor, especially in a prison chain-gang; a road, quarry or canebrake gang; any prison or prison camp where hard labor is enforced. "Man! That roach (guard) is always got his glimmers (eyes) on me. This is sure a sorry jook."

Joss-house. A Chinese gambling house, especially a lottery establishment; (less frequently) an opium-smoking establishment.

Jostler. A pickpocket's helper who jostles and distracts attention of victim.

Joy-rider. 1. An occasional user of habit-forming narcotics. "Yeah, this joy-rider screwed (fooled) around with the whizz-bang (narcotics) until he got hooked right (became a hopeless addict)." 2. A non-professional thief, especially of automobiles.

Juanita. A prostitute.

Jug. 1. A bank. "These cheap heist-men (holdup men) will throw (hold up) a store and get five clams (dollars) for their end. But they won't take a small jug that's a cold lay (easy thing). The big dough chills (scares) them." 2. A county jail. 3. (Rare) A prison. "Funny about these mastermind hoods (hoodlums), they're always in some jug."

Jugged. 1. Arrested and awaiting trial on a criminal charge. "Spunky was jugged throwing (holding up) a nautch-joint (brothel) in Brooklyn." 2. (P) Locked up for rule violation, protection, or psychopathic observation.

Jug-heavy. A specialist in blowing or ripping open bank safes or vaults.

Jugman. A specialist in bank robbery or burglary.

Jug-mob. 1. A crew of pickpockets who operate out of banks where they select their victims. The victims are usually followed and robbed. "Too many jug-mobs getting glommed (arrested). The grift (racket) is washed up for a while." 2. Bank burglars or bandits. 3. A gang of forgers who specialize in defrauding banks with forged cashier's checks. [Note: Accounts are opened and deposits of forged checks made. Large amounts of money are withdrawn by drafts before the checks clear the clearing house.] 4. Confidence game operators who select their victims at banks, especially savings banks patronized by aliens. [Note: Jug-mob swindlers usually speak several languages and specialize in victimizing foreign-born Roman Catholics, using scapulas, religious medals, rosary beads, etc., to disarm their victims.]

Jug-rap. A bank robbery charge.

Juice-joint. Any cheap drinking establishment.

Juke-joint. Any cheap establishment featuring juke-box music and soft drinks, "home brew," corn whiskey, or **jake.** Prostitution and gambling are frequent attractions.

Jump-steady. (Borrowed from Negro jargon) Gin. "Nine or ten jump-steadies and a couple of muggles (marijuana cigarettes) and up goes your gage (emotion reaches a peak)."

Jumper. A wiring device used by burglars to divert the alarm circuit during a robbery, or to defeat the protection of locked ignition in stealing automobiles. "Throw the jumper on that bug (alarm), and I'll put the barspreader on the windows."

Jungle. Any isolated clump of woods, patch of prairie, or stretch of plain where hobos congregate and exchange yarns before returning to the road. Jungles are also convenient hideouts for vagrant thieves.

Jungle buzzard. A hobo, especially a thieving hobo who prefers to remain around the **jungle** either because he is in fear of police, or because he finds it easier to chisel from other jungle residents and transients.

Jungle up. (Hobo) To spend the interval between travels in the **jungle.**

Junk. 1. Narcotics; drugs. "That junk pushing (selling) grift (racket) is a creep's (unprincipled fellow's) racket." 2. Any cheap imitation, as imitation jewelry; a **stiff.** 3. Any stolen goods other than cash, especially jewelry.

Junk, on the. Currently addicted to the use of narcotics.

Junked up. Under the influence of narcotics.

Junker. A narcotic addict; (rarely) a purveyor of narcotics to addicts.

Junkey. A narcotic addict. "I done everything on the calendar, but I don't want no rep (reputation) as a junkey."

Junk peddler. A seller of, or trafficker in, drugs for addicts. "They hit Joe with the book (sentenced him to life) for chilling (killing) some fink (unprincipled) junk peddler."

Junk pusher. See **Junk peddler.**

Junk-pushing. The narcotics traffic. "Junk-pushing and pimping are two rackets I don't go for. I'd sooner be a dinner-pailer (honest working man)."

Jury's out. (P) An idiom implying that one is awaiting a decision, hence, in doubt. "I dropped the D. A. a tab (note) asking him to yank (remove) my sticker (pending warrant). The jury's out yet."

Jute mill. (P) The hated prison factories where jute (burlap) bags are made. [Note: Convicts often contract tuberculosis while engaged in such work.] "Tom hit the jute mill, kicked over (refused to work) and wound up being bugged (committed to institution for the insane)."

K

Kale. (Obsolete) Money.

Kangaroo. 1. To convict on trumped-up evidence or without due process of law. 2. To subject to the practices of the kangaroo court.

Kangaroo court. (Some large and many small county jails) An inmate "court" that tries and fines all newcomers. Convicted of such deliberately nonsensical charges as "being lousy and attempting to scratch," "having two left feet," and "breaking into jail," the "defendant" is often šubjected to vicious penalties. The prăctice which began as a source of fun developed into a dangerous game in which the prisoner-victims suffered severe beatings or were forced into acts of degeneracy. In most areas the custom has been eradicated by public pressure.

Keen. (Obsolescent except in scattered areas of Central States) Perfect; ideal; all right.

Keeno. See **Keen.**

Keep a meet. To keep an appointment, especially to commit a crime. "Me and Big Mouth was supposed to take (rob) a couple of bookies (professional bet-makers), but he didn't keep the meet."

Keep-locked, n. (P) A formal locking-up of rule violator.

Keep locked, v. (P) To report or chalk in, while convict awaits decision of prison authorities. A sign "keep locked" is hung on the cell door.

Keep-locked banner. See **Keep-locked shingle.**

Keep-locked shingle. (P) The tin sign hung on the cell door of a convict awaiting trial by prison authorities, bearing the inscription, "keep locked."

Keep one's nose clean. To abide by the rules; to live in conformity with laws and conventions of the underworld; to go to work for a living, forsaking underworld associates.

Keister. 1. A safe; a strong-box inside a safe. "Easy on the soup (crude nitroglycerine) with that keister or she'll jam (the tumblers will get out of line so that the safe cannot be opened)." 2. A satchel, or bag, especially a burglar's kit. "Ditch that keister. It draws heat (attracts police attention)." 3. (Carnival) A small county jail; a local jail. 4. (P) The buttocks. "You know how to pull a bit (serve a sentence easily), always on your keister." 5. (N. Y. State prisons) Luck. "What a keister you got, making parole the first time up!"

Keister bandit. 1. An active homosexual, especially one who uses threats or force. 2. (By extension) A seducer or rapist.

Keisterman. A luggage thief.

Keister mark. A prospective victim of luggage thieves.

Keister, on one's. See **Pratt, on one's.**

Ketchup-dogs. Bloodhounds, used to hunt escaped convicts. "The ketchup-dogs were hot on his pratt (in close pursuit) as he lammed (attempted escape) over the hill."

Ketchup-hounds. See **Ketchup-dogs.**

Kettle. (Obsolescent) A large, heavy or old-fashioned man's watch.

Keystone cop. A small-town or curiously uniformed private policeman. [Note: Harking back to the Keystone moving-picture comedies in which the policemen were uniformed in a manner to provoke laughter.]

K. I. (Among "respectable" international thieves) Literally, a Knight of Immunity; hence a thief whose connections, money, or value as a police informer keep him out of prison.

Kibitzer. 1. A thief who attracts attention by superfluous movements and actions while at or near the scene of crime. "That kibitzer is poison. He'll get us all in a mopery jackpot (foolish trouble)." 2. (P) A convict who makes a nuisance of himself by playing pranks, or by being jovial at the expense of others. "I'm going to get a bug on (get angry) some day and dump (assault) that kibitzer."

Kick, n. 1. Pocket. 2. A thrill. 3. (Plural) Shoes. 4. (Near-South) The **third degree.** "Reuben couldn't take the kick when the clamper fell (he was arrested). He put the cross on (betrayed) the jokers (fellows) he was with."

Kick, v. To get rid of, as someone or something undesirable or incriminating. "Kick that creep. He's getting you all loused up (ruining your reputation)."

Kick a habit. To cure oneself of addiction to narcotics. "Cadillac Mike is kicking a tough habit in the pen."

Kick a hooker. To have a warrant dropped.

Kick a parole. To break parole contract, as by flight, bribery, political pressure, etc.

Kick around. To subject one to a **kicking around.**

Kick-back, n. 1. Restitution of stolen goods, usually for leniency, suspension of sentence, or other benefits. 2. An undesired reaction; the return of a cured drug habit; physical resistance of a victim of crime; a complaint to police, or refusal to pay, by victim of extortion. 3. (Loosely) The return of anything borrowed or previously accepted as a gift. 4. Repression.

Kick back, v. 1. To make restitution, especially of stolen goods; to restore gambling losses under threat of mob violence. "The D. A. will let us cop (accept) a low plea (guilty plea to lesser offense) with no beef (complaint) from the insurance company if we kick back all of the gullion (stolen jewelry)." 2. To retaliate; recoil; re-

spond violently. "His mouthpiece (lawyer) wants to take Joe out on a writ, but he figures the D. A. will kick back with a couple of hookers (lodge additional charges) if he springs (goes free) on this rap (charge)." 3. (Loosely) To return anything borrowed or received as a gift. "Kick that hoop (ring) back to that crumb. It's probably hot as a forty-five (stolen lately and vigorously sought by police)."

Kicker. An additional threat, as a warrant held over a prisoner's head by the district attorney, or an extra pistol concealed on the person by a hold-up man or a gangster; anything held in reserve for an emergency. "The D. A. thinks he's got me buried (convicted) on this rap, but I got a witness I'm holding for a kicker that'll knock his case dizzy."

Kick in. 1. To pay, especially as tribute to terrorizing racketeers, or venal police. "If you don't kick in, this joint (establishment) has got to fold (close)." 2. To force an entry into premises to be robbed; to smash a shop window and plunder the contents; to break into. "Them window crashers kicked in the show-glass and lammed (escaped) with a ten-G ($10,000) coat." 3. To kick while beating with fists and weapons; to beat unmercifully. "The coppers kicked his lemon (head) in till he opened up." 4. To produce all the loot, withholding none. 5. To die.

Kicking around. A beating; a raw deal.

Kick in with a buck. To contribute, as towards counsel fees of one awaiting trial; to send sums of money periodically, as to a friend in prison. "This single-o (selfish) muzzler won't kick in with a buck to ghees in stir (prison) like the old-timers done."

Kick loose. To give up or hand over a sum of money or quantity of collateral, as the victim of a swindle or robbery; to be robbed or cheated. "We clipped a gullion (jewelry) peddler in Chi., and he kicked loose with 20 G's ($20,000) in ice (jewelry)."

Kick-off, n. The start; the beginning. "I had a chill on that caper (feared that robbery) right from the kick-off. Every time I buck (go against) a hunch, I wind up in the satchel (arrested)."

Kick off, v. To die.

Kick one's cruller in. To assault; to beat severely. "That's the second time that crumb went South with dough (held out a share of the loot). I gotta kick his cruller in."

Kick one's lemon in or **off.** See **Kick one's cruller in.**

Kick one's sconce off. See **Kick one's cruller in.**

Kick out. To leave a prison, as a result of parole, discharge, transfer, or felonious escape; to discharge or parole a convict. "I gotta kick out of this stir (prison) somehow. A connection can (prison where bribery and influence win privileges) ain't no good to pull a bit (serve time) unless you got a buck (money)."

Kick out of. See **Kick out.**

Kick-over, n. 1. Any act of resistance to criminal force. 2. Any disagreement or quarrel among gangsters concerning the sharing of loot, spheres of influence, etc. 3. (P) Refusal to work; resistance to any official order; a riot; any deliberate breach of discipline. "I hear some screw (guard) got his lemon kicked in (beaten) in that mess-hall kick-over."

Kick over, v. 1. To refuse to submit, as to robbery or extortion. "I don't know what they're feeding them rabbits (victims of usurers); they got the shylocks (usurers) wacky the way they're kicking over on the vigerage- and (interest compounded weekly on loans)." 2. (P) To riot or refuse to work. "Three jigaboos (Negroes) kicked

over in the mess-hall and hit the bing (were placed in solitary confinement)." 3. (P) To refuse to tolerate another's aggressiveness, belligerency or abuse; to cease to serve as a menial or a pawn for bullying fellow inmates; to refuse to meet one's obligations, especially gambling debts.

Kick the engine around. To smoke the opium pipe.

Kick the gong around. 1. To smoke opium. 2. (Less common) To smoke marijuana. 3. (P) To indulge in aphrodisiac daydreams in a prison cell; to masturbate. "There's only one way to pull time (serve a prison sentence): keep your mind off the street (the outside world) and don't kick the gong around." 4. (Rare) To tell cock-and-bull stories of one's exploits.

Kick the mooch around. To smoke the opium pipe.

Kick-up, n. 1. (P) Any deliberate defiance of authority, as refusal to work, a hunger strike, or other breach of discipline. "That dude (fellow) loused himself up (ruined his reputation) when he wouldn't stick (participate) in that kick-up in the barber shop last year." 2. Any resistance to force or to the threat of force; defiance; rebellious reaction toward intolerable conditions to which one has been forced to submit in the past. "We can't stand for a kick-up. Them suckers (extortion victims) gotta be kept in line (compelled to continue to pay)."

Kick up, v. 1. (P) To riot or incite to riot; to refuse to submit to discipline, especially to refuse to work. "Those ghees (fellows) will be buried in the box (locked up indefinitely in punishment cells) if they kick up." 2. To resist force or the threat of force, especially to refuse to submit to blackmail or extortion. 3. To refuse to meet one's obligations, especially gambling debts.

Kid. (Prison and Hobo) Immature youth, or small person of youthful appearance. [Note: When preceded by the possessive pronoun, as "my," "your," etc., the word implies the existence of an improper sexual relationship and is synonymous with **punk; gunzel.**]

Kife, n. 1. (Pl.) Prostitutes; loose women. 2. (P) Passive pederasts; male oral sodomists.

Kife, v. 1. To swindle; to rob. "We had to play the deuce of clubs (use force) to lug the mark (get rid of the victim) them thimble-riggers (shellgame operators) kifed." 2. To deal with unjustly.

Kifing. A raw deal; a swindle; a **hosing;** a **humping;** a **screwing.** "What a kifing my shyster (cheap lawyer) gave me!"

Kill a bug. To short-circuit or otherwise silence a burglar alarm prior to the commission of a crime; to put a **jumper** on the alarm. "Kill the bug and make the entry. I'll take (force open) the keister (safe)."

Kill a rap. 1. To withdraw or indefinitely postpone prosecution of a criminal charge. 2. To employ influence or bribery to effect the withdrawal or indefinite postponement of prosecution of a criminal charge.

Kill the Chinaman. (Often varied: "To kill a Chinaman" or "to kill a (the) monkey"; or "to get the monkey off one's neck.") 1. To break a drug habit completely. 2. (By occasional extension) To score a big success, as in accomplishing a lucrative crime, or in winning a large sum in gambling.

Kindergarten. A reform school; any juvenile place of detention or institution for adolescents.

King. (Rare; South) A prison warden. [See note on **big noise.**]

King Kong. (South) A potent drink made from the skimmings of boiling sugar cane. "Yeah, some pink-chaser (Negro who seeks white women) got tanked up (drunk) on King Kong and

got into a necktie party (a lynching) over a short-arm heist (rape)."

Kingsnipe. (Central and mid-Western States) A section-gang foreman.

Kink. (Scattered areas of East and near South) A thief, especially an expert in stealing automobiles.

Kinky. (Scattered areas of East and near South) Stolen, especially stolen automobiles.

Kip. 1. Sleep; a bedroom; a bed. 2. (San Quentin, Folsom, N. Y. City Penitentiary, and scattered prisons) A cell. 3. (Central and Western U.S. chiefly) A night watchman, especially one who sleeps on the premises. "That's a nice lay (place to rob) if you can corral the kip and tie him up." 4. A house; a hotel.

Kip, on the. Asleep; in a drunken or narcotic stupor; not on the alert. "Everyone in the slough (house) was on the kip when Noiseo Joe put the shot (explosive) in the pete (safe). He blew the keister (safe) door right off without a flop (sign of having attracted attention) from anyone."

Kipped. (Central and Western U.S.) Guarded by watchman, especially one who sleeps on the premises; (by extension) occupied by sleeping residents.

Kisser. The face; a photograph of one's face. "Four rappers (complainants) made (identified) my kisser in the gallery (bureau of criminal identification) according to a right copper (policeman friendly to underworld). I'm pulling a Greeley (leaving town)."

Kiss-off, n. Any tactic to rid oneself of the victim of a swindle or any undesirable person without giving offense and without arousing suspicion.

Kiss off, v. To rid oneself of unwelcome company without giving offense; to leave a victim after swindling him. "As soon as the sucker dukes me the soft (gives me the money), I'll dust (leave) and you kiss him off."

Kiss the dog. (Pickpocket jargon)

To face a victim while in the act of picking his pocket.

Kitchen mechanic. A male or female cook.

Kite, n. 1. (P) A letter that has been smuggled in or out of prison without being censored. "Drop Moe a kite to have a hot boiler (stolen car) with legit plates (properly registered plates) up here for the crash-out (attempted escape)." 2. (Loosely) A note to any prison official; (very rarely) a **tab** or note from one inmate to another. "That fleabag (informer) dropped another kite to the man (the warden) this morning. I wonder who's being buried (informed upon) this time." 3. (Loosely) A forged check; (more accurately) a good check with insufficient funds on deposit to cover it. 4. A prostitute.

Kite, v. 1. To issue or pass, as a forged check or bond; (more accurately) to issue or pass a check against insufficient funds. "Some old fire-proofer (bogus clergyman) kited enough stiffs (bad checks) around town to paper the city hall." 2. (P) To send through devious illegitimate channels, as a letter, with the intent to evade censorship. "I want to kite a tab (letter) to my old fence (buyer of stolen goods) for some dough, but my connection (contact man) has a chill (is afraid of the risk). They're frisking (searching) the screws (guards) going off duty."

Kite checks. (New England States) 1. To issue forged checks. 2. To write checks, usually post-dated, against insufficient funds. 3. To raise illegally the face value of otherwise good checks.

Kiteman. A passer of bad checks, or of checks backed by insufficient funds.

Kite stiffs. (New England) See **Kite checks.**

Kite stocks. 1. To forge and issue spurious stock certificates. 2. To engage in pools or syndicates to control larcenously the price of stocks or other securities.

Kitty, the. 1. A prison; a jail; a reformatory. 2. (P) Confinement in segregation, observation, or punishment cells on a bread-and-water diet.

Knob. The human head.

Knock, n. An arrest; a criminal charge; a prison sentence. "We got a knock down in the Bayou Country in Louisiana. Them longline skinners (canebrake foremen) like to kill me till I up and beat the pups (escaped the prison camp and the bloodhounds)."

Knock, v. (Central and Western U.S.) 1. To press a criminal complaint against; to testify against. 2. To inform against an underworld associate; to betray to the police. 3. To arrest; to prosecute; to sentence or commit to prison. 4. To slander; to make derogatory reference to.

Knock-around. Sophisticated, as a result of long underworld experience; belonging to or connected with the underworld.

Knock-around broad. Any girl belonging to, connected with, or experienced in the ways of the underworld; any woman of loose morals, not necessarily a prostitute, especially one who lives successively with thieves or racketeers.

Knock-around ghee. Anyone belonging to, connected with, or experienced in the ways of the underworld; a professional thief or racketeer.

Knock dead. To beat into unconsciousness with fists or weapons.

Knock down. 1. To shoot and kill. "Pass that joint up. The sucker (prospective victim) is heeled (armed). He knocked down a heist-man (holdup man) last summer." 2. To arrest; to seize one in the commission of a crime.

Knocker. 1. (Carnival) Anyone in a crowd who loudly denounces a game as crooked but becomes silent when **shills** become rough with him; a troublemaker. 2. A complaining witness in criminal proceedings.

Knock-man. A policeman; an informer; a complaining witness in criminal proceedings.

Knock-off, n. 1. A killing. **2.** An arrest while in the act of a crime or under circumstances which insure conviction, as when a criminal is seized trucking stolen goods or contraband, or on the way to the scene of a crime; any arrest. "If you get a knock-off with them tins (police badges) and creeds (bogus credentials), the bulls (police) will sap (blackjack) you into the ground." **3.** (P) Seizure and report of an inmate while in the act of trafficking in stolen stores or contraband; any report or lock-up for rule violation. **4.** A raid of premises by the police. **5.** The cost, fee, or price—of any service, commodity, or "protection." **6.** (P) An order by one inmate to another to stop fooling, talking, etc., usually snarled at someone who is annoying others.

Knock off, v. 1. To kill. **2.** To rob, especially at pistol point, as trucks, stores, etc.; to hijack; to burglarize. "Someone had to be the fall guy (take the blame) for all them beer joints being knocked off, so Gabbo took the rap (pleaded guilty) and the bulls cleaned up the calendar (wrote off unsolved robberies)." **3.** To seize and arrest; to raid premises with seizure and arrest in view. "I'm backing out of the spot with the rod (gun) on the suckers when the bulls come from behind and knocked me off." **4.** (P) To seize anything in the act of being smuggled into or out of prison, or concealed on the person or anywhere in the prison, as contraband or stolen stores. "They frisked (searched) the cells this afternoon and knocked off my hot boiler (contraband cooking stove). I'm liable to hit the box (segregation)." **5.** To surprise; to find, as evidence; to seize. "I knew that creep was burning (watching) me, so I heisted him

(held him up) and knocked off the tin (policeman's badge) in his kick (pocket)." **6.** To set a price upon, as a service, commodity, or "protection." **7.** (Imperative) Stop! Danger! Police! **8.** To discover in illicit operation, as a tax-evading still, a counterfeiting plant, etc. **9.** To indulge in for a brief period, as in sleep, drink, marijuana, play, etc. "I was just gonna knock off a kip (sleep) when the coppers kicked into the joint and put the glom on (seized) me."

Knock off a kite. (P) To seize a letter being smuggled in or out of prison. "If they knock off that kite, you're buried (in serious trouble). They'll slap you in the box (segregation) and throw the key away (never let you out)."

Knock out. 1. To arrest. "Shorty never did live down that time he was knocked out by that lady bull (policewoman). He lammed (attempted to escape) on her, and she pooped (shot) him." **2.** (P) To surprise in the act of rule violation and report or lock up. "Some muzzler is got the horns on me (has me jinxed) all right. I'm rushing the growler from a batch (quantity of home brew) I had stashed (hidden), and the P.K. (principal keeper) himself knocked me out." **3.** To inform on an associate. "I got away clean but that fleeper (unprincipled) partner of mine knocked me out. Yeah, he spilled his guts (confessed and implicated me)."

Knock over. 1. To rob, usually by force of arms. "Joe and Stubby took a fall (were arrested) knocking over a small jug (bank) in Kansas." **2.** To arrest. **3.** To execute a police raid on suspicious premises. "The dicks (police) knocked over four of Nigger Nat's dice joints. His wires (connections) must be slipping."

Knock up. 1. To exhaust a lucrative racket or area by excessive exploitation; to render unprofitable for further criminal exploitation. "The shake (extortion) racket is knocked up with muscle men (strong-arm operators) and phonies (unskilled racketeers) putting the bite on (taking sums from) the suckers every day. They don't get time to get fresh (replenish their supply of money)." 2. To use up; to wear out; to exhaust one's welcome among influential friends; to abuse one's good nature. "My mouthpiece has got the pollies (politicians) down at the club knocked up putting the bite on (asking) them to square raps (quash criminal charges) for me." 3. To contaminate; to bring disgrace upon; to infest. "This can (prison) is knocked up with creeps (unprincipled persons). It used to be a swell stir (prison) to pull a bit (serve a sentence)."

Knock up a stir. (P) To take sly advantage of every means to circumvent prison rules and discipline; to master the art of reducing the discomforts of prison life to a minimum. "Yeah, Senator, you're one connie (confidence man) who found a home. You got this stir (prison) knocked up."

Knock up with contracts. (P) To take advantage of an obliging fellow convict who is in a position to do small favors, such as to secure books, do one's laundry, steal small parcels of food, and the like. "I'm gonna wrap up (quit) my job. These phonies supposed to be my friends knock me up with contracts. I gotta wind up in a jackpot (trouble) sooner or later."

Knock up with 48's. To harass a notorious criminal by arresting him on short affidavits, holding him for forty-eight hours' questioning, time after time, until he leaves a community in disgust. [Note: The degree of rough handling by the police depends upon the policy of the administration and the degree of influence of the criminal's friends.]

Knowledge-box. Any school or seat of learning.

Knucks. Brass knuckles worn by strong-arm men of the old school.

Kokomo (often, **the kokomo kid**.) 1. A cocaine addict. 2. Any drug addict.

Kosher. (Hebrew) Loyal; trustworthy; okay; right. "Solly's strictly kosher himself but that ain't saying this touch (robbery) he's got lined up is kosher."

L

L. A. (Carnival) A legal adjuster. [Note: Legal adjusters are professionally suave fellows, usually lawyers, who pacify irate swindle victims and handle all matters between carnival operators and the local police authorities. It is they who fix the limits of play and determine the maximum degree of swindling to be tolerated.]

Label. A person's name, whether genuine or fictitious.

Labor-skate. (South; borrowed from Negro jargon) A delegate or official of a labor union; (rarely) any unionized worker.

Lace. To beat or assault with or without weapons. "The cops laced the Greek and put the nuts on (subjected him to a rigorous **third degree**), but he stood pat."

Lady-lover. A lesbian.

Lag, n. (Southern, Central, and mid-Western U.S.) 1. A convict. 2. Any jail or penal institution; a road gang or prison camp. "The Johnny Creeps (guards) and ketchup-hounds (bloodhounds) sure keep these lags tight (make escape impossible)."

Lag, v. (Southern, Central and mid-Western U.S.) To jail or imprison. "They lagged that tipeasy (burglar) for ten spaces (years)."

Lake, on the. (Rhode Island and environs) See **Earie, on the.**

Lam, n. 1. The state of being a fugitive from justice. "Being on the lam is as tough as doing a bit (serving a sentence) in these times." 2. Escape from any custody or jurisdiction while awaiting trial or prosecution.

Lam, v. To flee, as from the scene of a crime, a place of detention, or any area where one is wanted by the police; to jump bail or parole. "If they make my mugg (recognize my photograph) on this trick (robbery), I gotta lam. The bulls in town got me pegged (identified) as an ex-con already."

Lam, on the. 1. In flight from justice. 2. (Loosely) In the act of swift departure. "I gotta meet (appointment) with a couple of bags (women). Guess I'll be on the lam, Joe."

Lam-beam. (South; very rare) A device, no longer in common use, which is fastened about the leg of a road-gang convict; it has sharp curved projections, front and rear, that limit the movements of the convict to short distances at an extremely slow pace.

Lamb's tongue. (West, Central, Southwest) 1. A five-dollar bill. "Some hustler (prostitute) in a San Antonio panel-joint (brothel specializing in robbing patrons) beat George for a lamb's tongue and what a beef (complaint) he made!" 2. (Rarely) A one-dollar bill.

Lam-car. An automobile, usually stolen, which is used by criminals to escape from the scene of a crime. [Note: In professionally executed crimes, the lam-car is exchanged for a pick-up car after the immediate getaway is accomplished.] "A couple of cowboys (reckless thieves) snatched (stole) the dicks' (policemen's) prowl-car (patrol-car) and used it for a lam-car. What moxie (nerve)!"

Lamester. One who jumps bail, escapes from prison, or in any manner becomes a fugitive from justice. "Tony copped a mope (escaped) with sleeping time (very little time to serve), but he's a lamester on a Texas bang-job (murder)."

Lammie. See **Lamester.**

Lamp, n. The human eye.

Lamp, v. To look at; to cast one's eyes upon. "Lamp the roll on that dude (fellow).What a touch (a promising victim)!"

Larceny in one's heart. Inherent dishonesty. [Note: Confidence swindlers work on the theory that this trait is in everyone and they exploit it for their own ends.] "That hoosier (rustic) sure went on (succumbed to) the Rumanian box (money-making and raising-of-bank-notes machine) gag. The larceny in his heart duked him in (urged him on) better than we could."

Larry, n. (Carnival) A cheap or worthless trinket given as prize at a gambling game. "Weed (hand) me a larry for this jag (fool). The bree (girl) with him is putting the chill on him to pack in (advising him to quit playing)."

Larry, a. (Carnival) Bad; counterfeit; cheap; profitless; no good.

Last mile. (Texas) The few paces from the "last minute cells" to the electric chair.

Last waltz, the. The march of the condemned man to gallows, chair, gas chamber, or other place of execution.

Lather up. To insert the soap ream into a hole drilled in a safe for the charge of the explosive and the percussion cap. 2. To fill the crevices, especially of an old-fashioned safe, with the soap ream to hold the picric and the percussion cap. "Flop that keister (safe) on its back and lather it up."

Laundry, the. Chinese aliens. Used only in the following idiom: To move the laundry—to smuggle alien Chinese into the country.

Law, the. 1. A policeman. 2. Any branch or member of the law-enforcement body. 3. (P) A prison guard.

Lay, n. 1. A prostitute; a loose woman; an act of sexual intercourse. 2. (P) A passive pederast; an act of sexual perversion. 3. Place to be robbed.

Lay, v. 1. To stand, as to stand watch, when used in the following

idioms: to lay butso, to lay jiggers, to lay zex. 2. To have sexual intercourse with. 3. To pass, as a forged check or counterfeit money.

Lay, the. 1. The site of a proposed crime. "Case (survey) the lay and spot (locate) the sleeper (night watchman)." 2. The detailed plan of a proposed crime.

Lay a barker or rod on. (South, Central, and mid-West) To point a pistol at, i.e., to shoot.

Lay butso. To stand watch and be ready to warn accomplices of danger.

Lay down! (P) Shut up! Go to sleep! (This is one of the most common expresions in prison slang.)

Laying in state. (Near South) Serving a prison term.

Lay jiggers. See Lay, v., meaning 1.

Lay off. To cease any action or activity; to stay away; (Imperative) danger!

Lay on the hip. To assume the posture traditional to opium-pipe smoking; to smoke opium.

Layout, n. 1. A rendezvous and all the appurtenances, as for opium-smoking, gambling. 2. The detailed plan of the site of an intended crime. "There's your layout. No bugster (burglar alarm) and a drop-off (repository for stolen goods) all set." 3. (Pickpocket jargon) A watch and chain. 4. The general state of affairs; the prevailing conditions.

Lay out, v. To draft plans, as for a theft.

Lay paper. 1. To pass worthless checks or other fraudulent instruments. "We laid sour paper all through those jerkwaters (small towns)." 2. (Rare) To pass counterfeit currency. 3. (Rare) See Lay the note.

Lays it but can't handle it. The underworld equivalent of "dishes it out but can't take it."

Lay sour paper. To issue bad checks.

Lay the gaff. To explain a proposed

racket or crime, or the mysteries of a trick or the means of deception.

Lay the leg. To engage in an act of sexual intercourse.

Lay the note. To operate in any of the various short-change swindles, involving a large banknote, an accomplice, a cashier victim, and confusing tactics. "Moish is doing handy out laying the note with a broad who used to be a booster (shoplifter)."

Lay up. To closet oneself in an apartment or den in order to smoke opium or marijuana, to drink excessively, or to gratify any other private vice.

Lay zex. To stand watch while associates commit a crime or, as in prison, a violation of rules. "Lay zex while I make the in (entry) to this joint."

Lead pipe. (N. Y. Catholic Protectory) Spaghetti.

Leaps. Jumpy nerves, especially after the tension of having been on a risky criminal venture.

Leather. (Pickpocket jargon) A wallet. (Among purse-snatchers and purse-lifters) A purse.

Leather-glommer (Variant: **Leather-snatcher**). A pocketbook snatcher.

Leave. To desert an accomplice in time of danger; to flee from danger without warning one's accomplice, or without helping him to escape. "That muzzler is no jigger man (lookout) to use; he'll leave you if there's a blow (trouble)."

Leave one the bucket. (P) To take leave of one's fellow convicts in prison. [Literally, to leave one's fellow inmates the use of one's portable toilet.] "If the board (parole board) don't hit me with the works (make me serve the rest of my sentence), I'll be leaving my bucket to you guys in June."

Leeasaw! The law! Police! Look out! Run!

Leech. (Gulf State area prisons) An

informer; an underworld traitor.

Left pratt. (Among pickpockets) The left-hand rear trousers pocket.

Leg, on one. See **Ear, on one.**

Legal adjuster. See **L. A.**, and **Patch.**

Legal pimp. A loafer who either marries for money or lives on the earnings of a bread-winning wife.

Leg-cramper. A quick gouging blow on the leg muscle. "I beat Joe for two leg-crampers in handball. What a sucker's holler (complaint) he made!"

Legit. 1. Within the law; legal; legitimate; not of the underworld. "Pete's strictly a legit ghee (working man). He got this drop (arrest) gapping (as a mere onlooker at scene of crime)." 2. (P) In accordance with prison rules and regulations. "I got a habit of stashing (hiding) the newspaper when the hack (guard) makes his rounds. Only a weekly joint (magazine) was legit in that can. All rags (newspapers) were barred." 3. Justified; reasonable; as a "legit," or legitimate, complaint.

Legit beef. A legitimate, or just complaint. "You ain't got no legit beef. When the rumble came (trouble started), you copped a mope (fled) and left us to hold the sack. You'll get your end (share), yes you will, under the arch (a beating or a shot in the head)."

Legit broad. An honest working girl. "The Clipper was stepping out with some legit broad when he got dropped (arrested). She wrapped him up (deserted him) when she found out he was a hood (thief)."

Legit ghee. 1. An honest working person; anyone who refuses to have relations with the underworld; one who lives within the law. "I sprung (suggested a bribe) to that copper, but he won't take. He's a legit ghee and he ain't taking no chances." 2. An honest man; one who will not accept a bribe; an honest man accidentally in prison or with the underworld for a time.

Legit holler. See **Legit beef.**

Legit joint. An honest establishment, especially one whose habitues are not of the underworld.

Legit squawk. See **Legit beef.**

Legit stiff. 1. One who earns his living by honest labor. 2. (P) An inmate who is not of the underworld; a convict who is not a professional criminal. "These legit stiffs got the cans (prisons) loused up (contaminated). If they see something happen, they figure it's right to fink (inform) to the screws (guards). Doing time is a hurdy (ride on a merry-go-round) with crumbs like that."

Leg-puller. An extortionist; a blackmailer.

Leg-pulling. Extortion; blackmail.

Lemon. 1. See **Lemon game.** 2. The human head. "I wrapped Scotty up. A little rumble (trouble) on a trick (robbery), and he blows (loses) his lemon." 3. Anyone or anything that is unsatisfactory or worthless; a traitor; a faker; an inept crook; a poor prospect for thieves; a prosecution witness who cannot be intimidated or bribed; an unprofitable criminal venture or racket. "The pollies (politicians) tried to pull a squeeze on (force the hand of) that lemon who's rapping (complaining), but he won't chill (exhibit fear)."

Lemon, on the. 1. Engaged in, or swindling by means of, the **lemon game.** 2. On the head. 3. Exactly; precisely.

Lemon game. A confidence racket in which gullible victims are enticed to meet beautiful and accommodating girls. While awaiting the girls, they are inveigled into a card, dice, or pool-game swindle. "Benny took a fall (was arrested) on the lemon game and got settled (imprisoned) for a sawbuck (ten years)."

Lemon-mob. A group of confidence men who specialize in the **lemon game.**

Level. 1. To operate with relative honesty. "We're leveling this dice game all the way." 2. To approximate the truth within the limits set by the exigencies of a criminal career. "I'm leveling, Jim. Three C's ($300) was all there was in the keister (safe we robbed)."

Lice. (Carnival) People who come to carnivals to gape or criticize, but do not spend money. "No oats (money); no tips (crowds). How're you gonna make a buck clipping (robbing) these lice?"

License. ("A license to steal") 1. A guarantee of immunity from police interference within a given area, as applied to pickpockets, pimps, or other petty criminals. This immunity is purchased either with cash or with valuable police information concerning bigtime criminals. "No wire-mob (pickpocket gang) is hijacking suckers (robbing people brazenly) like that without a license." 2. Right; privilege. "This guy's got a license to beef (complain). That heater (gun) was planted on him (placed in his pocket to frame him up)." 3. (P) Special privilege, or immunity from prison discipline. (Usually ironic.) "What's that crumb got, a license? He's got the run of the joint, and everyone else is getting honey (abuse) from them screws (guards)."

Licensed grift. Any of the craftier forms of thievery enjoying complete or partial immunity from police within a given area. "I was hustling (stealing) with a mob of broad-tossers (card swindlers) that had a licensed grift in that tank (small town). A tough town though without an in (connections)."

Licensed gunning. Picking pockets with immunity from police interference within a given town, district, or area. "That mob gives up enough (betrays many criminals to the police) to rate licensed gunning."

License-spot. An area or premises immune from police interference, through bribery or barter of information valuable to police. "It burned me up (made me angry) when them dicks (police) used to come down to knock off (raid) my alky (alcohol) joint. On the way they passed a dozen license-spots running wide open."

Life or **life bit.** A life sentence. (Varies according to local laws) (a) A "natural life" sentence is one from which there is no parole. Release may be obtained only by gubernatorial or presidential pardon. (b) A "habitual offender life" is a life sentence usually imposed after third or fourth felony conviction. In many States parole may be granted in such cases after the convict has served the maximum time which might have been imposed for the last crime committed as a second offender. (c) When sentenced to such terms as "one-to-life," "five-to-life," etc., a convict is usually paroled after serving a few years, but return to prison for a parole violation carries very heavy penalties.

Life-boat. (P., rare) A pardon or commutation of sentence; a stay of execution in capital punishment cases.

Life on the installment plan. 1. Successive parole violations and return to prison. "That ghee (fellow) is always giving me needles (poking fun at me) about my big bit (long term), but he come back three times since I'm here on this stretch. Hell, he's doing life on the installment plan himself." 2. Recidivism. 3. (P) Any indeterminate prison sentence with a big maximum (five-to-fifty years; two-to-life).

Lifer. One serving any of the various types of life sentences.

Life-saver. See **Life-boat.**

Lift, n. 1. Pocket picking. "The Republican convention opens up tomorrow. A couple of Democratic cannons (pickpockets) like us oughta do handy on the lift, Fingers. What about it?" 2. Truck robbery, usually of petty consumers' goods; hijacking. 3. Shoplifting. 4. Armed robbery. 5. (Rare) A pickpocket. 6. (Rare) A truck robber or hijacker. 7. (Rare) A shoplifter.

Lift, v. 1. To pick pockets. "Throw him a hump (pin him into position) and I'll lift the skin (his wallet)." 2. To engage in truck robbery, especially in hijacking truckloads of loot or contraband from other criminals. 3. To rob at gun point; to hold up. 4. To shoplift.

Light artillery. The drug addict's hypodermic needle or its crude equivalent.

Lighthouse. (P) A salt shaker.

Lightning. (Prohibition) Rotgut whiskey.

Light time. 1. A brief prison sentence. 2. Any non-violent crime, such as forgery, or petit larceny. "The pete-racket (safe-cracking) is caught up (finished). I'm playing the light time."

Limb. To pose as an authorized advertising solicitor for a legitimate publication, fraudulently accepting payment and cashing the checks through a **clearing house;** to solicit and accept payments for advertisements in a non-existent publication. "I'm gonna limb this joint (magazine) till it gets too hot (dangerous)."

Limb, the. That phase of the **tap** racket in which a swindler solicits advertisements for a magazine which he is not authorized to represent, or for any non-existent publication. "That Police News is a good flash (deceptive paper). The suckers figure you are law (a policeman) when you spring with it. But the ghee that runs it (manager) took my creed (credentials) away for beating (robbing) him. I'll work it on the limb though and make a nice buck (good money)."

Limb, on the. See **Tap, on the.**

Limb a joint. See **Limb.**

Limber. Pugnacious; anxious to use one's fists. "That crumb ain't lousing me around. I'm limber enough for that brother, and I'm gonna give him a fat lip (a beating)."

Limb it. See **Limb.**

Limb-joint. Any magazine or publication used by unauthorized advertising solicitors for the purpose of swindling prospective advertisers; any non-existent publication for which advertising is solicited for the purpose of swindling. "The tap (fake advertising racket) is okay these days. The suckers (victims) pay on your squash (honest appearance). I scored for two yards ($200) on a lousy limb-joint yesterday."

Limbo. 1. Penal confinement; a prison. 2. (P., chiefly Middle Atlantic area) Punishment cells.

Line. 1. A smoothly deceptive sales talk, especially that used by confidence swindlers. 2. (Carnival) (When preceded by a number, 30 line; 50 line, etc.) The amount of money exposed in the hand of the prospective victim of a crooked gaming wheel. [The number prefixed to line is double that of the amount in dollars. Thus, a "30-line" would signify $15.] The words are used by the shill who operates in the crowd outside of the booth and puts the squint on the prospective victims when they count or expose their money before playing. The shill then shouts the information, concealed in a torrent of meaningless expressions, to the operator of the wheel so that he knows how much money may be swindled with safety. Such limits vary according to locality and the terms arranged by the legal adjuster. It is never considered "safe" to leave a victim penniless. "See what the mark's (victim's) line is before we beat (rob) him."

Line, on the. 1. In sight; in the open; aboveboard, as the amount of cash involved in a transaction. 2. Engaged in street walking or in working in a brothel; engaged in some form of criminality for a living.

Line, the. The red light district; the rough area of a city or town.

Line of crap. A persuasive line of talk saturated with impressive lies.

Line-up, n. 1. The daily parade of all arrested persons before officers and detectives at police headquarters in metropolitan centers. 2. Police procedure in which a suspect is placed in a line of men as a test for identification by the complainant. 3. Criminal assault upon a woman by a series of men.

Line up, v. 1. To form a line of arrested persons at police headquarters for inspection by officers and detectives; to take one's place in such a line. 2. To form, or take one's place in a line of suspects for identification by a complainant. 3. To form, or take one's place in a line of men for a series of criminal assaults on a woman. 4. To organize unions, or so-called "protective agencies" by force; to secure a list of potential victims of extortion, and to organize them into regularly paying groups. 5. To make all necessary plans and preparations for the execution of a specific crime.

Lingo, the. 1. The language of the underworld, part argot, part slang—spoken largely by thieves, gangsters, prostitutes, and hobos. 2. Any of the several varieties of pig-Latin used by prostitutes, petty swindlers, and carnival people. [Note: Words are usually formed by transposing the initial letters of a syllable to the end, with "-ay" affixed; as: "day—ay-day"; "dough" —"ough-day"; "lingo—"in-lay o-gay"; or, by the insertion of "-iers-" between the first and second letters of the word, as: "day"—"d-iers-ay"; "dough"—"d-iers-ough"; "lingo" — "l-iers-in-g-iers-o".] When spoken rapidly, this "lingo" baffles the uninitiated, but it has the weakness of arousing suspicion and placing people on the alert.

Lion tamer. A leader among tough underworld members who effectively controls them. [Note: Often used sarcastically.] "Get that lion tamer, Bobo, to front for (pose as the owner of) the joint. He'll handle them shake-men (extortionists) and badeye ghees (strong-arm men)."

Lip. A lawyer. "The lip took a hundred skins (dollars) and never showed (appeared) in court."

Lip-burner. A very short cigarette butt.

Lip in. To break into a conversation rudely.

Live one. A gullible victim who has plenty of money; any promising victim of thieves, gamblers, or other professional criminals. "Them lemon-mobs (swindlers using promise of girls for lure, pool game to defraud) knock off (rob) some real live ones."

Live-wire. 1. A sober and alert victim of a robbery, in contrast to an intoxicated, drugged, or sleeping victim. 2. An apparently prosperous victim chosen by thieves, gambling swindlers, and the like.

Lizzie-lousy (or **Lousy Liz**). A policeman who tours his beat in a two-seater car.

Load, n. 1. A clumsy and inept thief. "Chill (discourage the presence of) that load. He's stir wacky (prison crazy)." 2. A stolen automobile. "Roll that load into the dog-house (garage) till the touch (robbery) is ready." 3. A clumsy or awkward fellow. 4. Skill, dexterity. "Joe was an ace (very good) wire (pickpocket) till he did that stretch (prison term). Then he blew

his load." 5. (P) Luck. "There goes your load; the cards gotta run my way now." 6. A dose of narcotics; a quantity of stolen or contraband goods; a term of years' imprisonment; a great quantity or amount (of anything).

Load, v. To crowd a victim skillfully, compelling him without his knowledge to mount a staircase or to enter any narrow passageway, as on a bus or train, in order to make it possible for one's accomplices to snatch the victim's purse or wallet without his taking notice of the necessarily rough pocketpicking operation. "We loaded the mark (victim) on the streetcar and the cannon (pickpocket) put the duke down (reached into his pocket) too heavy and ripped the guy's pants. The sucker rounded (turned around), and I had to split him out (step between him and my accomplice unobtrusively) while the rest of the mob mooched (fled). Then I had to help the sucker describe the ghees (men) who made (robbed) him when the bulls showed (appeared)."

Loaded. 1. Having stolen goods, a weapon, or contraband on one's person, in one's car, or at one's quarters. "If they ever give me a frisk (search), I'm buried (good for a prison term). I'm heeled (armed) and loaded with swag (loot)." 2. Having a great sum of money on one's person or in one's possession. "Put the squint on (look carefully at) that mark's (victim's) boodle (roll of money). If he's loaded, give him the push (crowd him into position) and we'll hustle (swindle) him."

Load up. To place concealed firearms upon one's person; to arm oneself. "Load up. Some of Butch's hoods (gangsters) are tryin' to muscle in on us (take over our territory)."

Lob. A dull-witted flunkey to thieves and racketeers; a prospective **fall guy.** "Send that lob out to pick up a load (steal a car) for the job (robbery) and switch the plates (put other license plates on the car)."

Lobby (variant: **Lobby-gow.**) See **Lob.**

Lock. (P) To occupy a cell. ("Where do you live?" is commonly translated in prison usage into, "Where do you lock?") "Where did you lock when you were in the pen, Mack?"

Lock-in, n. (P) A routine or emergency confinement of all inmates to their cells. [Compare: **Lock-up,** n.]

Lock in, v. (P) To lock convicts in cells as a routine matter or in a general emergency; to enter one's cell to be locked in. [Compare: **Lock up,** v.] "I gotta lock in for the count (routine check-up). Send that hard-covered book (novel) over on the trolley (improvised device for making cell-to-cell delivery)."

Lock oneself up. (P) To request officials to lock one up in a segregation cell in order to protect oneself from the anger of one's fellow convicts. [Note: Informers and debtors often ask for such protection against threatened violence.] "Lippo went in the barrel (in debt) for twenty cartons (of cigarettes) and locked himself up."

Lock up. [Compare **Lock in.**]

Lock-up, n. The act of locking up a convict for a violation of rules. [See **Lock up.** Compare **Lock in.**]

Lock up, v. 1. To remove a convict from his work assignment and confine him to his own cell or to a punishment cell, pending formal hearing on a report for rule violation. 2. To lock a cell door. [Compare **Lock in.**]

Loft-man. A burglar who specializes in robbing silk and fur vaults in loft buildings.

Loft-mob. A gang of loft-thieves who force entry into silk and fur vaults, usually through floors, ceilings, or sidewalls.

Loft-work. The burglarizing of mercantile lofts, especially to steal silk, usually by burrowing through walls from adjacent buildings which lack alarm systems.

Loft-worker. One who does loftwork.

Lone wolf. 1. (Probably a journalistic creation, seldom heard in the underworld) A clever thief who operates alone. **2.** (P) An active pederast who selects **undercover** perverts and maintains secrecy.

Long-chain Charley. (South) **1.** The prison camp officer who drives a truck or bus to bring chain-gang convicts to quarters at night. **2.** (P) A chain-gang boss.

Long-cut-short. (Rare) A sawed-off shotgun.

Long-haired. Artistic; religious; esthetic. "That long-haired business is part of his act; he's the front ghee (show-piece) for a mob of abbeys (swindling impersonators of clergymen)."

Long-haired boys. Artists; clergymen; psychiatrists working in prisons and court clinics. "That guy sure acts funny. He's giving them long-haired boys too much of a play. Dudes (fellows) like that go wrong (turn traitor)."

Long-line skinner. (Gulf State area prisons) The boss of a convict gang of workers in canebrakes or cotton fields.

Long rod. A rifle.

Long-timer, A convict serving a long sentence.

Look to. To try (to); to hope (to). "The D. A. is looking to pin that rap (charge) on somebody."

Lookout. (Obsolete) A criminal who stands watch during the commission of a crime. "The lookout lammed (fled) when the rumble (trouble) came and left us holding the bag (to face the danger alone)."

Look out for the man in the white

coat. (P) A half-humorous, half-serious warning to one who is acting queerly to watch out lest the prison psychiatrist commit him to an institution for the criminally insane. "That stir-bug (prison-crazed fellow) in cell thirteen is fishing in the bucket (portable toilet) again. He better look out for the man in the white coat."

Loop, on the. In a hurry; at top speed; on the button.

Lose a man. To suffer a member of one's gang to be wounded and seized. "We got a rumble (were interrupted) and lammed (fled). The blow-off (trouble) really came though when the bulls headed us off and started tossing lead (shooting). We lost a man getting to the pickup car (second car used when getaway car is abandoned)."

Loser. (P) Anyone convicted of a felony. [A second felony conviction makes one a "two-time loser"; a third conviction, a "three-time loser," etc.] "I'm a four-time loser on the next pinch (arrest) so I gotta wrap up (quit). I can't grift (steal), I can't do nothing legit (honest). I might as well hang up (hang myself)."

Lose out. (P) To forfeit one's work assignment for violation of rules. "Skinny got a keep-locked (report) for a batch (quantity of home brew). He's gonna hit the cooler (punishment cells) and lose out on that pinch."

Lost time. (P) Any curtailment, because of rule violation, of the time credited to a convict for good behavior. [Note: In no case may "lost time" be extended beyond the maximum term of sentence imposed by the Court.]

Loud talk a ghee. (P) To inform upon a fellow convict by indirection, as to utter such information while within earshot of a guard or a known informer.

Louse around. To treat badly, as to cheat, persecute, or betray. "That creep loused me around for my broad (girl) and my case dough (the last of my money) while I was waiting to go to bat (stand trial)."

Louse oneself up. To besmirch one's reputation by flagrant violation or betrayal of underworld conventions. "You loused yourself up when you copped a plea (pleaded guilty to a lesser offense) and left your partner go to bat (trial) alone."

Louse trap. A cheap lodging house; a verminous prison or jail.

Louse up. 1. (P) To slander; to ruin one's reputation by slander. "Get it up (pay off) or I'll louse you up so your own mother won't rumble (talk to) you." 2. To besmirch the reputation of a place by allowing informers, drug addicts, and even police and honest working people to frequent it. "Them p. i.'s (pimps) and finks (informers) giving your joint a play (patronizing your place) are sure lousing it up." 3. To blunder and fail in a criminal enterprise.

Lousy. Characterized by a lack of principle according to underworld standards; dirty; mean; undesirable; unsuitable for criminal purposes. "That's one lousy can (prison) to get a bit in."

Lousy and attempt to scratch, to be. (P) To be guilty of attempted forgery. [Note: The idiom was originally applied humorously to this offense. It has since been extended to apply to any petty crime which the culprit is unwilling to dignify with its proper legal name.] "I don't mind getting knocked off (arrested) for doing something to score for a buck (make money crookedly) but getting glommed (picked up) for being lousy and attempting to scratch, that's bad. Suspicion of I. M. M. (impairing the morals of a minor). If the mob ever hears this. . . ."

Lousy caper. Any mean or contemptible trick; any crime beneath the dignity of a self-respecting member of the underworld, such as robbing poorboxes, impairing the morals of a minor, rape, etc.

Lousy with. Swarming with; filled with; teeming with. The court was lousy with suckers (complaints) putting the finger on (identifying) me."

Lover. 1. (P) (Ironic) A rapist; a bigamist; a seductionist; any criminal offender against the person of a woman. 2. (P) (Humorous) A peaceful convict. "Yeah, you're a muscle man, Jake. Me? I'm just a lover." 3. A ladies' man.

Lowdown, the. The facts, especially the details of a projected crime.

Low number. (P) An old timer; one who has been in prison a long time; one returned for parole violation on an old prison sentence, and therefore registered under the old low serial number in prison.

Lug, n. 1. One who has a strong back and a weak mind; a thief whose assignments are of the strong-arm variety; a clumsy, inept thief. 2. (Rare) An automatic pistol of German Luger manufacture.

Lug, v. (Carnival) To eject forcibly. [A warning or order given by the operator of a gaming wheel to **shills** to force if necessary the ejection or removal of a victim after he has been swindled.] "Lug him, Legs. Play the deuce of clubs (use any force required)."

Lug a chiv. To carry a knife, razor, or other edged weapon. "It ain't no good being a dukester (fist fighter in a can (prison) where everyone lugs a chiv. Take a tumble (wake up) before you get clipped (knifed)."

Lug a mark. See **Lug,** v.

Lug a rod. To carry a gun.

Lug iron. To do dirty work (with a

pistol), especially for a criminal syndicate; to serve as a bodyguard.

Lug swag. To carry or deliver stolen goods.

Lulu. The male organ freshly infected with gonorrhea; a bad case of gonorrhea.

Lumber. (Carnival) A general term for **shills** and other **grifters** working on carnival grounds. "Gotta get some new lumber around here. We can't scorf (eat) unless we score (make money)."

Lump, n. (Hobo) 1. A handout of food, money or clothing. 2. An appreciable sum of money. 3. A sum of money, especially the proceeds of begging or theft.

Lump, v. To beat and kick viciously. "I'm gonna lump that crumb till his head looks like a sock full of doorknobs for copping a heel on me (hitting me when I didn't expect it)."

Lumping. A beating, with or without weapons. "Timmy got a sweetheart of a lumping for taking (robbing) the Swede with strippers (cards trimmed for cheating)."

Lumps. See **Lumping.**

Lump up. See **Lump,** v.

Lunger. 1. A victim of tuberculosis. "That lunger from L. A. kicked off (died) last month. The jute mill in stir (prison) did it." 2. The act of expectorating noisily, a studied token of belligerent contempt. 3. The act of clearing one's throat as a signal that one of the company is a plainclothes detective or a police informer; also used by pickpockets as a danger warning.

Lush, n. 1. A drunken person. 2. One easily victimized; a gullible person; a stupid fellow. "Nurse that lush along; don't clip (rob) him for all his coin now. He'll be good for a rehash (another substantial swindle) when he gets some fresh (additional money)." 3. Alcoholic drinks.

Lush, v. To drink to excess.

Lush-dive, n. A drinking establishment or district frequented by drunkards, especially by those who drink the cheapest alcohol, as **smoke, skee,** etc.

Lush dive, v. To rob drunkards.

Lush-diver. One who robs drunkards.

Lusher. See **Lush-diver.**

Lush roll. See **Lush dive.**

Lush-roller. See **Lush-diver.**

Lush up. See **Lush,** v.

Lush-worker. See **Lush-diver.**

M

M. Morphine. "I started chippying around (indulging experimentally) with C (cocaine) and got hooked (developed a habit). After a while, I couldn't get my gage up (find satisfaction) on that so I went for the M."

Mac. 1. A pimp. 2. A loafer supported by a working girl. [Note: This word is often prefixed to any fictitious name, to convey meanings of both 1. and 2., as: MacGimp, MacGluke, Mac-Kife, MacKoozey, etc.]

Macaluccis. (Ital. Amer.) Blows on the forehead delivered by grasping the middle finger of the left hand with the finger tips of the right hand, drawing it back stiffly and releasing it to snap a thumping blow. Macaluccis serve as forfeits in wagers in lieu of money and its equivalent among friends and penniless fellows.

Mace. (Scattered Southern areas) A blackjack.

Madam. 1. The proprietress of a bawdy house. "That barnacle (woman) who gave me my bit (prison sentence) on the skin-heist (for rape) was a madam in a nautch-joint (brothel) in Elcart." 2. An old male oral sodomist or passive pederast.

Made. 1. Lifted out of mediocrity to a position of wealth or influence in the underworld. "If this score (robbery) goes over we're made. No more scuffling (crude run-of-the-mill crimes) for nut-money (bare expenses)." 2. Robbed, especially by pickpockets. "Where's my poke (wallet)? I'll bet you I've been made." 3. Recognized; formally identified as the perpetrator of a crime.

Made fag, gunzel, or punk. (P) A male oral sodomist or passive pederast who has been perverted by persuasion, inducements or force, as differentiated from a congenital invert.

Mad hatter. Any person whose behavior is erratic, unpredictable, and reckless, especially in criminal activities. "The way that mad hatter cowboys around on the heist (hold-up), banging (shooting) people, I can't figure how he ain't hit in the head (shot to death) or settled (in prison)."

Magic. A process by which a cheap alcoholic beverage is made to pass for whiskey. [The whiskey is usually poured into an empty barrel in which genuine bonded liquor has been aged, and permitted to remain there for about two weeks. Caramel coloring is added and the product is then bottled and labeled with counterfeits. The finished product is deceptive to all but the trained eye, nose, and palate.]

Mahoska. 1. Habit-forming drugs. 2. A pistol or revolver. 3. (P) A knife or similar weapon. 4. Anything illicit or necessarily secret, known only to the parties involved, as stolen goods, combustibles, and counterfeit money. "Ditch (get rid of) the mahoska, Squint. The bulls (police) are gonna crash (raid) the joint (place)."

Mahoska, on the. See **Junk, on the.**

Main drag. The principal avenue or thoroughfare. "A relief bull (policeman) was on the beat when we took (robbed) this skin-joint (fur place). He mooched up (walked over) when we opened the joint with a double (duplicate key) and stood there cutting up jackpots (talking) with the limey on the main drag while we cleaned the spot (took out all the furs) and loaded the swag (loot) on a truck."

Main ghee. A gang leader; the head of a criminal organization; a prison warden; the chief prosecution witness in criminal proceedings.

Main line. (P) The regular prison

mess, as differentiated from the hospital mess, road gang kitchen, etc. ("What's on the main line today?"— what have they on the bill of fare today?)

Main-line bang. A hypodermic injection of a narcotic solution in the median cephalic vein in the forearm.

Main stem. The principal avenue or street of a city or town.

Majonda. Narcotics. "Duck (avoid) The Midget. He's still hooked (addicted) on the old majonda."

Make, n. 1. Professional thievery in general. "I took a wack at (made a try at) the legit (working for a living) but all the dudes (fellows) I knew was earning big dough, and I couldn't hold my end up (meet my share of expenses). The make looked pretty good to me from there." 2. A specific robbery, especially by the craftier methods, as in confidence games, picking pockets, etc. "That was a nice make, eight bills ($800) for my end (share)." 3. "On the make." Actively pursuing a criminal career; ready to participate in any lucrative criminal venture.

Make, v. 1. To succeed in robbing, especially by crafty methods, as in swindling, shop-lifting, pocket-picking, etc.; to succeed in any endeavor. "The bus pulled up, and Matty put the mark on (forced the victim to mount the step by jostling). I made the poke (wallet) without a blow (anyone's knowledge)." 2. To identify formally as a criminal in a police line-up; to recognize; to identify any person or place. "The sucker got one gander (look) at me in the dark on a heist (holdup) and he makes me a year later in court. That rap (charge) oughtn't stick."

Make a beat. To escape from custody. "Gyp tried to pull a Dillinger. He got a wooden biscuit (gun), figuring

to make a beat from the county (county jail))."

Make a boat. (P) To succeed in securing a transfer from one prison to another which may be more desirable.

Make a break. See **Make a beat.**

Make a bum beef. To complain unjustifiably, especially to the authorities.

Make a deal. 1. To conclude a bargain with a district attorney, judge, or other official whereby leniency or immunity is granted in exchange for a plea of guilty or for information leading to the arrest or conviction of other criminals. 2. To purchase by bribery or other means immunity from law-enforcement agencies.

Make a grab. (Among loan sharks) To take over the business or property of a victim caught in the incredibly usurious **vigerage-and** loan racket [usually, 20 per cent compounded weekly.]

Make a joint. 1. To succeed in robbing an establishment. "I'd like to make that slum (jewelry) joint. It's a nice score, but the place is all bugged up (equipped with elaborate alarm system)." 2. (P) To succeed in securing a transfer to, sentence to, or commitment to a specific institution. "They are opening a new can (prison) up-state with a good main ghee (warden) running it. I'd like to make the joint when a boat (transfer) goes out." 3. To succeed in escaping from any place of confinement. "You could make this joint with a couple of rods (guns) and a lam-car (car in which to flee)."

Make a kisser. 1. (P) To grimace an expression of distaste, contempt, or annoyance. "He made a kisser when I told him off (called him down) but he never opened his bazoo (mouth)." 2. To recognize a person's face.

Make a mark. 1. To succeed in robbing a victim. 2. (Very rarely) To succeed in robbing a place.

Make a meet. 1. To make an appointment. 2. (Occasionally) To keep an appointment. "I'm gonna cop a mope (leave). I gotta make a meet with the fence."

Make an entry. See **Make an in.**

Make an in. To gain entry either by force or guile preliminary to the commission of a crime, especially burglary. "The joint is bugged (equipped with alarms) on the doors and windows. But there ain't no bug on the coal chute. We'll make an in there."

Make a pass. (P) To deliver messages, reading matter, food, or other articles from one cell to another.

Make a pinch. 1. To make an arrest. 2. (P) To report or lock up, as a convict for rule violation.

Make a play for. 1. To try, especially by subtle and devious methods, to rob a prospective victim. "Every mob in town is making a play for that ghee (fellow) to beat (rob) him for that ice (diamond jewelry) of his, but he's a pretty hip (alert and sophisticated) gent. He done a bit (served a prison term)." 2. To attempt to win the favor of, especially to seduce, a woman or homosexual.

Make a poke. 1. To succeed in picking a wallet from a victim's pocket, or a purse from a store counter, a baby carriage, etc. 2. (Less commonly) to succeed in removing money from a woman's purse by stealth; to snatch a purse and flee.

Make a riffle. (Rare) To panhandle or steal successfully in one single instance.

Make a score. See **Make a touch.**

Make a stir. 1. To succeed in having oneself committed to, sentenced to, or transferred to a relatively lenient prison. "If I had to do a bit (serve a prison term), why couldn't I make a stir like Pleasant Haven where the screws (guards) aren't ball-breakers (marti-

nets)?" 2. (P) To succeed in escaping from prison.

Make a sucker. See **Make a mark.**

Make a touch. 1. To succeed in the execution of a profitable crime. "What a sweet mark (victim)! We made the touch right on the main stem without a rumble (interference)." 2. (P) To acquire anything by means of guile, cleverness, or outright thievery. "We got Mickey to chop it up (talk) with the screw (guard) about baseball while I made the touch for a ham and a bag of spuds (potatoes) from the storehouse."

Make book. 1. To accept bets on horse races. 2. To bet. "I'll make book you don't rehash (rob a second time) that sucker. He's all hipped up (smartened up) now."

Make citizens. To practice extortion among aliens not yet admitted to citizenship, by offering to hasten the process for a consideration, and threatening deportation as an alternative. [Frequently victims are brought before a bogus "federal judge" or other distinguished-looking impostor as a means of intimidation.]

Make one for. To steal from. "Can you tie (imagine) that? Some muzzler made me for my poke (wallet)."

Make one on his prints. To discover the hitherto obscure criminal record of a prisoner by comparison of fingerprints with those in official criminal files.

Make one's kisser. To recognize one's face, especially in police procedure governing identification of suspects. "The rapper (complainant) made my kisser all right, but he couldn't peg (formally identify) me as the guy that clipped (robbed) him."

Make one's mugg. See **Make one's kisser.**

Make one's prints. To identify one's fingerprints left at the scene of a crime with those on file at the Bureau of Criminal Identification. "Wise guy, you wouldn't mitt up (wear gloves). Now they made your prints, and your mugg is on the board (your photograph is on a 'wanted' circular)."

Make parole. (P) To have parole application granted.

Make the arrival and screw. To report to the parole officer upon being released from prison and then flee jurisdiction.

Make the board. (P) To be granted parole by the Parole Board. "Only four out of thirty first-time losers (first offenders) made the board last month."

Make the boast. (P) (Scattered near-West and Central States) To agree to carry out one's parole commitments; hence, to be paroled.

Make the bughouse. 1. To escape capital punishment or a very long prison term by successfully feigning insanity and being committed to an institution for the insane prior to completion of trial. 2. (P) To succeed in being committed from prison to an institution for the criminally insane. [Note: In many states, a prisoner whose aggregate loss of good time for rule violations is great may thus seek its restoration. If he is later adjudged sane, he may be returned to prison and absolved of the time penalties, since presumptive proof exists that he was irresponsible mentally when he committed the offenses for which the penalties were imposed.]

Make the nut. To clear expenses and show a profit on a transaction.

Make the rounds. (P) To be interviewed by the doctor, chaplain, school officials, deputy warden, psychologists, etc., prior to a parole hearing. "Yeah, I'm getting real short (nearing the end of my term) now, making the rounds."

Make-up. Any radical change in appearance, particularly when effected by

wearing eyeglasses, a moustache, unusual clothing, etc. "How come the make-up? Ain't nothing wrong with your glimmers (you don't need eyeglasses)."

Makin's. Tobacco and paper for making hand-rolled cigarettes.

Makko. Macaroni.

Mama bull. See **Mother bull.**

Man. 1. Policeman; any representative of the law. "Case (watch) the man ringing in (phoning in his report). I'll make the in (force an entry in the place)." 2. (P) Prison keeper, warden, or other prison official. "Lay zex (be-ready to warn me) for the man, I'm gonna cop a heel on (beat) that new fink (informer) in the shop."

Man behind the gun. See **Man behind the stick.**

Man behind the stick, the. 1. (Carnival) The operator of any gaming wheel. 2. The operator of any gambling game; a cashier; a croupier.

Mangey, a. Lacking in underworld principle and pride; dirty; mean.

Man with the brass nuts, the. (P) (California and scattered prisons) The chief disciplinary officer of a prison; the principal keeper; the deputy warden; or the captain. "I'm hitting the porch (going to be tried for rule violation) today and the man with the brass nuts is gonna throw me in the hole (solitary confinement) sure pop (certainly)." 2. A leader of a gang or criminal syndicate.

Man with the white coat, the. A prison psychiatrist; an attendant at an institution for the criminally insane. "What a wack this dude (fellow) is; he wrote a letter to Stalin asking him to get him sprung (released). The man with the white coat dropped the net on him yesterday and put him in obso (an observation cell)."

Marbles. (P) Eggs.

Mark, n. 1. A person easily victimized; the victim of a robbery or blackmail. 2. Anyone selected to be victimized by pickpockets or confidence men. "What a sweet mark! He goes (yields) like a clock." 3. (Rare) A place selected to be robbed. 4. The scar of a knife, usually from cheekbone to mouth, the traditional mark of the informer. "I don't want no part of that joker (fellow). He didn't get that mark on his kisser for being a right ghee (loyal person)." 5. A fool; one incapable of protecting his own interests.

Mark, v. 1. To select, or **put the finger on,** as a prospective victim of murder or robbery. 2. To denounce or stigmatize, as an informer or pervert. "Any guy that don't mark a fink (informer) that he knows is a wrong ghee himself." 3. To mark one with a knife as the stigma of a traitor.

Marked. (P) Classified by prison officials as a troublemaker: an agitator, hater of authority, knife-wielder, etc. "Don't get marked as a chiv-man (knife-wielder) here or you'll be screwed up (in constant trouble) the rest of your bit (prison term)."

Marker. A spotter of victims for criminals.

Markers. Automobile license plates.

Market. The rendezvous of male oral sodomists and pederasts—with robbery and extortion as an indirect objective of youths frequenting these sections. "Guess I'll hit the market and give the fruit (perverts) a play."

Mark lousy. 1. To publicize another's betrayal of underworld honor, ruining his reputation; to slander or defame. "That fleabitten muzzler (good-for-nothing) opened up (informed) on me. Now he's marking me lousy to cover up for himself. I'll show you the trial minutes. Then see who's wrong." 2. To ruin the reputation of an establishment, as by labeling the proprietor an informer or conscious host of police or stool-pigeons. "Groggo John's scatter (underworld rendezvous) is marked lousy, I hear. The dicks (detectives) are grabbing too many guys on right raps (charges of which they are guilty) in there."

Mark one's kisser. To slash one's cheek from jawbone to mouth, as in branding an informer. "That rat (informer) ate all the cheese (gave all the information) he's gonna eat for a while. I'm marking his kisser for him."

Mark wrong. See **Mark lousy.**

Married. (P) Bound by illicit or perverse sexual relations. "I ain't gone for none of them punks (pederasts) yet. Now the bit (sentence) is almost done, I ain't gonna get married."

Married to Mary Fist. (Coarse prison humor) In prison; hence, by implication, addicted to the practice of masturbation.

Mary Ann, the. The robbery of drunkards by combined crude pocket-picking and suave talk; frequently the thief pretends to be a sexual pervert to throw off suspicion that he is feeling for the victim's wallet. Discovery of the ruse by the victim results in the **mugg** of which the Mary Ann is a refined New England variant.

Mary Ellen. See **Mary Ann.**

Mary Magdalene. A reformed prostitute. "Legit broads (girls not of the underworld) all want something. It took a Mary Magdalene to kick in (produce the money) when I needed fall dough (money for lawyers and bail)."

Mastermind, n. (Ironically) A fool. [Note: The word originated with its usage in the press as descriptive of "clever criminals," most of whom were discovered to be fools upon arrival in prison.]

Master mind, v. (Ironically) To plan a crime stupidly; to lead others in the execution of a clumsy and inept plan. "Who ever master minded that trick (robbery)? You shlubs (fools) worked all night ripping a crib (forcing open a safe) that wasn't even locked? Nice going!"

Mat. A prostitute or a very promiscuous woman.

Match. See **Play the match.**

Match-game, the. A swindle in which the victim is shown three match boxes, one of which is filled with matches and two of which are empty. The victim is induced to wager that he can select the full box after all three have been manipulated by the operator. The operator then deftly removes the full box and substitutes a third empty one. The illusion that the third box—the full one —is still in play is maintained by the operator by rattling a partially filled match box which is taped to the underside of his wrist. Aides stand by with full boxes of matches and an array of clever diversions to off-set any awakening suspicion. Sometimes the local sheriff plays openly for a few hands. Frequently he is permitted to win ten or twenty dollars as an indirect bribe for his tolerance.

Matinee. A second crime committed upon the same person or establishment; a second crime committed within one day. "One good heist (hold-up) a day ain't enough for these cowboys (reckless thieves). They got to play matinees like they got a license (official immunity)."

Max. (P) The maximum limit of an indeterminate prison sentence; the maximum penalty, other than capital punishment, provided by law for any specific crime.

Max less comp. (P) The maximum limit of an indeterminate sentence with time off (compensation) for good conduct. [Note: The most severe decision of any parole board is: "full max." "Max less comp" is slightly less severe.]

McCoy, the. The real thing; a genuine article; a fully trustworthy person; the truth. "These kids got a swag of (lot of) happy dust (cocaine), the real McCoy, they clipped (stole)."

Mean scorfer. A gluttonous trencherman.

Measure. To knock down or out, with or without a weapon. "The first dude (person) who beefs (complains), measure with the butt of your biscuit (gun)."

Meat-ball. 1. (Chiefly N. Y. State prisons; Ital.-Amer.) An inept person; a dolt; (applied derisively) a Negro. 2. (Same area; adopted by Irish-Amer. convicts) An Italian.

Meat-hooks. The fingers; the hands.

Mechanic. 1. An expert card swindler. "I seen some ace (expert) tubworkers (card sharps traveling ocean liners), but this guy is one bitch of a (very good) mechanic." 2. A safe-burglar who specializes in forcing safes without recourse to explosives or oxyacetylene burning.

Mechanic's grip, the. The card cheat's most effective method of holding the deck when dealing: Three fingers of the left hand are spread apart under the deck; the index finger overlaps and covers the forward edge; the thumb is kept free to draw back the top card which is then slid sufficiently forward to screen the dealing of another card, usually the second from the top, or one of the first two cards at the bottom of the deck.

Meet. 1. An appointment. "I gotta keep a meet with Dan's shyster (lawyer) and the rapper (complainant) to try to square the beef (quash the criminal charge against Dan)." 2. A thieves' meeting place.

Meet the board. (P) To appear before the board of parole for a hearing. "When do you meet the board again, Country?"

Meg. (Sing. and pl.) A cent; a penny. "That rat (informer) ain't worth banging (shooting to death) at three meg a pill (three cents a bullet)."

Menagerie. (P) A cell-block, especially one in which Negro inmates are numerous.

Merchandise. 1. Stolen goods. 2. A prostitute.

Merry-go-round, on the. (P) Dizzy; groggy; usually as a result of long imprisonment or parole uncertainty; shunted from "pillar to post." "The parole board gave me three hold-backs (denials of parole) and I'm on the old merry-go-round now."

Mess up. To involve, or become involved, in trouble, especially with the law; to bungle.

Mess with. (South) To annoy; to irritate; to take liberties with; to have relations with; to do. "I ain't messing with no barkers (guns) when they lag (imprison) you for that big stretch (term)."

Meter. (Among thieves who steal packages from automobiles) A bag; a suitcase.

Mexican. Inferior; counterfeit; phony, as "Mexican money," a "Mexican payoff," etc. "That spotter (thieves' tipster) is giving us them Mexican steers (leads) that don't even get us off the nut (meet expenses). Tell him to hip up (wake up)."

Mexican bankroll. See **Michigan bankroll.**

Mexican diamond. An inferior diamond, or any other stone cut or polished to pass as a genuine gem for the purpose of defrauding.

Michigan bankroll. 1. A roll of paper with a bank note of large denomination wrapped around the outside to simulate a bankroll—for use in swindling. 2. A roll of single bills wrapped inside a bank note of large denomination to be exhibited for effect.

Mick or micky. (P) An inmate of a penal institution. 2. A person.

Middle, in the. In an untenable or precarious situation. "My partner copped out (pleaded guilty.) and left me in the middle. What jury will spring (acquit) a guy then?"

Midnight. An armed burglar who prowls inhabited dwellings. [Note: This crime is punishable by death in several States.]

Midnighter. See **Midnight.**

Midway. 1. (Carnival) The main thoroughfare on carnival grounds. 2. Any main thoroughfare or street. "Mickey was burned down (shot) copping a heel (fleeing) across the midway to the heap (car for getaway)."

Mike and Ike. 1. (Obsolete) The uniformed team of officer and sergeant in a police car, formerly common in metropolitan centers. 2. A pair of detectives who work together regularly.

Mill. (Chiefly Central and mid-Western) A prison; a jail; reformatory; penitentiary. "Jed threw snake-eyes (was arrested) on a cold slough prowl (burglary of an empty house). He's back in the mill."

Miss a bit. To escape a prison term. "I just missed a bit with the Jammer and his mob. I was supposed to fill (in), but I passed up the trick (robbery) on a hunch."

Miss a meet. To fail to keep an appointment. "I missed a meet with Pippy to step out on a nice score. To make it worse he got a pick-up (arrest on suspicion) waitin' for me on the stem."

Mission-stiff. 1. A petty thief or hobo who accepts meals or lodgings from missions. 2. (P) A religious hypocrite. 3. (Contemptuously) A reformed criminal who accepts aid from religious organizations, in either good or bad faith.

Miss-outs. Crooked dice, loaded or shaped in such a way that the roller is unable to turn up winning numbers.

Miss-up, n. A completely bungled crime; a criminal fiasco; a failure to execute a prearranged plan.

Miss up, v. To suffer a **miss-up.**

Mister fix. A go-between, especially one who shuttles between the underworld and the overworld, handling bribes, ransom payments, etc.

Mitt. 1. The human hand. 2. One's holding in a card game.

Mitted. 1. (Rare) Armed with any weapon capable of being used with one hand, especially firearms, a knife, or a bludgeon. 2. Gloved, as protection against leaving fingerprints.

Mitt-glom. A handshake, i.e., a cordial reception.

Mitt-glommer. A hand-shaker; a "yes-man."

Mitt-joint. (Carnival) A palm-reader's booth or tent.

Mitt up. To put on gloves in order to avoid leaving fingerprints. "You mitt up and scheme not to give your kisser up (show your face), then you shoot your bazoo off (talk indiscreetly) to some broad. I'll be seeing you in the big house (prison)."

M-joint. An establishment where morphine is sold to addicts.

Mob. A number of persons nefariously engaged.

Mob-ghee. One who works with a gang in preference to operating alone; a member of a criminal gang.

Mob-marker. One who marks or selects prospective places to be robbed by a mob.

Mobster. See **Mob-ghee.**

Mob up. To associate oneself with a criminal gang in preference to operating independently; to ally oneself with a criminal gang, syndicate, or faction. "Mobbing up in the can (prison) is peasoup (unwise) if you wanta stay out of swindles (fights)."

Mojo. Drugs; narcotics.

Moke. Coffee, usually of indifferent brew.

Moll. 1. A woman accomplice of a gunman; a gun-woman. [Note: Rarely used in the East; **broad** or **head** is much more common.] 2. Any prospective woman victim of purse-snatchers or moll-buzzers. 3. (Loosely) A woman.

Moll-buzz. A technique of snatching women's purses from baby carriages. [Note: The theft is accomplished in the following manner: An accomplice, known as the **buzzer,** accosts a victim and asks to be directed to a given place in the neighborhood. The destination is so chosen that the victim must turn her back to the carriage to point. The purse-snatcher now advances from the direction which the victim is facing and deftly seizes the purse. The victim seldom discovers her loss until the thieves have disappeared. Premature discovery requires the **buzzer,** feigning solicitude, to block pursuit and delay any outcry until the snatcher has escaped. Very youthful operators are most successful.

There are several variations of this technique. Sometimes a second accomplice is used, a boy who sells paper market-bags. He and the snatcher converge on the baby carriage from opposite directions so that the seized purse may be swiftly dropped into an open market-bag. Arrests in this form of thievery are infrequent, and the thief is rarely found in possession of the stolen purse.]

Moll buzz. To operate in the **moll-buzz** racket.

Moll-buzzer. One who practices the moll-buzz.

Moll-buzz, on the. Engaged in, or swindling by means of, the **moll-buzz.**

Moll-whiz. (Very rare) A female pickpocket.

Momma. (P) (Often prefixed to the subject's name) Any convict who assumes mother-like protection over youthful or less self-reliant inmates. [There is no implication of effeminacy or perversion in the use of this term.] "Get Momma Russo to square Peanuts with the shop screw (to mend their relations). The kid's getting honey (abuse)."

Money! The announcement of the **stickman** or **book** of a craps game that the roller has thrown a winning number.

Money machine. Any of various devices sold to the gullible as machines for printing genuine currency or for raising the denomination of genuine currency; the **Rumanian box.** [Note: These machines are usually elaborate affairs into which plain white bond paper is fed. The paper then seems to emerge in the form of perfectly duplicated United States Treasury notes. Actually the bond paper disappears into a concealed chamber from which previously deposited genuine new bills emerge. The victim is then urged to spend several of the Treasury notes to convince him that they will be accepted as genuine. Aliens are usually selected as the most likely victims of this type of confidence swindle.]

Monicker. One's real name, not an alias.

Monk. (Near South and scattered areas) A supreme court judge, especially of a State court.

Monkey. 1. (Near South and Central U. S.; prohibition era) A prohibition agent. 2. (Chiefly among smugglers of aliens) A Chinese, sometimes extended to include any Oriental. 3. (Rare) A Negro.

Monkey-runner. One engaged in smuggling Chinese into the country. [Note: In case of sudden danger of discovery, monkey-runners often literally destroy the evidence of their crime by tossing their charges into the sea.]

Mooch, n. 1. A person with no sales resistance; an easy victim for peddlers of watered stocks and securities, imperfect diamonds, and other commodities of dubious value. "There's the mooch. Duke (hand) him the stiff (bad check) to smash (cash)." 2. The victim of a swindle. 3. Habit-forming narcotics. 4. A drug addict. 5. A beggar or a petty thief; a chiseler; the panhandling profession; the act of panhandling. 6. An idler or passerby; a pedestrian; the act of walking around aimlessly; jay walking; the art of walking away from the scene of a crime with studied casualness. "Some shlub (fool) gunned us over (looked at us) coming out of the joint with the swag (loot), but we gave it the old easy mooch and never got a rumble (a sign of suspicion)." 7. The act of stealing petty things in passing.

Mooch, v. 1. To steal, beg, or otherwise get something for nothing. 2. To move quietly away from any source of danger or unpleasantness. "I think I got a tail (was followed) tonight. I better mooch till the heat (police activity) dies down." 3. To move about stealthily; to skulk; to slip in and out of unfamiliar places and social circles without attracting notice, usually as part of a planned criminal operation.

Mooch around. 1. To move subtly and craftily in and out of places generally considered inaccessible to criminals. 2. (P) To succeed in moving freely from one place to another in a prison, chiefly as a means of procuring stolen stores or contraband. "This can (prison) is sure loused up (spoiled). A promoter (clever fellow) can't even mooch around no more."

Moocher. 1. A beggar; a petty borrower who never repays loans; an expert chiseler, or anyone who travels without paying fares. 2. (Obsolescent) A narcotic addict.

Mooch in. 1. To walk in unconcernedly where one does not belong. **2.** To enter and stroll about, as police casually investigating suspicious premises. **3.** To make a planned entrance, as a **capper,** in a confidence swindle. **4.** (Loosely) To enter; to walk in. "Look who just mooched in! Pickles! He must have beat the rap (been discharged) on that knock-off (murder)."

Mooch-joint. An establishment where narcotics are retailed or distributed to addicts; an opium den; a rendezvous of drug addicts.

Mooch, on the. 1. Currently addicted to the use of narcotics. **2.** Begging; engaged in petty thievery; earning a precarious criminal livelihood. **3.** Moving about with studied nonchalance, especially while engaged in a criminal pursuit; to get around on the **squash.**

Mooch out. 1. To slip out of a place with studied casualness, especially after a theft, or when escaping from custody. **2.** To walk out; to saunter forth.

Mooch-pusher. A trafficker in narcotics to addicts.

Moonlighter. See **Midnight.**

Moonshine. Illicit whiskey.

Moosh. 1. The human face. **2.** The mouth.

Mope, n. 1. A stealthy departure, especially from custody or from any area made dangerous by the presence of police. **2.** (P) An escape from custody effected without the use of force, especially while engaged in a work assignment outside of prison walls.

Mope, v. 1. To depart quickly, especially from an area in which police are active. **2.** (Imp.) Danger! Run! Police! **3.** (P) To escape from custody, especially while on the outside of prison walls, without the use of force. "Some dude (fellow) moped with only two months to go (serve). On a good screw (kindly guard) too."

Mopery. 1. Suspicion; vagrancy; any petty offense; any criminal act which, even if successful, would be so unprofitable that its commission must be considered an absurdity; hence, stupidity. "That saperoo (fool) never gets glommed (caught) for any rap (charge) but mopery." **2.** (P) Any stupid or petty rule violation which results in report or **lock-up.**

Mopery-collar. See **Mopery.**

Mopery in the first degree. (P) Any exceptionally stupid or petty crime or rule violation. [Note: This is one of the stock answers to inquisitive fellows who want to know the crime for which one has been imprisoned.]

Mopery-pinch. Seizure for **mopery.**

Mopery-rap. Any formal preferment of charges against one for **mopery.**

Morph. 1. A hermaphrodite. **2.** Morphine.

Morphodite. (Erroneous for hermaphrodite) A hermaphrodite; (loosely in prison usage) a pederast; an oral sodomist. [Note: The word is often used in gross humor rather than literally. When said good-naturedly, inmates rarely take offense.]

Mosey. To move slowly; to come upon stealthily. "Stick and slug (stand and fight), Slim. The bulls (police) are moseying outside."

Mota. (Spanish-American underworld) Marijuana. "Some Spik all charged up on mota chivved (knifed) Johnny the Mugg and the juanita (prostitute) he was with."

Mother Bull. (N. Y. City localism) A policeman or detective who pretends to befriend a prisoner, protecting him from threatened police violence in order to obtain a confession. [Note: The "maternal" technique often includes the proffering of cigarettes and coffee and other tokens of good will. Accomplices are held in separate rooms, each threatened with violence and subsequently "protected" by the **Mother Bull** who shuttles back and forth from one accomplice to the other. He knows how to make full use of any trivial admission a criminal may make, leading each one to believe that he has been betrayed by his associates. Together with the threatened, and often applied, **third degree**, the **Mother Bull** technique will break down most weak suspects.]

Mountain goat. (P) Sliced mutton or roast beef.

Mouse, n. An informer. "There's that mouse cutting it up with the bulls (detectives) again. I wonder who's buried (betrayed) now."

Mouse, v. To inform against associates. "There was a right bull (policeman friendly to underworld) till the fleas (informers) moused on him."

Mouthpiece. A lawyer.

Mouth-wash. (P) Coffee served in the prison mess-hall.

Move, on the. Going on; in the process of development.

Move a job. To transport or dispose of a stolen automobile.

Move the laundry. To smuggle alien Chinese into the country.

Moving. Developing; going on; in the process of development. "What's moving, Tippy? I could use a buck (some money)."

Moxie. 1. Nerve; courage. "Red had moxie enough to hit himself out (commit suicide) instead of waitin' for the chair (electrocution) on that heist (hold-up) knock-off (murder)." 2. Effrontery; gall. "That crumb is got some moxie! After lousing Slim up (slandering him), now he's hanging out with the ghee (fellow)."

Muckstick. A shovel.

Mud. Coffee.

Mud-fence. An enclosure of soap or any similar plastic substance in which crude nitroglycerine is poured and allowed to seep into the crevice of an old

style safe or a hole drilled into a modern safe under the dial. The safe is tilted on its back for the operation.

Muff. (South) A prostitute or very loose woman.

Muff diver. See **Bumper.**

Mugg, n. 1. The human face. 2. A photograph, or other likeness of one's face.

Mugg, v. 1. To assault by crushing the victim's head or throat in an arm-lock; (by loose extension in New York City) to rob with any degree of force, with or without weapons. "Joe mugged the sucker (victim), and I went through him." 2. To photograph, especially for the Criminal Bureau of Identification. 3. To express annoyance or convey a message by grimacing.

Mugg, the. A form of assault in which the victim's head or throat is crushed in an arm-lock; (loosely in New York City by extension) any robbery with any degree of force employed, with or without weapons. "Tom was heeled (armed) so we had to throw the mugg on him and get him out of the joint (place)."

Mugg artist. A specialist in the use of the mugg.

Mugger. 1. A specialist in the use of the mugg. 2. A lawyer .

Mugg-joint. 1. (Carnival) A photograph gallery concession. 2. Any establishment notorious for applying the mugg on unwelcome guests or on those who protest against bill-padding.

Muggles. Cigarettes containing marijuana; the marijuana weed.

Mugg on the board, to have one's. To have one's photograph posted by authorities as "wanted." "I gotta lam (flee). My mugg is on the board for a tough beef (serious charge)."

Mulligan. 1. (La. and other Gulf State prisons) A prison guard. 2. Stew, usually of whatever ingredients can be stolen or begged, and cooked in a hobo

jungle, often in an old tomato can. 3. Crude nitro-glycerine extracted from stick dynamite by boiling. [Note: The word was borrowed from Mulligan stew because of the similarity of appearance of the two.]

Mulligan joint. An eating establishment.

Murder, v. To bungle; to ruin. "You sure murdered that trick (crime). We had the joint readied up (all ready), and you had to start an argument with some legit dude (honest workman) and get yourself pinched (arrested) for mopery (disturbing the peace)."

Murder, a. Awful. [Note: Murder is equally applicable to clumsiness, stupidity, disloyalty, gullibility, injustice, severity, the weather, and all kinds of human or natural phenomena. It corresponds to "awful" in the colloquial sense of the term.]

Murder-grift. Criminal operation with a license, i.e., with immunity from police intervention. "I hustled (worked) with a wire-mob (pickpocket group) that had the alzo (immunity from police intervention) in Chicago for a four-year run. That was a sweet murder-grift."

Muscle, the. 1. Force, or the threat of force. 2. The **mugg.** 3. The strong-arm man of a gang.

Muscle in. To use force or the threat of force to gain control or partial control of a racket.

Muscle man. A gangster who makes professional use of the **muscle.**

Muscle, on the. 1. By strong-arm methods; engaged in any criminal activity requiring strong-arm methods. 2. Acquired without paying as the result of a reputation for violence. "All the hoods (thieves) are free loading (eating and drinking) in Mike's joint (place), payin' off on the muscle." 3. Belligerent. "What's this bum, on the muscle, now? Root (kick) him in the keister (buttocks)."

Muscle out. To expel by force or threat of force an individual or gang from any racket or area in order to augment one's own revenues.

Muscle work. Any crime or racket requiring physical labor or violence.

Mush. A stolen umbrella.

Mush-faker. An umbrella thief who solicits umbrellas for repair and fails to return them.

Mutt. An utterly contemptible fellow. "That lousy mutt dogs it (cringes) in a tight spot (face of danger). He's strictly first baseman (playing safe at the expense of others)."

Mutt up. To keep a dog as burglary protection.

Muzzler. (P) A contemptible fellow, as an informer or a degenerate; an unpopular prison keeper or other official; "That muzzler is a copper-heared rat (born informer)."

N

Nail. 1. To seize [one] in the commission of a criminal act; to arrest with incontrovertible proof of guilt. 2. (P) To seize [one] in the act of violating prison rules. "Some bug (fool) with sleeping time (very short term to serve) was nailed copping a mope (while attemping to escape)."

Nailed. (Pickpockets) Buttoned or pinned securely (speaking of a pocket).

Nance. A male oral sodomist or passive pederast; any man or boy pronouncedly effeminate in manner.

Nautch-broad. A prostitute working in a brothel, not soliciting on streets.

Nautchery. A brothel.

Nautch-joint. A house of prostitution.

Necktie-bum. 1. A type of tramp who strives to be foppishly neat—hence suspected by others. 2. (P) A convict who insists upon wearing a black tie [this is permissible in some prisons], thus provoking dislike and suspicion.

Needle. 1. To agitate; to stir up, especially by crafty means; to prod unduly. "Keep on needling that wack (mentally unbalanced person), and he'll pull a sneak on you (assault you when you least expect it)." 2. To inject ether or alcohol into beer. 3. To beg or borrow a small sum of money with no intention of repaying it.

Needle, the. The hypodermic needle, or any crude substitute as an instrument for the injection of drugs.

Needle-knight. A drug addict who uses a hypodermic needle or any crude substitute. "Nix (don't trust), Jeff, a needle-knight, lamp (look at) them peepers (eyes)."

Needle-man. 1. A drug addict who uses a hypodermic needle. 2. (Especially prohibition era) One who **doctors** beer by charging it with ether or denatured alcohol. 3. An agitator or troublemaker; one gifted with a clever and sharply critical tongue.

Needle, on the. 1. Addicted to hypodermic injections of narcotics. "Nozzo spent a lotta time gettin' that pig (woman) he's doubled with (living with) to kick the habit (to cure the drug addiction). Now she's back on the needle." 2. Engaged in stirring up trouble between others; bantering. 3. Seeking to beg or borrow.

Needles. 1. Humorous or ill-natured criticism or ridicule; deliberate agitation. "Knock off (stop) the needles. That guy will bug up (grow angry) and there'll be a come-off (you'll have a fight on your hands)." 2. Statements or information prejudicial and detrimental to a criminal defendant, parole applicant, supplicant, or petitioner. "Somebody stuck the needles in on me to the P.K. (Principal Keeper). He says I'm an adjy (agitator) and the first pinch (report for rule violation) I get I'm goin' to the box (segregation building)."

Nephew. A youth who is maintained by male oral sodomists and active pederasts. [See **Uncles**.]

Net on, to drop the. (P) To place under observation as a psychopath; to commit to an institution for the insane; (often humorously intended). "The man in the white coat (psychiatrist) will drop the net on you if you keep cabareting (indulging in erotic dreams) every night."

New bit. (P) A prison term added to the unexpired parole time of a previous sentence.

New fish. (P) 1. A newly arrived convict. 2. (Sometimes by loose extension) A new prison guard.

New jice. (Scattered Western, Central, and near-Western prisons) A newcomer to prison, especially a first offender unacquainted with prison life. **New mick** or **mickey.** (P) See **New fish.**

Nibbler. A male oral sodomist.

Nice buck or **dollar.** A satisfactory income; plenty of money; a good thing. "Lippy made a nice dollar lifting (robbing) trucks, until he got this drop (sentence)."

Nice thing. Any lucrative racket or criminal venture; any position of advantage.

Nick, n. 1. (Briticism, heard rarely in American coastal cities) Jail; prison. "Limey, here, was in nick over there—the Borstal (reformatory for boys in England; world-famous because of the revolutionary reforms attempted there)." 2. (Heard rarely but over widely scattered areas) A successful criminal coup; the proceeds of a crime; anything borrowed or begged; the act of obtaining anything by begging or borrowing.

Nick, v. 1. (Briticism, heard rarely in American coastal cities) To arrest; to commit to jail or prison. 2. To beg, borrow, or steal from; to obtain something for nothing.

Nickel bat. A wooden bludgeon.

Nickel note. A five-dollar bill.

Nicks. Walnut shells used in the shell-and-pea swindle in which the victim must select one of three shells under which a pea is supposed to be concealed. Actually the pea is hidden in the crook of the operator's finger. [See **Shell game.**]

Nigger heads. (N. Y. Catholic Protectory) Prunes.

Night club. (P) See **Cabaret.**

Night clubbing. (P) See **Cabaret.**

Night on the rainbow. (Near West) A period of indulgence in narcotics. "Yeah, Clipper, I feel low, like a hophead (drug addict) after a night on the rainbow."

Night ride. The process of tiring a race horse by riding him or sitting on him in his stall the night before the race.

Nine of hearts, to play. (Carnival) To withhold money or loot that should be divided among accomplices. "Come on get up the oats (money). Playing the nine of hearts on me, hey?"

Nip. (Rare) To arrest.

Nippers. 1. (Among burglars) An instrument for cutting wire or bolts. 2. A pickpocket's instrument for slashing clothing in order to reach otherwise inaccessible valuables on a victim's person; (formerly, in stealing tiepins) a device to snip off a victim's tie while an accomplice thrusts an open newspaper before the victim's face. 3. Handcuffs; leg-irons. "We hit a scorf joint (went into an eating place), and the dick (detective) took the nippers off. I lammed (ran) out the back."

Nix. 1. Look out! Stop! Danger! Beware! 2. (South) To acquit; discharge from custody. "Mike got a collar (was arrested) pistol whipping (for assaulting with the butt of his gun) a creeper (prostitute) that rolled (tried to rob) him, but he got nixed out." 3. (South) to deny an application for parole, pardon, commutation, or reprieve; to reject a legal appeal.

Nix, the. Any gesture, sound, or exclamation signifying danger.

No bargain. (P) A thing of dubious worth; a person not to be trusted or relied upon. "That dude (fellow) is no bargain. He don't act so hot."

Noble. (Rare) A guard hired to protect strike-breakers.

Nod, on the. 1. In an opium stupor; drugged. 2. Asleep; not fully awake or conscious. "The damper (bank) is kipped (has a burglar alarm), but the bugster (night watchman) is strictly on the nod."

Noggin. Head.

Noggin, on the. (P) Exactly; precisely.

Noise. 1. Dynamite, or crude nitroglycerine, used by safe-blowers. [More commonly: **soup.**] 2. The narcotic heroin.

Noise off. To talk excessively, especially in a boastful or belligerent manner. "There's that jerk (imbecile) noising off and bad-eyeing (glaring at) people again. Keep him out of here, or he'll louse the joint up (give the place a bad reputation)."

Nola. (South) A passive pederast.

North-and-south. The mouth. "Don't crack (say anything) with this punk (youngster) on the earie (listening). Too much north-and-south (he talks too much; has too much mouth)."

Nose, the. A police spy who has entree to the underworld; stool pigeon.

Noses. (P) Sharp blows on the nose with playing cards, as a forfeit in prison games. "C'm'on; I'll play some dominoes for noses."

No spinach! No use! No good! A failure.

Note-dropper. (P) An informer who drops his reports to prison authorities in their official intramural mail boxes.

Note-layer. (Carnival) A short-change swindler. [Note: The note-layer usually works with an accomplice. He makes several purchases and offers a large bill in payment. While the merchant counts out the change, the swindlers bewilder him by constant rapid-fire conversation. They then request the return of the bill in exchange for smaller currency. While the money is shuttled back and forth, the short-change is accomplished.]

Note-man. See **Note-layer.**

Not so hot. Unsatisfactory; not so good. "That can (prison) ain't so hot to pull time (serve a term in). Ain't enough them screws (guards) ain't got no use for a con (convict). They're hoosiers (rustics) anyhow that don't like the city ghees (fellows)."

Not so kosher. Of questionable loyalty; untrustworthy; not genuine; suspect.

Nozz. Nose; any person with a prominent nose.

Number. (P) 1. (Ironically) An inmate who poses as a **big shot.** "This new mick (newcomer) thinks he's a number." 2. The prisoner's number, as a symbol of imprisonment. "You got a number the same as me. What do you think, you're a big ghee (big shot)?"

Number-baron. A powerful and wealthy operator in the policy numbers game. "The Big Frog used to work shorts (pick pockets) with me. Now he is a number-baron in Chi. (Chicago)."

Number-man. Anyone engaged in the policy numbers racket.

Numbers, the. The policy numbers lottery, based upon pari-mutuel race track reports for the day.

Nursery. (P) A reformatory or protectory. "All the young punks (youngsters) hitting (sent to) state's (State's prison) now, you can't tell it from the nurseries."

Nursery stretch. A term served in any juvenile institution or reformatory.

Nut. To castrate; to sterilize one by surgical operation; deliberately to mutilate by castration. "The way they're hitting (sentencing) hoods (criminals) with the works (maximum terms of imprisonment) they don't need to nut them. These bits (prison terms) do it slow."

Nut, the. The basic operating expenses of any given criminal enterprise or racket. "We got to pay the mouthpiece (lawyer) and the connection (political fixer). I got a couple of scores (crimes) lined up (in mind) to meet the nut."

Nut, on the. In poor financial straits; compelled to draw upon one's investment, expense, or emergency money; living on credit.

Nut-house. A hospital for insane or defective delinquents.

Nut-money. Expense money.

Nuts, the. 1. Anything excellent or desirable; perfection. "That score (theft) was the nuts. No heat (police outcry) and a nice dollar (good profit)." 2. (P) (Ironically) Any thing or event that is thoroughly disappointing; a total failure. "This joint (prison) is the nuts. The screws (guards) are murder (awful), and it's loused up (full of informers and perverts) anyway." 3. The three nut-shells used in the **shell game.** 4. The edge; the advantage; the upper hand. "We got the nuts on the D. A. (District Attorney) when we got to bat (went to trial). Nobody made (identified) us in the line-up (police line-up)." 5. Pressure; force; influence. "Put the nuts on him and make him spill (talk)." 6. Testicles. ["To have by the nuts"—to have in a helpless or disadvantageous position; to have so involved that withdrawal is impossible, as a bank teller drawn from minor speculations into deep involvement, or a prison guard from petty favors to serious breaches of his oath.]

Nut-squealers. Operators of the **shell game.**

Nuttery. An institution for the criminally insane or for mentally defective delinquents.

Nux. (Leavenworth Federal Prison) The tea served in the prison mess-hall.

O

Oats. (Carnival) Money, especially money withheld from a boss or an associate.

Oblay. Blow! Flee! Danger, get out of here! Police.

Observation. (P) See **Obso.**

Obso. (P) A cell or cells reserved for the observation of recalcitrants suspected of mental deficiency.

Oday. Money. "This rap (charge) would be a cinch to beat if I had the oday to get a good mouthpiece (lawyer). I'll have to settle for (be satisfied with) one of them two-bit shysters (some cheap lawyer)."

Off the nut. 1. Financially sound, all expenses having been cleared, and all future revenues to be considered as net profit; free from monetary obligations. "This caper (theft) will keep us off the nut for months." 2. Released from emotional tension. "Getting my gage up (smoking marijuana) gets me off the nut."

Off the pop. Immediately; from the start; at once. "The shyster (lawyer) told him to cop out (plead guilty). He told the Blackstone (judge) to give him the bit (sentence him) right away, so they settled (sentenced) him for a pound (to five years' imprisonment) off the pop."

Office, the. Any signal or cue for action. "There's the office to blow (flee); cop a mope (go)."

Oh, sing it, sucker! (P) A common reply to the boring complaints of a fellow convict.

Oil. 1. Suspiciously smooth talk, as the words of a confidence swindler; sycophancy.

Oil business. (Pennsylvania and environs) The lucrative racket based on false automobile accident claims. "Benny's the best flopper (pretended victim) in the oil business today."

Oil merchant. 1. A confidence man; a clever swindler who disarms his victims by a smooth line of talk. "This oil merchant thinks I'm a square-John (legitimate citizen). Watch the play (his efforts to swindle me)." 2. A liar.

Okus. (Chiefly mid-West pickpockets' jargon) A wallet. "Okus in port pratt (left rear trousers pocket). Put his back up (jostle him into position)."

—Ola. A noun suffix appended for emphasis, as crap (lies), crapola; sap (blackjack), sapola; scratch (money), scratchola.

Old bit. (P) A previous prison term, the maximum of which has not expired. "Smiley's gotta finish up his old bit before he starts this double-sawbuck (twenty years)."

Old clap. A neglected case of gonorrhea.

Old dog, the. Syphilis (sometimes extended to gonorrhea).

Old dose, the. A neglected case of gonorrhea or syphilis.

Old monkey. (South, scattered) The electric chair.

Old number, (to have) (P) An old-timer in prison.

Old-timer. A veteran criminal or convict.

Old touches. One's past crimes; stories of one's past crimes. "I'm goin' up and smoke a few muggles (marijuana cigarettes) and chop up old touches."

Ole Man Cole. (Chiefly Utah State Prison) Capital punishment by firing squad.

Once-over. 1. A quick touching of pockets in superficial search for weapons, stolen goods, or contraband; a light **frisk.** 2. A mild **third-degree** examination. 3. A relatively mild beat-

ing, usually with fists. 4. A quick searching examination or glance. "Give the
joint a once-over. If it shapes up okay,
we'll throw (hold up) the cashier."

One-arm bandit. 1. A slot-machine for
gambling. 2. (By extension) A pin-ball
machine or any similar device in which
the odds are grossly against the player.
"Chick is on the legit (honestly occupied). He's got forty one-arm bandits
and a few hoods (strong-arm men) on
the payroll."

One of the Brown family. ("One of Mr.
Brown's kids," or any similar phrase
with Brown as the key word) A catamite.

One-two, n. A swiftly executed crime.

One-two, adv. Quickly; immediately.
"We crashed the window, snatched
(stole) the skin (fur-piece) one-two
and blew (fled)."

One-two play. Any quickly consummated criminal venture.

One-way ghee. 1. A thoroughly selfish person. "That flea is strictly a one-
way ghee, hustling (stealing) outside
and peddling (selling stolen prison
stores) in the can (prison). What a
wrongo (unprincipled fellow)." 2.
(Rare) A forthright, dependable person. "Them screws (guards) that kibitz around with a con and then slough
him up (report him) are crumbs. Give
me a hundred-percent screw that's a
one-way ghee."

On the. (Succeeded by any term signifying a specific criminal activity) Engaged in, or by means of. ("On the
hustle"—engaged in stealing, or by
means of theft.)

On the bend. Engaged in, or open to,
a criminal proposition; **on the make;
playing the field.**

On the button. In a hurry; at top
speed; exactly.

O. O., the. The once-over; a quick
searching glance. "Round easy and give

this dude (fellow) the o. o. Looks like
law (a policeman)."

Ooscray. Danger! Get away!

Open up. 1. (Western and mid-Western prisons) To stab or slash with a
knife. 2. (Eastern prisons and general
underworld) To confess and inform
against accomplices. "That punk had
no guts. He got a lousy once-over
(mild third degree) and opened up on a
dozen scores (robberies)."

Oregon boot. Any of the various
heavy metal, shoe-like devices encasing
the ankle and foot, secured by padlock,
used in transferring convicts from one
prison to another, on road-gang convicts and in transferring extradited
fugitives from justice. [Note: A pair
of such boots joined by a thirteen-inch
chain is used on road-gang convicts in
some states; in one or two prisons and
reformatories, a similar pair of boots
must be worn during military drills as
a form of punishment.]

Organ-grinder. A machine-gunner.

Oscar. (Rare) A pistol or revolver.

Out. 1. A means of swift egress from
premises or area where a crime is
committed. [Note: Careful criminals
seek one main and one or two alternate
exits before committing crime.] 2. Any
means or method of escape from danger
or from an unpleasant predicament; a
way out. 3. Any means of achieving
freedom from custody or confinement,
whether by violence, bribery, or extension of leniency or legal relief. "There's
no out on that knock-off rap (murder
charge) unless he buries (informs upon)
a few for the D. A." 4. In craps, the
houseman's cry when the roller has
thrown a losing number. 5. An excuse;
means of retreat from an untenable
position.

Out. 1. At liberty; not in jail or prison. 2. Unconscious; intoxicated. 3. Not
entitled to a share, as of loot.

Outfielder. (Contemptuous) A profes-

sional criminal operator who habitually seeks the least dangerous assignments, especially that of the **outside
man** in order to have the best chance
to escape; (by implication) a chauffeur
who in the event of danger would drive
away and desert his accomplices, an
inexcusable underworld offense. "I ain't
steppin' in any joint on a trick (robbery) with that lousy outfielder laying
zex (watching for police)."

Outfit. A group of organized thieves
or racketeers.

Out for a buck. Looking for easy
money, by theft, bribe-taking, prostitution, etc.

Out for a rep. Seeking to achieve a
reputation for violence and the use of
terror in order to gain underworld prestige. "That young punk is out for a
rep. He'll bang (shoot) anybody to make
himself a big ghee (leader)."

Out of turn. In indirect violation of
the traditional rule of observing the
underworld code. "That weasel don't
put the finger on (overtly inform) no
one, but he cracks (talks) out of turn."

Out on the shorts. Picking pockets
as a member of a gang on crosstown
bus and trolley lines.

Outside man. 1. A lookout; a **zex-
man.** 2. (P) A trusty.

Outsiders. 1. (P) Visitors to, or
civilians working in, prison. 2. Narrow
pincers used to turn a key in a lock from
the outside.

Out to get even. (P) A passive pederast seeking to even the score by becoming an active pederast and looking
for **punks.**

Over-issue, the. A swindle in which
the victim is induced to participate in
cashing genuine currency which the
swindler describes as having been printed illegally by venal employees in the
United States Bureau of Engraving and
Printing. Threat of arrest by a bogus
Federal Agent is followed by extortion.

Overnighter. See **Overnight job.**

Overnight job. An automobile stolen
the previous night to be used in the
commission of a crime.

Over the hill. Away from custody, as
in a jail-break, jumping bail, or flight
from criminal prosecution.

Over the hump. (P) 1. Over the prison wall, or over the nearby hill, in an
attempt to escape. 2. (P) Past mid-
point of prison sentence; at the beginning of the second half of one's prison
term.

Owe time. 1. To be on parole from a
prison or reformatory and subject to
return to serve the unexpired portion
of the sentence. "Guys don't fall (get
arrested) owing much time now. Too
many finish up (serve the full term) in
stir (prison)." 2. To have yet to serve a
portion of a previous sentence. "That
old ghee has a new bit and he owes time
from a jolt (prison sentence) he got
in 1910."

Owl. (Rural) A sunset-to-sunrise
burglar.

Owl-job. (Rural) A sunset-to-sunrise
burglary.

Owner's job. The act of stealing an
automobile in collusion with owner to
defraud insurance company.

O. Z. An ounce of any powdered narcotic.

P

Pack. To carry on one's person, as firearms.

Pack a chiv. 1. To carry a knife, razor, or other edged weapon. 2. "To pack a chiv for"—to carry a knife or razor with intent to assault a definite enemy.

Package. 1. A venereal disease, usually gonorrhea. 2. (P) A long prison sentence; any prison term. "I'd wrap up (commit suicide) if I had a package like yours to carry."

Pack a rod or **heater.** 1. To carry a revolver. "To pack a heater for"—to be armed with a revolver with intent to shoot a specific enemy, or to defend, as a bodyguard, one's employer. "Dasher Dan is packing a heater for the fink (informer) that got him settled (convicted) on his last bit (prison term)."

Pack away. (P) To serve, as a prison sentence. ["To pack away a bit"— to serve a prison term.] "That's half the bit packed away. I'm over the hump (halfway mark) now. All I gotta do is slide down the other half."

Pack heat. See **Pack a rod.**

Pack horse. (West) A person who assumes the full onus of criminal guilt to protect others; a **fall guy.**

Pack-in, n. 1. The act of quitting a place, business, kind of enterprise, etc. 2. (P) The act of refusing to continue to work.

Pack in. 1. To give up; to resign; to quit. "One good touch (profitable robbery) and I'm packing in hustling (stealing)." 2. (P) To quit one's assignment in prison as a form of protest. "Nervo packed in and hit the hole (went into solitary confinement). That screw (guard) in his shop was giving him

buckwheats (persecuting him)." 3. See **pack away.** 4. (Ironic) To commit suicide. "The Board (of Parole) is gonna hit you with the max (maximum term). Why don't you pack in? Want a nice hunk of rope?"

Pack time away. (P) To serve a prison sentence.

Pad. (Chiefly in South; borrowed from Negro jargon) 1. A bed; a bedroom; an apartment. 2. (P) A cell.

Padded. Having stolen goods or contraband secreted on one's person. [Note: Drug smugglers, often disguised as uniformed messenger boys, board and leave docked ships after being padded with several kilos of drugs, usually taped about their bodies.]

Pad-dough. (Central and Southern U. S.) Money for rent or lodgings. "Some old geezer prowling (burglarizing) for pad-dough just got pooped (shot). The joker (fellow) in the slough (house) put a smoke-wagon (heavy-calibre gun) on him."

Paddy. A padlock.

Paddy-wagon. (Obsolete) A patrol wagon.

Pad roll. To swindle in craps by controlling the turn of the dice, rolling them on a blanket or other soft, even surface.

Pads. (Relatively rare) Automobile license plates.

Paid off. 1. Bribed. "We kicked back (made restitution) to the rappers (complainants), and the pollies (politicians) are paid off. The mouthpiece (lawyer) says we'll draw an s.s. (suspended sentence) with a floater (order to get out of town)." 2. In possession of loot.

Panel-joint. A cheap house of prostitution in which the patrons' valuables are stolen from their clothing through the panel of a wall in an adjoining room. "Turk was settled for heisting (holding up) some panel-joint after the hustlers (prostitutes) reefed (robbed) him."

Panic is on, the. A common idiom implying that: 1. Things are at their worst; the expected trouble has come; money is urgently needed; no drugs are to be had; arrest is imminent. 2. (P) There is a scarcity of tobacco, money, food; there is sufficient cause for protest or actual rioting.

Pansy. A male oral sodomist; a man of effeminate appearance, speech, or manner.

Papa. A Lincoln automobile; **daddy.**

Paper. 1. Forged checks, stocks, or bonds. "It was murder the way we pushed (passed) the paper in those jerkwaters (small towns)." 2. (Among impersonators of law enforcement officers) A bogus police warrant, as a means of extortion. "Spring with (exhibit) the paper and flash (show) the tins (badges). This guy will go because he can't stand a pinch (arrest)." 3. (Among card cheats) Playing cards which have been marked, trimmed, slicked with wax, or otherwise prepared for use in swindling. 4. (P) A court writ, especially one of habeas corpus.

Paper-hanger. One who issues or passes worthless checks.

Paper-hanging. The act of passing or issuing forged checks.

Paper-layer, or **-pusher.** See **Paperhanger.**

Paralyzed. Intoxicated.

Park the biscuit. 1. To sit down. 2. To get rid of a pistol or revolver on one's person.

Parole time. (P) The unexpired portion of a sentence still remaining when a convict is released on parole.

Parolitis. (P) The acute anxiety that besets convicts during the period just before they meet the Parole Board.

Pass. (P) A cell-to-cell delivery. "What's the matter with that flea

(good-for-nothing) .locking next door to you? Won't he make a pass?"

Pass-can. (P) A sheet-metal can with an open top, about seven inches long, six inches deep, for passing hot coffee or other food from cell to cell.

Pass-line. (P) A cord, weighted at one end, which is tossed from one cell to another and used for exchanging newspapers, cigarettes, books, etc. [Note: The simplest method of passing articles, such as contraband food or messages, from one cell to another, is to induce a trusted inmate (water-boy, radio repair man, or cell hall clerk) to act as go-between. When such aid is not available, pass-lines are used. These are simply weighted strings, the weighted end being tossed to a neighboring cell. The object to be passed is slipped over the cord and slid down the cord's length to its destination. Passes may even be made successfully from one gallery to another. The object is tied to the end of the pass-line, lowered over the edge of the gallery floor, and with the aid of a broomstick swung pendulum-like within reach of the receiver. If all else fails, one sends for the inmate nurse or the plumber to make the delivery. In illiberal prisons, inmates sprinkle salt or sand on the floor just around the corner of the gallery. The approach of the guard is thus signalled by a scraping gritty sound which forewarns the passer. A "gapper" or small mirror gives the passer a clear view of the gallery as a precaution against the intrusion of a guard.]

Pass up. 1. To exclude from consideration; to do without; to avoid. 2. To overlook; to neglect. "That jerk passed up a G ($1000) in stones (gems) frisking them suckers (victims)." 3. To fail to recognize, as a criminal in a police line-up. (a) "I think the rapper (complainant) pegged (recognized) me, but he passed me up." (b) "I'm in a hot boiler (stolen car) when the bulls (police) rode up. They passed me up but they crashed in on Shorty and Moe in the corner lush-joint (saloon) and dropped (arrested) them." 4. To snub; to ignore. "Pass that fink (informer) up. He's marked lousy (branded untrustworthy)."

Paste. Imitation diamonds or other gems so finely designed to resemble genuine jewelry that only connoisseurs can distinguish the difference.

Pat, n. 1. A superficial examination of the contents of pockets by running one's hands over the surface in search of weapons, stolen goods, or other articles. "The coppers flagged (stopped) me and gave me a little pat for a rod. If they knew my skin (wallet) was full of queer (counterfeit money), I'd been a dead-pigeon." 2. (Pickpocket) The act of running one's hand gently over the pockets of an intended victim in search of a wallet or wad of bills.

Pat, v. To give one a **pat.** "There's a muscle-man in that joint who helps you off with your benny (overcoat). He pats your pratt-kick (back pocket) to see if you're heeled (carrying a pistol)."

Pat, a. Okay; trustworthy.

Patch. (Carnival) The **legal adjuster** of a carnival troupe; the contact man between carnival operators and local police authorities; he determines the legal limits of operation and adjusts complaints. "We gotta pull a few sneaks (unauthorized sharp operations) to get off the nut (meet expenses). Give us six-to-five on (warning of the approach of) the patch."

Patsy, n. A pistol; a revolver.

Patsy, a. (Rare) All right; okay; trustworthy.

Pavement, on the. Free; not in confinement.

Pay-off, n. 1. Any of the various swindles in which the victim is led to believe that he has won a large sum in gambling. Before he "collects," he is required to exhibit, as evidence of good faith, a sum equal to that which he had risked losing. The victim's money is examined and palmed; a wad of worthless paper is substituted for the genuine currency. The victim is thus swindled both of his own money and of his supposed winnings. 2. The successful termination of any criminal action; the actual transfer of money or loot from victim to criminal. 3. The climax, especially one which is not expected. "The rapper (complainant) stepped in on the line-up (police review of suspects) to put the finger on (identify) me. The pay-off came when he picked one of the bulls (policemen) and passed me up."

Pay off, v. 1. To hand over money or valuables as the victim of a crime or racket; to yield to blackmail or extortion; to pay money as bribery. 2. To yield a profit; to bring results. 3. To repay a debt. 4. To assault or kill in retribution.

Pay-off ghee. The prospective payer of extortion money, ransom, or other enforced payment of criminals or racketeers; the banker in a policy-numbers racket; the proprietor of a shady establishment, or his agent, who dispenses bribes. "Don't flash (exhibit) the button (police badge) till I make (recognize) the pay-off ghee in this joint."

Pay off in the alley. To use violence against a creditor who insists upon payment of a debt. "Screw (get out of here), bum. You'll get your cut (share). I'll pay you off in the alley."

Pay off on the squash. To submit to extortion without having been subjected to any threat of violence or evidence of authority other than that which is implicit in the appearance or demeanor of an extortionist. "This rabbit-snatcher (abortionist) is a sweet mark. He'll pay off on the squash."

Pay off on the tin. To submit to extortion when confronted with a counterfeit or a stolen police badge. "You don't need no pressure on these schmeck-pushers (dope peddlers); they all pay off on the tin."

Pay off under the arch. See **Pay off in the alley.**

Peach. (Obsolescent) To inform; to confess guilt and implicate associates.

Peanuts. Anything, especially loot, of trivial value, anything trivial or negligible. "Ten boffos (years' imprisonment) for a lousy mopery rap (relatively minor felony)! What's that, peanuts?"

Peasant. (Broadway and general underworld) Anyone who works for a living; an honest citizen.

Pea-shooter. A small-calibre pistol or revolver. "Dump (get rid of) that pea-shooter. Here's a toy (substantial gun) to make the suckers reach (put hands up promptly)."

Pea soup. (General underworld, and chiefly prisons in Northeastern industrial area) 1. Anything that is worthless or good for nothing. 2. Anyone disloyal to the underworld. "That flea is pea soup. Chill (ignore) him."

Peddle. To sell, as a **peddler.**

Peddler. 1. A seller of drugs to addict trade; a prostitute. 2. (P) A trafficker in stolen food or other goods belonging to the State; one who trades in contraband which has been smuggled into prison. [Note: Convicts who sell anything at all—even such products of their own labor as paintings, carved boxes, etc.—are often contemptuously labeled **peddlers.** In some prisons, only the sale of State-issued articles brings opprobrium. "That lousy peddler wants two skins (dollars) for tailor-made State-os (issue pants)."

Pedigree. The formal police record of a criminal.

Peekaboo, the. (Obsolete) A racket involving the use of a ring containing a semi-precious stone, such as a zircon, which resembles a diamond or other gem. The swindler places the ring where it may be conveniently discovered by a victim. As the victim approaches the ring, the swindler with a show of feverish excitement snatches it from under him. Then, pretending to be conscience-stricken, the swindler grudgingly admits that the victim is entitled to a share of the prize as co-finder. Impressed by the swindler's show of honesty and enthusiasm, the victim is easily persuaded to buy out the swindler's share, paying several times the real worth of the ring.

Peeled. Open, as the eyes. "Keep your lamps (eyes) peeled while I kill the bug (burglar alarm)."

Peeler. (Obsolete) A policeman.

Peep. To betray associates; to give information to the police.

Peepers. The eyes.

Peg. 1. To recognize; to identify; to appraise or categorize at a glance. (a) "There goes the copper that gave me my first bit (prison term). He didn't make (recognize) me, but I pegged him right off the pop." (b) "You guys said Harpo was a right ghee (loyal associate), but I pegged him right months ago. Now the fink (informer) is singing to the D. A." 2. To commit active pederasty. 3. To fornicate.

Peg-house. 1. A house of prostitution which includes or specializes in the services of passive pederasts. 2. (P) Any prison where pederastic degeneracy is common.

Peg slugs. To fire shots.

Pen. 1. (West) A State or county penitentiary. 2. (East) A county or city penitentiary. "Mickey copped out (pleaded guilty) on a phony rap (charge of which he was innocent) to make State's (State prison) and duck that crummy pen. That's a fleabag (full of degeneracy and filth)." 3. The —. (New York City) The New York City Penitentiary at Riker's Island; a sentence to that institution.

Penance. (P) 1. (Rare) A term of penal confinement. 2. (Rare) A period of detention in punishment cells.

Pen bit. A sentence to a city, county, or state penitentiary, hence, generally, a comparatively short sentence. "You can keep them big touches (lucrative thefts) on the heist (holdup). You fall (get arrested) and get a double-saw-buck (20 years) for low. Me, I drop on the cannon (picking pockets) and score for a pen bit."

Pencil. (Scattered prisons) To write a formal report against a convict for rule violation.

Penciler. A term of mild contempt applied by skilled free-hand forgers to any inept forger who first traces signatures in pencil and then goes over the tracing in ink.

Penitentiary highball. (P) A mixture of strained shellac and milk. [Note: The shellac is run through cheesecloth or through the pithy part of a loaf of bread; the denatured alcohol is thus almost freed of gums and resins. Milk is added as an antidote.]

Penman. 1. A forger, especially one skilled in free-hand forgery. Compare: **penciler, tracer.** 2. (P) A convict who writes messages to prison officials, especially notes betraying fellow convicts.

Penny-weighter. A thief who specializes in stealing uncut and unset diamonds.

Perfects. Honest dice.

Persuader. 1. A blackjack; a bludgeon. 2. A pistol or revolver.

Pete. A safe or vault.

Pete-job. A safe or vault burglary.

Pete-man. A safe-cracker, especially one who uses explosives, as distinguished from a **ripper.**

Peter. 1. A safe or vault; a strongbox; an iron-chest; a trunk, suitcase. 2. Crude nitroglycerine. 3. (Juvenile) The penis.

Pete-work. See **Pete-job.**

Phony, n. A pretender; a hypocrite; a traitor who feigns loyalty to the underworld; anything artificial.

Phony, a. Artificial, counterfeit; insincere, disloyal to the underworld.

Phony-baloney. See **Phony.**

Phony-baloney bit. (P) Any prison sentence which is manifestly unjust or discriminatory, especially one based on a legal technicality rather than on a sound principle of law. "I got hit with one of them phony-baloney bits, nineteen to twenty years. Maybe I'll go down on a writ if I can get up the dough for a mouthpiece (lawyer) with an in (influence in the courts)."

Phony-baloney life. (P) Any sentence of life imprisonment which may be appreciably shortened by parole. See **Life.** "Chucklehead Murphy is doing one of them phoney-baloney lifes. He can spring in a saw (ten years)."

Phony collar, drop, fall or **grab.** See **Phony pinch.**

Phony handle. An alias.

Phony knock. See **Phony pinch.**

Phony line-up. Police malpractice of placing a dishevelled and often bruised prisoner among well-groomed detectives—often with badges pinned to outer lapels—and allowing the victims to pick the suspect as their assailant. Technically, they have conformed with police line-up regulations. "They gave me a phony line-up with half a dozen fresh shaved bulls (policemen), and the sucker (victim) had to peg (identify) me."

Phony monicker. See **Phony handle.**

Phony pinch. 1. An arrest on a charge of which one is innocent; an arrest for a petty violation which, nevertheless, involves serious punishment because of prisoner's criminal record or current parole status. 2. (P) A report or lock-up for a rule violation of which one is innocent; a report for a petty offense, usually by an officer who is giving the victim **buckwheats** or **honey.** 3. A pretended arrest made by extortionists impersonating police officers.

Phony rap. A criminal charge of which one is innocent; a charge which results in punishment disproportionate to the triviality of the offense committed; a charge which results in a conviction obtained in violation of due process of law, or the prison sentence resulting therefrom. "What am I, the only dude (fellow) in here with a right rap (deserved term)? Every con in this can (prison) is beefing about the phony rap he got."

Phony snatch. 1. See **Phony pinch.** 2. A faked kidnapping.

Phony steer. False information, especially that which is supplied by **tipsters** concerning the details of a projected crime or the exaggerated proceeds likely to accrue therefrom. "Toby's sure hot in the biscuit (angry) over that phony steer the ten-percenter (spotter) gave us. We almost got banged in the noggin (slain) pulling out of that joint."

Phony super. A very cheap or imitation watch.

Phony tag. An alias.

Phony up. To counterfeit; to set up an impressive **front** or agency for purposes of swindling; to alter the amount of money indicated on a check; to change the serial number of a stolen bond or commit any similar criminal act; to turn traitor to the underworld. "I got a chill on (doubt the courage of) this dude we're working with. He might phony up on a drop (under police pressure coincident with arrest)."

Phutz. To rob; to swindle; to cheat; to use badly; to **screw, screw around** or **screw up.**

P. I. 1. A pimp. 2. Anyone who accepts money from a woman; one who loafs at street corners or dance halls, serving as a non-professional pander. "Some lousy street-corner P. I. was on the gog (looking) when we made the score, and he beefed (informed the police)."

Pick a berry. (Central and mid-Western States) To steal clothes from clotheslines.

Pick fruit. To seek out male oral sodomists or pederasts for purposes of robbery or of indulgence in perversion.

Pickle. (Chiefly Jewish-American) A pistol or a revolver.

Pick one's spots. 1. To choose carefully the crimes in which one will agree to participate, avoiding ordinary risks; to proceed with an unwarranted degree of caution. 2. (P) To attempt to win a reputation in prison as a tough guy by bullying and assaulting relatively helpless victims. "A chiv (knife) chills (frightens) that dog (coward). He strictly picks his spots."

Pick-up, n. An arrest on suspicion with no formal charges preferred.

Pick up. To subject to a **pick-up.**

Pick up a tail. To begin to be trailed, as by a policeman; to begin to follow, as a prospective victim. "One of you guys must have picked up a tail when you was hitting the scatter (hangout). The bulls just crashed the joint and give everyone a stand-up (personal search)."

Pick-up car. The second of a series of automobiles used to effect an escape from prison or from the scene of a crime. [Note: The first car, usually stolen and marked with counterfeit plates, is abandoned or destroyed at a safe distance from the point of departure. Flight is resumed in the **pick-up car.** Compare **lam-car.**]

Pick-up man. See **Horseman.**

Picric. Crude nitroglycerine extracted from stick dynamite by boiling.

Piece. 1. A small folded piece of paper containing approximately one ounce of morphine, heroin, or cocaine. [See **Deck.**] "What's the knock-off (price) for a piece of H (heroin) today?" 2. A pistol or a revolver. 3. A share of loot or of any criminal income. 4. Part ownership of any establishment or racket. 5. (P) A knife, a razor or any similar weapon. "There's a couple of pieces stashed (concealed) under the stairs. Get 'em quick, I'm in a swindle (trouble)."

Piece of a joint. Part ownership, especially of an illicit establishment. "A couple of tub-workers (ocean-liner card sharps) clipped Jonesy with the hog-box (crooked dealing device) and settled for a piece of his alky joint (gin mill)."

Piece of pratt. (Obsolete) See **Piece of snatch.**

Piece of snatch. 1. A loose woman; an epicene. 2. A male pederast; a male oral sodomist.

Piece of work. Any criminal venture. "Get me a good wheelman (driver) to fill on a piece of work we've got— a jug (bank) in an upstate tank (small town)."

Pig. 1. A loose woman; a prostitute. 2. (Abbreviation of **blind pig**) An illicit establishment with a deceptively innocent exterior, as a cheap barroom or roadhouse often housing prostitution and gambling units. 3. Any burglar's tool, piece of firearms, or sharp-edged weapon.

Pigeon, dead. Anyone faced with imminent and unavoidable disaster. "I got to cop a plea (plead guilty) and this is a bum rap (unjust charge). But I'd be a dead pigeon going to bat (trial) with my record."

Pig-joint. An establishment (hardware store or blacksmith's shop) where burglar's tools may either be bought or made to order.

Pike. A look; a glance. "Take a pike at that box (safe) for a bug (hidden alarm) before you lather it up (make the soap ream to hold explosives)."

Pike off. To watch, often surreptitiously, as in preparing for robbery or blackmail. "Plant (hide) and pike the sucker off when he stashes (hides) the chunk (money)."

Pill. 1. A pellet of opium or other habit-forming drug. 2. A bullet. 3. (P) A cigarette.

Pill-joint. A poolroom where a pill pool game (one of the liveliest games to stimulate gambling at pool tables) runs open to anyone; usually a rendezvous of the cleverer thieves.

Pill-roller. A doctor. [See **Croaker.**]

Pin. To cause indictment and conviction, justly or unjustly; to stigmatize; to make a **rap** stick.

Pin a rap on. To make an accusation against, and secure the conviction of, an alleged criminal on a specific charge; to put the blame on, with or without justification. "Them bulls (policemen) are out to pin the rap on some fall guy (luckless fool) for that mess of slum-heists (jewelry robberies)."

Pinch, n. 1. An arrest. "Pat couldn't stand another pinch with the book (life imprisonment) waiting so he hit himself out (committed suicide)." 2. (P) A lock-up or report for violation of rules. 3. Any gambling wheel which is crookedly controlled by a device capable of stopping it precisely as desired; a **gaffed** wheel.

Pinch, v. To subject to a **pinch.**

Pineapple. 1. A bomb. 2. (Rarely) An un-Americanized Italian. 3. A pimp.

Pink. 1. (South; obsolescent) A member of the white race, especially a white woman. 2. A Pinkerton—or any other —private detective.

Pink pants. (Rare) A young passive pederast or male oral sodomist.

Pins. Legs.

Pinwork. Needle or pin pricks marking playing cards for cheating—a crude variation of **edgework.**

Pipe, n. Anything capable of accomplishment with little risk or effort.

Pipe, v. (Carnival) To look; to see.

Pipe, on the. Addicted to smoking the opium pipe.

Pipey. 1. One who smokes an opium pipe habitually. 2. (Rare) An occasional smoker of opium. See **Pleasure smoker.**

Piss and punk. (P) The bread-and-water ration served in punishment cells in prisons where the custom has not been abandoned.

Piss away. To spend prodigally, as time, money, or health; to throw away, as an opportunity; to waste or squander.

Piss-can. The station-house, or local jail. Any place where suspects or accused are held while awaiting hearing. "Tommy the Heel got a pickup (arrest on suspicion). He's down in the piss-can."

Piss-cutter. See **Pisser.**

Pisser. Any extraordinary person or thing; anything affording extreme satisfaction or dissatisfaction; an unusual occurrence or predicament. "That guy Solly is sure a pisser on the cannon (picking pockets). Some dick tailed (followed) and questioned him, and Solly wound up reefing (stealing) his tin (badge) and poke (wallet)."

Pisseroo. An emphatic variant of **pisser.**

Pisshouse. See **Piss-can.**

Piss in a snowbank. To bungle.

Piss-up, n. A fiasco; a bungled or unremunerative crime.

Piss up. v. To suffer the disappointment of a **piss-up.**

Pistol whip. (South chiefly) To beat with butt or side of a pistol.

Pit. (Among pickpockets) The vest pocket; or, less frequently, the inside breast pocket of coat.

Pitchman. Any peddler of novelties who sells from a small pitch or collapsible stand; one who operates the **three-card monte** swindle from a pitch, especially at carnivals.

Pit-score. A vest or inside-pocket robbery by pickpockets.

Pit-touch. See **Pit-score.**

Pivot. To beg on the streets or highways.

P. K. (P) A prison principal keeper; a **dep.**

P. K.'s box. See **Dep's box.**

P. K.'s man. (P) 1. A convict assigned to important inmate prison work by the principal keeper or deputy warden. 2. An informer who reports convicts, guards, or other officials directly to the principal keeper.

Plant, n. 1. A frame-up; an arrest based upon incriminating evidence deliberately placed on the person or property of innocent or guilty. 2. A place where weapons, stolen goods, contraband, etc. are concealed. 3. An establishment for the production of illicit commodities, as tax-evading whiskey, counterfeit labels or currency. 4. Any article, as a gun, counterfeit money, etc., used or placed in such a way as to incriminate an innocent person. "That rod (gun) was a plant. I wasn't heeled (armed) when I took this drop (was arrested)." 5. A plainclothesman or informer deliberately placed in a position to spy upon a suspect; a provocateur. "Dummy up (shut up), Chick, this ghee (fellow) on the earie (listening) shapes up (looks) like a plant." 6. A place of concealment for fugitives, kidnap victims, etc. 7. A rendezvous of thieves, as a drinking place, apartment, or isolated shack. 8. (In scattered prisons, especially in Massachusetts State prison) The segregation block where recalcitrants and convicts requiring protective custody are housed. 9. (Rare) An isolated place where gangland murders are committed, or where the bodies are concealed or otherwise disposed of. 10. A place marked to be robbed.

Plant, v. To incriminate by deliberately placing evidence on the person or property of anyone, innocent or guilty; to commit to prison, especially by other than due process of law. 2. To station, or stand, as a watch, guard, or spy. 3. To conceal or hide, as a fugitive from justice, a victim of kidnapping. 4. (Scattered prisons) To place in a segregation cell. 5. To remove to an isolated area, slay and secretly dispose of the body; to murder.

Plaster. A dollar bill.

Platinum loaders. Dice loaded with a platinum base beneath the enameled number spots.

Play, n. 1. The total sum wagered on a given event or during a given period of time; the total income for any given period of time from any racket or enterprise. "I'd sure like to cut in for a piece (share) of that skee-joint (distillery). The play comes to a nice buck." 2. Patronage. "Good people got that spot, a couple of ex-cons. Give them a little play." 3. Attention given to a person or place as the intended object of a crime. "That jug (bank) has never been taken. Case (study) it and we'll make a play for the score." 4. The complex pattern of a criminal plot. "What are you, asleep? Hip up (follow) to this play. The Harp is looking to fill (to become a partner) on this score (theft) and he's pea soup (no good)." 5. The culmination of a swindle. "The mark (victim) is all readied up for the take (theft). Spring with the play." 6. (P)

Feigned insanity, to effect transfer to a liberal institution. 7. Feigned friendship or devotion lavished on one to be victimized or used for personal advantage. 8. Concentration upon the achievement of any purpose or goal.

Play, v. 1. To prepare to victimize, especially as the victim of a swindle; to mulct slowly and with restraint, as a victim of swindling or extortion. 2. To execute one's criminal operations within a specific area or in a particular field of criminal activity. "Tomorrow we'll play the breaks (rush hour crowds) in the hole (subway)." 3.—**for.** To make the direct and final bid in a swindle to rob the victim of his money. "We gave the sucker a quick hipe (increase in gambling stakes) and played for the boodle (the whole of his money) fast 'cause he was hipping up (becoming suspicious) on us." 4. To patronize, as an habitue; to frequent; to show partiality towards. "You're playing the county (jail) regular. That's four bits (terms) you pulled there." 5. (P) To be regularly present at, as church services, recreation yard, etc. "I'm playing the cell today. There ain't nothing in that yard but short-conners (liars) and jerks cutting up touches (telling boastful stories)." 6. (P) To plan or seek to victimize, as the object of a swindle or of pederastic seduction; to act the role of the sycophant; to lavish attention on, with criminal intent. 7. (Loosely) To concentrate on; to lay plans, as for the achievement of any goal.

Play a bloomer. 1. To bungle a crime; to waste one's efforts on a profitless criminal venture. 2. To fail; to fall short of expectations; to make an unwise choice or plan, resulting in failure or disappointment.

Play a matinee. To rob the same victim twice; to commit a second crime within a single day.

Play ball. To work together for mutual advantage despite hostility; to make a mutually beneficial bargain with an adversary or enemy, especially through bribery, exchange of information, or division of spoil. "Them coppers that glommed (arrested) you will play ball. Crack (suggest) business (bribery) to them."

Playhouse. (P) Any prison in which discipline is less rigorous and living conditions more congenial than in most prisons.

Play the bird with the long neck. (Rare) To pry into other people's affairs; to look over, as the site of a proposed robbery or an intended victim.

Play the deuce of clubs. (Carnival) To use drastic measures to prevent a complaint from reaching the police; to assault or use violence against a complainant in order to quash a charge. "That beef (complaint) has got to be chilled (checked by intimidation). Play the deuce of clubs if you gotta."

Play the dozens. 1. To insult in such a manner as to cast doubts on the legitimacy of one's birth. "Someone's gonna kick that flea's lemon in (beat him), going around playing the dozens." 2. To force unwelcome advances upon the wife, sister, cousin, etc., of a friend or associate.

Play the field. To engage generally in crime without specialization.

Play the fruit market. To visit the haunts of male oral sodomists and pederasts, especially to rob them.

Play the iggy. (Carnival) 1. To snub; to ignore. 2. To feign ignorance; to withhold information, fearing exposure. "I don't know whether this ghee (fellow) is wrong (a traitor), but play the iggy to him till we see how he shapes up."

Play the level. 1. To abandon a criminal career for socially approved means of livelihood. "I'm getting tired of pulling time (going to prison); I think I'll play the level a while." 2. To tell the truth; to deal fairly in a given instance. "Them schmeckers (drug addicts) never play the level. I'm going to frisk (search for withheld loot) that guy after every trick (robbery)."

Play the match. To engage in the old coin-matching swindle in which the victim is never permitted to hold the odd coin. [Note: The two swindling conspirators simply arrange in advance never to turn up "heads" or "tails" simultaneously, thus guaranteeing that one of them must be "odd man" at every play.]

Play the numbers. To place a wager on policy numbers which are usually based on pari-mutuel race-track figures; see **Policy game.**

Play the schweinet. To commit the act of male oral sodomy

Play with the squirrels. (P) To be insane; to be an inmate of a hospital for the insane.

Plea. (P) A plea of guilty, usually entered by a defendant as part of a bargain wherein the accused saves the State the expense of a criminal trial by acknowledging guilt of a crime of lesser degree than that named in the indictment, thus incurring a lesser penalty. "There ain't no way for this rap (charge) to stick (end in conviction). I'm going to bat (trial) with a lousy State (appointed) lawyer, and I ain't taking no plea, even spitting on the sidewalk (the lowest of misdemeanors)."

Pleasure smoker. A person who smokes an opium pipe occasionally, but who is not an addict. Compare **Habit smoker.**

Plenty of numbers, to have. 1. To have a penchant for imposing extremely long prison sentences, as a harsh judge. 2. (P) To have a reputation for severity in imposing time penalties for violation of prison rules, as any disciplinary officer. 3. (P) To have a long prison term to serve, as several consecutive sentences.

Pling. To beg on streets or highways.

Pling, on the. Engaged in, or by means of, the panhandling art.

Plinger. One who **plings.**

Plough the kip. To sleep soundly.

Plow. To rape; to have sexual intercourse or pederastic relations with.

Plow-jockey. A farmer; farmhand; a rustic.

Pluck. To rob a victim, usually in some form of swindle.

Plug. To shoot. "Gyp was plugged taking a powder down the stem (fleeing down the avenue)."

Plum-picker. (Southern carnivals) 1. An armed guard who collects concession money for banking. 2. (By extension) Anyone connected with a carnival who carries firearms for illegal purposes. "There was a bad beef (complaint) to the fuzz (police) about a plum-picker turning his heater (gun) on some jokers (people)."

Plunge out. To leave a rendezvous of thieves or beggars to ply one's trade.

Pocket touch. A swindle or robbery that relieves the victim of all the money he has on his person, especially in the **lemon game.** "That dude (fellow) that Joe marked for a stiff (a poor prospect) kicked loose (surrendered) with a C-note (hundred dollars) pocket touch."

Poger. (Among hobos and traveling thieves) A passive pederast.

Pogey. 1. A county farm or poorhouse. 2. A hospital, especially a prison hospital. 3. A **poger.**

Pogie. (Scattered prisons) See **Pogey.**

Pogie-bait. (Scattered prisons) Candy or other small luxuries offered as inducement to degenerates.

Poison. 1. Any thing, place, or circumstance that is extremely undesirable, as an unprincipled or stupid person, a harsh law, a vicious prison guard, or a particularly severe prison. 2. Any thing, place, or circumstance fraught with danger, as an area too well policed, a type of crime incurring heavy penalties.

Poke, n. 1. A wallet; a handbag or purse; (by extension) a roll of bills. 2. A pocket. 3. A fist blow.

Poke, v. To assault with fists.

Pokey. The county jail. "The clatter (patrol wagon) backed up to Sadie's nautch-joint (brothel) and whipped the broads down to the pokey."

Policy bank. The central office of a syndicate operating a policy-numbers lottery.

Policy game, the. The policy-numbers lottery, usually based on pari-mutuel aggregate race track wagers for the day.

Polly. 1. Any political office holder or hanger-on, especially one who accepts bribes or in any way deals with the "overworld" in the interests of the underworld. "A couple of pollies are putting the zingers (arranging things) for an s.s. (suspended sentence) for me, if I cop out (plead guilty)." 2. (P) Any prison inmate holding a position of trust, especially one who exerts his influence for the benefit of fellow-convicts. "Don't let any of them can (prison) pollies front for (represent) you with the Dep (Deputy Warden). Put the handle on (ask) him yourself and you might score for (secure) the job."

Pontius Pilate. (Rare, except among transient old-timers) A judge; a **wig.**

Pooch-snatch. The kidnapping and holding for ransom of an expensive dog; stealing and selling a dog. [Note: The criminals first find a customer who wants to obtain a pedigreed dog but who is not too scrupulous about the method of obtaining it. Let's say he wants a male Great Dane. A spotter locates such a dog. Two dog thieves bring a bitch in a car to the scene of the theft. As soon as they pull up near enough for the male dog to smell the presence of the female, the door of the car is thrown open. Invariably the dog, however pedigreed and trained, will enter the car after the female. A bag is thrown over its head. Brought to a **plant,** the male is dyed much as a woman tints her hair. The color will hold until the dog sheds its fur. By that time, the search for the animal has ceased and the thieves are safely out of the area. Dog thieves usually cater to an underworld clientele and operate in a very wide sphere. A dog seized in Illinois may be sold in Georgia, etc.]

Poop. To shoot a person.

Pop. Opium.

Popcorn. A fool; a person mentally deranged or feeble-minded.

Pop a nut. To feel extremely gratified or delighted; to find sexual gratification. "Boy, I'm sure popping a nut! I just see in the home town rag (newspaper) where my rapper (complainant in criminal proceedings) got pinched (arrested)."

Pop-joint. (Variation of hop joint) An opium den.

Pop-off, n. 1. The beginning; the start. "I pegged (recognized) that rapper (complainant) for a business man (one who would accept a bribe) right at the pop-off. Most of them guys that go for a short-con (fast confidence game) got plenty larceny in their hearts)." 2. The explosion of the charge in safeblowing; an explosive exhibition of temper or temperament.

Pop off, v. 1. To fly into an uncontrolled rage; to jump with delight or any emotional stimulus. "You should have seen Chris pop off when the jury

sprung (acquitted) him!" 2. **To pop one's nuts.**

Pop one's nuts. To have a sexual orgasm; to be so exhilarated by anything that the experience is equal to a sexual orgasm.

Poppy. Opium.

Poppy-pipe. An opium pipe.

Population. (P) The general body of inmates as differentiated from convicts in trusty jobs, hospital patients, and occupants of punishment or psychopathic observation wings.

Porch-climber. A second-story man.

Port. (Pickpocket jargon) On the left side, as a "port-kick"—left-hand pocket.

Port britch. (Among pickpockets) The left-hand trousers pocket.

Port pratt. (Among pickpockets) The left-hand rear trousers pocket.

Potato. (Usually in the phrase, "a big potato") A **big shot;** anyone who has money, influence or the appearance of having either. "That new mickey (newcomer) is a big potato already. What is he, a fleeper (informer)?"

Potato water. (P) A vile alcoholic beverage made of fermented potato-peelings and sugar.

Pound. 1. Five dollars. 2. (P) Five years' imprisonment.

Pound the bell or **ear.** To sleep.

Pour it on. To fire; to shoot.

Powder, to take a. To flee, as the jurisdiction of a court, official custody, confinement or danger. "All right, take a powder; you're lousing up (spoiling the reputation of) this joint."

Pox. An opium pill.

Pratt, n. 1. Rump; posterior. 2. (Among pickpockets) The rear trousers pocket area. "Fan (search) the pratt for the leather (wallet). I'll stick the mark up (lurch against the victim and pin him in position)."

Pratt. 1. To have sexual intercourse. with, normally or—usually—abnormally. 2. To take advantage of, as of an abject flunkey; to abuse or cheat.

Pratt, on one's. 1. On one's tail; in close pursuit. "The dicks' (detectives') prowl-car was hot on our pratt when Skipper broke out a swag (lot) of big tacks and threw them on the road." 2. Under surveillance, especially as a prospective victim of robbery or other criminal action. "This ghee (fellow) who is filling in is supposed to be a good rod (gunman). Keep on his pratt till we see how he shapes up." 3. Sitting down; idle; ill. 4. In financial difficulty. 5. (P) Nagging, as a guard who plagues a convict with undesirable assignments or remarks—giving him **buckwheats** or **honey.**

Pratt-digger. (Rare) A pickpocket.

Pratt-kick. (Among pickpockets) Rear trousers pocket.

Pratt-leather. A wallet or billfold carried in the rear trousers pocket.

Pratt-man. 1. A pickpocket. 2. An employee of an underworld rendezvous who, while helping patrons off with coats, manages to feel pockets to learn if they are armed. 3. A **turk;** a **wolf.**

Pratt-score. (Among pickpockets) A theft by pocket-picking of rear trousers pocket. "You better get a grindstone (someone to practice on) and sharpen it (perfect your touch). Since you did that sixer (six-month term in jail) you ain't even made a pratt-score (easiest of assignments)."

Pratt-wise. Alert to pickpockets.

Press. (Rare) A tip on a prospective victim for robbery or any form of theft or racket.

Press the bankroll. (Carnival) To increase the bank, or the sum of money in play in a gambling game. [Note: The gambling operator presses the bankroll to build up the play, paying out increasing amounts of temporary losses until he is ready to swindle the victims of a lump sum. The operator

notifies his aides in the crowd of the amount added, mixing it in a patter of double-talk, so that they will not suspect him of double-crossing them and withholding sums of money.] "Getting a nice play on this wheel. Hip (inform) them shills (aides) up that I'm pressing the bankroll a hundred for the big take."

Pressure. The utilization of drastic methods to defraud, swindle, or rob a difficult or unwilling victim; force or the threat of force.

Pretzel. (Usually in negative expressions, such as "ain't got a pretzel") Anything of little or no value. "The fence (buyer of stolen goods) won't give you a pretzel for that slum (cheap jewelry)."

Primed. Under the influence of alcohol or drugs. ("Primed to the ears or nuts"—very drunk; exhilarated by drugs).

Print. To take one's fingerprints.

Prints. Fingerprints.

Prison hustler. (P) A convict who pretends to occupy a position of importance in prison. "Look at that prison biggie (big shot) hustling for peanuts (scheming for trifles). That saying, 'prison hustler, street bum,' is the McCoy."

Prison tough guy. (P) A bully, especially one who assaults his fellow inmates in the presence of guards so that his victim may not retaliate; one who abuses fellow convicts seeking parole, knowing that they will not retaliate.

Prod. 1. A pistol or revolver. 2. (P) A knife or stiletto. "Cappy just hit the hole (punishment cells) for lugging (carrying) a prod." 3. (In scattered areas) A county jail, penitentiary, prison, or reformatory.

Professor. (Hobo) A panhandler with a clever **story,** especially one who makes pretenses of erudition.

Prohy. (During the Prohibition era) A prohibition agent of the Department of Justice or Treasury Department.

Promote. 1. To swindle by high pressure means; to give, or use the **promote.** 2. To raise money through persuasion and guile; to procure anything without payment, merely on the strength of words and persuasion. "The panic is on (things are bad). I gotta get out and promote some makin's (tobacco and cigarette papers) before we lock in (are locked up for the night)."

Promote, on the. 1. Engaged in, or swindling by means of, any of the various confidence games. 2. Seeking to obtain something for nothing. "Are you going for that short-con (persuasive talk) of his? Don't give him a flop (a serious hearing); he's strictly on the promote."

Promote, the. 1. The swindling profession; the confidence game generally, or any of its subdivisions; the practice of any of the various confidence swindles. "The promote ain't so bad. We made a couple of good scores on the spud (exchanging sums wrapped in handkerchief, bill fold, etc., for wad of worthless paper) last week." 2. The persuasive talk and guileful actions of the high-pressure confidence swindler; persuasion and guile as a means of securing an object. "We gave that rapper (complaining witness) the old million-dollar promote. He's pulling off (withdrawing his complaint)."

Promoter. One who **promotes.**

Promotion. Any transaction based on the use of persuasion and guile; a confidence swindle.

Prop. (Chiefly among pickpockets) 1. A tie-pin. 2. Any flashy but cheap article used to deceive the uninitiated, as cheap dolls at carnivals, impressive furnishings, etc.

Protection. Immunity from threatened arrest, violence, slander, defamation, or from any other action by criminal or law-enforcement agents, purchased by bribery, information, or other favors; protective custody or surveillance by police; freedom to steal or engage in rackets with purchased immunity.

Protection town. (Chiefly Central, South-Central and South-Western areas) A town in which a fugitive from another State or from Federal authorities may find a haven, usually under the sheriff's care, in return for a consideration, provided the fugitive keeps the peace during his stay; a town operated by members of the **Johnson family.**

Prowl. 1. Burglary, especially when executed by stealth rather than force. 2. Any furtive or stealthy prowling in search of loot, prey, information, etc. "Keep away from the drop (hideout). I gave it a gunning (inspection) yesterday, and someone must have give the joint a prowl. It don't look kosher (safe)."

Prowl. 1. To subject a place to a **prowl.**

Prowl, on the. 1. Engaged in, or by means of sneak-thievery, especially in private homes or apartments. 2. In the act of prowling about in search of loot or information.

Prowl car. A police car roving through a district in search of lawbreakers. "Hit the drop (hideout) fast. This spot will be lousy with (full of) prowl cars in a minute account of that heist (holdup)."

Prowler. A sneak-thief; a burglar; anyone who **prowls.**

Pruno. (P) An alcoholic home brew concocted of prunes and sugar.

Prussian. (Chiefly among hobos and traveling thieves) An active pederast, especially one who moves about in company with a passive partner.

Pry. A burglar's tool, especially for safe-cracking, having a strong pronged tip capable of biting into the protective sleeve around the combination spindle of a safe, employed after a drill, or a hammer and chisel, have penetrated the frontal combination plate.

Psalm-singing muzzler. (P) A religious hypocrite. "That psalm-singing muzzler didn't pray his way into this swindle (trouble), but now he wants to pray his way out of the can (prison)."

Puff. Crude nitroglycerine or **picric**, used by safeblowers. [More common: **soup** or **grease**.]

Puke on. To inform upon self and associates under police questioning; to turn underworld traitor.

Pull. 1. To commit or execute, as a robbery, burglary, or escape. "Here's a ghee (fellow) pulled twenty heists (holdups) and got dropped (arrested) once. He's a first offender with a nice short bit. Some other jerk pulls five tricks (crimes) and drops four times. He's a four-time loser (fourth offender) with a life bit. Screwy set-up, ain't it?" 2. To serve, as a prison sentence. 3. To withdraw, or cause to be withdrawn, as a criminal charge or complaint. "To pull a rap or warrant." 4. To do.

Pull a beef. See **Pull a pinch.**

Pull a bit. (P) To serve out a prison or a penitentiary sentence. "There's a mick (convict) ain't gonna pull his bit; he's blowing his roof (going insane) fast."

Pull a bloomer. See **Play a bloomer.**

Pull a chiv on. To draw a knife on.

Pull a crater. To disappear; to leave town.

Pull a deuce. To serve two years in prison.

Pull a double saw, or sawbuck. (P) To serve twenty years in prison.

Pull a fast one. To take advantage of by use of chicanery or treachery. "Imagine that crumb duking me in (getting me) to hold swag (his loot)

for him when he knows a frisk (search) is comin'? That's the last time he'll pull a fast one on me."

Pull a fin, or a **finif.** (P) To serve five years in prison.

Pull a Greeley. To go West, i.e., turn fugitive. "The Greek was red hot (wanted by the police with conviction almost certain) for that knock-off (murder charge); had to pull a Greeley."

Pull a Jesse James. (West and near South) 1. (Rare) to take over an entire town by banditry. 2. To commit train robbery. 3. To commit robbery in a reckless manner. "These punks (young kids) pullin' a Jesse James screw the racket (make it hard for 'good' thieves to make a living)."

Pull a job. To commit a crime of professional character, as distinguished from crimes of passion.

Pull a joint. To execute a police raid on premises and make arrests.

Pull an ace. (P) To serve one year in prison.

Pull a pinch. 1. To have a criminal charge dropped as a result of coercion, bribery, or political influence; to withdraw a charge or complaint. 2. (P) To withdraw, or cause to be withdrawn, a formal report against a convict for rule violation. "Buzz (talk to) that screw (guard) to pull this pinch. Tell him I meet the Board (Parole Board) next month."

Pull a pisser. To do something exceedingly stupid or embarrassing. "We sure pulled a pisser copping a plea (pleading guilty to a lesser offense) while the jury was out. The mouthpiece (lawyer) got the wire (inside information) that they were gonna give us a turn-out (acquit us)."

Pull a quickie. See **Pull a fast one.**

Pull a rabbit. To perform an abortion.

Pull a rap. See **Pull a pinch.**

Pull a saw, or **sawbuck.** (P) To serve ten years in prison.

Pull a sneak. 1. (Carnival) To exceed the gambling limits set by the **legal adjuster** for a local carnival swindle. 2. To escape; to commit any crime using the tactics of a sneak; to seize an opportunity to commit a theft without plan. 3. To take one at a disadvantage in assault, betrayal, cheating, etc.

Pull a soft bit. (P) To serve a prison sentence with minimum hardship.

Pull a tough bit. (P) To serve a most unhappy prison sentence. [Note: Ill health, family difficulties, lack of money from outside friends or relatives, a harsh prison routine—all go to make up a **tough bit.**]

Pull a treyer. To serve three years in prison.

Pull a trick. 1. To commit a crime for gain. 2. (Usually with the word "trick" modified by such adjectives as "lousy," "dirty," "smelly," or "crummy") To commit any unethical or treacherous act against another. "Nobody but a crumb (exceedingly low fellow) would pull a lousy trick like that, ranking my play (ruining my attempted robbery) 'cause you couldn't make (rob) the sucker yourself." 3. To engage in an act of oral sodomy or pederasty.

Pull a wire. To use one's influence, especially political influence, to achieve an objective. "The pollies (politicians) are pulling a wire to get Biff bugged (adjudged insane) so he won't burn (be electrocuted) for that knock-off (murder)."

Pull . . . boffos. (P) To serve . . . years in prison.

Puller. See **V.**

Pull off. 1. To withdraw, or effect the withdrawal of, a complainant or a witness in criminal proceedings. 2. (P) To withdraw, or to effect the withdrawal of, a report for rule violation or

a pending warrant. 3. To masturbate. 4. To accomplish by chicanery or treachery. "What are you tryin' to pull off? You ain't short-connin' (using flattery) and glommin' (handshaking) for practice."

Pull one's leg. To extort from; blackmail.

Pull out of the bag. To recover; to salvage; to effect reversal of a trend previously adverse, as in a criminal trial, in gambling, etc. "My spouter (lawyer) sure pulled that case out of the bag for me."

Pull the nut. (P) To wish with all one's might for good luck. "Some polly (politician) is trying to jerk the hooker off me (withdraw pending warrant). I'm pulling my nut to get a break on it."

Pull time. To serve a prison sentence.

Pump, n. The heart.

Pump, v. To employ guile to wheedle information; to examine in ordinary police routine.

Pumpkin. (Pronounced "punkin") The head. "They knocked some guy's pumpkin in with a sap (blackjack) for a lousy sawbuck (ten dollars)."

Punch. To burglarize a safe by means of a heavy steel punch and a hammer with which the combination dial is knocked off, and, after the tumblers are lined up, the old-style locking mechanism smashed.

Puncher. A crude safe-burglar who burglarizes by **punching.**

Punch the gun. (Chiefly carnival) To talk in underworld slang. [Compare: **Sling the lingo.**]

Punch the guts out. To burglarize a safe by **punching.**

Punk. 1. (P) A passive pederast or oral sodomist. "That kid chivved (knifed) three wolves (active pederasts) who tried to mug him (employ a crushing headlock) and make a punk out of him." 2. (Rare, because of confusion with implications of degeneracy) A young boy. 3. (P. and hobo) Bread.

Punk and plaster. (P. and hobo) Bread and butter.

Pup. 1. The phallus. 2. A despicable fellow.

Push, n. 1. A crowd of people, especially as potential victims of pickpockets. 2. (P) A prison-break, especially one involving numerical rather than armed force. 3. (Carnival) The process by which aides crowd a prospective swindle victim close to a stand or game. "I just put the squint on (looked at) this hoosier's (prospective victim's) poke (wallet). Give him the push, he's loaded (has plenty of money)."

Push, v. 1. To sell, especially stolen or contraband goods. 2. To pass or issue, especially counterfeit currency or negotiables. 3. To burglarize.

Push a can. To escape from any place of imprisonment or detention.

Push a joint. To burglarize.

Push a kite. 1. (P) To smuggle an uncensored letter out of prison. 2. To pass a forged check or other forged instrument.

Push and slide. (Chiefly Carnival; rare) See **Hipe,** 1.

Push around. 1. To abuse, persecute, rob, or to extort money from by force or the threat of force. "The joint is goin' great when the coppers (police) goin' to the man (complaining to the warden) when guys were pushing him start pushin' me around. I won't stand for a shake (submit to extortion), so they crash the spot (force their way into the place) one night and wreck it." 2. To take advantage of or abuse in any way. "This jerk (fool) loused himself up (ruined his reputation) around. He just come off the street (come to prison) on his first bit (sentence) and didn't know what the score was (the ropes)."

Push a stiff. To issue a forged check or bond.

Pusher. 1. One who passes counterfeit money. 2. A retailer of narcotics to addicts. 3. A leader of an organized gang, especially one handling drugs, stolen cars, counterfeit money, etc.

Push flats. To burglarize flats and apartments when occupants are out.

Push gage. To sell narcotics.

Push hot ones, or **boilers.** 1. To market stolen automobiles after appearance and motor-block numbers have been altered. 2. (P) To make and dispose of contraband electric stoves.

Push in. 1. To burglarize. 2. To seize control, as of a racket or a shady establishment, by force or the threat of force; to **take over** a racketeering labor union; to achieve any end by brazen aggression. "I got the wires (necessary influence) to chill (quash) any beef (police complaint). Push in and make them people get in line (comply with our demands)."

Push junk. To sell narcotics to the addict trade.

Push kites. To issue or pass forged or illegally altered checks. "Some scratch-mob (forgery gang) has the whole town stiffed (defrauded), pushing kites."

Push muggles. To sell cigarettes containing marijuana.

Push out. 1. (P) To escape from any place of confinement by force. 2. To leave a place; to go out. 3. To leave on a criminal venture or mission.

Pushover. 1. A woman of extremely easy virtue. 2. Anything exceedingly easy to achieve; anyone easily victimized; any place capable of being easily robbed; a simple task. "The touch (robbery) is a pushover but the out (means of escape) won't stand up (serve us in case of danger)."

Push paper. To issue or pass forged

checks or other fraudulent instruments of exchange.

Push queer. To pass counterfeit money.

Push reefers. See **Push muggles.**

Push schmeck. To sell drugs.

Push stores. To burglarize stores and shops.

Push swag. 1. To sell stolen goods. "You can push that swag to blind fences (innocent buyers). It ain't so hot (readily identifiable, with the police hunting for it)." 2. (P) To sell prison stores or contraband.

Push the mooch. See **Push junk.**

Push the note. See **Lay the note.**

Push up. To hold up.

Put, to be. 1. To participate in sexual intercourse. 2. (P) To engage in pederasty; to be intimate with an oral copulator.

Pussy-bumper. See **Bumper.**

Put a buck one's way. To provide opportunities for one to make money in a crime or in a racket.

Put a bug on. 1. To install or set a burglar alarm. 2. To tap a telephone line.

Put a chiv on. To place a knife against one's body, often across the throat, in coercion. [Note: This is a common method of forcing young convicts to submit to acts of perversion.]

Put a mark on. To jostle a victim onto a car or bus step when picking his pockets.

Put a prowl on. To ransack; burglarize.

Put a spot on. To detail one to follow another; to dispatch, as a spy.

Put a stiff on the buck. To put a fresh keg of beer on the ice. "What a score (profitable crime)! Plant (put away) the gullion (jewelry) and the biscuits (guns). I'll put a stiff on the buck at the scatter (meeting place)."

Put a tail on. To cause a person to be followed.

Put in. (P) To make a formal request or petition, as for transfer to another prison, change of work assignment, etc. "I'm puttin' in for a boat (transfer) to some other joint. This can (prison) ain't got no system. You blow your top (can go insane) here."

Put in a beef or a pinch. See **Put in a rap.**

Put in a rap. (P) 1. To report an inmate formally for rule violation. 2. To enter a complaint.

Put in the hole. 1. To conceal, as a kidnap victim, in a place of detention. 2. (P) To place a convict in solitary confinement on a bread-and-water diet.

Put in the middle. To place [one] in an untenable position.

Put it on one. To turn a gun, knife, or any weapon against one; to seize one in a strangle hold. "Put it on the dick (policeman), and I'll frisk (search) him for his rod (revolver)."

Put-off, n. 1. The act of jostling a victim, forcing him to descend bus or car steps while a skilled pickpocket robs him. 2. A point at which people leave cars, trains, or buses where pickpockets may operate profitably. 3. The act of jostling a pickpocket victim through the closing door of a train or bus at the instant of robbing so that recovery is rendered impossible.

Put off, v. 1. To pick pockets at train, bus, or car stop. 2. To pick pockets using the **put-off.**

Put on an act. To feign, as illness; to make any pretense with an ulterior motive.

Put one's back up. To jostle one into a fixed position in a crowd while a skilled accomplice picks his pocket. "Pit touch (inside pocket snatch), Lefty. Put his back up tight."

Put on the arm. To take something on credit without any intention of repaying, the credit being given as a result of intimidation—indirect petty extortion. [Compare **Put the arm on.**] "Them bulls (policemen) got the joint knocked up (rendered it unprofitable) puttin' drinks on the arm."

Put on the cuff, or **muscle.** See **Put on the arm.**

Put on the spot. 1. To lure a victim to a murder tryst. 2. To put one in an untenable or embarrassing position. 3. To subject one to the **spot** punishment. [See **Spot,** def. 5.]

Put out. To give; share; lend; to be prodigal. "You got a swag (lot) of makings (tobacco and paper for rolling cigarettes) and tailor-mades (machine-made cigarettes) in your cell, but you ain't puttin' nothin' out, you single-o muzzler (selfish fellow)." 2. (P) To submit to active pederasty. 3. To be promiscuous, as a prostitute or woman of loose morals.

Put the arm on. 1. To assault by seizing the victim's head in a crushing armlock. 2. To coerce; to threaten directly or by implication.

Put the "B" on. 1. To solicit money on the streets or highways. 2. To beg or borrow; to request any favor or concession; to press for payment of an obligation; to extort or blackmail; to ply with questions seeking information. "A couple of dicks were mooching (skulking) around putting the 'B' on to know where you were."

Put the bend on. To bend the corner of the winning card in the **three-card-monte swindle,** thus leading the victim to believe that he is in league with the swindlers against the operator; after several winning plays, the bend is transferred to a losing card, and the victim pays.

Put the bite on. 1. To extort money from. 2. To beg or borrow from; to solicit a favor or concession from. 3. (Rare; scattered South, West, and Central States) To arrest.

Put the blocks to. 1. (P) To be car-

nally intimate with. 2. To cheat; to betray; to inform against; to take unfair advantage of. "The bulls (police) agreed to spring (release) my partner if he'd put the finger on me (inform against me). Then they got the D.A. (District Attorney) to put the blocks to him and he got a fin (sentence of five years in prison)."

Put the boots to. 1. To kick a victim, especially after knocking him down. 2. To know carnally. 3. To cheat; take unfair advantage of; betray. "I copped a plea (pleaded guilty) to one rap (charge) in a deal to cover all the beefs (other charges would be quashed). But they put the boots to me right. I got a sawbuck (sentence of ten years in prison) and they still got three hookers (warrants) against me."

Put the chill on. 1. To snub; to get rid of; to avoid. 2. To discourage, intimidate, or otherwise influence one to desist from the execution of an act. 3. To kill; to knock unconscious.

Put the chuck on. (East; except N.Y. and N.J.) To assist police in railroading an underworld associate. "This geepo (weakling) put the chuck on his partners. They're all pegged for a big stretch (serving long sentences)."

Put the clown to bed. To follow a small town cop home before committing crime.

Put the cross on. 1. To betray; cheat. 2. To order the murder of. 3. To point out one to be murdered; to lure an intended victim to his death.

Put the duke down. (Among pickpockets) To reach into a victim's pocket for the robbery. "What a rowdy-dowdy (rough-and-tumble) score (robbery)! The mark (victim) rounded (turned around) when I put the duke down and beefed murder (shouted for the police). We didn't cop a mope (make a getaway) till he was beat (robbed)."

Put the finger on. 1. To direct police to one's accomplice; to inform against; to give state's evidence; to identify formally in a police line-up or court as the author of a specific crime. "That rapper (complainant) was a right ghee (good fellow). He pegged (recognized) me in the line-up (police line-up) but he wouldn't put the finger on me so I got a turn-out (was released)." 2. To point out, or suggest, as a prospective victim or objective for thieves. "Bootsie got a bum rap (was falsely blamed) for putting the finger on that policy number bank (lottery syndicate office) for a heist (holdup)."

Put the frame on. 1. To cause one, guilty or innocent, to be sent to prison. 2. (P) To cause one to be convicted falsely on any charge; to convict one who is guilty but by improper methods.

Put the glom on. See **Put the snatch on.**

Put the grab on. 1. To seize, as a loan shark, the property of a victim in satisfaction of a debt. 2. See **Put the snatch on.**

Put the gorill on. 1. See **Put the shake on.** 2. To threaten; to intimidate.

Put the handle on. See **Put the bite on.**

Put the hat on. To affect an air of superiority. "Get a load of (look at) that punk (young nobody) puttin' the hat on. What'd he do, get a money order?"

Put the heat on. 1. To point a pistol at. "I threw the benny (overcoat) over the arm to cover the biscuit (gun), put the heat on him right on the stem (street) and snatched the boodle (money)." 2. To intensify police activity within a given area or throughout the underworld generally; to spur an anti-crime campaign; to publicize racket operations; to begin a widespread hunt for a wanted criminal. 3. To apply drastic measures, especially upon prospective victims of extortion.

Put the hipe on. To subject to any phase of the **hipe.**

Put the horns on. 1. To cheat. 2. To jinx; to give one bad luck. "Someone's puttin' the horns on us. We get a rumble (find trouble) every trick (robbery) we go on."

Put the hustle on. 1. To strive to lure a prospective victim into a swindle trap. "Get out and put the hustle on these lushes (fools). It's scuffle (use drastic measures) or get skunked (go penniless) here." 2. To use guile rather than force in overcoming the reluctance of a victim or tool.

Put the lug on. To remove forcibly with the aid of strong-arm accomplices an irate victim from the scene of the swindle, as at a carnival. [Note: Such tactics are possible only when the local police have been bribed into immobility.]

Put the mugg on. See **Put the arm on.**

Put the muscle on. To employ force or the threat of force. "You're on the payroll for a hundred clams (dollars) a week. When these joints don't kick in (pay), put the muscle on them."

Put the needles in. To agitate subtly; to prejudice the case of another by any secret word or act. "That rat ain't gettin' no work (opportunities for profitable crimes) from good people (good underworld citizens) around here. I'm puttin' the needles in to louse him up (ostracize him) right."

Put the nuts on. To apply pressure or force.

Put the pencil on. (P) To report for a rule violation. "Whitey got the pencil put on him for bad-eyeing (glaring viciously at) some screw (prison guard)."

Put the promote on. See **Put the hustle on.**

Put the prongs on. To cheat, swindle,

or inform against; to rape. "That swaggie (buyer of stolen goods) put the prongs on us plenty. We'll screw (get even with) him on this stuff and fence it blind (sell it to innocent buyers)."

Put the shake on. 1. To subject to extortion or blackmail. 2. (P) To coerce another into serving one in menial capacity; to exact petty favors from another. "Lefty, you are sure hitting me with contracts (asking me for too many favors). Now you gotta get a kite out (smuggle an uncensored letter out of prison). What are you, puttin' the shake on me, Bud?"

Put the skids to. To get rid of.

Put the sleeve on. To beg or borrow; to defer payment of an obligation, especially a gambling debt. 2. To solicit any favor or concession from [anyone].

Put the slough on. 1. To arrest. 2. (P) To lock up for rule violation. 3. To assault, usually with fists.

Put the slug on. To assault with fists or a bludgeon; to render unconscious. "Don't get knocked off (arrested) with that tin (police badge on your person). Some hoods (rowdies) beat (robbed) a bull (detective) and put the slug on him for it."

Put the snare on. 1. To arrest; to seize, especially in the act of committing a crime. 2. (P) To report or lock up for a violation of rules; to seize in the act of a rule violation. 3. To grab; steal. "The P. K. (Principal Keeper) busted in on the crap game with about twenty clams (dollars) on the deck (table). He asked whose dough it was and nobody rumbled (answered). 'Humph! It must be mine, then,' he cracks (says), puts the snare on it and lams (leaves the room)." 4. To stop one for the purpose of soliciting alms, a favor, or any concession.

Put the snatch on. 1. To kidnap. 2. To arrest; to seize in the act. "Get the shyster (lawyer). They put the snatch on Bolo for a forty-eight (forty-eight-hour police examination)." 3. (P) To seize in the act of a rule violation; to hold for psychopathic observation. 4. To commit a theft.

Put the squeeze on. To coerce; extort from; to wear down resistance.

Put the tap on. 1. To defraud by means of the **tap.** 2. To swindle or attempt to swindle of a moderate sum.

Put the zingers on. See **Zingers.**

Put-up, n. 1. The act of pinning a victim so that his pocket may be picked. "I just gave the mark (victim) the old put-up and Fingers is putting the duke down (reaching into his pocket) when a cannon squad (pickpocket squad) bull (detective) made (recognized) me. What a tumul (commotion)!" 2. (Obs.) An armed robbery; a holdup.

Put up, v. 1. To jostle, stall, or otherwise place a victim into a position in which his pocket may be picked. "Put him up. Gotta use nippers (instrument for cutting wire). The wad (money) is anchored (fastened)." 2. To return a pistol or other weapon to pocket or holster. 3. (Obs.) To rob at gun point.

Put up a beef. 1. To complain, especially to police; to protest. 2. See **Put up a sucker's holler,** 2.

Put up a holler. 1. To shout for police; to complain; to protest. 2. See **Put up a sucker's holler,** 2.

Put up a squawk. See **Put up a holler.**

Put up a sucker's holler. 1. To complain to police. 2. To commit the unpardonable sin, as a member of the underworld, of carrying one's just grievances to non-underworld authorities.

Q

Queen. A passive oral copulator.

Queer, n. 1. Counterfeit money, especially paper currency. 2. An oral copulator; pederast.

Queer, v. To ruin or spoil, as the execution of a crime, especially by a blunder. "Cop a mope (get away), Happy, you're queering the play (my plans)."

Queer, a. Erotic; abnormal.

Queer pusher. A passer of counterfeit paper currency.

Quetor. A quarter; twenty-five cents.

Quickie. An unexpectedly rapid strategic move; any swiftly executed piece of trickery. "They gave him a quickie, rushed him to bat (trial) with a State lip (lawyer)."

Quick one. Any swiftly executed piece of trickery; double-cross. "Spider pulled a quick one on the D. A. (District Attorney); took the stand (witness stand) to open up (testify against his accomplices), turned (changed his testimony) and sprung (effected the acquittal of) his partners."

Quiff. Generic term for women of loose morals; epicenes.

Quiff, on one's. See Pratt, on one's.

Quinine. (Scattered South and West, especially in prisons) See Buckwheats.

R

Rabbit, n. 1. (Loan shark racket) A steady borrower who pays promptly. 2. An abortion.

Rabbit, v. (South, Southwest, Central and West) To scurry away. "You're throwin' snake eyes (running into bad luck), Smoky. Better rabbit for Indian Gulch and hole up (hide). Them people's all Johnson family (loyal to the underworld) up there."

Rabbit blood. (P) A constant and "instinctive" readiness to escape from prison. "I tried to duke in (induce) the P. K. (Principal Keeper) to put me on the (prison) farm, but he says he can smell rabbit blood a mile."

Rabbit out. (Rural areas) To flee.

Rabbit-snatcher. An abortionist. "You might as well hit (shoot) your barnacle (girl) in the noggin (head) as let those two-bit (cheap) rabbit-snatchers work on her."

Racket, n. 1. Any illegitimate business or occupation. 2. A technically legitimate business that violates the spirit of the law. 3. Any "easy," lucrative occupation or business. 4. Any dance, party, or social function. "The bulls (detectives) crashed a racket uptown and snatched (arrested) Foxy and two other lamesters (fugitives from justice.") 5. (Loosely) Any means of livelihood.

Racket, a. Of the underworld.

Racket broad. A girl criminal.

Racket dude. A thief or racketeer.

Racketeer, n. One who is engaged in any illegitimate business.

Racketeer, v. To operate as a racketeer.

Racketeering. The operation of any illegal business; crime as an organized means of livelihood. "Racketeering gets you peanuts today. Your partner squeals on you. The D.A. can't be reached (bribed), and your shyster (lawyer) sells you out. A thief can't make a living no more."

Racket ghee. Anyone who earns his living by stealing, extortion, running doubtfully legal establishments, or similar means.

Rag. 1. Newspaper. "The rags are always beefing (complaining) how cons (convicts) are pampered in stir (prison). I wish one of them crumbs (contemptible fellows) would pull a bit (serve a prison term)." 2. A one-dollar bill. 3. Paper currency.

Rag-bag. 1. (Hobo) A badly tattered bum. 2. (Carnival) A very small carnival.

Rahl, the. Syphilis.

Rahled up. Afflicted with syphilis.

Railroad. To send to prison on trumped-up charges; to convict without due process of law.

Rain-check, (P. Scattered areas; not very common) A parole.

Raise heat. To cause police activity to be intensified.

Raiser. 1. A forger who specializes in altering the amounts on otherwise legitimate checks or money orders. 2. A specialist in counterfeiting who bleaches one-dollar bills and, by photo-engraving, raises their denomination; one who uses any device to raise the true denomination of securities or other negotiable instruments. 3. A specialist in raising the denomination of securities or other negotiable instruments.

Rake-off, n. 1. Bribe. 2. Money realized from share of loot, or proceeds from any racket. 3. Money stolen from employer. 4. A percentage of the proceeds of a crime or racket—less than a full participant's share—given to any minor accessory. [Note: An end, or cut, or piece is a full partner's share or that which is given to the **tipster**. A rake-off is given to one who furnishes minor items of information or otherwise serves in a minor capacity. Compare **Gapper's cut**.]

Rake off, v. To draw a **rake-off**.

Range. (Western prisons) A gallery or a tier of cells. "That weasel (informer) on six range fingered (informed the authorities) that crash-out (of the planned escape)."

Rank, n. 1. An unsuccessful crime, especially one caused by interference during commission; a thwarting of plans. 2. Notice.

Rank, v. 1. To frustrate or ruin the execution of a crime by blunder or intention. 2. To betray; to double-cross.

Rank a joint. 1. To render a place unfit for criminal operations; to render a place unsafe for robbery. "That score (robbery) is screwed up (ruined). You ranked the joint makin' all that noise." 2. To alter the character of a place for the worse, as by abuse of privileges or by the presence of disreputable guests or occupants. "Them fleas (informers and petty thieves) are rankin' this joint. Ain't you got no respect for the good people (decent underworld citizens) givin' you a play (who patronize you)?"

Rank a mark. To arouse the suspicion of an intended victim, thus bungling or thwarting the execution of the crime.

Rank and lam. 1. To bungle a crime and flee. "Tough break. We ranked and lammed. Some sucker rumbled (became suspicious and thwarted) the play (crime)."

Rank a play. To bungle or thwart the execution of a crime. "This sucker (victim) is a pretty hip ghee (smart fellow). Don't spring (act) too quick or you'll rank the play."

Ranked. Thwarted, as by police interference; spoiled, as the execution of a crime, by a blunder or by an unfortunate turn of events.

Rap, n. 1. A criminal charge. "There ain't no way for a city ghee (fellow) to beat (to be acquitted of) a rap in them jerkwater (small town) courts." 2. A prison sentence. "A tenner (ten-year prison sentence) is a big rap for a prowl (burglary)." 3. The blame; stigma.

Rap, v. 1. To press a criminal charge; to testify against. "The sucker (victim) ain't gonna rap. We hit him with (we gave him) five C's (five hundred dollars) to take a powder (to flee the jurisdiction of the court)." 2. To blame; to stigmatize.

Rapper. 1. A judge. 2. A complainant; the chief witness for the prosecution in a criminal proceeding. "Snatch (kidnap) that rapper and stick him in the hole (keep him in hiding) or we're buried (put in prison for a long time.)"

Rap to. To recognize; greet; reply to a greeting or salutation; take notice of. "Don't rap to that rat (informer); he's a fink (stool pigeon) for the cops."

Rat, n. A stool pigeon; betrayer; an informer; one who secretly aids the police to apprehend criminals.

Rat, v. 1. To assist authorities secretly in bringing criminals to justice. 2. (P) To act as a stool pigeon or informer for officialdom, either openly or covertly. "If he rats on me, I'll mark his kisser (cut his face). With my bit (long prison term), I got nothing to lose."

Rat caper. A theft or any act characteristic of a contemptible person.

Rat-crasher. A thief who breaks into and robs freight cars.

Rat-mark. A knife scar from cheekbone to mouth, often v-shaped, inflicted as a stigma upon informers.

Rats. 1. Freight cars. 2. Any railroad train; street cars.

Rats, on the. Engaged in, or by means

of, freight-car robberies.

Rat-shackle. (Southern prisons) A fifteen-inch standard chain between riveted ankle-bands which severely limits a prisoner's movements. [Note: At night a long chain is usually passed through each individual rat-shackle, binding prisoners together in such a manner that there is barely enough slack to permit them to move about in sleeping quarters.]

Rat stand. A rural railroad station.

Rattle. To extort money from; to rob freight cars.

Rattler. 1. (South) The chain by which chain-gang convicts are fettered. 2. A freight or passenger train; a trolley or other surface car.

Raus, n. 1. The use of rough jostling amounting to force in pocket-picking operation where money or valuables are not readily accessible. "The mark (victim) was loaded (had a large sum of money), but he had a boodle-belt (money-belt). What a raus we had to give him!" 2. The act of prodding one into action; the application of pressure or force, especially in removing a victim from the scene of a swindling operation, as at a carnival.

Raus, v. To give one a **raus.**

Raust. See **Raus.**

Reach. 1. To bring influence to bear upon any official by bribery or other means in order to obtain favors or concessions not provided for by law. "We can reach the wig (judge) with five C's (five hundred dollars), but he'll only do business (accept bribes) with Big Kelly." 2. To put one's hands up at the order of armed robbers or police. "Make them all reach and belly (face) the wall." 3. To reach for a pistol or other weapon. "The bull (detective) reached, and Buzz banged (shot) him in the conk (head)."

Read. To note and interpret markings on the backs of crooked playing cards; to use any illegitimate device for reading an opponent's cards.

Read a shirt. To examine a shirt for vermin.

Reader. 1. A printed "wanted" circular, bearing the picture, fingerprints and record of the fugitive. 2. A warrant for one's arrest. "Better blow (take to your heels), Blue. They got a reader on you, mugg (photograph) and all."

Readers. Cleverly marked playing cards, often requiring the use of a colored eye-shade or tinted eyeglasses to be read. "If the mark (victim) chills (becomes suspicious) on the readers, spring (bring out) the shoe (crooked dealing device) on him."

Reader with a tail. A "wanted" circular offering a reward for information leading to the arrest and conviction of the fugitive.

Ready. Ripe for robbery. "I just put the squint (caught a glimpse) on the boodle (money). That mark (victim) is loaded (has plenty of cash) and ready."

Ready up. To prepare, as a victim, for a swindle operation, a robbery, or pocket-picking. "Spring (go to it), Nate, this square (workingman) is all readied up for the take (to be robbed)."

Rebel. (P) A Southerner.

Receive. 1. To buy or deal in stolen goods. 2. (P) To serve as a passive oral copulator or pederast.

Reception. (Sing Sing and many other prisons) Euphemism for the unpleasant quarantine procedure to which newly arrived prisoners are subjected. "Two weeks in reception and a root in the keister (kick on the rump) would cure half of them punks (young rowdies)."

Reck. (P) An indoor recreation room. "Skip the reck today. There's a come-off (trouble) due, a chivving-match (knife fight)."

Record. A police record of one's previous arrests and convictions. "The wheelman (driver of the car) on the trick (in the robbery) had no record, so he took the fall (full guilt) and turned us out (exonerated us)." [Note: The existence of a criminal record prejudices the court's sentence and compels operation of increased penalty laws for second, third, or fourth offenses].

Red, n. A penny. "That crumb ain't got a red, and he's puttin' on a million-dollar front (appearance)."

Red, a. (Carnival) Lucrative. "Nice tip (crowd). If it ain't red today, we might as well pack in (close up)."

Red-hot, n. (South, scattered) 1. A thief; crook. "That redhot's gonna wind up in lag (prison) if he don't take a powder (go away from here)." 2. A gunman or professional killer. 3. A fugitive from justice.

Red hot, a. 1. Recently stolen; hence, easily identifiable. 2. Actively sought by police. 3. Teeming with police activity. 4. (P) Characterized by a tense atmosphere, as a result of an escape, riot, general search, or similar serious occurrence. 5. In a state of intense readiness or preparation, as for the commission of a crime; working with abnormal skill or intensity.

Red lead. (P) Jelly served in prison mess-hall.

Red one. (Carnival) Any thing, place, or person that offers especially lucrative opportunities for carnival swindle, as a game, town, or particular crowd of patrons. "Man, this tank (little town) is a red one! Start weeding (choosing the victims)."

Reef. 1. To swindle; rob. 2. (Among pickpockets) To withdraw a victim's wallet by manipulating the pocket lining from inside the coat or trousers. "The best pocket-touch (pocket-picking) I ever made, the mark (victim) was on the nod (half asleep). Didn't have to stick him up (to be jostled or pinned into position). I reefed, weeded (took what I wanted), and stuck the leather (wallet) back without a rumble (his knowing anything about it)."

Reefer. A cigarette containing marijuana.

Reformed. (P; seldom used in any other sense but this) Freed of addiction to vicious practices of passive degeneracy.

Reg'lar feller. A newborn male infant, as distinguished from a **split-tail.**

Rehash, n. A repetition of a crime committed upon the same victim. "That square-john (innocent workingman) ain't hip (does not know) how he was beat (robbed). Hit him with a rehash later."

Rehash, v. To victimize a second time, as by repeated extortion, robbery, or swindle. "I got a steer (tip) on them dudes (fellows) moving the laundry (smuggling alien Chinese into the country) again. Get the tins (counterfeit badges) out, and we'll rehash 'em on the shake (extortion)."

Reindeer dust. Powdered morphine or heroin.

Relief, one's. (Elmira, N.Y., Reformatory, and scattered penal institutions) The inmate whose number is one thousand and higher than one's own. [Note: An Elmira inmate's sentence usually approaches completion at the time of his relief's arrival. It had become traditional at that reformatory for one to present his relief with some small gift, such as a package of cigarettes or a bar of candy. The custom is gradually passing into obsolescence. See synonym: **Fish, one's.**]

Reload. To sell a second lot of worthless stock to a previously victimized person, especially by accepting the first lot as part payment for the second at a "liberal" exchange value.

Rep (Abbr. of reputation). A reputation for being dangerous to trifle with.

[Note: A rep is a distinct underworld asset.] "Get some dude (fellow) with a rep to front for you (whose name you can use for purposes of intimidation) and shylocking (the loan-shark racket) is candy (easy and lucrative)."

Repeater. 1. A specialist in the automobile accident claims racket who has posed as the "victim" of many accidents and has several suits pending concurrently in the courts. 2. (P) A recidivist. 3. A second criminal act committed against the same victim. "Think we oughta play a repeater heisting (try second armed robbery) in that croaker's joint (doctor's office), or give him a shake (extort money from him) for pushing junk (selling drugs to addicts)."

Re-run. Denatured alcohol made potable by redistillation.

Rib, n. The preparatory persuasion in a confidence swindle. 2. (P) Coarse jocularity at another's expense. "Nix on the rib (stop joking). I'm all bugged up (in a bad mood) today."

Rib, v. 1. To prepare victim in a confidence swindle by smooth and persuasive talk. "The mark (victim) is all ribbed up. Spring the duke (take his money)." 2. (P) To subject to coarse jocularity; to poke fun at; to tease.

Rib-joint. A brothel.

Richard (Variant of **Dick**). A detective or plainclothesman; (loosely) any policeman.

Ride, n. 1. The procedure by which a victim is taken by automobile to an isolated spot and murdered. 2. Conviction and imprisonment on trumped-up charges, or without regard to due process of law, of anyone guilty or innocent. 3. (P) Summary transfer, usually from a liberal to a harsh prison.

Ride, v. 1. To abuse; persecute; agitate. "That bull (policeman) is looking to (looking for a chance to) give me a bit (to send me to prison). The crumb (unscrupulous fellow) has been riding me ever since I beat (was acquitted of) that heist rap (hold-up charge.)" 2. To give one a ride (2 and 3).

Ride old smoky. (Scattered; South) To die by electrocution in capital punishment.

Ride on the green. (Chiefly through far West) To give railroad brakeman a dollar or two in lieu of an I.W.W. card as authority for stealing a train ride.

Ride on the red. (Chiefly through far West) To exhibit an I.W.W. card to brakeman as authority for stealing a train ride.

Ride the deck. 1. (Central and Western prisons) To practice active pederasty. 2. (Hobo) To ride the top of a freight train or passenger train.

Ride the earie, or **Erie.** To eavesdrop. "Round (turn around) slow and get a load of (take a look at) that mugg ridin' the earie."

Ride the rods. (Hobo) To ride the understructure of freight trains; to ride railroads illegally.

Ridge. (Obsolete) Any gold coin.

Riding a wave. Under the influence of drugs. "Don't rumble (go near) Lou when he's ridin' a wave. The jerk (stupid fellow) is liable to bang (shoot) you just for a kick (thrill)."

Riffle, n. The act of **reefing.**

Riffle, v. 1. See **Reef.** 2. To rifle.

Rig. An automobile.

Rig, or **Rigout.** An outfit of clothes.

Rigged joint. A crooked gambling house or carnival concession, especially the gambling wheels.

Right. Conforming to underworld ethics and standards; [applied to non-members of the underworld] willing to cooperate with the underworld; ready to trade moral scruples for relatively safe cash; capable of being trusted by the underworld. "High Hat runs a right joint. All hoods (crooks) hit (go) there.

No dicks (policemen), no finks (informers.)"

Right buck. (P) A prison chaplain (esp. Roman Catholic) whose sympathies with the convicts exceed his sense of obligation to the authorities.

Right copper. A policeman who will accept bribes or offer limited cooperation to the underworld; a policeman who shuns use of **third degree** methods and is scrupulously fair in his relations with criminals. (See **Square Bull.**)

Right croaker. A physician who does business with the underworld, treating wounds without reporting to police.

Right dice. Dice so constructed that they are capable of being controlled, when thrown, to turn up a succession of winning points.

Right fall. An arrest on a charge which is certain to be sustained in court; an arrest for a crime of which one is guilty. "Yeah, Cap, it's a right fall. No use goin' to bat (trial). I'm gonna cop out (plead guilty to a lesser offense.)"

Right ghee, or **guy.** 1. A loyal member of the underworld. 2. Any non-member of the underworld who transacts business with the underworld and is friendly to its members.

Right joint. Any establishment or prison operated in conformity with the established ethics of the underworld, as a saloon from which police and stool pigeons are excluded.

Right mouthpiece. A lawyer who is an ally of his underworld clients, insensitive of any duty to the overworld.

Righto. (P) A loyal member of the underworld.

Right people. A person or persons loyal to the underworld; any non-member of the underworld who is friendly to it. "That dude (fellow) is right people. He pushed queer (passed counterfeit money) years ago and wrapped up

(quit) when he got his lump (became sufficiently rich)."

Right polly. A politician who may be relied upon to help underworld members, often without monetary compensation.

Right rap. 1. A criminal charge, an arrest, a conviction, a sentence, or a commitment to prison which is legally and morally justified. 2. Any justified accusation. "You have no out (way out), crumb (contemptible dog). That's a right rap. You were knocked off (seized) peddlin' [stolen prison stores to fellow convicts]."

Right screw. (P) A prison guard who handles smuggled letters, contraband, etc., often for bribes, sometimes gratis.

Ring. An occasional variant of **ring in.**

Ringer. 1. An obvious imitation, as a paste imitation to be substituted for a real diamond. 2. A substitute. 3. A double; one who closely resembles another; hence, one easily mistaken for another. 4. (P) An expert posing as an amateur. "The Hatter'll go down the line for you (will stand by you whatever happens), and he's a ringer with a chiv (knife-wielder)."

Ring ghee. (Elmira, N.Y., Reformatory and Eastern prisons) An inmate holding a desirable work-assignment; a trusty; any inmate favored by the authorities. [Note: The term ring ghee originated several decades ago when State's prison inmates, transferred to Elmira Reformatory, were permitted special privileges to compensate for the more rigorous reformatory routine. They were granted the use of a separate recreation yard during periods when other inmates were locked in their cells. No sport or breaking of ranks, however, was allowed. In cold weather, these privileged inmates would run around in circles to keep warm. Hence, there developed the ironic term ring ghee. Today, the term has no ironic con-notations.]

Ring in. 1. To make any substitution in a game, without the knowledge of one's opponents, as to substitute crook-ed dice or marked cards; to bring an expert swindler into a game with un-suspecting adversaries; to pass off a master as an amateur; to enter a horse in a race after altering his identification marks in order to fake the odds. **2.** To substitute an outsider for an absent member of a gang; to bring in a speci-alist to execute a difficult assignment; to force [oneself] into a desirable posi-tion in a game or racket. "We got to ring in a good wheelman (chauffeur) on this score (robbery). The town is lousy with (teeming with) squad cars (police squad cars)." **3.** To report by telephone, as a policeman on beat; to punch a clock, as a watchman.

Ring job. (Scattered Eastern pris-ons, especially N.Y. and N.J.) Any pref-erential work assignment in prison, usually entailing special privileges, ex-tra food rations, and a small additional compensation.

Ringman. A small-time confidence man who pretends to find a flashy but cheap ring before the victim, then sells him his share.

Ringtail. A passive homosexual.

Ring the bell. To succeed handsome-ly. "We sure rang the bell on that touch (robbery). All cabbage (cash) and no fence's cut (no share to give to a buyer of stolen goods)."

Rip. (P) Luck; lucky fellow. ("What a rip!"—"What a lucky fellow!")

Rip, the. A technique of safe burglary by mechanical force without the use of explosive or oxy-acetylene equipment. [Note: The combination dial may be knocked off to furnish a hole for the in-sertion of the ripping **can-opener**; or, a rivet head may be driven away from the steel sheeting to furnish the start-ing point. Often a slip pasted on the back of a safe may reveal recent re-pairs, betraying the weak point. The **can-opener** is inserted, a length of pipe slipped over it to give increased lever-age, and the other plating is ripped loose. Hammers and chisels remove the fire-brick and clay inside. If a **duster** or inner door is encountered, the same ripping process is used, provided the locking mechanism is not readily ac-cessible. Usually, ripping the other plate enables burglars to get at the tumbler box, line up the tumblers on their rod, smash them with a hammer blow, and open the door. A crew often works over the weekend, having two or three days to work on difficult safes and vaults.] Compare **Punch.**

Rip, v. To burglarize a safe by the **rip** technique.

Rip-job. A safe burglary committed by means of the method known as the **rip.**

Ripper. A safe-burglar who operates by using the **rip** method.

Roach. 1. (P) A prison guard. **2.** A cigarette containing marijuana. "What kind of gage (marijuana) was in that roach? Kicked like a mule." **3.** (South; chiefly among Negroes) A policeman.

Road agent. A tramp; any seasoned veteran among hobos.

Road kid. (Hobo) A youthful transi-ent bum, occasionally passively pede-rastic.

Roar, n. Any obstreperous protest; testimony against an accomplice. "What a roar that muzzler (traitor) put up when I got an s.s. (suspended sentence) and he got hit with a bit (sentenced to prison)."

Roar, v. To protest loudly; to com-plain; to testify against accomplices or to furnish authorities with information leading to their arrest. "That sucker (victim) loved it when I put the bend on (turned down the corner of the key card). But when I hiped him (induced to increase his bets) and took (swindled) him for two yards (two hundred dollars), he roared murder."

Rocks. 1. (P) Dominoes, used in lieu of playing cards in institutions where the latter are contraband. 2. Diamonds, or diamond-studded jewelry. 3. (Rare) Money.

Rod. 1. A revolver. "Don't get glommed (caught) with a rod in that tank (town). They'll slap you in the can (jail) and throw the key away." 2. An armed thief; a gunman. "We need two good rods to cover this joint. The owner is heeled (armed), and he is a tough giver-up (won't give up his money without a struggle)."

Rodded up. Having one or more revolvers concealed on one's person. "The combo (rival gang) got (shot and killed) Slim. Get rodded up for the fireworks (shooting that is bound to follow)."

Rodman. One who carries a gun.

Rods. (Chiefly hobo) The undercarriage of railroad cars.

Roll, n. A sum of money; all of one's money.

Roll, v. To rob a drunken victim or one previously rendered unconscious by any means.

Roll a pill. 1. To hand-roll a cigarette. 2. To pick opium or **yen hok** and roll it over lightly until ready for smoking; to smoke opium.

Roll around! Expression equivalent in meaning to "Time, please pass quickly!"

Rolled over the barrel. (Southern prisons) Subjected to the brutal **barrel** punishment in which the victim is placed over a barrel and lashed. "Some Poger (pederast) got rolled over the barrel for going over the hill (attempting to escape)."

Roller. 1. (South; loan word from

Negro jargon) A policeman. 2. The station house or local jail.

Rollin's. (P) The ingredients of hand-rolled cigarettes.

Roll out the barrel. (Southern prisons) To prepare for the **barrel** punishment.

Roll-over. (P) The last night's sleep of a prison term. "This three days and a roll-over is worse than the whole bit (prison term). I'm blowing my roof (going crazy)."

Root. To kick. "If that broad (girl) puts the horns on me (cuckolds) me, I'll root her out on her biscuit (rump)."

Root in the keister. A kick in the pants. "If that little punk (squirt) gets flip (tries any clever tricks) root him in the keister."

Rope. 1. Capital punishment by hanging; (loosely) capital punishment by any means. 2. A necklace. 3. Suicide by hanging.

Rope in. To persuade [one] to participate in any disadvantageous enterprise; to involve [one] against his will; to ensnare.

Ropes. (Those States where hanging is the prescribed form of capital punishment) A substituted term for Mister, as Ropes Jones, Ropes Smith, etc., applied to district attorneys with a reputation for having sent many defendants to the gallows, and to any lawyer, many of whose clients have died on the gallows.

Rosary, the. (P) A life sentence in prison. "That old jig (Negro) in B-block, doin' the rosary, took a rope (hanged himself) last night."

Roscoe. Pistol or revolver. "Any grift (form of thievery) you gotta pack (carry) a roscoe on is pea soup (isn't worth while)."

Rot in stir. To grow decrepit and simple from a very lengthy prison term.

Rough. 1. (To look **rough**) Pale;

sickly; poorly garbed; drunken. 2. (To go **rough**) Bad; fraught with danger; unsuited to criminal aims; unsatisfactory. "Things are goin' real rough since I hit the pavement (left prison). I ain't made a score (robbery) big enough to get me off the nut yet (to cover the costs of my criminal operations)."

Roumanian box. See **Rumanian box.**

Round. To turn around; to turn and rapidly retrace one's steps. "Don't round. Cop a mope (walk away) slow. A hip (alert-looking) ghee (fellow) is gunning the play (watching everything we're doing)."

Rounder. An unimportant underworld character who has a multitude of interests, often in the employ of several different gangs.

Roundeye. 1. (P) General term for passive pederasts; any passive degenerate. 2. (P) The anus.

Round-heeled. To be easily victimized or used.

Round-heels. Anyone easily victimized; a promiscuous woman or epicene; (obsolescent) a policeman or detective.

Route the grift. To arrange a schedule of operations in pocket-picking or any of the craftier forms of crime. [Note: A "route" usually includes scheduled conventions, rallies, fairs, rodeos, and similar events.]

Rowdy-dowdy. Rough-and-tumble. "We couldn't put the hoosier's back up (pin the victim while his pocket was being picked) so we gave him the old rowdy-dowdy hijack (rough jostling)."

Rubadub. Rubbing alcohol.

Rubadub bum. One addicted to drinking **rubadub.**

Rubber. 1. Forged checks or other instruments. "Cop (steal) some damperpads (checkbooks) and we'll bounce (issue) a little rubber." 2. (P) Steak. 3. A latex contraceptive. 4. (Rare) A stolen car.

Rubber bum. A hobo or panhandler who travels in an old automobile and is regarded as something of a snob in consequence.

Rubber-hustler. A condom peddler.

Rubdown. 1. A search of one's person in which the hands are passed over the body and limbs outside the clothing. [Note: In the order of thoroughness, body searches are termed: 1. **strip frisk;** 2. **frisk;** 3. **rubdown;** 4. **fan;** 5. **once-over.**] 2. (Rare) A beating administered in the course of an illegal **third degree.** "I'm lamming (fleeing the area) till the heat is off (police activity lessens). Them pick-ups (arrests on suspicion) and rubdowns ain't doin' me no good."

Rub out. (Prohibition era; obsolete) To slay, especially in gangland rivalry.

Ruffy. (Carnival) Any roughneck or common laborer employed at a carnival. "Them shills (aides) can't scuffle (bring customers to be swindled). What are they, ruffies out of gillies (very poor carnivals)?"

Rumanian box. The swindle by which a victim is induced to invest in a machine supposed to alter currency denominations; the machine itself. [Note: The prospective victim is persuaded to insert a dollar bill into a complicated device which then issues a previously concealed five-dollar bill in its stead. The five-dollar bill is then "transformed" similarly into a ten-dollar bill. The eager fool is then told that the device works only a limited number of times in succession. Swindlers and victim agree to pool all their available money and a date is set for the "transformation" of the new currency. At the prescribed time, a few large bills are "run off," during which a short celebration party is proposed. The money-stuffed machine is locked carefully in the apartment, the keys being entrusted to the victim. A confederate enters soon after with the aid of duplicate keys. The victim is easily disposed of during the celebration.]

Rumble, n. 1. Any interruption in the course of criminal activity, as the result of police intervention, or by the presence of bystanders, the sounding of an alarm, etc. "We got out of the joint after the score (robbery) clean (undetected), but I got a rumble from the prowl-car (patrol car) dicks (detectives)." 2. Press and radio reports of a crime; any general alarm raised against criminals or criminal activity. "A tough beef (clamor) on the trick (about the robbery), Joe. The rumble's got the heat (intensified police activity)." 3. Recognition, especially of a suspect by a complainant viewing a police line-up; a greeting. 4. Notice taken of a place, thing, or event. 5. A thought; consideration. 6. A general complaint or report to authorities.

Rumble, v. 1. To interrupt the execution of a crime by mere discovery, by raising an outcry, or by physical violence. "Some stiff (loiterer) rumbled the come-off (criminal act) and raised a beef (an alarm)." 2. To awaken to the fact that one is being victimized. "Duke was reefing the sucker (picking the victim's pocket) when he rumbled. What a tumul (uproar)! It was murder (awful)." 3. To publicize or broadcast as a means of spurring police activity. 4. To show signs of recognition, as a victim about to identify a criminal in the police line-up or court. "The rapper (complainant) rumbled, but I knew he wouldn't finger (formally identify) me 'cause he had the chill (a scare) put on him." 5. To view or note with suspicion. 6. To recognize; to greet or hail; to have relations with; to pay attention to. 7. To complain to police; to instigate police activity against the underworld. 8. To engage a policeman or a bystander in conversation during the commission of a crime by one's accomplice.

Rum-dumb. A chronic drunkard; any stupid or inept person.

Rum-row. (Prohibition era term) The line of vessels lying outside the twelve-mile limit purveying alcoholic liquors for the illicit trade.

Rum-runner. (Prohibition era term) A fast boat engaged in smuggling alcoholic liquors from **rum-row** into the United States; one engaged in smuggling alcoholic liquors across the border.

Run. A period of criminal activity before arrest and conviction or between prison terms. "He had a nice three-year run before he took his fall (was arrested and sentenced)."

Rundown. Recapitulation; brief account of what happened.

Run-in, n. 1. A disagreement or dispute. 2. An arrest. 3. (P) A report or lock-in for rule violation.

Run in, v. To arrest. 2. (P) To report or lock up for rule violation.

Runner. A policy-numbers agent or collector. [Note: Runners often build up a large personal following of players, receive as much as twenty-five per cent of the money collected from bettors and an additional ten per cent as a bonus to be deducted from the bettor's winnings.]

Run-out powder. Flight; escape; a hasty departure.

Run rum. (Prohibition era term) To engage in liquor smuggling.

Run the roads down. To drive swiftly along roads adjacent to the scene of a prospective crime to plan methods for a getaway.

Run the tier. (Leavenworth Federal Prison) To move about cell-block galleries in search of a passive pederast.

Rustler. A beggar or thief, skillful in securing small sums quickly; one who is quick to find essential people as soon as their presence is needed.

Rustle out. To dispatch hurriedly, especially out of a home or rendezvous, for criminal purposes. "Rustle the mob (gang) out and make a meet (have them meet) here in an hour heeled (armed)."

Rustle up. To raise money; to locate influential friends in an emergency; to round up. "Them pollies (politicians) at the club can spring me (secure my release) before the bulls (police) dig up on me (dig up my criminal record). Get out and rustle them up quick."

S

Sack. 1. To murder by tying a drugged or beaten victim in a gunny-sack, his body cramped in jackknife fashion, a noose drawn loosely about his neck, one end tied to his ankles. As he regains consciousness, his effort to straighten out draws the noose tight enough to make strangulation inevitable. 2. To prearrange and predetermine. "The jury is spiked (bribed) and the rapper (complainant) is squared (appeased). A turn-out is all sacked for you, Guzzler." 3. To murder and place body in a sack as a means of disposal.

Sack, in the. Fixed; prearranged; bribed; murdered; disposed of.

Sad. 1. Inept; clumsy; stupid. "Man, he's a sad grifter (thief)." 2. Bad; crude; bungled. "They did a sad job on that jug-heist (bank robbery) in Miami."

Saddle ("In the saddle"). A position of control, especially behind a gun.

Sail, on the. On the move; engaged in criminal action.

Sailor. One who spends money freely, hence, an easy prey of swindlers or other criminals.

One's sails are flapping. One is eavesdropping. (More common: riding the earie, to be). "Dummy up (stop talking); that ghee's (fellow's) sails are flapping wide."

Salt. To set as bait; to place ores or minerals in a mine, oil in a well, or to do any similar act, in order to deceive a prospective buyer or investor; to swindle by baiting, as by placing genuine currency in a "money-printing" machine.

Salt creek, up. In a precarious or hopeless position; checkmated; stalemated; in prison; awaiting execution; facing inevitable disaster.

Salted. (Rare) 1. In prison for a long time. 2. (P) Under long imprisonment in an isolation cell.

San Bardoo. San Bernardino, Calif.

Sand. (P) Sugar.

Sandwich. To put in the middle.

Sap, n. 1. A blackjack; a light bludgeon easily wielded. "The rapper (complainant) got his cruller (head) beat in with saps. Next time he won't be so anxious to put the finger on (testify against) people." 2. A victim of thieves.

Sap, v. To beat with a sap. "The bulls (detectives) nearly sapped Pat's brains out, but the kid stood up (refused to turn informer)."

Sapadilla. A fool.

Saperoo. A very stupid person, especially one unable to protect himself from shrewd criminals.

Sap-stick. A club or bludgeon. "The big ghee (big shot) down at the club wants some work done with sap-sticks. A strike in a joint he's got a piece of (has financial interest in)."

Sap up. See Sap, v.

Satch. Narcotic sent in a letter by saturating paper, or by placing a tiny piece of saturated paper under stamp; narcotic saturated in shirts, or underwear. (Hence the prison custom of laundering new clothing before giving it to inmate.)

Sausage. (P.; mildly contemptuous) A good-natured fool; a willing but inept fellow. "That sausage is always getting mopery collars (being reported for petty rule violation). Who made the pinch (report)? Maybe we can square it (have it recalled)."

Savage. Any newly appointed police officer overeager to make initial arrest.

Save one for oneself. To shoot it out with police, keeping one bullet for suicide in preference to arrest. "One good touch (lucrative crime) and I wrap up (stop stealing). I can't stand a fall (another arrest); so I'm saving one for myself."

Saw. (Abbrev.) See **Sawbuck.**

Sawbuck. 1. Ten dollars. 2. (P) Ten years. "Snakes got the book (sentenced to maximum term). Ain't no way to hit the sidewalk (to get out of prison) in less than a sawbuck, 'cept in a box (coffin)."

Sawed-off. A shotgun with a sawed-off barrel, deadly at close range.

Sawski. See **Sawbuck.**

Scalp. (P) To shave the head, especially at the time of the convict's first arrival at prison. [Note: In New York and various other States **scalping** is no longer prescribed by prison rule. So many convicts, however, desire their heads to be shaven that **scalping** is in some states forbidden except on physician's order.]

Scat. Whiskey, especially of the cheapest grade. "You better wrap up (stop) guzzlin' (drinking) that scat. That puts more hustlers (thieves) in stir (prison) than the dicks (detectives)."

Scatter. A rendezvous for thieves, especially a place where drinks are sold. "The mob (gang) is over at the scatter cutting up touches (exchanging tales of criminal accomplishment). C'mon (let's go there)."

Scenery bum. A tramp who wants to ride the top of freight cars to view the scenery, hence, an object of derision.

Schmear, n. 1. A bribe. 2. Mollifying talk or flattery. "Give the rat (informer) the schmear till we can cop a heel on him (beat him up)."

Schmear, v. To bribe. "Schmear. He's a businessman (he'll do business with crooks)." 2. To flatter; mollify. "Schmear the screw (guard). Maybe we can get him to pull off (withdraw) Harry's pinch (report against Harry)."

Schmeck. (Yiddish - American) Narcotics, especially powdered drugs in the form of snuff.

Schmeck, on the. Under the influence of, or addicted to the use of, narcotics.

Schmecker. (Yiddish-American) User of narcotics, especially a snuffer of powdered drugs.

Schnozzo. A long-nosed person; the nose.

Schoolmate. An ex-convict with whom one previously served a prison sentence.

Schweiner. (N.Y. State prisons and lower West Side Manhattan) The Sing-Sing death-house; the electric chair. "If the schweiner rap (murder charge) stuck (was sustained), I was a dead pigeon (sure to be electrocuted); so I copped out (pleaded guilty) on a phony (to a false charge as a compromise with the District Attorney)."

Schweinet. See **Play the schweinet.**

Scissorbill. (Near West, mid-West, and Central U.S.) 1. Any workingman. 2. A victim or a potential victim of thieves.

Sconce. The head. ["To kick one's sconce in"—to beat one unmercifully.]

Score, n. 1. A profitable crime. "There's too many ends (shares) comin' out of our scores. We're hustlin' (stealing) for the shysters (lawyers) and the swaggies (receivers of stolen goods)." 2. (P) Anything stolen from prison stores; gambling winnings; a gift from home; any fortunate event. 3. Anything unexpected or unearned; anything secured by skill or craftiness; the act of obtaining by cleverness or craft. 4. A criminal action or operation, as a robbery, burglary, etc. 5.(P)(Loose extension) Anything borrowed or begged; the act of borrowing. "This is my case (last) bag of dukes (tobacco). Gotta make a score for some."

Score, v. To make a **score.**

Score, the. 1. The general scheme of things in the underworld as known only to the initiate. "That stiff (fool) doesn't know what the score is. Ditch (get rid of) him." 2. The plans or details of a given crime or action. "You better hip me up (let me in on the facts). I heard Stretch cracking (talking about the crime), but I don't know the score yet."

Scorf. To eat.

Scorf-joint. A restaurant; lunch-counter, or any eating place.

Scoring job. (P) Any work assignment on which a special food ration is issued or through which extras may be stolen. "I gotta promote (manage to get) a scoring job. Ain't no way for me to pull my bit (serve my sentence) unless I'm beating the State for some swag (stealing prison stores)."

Scram. To flee precipitately.

Scratch, n. 1. Money. 2. A check, usually forged. 3. A signature, especially forged. "There's a scratch you can spring (present) in the bank without a rumble (arousing suspicion)." 4. (Loose extension) Any letter, signature, or handwriting; anything written.

Scratch, v. 1. To duplicate a signature in forgery, especially by free-hand skill. 2. (Loose extension) To sign or write anything.

Scratch, the. The forgery racket.

Scratch, on the. Engaged in, or by means of, forgery or issuing spurious checks and other negotiable instruments.

Scratcher. See **Scratch-man.**

Scratch-house bum. 1. A seedy vagrant who sleeps in the cheapest quarters obtainable. 2. A petty thief, dirty and unkempt, unable to live on his paltry gains. 3. (P) A term of profound contempt implying that one is no thief at all but a mere vagabond.

Scratch-man. A skilled free-hand forger. "Gus is one scratch-man that gives you paper (checks) you can lay (pass) without a chill (being afraid)."

Scratch-mob. A band of forgers or passers of bad checks.

Scratch paper. To forge checks. "I'm scratching paper for an old abbey (a thief who impersonates a priest). He pushes them stiffs (passes those checks) like they were legit (genuine)."

Scratch park, the. (Hobo) A rendez-vous of bums near the Old Sailors' Home, New Haven, Conn.; Bryant Park, N.Y. City; any similar gathering place in a large city.

Screasew. Flee! Get away, police! Keep moving!

Screen. 1. A false front on which the likeness of a safe is painted. [Note: Placed before a real safe in line of vision of passers-by, the screen enables safe-crackers to work with maximum privacy.] 2. Any deceptive exterior which conceals an illicit establishment or criminal operations.

Screen-cell. (P) A cell whose door is covered with heavy, closely knit wire-mesh where recalcitrants and mental cases are segregated for observation or punishment. "Toddo was dropped (reported) for giving dust (tobacco) to the ghees (fellows) in the screen-cells."

Screw, n. 1. (P) A prison guard. "Zex (be careful), the screw is on the earie (eavesdropping)." 2. (Carnival). A key.

Screw, v. 1. To abuse; misuse; take unfair advantage of; cheat; inform upon; railroad to prison; sentence to an unduly harsh term; to swindle. "That tongue (lawyer) sure screwed me proper. He took five yards (hundred dollars) and duked me in (induced me) to copping out (plead guilty). He said if I got a day he'd kick back (return) my dough (money). I got twenty boffos (years) and he won't answer my tabs (letters)." 2. To escape; to flee; to move on; (imp.) get out of here! "Screw! The shamus (guard) is on the prowl (looking for someone to report)."

Screw around. 1. See **Screw, v.** 2.

To engage in any crime or racket. "I can't screw around no more. I'm a three-time loser (convicted of three felonies) and the next bit (sentence) is the works (will be for life)." 3. To clown and play the fool, paying scant attention to business. "Don't you screw around when you're hustling (stealing) with me. I ain't askin' for no fall (looking for an arrest)."

Screw-baiter. A convict who enjoys twitting prison keepers who invite familiarity.

Screw-ball. (P) Any mentally defective person, especially one afflicted as a result of prison routine.

Screw-fighter. (P) A convict who delights in the unhealthy practice of assaulting guards.

Screw-hater. (P) A convict obsessed with hatred for prison guards. "Jack's got the rep (reputation) for being a screw-hater and they're hitting him with buckwheats (persecuting him for it)."

Screwing. A raw deal; unwarranted abuse; a swindle; a betrayal. "I got a screwing on my end (share) of that score (profitable crime). The partner musta burned me (held back part of the money)."

Screwing around. See **Screwing.**

Screwman. A burglar who works with skeleton keys, each of which operates a variety of locks of one type.

Screw out. To go out; to leave. "I'm gettin' the leaps (nervous) around this camp (waiting here in this flat). Let's screw out and case (look over) that job (the place we are going to rob)."

Screws' man. (P) A prison administrator who consistently supports his officers in any dispute with the inmates.

Screw town. To leave town, especially as a fugitive from justice. "I'm gonna screw town till the rumble on crime (reform campaign) stops in the snitch-sheets (newspapers)."

Screw-up, n. A mix-up; any disruption of plans as the result of a blunder, treachery, or ill luck. "The screw-up came when Chesty's broad (girl) took a powder (ran away) with fall dough (money set aside for lawyer's fees and possible bribery)."

Screw up, v. 1. To bungle. 2. To place in jeopardy by treachery, cowardice, or negligence; to betray; to ruin. "One of them two-for-one shysters (lawyers who betray two poor clients in order to save one with money) screwed me up. He put me in the sack (I was sentenced to prison) when I should of hit the sidewalk (have been acquitted)."

Screw with the works. To flee with all of the loot, cheating accomplices of their share.

Screwy. Crazy; insane; eccentric; garbled and inconsistent; incoherent; queer. "What a screwy joint! The doors and windows are bugged (have burglar alarms) and the walls are like paper. Oughta be soft for gopher work (easy for a tunneling gang to get inside)."

Screwy bit. (P) Any irregular or unusual prison sentence.

Script. (Chiefly West and far West) Forged checks.

Script-writer. (Chiefly West and far West) A forger, especially of checks.

Scrub, n. (Middle Atlantic area) A dolt; an inept fellow. "Get under the bed (keep quiet), scrub, and bag your head (stop talking)."

Scrub, v. To rob of everything, overlooking nothing of slightest value. [More commonly: **clean.**]

Scuffle, n. The act of using drastic and crude methods to rob one's victims, using much energy for little gain.

Scuffle, v. To use the **scuffle.**

Scuffle, on the. Engaged in, or by means of, the **scuffle.**

Sea-food. (Pacific Coast) Degenerates' term for sailors.

Seal, the. Poker, or other, hands

dealt to a victim in a card game on which he wants to bet to the hilt. The hand is sealed in an envelope by swindlers and given to one of the hoods (thieves) to hold while associates of the victim wire for money to support heavy bets. Ultimately the switch gives one of the crooks an unbeatable hand.

Seal-buster. A burglar who robs freight cars after breaking the door seals.

Seam-shot. A crude safe-cracking method by which explosive is introduced through a crack between safe doors.

Seam-squirrel. (P) Any vermin that infests clothing or bedding.

Sechs. See **Zex.**

Second baseman. Same as **Baseman.**

Second-count. The short-change artist's trick of counting change into victim's hand while switching small coins for large ones.

Second-deal. To deal the second card from the top of a stacked pack of playing cards.

Second-story worker. Burglar who works while family is at dinner downstairs in private dwelling.

See. To pay a bribe, or obligation, or tribute, especially under coercion; (loosely) to make any payment. "See me with a fin (five dollars)."

Sell-out, n. 1. A bargain consummated with authorities by which one gives information or testimony against one's accomplices in exchange for personal immunity or leniency. 2. Failure by counsel to discharge fully his duty toward a client. 3. Any unscrupulous deal by which one injures or prejudices another's interests for personal gain.

Sell out, v. 1. To betray; to give police information, or to testify against accomplices in exchange for leniency or immunity. "We can't go to bat (trial), Bing; the fence (receiver of stolen goods) is selling out." 2. To fail, as a lawyer, to defend one's client

properly, yet fulfilling the bare requirements of the law.

Send-in. 1. A crime carried out on the advice of a **tipster.** "That ghee's (fellow's) send-ins are always stiffs (no good), and I get a chill (I'm afraid of them). Count me out." 2. Any person or place, as the object of a crime suggested by a **tipster.**

Send one a buck. (P) To send money to one in prison, providing him with a steady, though small, income, sufficient for purchase of tobacco, toilet articles, etc.

Send-up, n. A sentence to prison.

Send up, v. To have any part in sending one to prison; to inform upon, or testify against.

Serve time. To spend a term in any penal institution.

Set. Established security in the underworld or in prison. "Mike is packing heat (a gun-carrying guard) for the union. As soon as he hit the pavement (was released from prison) he got an in (introduction) there. Yeah, he's set."

Set-down. (Hobo) A hot meal to which a hobo is invited.

Set down. To give one a set-down.

Set-in, n. A grant of immunity to engage in petty crime, such as picking pockets, in a given district, obtained by bribery or in exchange for valuable police information. "C'mon, I'll ring you in (include you) on a set-in we got on the spud (confidence swindle). Everything is gimmicked up (prearranged)."

Set in, v. To provide with a **set-in.**

Set in, a. To have a **set-in.**

Set[one]up. 1. To maneuver a victim into a position in which his pockets may easily be picked. 2. To expose to danger or death. 3. To infect with a venereal disease.

Settle. To sentence to prison. "Bing was settled for the book (life imprisonment) as a four-time loser (for a fourth felony conviction)."

Settled right. Committed to prison on a charge of which one is guilty, all procedure having been in accordance with due process of law.

Settled wrong. Committed to prison for a crime of which one is innocent; convicted and imprisoned in violation of due process of law. "The wig (judge) and the D.A. know this ghee (fellow) is settled wrong. His kid brother pulled (executed) the heist (robbery), but the rappers (complainants) can't make (identify) him, so they can't do nothin'. Screwy (crazy) laws, huh?"

Settle for. To accept as compromise; to conclude as a bargain.

Set-up, n. 1. The detailed plan of a projected crime. 2. Any person or place that can be easily robbed. 3. A frame-up; any false information designed to lure a criminal into a police trap. 4. (Jails and workhouses) A one-day sentence. 5. A crime, especially robbery or arson, planned in collusion with the supposed victim to defraud insurance underwriters.

Set up, v. 1. To survey the site of a projected crime in order to lay plans for action. 2. To prepare a place for robbery by any inside work, as by unlocking of doors or the disconnecting of burglar alarms; to prepare a victim for robbery. 3. To frame; to lure into a trap; to give false information as a means of entrapping a criminal. 4. (Jails and lower courts) To sentence to a one-day term. 5. To arrange a collusive crime to defraud insurance underwriters. 6. To infect with a venereal disease.

Seven-up. (Rural areas) A general store.

Shack, n. 1. Any pretentious dwelling, considered for burglarizing by **dinner burglars.** 2. The **dinner burglar's** profession. 3. (Hobos and thieves) A railroad brakeman.

Shack, v. To operate as a **dinner burglar.** "Let's shack the Park Drive shanties (homes) for a few touches (robberies)."

Shacker. A burglar who robs the homes of the well-to-do during dinner hours.

Shacking touch. A house burglary during dinner hours; the loot taken in such a robbery. "A couple o' good shacking touches and I'm goin' legit (stop stealing). Get a spot (business), run a small book (book bets), mebbe push some junk (sell narcotics)."

Shack, on the. Engaged in burglarizing homes or apartments during the dinner hour when occupants are engaged in eating and confined to one room of the dwelling.

Shade. 1. A pickpocket's aide who, by moving his body cleverly, covers the activities of his accomplice. 2. (Scattered; Central and Western U.S.) A place of concealment from police. "The C.O. dicks (Central Office detectives) are on my pratt (following me). I gotta shake (get them off) the tail (my trail) and rabbit (scurry) for the shade."

Shadow. (Among loan sharks) The strong-arm collector who exerts various forms of pressure on delinquent borrowers.

Shady. Of questionable legality; on the shadowline of the underworld.

Shafts. (Obs.) Legs.

Shag. 1. (Obs.) See **Screw,** v. 2. (Rare) To discover in a criminal act; to call police attention to; to identify formally, as a complainant in a criminal proceeding; to follow or pursue.

Shake, n. An act of extortion, especially by threat of arrest or physical harm.

Shake, v. 1. To get rid of, especially a tenacious victim who has been swindled or a persistent pursuer. 2. To practice extortion; to extort from. "Get the tins (counterfeit police badges) and we'll shake some of them pineapples (Italian aliens)."

Shake, the. The extortion racket in general.

Shake, on the. Engaged in, or by means of, any form of **shakedown.**

Shake a joint. To extort money from proprietors of shady establishments by impersonating police and threatening arrest. "What a workout (beating) we got when we tried to shake a joint uptown on a white tin (with a uniformed policeman's badge). The cop (officer) who got beat (robbed) for the button (badge) was the owner's brother. Murder (awful)!"

Shake a parole. To rid oneself of parole surveillance by strict adherence until the expiration of the parole term; to escape parole surveillance by bribery, flight, or other irregular means.

Shake a tail. To elude pursuit. "That boiler (car) is still on our pratt (close behind us), Pewee. Looks like a prowlcar (police car), and we're red hot (badly wanted by the police). C'mon, shake that tail or it's curtains (go to prison on a long sentence)."

Shake-down, n. 1. Extortion; blackmail. 2. (P) A search of prison shops and cells for stolen stores, weapons, and contraband. "Dump (get rid of) that batch (home brew). I got a hot wire on (news of) a shake-down."

Shake down, v. 1. To extort from; to blackmail. 2. (P) to search prison shops cells, etc., for stolen stores, weapons, and contraband.

Shake-man. A specialist in extorting "protection money" from shady people by threats of violence or of exposure; an extortionist who impersonates a police officer.

Shakester. See **Shake-man.**

Shamus. (Jewish-American) 1. Policeman. 2. (P) Guard; any prison official. "Zex (Watch out)! The shamus

is out to glom (report) somebody."
3. (Rare) A jimmy used by burglars.

Shanty. Any private dwelling place, especially in the argot of the **shackers.**

Shapes. Dice, not true cubes, shaped to decrease crapshooters' chances to win against the establishment. Shapes are placed in and withdrawn from play by employes of the establishment at propitious moments.

Shape up. 1. To appear; to be on hand for action, especially of criminal character. "Shape up at that plant (apartment) tonight. The tipster (informant) got some work (a criminal job) for us." 2. To become manifest; to develop; to materialize. "I ain't gettin' duked in (to be drawn) to no swindle (trouble). Keep that new mick (inmate) away till we see how he shapes up." 3. To be satisfactory, as the method or object of a crime.

Shark. 1. An extremely shrewd or talented person; an expert. 2. A "loan shark" who lends sums at exorbitant weekly interest rates without security. [Note: A week in the loan shark racket means any fractional portion thereof. A loan made Monday and repaid the next day is still subject to weekly interest rates. See **Vigerage.**] 3. A professional card, dice, or pool player, very expert and often a master crook.

Sharp or **Sharper.** 1. A skilful card cheat; a crooked gambler. 2. An expert.

Sharpie. A swindler; a card, dice, or pool expert with a talent for cheating.

Sharpshooter. A crooked gambler.

Sharp stuff. 1. A handsome or trim person; a clever, personable or alert person. 2. A thing of superior quality; any thing or place capable of exciting admiration. 3. Anyone skilled in the ways of the underworld.

Shebang. 1. A saloon, poolroom, or

brothel, as a rendezvous of thieves. [More common: **scatter.**] 2. (Contemptuous) A jail, reformatory, or prison; (rare) a cell.

Shed. A closed car.

Sheepherder's wife. A sheep.

Sheet. (P) A newspaper, especially one used as a bed-sheet where linen is not supplied.

Sheet-passer. (Scattered areas of U.S.) One who issues or passes forged checks.

Sheet-writer. A swindler who solicits signatures to popular causes, usually patriotic, defrauding the signers by short change, demanding mailing costs—and occasionally a subscription fee—for periodicals connected with the cause. [Note: The principal victims of sheet-writers are aliens who are led to believe that the solicitor is a government employe who can facilitate the securing of citizenship papers.]

Sheik. A thief who specializes in victimizing women.

Shelf, hit the. To cease operating criminally; to abandon a criminal career for legitimate pursuits. ["Legitimate pursuits" in underworld terms include bookmaking, shylocking, procuring, etc.]

Shell. A safe or vault with a thin door.

Shellack. 1. To beat severely. "The rapper (witness) beefed (complained) that he was shellacked and clipped (robbed). 2. To ruin; to defeat; to beat, as in a game of chance.

Shell game. A swindle in which the victim is required to locate a pea-like pellet which, after dexterous manipulation, is supposed to be concealed under one of three walnut shells, but which in reality is hidden in the bend of the manipulator's small finger.

Shell-V. An easily robbed steel vault with a thin single-plate steel door.

Shield. (Hobo; Far West) A young hobo who protects and begs for an old veteran associate.

Shifter. (East and near South, except New York and New Jersey) A go-between from thief to buyer of stolen goods.

Shill, n. A carnival swindler's aide who mingles with the crowd, luring victims to be swindled by guile and by ostentatious prearranged winnings; any swindler's accomplice.

Shill, v. To lead on; to serve as aide to pickpockets, auctioneers, etc., luring victims into untenable positions.

Shillaber. See **Shill,** n.

Shiller. (Southern variant) See **Shill,** n.

Shimmy lizard. (Leavenworth Federal Prison) A body louse.

Shine. 1. (Far West, hobo) A plainclothesman who wears his police badge in plain view. 2. A Negro.

Shiner. 1. A flashlight. 2. A black eye.

Shingle. (N.Y. State prisons) 1. A tin sign bearing the inscription "keep locked" hung on the cell door of a convict who has been locked in for a rule violation. [Note: "Detention" shingles indicate that a convict has been confined to a punishment cell.] "That new hack (guard) is a nice fink (rat); he's givin' out shingles for mopery (petty rule violations)." 2. (Loosely) A report; a lock-up for violation of rules. 3. Toast; dry bread.

Ship. (P) To transfer a convict from one prison to another, often as a punishment.

Shipment. (P) A transfer of convicts from one prison to another.

Shit creek, up. In a precarious or hopeless position; checkmated; stalemated; in prison; awaiting execution; facing inevitable disaster.

Shit-heel (Variant, **Shit-heeler**). A contemptible person.

Shiv. See **Chiv**.

Shivving-match. See **Chiv**.

Shlepp, the. The act or profession of stealing packages from automobiles. "They clipped (stole) a slum-peddler's (jewelry salesman's) turkey (satchel) full of ice (diamonds) on the shlepp."

Shlepp, v. To operate the **schlepp**.

Shlepper. A professional thief engaged in the **shlepp**.

Shlub. (Yiddish-American). A dolt; a fool.

Shoe. A card-dealing box devised to prevent false dealing by card-cheats, but which has itself been transformed by swindlers into a means of cheating by the addition of a bottom where extra cards are concealed. [See also **Hog-box**.]

Shoot. (P.; Central and mid-Western States and scattered areas) To make a formal charge against a convict for violation of rules. [See **Shoot with square chalk**.]

Shoot a jug. (Mid-West and near South) To dynamite a bank safe or vault. "Hank took a fall (was arrested) cracking his jaw (after boasting) that he shot a jug in Tucson."

Shoot a snipe. To pick up a partly smoked and discarded cigarette butt.

Shoot one's bazoo (or **kisser**) **off.** [See **Shoot one's yap off**.]

Shoot one's load or **lump.** To expend one's courage and energy to the point of exhaustion. "Schnozzo shot his lump pullin' (serving) that last bit (prison sentence). He's chilled too bad (too much afraid) to get back on the turf (to a life of crime)."

Shoot one's mouth off. See **Shoot one's yap off**.

Shoot one's yap off. To talk indiscreetly or belligerently; to inform authorities. "Why don't you turn yourself in (to the police) and get it over with? You're shooting your yap off to every fink (informer) in town."

Shoot the lemon. (Leavenworth Federal Prison) To sit around telling stories, especially of exploits.

Shoot the pin. To prick the skin with a safety pin prior to dropping drug from eye-dropper into perforation, as a crude substitute for a hypodermic injection among addicts.

Shoot with square chalk. (Central and mid-West scattered prisons) To report for a rule violation.

Shop, the. (Many prisons) Any industrial, maintenance, or personal service unit or office. [Note: Almost every indoor work unit, except such departments as the school or hospital, are called the shop by their respective inmate personnel. The officer in charge is the "shop screw" or the "shop hack."]

Short, n. (Among pickpockets) A crosstown trolley or bus line.

Short, a. (P) Approaching the end of one's prison term. "Three months and a wop (fraction) to hit the pavement (before I go free). I'm short now."

Short-arm bandit. See **Short-arm heister**.

Short-arm heist. A criminal assault; rape. "Don't rumble (have anything to do with) that creep (unprincipled fellow); he's in (serving a sentence) for a short-arm heist."

Short-arm heister. A rapist.

Short-arm inspection. (P) Organic examination for venereal infection.

Shortcake. The shortchange racket or the proceeds of the same.

Short-con. 1. A combination of persuasive lies and deceptive actions as a means of swindling a victim. 2. Any smooth line of persuasive talk with an ulterior motive. "That screw (guard) is givin' me a short con why he had to pinch (report) me. Makin' himself a good feller."

Short-con, the. Any of the less elaborate swindles, as **the spud, the match game, the lemon game, the overissue. the shell game,** etc.

Short-con, on the. Engaged in, or swindling by means of, any of the **short-con** games.

Short dough. 1. An insufficient sum of money as working capital in any illicit enterprise or venture. "He started his policy bank on short dough and the muscle (intimidation)." 2. Money obtained in hastily executed crimes for the purpose of financing a larger planned crime or racket, or in order to meet such immediate expenses as lawyer's fees or necessary political bribery; trivial loot which would ordinarily be spurned by a professional thief but which necessity makes welcome.

Short end. A relatively small share of loot given to participants having less than a full partnership status in a gang.

Short hustler. A pickpocket who works on short-run buses or trolleys.

Shortitis. (P) The nervous anticipation and impatience that affect convicts who have only a few more months, weeks, or days to serve.

Shorts, having the. Out of funds; "broke," or very nearly so.

Shorts, on the. Engaged in, or by means of, pocket-picking on crosstown buses or tram cars, or other familiar "short distance" transportation vehicles.

Short story. A forged check.

Short story writer. (Rare) A forger of checks or other instruments.

Short time. 1. (P) The unexpired portion of a paroled convict's prison sentence which he must serve when re-

turned to prison for violation of parole, or upon subsequent conviction for a new offense. 2. The period of time spent in visiting a prostitute.

Short-timer. (P) A prisoner whose sentence is nearing expiration.

Sho-Sho. A machine gun. [More common: **spray** and **tommy.**]

Shot. 1. A sufficient dose of any narcotic to stimulate an addict. 2. A pickpocket, especially one who can work alone successfully. 3. One whose position or affluence entitles him to underworld respect; a person of importance. "Scootch never scored (successfully stole for) a quetor (quarter) till that nautch-joint (brothel) made him a shot." 4. The quantity of explosive used in safe-blowing or the actual detonation. 5. (P) A report or lock-up for rule violation.

Shot for shot. (P) Tit-for-tat; an immoral relationship between two prison degenerates.

Shot in the arm. A hypodermic injection, literal or figurative.

Shove. To issue or pass, as bad checks or counterfeit money; to sell, as contraband; to peddle, as drugs.

Shove a buck one's way. To favor another by employing him or directing him to employment in any criminal venture from which he will profit.

Shove-down, n. A theft of a portion of loot from one's thieving accomplices.

Shove down, v. To pocket a portion of loot surreptitiously, cheating one's accomplices of their full share. "This ain't all the swag (loot). Whoever's shoving down, better get hip (stop being a fool) before he gets dumped (murdered)."

Shove over. (Rare) To die naturally or at the hands of slayers; to slay.

Shove queer. To pass counterfeit money. "We can shove queer till we get off the nut (clear expenses). Then we'll pack in (quit) because whiskers (Federal Government) gets on your tail (tracks you down) too quick."

Shover. 1. A passer of counterfeit money. 2. (Less common) A passer of worthless checks. 3. (Rare) A peddler of narcotics to addicts.

Shove the note. See **Lay the note.**

Show. To appear; to keep an appointment. "The mouthpiece (lawyer) didn't show so I went to bat (stood trial) with a State lawyer (lawyer appointed by the State). I sure got a gurdy (raw deal). That beef shouldn't o' stuck (I should have been acquitted)."

Show-boat. (Sing Sing Prison) The habitual transfer of inmates to more remote prisons after misconduct at annual inmate Christmas shows for outside audience. [Note: These performances have been discontinued in recent years.]

Show for one's money. A fair chance to win in a gamble where odds are not stacked against the player; a gambler's chance; a square deal.

Show-up. The daily line-up of arrested suspects before police and detectives. [Note: All suspects picked up in metropolitan areas are supposed to be presented for possible identification at such "line-ups."]

Shrubbery. (P) Sauerkraut.

Shuffle. Counterfeit paper money.

Shut-eye. (Rare) An easily robbed victim.

Shylock, n. A racketeer-usurer who lends money, usually in moderate sums without demanding collateral, at usurious rates. [See **Vigerage.**]

Shylock, v. To operate as a **shylock.**

Sidekick. 1. (Among pickpockets) Outside coat pocket; vest pocket. 2. A partner in crime; pal; buddy.

Sidewalk, the. (P) The world outside prison walls. "Mickey had a fin (five-year sentence) and short time (the remainder of his previous term to serve); he oughta be on the sidewalk now."

Sidewalk, on the. See **Pavement, on the.**

Sign. (N.Y. State prisons). See **Shingle.**

Silent insolence. (P) Disrespect towards an official implied in a glance or gesture; refusal to answer a direct question. [Note: In many prisons silent insolence is punishable as a serious infraction of prison rules.]

Silk. 1. (Especially among loan sharks) Money, especially paper currency. "That rabbit (usury victim) sure gets the silk up (manages to pay on time)." 2. (Scattered; South) A swindler.

Simoleon. A dollar.

Simple Simon. (Obs.) A diamond tiepin; any expensive stickpin.

Sing. 1. To inform; to turn State's evidence against one's associates. 2. (P) To complain of one's ill fortune. "Go and bag your head (shut up). You stiffs (fools) with sleeping time (short terms) are always singing to people that's buried (have long terms to serve)."

Sing 'em. (P) To complain of trouble.

Singer. (South) The convict on a chain- or other road-gang selected to lead the singing for the day, a custom that lessens the deadly monotony of the rise and fall of the sledges.

Single-o, n. 1. A thief who works only alone. 2. (P) A thoroughly selfish person, especially one not overscrupulous in his dealings with others. "That single-o muzzler (unprincipled fellow) bites (is trying to borrow from) everyone for stuff while he's swagged up (has stuff piled up) in his cell."

Single-o, v. To work solely in one's own interests; to withhold portions of loot from one's accomplices; to beg and borrow from others while hoarding one's own possessions. "Break out (bring out) them tailor-mades (cigarettes) you got stashed (hidden). You're single-o-ing around here smokin' my makings (tobacco for hand-rolling cigarettes). I just give it a flop (realized that)."

Single-o, a. Unscrupulously selfish; egocentric. "My partner was single-o as soon as we fell (were arrested). He didn't rat (inform against me), but he got his own mouthpiece (lawyer) and copped out (made a deal with the District Attorney) alone."

Sing the weeps. (P) To complain bitterly.

Sin-hound. (P) A prison chaplain.

Sinker. A thief who withholds a portion of loot, thus cheating his accomplices. "Better strip and frisk (disrobe and search) that crumb after the touch (robbery). He's a sinkeroo [See suffix: —eroo]."

Sissy rod. Any piece of firearms fitted with a silencer. "You'll get hit with the book (sentenced to life imprisonment) if you get dropped (arrested) heeled (armed) with that sissy rod."

Sister-in-law. A woman who supports a man by prostitution or thievery. "That p. i. (pander) is doing handy (making a good living). Musta got a new sister-in-law."

Sit-down. (Hobo) An invitation to come in and sit down to a meal.

Sit on it! (P) (Always spoken sharply or sarcastically) Keep it! Save it! Hoard it! [Note: This gross idiom is a favorite reply to convicts who are reluctant to lend or give when asked.] "You are a tough giver-up (stingy man), Stubbo. I was in a jackpot (in for a fight) and needed a chiv (knife). You can sit on it now. The thing's squared (straightened out)."

Sixer. 1. A six-month term in any

place of confinement. 2. (Rarely; when discussion is limited to terms of years) A six-year term of imprisonment.

Six hat and fifty shirt. (Rare) Having a strong back and a weak mind.

Six-to-five! (Carnival) [Variant: "65," "65th Street," "six-fifty," "six and a half bucks," or any compound numeral including "six."] Look out! Police! You are in danger! "Put my money on fuzz at six-to-five"—"There is a policeman in the crowd. Be careful!"

Sixty-forty. To secrete and withhold a portion of loot to cheat accomplices; to demand more than an equal share of loot. "You ain't sixty-fortying me. Get up (produce) my full end (share of loot), or you'll find your head behind the ash-barrel."

Sixty-nine. A form of degeneracy in which two parties exchange oral service simultaneously.

Sixty-niner. One who practices the sixty-nine act.

Sizzle. 1. To enrage; to become enraged. 2. To disseminate scandal about [anyone]; to slander one who is absent.

Sizzling. 1. Enraged. 2. Under fire, as the subject of scandal-mongers. 3. Strenuously sought by police, as a criminal, or as recently stolen loot. 4. Too dangerous to handle, as readily identifiable loot.

Skee. Whiskey, especially cheap grade.

Skee-joint. A cheap drinking establishment.

Skibo. 1. An Oriental. 2. (Rare) A Negro.

Skid. To get rid of. "Skid them plates (printing plates) and burn the boodle (counterfeit money). Nate was collared (arrested) by the feds (Federal agents)."

Skid row. (Probably a corruption of "skid road," term for street or area where loggers relax) The Bowery in New York City; any similar street or avenue in other regions of the country where the dregs of humanity tend to gather. (The original "skid road" is Yesler Way, Seattle, Washington).

Skilly. (P) Gravy; stew.

Skin. 1. (P) A one-dollar bill. "The screw (guard) wants a skin for his end (share) to bring in stickers (contraband stamps)." 2. Loose women or degenerates generally; a loose woman; a degenerate. (A **hunk of skin.**) 3. (Pickpocket jargon) A wallet. "Weed (take the money out of) that skin and whip (get rid of) it."

Skin, the. The fur-stealing racket.

Skin, on the. Engaged in, or by means of, any of the various forms of the fur-stealing racket.

Skin a skin. To remove money from and dispose of a stolen wallet.

Skin-heist. (P) A rape or criminal assault. "This joint (prison) is crumbed up (full) with fleas (low fellows), squares (victims of economic depression) and them dudes (fellows) in for skin-heists."

Skin-joint. A fur store or loft.

Skinful. 1. An intoxicating quantity of intoxicating drink. 2. (By rare extension) A full charge of narcotics, especially drugs subcutaneously injected.

Skin-plaster. An inside money belt.

Skins. Pelts; furs. "Izzy was knocked out (arrested) on a loft job (burglarizing a warehouse) with a swag (batch) of skins."

Skin-worker. A **loft-man** who specializes in stealing furs.

Skip, n. 1. A thief who obtains articles on the installment plan, using a false home address and a false claim to employment, and then moves away with the goods in his possession. 2. A petty thief who defrauds hotels and rooming houses by evading payment of rent.

Skip, v. To leave; run away. (Commonly, to skip town, skip bail, skip parole.) "It was a bum rap (false

charge) but Angie skipped the collar (evaded arrest) 'cause the D. A. (District Attorney) might make it stick (have won a conviction against him)."

Skipper. 1. (P) The warden of a prison, penitentiary, reformatory, or jail. [See note attached to **Big Noise.**] 2. The ranking police officer in charge of a precinct.

Skivvies. Underwear.

Skunk. A criminal venture netting little or no gain.

Skunked. Disappointed or cheated in an abortive or profitless criminal venture. "We hit (tried) four junk (narcotics peddlers') joints on the shake (to extort money). Scored (were successful) in three and got skunked on the fourth."

Skunker. (Rare) A cheat.

Sky pilot. (P) A prison chaplain; any clergyman.

Slab, on a. Dead; slain. "That ghee (fellow) will wind up on a slab if he keeps on bucking that combination (defying that criminal syndicate)."

Slam. (Scattered Western and Central prisons) To refuse a specific work assignment; to refuse to do any work whatever.

Slam off. To die.

Slap down. 1. To knock down with a blow of one's fist. 2. To pay, as a sum of money; to pay cash; to hand over. "I had to slap down twenty skins (dollars) for that rod (gun)."

Slap in. To place summarily, as in jail, prison, or a punishment block in prison. "The dep (Deputy Warden) slapped three new mickeys (inmates) in the cooler (punishment cells) for that come-off (occurrence) in the yard."

Slap in the kisser with. 1. To sentence to. "We got slapped in the kisser with seven boffos (years) for packing heaters (carrying guns)." 2. (P) To sentence to additional time as a punishment for rule violation. 3. To hurl in one's face, as an insult or accusation.

Slapman. (Penn., N. J., Maryland, and scattered areas) A plain-clothesman or detective.

Slap out. (P) To write and send out, as a letter or legal writ; to write and direct, as a note, to an official or a fellow convict.

Slap with. To sentence to a specific prison term. "Firpo got slapped with the book (life imprisonment) as a four-time loser (for fourth felony conviction)."

Slats. 1. (P) Window or door bars in prison. ["To kick a slat out"—to escape by cutting or screw-jacking a bar.] 2. The human ribs. "I'd be a bad ghee (fellow), I suppose, if I gave you a fat lip (punched you in the mouth) and booted (kicked) your slats in. Don't screw around (clown around). I got a bug on (am in no mood for fun)."

Slave. (P.; rare) A passive pederast.

Slave-bracelets. (Rare) Handcuffs.

Sleeper. 1. A sly trick. ["To pull a sleeper."] 2. A supposed easy victim who suddenly shows life and fight. 3. A short prison term; the rump end of a term, the greater part of which has been served. "Fritz can pull (serve) a fin (five-year term) on one ear (easily). That's a sleeper for an old-timer (veteran)." 4. A night watchman.

Sleeping-time. See **Sleeper** (3).

Sleep off. (P) To serve a prison sentence, especially a short one, with ease. "There's a ghee (fellow) can do a bit (who knows how to serve a prison term) without taking his shoes off (as if he were taking a short nap)."

Sleigh-ride, n. (P) A run-around. "You ain't playing me pinochle on the arm (using I.O.U.'s instead of money). Put it on the line (cash on the table).

I got hooked (tricked) for one sleigh-ride."

Sleigh-ride, v. (P) To send on a wild goose chase; to mock and mislead. "That phony parole board is sleigh-riding me. Five hold-backs (denials of parole) they boffed (hit) me with so far."

Slew. A great many, as a slew of rappers (a large number of complainants).

Slewfoot. A detective.

Slice, n. A share, as of loot or income; part ownership. "A full slice of this touch (robbery) gotta go to Patch's mouthpiece (lawyer) to square that beef (criminal complaint)."

Slice, v. (P) To wound with knife, razor, or any sharp-edged weapon.

Slick-backs. A deck of playing cards in which the backs of certain cards have been waxed for swindling.

Slicker. 1. A stolen automobile freshly painted and cleared of identification markings and numbers. 2. A shrewd person sophisticated in the underworld; a city dweller as differentiated from a **hoosier.**

Slim. A gun.

Sling. To talk, especially in the persuasive manner of a confidence swindler; to speak braggingly; to use slang.

Sling the crap. To tell grossly exaggerated stories; to lie artfully; to boast.

Sling the lingo. To speak in a manner unintelligible to all but one's accomplices or friends; to use the language of the underworld. "Who is that hip ghee (experienced fellow) that slings the lingo? Got a front (looks) like a square (one not of the underworld)."

Slip, the. (P) The formal announcement of the decision of the Parole Board, brought to a convict's cell after a hearing. "How'ja do, Windy? Get the slip yet?"

Slip one the heat. To shoot a person, especially to death.

Slob, n. 1. An honest workingman. 2. A fool; dupe; hireling; any petty thief. "That slob got a blast (was written about in all newspapers) like he was a biggie (underworld celebrity). He's only a fall guy (taking the guilt for the gang that hired him)." 3. (P) One who lacks cunning and aggressiveness, hence suffers in prison.

Slob, v. To be a **slob.**

Slobber, n. (P) A kiss squarely on the mouth.

Slobber, v. To give a **slobber.**

Slop up. To gorge oneself on liquor; to become intoxicated. "You ain't goin' on no heist (armed robbery) with me slopped up. What is it, the chill (what's the matter, scared)?"

Slough, n. 1. A jail, workhouse, station house, penitentiary, or prison. "Jim the Gimp just got tossed in the slough as a lamester (fugitive) on an old scratch rap (forgery charge)." 2. (Chiefly among house burglars) A dwelling place; a house. 3. Any small bag or package, containing loot, weapons, or burglar's tools that can be thrown away in case of sudden danger of arrest.

Slough, v. 1. To arrest; to imprison. 2. To subject to police raid and put out of business. 3. To beat, usually with the fists. 4. (P) To lock a convict in his cell. "About time to get sloughed, and I got a funny yen (urge) to hit the street (be free) tonight. Roll around, '56!"

Slough a joint. 1. To close a carnival concession or any illicit establishment by police raid. 2. (By loose extension) To discontinue one's business; to shut up shop.

Slough around. To beat with fists or weapons.

Slough in. (P) To lock in a cell as routine or because of a general emergency, but not as a form of punishment.

Slough-up, n. 1. An arrest. 2. A police raid and closure of premises. 3. (P) A lock-up for rule violation; a general locking in of all inmates as routine or in the event of an emergency. "Looks like a beat (attempted escape). It's a slough-up for the whole joint."

Slough up, v. To effect a **slough-up.**

Slough-worker. A house burglar.

Slow burners. (P) Slow burning, hence, fresh cigarettes. [Note: Cigarettes are used as a medium of value in almost all prisons. Cartons of cigarettes may pass in circulation for a long time and grow stale. To avoid deception, cartons are generally dated when purchased. Compare **Fast burners.**]

Slug, n. 1. A bullet. 2. A dollar.

Slug, v. To assault; to strike with a bludgeon or with one's fists. "Tail (follow) that bugster (watchman) till he rings in, then slug him and tie him up."

Slugging. A severe beating with fists or weapons.

Slum. 1. (P) Stew; prison food generally. 2. (Carnival) Cheap prizes at concessions substituted for **flash,** the prizes displayed to the gullible public. 3. Jewelry, in general; imitation jewelry. "That prowl (burglary) was a bum steer (bad tip). We won't get a yard (hundred dollars) for that slum."

Slum-bum. 1. One who, lacking talent for soliciting money, begs for food. 2. (Loose extension) A petty and contemptible thief.

Slum-gullion. See **Slum.**

Slum-heist. A jewel robbery at pistol point. "They gotta reader (police circular) out for us on them slum-heists. It's a tough beef (charge). We better hole up (go into hiding) a while."

Slum-hustler. One who traffics in cheap or imitation jewelry.

Slum-joint. A jewelry store. "That slum-joint is ready (a ripe plum for us)'. A little soup (nitro-glycerine) will crack the crib (safe) pretty."

Slum-peddler. A jewelry salesman. "Two heist-men (armed robbers) tailed (followed) the slum-peddler to Chi (Chicago) and beat (robbed) him for a hundred G's (thousand dollars) in ice (diamonds)."

Slum-poke. A jewel salesman's gem wallet.

Slum-worker. A specialist in selling cheap jewelry as genuine valuable pieces.

Smacker. 1. One dollar. 2. (P) A year. "Pinky got hit with two smackers by the Board (Parole Board)."

Smack in the kisser with. See **Slap in the kisser with.**

Smack with. See **Hit with.**

Smart buck or **dollar.** Money obtained by cleverness, skill or guile. "He packed in (gave up) the heist (armed robbery) and steps out (engages) only for a smart dollar."

Smarten up. 1. To become, or to help another to become, sophisticated in the lore of the underworld. 2. Wake up! Do as you are told! 3. To warn. "If you know that ghee (fellow), smarten him up to hustle (steal) somewhere else. This is our set-in (private reserve)."

Smart money. A clever and successful racketeer; any shrewd person. "That ghee (fellow) is real smart money."

Smash. To convert into cash, as a check or other negotiable instrument. "C'mon, get busy and scratch (forge) a few stiffs (checks). I got a couple of suckers that'll smash 'em when they're so bad they smell."

Smash a stiff. To pass a forged or raised check.

Smoke, n. Denatured alcohol and water, mixed and shaken up to form a cheap, smoky concoction.

Smoke, v. (South: borrowed from Negro jargon) 1. To take a look at; observe. 2. To shoot at. 3. (Rare) To flee.

Smoke a joint. (Chiefly South and southernmost Middle Atlantic States) To survey a place carefully as the site of a future crime; to glance about a place in search of a victim. "That fink (stool pigeon) that's rapping us (pressing the criminal charge against us) hits (hangs out at) Dago Joe's place. Go up and smoke the joint for him. He's gotta be banged (shot) if he won't chill (can't be intimidated by threats)."

Smoke-bum. A penniless vagrant, chronically besotted with **smoke.**

Smoked Irishman. (P) A Negro. [Note: The expression is used to poke fun at Irish-American convicts.]

Smoke-joint. An unlicensed dive that sells **smoke.**

Smoke-poke. (South; scattered Central and West) A holster or deep pocket for carrying a heavy-calibre pistol. [See **Smoke-wagon.**]

Smoke-pole. (South; scattered Central and West) See **Smoke-wagon.**

Smoke-wagon. Any heavy calibre— usually .45-calibre—non-automatic revolver.

Smoky City. Pittsburgh, Pa.

Snaffle. To steal, especially by highway armed robbery.

Snaffler. A highwayman, as distinguished from holdup men who rob stores, apartments, banks, and the like.

Snag. 1. To snatch, as a scavenger; to pick up discarded things; to steal trivial things. "The stirs (prisons) are full of depression bums (victims of an economic crisis). Half of them snagged mats out of doorways." 2. To arrest; to seize red-handed. 3. (P) To report for rule violation; to seize in act of violating rule.

Snake. 1. An habitual smoker of

marijuana. 2. An informer; any disloyal or unprincipled person.

Snake, v. See **Snake out** (2).

Snake-eyes. (Scattered rural areas) A double-ace in craps; hence, hard luck.

Snake out. 1. To escape from any predicament by dishonorable means. 2. To wheedle, cajole, or flatter as a means of obtaining secret information. 3. To escape from surveillance or from the scene of a crime by guile rather than by headlong flight.

Snap out of one's hop. To snap out of one's lethargy; to awaken to danger; to regain one's self-control. "You better snap out of that hop or that bug-doctor (psychiatrist) is gonna put the snatch on you (put under observation)."

Snap the rubber or **whip.** To masturbate.

Snare, n. 1. Any adroit piece of thievery. "That was a sweet snare glomming (stealing) that ice (diamonds)." 2. Arrest; seizure in the act of a crime or violation of prison rules.

Snare, v. 1. To acquire adroitly by thievery. 2. To arrest; to seize in the act of a crime or violation of prison rules. "Puggy was snared gandering (looking) through the jackets (case-history files) up front (the administration office)."

Snare flat-footed. To seize and arrest a trapped suspect. "I hit the kip (went to bed) and I'm just on the nod (dozing off) when the dicks (police) crashed the joint (broke into the apartment) and snared me flat-footed."

Snatch, n. 1. A kidnapping; the kidnapping racket. 2. A snatch-and-run robbery or theft. 3. (P) A report or lock-up for violation of prison rules. 4. Seizure in the commission of a crime; arrest. 5. (Coll.) Loose women; degenerates. 6. (P) The buttocks.

Snatch, v. 1. To kidnap. "Count me out. The feds (Federal agents) will glom

(arrest) you sure as hell if that ghee (fellow) gets snatched." 2. To steal by quick seizure and flight, as in the snatching of a purse. 3. (P) To seize in the act of violation of prison rules; to lock up. "Benny was snatched on a finger (informer's tip) with a couple of stickers (contraband postage stamps) and kites (letters intended to be smuggled out of prison)." 4. To seize in the commission of a crime; to arrest. "The G-men (Federal agents) snatched us for pushing queer (passing counterfeit money), but the plant (printing plant) was clear (free of incriminating evidence)."

Snatch, on the. 1. Engaged in, or by means of, kidnapping. 2. Engaged in, or by means of, purse-snatching or any similar snatch-and-run thievery.

Snatch-man. A kidnapper.

Snatch-peddler. 1. A prostitute. 2. (P) A catamite.

Sneaker. 1. An illicit still run independently of local criminal syndicate. 2. (South; close to the Atlantic coast) A motorboat equipped with a muffled motor.

Sneak-gate. A steel-barred openwork vault door, used as a daytime barrier when many doors must remain open, especially in banks, large jewelry stores, etc.

Sneeze. 1. To arrest. 2. To kidnap. 3. (Scattered South) To subject a witness to strong-arm police examination; to subject to **third degree.**

Sneezer. 1. Local jail; station house. 2. A hideout in which a kidnaped victim is held pending ransom payment. 3. (Rare) A kidnaper. 4. (Scattered South) Any police officer who uses **third-degree** methods.

Sniffer. A drug addict who sniffs powdered narcotics, usually with the characteristic addict's grimace. "That sniffer they used as a wheelman (chauffeur) left them in the sack (lurch) when the rumble (trouble) came."

Snipe. A discarded cigar or cigarette butt.

Sniper. A bum who picks up discarded cigar or cigarette butts.

Snitch, n. (Obs.) An informer. "That buck (chaplain) I worked for in the big house (prison) was a right ghee (regular fellow). He knocked me off (caught me) with a swag (stolen prison stores) one day and never beefed (reported me). All he says was 'I'm no snitch, but put that back.'"

Snitch, v. (Obsolete) To inform against a member of the underworld.

Snitcher. 1. (Alcatraz) An electrically controlled device that sounds an alarm when passed by anyone carrying concealed steel weapons as a revolver or knife. 2. (N.Y. State Prison) Walter Winchell, columnist and radio commentator. 3. (Obs.) One who gives information to authorities; a squealer.

Snitch-sheet. Any newspaper, especially one which makes a practice of sensationalizing criminal cases. "Them lousy snitch-sheets don't give no play to all cons (ex-convicts) that stay out, but they sure put up a sucker's holler when one bangs (shoots) someone on a heist (holdup)."

Snoose. Snuff.

Snorky. Irascible; belligerent; quarrelsome; surly. "That snorky bum goes around heeled (armed), bad-eyeing (glaring belligerently at) everyone. He'll get his lemon (head) kicked (bashed) in yet."

Snot-rag. A handkerchief.

Snow. Cocaine; cocaine-morphine mixture.

Snowbank. An establishment frequented by users of cocaine and heroin.

Snow-bird. 1. A user of cocaine or morphine. 2. (By extension) any drug addict.

Snow-digger. (Gulf State area pri-

sons) Any person from the Northern States.

Snub-noser. A short barreled .38-calibre revolver.

Soak, n. 1. (Rare) prison or county jail. 2. Pawn; pawn shop.

Soak, v. 1. (Rare) To sentence to prison or county jail. 2. To sentence to an excessive term in prison. 3. To pawn.

Soaker. (P.; mid-West, Central, and East Central U.S., some sections) A brutal prison guard. "Don't fall (get arrested) around here. The soakers in lag (the jails) are murder (brutal)."

Soap up. See **Soup up.**

Sock. A large sum of money. "The Deacon got his sock playing the abbey (impersonating a clergyman)."

Sock away. To hoard; to put aside for safekeeping; to hide, as loot.

Soft. (Carnival) Paper currency; bills.

Soft bit. (P) A prison sentence capable of being served with a minimum of discomfort. "You pull (serve) a soft bit, bum. You struck a home in this can (jail)."

Soft giver-up. 1. One who yields easily to extortion or holdup. 2. One generous to excess.

Soft-heel. (Hobo) A railroad detective.

Soft touch. A very easily accomplished theft; a person or place very easily victimized; the loot of an easy crime.

Sol. (P) See **Solly.**

Solid. Loyal; dependable. "Don't lam (run away); Boston is solid. He won't open up (talk to police under grilling)."

Solly. (Scattered mid-West and East Central U.S. prisons) Solitary confinement in punishment cells, usually on bread-and-water diet. "Someone put the finger on (informed the authorities) Cappy for a crash-out (attempt to escape). He's in solly."

Sound. 1. To search cursorily for

concealed weapons or contraband by patting the pocket surfaces. 2. (Pick-pockets) To pat the pockets of a prospective victim to locate concealed valuables.

Sound off. To talk boastfully or belligerently; to complain loudly. "Are you sounding off, scrub (you dolt)? Why don't you hang up (commit suicide)?"

Soup. 1. Crude nitroglycerine. [Note: Soup is generally made by cooking fragments of stick dynamite in water until the **picric** extract can be skimmed. Camphor masks are worn to counteract the odor.] "I got a peterman (safe-cracker) to fill on the score (join us in the robbery). He's a ringer (expert) with soup." 2. Narcotics used on race horses to impair their coordination in crooked races.

Soup-man. A safe burglar who employs explosives, usually **picric**.

Soup up. To place **picric** in a soap ream which is then inserted in a hole drilled into a safe, preparatory to blowing it open; (Obs.) to build a small soap enclosure around a crevice of an old-fashioned safe, the **picric** being allowed to seep through before touching off the explosion.

Sour paper. Forged checks.

South (to go—with). To conceal, as a portion of loot, in one's pocket in order to defraud accomplices of their just share.

Spaces. (South) Years, especially years in prison. "Ten spaces on the rattler (chain gang) is sad pullin' (hard to bear)."

Spark. (West, Central, and Southwest area) A professional arsonist in the employ of a gang; (loosely) a pyromaniac.

Spear. To cadge, as drinks in a saloon.

Spearer. (Obs.) A thief who uses grease to steal rings from the fingers of his victim.

Specker. A prison term; as, a two-specker (two years), a five-specker (five years), etc. "That spider (porch-climbing thief) never pulls (serves) more than a three-specker in stir (prison) and he makes nice scores (lucrative burglaries)."

Speed ball. A shot of narcotics in addict dosage.

Spider. 1. (West, Central, and West-Central U.S.) A burglar who is skilled in acrobatic modes of entry and egress; a second-story man. 2. (Among automobile thieves) An old-fashioned Ford car.

Spiel, n. 1. A talk or speech delivered convincingly with an ulterior motive; a sales talk; a confidence man's line of talk; the appeal of a panhandler. 2. Any cryptic speech concealing a message to accomplices, especially as a warning. 3. (Loosely) Any long-winded and convincing argument or narrative.

Spiel, v. To deliver a **spiel**.

Spieler. 1. A criminal lawyer, especially one in close touch with the underworld. 2. Anyone who delivers a **spiel**.

Spig, or **Spik.** A Spanish, Portuguese, Mexican, or Latin American type.

Spike. 1. To etherize alcohol or beer. 2. To thwart. 3. To bribe or intimidate as a means of circumventing justice. "Go to bat (stand trial). The jury's spiked for a turn-out (an acquittal)."

Spill, n. (Among pickpockets) A railway, subway, or elevated station.

Spill, v. To give incriminating information to authorities; to inform; to confess. "The dicks (policemen) dusted that mouse off (struck that informer once or twice), gave him a short con (persuasive talk), and he spilled."

Spill one's guts. To confess one's guilt, usually implicating accomplices; to talk indiscreetly. "I put the chill on (frightened) the fence (buyer of stolen goods). I kited (smuggled out) a tab (letter) telling him I'd spill my guts if he didn't kick in (contribute money) for my appeal. He'll stand for the shake (yield to the extortion)."

Spinach. Money.

Spindle. (Scattered: South, mid-West, and Central U.S.) A prison guard. "That old spindle that was chivved (knifed) in the big crush (prison-break) slammed off (died)."

Spinners. (P) Window and door bars so constructed that they cannot be hacksawed. [Note: Spinners contain one or more steel sleeves encasing a tool-proof core.]

Spit! (N.Y. State prisons) Shut up! "Spit, you bum, spit."

Spitting on the sidewalk. Any trivial crime, the punishment for which is other than trivial; technical charge. "They gave me a fin (five-year sentence) for a nail file, called it burglar's tools. It's tough pullin' time (serving a sentence) for spitting on the sidewalk." [Note: Among prisoners, "spitting on the sidewalk" is a common answer to inquisitive persons who ask the nature of one's crime.]

Split, n. 1. A division of loot. 2. A share of loot. 3. (Rare) A betrayal to police.

Split, v. 1. To share, especially loot. 2. (Rare) To betray to police.

Split bit. An indeterminate prison sentence, subject to the arbitrary decision of the parole board.

Split out. To place oneself between the pickpocket and his victim in order to block seizure or pursuit.

Splits. (P) Matches split in halves or thirds for purposes of economy. "These can (prison) big shots use splits and dust (loose tobacco) in the cell and tailor-mades (machine-made cigarettes) in the yard. The weasels (sneaky fel-lows) stash the tailor-mades and flash (exhibit) the dust."

Split-tail. A newborn female child, as differentiated from a **reg'lar feller.**

Split-up. The division of loot.

Splurge on the line. To spend money very freely.

Sport a bug on. (P) To nurse an evil mood.

Sporting-girls' manager. A pimp.

Spot. 1. A site selected for the commission of a crime. "I got the spot all cased (examined). It's a cannonball peter (hard safe to crack), but the joint is okay for a weekender." 2. An advantage conceded to an opponent. "Them fleas (low fellows) ain't lousing me around (taking advantage of me). Give me a guinea wrench (baseball bat), and I'll give them a spot of all the chivs (knives) they want." 3. A purposeful surveillance, as of a place or person selected as the object of a crime. 4. An assignment to a specific place in a carnival operation. "That out (exit) is your spot. Plant (stay there) and heist (hold up) anyone comin' in." 5. (P) An obsolete form of punishment in which the prisoner is made to stand—sometimes for as long as two days—on an 8-inch-square carpet or painted floor space. [Note: One of the many variations was that in which the prisoner was made to stand facing a wall, his nose pressed against a painted spot. Compare **Walk the line.**] 6. An untenable position or predicament. 7. A business; an exploitation area; (loosely) one's home or any place under one's occupancy, control, or proprietorship; a rendezvous of thieves. 8. (P) One's work assignment; the shop or office in which one works; one's housing quarters; the part of the recreation yard which one frequents with his friends.

Spot, v. 1. To select and mark for robbery; to examine movements of a person or the site of an intended crime. 2. To concede an advantage to an opponent.

Spotter. 1. (Southern chain gang) A convict assigned to tend bloodhounds and watch from a vantage point for convicts attempting to escape. 2. One who selects sites and victims for criminals. 3. A departmentstore or hotel detective. 4. A term of imprisonment, as a two-spotter (a twoyear term), a five-spotter (a five-year term), etc.

Spouter. A lawyer, especially one in criminal practice. "There's the spouter for a knock-off rap (murder case). You'll spring (be acquitted) or get bugged (be adjudged insane)."

Spow. (N.Y. Catholic Protectory) Coffee.

Spray. A light machine gun; a tommy-gun. "Rocky gave up (paid) two yards (hundred dollars) for a spray, two biscuits (revolvers) and some pills (bullets)."

Spread. 1. A layout or setting for a prosperous crime. 2. (P) The buttocks; luck. "What a spread you got, gettin' a commute (grant of clemency)!"

Spreader. A screw-jack or heavy pry-bar for spreading windows or doorbars.

Spread the eagle. (South) To escape from prison or other official custody. "Couple of dusters (jailbreakers) grabbed a kinky (car) and spread the eagle from the clink (jail)."

Spring, n. 1. The decisive or criminal act in the unfolding of a crime. "This rabbit-snatcher (abortionist) is plenty hip (very shrewd). Hold back the spring till I crack (feel him out)." 2. The release before the expiration of the maximum term of imprisonment; a suspension of sentence; an acquittal; a reversal of a court decision; a discharge from custody; an escape.

Spring, v. 1. To take the decisive step in criminal operation; to consummate a crime; to produce one's weapons, as in a holdup. [Note: Often used negatively, as, Don't spring!— Wait!] 2. To release or discharge; to acquit; to be released or freed from custody; to be acquitted; to escape; to cause to escape. "The board (parole board) won't spring Rico till he beefs on the fence (tells them who brought the stolen goods)." 3. To produce or exhibit, as a weapon, a police badge, or other show of force or authority. 4. To make a remark; to reveal one's identity cautiously while seeking to discover the character or identity of another. 5. To give evidence of recognition; greet. 6. To yield, as to criminal overtures or coercion.

Springer. Bail bondsman; lawyer; any political or other fixer. "Get fall dough (lawyer's and bondsman's fees) ready in case the springer makes bail for Joe."

Springfield. (Carnival) A victim about to be swindled. "Stall (hold) that springfield till I toss him some doublewillie (two chances for the price of one) for a duke-in (as bait to continue)."

Spring one's duke. To reveal one's plans or intentions; to force or outmaneuver another into disclosing his plans or intentions.

Spring on a teck. To free, or be freed, from custody on a legal technicality. "The fingerman (salesman of robbery leads) steered (directed) me into a plant (police trap) and the coppers (policemen) waited till I shook the joint (extorted the money from the owner of the establishment). The judge had to spring me on a teck 'cause they shouldn'ta let me pull the trick (carry out the crime)."

Spring the gaff. To play the trump card, i.e., to deliver the confidence talk or get right down to playing the trick intended to fleece the victim.

Spring with. To produce and confront a victim with, as a weapon, bogus credentials, a forged check, etc.; to take any decisive action in the execution of a planned crime; to consummate a criminal operation, as by threat or demand; to trick one into disclosing a secret. "Them dicks (policemen) ain't givin' us a flop (are paying no attention to us). Spring with the spiel (stock confidence talk); this guy's begging to be clipped (robbed)."

Spring with a crack. 1. To say anything that proves damaging or incriminating. "A lot of wrong ghees (stool pigeons) in this scorf-joint (restaurant). Watch the earie (eavesdroppers) and don't spring with a crack." 2. To make some revealing remark, meaningless to one not of the underworld, as a means of sounding one out. "That broad (girl) looks like a booster (shoplifter) I met once. I think she made (recognized) me too. Spring with a crack when we get near her." 3. To make a purposeful remark in verbal fencing, as in a swindle.

Spud. (Obs.) A pistol or revolver.

Spud, the. Any of various confidence swindles in which the victim is persuaded to invest money in a common pool with the swindlers, the money never being recovered by the victim.

Spud, on the. Engaged in, or by means of, any variation of **the spud.**

Squad car. A police department car carrying a detail of plainclothesmen or detectives.

Square, n. See **Square-John.**

Square, v. 1. To straighten out any difficulty, complaint, report, difference of opinion, quarrel, etc. 2. To settle, as a criminal complaint, by placating those aggrieved; to bribe or bring political pressure to bear upon anyone in authority. "Things gotta be squared before we go to bat (trial) or we're gonna get settled (imprisoned) for a swag of time (many years)."

Square a beef, or a collar, or a pinch. See **Square a rap.**

Square a rap. 1. To cause a criminal charge or complaint to be dropped with the consent of the complainant and the authorities. 2. (P) To bribe or otherwise persuade a prison officer to withdraw a report entered against one, or to withhold the filing of such report. "That hack (prison guard) is a businessman (can be bribed or persuaded). Square this rap with him before he writes the beef (formal report)."

Square a rapper. To cause the author of criminal complaint to withdraw his charge by means of bribery, restitution, or any other than open coercion.

Square bull. A police officer who will not accept a bribe; a police officer who, if he takes a bribe, will not double-cross the briber; a police officer who will not stoop to **frame up** a criminal, use **third degree** methods, or otherwise abuse his position.

Square egg. A loyal and trustworthy person.

Square-John. 1. A workingman; one not of the underworld. 2. Any thoroughly law-abiding citizen. 3. (Among drug addicts) A thief who never touches drugs. [Note: Anyone but a professional criminal or a peace officer may be termed a square-John. In underworld concept, police and criminals are soldiers of contending armies, equally dishonest. Civilian noncombatants are square-Johns.] 4. (P) Derisive term for accidental criminals whose behavior in prison betrays their alien status in the underworld. "These cans (jails) are gettin' crumbed up (infested) with square-Johns collared (arrested) for waiting for a streetcar (trivial and senseless crimes)."

Square-John pinch. 1. An arrest for a crime not specifically of an underworld character, as rape, desertion, and non-professional fraud. 2. (P) A report for any technical violation of prison-rules, such as making one's bed improperly, or failure to clean one's cell-bars.

Square oneself. To mend one's ruptured relations with others, as by apology, conciliation, indemnification, bribery, employment of venal political go-between, etc.

Square plug. See more common **Square-John.**

Square skirt. A thoroughly loyal woman; a woman who can be trusted. "Lefty's broad (girl) is one square skirt, got up fall-dough (raised a defense fund), and stuck (remained true to him) through a sawbuck bit (ten-year prison term)."

Square Willie. A person familiar with narcotics and users but having scruples against engaging in the business or using drugs.

Squash. (New England) The face; the head. ["To use one's squash"—to proceed with caution; to act cleverly.] "Take a flash (look) at that squash. If that ain't fuzz (a plainclothesman), I'm a jag (fool). Mooch (go over) and crack (talk) to him. I'll look for the office (signal from you)."

Squash, v. 1. To quash, as a criminal complaint or indictment. 2. (P) To quash a formal report for rule violation.

Squash, on the. (New England) Inspiring fear in one's victim merely by one's facial expression.

Squat. To execute in the electric chair; to be electrocuted. "They're squatting three ghees (criminals) tonight for that heist (holdup) knock-off (murder) in Harlem."

Squawk, n. 1. A confession, especially one implicating accomplices; the act of testifying against one's accomplices. "There musta been a squawk

in his rap (criminal charge). His partners are all in different cans (prisons), and he louses them up (slanders them) when you mention them." 2. A betrayal of one's fellow convicts to prison authorities. 3. A complaint or protest; an alarm; any radio, newspaper, or church crusade against crime and the underworld. "You ain't got no squawk comin' for that pinch (arrest). What do you think, you got a license (guarantee of immunity) to shake (extort money from) them junk-pushers (drug-peddlers)?"

Squawk, v. To make a **squawk.**

Squawk murder. 1. To make a full confession, implicating one's accomplices in a bid for leniency. 2. To complain bitterly to authorities demanding drastic action; to protest vigorously.

Squeeze. 1. A difficult predicament; sudden trouble; a crisis. "The Slugger's got a good wheelman (chauffeur) when things is okay, but he's murder (awful) in a squeeze." 2. Pressure; coercion. "Put the squeeze on the tipster (criminal agent) for some steers (good leads)."

Squeeze rates. Abnormally high extortion rates enforced by gangs selling "protection." "It's gonna cost plenty squaring that beef (to quash this indictment). Put the squeeze rates on them joints."

Squint. (Carnival) The appraising glance at a prospective victim's money to see if he is worth swindling. "This hoosier (hick) looks ready (gullible). Put the squint on and see what he's holding (how much money he has)."

S. S. A suspension of sentence by the court. "The shyster (lawyer) made a deal for me to cop out (plead guilty to a minor offense) and settle for an s. s."

Stab, n. 1. The act of copulation. 2. Effort; any desperate attempt. "I can't figure how these ghees (fellows) hang up (hang themselves) when they can't pull a bit (bear a prison term). Why don't they make a stab at a beat (an escape)?"

Stab, v. To copulate.

Stabbing a horse and stealing his blanket. (N.Y. State Prisons) Any trivial or absurd crime. [Note: A commonly heard satirical reply to inquisitive persons who ask the reason for one's imprisonment. The phrase is tantamount to "mind your own business."]

Stable. A chain of houses of prostitution under one central management.

Stable boss. A keeper of a **stable**.

Stack up. To reveal one's true character; to prove oneself. "The first touch (robbery) we took this dude (fellow) on, he stacked up like a good man. He stuck and slugged (stood and fought) when we got rumbled (trouble started)."

Stage name. (Carnival) The current alias used by an operator in a carnival. [Note: Carnival-wise veterans never ask, "What's your name?" The correct form is, "What's your stage name?"]

Stagger-bit. (P) A long prison term, usually more than ten years.

Stake, n. Anything given to **stake** another.

Stake, v. 1. To give a sum of money, as a bribe, a gratuitous share of loot from a crime in which one had no active part, a token of underworld good will, etc. "Them bulls (policemen) ain't got no beef (complaint coming). They was on the payroll for twenty clams (dollars) a week, and I was always staking them for a few extra." 2. To advance expense money for launching a crime or racket; to lend money as a favor, especially to a newly released convict, as for the purchase of clothes. 3. (P) To lend small sums of money or such articles as tobacco to a needy

fellow convict without expecting or desiring repayment.

Stakeman. Financier of criminal venture; one who advances money against future criminal gains. "Who's the stakeman behind that gaff-joint (crooked gambling house) on the stem (main street)?"

Stall, n. 1. A pickpocket's aide whose task it is to distract or maneuver a victim so that he may be robbed, or to prevent or delay pursuit of the thief; any criminal accomplice with similar tasks to perform; the act of delaying or preventing pursuit; any of the various maneuvers employed by a pickpocket's aide. 2. Any maneuver to win postponement or delay. 3. Feint or pretense with an ulterior motive, as feigning illness as a means of winning release from a work assignment in prison.

Stall, v. 1. (Carnival) To stop; to hold or detain, as a prospective victim. 2. To serve as a pickpocket's aide by jostling, distracting, or pinning a victim; to render similar assistance to any kind of robbery. 3. To safeguard an accomplice's escape from the scene of a crime by pretending to aid, while actually hindering assistance to the victim. "Cover that out (exit) till the getaway (escape) rig (car) is rollin'. Stall the squares (people), then lead the suckers' holler (hue and cry)." 4. To hesitate; show reluctance; stand; wait. 5. To delay or restrain by skilful action or use of words.

Stall a beef. To prevent or delay pursuit of an accomplice by any means, especially by pretending to aid the victim while actually impeding his movement.

Staller. A shirker.

Stand, on the. In the witness chair in criminal proceedings. "If my partner ever gets on the stand with all them bits (arrests) and pinches (convictions) on his pedigree (police record), we're buried (certain to be convicted)."

Stand a bull on his ear. To talk unconcernedly with a policeman while one's accomplices execute a crime.

Stand a pinch. To accept an arrest without complaint, usually under circumstances which offer the excused a fair chance of acquittal or leniency; to be able to afford an arrest. "I ain't goin' on no shakes (to extort money) heeled (armed). I can stand a pinch and maybe get sprung (win a release) if it ain't a bad rap (serious charge)."

Stand for. To yield without resistance, as to robbery, arrest, etc.

Stand for a heist. To suffer a holdup without attempting to resist. "I'd a' stood for the heist, but them muzzlers (contemptible fellows) started to sap (blackjack) me up, so I snatched one of their rods (guns) and ran 'em out."

Stand for a pinch. To submit to arrest without resistance. "I can't stand for a pinch with them bits (prison terms) they're givin' out. Might as well throw slugs (shoot it out with the police) and save one for myself (to commit suicide)."

Stand for a shake. To submit to extortion without resistance. "This joint is making me a nice buck (bringing me a good living), but ex-cons (ex-convicts) are biting me to death (are demanding every penny of it). If I stand for all them shakes I gotta wrap up (get out of business). If I holler copper (complain to the police), I'm a fink (traitor)."

Stand one on a corner. To fail to keep an appointment, especially of a meeting at a street-corner.

Stand pat. To refuse to give information to police or other authorities.

Stand the gaff. 1. To withstand legal prosecution and persecution without confessing or involving one's accomplices. 2. (P) To serve a prison term without compromising one's underworld principles.

Stand-up, n. 1. A quick, unexpected search of one's person by police, especially a superficial search for concealed weapons. "My kick (pocket) was packed with queer (counterfeit currency) when the dicks (police) gave me a stand-up, but they were lookin' for rods (guns). They told me to cop a mope (move on)." 2. A line of suspects at the police station where victims of crimes seek to identify their assailants. [Note: Policemen in plain clothes usually stand in line to lessen chances of false identification. Victims pointing out policemen as their assailants reveal their confusion by the error.] 3. Presentation on a platform before assembled policemen and detectives to enable them to note professional criminals.

Stand up, v. 1. To remain valid, as an alibi, a legal defense, an indictment, or the testimony of a witness. 2. To hold to one's testimony under fire. "It means short time (serving the unexpired portion of your previous sentence) and a new bit (term), Benny. You gotta stand up or you're all caught up (sent to prison for life)." 3. To be deemed genuine, as bogus credentials, forged checks, or anything counterfeit. 4. To prove steadfast and loyal.

Stash, n. 1. A cache; a hiding place for loot, contraband, weapons, etc.; a hideout, especially for fugitives from justice. 2. Anything hidden away, as the paraphernalia of the drug addict, pistols, burglar's tools, stolen goods, etc.

Stash, v. To conceal, as a fugitive; to cache; to hide, as money, loot, or weapons. "Stash all that junk (narcotics) at the drop (hideout) till the pushers (drug-peddlers) call for it."

Stash oneself away. To take cover when sought by police.

State. (P) Supplied [to convicts] by the State, as cheap tobacco, soap, towels, clothing, etc. [Note: The term is generally synonymous with "contemptible" or "shoddy."] "Sit on that state. I wouldn't smoke that for a commute (commutation of sentence)."

State grad. An ex-convict, "graduate" of a state prison.

State lawyer. A counsel appointed by the court to represent defendants too poor to retain their own attorneys. [Note: Regarded as minor aides to the District Attorney, state-lawyers are never trusted by members of the underworld.]

State man. (Gulf State area prison) A convict who serves as an armed guard, notoriously quick to shoot to kill any fellow-convict who attempts to escape.

State mouthpiece. See **State lawyer.**

State-o. (P) Variant of **State.**

State's. 1. Clothes given a convict by the state upon his release from prison. 2. Any state prison, as differentiated from reformatories, county penitentiaries, jails, and workhouses. "Pete is pullin' (serving) a big bit (long sentence) in state's."

State stuff. See **State.**

Statey. (Carnival) a state trooper.

Steamed up. 1. Erotically stimulated. 2. Angered; belligerent. "Every time I gun (look at) that crumb I get steamed up. He sent two dudes (fellows) to the chair."

Steam-up ghee. An agitator who stirs up friction between gangs or individuals to further his own interests; a trouble-maker. "That steam-up ghee is gonna wind up on a slab (in the city morgue). He's got the heat (attracted police attention) on the racket and the combo (gang) is bugged up (enraged)."

Steel. (P) A knife, razor, or a similar edged weapon.

Steer, n. 1. The desired information; the details of a proposed crime; the inside facts. 2. A lead or a tip in a criminal enterprise. "That big score (robbery) in St. Louis was Sam's steer.

He's a good **tipster.**" 3. Direction; reference; recommendation; suggestion. 4. See **Steerer.**

Steer, v. 1. To act as a **steerer.** "Don't steer them bums to mooeh (ask for) my makin's (tobacco). The next one bites me (begs of me), I'll heist (kick him) in the biscuit (buttocks) and be a bad feller."

Steerer. 1. Anyone, especially a taxicab driver, policeman, or bellboy, who directs prospective customers to houses of prostitution, **clip joints,** gambling establishments, etc. 2. A pimp. 3. A specialist in selecting sites or victims for robbery. 4. See **Shill.**

Steer-joint. Any gambling establishment, night club, brothel, or the like, that uses **steerers** to attract persons.

Stem, n. 1. Street; avenue; thoroughfare. 2. Professional beggary. 3. A request for a loan that will not be repaid; a solicitation for food or money. 4. A steel drill used by safe- and vault-burglars.

Stem, v. To beg; cadge; panhandle. "Them grifters (thieves) are all stiffs (fools). I can stem more than they can clip (steal)."

Stem, on the. 1. On the main street of a town or village; on the highway. 2. Engaged in, or by means of, panhandling. 3. (P) Engaged in, or by means of, begging or borrowing. "I gotta get on the stem for makin's (tobacco) before we lock in (go to our cells). I ain't holdin' (have) nothing."

Stem in. To drill a hole in the door of a safe before inserting explosives or forcing the combination; to drill an opening for the insertion of a **can-opener.** "The suckers (fools) oughta leave these gingerbread petes (fancy but easily cracked safes) open. Save them dough (the money they have to pay for a new one). Stem in and we'll rip."

Stemmer. 1. (Hobo) A panhandler. 2. (P) A cadger.

Stem-shot. A shot of explosive introduced into the hole in which the combination spindle of a safe turns.

Step. See **Step out.**

Step out. 1. To go out to engage in criminal action. 2. To graduate from petty to major crime or racketeering. "The Gigolo's stepping out, eh? I knew the chump when he was a two-bit mooch-pusher (peddler of cheap narcotics)."

Step out blind. To commit a crime without plan or previous information. "If you gotta steal, remember one thing: the cans (prisons) are full of heist-men (holdup men) who stepped out blind and got themselves thirty boffos (thirty-year prison sentence)."

Step out in bracelets. (P) See **Step out in cuffs.**

Step out in cuffs. (P) To be released from prison, after serving a sentence, in handcuffed custody to face another pending charge. "I got twelve more boffos (years) to do, then I step out in cuffs. Might as well hang up (commit suicide)."

Step out in irons. (P) See **Step out in cuffs.**

Stepping dough, looking to glom. Ambitious.

Stern-wheeler. (Mississippi Valley) A passive pederast.

Stew. Crude nitroglycerine, or **picric,** made by stewing sticks of dynamite, freeing the sawdust and clay base of the explosive, after which the **soup,** or picric extract, is skimmed and placed in vials.

Stew bum. (Hobo) A besotted bum who panhandles sums of money to buy drinks.

Stew for beans. (P) See **Shot for shot.**

Stick, n. A pistol; revolver. 2. A burglar's jimmy or pry-bar. [Note: Sticks are often assembled in sections for pur-

poses of concealment on one's person.] 3. A cashier's cage; a cash register; a croupier's booth; any place where money is received. 4. (Carnival) See **Shill.** 5. (P) A match. 6. (P) A bludgeon. 7. The stem of an opium pipe.

Stick, v. 1. To be sustained, as a criminal charge or indictment. "With your record (criminal record) the coppers (police) can make any rap (charge) stick." 2. (Among pickpockets) To jostle a victim and pin him into position to be robbed. 3. To remain staunch, especially in a crisis; to remain loyal. "Don't lam (run away). Stick and we'll bang out (shoot our way out)." 4. (P) A knife.

Stick a mark. (Among pickpockets) To jostle and pin a victim into position while his pocket is picked by a skilled accomplice; to render a victim incapable of defending himself from pocket-picking operation. [Note: Pickpocket aides have developed many a device for sticking a mark. A common method is to spread open a newspaper in such a way that the victim cannot help but become angry and push it aside, thus rendering himelf even more vulnerable to any crude robbery. Sometimes aides will resort to the rough-and-tumble tactic of seizing a victim and engaging in a violent argument with him while the pickpocket accomplishes the theft. Such methods are generally termed hijacking.]

Stick and slug. To stand and fight, with or without weapons, especially in resisting arrest.

Stick, cop, and blow! (Carnival) Take the victim's money and leave him. A common command given by the operator of the game to a **shill** or a **stick.**

Stick croaker. A doctor who specializes in treating venereal diseases, chiefly on male clientele.

Sticker. 1. (P) A knife as a weapon. 2. (P) A detainer or warrant on a pending charge. 3. (P) An uncancelled postage stamp [contraband]. "Get the kite (letter to be smuggled out) ready. The connection (guard) will put the sticker on." 4. Anyone who is loyal in all exigencies, especially to one in prison.

Stick in the hole. To seize a kidnap-victim and place in hiding.

Stick it in and break it off. (P) To exact the last ounce of vengeance. "That creep (unprincipled fellow) tried to bury me (send me to prison). Now he wants me to be the fall guy (to assume the full burden of guilt) and turn him out (exonerate him). What moxie (nerve)! I'll stick it in and break it off."

Stickman. 1. An expert at ripping safes with a **stick** or **can-opener.** [See **Ripper.**] 2. (Carnival) The operator of a concession, especially of any crooked gambling wheel. 3. A cashier. "There's a hip (smart) broad (girl) that works (steals) single-o (on her own) laying the note (working the short change swindle). She's got them stickmen blowing their tops (crazy)." 4. (Rare; limited to those areas where stick is synonymous with gun; especially New York City) Gunman. 5. A croupier in a gambling place.

Sticks. 1. Feminine legs. 2. Matches, in prison where they are contraband.

Stick the heater on. To level a gun at.

Stick-up, n. 1. Armed robbery; holdup. 2. Pocket-picking operation. [See **Stick,** v., def. 2.]

Stick up, v. 1. To rob at gun point. 2. See **Stick,** v., def. 2.

Stickup man. A holdup man.

Stiff, n. 1. A person; fellow. [Note: The inflection of the speaker determines whether the particular stiff is an excellent or contemptible fellow.] 2. A profitless criminal venture; a poor prospect for robbery; a dud. "That score (robbery) turned out to be a real stiff. It took four hours to punch the guts out (smash the mechanism) of the crib

(safe) and there's nothin' but books in it." 3. (Trenton state prison, and scattered prisons where newspapers are contraband) Any contraband newspaper or magazine, especially an old one. [Note: A hot stiff is a daily newspaper of recent date; hence, possession of one is especially punishable.] 4. A worthless check; a good check that thieves cannot afford to cash; an I.O.U.; any non-negotiable medium of payment to thieves or swindlers. 5. Anything of little or no value; a mere formality or token; counterfeit money. 6. (P) A note from one inmate to another, or from an inmate to officials; a smuggled letter sent into or out of prison. 7. A hobo. 8. A victim of thieves. 9. A corpse.

Stiff, v. 1. To pass a bad check. "We'll have a swag (lot) of hookers (warrants) for stiffing these dampers (banks), if we fall (are caught)." 2. To evade payment of an obligation. 3. To get little or no loot in a robbery. "That mob was stiffed on that Cleveland trick (robbery)." 4. To pay by check which the recipient cannot risk cashing.

Stiffed. 1. Cheated, especially of loot, or in an abortive or profitless criminal venture; paid off in a swindle with a good check which one dares not cash; defrauded, having cashed a bogus check. 2. (Rare) Denied or rebuffed, as in a parole application or court appeal.

Stiffed in. Surrounded; hemmed in; in a hopelessly untenable position.

Stiff-joint. 1. A town, establishment, or location unsuitable for work of careful and discriminating thieves; a hangout of petty thieves, panhandlers, etc.; any place which is disliked or held in contempt. 2. An illegal clearing house through which valid checks, made to the order of other than the bearer, may be cashed at a discount. 3. A brokerage house through which stolen or counterfeit stocks, bonds, or other negotiable paper may be marketed. 4. Any establishment, especially a prison, which is regarded with contempt by the underworld because of the low character of those who are to be found there. "This is a real stiff-joint to pull a bit (serve a sentence). I'm dropping a tab (note) to make a boat (requesting a transfer to another prison)."

Stiffo. See **Stiff**, n.

Stiff rap. 1. A severe sentence. 2. A criminal charge of which one is innocent; a criminal charge which is certain to result in discharge, acquittal, or extremely mild punishment. [Note: In the latter deprecatory sense, the emphasis is on stiff; in the first sense an even accent is heard.]

Stiff with. Infested with, as with thieves, informers, or police, or other undesirables. "That scatter (rendezvous) is stiff with fleas (informers, policemen, pimps, etc.). Wrap the joint up (stop going there)."

Sting, n. A theft; touch; wallet.

Sting, v. (P) To report a prisoner for rule violation. 2. (Very rare) To make a successful theft.

Stinger. 1. The tongue. 2. (P) A report for rule violation.

Stinko, n. (Hobo; far West) A hobo who drinks **canned heat.**

Stinko, a. Helplessly intoxicated.

Stink weed. Marijuana.

Stir. A federal or state prison or penitentiary; any place of imprisonment for felons. "Any dude (fellow) that pulls (serves) more than a sawbuck (ten years) in stir is a bug (insane)."

Stir-agent. (P) A cheap lawyer or his soliciting agent, who seeks clients in prisons promising to obtain their release on technical constitutional grounds. [Note: The activities of stir-agents have been curtailed in many of the progressive states.]

Stir-belly. (P) A common type of nervous indigestion that affects many convicts after years of nerve-racking routine and prison diet.

Stir-bug. A convict or ex-convict whose mind and nerves have been affected by years of prison routine. [Note: Commonest superficial symptoms are glazed eyes, a nervous, preoccupied manner, and frequent suffering from delusions.]

Stir-buggy. (P) An occasional variant of **Stir-bugs.**

Stir-bugs. Affected mentally by years of routine; suffering from prison-induced stupor. "I must be gettin' stir-bugs or blowing my top (going insane) altogether. I bust out laughing over nothin' and when somethin' funny makes other ghees (fellows) laugh, I bug up (get mad)."

Stir-chop. A prison haircut.

Stir-crazy. (P) See **Stir-bugs.**

Stir-hustler. (P) One who exhibits a talent for serving a prison term comfortably; hence, by implication, a failure as a thief outside of prison.

Stir-nuts, or **Stirry,** or **Stir-simple,** or **Stir-wacky.** See **Stir-bugs.**

Stirwise. (P) Familiar with complexities of prison life, hence able to serve time with a minimum of discomfort insofar as rules and regulations are concerned.

Stockholder. (P) A convict who works so zealously in the state's interest that he is held in contempt by fellow prisoners.

Stomach. Courage.

Stones in the head, to have. (Chiefly in New York and environs) To be very stupid.

Stone-tail. The act of pursuing wealthy opera or night club patrons—especially those decked in jewels—to a place where they can easily be robbed at pistol point. "Whitey and Gimp got a pickup (were arrested) on a stone-tail, heeled to the hilt (heavily armed)."

Stool or **Stoolie,** n. An informer; a stool pigeon.

Stool, v. To inform authorities.

Stool-mark. A knife-scar, usually slanting down from cheekbone to mouth, frequently inflicted on **stool pigeons,** cheaters, and other traitors to the code of the underworld. "I'll get hit with a bit (be given a new sentence) for givin' this crumb (traitor) a stool-mark, but it is worth a deuce (two-year term)."

Stoolo. See **Stool pigeon.**

Stool pigeon. One who barters underworld secrets for immunity from police interference in petty rackets. [Note: In the strict sense of the term, a stool pigeon is not, as is generally supposed, one who informs under extreme police pressure; he is not a casual informer.]

Stop. (Extremely rare) A buyer of stolen goods. [Most common: **fence** and **swag-buyer.**]

Stored away. In prison.

Story. Any lengthy preface to a request for a loan; a build-up for a confidence swindle; any narrative told with an ulterior motive. "Tell your story walkin', bum. I left my tear-duster (handkerchief) home."

Stowaway. A political hireling holding one or more local government jobs under various aliases.

Stowed away. See **Stored away.**

Straighten out. 1. To provide one with an introduction to the proper underworld people, especially one who is a stranger in the community or who has recently been released from prison; to rehabilitate in criminal circles. 2. To correct; to check the belligerent or insulting behavior of [another]; to change [another's] course of action to accord with one's own concept of right; to restore one's reputation by refuting a slander. "That flea (contemptible fellow) thinks he's got me scared. I'm gonna straighten him out so he'll never

bad-eye (glare at) me again." 3. (P) To arrange [affairs] to one's satisfaction; to quash a formal report by influencing the guard by bribery, flattery, or intimidation.

Stranger. (Limited to professional car thieves) An automobile stolen at a distant point.

Strange weed. (West) A stranger of doubtful underworld status. "Strange weed in one's garden"—a stranger in one's town or neighborhood. "Don't crack your jaw (talk). There's a strange weed in the scatter (rendezvous)."

Straw hat and red tie. (P) Formerly, standard accessories to civilian attire in which inmates, committed from prisons to mental institutions, were dressed. [Note: The term survives the custom.]

Street, the. (P) The world outside, especially one's home-town or neighborhood.

Street, on the (P) Not in confinement; at liberty. "I got a run (criminal activity) for two years on the street till I got this fall (arrested on this charge)."

Strength. (Carnival) The amount of money seen in the possession of a prospective swindle victim. "What strength is the iron?"—How much money has he?

Stretch, n. A prison term. "The last stretch was murder (terrible). Them screws (prison guards) was sure ball-breakers (persecutors), on your pratt (tail) all the time."

Stretch, v. 1. To kill or knock unconscious. 2. To hang; to lynch. "They stretch you for stepping on the prowl (committing burglary) heeled (armed) in them rebel (Southern) states."

Stretch hemp. To pay extreme penalty by hanging.

Stretch the rubber. To practice infidelity to one's wife or mistress.

Strictly on the legit. Completely honest and free of guile.

Strides. Trousers. "Mickey makes a nice buck (good living) prowling outside hot sloughs (houses), stickin' a cane in the kip (bedroom) window after (to get) the strides. He weeds them (steals all valuables) and then puts them back. Then the sucker (victim) lumps (beats) his wife for clipping (robbing) him."

Strike a home. (P; ironic) To find prison life congenial. "Yeah, 'big shot,' you struck a home. You were mooching (begging) coffee-and (cake) and flopping (sleeping) in barnacles (cheap rooming houses) outside."

Striker. (P) A match-box or a torn-off portion of the sulphur-coated surface of a match-box.

String. (Obs.) 1. Fuse for exploding percussion cap in safe burglary. 2. The lead wire from the electric socket to the percussion cap in safe burglary. "Okay, Chuck, hang (connect) the string. One shot oughta crack (open) this crib (safe)."

—String. (Combination form, as three-string, four-string, etc.) Together, as numbers of a gang. "We hustled (worked) three-string tossing the broads (playing the **three-card monte** swindle) and never got a drop (arrested)."

String of hustlers. A group of prostitutes operating for the same house or syndicate. "Broadway Al's got a string of hustlers. That's where his dough comes from."

String up. 1. (Scattered prisons) To handcuff a prisoner by his wrists to the upper part of the cell-door, compelling him to stand on tiptoe, as a form of extreme punishment. 2. To hang; to lynch; to commit suicide by hanging.

Strip a crate. To jack up a car and steal the tires and accessories. 2. To remove license plates and other identification marks before abandoning a car which has been used for criminal operations.

Strip frisk, n. A search of the person, all clothing having been removed.

Strip-frisk, v. To disrobe and search minutely, as a criminal or a convict suspected of concealing contraband. "Get clean (get rid of anything incriminating), Tom. Some geezer (fellow) was chivved (knifed) and they're strip-frisking."

Stripper. (Mid-Western area; rare) A pickpocket.

Strippers. A deck of cards in which all but the key-cards have been trimmed, for swindling. "What a lush (easy victim)! We took him to the driers (robbed him of every penny) with strippers."

Strong-arm squad. 1. (In large cities) A hand-picked police detail whose duty is to provoke and use violence against criminals, seeking them out in their habitual rendezvous. [Note: Strong-arm squads make relatively infrequent arrests, contenting themselves with dealing out rough treatment.] 2. (P) A riot squad consisting of prison guards.

Studie. A Studebaker auto.

Stuff. 1. Narcotics; contraband; loot. "Ditch (hide) the stuff. A swag (lot) of screws (prison guards) is comin' over to fan (search) the joint." 2. Talent; skill. "Ring (arrange for) that dude (fellow) to hustle (steal) with us. He's right (loyal) and he's got plenty of stuff." 3. Action; behavior. "That's foolish stuff, luggin' (carrying) a roscoe (gun) when you ain't out to pull a trick (commit a robbery)."

Stuff, on the. Under the influence of, or addicted to the use of, narcotics.

Stumble bum. 1. (Among hoboes) A worthless hobo incapable of panhandling or stealing. 2. (P) A clumsy and stupid fellow. "They oughta put higher walls around stirs (prisons) to keep stumble bums like Sloppy Mike out. Don't know what these joints are comin' to."

Stumer. 1. (Among race-track gamblers) A horse with no chance to win. 2. A bullet of large calibre. 3. A counterfeit coin. 4. A forged check. 5. A phony; a sham.

Stunkey. (Carnival) A smugly righteous, chronic complainant to police.

Sub. A sub-machine gun.

Sucker. Any prospective victim of thieves or swindlers; one easily cheated or victimized; a gullible fellow; a fool.

Sucker for a left, to be a. (Extended from prize-fight parlance) See **Wide open.**

Sucker list. A list of names and addresses of persons capable of being profitably victimized. [Note: Sucker lists are often marketable commodities, bringing high prices to their compilers.]

Sucker's holler. 1. The outcry or the complaint of a victim of crime. "What a sucker's holler the mark (victim) made for half a C (fifty dollars)." 2. Any protest by a loser in any game of chance. 3. (P) Whining and pleading following a report for a rule violation; complaint; protest.

Suck in ones' guts. (Central and mid-Western States) To keep quiet; shut up; to refuse to talk under police interrogation.

Suey-pow. A sponge or rag for cleaning, cooling and holding opium pipe.

Super. (Especially among oldtime pickpockets) A watch.

Super-twister. A pickpocket specializing in stealing watches.

Sure-thing ghee. 1. A crooked gambler. 2. An excessively cautious thief. "A sure-thing ghee this dude (fellow). Wants his touches (robberies) sacked (prearranged) for him."

Swag. 1. Loot; stolen goods. 2. (P) Contraband; stolen prison stores; (loosely) anything unearned. "What a

swag in that package you got! What's the broad (girl) out of the workhouse again?" 3. A lot; a large amount. ["A swag of time"—a long prison sentence; "a swag of lumps"—a bad beating; "a swag of hookers"—many pending warrants.] "Pete's got a swag of shacking (robbing houses at dinner time) collars (arrests)."

Swag-bag. (P) Any cloth or paper bag capable of being used as a receptacle for stolen goods. "You mooch (walk) around with them swag-bags like you had a license (to steal). What kinda short-con (convincing talk) you give them screws (prison guards) anyhow?"

Swag-benny. A loose coat with large pockets to hold stolen goods, especially used by shoplifters.

Swag-buyer. A receiver of stolen goods; a fence. "The swag-buyer won't touch that ice (jewelry); the beef is too hot (the police are watching for it). Take the rocks (diamonds) out and stash (hide) them, and you can fence (sell) the break-up (gold and platinum settings) for the nut-money (expense money)."

Swag-flogger. See **Swag-benny.**

Swagged-up. 1. Laden with stolen goods; stolen prison stores, or contraband; having a large quantity of any goods in one's possession. 2. (P) Filled with; infested with. "This can (prison) is swagged-up with fleabags (informers and degenerates)."

Swagger. 1. A receiver of stolen goods. "There's a swagger to buzz (talk to) about a hot boiler (stolen car). Flag (call) him." 2. (P) A convict who sells stolen prison stores or contraband.

Swaggie. See **Swag-buyer.**

Swagman. See **Swagger.**

Swag-pocket. (P) Any large pocket, especially one inside the coat of the convict's uniform, regarded as a convenient place for concealing stolen goods or contraband.

Swamp-angel. (Central and mid-Western States) One whose manners and appearance are rustic or outlandish.

Swamped. Surrounded by police and hopelessly outnumbered; trapped in a hopeless predicament. "Unload (get rid of everything incriminating) quick, Turk. We're swamped."

Swap spits. 1. To kiss lingeringly. 2. (P) To engage in mutual pederasty.

Sweat. To apply **third degree** methods; to employ duress in securing an admission of guilt or a confession involving accomplices. "The bulls (police) sweat him into opening up (confessing)."

Sweat-box. (South) A chain-gang or other road-gang punishment chamber of corrugated steel, usually 7 ft. high by 4 ft. square, with a peaked roof. Inside, from the roof apex, hangs a heavy strap with leads to be fastened to the prisoner's wrists. [Note: Hung by his wrists, the prisoner is left in the sweat-box which is heated by the blazing sun, until a guard discovers that the convict is thoroughly limp and unconscious. Fortunately, the vicious practice is being eradicated.]

Sweet. Simple and profitable, as a specific crime or type of crime; exceedingly gullible, as a victim of crime; extremely satisfactory, as an area of criminal exploitation.

Sweeten. To increase the stakes in gambling swindles; to offer more bait to a prospective victim to hasten a swindling procedure.

Sweetheart. 1. One easily victimized; a place easily and profitably robbed. "That jug (bank) is a sweetheart for a pete-job (safe-robbery)." 2. An extremely desirable person or thing.

Swindle. Trouble; difficulty; anything to be avoided, as a fight, a report for prison rule violation, etc. "I'm in so many swindles with the dicks (police), I'm gonna cop a sneak (slip quietly away) till I cool off (they lose interest in me)."

Swindled up. In serious trouble or difficulty. "Peppy's swindled up bad, got a big bit (long prison term) and a swag of hookers (a lot of warrants pending on other charges)."

Swing. To hang; to hang oneself.

Swipe. To steal (usually something petty by juveniles).

Switch. 1. To substitute imitations for genuine articles in any confidence swindle. 2. (Rare) To be disloyal to the underworld.

Switch, the. Any of the various swindles in which imitations are substituted for genuine articles purchased by a victim.

Switch plates. To remove the license plates from a stolen car, replacing them with a genuine or counterfeit set not listed by police. "Pull that hot load (drive the stolen car) in the drop (hideout). Get the daubers (painters) busy and switch the plates."

T

Tab, n. 1. (P) A written note passed from one convict to another; an informer's note to officials. 2. Any note or letter. 3. (Rare) An uncensored letter smuggled in or out of prison.

Tab, v. To book formally, as at police station, police headquarters, prison, etc.

Tab a kite. (P) To write a letter to be smuggled out of prison, evading censorship.

Tag. 1. One's name, whether genuine or an alias. 2. (Rare variant) See **Tab,** n.

Tail, n. 1. Pursuit; the act of following. ["To give a tail"—to follow.] "Give that ghee (fellow) a tail to the jug (bank)." 2. (Collectively) Loose women or degenerates. 3. Reward for capture of a criminal. "They got a five-G tail for you, Tobby. You better get a swag of ticket (railroad ticket for a distant place) and hole up (go into hiding)."

Tail, v. To follow. "There's a prowl-car (police patrol-car) tailing us. Give it the gun (step on the gas)."

Tail down. To track and overtake.

Tail, on one's. See **Pratt, on one's.**

Tailor-mades. (P) 1. Machine-made cigarettes, as distinguished from **makin's.** 2. Uniform trousers made to one's measure, as differentiated from ill-fitting ready-made trousers. "Them peddlers (sellers of prison stores) want two skins (dollars) for tailor-mades."

Take, n. 1. The proceeds of a crime; the income from a racket. "That skin-mob (gang of fur thieves) made a nice take." 2. The consummation of a crime. "Get the patsies (revolvers).

That bookie-joint (betting establishment) is ready for the take."

Take, v. 1. To consummate a crime. "Case (look over) that joint. We can take it Friday." 2. To accept a bribe. "Spring (talk) to the sheriff. He takes if he knows you are right (loyal to the underworld)." 3. To be sustained, as a criminal charge; to remain in effect. "I fell (was arrested) on the heavy (committing a robbery), but the rap (charge) didn't take." 4. (P) To be passively homosexual. 5. (P) To accept payment from a fellow convict for favors, services, or the securing of stolen goods. [Note: Taking is regarded as contemptible practice. Offering payment to a **right** person is considered a very grave insult.]

Take a bit. 1. To be sentenced to prison. "There ain't no way to spring (escape) on this rap (charge). We gotta take a bit. Grab a low plea (plead guilty to the least severe offense charged in the indictment)." 2. To accept sole burden of guilt to exonerate one's criminal associates.

Take a brodie. 1. To take a gambling chance; to steal without plan or prior information. 2. To be arrested. 3. To collapse; to fall down.

Take a bum beef. To take the blame for something one has not done; to go to prison for another's crime.

Take a bum rap. See **Take a bum beef.**

Take a collar. 1. To be arrested. 2. To plead guilty, exonerating one's accomplices. 3. (P) To be reported or locked up for a rule violation; to plead guilty to a charge of rule violation to shield others.

Take a dive. (Hobo, far West) To accept "salvation" at revival meeting or mission, usually to secure food, lodging, etc.

Take a drop. See **Take a fall.**

Take a fall. 1. To be arrested. 2. To

plead guilty with the understanding that one's accomplices will be exonerated. "The D.A. told the lip (lawyer) two of us gotta take the fall and two of us will spring (be acquitted). The rags (newspapers) are squawking murder (calling for a conviction)."

Take a flier. 1. To commit a crime of gain impulsively, with no foreknowledge or plan. 2. To act impulsively or without plan.

Take a flop. See **Take a tumble.**

Take a joint. To rob a place.

Take a joint apart. To wreck; to frisk thoroughly.

Take a jolt. To be sentenced to a prison term. "It's a right fall (proper charge), Red. Guess I'll have to take a jolt."

Take a mark. To rob a person.

Take a pinch. 1. See **Take a fall.** 2. (P) To be reported or locked up for rule violation; to plead guilty to a charge of rule violation to shield others.

Take a powder. 1. To flee; to make a getaway. 2. (Imperative) Get out! "Take a powder, crumb! We don't want you lousing up (ruining the reputation of) this joint."

Take a rap. 1. To accept the full burden of guilt for a crime in order to exonerate one's accomplices. "He's a right (loyal) kid. He took the rap alone and turned out (exonerated) his partners." 2. To be sentenced to prison. "I hear Luke took a rap in some stir (prison) down east." 3. To accept any blame.

Take a rope. 1. (P) To hang oneself. 2. (Loosely) to commit suicide.

Take a snare. See **Take a fall.**

Take a stab at. To try; attempt. "The legit (honest work) looked good when I hit the pavement (was released from prison), so I took a stab at it. But I done (served) too much time. A day's work was murder (unbearable)."

Take a toss to oneself. (P) (Northeastern industrial area) To become aware of one's shortcomings.

Take a tumble. 1. (P; Northeastern industrial area) To become aware; to take notice. "Why don't you take a tumble, bum? You're biting (cadging) me to death. I ain't married to you, you know." 2. To be arrested.

Take a whack at. 1. To make an attempt at; to concentrate one's attention and effort upon.

Take care of. 1. To assault; kill. 2. To pay a bribe to; exert political pressure upon; to coerce or intimidate. 3. To assist, as a person awaiting trial; to aid, as a prisoner or his dependents.

Take clemo. (Leavenworth Prison) To escape prison.

Take for a ride. 1. (Prohibition era term, now obsolescent) To force a gangland enemy into a car, drive him to a desolate spot and murder him. 2. To raise one's expectations and then to dash them abruptly; to nurture on empty promises; to poke fun at.

Take for a sleigh-ride. 1. To swindle; to outwit; to bait with false promises and expectations; to poke fun at. "If that crumb (unprincipled fellow) don't pay me them butts (cigarettes) on the next buy (commissary purchase), he better get himself locked up (in the segregation block). He ain't takin' me for no sleigh-ride." 2. To bring under the influence of drugs.

Take it easy. (N.Y. State prisons; less frequently in surrounding states) A common leave-taking expression among convicts. Take care of yourself!

Take it on the duff. (Obs.) To run away; to slip away quietly; (imperative) get out of here!

Take it on the lam. 1. To become a fugitive; to flee. 2. (By loose extension) To go away; to move on; to leave; (imperative) get out of here!

Take-joint. A crooked establishment.

Take (one) out in the country. See **Take for a ride,** def. 1.

Take (one) over the hurdles. 1. To subject to an ordeal, as in a **third degree** examination; to abuse or persecute; to use violence upon. "Did I get taken over the hurdles when the bulls (police) glommed (arrested) me! You'd think I started the war or somethin'." 2. (P) To subject a convict to abuse or persecution, as to a difficult or disagreeable work assignment; to cheat, abuse or harrass, a fellow convict.

Take one's number. (P) To report a convict for violation of prison rules.

Take one's shoes off. To rob one of everything. "Never give a **sucker** an even break; take their shoes off."

Take over. 1. To rob; to cheat. "A loft-mob (gang of warehouse thieves) took the joint over for twenty G's in skins (furs)." 2. To appropriate by threat or force.

Taker. 1. Buyer of stolen goods. [See more common: **Fence** and **Swag-buyer.**] 2. (P) A passive pederast; a male oral copulator.

Take the veil. To discontinue passive sodomous practices.

Take the bend off. To smooth the edge of the key card in the **three-card monte** swindle which has been deliberately bent by the swindlers. [Compare: **Put the bend on.**]

Take the knock. 1. To plead guilty to a crime; to accept full guilt in order to exonerate others. [Compare: **Cop a plea** and **Fall guy,** def. 1.] 2. To surrender and accept an arrest without resisting or attempting to flee. 3. To accept a loss or a reverse and retire without protest or complaint.

Take the stand. To enter the witness stand; to testify in court. "Yeah, the partner ratted on (informed against) me when we got dropped (were arrested), but he kicked over (refused to testify against me) when they wanted him to take the stand against me. I beat the rap (was released)."

Take to the cleaners. 1. To win all of one's opponent's money, as in a gambling swindle. "We rung in miss-outs (substituted crooked dice) and took the suckers to the cleaners." 2. To rob and leave penniless.

Take to the driers. See **Take to the cleaners.**

Taking one's shoes off, to pull a bit without. (P) To serve a prison term without serious inconvenience, especially a brief sentence or the rump end of a long term.

Talent. (Carnival) 1. (Collective) The more highly skilled criminals attached to a carnival. "Get all the talent out on the hustle (working among the crowd) and make it red (a prosperous day)." 2. Natural aptitude among carnival thieves.

Talented. (Carnival) Very able, as a crooked operator or thief with carnivals.

Talk. 1. To confess one's guilt; to implicate or incriminate others; to inform to authorities. 2. To boast dangerously of one's criminal exploits. "Happy's talking too much. We better take him out in the country (murder him)."

Talk business. 1. To offer a bribe to arresting officers or other officials; to offer to barter information against the underworld for leniency or immunity. "That fink (informer) sent for the D.A. to talk business. Looks like he's goin' to sing (inform against us)." 2. To bargain with the District Attorney offering to plead guilty to a lesser charge than that named in the indictment.

Talk turkey. To state one's business bluntly and frankly; to talk to the point. "Yeah, yeah, you do that: talk turkey when you meet the Board (appear before the Parole Board). On your kisser (with your face) and pedigree (criminal record) you'll rot in stir (never be granted parole)."

Tampered with. Divested of virginity, especially applied to passive pederasts.

Tangle ass. To become embroiled in a fight or heated argument. "That hack (guard) ain't handin' me no more buckwheats (abuse) or me and him's gonna tangle ass. The judge didn't say nothin' about that bein' in the bit (my prison term)."

Tangle-jaw. (Chiefly in the Prairie States) A criminal lawyer.

Tank. 1. A small town. 2. A small local jail. 3. (P) A large barred enclosure where men awaiting court hearing are herded together.

Tanker. 1. One who sells out accomplices to police. 2. A prize fighter who accepts money for deliberately losing his bouts. "Ziggy's got a piece of (financial interest in) a couple of tankers chiselin' (making) a nice buck (good money)."

Tap, v. 1. To open and empty of money, as a cash register, or strongbox. "I'll throw the spot in the air (hold the place up at pistol point) and you tap the damper (cash-register) and the pete (safe)." 2. To work **the tap.**

Tap, the, n. 1. Any of the various swindles effected by fraudulent advertising solicitations. [Note: Solicitors working **the tap** game sell space in non-existing publications, in publications having negligible circulation and no responsible staff, or in bona fide publications which they are not authorized to represent. Magazines with some reference in their titles to the police, fire, or health departments, or to an influential political party, are most effective with shady businessmen who are led to believe that by purchasing space, they are buying political "protection" and "good will." Victims

are prepared in advance of the solicitor's visit by a telephone call from a bogus "police inspector" or politician who simultaneously flatters and intimidates the prospective victims. Checks paid to solicitors are cashed at a discount by underworld **clearing houses.** Variations of the **tap** include the sale of tickets to phony banquets and the solicitation of funds for non-existent charitable organizations.] 2. A successful swindling operation involving a moderate sum of money; an extortion of a small amount of money. 3. An establishment or its proprietor who submits to repeated victimization in **the tap** racket.

Tap, on the. Engaged in, or by means of **the tap.**

Tap-man. One who works **the tap.**

Tapped out. Out of funds; "broke"; on one's uppers.

Tappers. Platinum or otherwise loaded dice with weights in slotted interior, used by tapping shot in and out of desired face of dice.

Ta-ta. A machine gun.

Taxi-bit. (P) A five-to-fifteen-year prison sentence.

T.B. 1. A confidence man. 2. (Carnival —abbreviation of "total blank") See **Blank.**

Tea. Marijuana.

Tea'd (or teed) up. 1. Under the influence of marijuana. 2. Exhilarated from any cause.

Tea-hound. A marijuana addict.

Tea-man. A smoker or purveyor of marijuana.

Tea-pad. An opium or marijuana smoking den. "I'm hitting (going to) the tea-pad and get my gage up (indulge in narcotics)."

Tearaway. Flight. ["On the tear"— in flight.] "We got a rumble (interrupted red-handed) and Pippy got banged (shot) in the leg on the tear-away."

Tear-drops. Pearls.

Tear-duster. A handkerchief.

Tears. See **Tear-drops.**

Teck. A technicality; a legal loop-hole.

Telephone number. A fantastic sum; a long prison term.

Telephone number bit. Any prison term in excess of fifteen years. "Cheech has one of them telephone number bits. Forty-to-eighty for the heist (robbery) and ten boffos (years) short time (still to serve on a previous sentence). He oughta hang up (should commit suicide)."

Tell off. To answer belligerently; to silence; to stand up for one's rights. "Tell that muzzler (unprincipled fellow) off. I'll go to bat (fight) with you if he kicks over (attempts any violence)."

Tenner. 1. (P) A ten-year prison sentence. 2. Ten dollars.

Ten percenter. See **Tipster.**

Ten spot. 1. A ten-year sentence. 2. A ten-dollar bill.

Tent. (P; very common, scattered areas) A prison inmate's uniform, notoriously ill-fitting.

Thank the judge that sent you here. (P) You're welcome. [Note: A standard prison expression deprecating "thanks" by fellow-convicts for favors.]

There. Ready; capable; reliable. "Get Joe to fill (participate) in on the heist (robbery). He's there with a rod (gun)."

Thick-slung. Oily tongued. "Were you riding the earie (listening) on the short-con (smooth lies) that sucker (fool) was givin' me? What a thick-slung ghee (fellow) he is!"

Thief. (Carnival) The operator of a gambling concession. "The thief is giving us the nix (signal). Lug the mark (get rid of the victim). He's a t.b. (total blank—unfit for swindling)."

Thimble. (Industrial northern area; rare) A stolen watch. [More common: **turnip.**]

Thimble-rig. 1. To defraud in the shell game. 2. (By extension) To rob by trickery; to swindle.

Thimble-rigger. 1. One who works the shell game. 2. (By extension) Any swindler.

Thin one. A dime.

Think-pot. The head; the mind.

Third baseman. Same as **baseman.**

Third degree, the. Examination by police using any of various methods of coercion and duress.

Third-degree. To subject to the third degree.

Third-rail. 1. Strong raw whiskey. 2. A thief who works on railroad passengers, picking pockets or stealing luggage.

Thirty-three gallery. (P) The prison graveyard. [Note: The number 33 is not always arbitrary. The number given the graveyard is often one higher than that of the highest-numbered gallery or tier in the prison. Thus in a prison of twenty-four tiers of cells, "twenty-five tier or gallery" might be the graveyard.] "Thirty-three gallery is gonna catch that rat (informer) if he keeps dropping tabs (sending notes) to the man (officials)."

Thousand-mile shirt. (Hobo) A shirt of very heavy serviceable fabric; a bright-colored shirt.

Three-card monte. A card game of Spanish origin in which two red cards (hearts or diamonds) and one black (spades or clubs) are laid face down on the table after deft manipulation by the dealer. Players must draw the black card to win. In the three-card monte swindle, the black card is withdrawn from play during the manipulation. Aides are usually employed to distract the victim's attention. [Note: A common variation is that in which the swindler's aide pretends to become the victim's partner. The operator seems not to notice the aide bend the corner of the black card, which is now in play. After several winnings, the stakes being rapidly multiplied, the fold is transferred by the manipulator from the black to a red card. The victim's angry complaints are interrupted by a cry of "Cops!" All take flight, leaving the victim to protest unheard.]

Three-sheet, v. (Mid-West, upper Mississippi Valley, scattered Middle-Atlantic States area) To boast. "That gapper (onlooker) three-sheeted himself into a fall (an arrest) on a hummer (crime of which he was innocent)."

Three-tap joint. An opium-smoking establishment.

Three-tapper. A patron of opium parlors. [See **Three taps.**]

Three taps, the. The soft rapping with the fingertips that is the open sesame to opium dens. "Think I'll hit the tea-pad the three taps (pay a visit to the opium den)."

Three-time loser. A third offender, i.e., one who has had two previous felony convictions, hence is liable to increased penalty for a subsequent conviction. [Note: In a few States, a third felony conviction carries a mandatory life-sentence. In New York and several other States, second and third offenders are liable to identically increased penalties, and fourth offenders to mandatory **life.**]

Throw, n. **Throw-up.**

Throw, v. To rob at pistol point. "My partner held the door down (guarded the exit) and I threw the joint."

Throw a spot in the air. To hold up a place at gun-point. "That joint goes on (yields to) the tap (fraudulent advertising solicitation) regular. Plenty scratch (cash) and ice (diamonds) on the suckers (patrons) there every

night. I'd like to throw the spot in the air."

Throw a wing-ding. 1. To feign or exaggerate sickness in order to obtain drugs. 2. (P) To malinger or feign illness, in order to escape work or enjoy hospital fare which is sometimes only slightly better than regular prison mess. 3. To feign illness in order to impede court proceedings in a bid for leniency. "No moxie (moral stamina) in them pollies (politicians) and legit big shots (big business men). When the pinch (an arrest) comes, they all throw a wing-ding and crawl (plead most abjectly)."

Throw boxcars. (Chiefly rural; Central Western and Southwestern States) To suffer a stroke of misfortune; to run into hard luck. "I was doing a bit (serving a sentence) on the farm, and me and a couple of other cons (convicts) went over the hill (attempted to escape). They made it, but I threw boxcars when one of the posse pooped (shot) me in the leg."

Throw lead. To fire pistol shots; to exchange shots.

Throw one a hump. 1. To jostle and pin one in a position to be robbed by a pickpocket. 2. To engage in sexual intercourse with one. 3. To be intimate with, as with a passive pederast.

Throw one's weight around. To use rough tactics.

Throw-out. An arm or wrist which can be thrown out of joint at will in insurance frauds.

Throw slugs. To shoot. "We busted out of the joint on the tearaway (in flight), all the dicks (with all the police) in town throwing slugs at us, across the main drag (main street) into the boiler (car) and away. Gimpey was pooped (hit with a bullet) in the leg, but nobody was snatched (arrested)."

Throw snake-eyes. (Rural areas,

West and Southwest States) **To run into ill-luck.**

Throw the book away. 1. To conduct court proceedings without regard to due process of law. "The snitch-sheets (newspapers) had the heat on plenty (were raising a hullabaloo) and the rappers (complainants) were all screwed up (confused). The judge figured it was a right rap (justifiable charge) that hadda stick (upon which we should be found guilty), so he threw the book away." 2. To adhere to the letter rather than to the spirit of the law; to exercise undue severity in court proceedings.

Throw the key away. 1. To commit to prison for an exceedingly long term. 2. (P) To place in a punishment cell for a long period.

Throw-up, n. An armed robbery; a stick-up. "Might as well bang (kill) the sucker (victim) these days. If you don't get topped (electrocuted), you get a smaller bit (sentence) for a knock-off (murder) than a throw-up."

Throw up, v. See **Throw, v.**

Throw wood on the fire. 1. (P) To pretend to make peace between angered parties while slyly slipping in remarks that add fuel to the smoldering fire. 2. To agitate; to stir up trouble maliciously; to incite to riot.

Thumb. To approach and accost, as a prospective subject for swindling or panhandling; to accost.

Ticker. 1. Heart; nerve; boldness. "What a ticker that Dutch's got! Him and the bull (detective) laid on the street with slugs (bullets) in them banging it out (firing shots at each other)." 2. A bomb with a built-in timing mechanism.

Ticket. 1. (P) A formal report for rule violation; a warning to comply with a rule or be formally reported. 2. (Scattered prisons) A formal grant of parole. ["To get a ticket"—to receive a formal grant of parole.] 3. A war-

rant for one's arrest. 4. (P) A detainer lodged against a convict pending the completion of a current prison term. [See more common: **Hooker.**]

Tie up with. 1. To enter into criminal partnership with. 2. To become embroiled in a fight with; to quarrel with. "Looks like I'm gonna have to tie up with the fence (buyer of the goods we steal). He's clipping (cheating) us bad on that swag (loot)." 3. To marry; to live with.

Time. A sentence to any penal institution—To do . . . ; to pull . . . ; to serve . . . "Them judges that settle (sentence) us hand out time like it was peanuts (something trivial)."

Timer. A safe or vault equipped with a time-lock mechanism. "I cased the spot (looked around), and it chilled (discouraged) me plenty. It's all bugged up (filled with burglar alarms), the pete (safe) has a timer and the out (means of escape) is tough."

Tin. A policeman's or other law enforcement agent's badge; a stolen or counterfeit badge used by extortionists impersonating venal police.

Tin-ear. A studious eavesdropper, endeavoring to appear deaf or preoccupied. "Dummy-up (be quiet), tin-ear over there is tuned in."

Tin throne. (P) The cell slop bucket in unmodernized prisons.

Tip, n. 1. (Rare) A cashier's booth, desk, or cage. 2. A crowd at any carnival or curiosity exhibit. "Let's get on the whiz (start picking pockets), Whitey. That tip looks lousy with (to be full of) marks (prospective victims)."

Tip, v. See **Tip off, v.**

Tipeasy. (South) An expert burglar, especially one having acrobatic skill in making difficult entries. "If that dinghe (colored) tipeasy takes a fall (is arrested), they'll stretch (hang) him for luggin' (carrying) a barker (revolver)."

Tip-off, n. 1. Any word or gesture,

as a clue to cryptic pattern of words or actions; a key or an explanation. 2. Information given to thieves regarding prospects for robbery; information given to police concerning criminals.

Tip off, v. 1. To warn; advise; inform. "Tip Mickey off that his partner dropped (was arrested) and spilled his guts (made a full confession)." 2. To give information to thieves regarding potential victims for robbery; to inform to the police.

Tip one's duke. 1. To reveal one's purpose or plan. 2. To cause or force one to reveal the truth; to draw the truth from one; to cause one to reveal his purpose or plan. "Don't crack (say anything) till I tip the ghee's (fellow's) duke."

Tip-over, n. Police raid to break up a disreputable establishment, making no arrests.

Tip over, v. To rob an establishment or dwelling, especially by burglary; to raid premises, as by the police.

Tips. (Carnival) Sums of money withheld from a concessionaire; money withheld from associates.

Tipster. One who points out potential victims to criminals in exchange for a share of the loot (usually ten percent); a professional purveyor of information about persons or places which may profitably be made the object of criminal activity. "Them tipsters are all crumbs (unprincipled fellows). When they are hot in the biscuit for (in great need of) dough, they give you a send-in (send you out) on any steer (wild goose-chase)."

Tipster's bit. The share of loot paid the tipster—usually ten percent of the total.

Title-tapper. One who hypothecates forged property deeds.

Toad-skin. A one-dollar bill.

Toad-sticker. A knife, especially a long-bladed weapon.

Tomato can vag. A hobo, especially one with enough experience to cook good mulligan stew in a gallon tomato can over a bonfire.

Tommy. A light machine gun.

Tommy-ghee. A machine-gunner.

Tongue. A lawyer.

Tool, n. The skilled craftsman in a gang of pickpockets. "You better get the grindstone and sharpen it (practice pocket-picking on one of us), Fingers. Any tool gets three rumbles (troubles) in a day is slipping. 2. (Rare) a pistol or revolver. 3. The phallus.

Tool, v. (Leavenworth Prison) To shirk work.

Toot the tooter. 1. To ring the bell; to blow the automobile horn. 2. (P) To blow the steam whistle to stop work; to sound the escape siren. "Four, of them road-gang ghees (fellows) had a batch (jug of home-brew) stashed (hidden away). They got lushed up (drunk) and copped a mope (escaped). They'll be tooting the tooter any minute."

Top. To punish by legal hanging; (by general extension) to subject to any form of capital punishment.

Toppin's. (Hobo: far West; California prisons) Cake with icing, sugar-top, etc.

Tops. Crudely loaded dice, capable of being used only upon the most gullible of victims. [Note: Tops are manipulated in and out of play by the swindlers. They are so weighted as to guarantee the turning up of a single combination of numbers.]

Torch. A professional arsonist who sets fires to defraud insurance companies.

Torch a squib. 1. (Obs.) To light the fuse attached to the percussion cap in a safe-blowing operation. 2. To make electric contact with the percussion cap in safe-blowing.

Torch-man. A safe-cracker who special: izes in the use of oxy-acetylene equipment. "A good torch-man can burn through that outside door, but the keister (strong-box) inside won't go for nothing (yield to any force)."

Torpedo. A professional killer.

Toss, n. 1. An armed robbery. "That slum-joint (jewelry store) the **tipster** gave us ain't no good for a toss. The clerks is all heeled (armed), and the joint is lousy with bugs (full of burglar alarms)." 2. A hasty search of a place during a robbery that leaves it in wild disorder. 3. (P) A search of prison cells, shops, recreation rooms, etc., as differentiated from a search of the person. "The man (officer) gave my cell a toss, but he didn't fan (search) me. I figure it musta been a finger (information to authorities) on a big swag (stolen prison stores) or a hot boiler (contraband stove)." 4. A sign of recognition; a greeting. "I ain't givin' that fink (informer) a toss. He's a lousy peddler (of stolen stores)." 5. A second thought; notice. "I never gave it a toss till you cracked (spoke) about it. That's three times we seen that car on our pratt (behind us). It must be a tail (someone following us)."

Toss, v. To rob a place at gun point; to throw things about during a robbery while searching for valuables. "The next joint we toss, I'm frisking (searching) the suckers (victims). You missed a couple o' yards (hundred dollars) on the last score (robbery)." 2. (P) To search [cells] for contraband, stolen goods, etc. "Some new hack (prison guard) tossed our tier. He wrecked my coop (cell), gunning (looking) everywhere but under the paint on the wall, the creep (mean fellow)." 3. To search any place hurriedly, throwing things into wild disorder.

Toss lead. To fire shots.

Toss the book at. 1. To sentence to life imprisonment; to impose the maxi-

mum penalty provided by law. 2. (P) To order a parole applicant, or a convict returned to prison for parole violation, to serve the maximum term of his unexpired sentence. "I got a dead bang fall (arrested in the act) on parole and beat the rap (was acquitted of the charge). The Board (Parole Board) will toss the book at my noggin (head) all right."

Toss the broads. To operate the swindle-game **three-card monte.**

Touch. 1. A crime of gain; the loot from a specific crime. "We oughta have another rod (gunman) on that touch (robbery). If there's a rumble (trouble), three men can't control the joint." 2. (P) A successful raid on prison stores. "The screw (guard) is blowing his top (almost insane with rage). Some ghee (fellow) made a touch for a ham and mooched (sauntered) out with it right under the hack's (guard's) nose." 3. Anything especially desirable, as a letter or money from home, or a satisfactory work assignment. "I buzzed (talked to) the dep (Deputy Warden) for that bake-shop job. Nice touch if I get it. That's a good scoring job (a job with plenty of opportunity to steal)." 4. A victim of criminals. "I've got a touch readied up (prepared) to go (yield) on a little shake (extortion). Want to fill (take part in the deal)?"

Touch-off. An incendiary fire; the act of causing such a fire.

Touch-off man. One who starts the fires for professional arson-rings. [See **Torch;** compare **Firebug.**]

Tough bit. (P) An especially unpleasant term of imprisonment. [Note: Strict discipline, uncongenial inmates, personal poverty, and outside domestic difficulties are the most general characteristics of a tough bit.]

Tough can to do business. A place of imprisonment in which bribery, corruption, and disciplinary laxity are absent.

Tough gaff. A severe punishment; a long prison sentence; a hard ordeal; anything difficult of accomplishment.

Tough-giver-up. 1. One who stubbornly resists robbery, extortion, or other criminal attack. 2. A stingy person; a miser.

Tough man. (P) A difficult person to convince, curb, bribe, or otherwise influence; a stubborn fellow. "That guy got me knocked up (sick and tired), puttin' the handle on me (asking me for favors). He's a tough man."

Tough rap. 1. A serious charge punishable by severe penalty. 2. (Less common) A long prison term. 3. (P.; loosely) Any accusation of a serious character, directed against an inmate. "What do you mean I beat you (stole) for your dukes (tobacco)? That's a tough rap to give a pal. Frisk (search) yourself (about your person). I stuck it in your kick (pocket)."

Tough town. A town unsuitable for criminal activity, either because of its poverty or its effective police force.

Tough town to do business. A town in which there is little or no political corruption and where leniency or immunity cannot be bought.

Tout, n. 1. A race track swindler who induces bettors to place wagers for him in exchange for worthless "inside" information. 2. A pimp; one who directs gullible patrons to gambling houses, bill-padding night clubs, and other shady establishments.

Tout, v. 1. To operate as a **tout.** 2. To inveigle or induce (another) to carry out any planned action, seeking to obtain without risk a share of the profit or gain; to promote; to persuade; to cajole; to coax by word or action. "What are you touting me to heist (hold up) the joint (place) for? You ain't getting no tipster's bit (share of loot in exchange for information) 'cause I had it cased (that site inspected) before you cracked (mentioned it)."

Tower. (P) A guard turret on a prison wall. "If you're thinkin' of makin' a beat (escaping), Denny, hit (try going over the wall) six tower. The hack (guard) up there is a stiff with a gun (a very bad shot)."

Town clown. A marshal, constable, or policeman in a small one-cop town.

Toy. 1. A measure of opium, approximately one-twentieth of a pound. 2. A pistol; revolver.

Tracer. A crude forger who traces signatures in pencil and goes over them in ink. "That stiff (clumsy fellow) is a tracer. We gotta get an ace (expert) scratch-man (free-hand forger) for this trick (job)."

Tracer-chain. (South) A strong light chain threaded through the shackles of convicts returning to prison quarters from a labor assignment. [Note: Tracer-chains are often used illegally to beat men inured to the lash.]

Trade. (West) Youths who make a practice of submitting to or robbing degenerates. ("Rough trade"—the unkempt street urchin type of trade.)

Treyer. 1. Three dollars. 2. (P) Three years.

Tribe. A group of thieves or gangsters who operate together; a gang.

Trick. 1. A specific crime, as a robbery, burglary, or the like. "That stiff (fellow) fell (was arrested) on a two-bit (petty) trick, opened up (confessed and implicated others), and they cleaned up the calendar (and pinned on him every unsolved crime ever committed in that neighborhood)." 2. (Central and mid-Western States; rare) A term served in a prison, reformatory, or penitentiary.

Trigger. A gunman, especially for

gangland warfare or special murder assignment.

Trip. 1. An arrest or commitment to prison. 2. (P) A transfer from one prison to another.

Triple life. (P) A prison sentence to three "life terms." [Note: In states where a life-sentence carries parole eligibility after a specified number of years, more than one such term is imposed by a judge who wishes to thwart parole.]

Tripod. (Carnival) A device to control a crooked gambling wheel. "The patch (legal adjuster) can't do business with (bribe) the fuzz (police). Knock off (quit work). The tripod is staying down (cannot be used)." ["The tripod is up"—the tripod is being used.]

Trip up back, the. (P) The brief walk to the death chair. "Three were supposed to go (die) tonight. One ghee (fellow) got a commute (Governor's commutation of sentence to life imprisonment) and hit the population (was placed among the general inmate population). The other two's makin' the trip up back."

Trolley. (P) A line by which things are passed by inmates from one cell to another. "The screw (guard) just glommed (grabbed) a tab (note) off Prussian Pete's trolley goin' to that hunk of hat (passive pederast) in 20-cell (cell number 20)."

Tronk, n. (Penn. prisons and neighboring states) A state prison or penitentiary. "Jake did a tenner (served ten years) in tronk."

Tronk, v. (Penn. and environs) To imprison; commit to penitentiary. "I got tronked for a sixer (six months) on a bum rap (on a crime of which I was innocent)."

Troupe. (Carnival) A mob or gang of thieves.

Truck driver. (Ironically) One who is not perverted.

Truck-lift. An armed robbery of commercial trucks.

Trusty. (P) An inmate assigned to a position of trust, especially outside the prison walls. [Note: In·New York State prisons this term is rarely heard. Outside man is more common.]

Try to get even. (P) To practice active pederasty. (By implication: To try to balance one's previous passive pederastic record.) "There's the Turk gunnin' (looking) over the new fish (new inmates); still tryin' to get even, huh?"

T's. A variant of **Tops.**

Tub-worker. A card-sharper who operates on trans-oceanic liners. "Monty was hooked (inveigled into a card game) by an old tub-worker, and went for the works (was robbed of everything he had)."

Tumble, n. 1. An interruption by police or others during the commission of a crime; pursuit following a crime; outcry or complaint to police during or immediately after a crime; the newspaper and radio alarm and publicity following a crime. 2. Suspicious notice or attention, especially by police. "I'm hot as a forty-five (in grave danger of arrest), heeled (armed) and swagged up (carrying loot), and I breezed (sauntered) right by the bulls (policemen) without a tumble." 3. Recognition by a complainant of a suspect in a police lineup, not necessarily followed by formal identification. "The sucker (victim) gave me a tumble for a second, but he couldn't peg (identify) me for sure." 4. Any notice or recognition, usually followed by a sign or greeting. "I ain't got a tumble for any of them fleas (low fellows.) They're all copperhearted (policemen at heart)." 5. Sudden awareness or realization. (a) "Do you know, I just took a tumble to the score (realized what is going on)? I nearly ranked (spoiled) the trick on (robbery for) you." (b) "Why don't you take a tumble (realize you are not wanted) and cop a sneak (get out of here), you crum?" 6. (Rare) An arrest in the act of committing a crime. 7. (Rare) The act of accosting a person.

Tumble, v. To give or take a **tumble.**

Tumul, n. (Jewish-American, especially in N.Y. State) Any scuffle; rough-and-tumble tactics, especially in racketeering or in the commission of a crime; confusion. "The mark (victim) fanned (felt for) and missed his poke (wallet). He grabbed some square (innocent bystander) and in the tumul we blew (fled)."

Tumul, v. To commit a crime by rough-and-tumble tactics; to engage in a scuffle; to stir up a fight; to hustle energetically, with few or no scruples. for money. "I'm wrapping up (going straight) after this bit (this prison sentence is completed). Ain't nothin' but headaches tumulin' around."

Tumuler. 1. A criminal of the crude rough-and-tumble variety. 2. A noncriminal who enjoys a fight or free-for-all combat; a ruffian.

Tune in. To eavesdrop. "I just saw those ghees (fellows) get chivs (knives) slipped to them. Ease over and tune in. I think they're out to cop a heel (assault), Thumby."

Turf, on the. 1. Out of prison and engaged in a criminal career; engaged in criminal activity. "Max is back on the turf playin' the field (ready to try any sort of crime for money)." 2. (Hobo) On the road; operating professionally as a beggar. 3. (Prostitution) On the streets; in a bordello or callhouse.

Turf, the. The criminal arena; any criminal activity; the underworld.

Turf it. (Hobo) To leave town or a hobo camp to travel.

Turk. (P) An active pederast.

Turkey. 1. A suitcase; satchel; any

piece of luggage. "Cop a sneak (steal up quietly) and snatch the turkey when I stall (divert the attention of) the mark (victim)." 2. Anything worthless, especially a package of valueless substitute for narcotics sold to addicts; a failure; a profitless crime; a criminal victim with no money or valuables. 3. (Hobo) The handkerchief-wrapped roll of belongings carried by hobos and tramps.

Turn. 1. To turn traitor to the underworld and its code of criminal ethics; to betray one's criminal associates. "There is one ghee (fellow) no one figured he'd turn. They all go wrong (abandon the underworld code) these days." 2. To execute, as a theft or robbery.

Turn a trick. 1. To commit a crime. 2. To commit an act of prostitution. 3. (P) To submit to any act of degeneracy.

Turn copper. To desert the underworld and assist the authorities by informing against one's erstwhile associates. "Any hustling (stealing) I do is gonna be single-o (on my own) from now on. I ain't having no partner to turn copper on me. You can't trust these ghees (fellows) on the turf (in the underworld) today."

Turn copper-hearted. To lose one's courage; to confess one's guilt, especially in such a way as to implicate one's associates. "The bulls (police) were on our pratt (behind us) throwing slugs (firing shots), and this creep (weak-kneed fellow) turns copper-hearted on me."

Turn-down. 1. (P) A denial or refusal, as of a parole application, an appeal to a higher court, or a petition for clemency. 2. (Hobo) A refusal of alms.

Turn-in, n. 1. An arrest resulting from the treachery of one's associates. 2. (P) A report for violation of prison rules. "The shop (workshop) hack (guard) gave Bob a turn-in for a kick-over (refusing to work)."

Turn in. 1. To betray (one's accomplices) to the police. "That crumb turned in his partners in a deal for an s.s. (suspended sentence)." 2. (P) To report for rule violation.

Turnip. A watch.

Turn it loose! Shoot! Fire!

Turnkey. (P) 1. A guard or keeper in a penal institution. 2. (Various penal institutions) An inmate trusty who locks and unlocks cell doors under official supervision. "Watch them turn-keys, Chuck. They'd bury (inform against) you quicker than a screw (guard)."

Turn off. To rob a place; to burglarize.

Turn oneself in. To surrender oneself voluntarily to police or district attorney's office to answer pending charges or submit to examination. [Note: An act usually regarded with contempt by the rank and file of the underworld.] "There's a jerk (imbecile) must like the can (prison). He gets a commute (a governor's commutation of sentence) after pullin' (serving) a sawbuck (ten years in prison). Two weeks after he hits the pavement (was released) he turns himself in and says he's scared of the cars and noise out there. Them screwballs (half crazy fellows) get all the breaks (concessions)."

Turn on the heat. 1. To increase and intensify police activity, whether directed against specific criminals or against the underworld in general. 2. To threaten with a gun; to shoot; to apply drastic measures. 3. To subject to **third degree** police examination.

Turn-out, n. 1. A discharge in consequence of an accomplice's assuming the sole burden of guilt. "The shyster (lawyer) fixed it so I cop out (plead guilty to a lesser charge) and you get a turn-out." 2. A discharge from prison; an acquittal by due process of law.

Turn out, v. To secure the release of a co-defendant by pleading guilty and assuming full responsibility for the crime charged. "That fink (low fellow) promised me a fin (five dollars) a week if I'd be the fall guy (assume full guilt) and turn him out. I got a Christmas card four years after." 2. To parole; to acquit; to discharge from court or prison. 3. To reveal the contents of one's pockets after a robbery to prove that no loot is being withheld. "C'mon, let's turn out. I don't say nobody is h.o.-ing (withholding loot), but maybe someone forgot somethin'."

Turn the hose on. To beat with a length of rubber hose in police **third degree**, thus leaving no telltale marks.

Turn upside down and shake. To search an accomplice suspected of withholding a portion of loot.

Turret-man. (P) A guard posted in a gun-turret of the prison wall.

Tweezer. A woman's handbag; any old-fashioned purse with knobbed snap clasps.

Twenty-four. A warning by police to leave town within twenty-four hours or be arrested for vagrancy. "You're gettin' a tweny-four before your prints (fingerprints) are checked (in the General Bureau of Identification). Take a powder (leave) as soon as you spring (are released)."

Twenty-two-fifty men. (N. Y. City; Obs.) A term applied to taxicab drivers, and other people regarded as assistant policemen; informers. [Note: In the early 1920's the N.Y. City police department is alleged to have retained the services of such aides at a weekly salary of $22.50. Most of them were awaiting examination for positions in the police department. The term endures, although the conditions that gave rise to it are all but forgotten.]

Twidget [**A hunk of twidget**]. 1. Prostitutes; loose women. 2. (P) Passive pederasts as a group.

Twister. A beggar or a junkey who throws fits of convincing character; a **wing-ding.**

Twist one. (P) To roll a cigarette.

Two-and-over. (A prohibition era term, still used in the illegal alcohol racket) Rot-gut whiskey; green liquor.

Two-bit. Worth about twenty-five cents; contemptible; insignificant. "Them two-bit touches (robberies) you go on will get you a million boffos (years) in stir (prison). Might as well go after somethin' big."

Two-bit hustler. 1. Any petty thief or racketeer. 2. A prostitute who sells her favors cheaply. [Also Two-Bit Kitty; Two-Bit May; etc.] 3. (P) A passive pederast or male oral copulator who is promiscuous and cheap in the sale of favors. [Also: Two-Bit Willy; Two-Bit Tom; etc.]

Two-bit mouthpiece. A criminal lawyer whose retainer never exceeds the maximum of twenty-five dollars; a cheap or contemptible attorney. "All them two-bit mouthpieces do is duke you in (inveigle you) to cop a plea (plead guilty); phony rap (innocent) or right rap (guilty), they don't wanta know nothing, just to put the glom on (grab) your dough (money) and lam (get away from you)."

Two-bit score. 1. A contemptibly petty crime. 2. A loan, or request for a loan of twenty-five cents or twenty-five dollars.

Two-bit shyster. See **Two-bit mouthpiece.**

Two-for-one. Characterized by the legal malpractice of attorneys who bargain with the district attorney to secure leniency for one wealthy client in exchange for a guarantee that two poor clients will plead guilty. [Note: This malpractice augments the lawyer's prestige among moneyed clients and the district attorney's record for convictions.] "That two-for-one muzzler (unethical fellow) sold me out after he beat me for my last C-note (hundred dollars)."

Two-one. (A certain prison in N. Y. State) Two company, cell number one, a cell reserved for use as a lavatory in which rumors are born concerning all things from State legislation to personal gossip. [Note: Two-one is a constant source of convict humor. In answer to rumors of pending legislation favorable to convicts, prison cynics are prone to reply, "Yeah, that bill just passed in two-one." Reference is likely to be made to the kind of paper available in that cell for writing such legislation and the ultimate disposition of it. In most prisons there is a similar washroom or utility cell around which the humor revolves.]

Two-stemmer. A town with at least two principal thoroughfares, regarded as profitable area for panhandling or racketeering. "Them tanks (small towns) get you peanuts (no money at all). We'll hit (go to) two-stemmers where there's a nice buck (money to be had)."

Two-time. Double-cross.

Two-time loser. A second offender, i.e., one who has a previous felony conviction, hence is liable to increased penalty for a second felony conviction.

Two-way ghee. 1. A fence-straddler who travels with the underworld, but informs to police surreptitiously. 2. A hypocrite; one who is two-faced; a moody and treacherous person. "This bull (policeman) was supposed to be a businessman (man who accepts bribes), but he was a two-way ghee. He'd take (the bribe) and then put the finger on you (point you out) so his partner (brother officer) could make the pinch (arrests)."

Typewriter. (Rare) Machine gun.

U

Unbutton a box. To force open a safe or vault with an iron bar, sledgehammers and specially designed ripping instruments.

Uncle. 1. A buyer of stolen goods. 2. A pawn shop proprietor. 3. An active pederast or male oral copulator interested in young boys [nephews]. 4. (Plural) G-men; agents of the Federal Bureau of Investigation.

Undercover. Operating very secretively, as an informer, degenerate, withholder of loot on criminal accomplices. ["Undercover rat"—informer; "undercover punk or fag"—degenerate; "undercover sinker"—withholder of part of loot.]

Underneath. The woman shoplifter's place for concealing stolen articles under her dress.

Under one's belt, to have. Murders; notches in one's gun. "That Chicago torpedo (killer) had ten under his belt before they chilled him (he himself was murdered)."

Under the gun. 1. (P) Under armed guard, as prisoners working in gangs outside the prison walls. 2. In a helpless or untenable situation, as a result of being outmaneuvered; under close surveillance. "I can't clip (steal) no mess-hall swag (food). The hack (guard) has got me smack under the gun."

Under the light. Undergoing police questioning, often under **third degree** coercion.

Unload. 1. To sell, as stolen goods or contraband; to store away or conceal, as loot. "Okay, Tiny, on the tearaway (flight after crime) head straight for the drop (cache) and I'll unload this swag (the stolen goods)." 2. To rid oneself, as of weapons or of undesirable company. "Unload that muzzler (unprincipled fool). He ranks (bungles) every touch (theft) you bring him on." 3. To pick pockets as a member of a gang at any point where passengers leave or enter trains, buses, ferry-boats, public elevators, and the like.

Unslough. (Among pickpockets) To unbutton or unfasten, as watch and chain from a vest. "I thought I'd need a stick (burglar's jimmy) to unslough that mark's (victim's) boodle (money). Buttons, safety pins, and a deep pratt (trousers) kick (pocket)."

Untouchable. Will not accept a bribe.

Up. 1. Slated for pleading, trial, sentence, or other court proceedings. 2. (P) Scheduled to appear before the Parole Board for a hearing. "The shyster (lawyer) says I'm up to get my bundle (sentence) tomorrow."

Up against it. Addicted to, as to a drug habit. ["Up against the gonger" —addicted to the opium pipe; "up against the h"—addicted to heroin; and the like.]

Up-and-up. 1. Out of the underworld, making an honest living; honest; reformed. "Midge's got a couple of dice games and a string of hustlers (group of prostitutes) makin' him a nice buck (good money). He's strictly up-and-up." 2. Loyal; fair; trustworthy; not open to bribery. "Yippy aced it (has been showing his character) for years. Yeah, he's an up-and-up ghee (fellow) of the old school." 3. True, factual. "I ain't on the rib (fooling you). That's up-and-up. He got hit in the cruller (was killed) on the heist (attempting a robbery) in St. Louis."

Up-and-up, the. 1. An honest means of livelihood. 2. Loyalty to the underworld code and standards. "No, he ain't opening up (won't confess). The up-

and-up looks better to him than a spring (release) for ratting (in exchange for turning informer)." 3. The truth.

Up back. See **Back up.**

Up-and-downs. Playing cards slight-ly bent at the edges for swindling.

Upstairs. (Among pickpockets) Inside breast pocket.

Up the river. To prison; in prison.

User. An addict and purchaser of narcotics.

V

V. 1. A five-dollar bill. 2. A five-year sentence. 3. A safe; a vault. 4. A safe-burglar's implement to expedite the removal of the combination spindle of a safe with a minimum of noise and labor. It is a 4-inch-square steel plate of half-inch thickness with a deep v-shaped cut in the upper rim, large enough to slip over the combination dial plate of a safe. The sides of the v-cut are beveled to assure a snug fit as it is tamped into place. Four screw-bolts, one at each corner, are fitted in an 8-turn thread, $\frac{1}{16}$" thick. Gradual turns on the bolts are taken alternately until the terrific pulling power thus exerted yanks knobs, combination-dial, spindle, and inner sleeves free, exposing the mechanism.

Vag, n. 1. A vagrant. 2. Vagrancy. [Note: A charge of vagrancy is a legal device for arresting suspicious or undesirable persons who cannot be proven guilty of any crime, in order to rid the community of thieves who manage to escape conviction for theft. Such persons are sent to the workhouse on the ground that they lack "visible means of livelihood" or a legally fixed minimum sum of money. Regulations vary in different sections of the country.]

Vag, v. To sentence [one] to the workhouse, county jail, or road gang as a **vag.** "We got a pick-up (were arrested) in New Orleans and got vagged for a sixer (six months)."

Valentine. A clever safe-cracker whose technique is similar to that of "Jimmy Valentine" of fiction. [Note: Sandpapered fingertips and stethoscopes for "feeling out" tumbler com-

binations are complete fictions. Expert mechanics do operate weirdly to inexpert eyes; hence the romantic buncombe.]

Valentino. (Rare) A thief who specializes in preying upon women.

Varnished joint. (New York City) A furnished room or apartment.

Vegas. (Nevada and New Mexico) Las Vegas.

Vic. (Scattered prisons and reformatories) A convict. "The hacks (guards) snatched (intercepted) a rod (gun) shipped to the storehouse. They ain't got the vic it was for."

Vigerage. The loan shark's twenty per cent weekly interest rate. [Note: "Five dollars for six" is the usual weekly arrangement. Small loans are most frequent, although very large sums are sometimes borrowed by influential citizens who wish to keep their transactions secret.]

Vigerage-and. (Loan-shark racket) Principal and a week's interest on a loan, plus the interest compounded on the entire debt. "You borrowed $50.00 for $60.00 eight days ago; vigerage-and makes you owe $72.00 now."

Violation. (P) The formal charge of violation of parole.

Violator. (P) An ex-convict who violated parole contract; a parole violator who has been returned to prison. "How many violators hit (were sent back to) the joint (this prison) on the last boat (transfer of inmates)?"

Violin (Variant: **fiddle**). A portable machine gun.

Violin-case. A case for a machine gun.

Viper. An habitual smoker of opium or marijuana as distinguished from an occasional or periodic smoker. "That viper has always got the gage up (under the influence of drugs)."

W

Wack. See **Whack,** n. and v.

Wacky. Mentally unbalanced; queer; erratic.

Wad. A roll of paper money. "The sucker (victim) blew (lost) his wad on the lemon game (card swindle) and hollered copper (complained to the police)."

Wagon, the. The police patrol wagon.

Waiting for a dude. Said of a woman who is loyally awaiting the release of her husband or sweetheart from prison.

Waiting for a ghee. See **Waiting for a dude.**

Waiting for a street car. Any ridiculous or trivial offense involving serious punishment under the law. [Note: The phrase is constantly used in an ironic sense in reply to inquisitive inmates who ask, "What are you in for?" The implication is, "Mind your own business!" See **Spitting on the sidewalk.**]

Wake-up. (P) The morning of the day on which a convict is scheduled to be released. "Three days and a wake-up and I hit the pavement (shall be released)."

Walk into a collar. To step unsuspectingly into a police trap; a purely accidental arrest.

Walk-out, n. A criminal charge which is without foundation; an indictment which cannot be sustained. "Don't even buzz (call) the tongue (lawyer). This rap (charge) is a walk-out."

Walk out, v. 1. To be released in absolute freedom from court or legal custody. 2. (P) To leave prison by mandatory discharge without parole or other restraint.

Walk the line. (Many scattered prisons) To be compelled to walk along a prescribed path or chalk line for a specific period of time as punishment for a rule violation.

Walk-up. A brothel.

Wall flower. A saloon hanger-on who cadges drinks.

Walter Winchell. (P) An informer; one who gossips. [Note: Since he commenced championing the F.B.I., the columnist and radio commentator has been called **The Snitcher** in N.Y. State prisons. He is avidly heard and ardently hated by the underworld.]

Wampole. A liquid narcotic, highly aphrodisiacal, popular among marijuana and opium addicts. Alcohol, quinine, and strychnine (and, occasionally, tincture of cantharides) are chief ingredients. Used by opium eaters to counteract the bitterness of opium pills. [Note: The term is a survival of the proper name of an American drug firm, prosecuted and fined in 1912 for the use of this recipe in a quack cure-all.]

Wampum. Money, especially small change. "What am I gonna pay the shyster (lawyer) off with, wampum?"

War. A fight between rival mobs or racial factions in or out of prison.

Warbler. (Chiefly in the Prairie States) A criminal lawyer.

Warden's box. (P) A locked, slotted box in the prison cell-hall, into which inmates may drop notes requesting interviews, changes of work assignment, and the like. [Note: Frequently the Warden's box is used by inmates informing against fellow-convicts.] "That fleabag (unprincipled fellow) is always droppin' tabs (putting notes) in the Warden's box. I think he's an undercover fink (informer)."

Warden's court. (P) The prison tribunal, presided over by the Warden or his deputy, to try those charged with rule violation. [Note: Individual penalties, in most prisons, may not exceed 364 days. Neither a single penalty nor aggregate penalties may in any case exceed the maximum term of the convict's commitment. Punishment cells house recalcitrants not eligible for further time penalties.]

Warden's man. (P) 1. A convict assigned to an important work assignment by the warden. 2. An informer who communicates directly with the warden.

Washed up. 1. Useless in criminal enterprise, because of loss of nerve, old age, unrelenting police or parole surveillance, etc. 2. Exhausted of possibilities as a specific racket or field of criminal activity; no longer able to be used for criminal exploitation. 3. See **Bury,** def. 1 and 2.

Washers. 1. Coins; small change. 2. (Loosely) Money; currency. 3. (Usually negatively) A trivial sum of money. "What! You won't take a yard and a half ($150.00)? That ain't washers, Steve."

Washout. (Rare) A life-sentence with no parole; a death-sentence.

Waxer. An excessively talkative person. "That waxer is gonna be loused up (earn himself a bad reputation) if he don't dummy up (keep quiet)."

Weasel. 1. A crafty person without scruples. 2. A borrower from a loanshark who must be persuaded to pay.

Weave a mark. To sandwich a victim between two pickpockets' aides who jostle him simultaneously while the pickpocket snatches his wallet.

Wedges. Playing cards slightly trimmed or tapered in such a manner that cheats may feel the key cards as they handle them.

Weed, n. 1. Marijuana. 2. (P) Tobacco. 3. The act of searching a crowd for prospective robbery victims. 4. (Ohio, especially Columbus penitentiary) A person. ["Strange weed in the garden" —a newcomer or stranger.]

Weed, v. 1. To single out as a prospective victim of theft. 2. To remove a

sum of money from so large a package of bills that the loss will not be noticed immediately; to withdraw sums stealthily, as from a cash drawer or register. 3. To steal piecemeal. 4. To remove valuables, as from a wallet, leaving other contents untouched. 5. To remove a portion of loot in order to cheat one's accomplices. 6. To transfer or pass surreptitiously, as a pickpocket might pass a stolen wallet to a confederate.

Weed a poke. (Among pickpockets) 1. To remove money from a wallet before discarding it. "It's a rumble (we have been seen), Hink. Weed the poke on the duff (on the run)." 2. To pass a stolen wallet to a confederate immediately after a theft.

Weed a tip. To go through a crowd selecting victims to be swindled or robbed by pickpockets.

Weeding. 1. Petty thievery, as differentiated from organized racketeering. 2. The act of selecting one's prospective victims on the spot, as distinguished from planned robbery based on information furnished by professional **tipsters.**

Weekender. A difficult safecracking operation started on a Saturday night and completed on Sunday night.

Welch. To betray a promise or obligation; to go back on one's word; to desert in a time of crisis.

Whack, n. 1. A share or portion, as of loot. "Stash (bank) your whack on this score (robbery) for fall dough (expenses to be met in case of arrest)." 2. A trial effort; attempt. "Did you ever take a whack at boosting (shoplifting)?" 3. (P) A rash or erratic person; one mentally unbalanced. ["Stir-whack"—one mentally affected by years of prison monotony.] "Some whack hit the wall (attempted to escape over the wall) cold turkey (without any plan), and got hit in the noggin (was killed)."

Whack, v. 1. To declare; to give, as a

portion of loot. "Whack Joe in for a full end (share of loot) till he cuts out (gets out) of stir (prison)." 2. To hit; to strike; to sentence to a long prison term. "The Board (Parole Board) whacked Al with all of it (to serve balance of his term)." 3. To make an effort; to attempt. "Boston Bill wants to whack the legit (honest work) but he's too old."

Whacks. (Obs.) A beating; force. (More common: **lumps, or works.**)

Wheel. (P) One mentally unbalanced; a queer or erratic person. "How come they bug (commit to the insane asylum) some guys and don't drop the net on (place under psychiatric observation) that wheel?"

Wheelman. 1. An expert chauffeur and gunman. 2. (P) An active pederast.

Whip. (P) 1. An exceedingly clever or talented person; (sarcastically) a dolt; an inept fellow. 2. Anything extraordinary.

Whip it. (P) 1. To junk it. [Note: The term whip it is commonly used angrily or contemptuously to signify one's disdain for anything offered or withheld.] "I got one and a wop (a year and a fraction) to finish up (left to serve). Parole? They can whip it." 2. To rid oneself of anything worthless or incriminating. "If you got anything hot (contraband), whip it. I just got the wire (heard) there's a frisk (search) comin'."

Whip over. 1. To smuggle, especially liquor, across a border. 2. (P) To send from one cell to another. "Take a tumble (wake up) and whip some weed (tobacco) over on the trolley (pass-line). The panic is on (we are poverty stricken) over here."

Whipsaw. To rob or swindle a difficult victim; to employ extreme resourcefulness in robbing such victim.

Whiskers, n. Uncle Sam; any officer of the Federal government. "Whiskers

gave Mike a collar (arrested) pushing junk (selling narcotics) in Kansas City."

Whiskers, a. (As applied to women) Loose morally; (as applied to men) sexually perverted.

Whistle, to blow the. 1. To complain to the police; to inform on one's criminal accomplices; to testify in court against one's accomplices. 2. (P) To complain or to give information to prison authorities. "These finks (informers) will blow the whistle quicker than the screws (guards)."

Whistler. (South) A police car. (More common in large cities: **prowl car.**)

White. (Prohibition-era term used between retailers and customers) Gin.

White gold. Sugar.

White line. Alcohol. "Lam (get out of town). Whiskers (Federal Agents) is kicking in (raiding) all the white line plants in the county."

White-liner. One who deals or traffics in illicit alcohol; an habitual drinker of same.

White mule. Raw alcohol.

White stuff. Any of various powdered narcotics, as cocaine, heroin, and morphine. "There's a nice buck (good money) pushin' (selling) white stuff. Junkeys (addicts) are easy to clip (swindle)."

White tin. The silvered badge worn by uniformed policemen and precinct plainclothes men. [Compare **Yellow tin.**] "The bulls (detectives) that grabbed (arrested) him are supposed to be from downtown (Police Headquarters), but they only flashed (showed) white tins."

Whiz, n. A pickpocket.

Whiz, v. To pick pockets.

Whiz, the. The pocket-picking profession. "The best score (profitable crime) we made in the whiz, I near whipped (nearly threw away) seven G's (thousand dollars). The wire (skilled pickpocket) made the mark (robbed the victim) and weeded me the poke (handed me the wallet) and there ain't nothing but old stamps in it. Zappy put the glom on (grabbed) the skin (wallet) before I could ditch it (throw it away)." [The stamps, of course, were valued at seven thousand dollars.]

Whiz, on the. Engaged in, or by means of, picking pockets.

Whiz-bulls. The pickpocket squad.

Whiz-mob. A gang of pickpockets.

Whizz-bang. (Among addicts and purveyors) A potent mixture of cocaine and morphine.

Whore's bath. (P) A light sponge-bath, usually with cold water, taken in one's cell. [Note: A bath once a week is still standard prison routine even in the most progressive prisons.]

Wide open. 1. Unhampered by police restrictions or law enforcement, as an area where crime is permitted to flourish. 2. (Northeastern industrial area) Extremely lucky. "How come you scored (secured) for a break (leniency) with a hanging (harsh) judge like that when I couldn't get crabs (any consideration) off him? Boy, you're wide open." 3. Extremely vulnerable; off guard.

Wide-open joint. A town or an establishment which is admirably suited to purposes of criminals—money, pliable police, corrupt officials, vice, etc.

Wig. (Scattered areas in the U.S.) A judge, especially in criminal courts.

Wiggle out. To beat a **rap.**

Willie. (Many scattered areas) A passive pederast.

Window-crash, the. 1. Robbery by smashing display windows and snatching valuables. [Note: The usual technique is to use a brick wrapped in cloth, or the heel of one's foot to shatter the plate glass with a minimum of noise. The theft must be carefully timed. The thief usually strikes when the policeman on beat is calling in his report to the precinct house, and when thunder or passing trucks can drown the crash. Mink, sable, and jewelry are frequently chosen as loot.] 2. The profession of the **window-crasher;** any robbery committed by a **window-crasher.**

Window-crasher. A thief who smashes store windows, seizes valuables and flees.

Wind up with your joint in your hand. (Literally, to wind up in prison masturbating for sex relief.) To end a criminal career by going to prison; to complete an involved criminal venture with no profit and with either a prison term, or shooting by rival gangs or police, or similar misfortune. "There's a dude (fellow) supposed to be a hipster (underworld sophisticate) out on the heist (committing holdups) with two junkeys (drug addicts). He's got to wind up with his joint in his hand."

Winey, or **big winey.** (P) Underworld celebrity. "Take a gander (look), Polack; Tom was a street bum, now he's a stir (prison) big winey."

Wing. To shoot someone.

Wing-ding. 1. A beggar; the act of begging. 2. (P) A feigned attack of illness, especially by an addict to obtain drugs; illness feigned by a convict to shirk work. 3. A fit thrown by beggar or narcotic addict. "Some junkey (drug addict) in the pen (penitentiary) used to throw wing-dings funny as hell."

Wire. 1. A pickpocket, especially an expert as distinguished from his aides. 2. Any person or means by which political influence may be brought to bear to obtain extra-legal advantages; any influential person. "That wire you fixed (spoke to) scored for me (was successful). The screw (guard) says I'll be back in the shop tomorrow." 3. (P) A signal; any piece of confidential information; a warning. "I just got a wire that all the brass (officials) in the joint (prison) is on the prowl (snooping)."

Wire, the. 1. (Erroneously termed "the grapevine") The prison and underworld channels by which rumors and gossip are disseminated. "The big Polack was chivved (knifed) in a come-off (an argument) over some punk (passive pederast) in the county (county jail). The shop screw (guard) just got it off the wire." **2.** The specific and confidential report of an incident. "Where did you get the wire on that beat (prison escape), in two-one (prison washroom)?"

Wire (To have a . . . in). To have connections made so that a desired result is almost sure of achievement, as in fixing a jury; bribing of any public official.

Wired. 1. Back-to-back, as a pair of aces, in a stud-poker game. **2** Marked, as playing cards used by swindlers.

Wire ghee. (P) A convict who has influential friends among inmates and officials and who is therefore able to secure favors and concessions for himself and others. "I ain't gettin' crumbed up (earn myself a bad reputation) bein' seen with that fink (informer). I don't care how big a wire ghee he is."

Wire job. (P) A choice work assignment secured with the aid of influential friends; an assignment enabling a convict to exert influence for himself and others. "The new Warden says there's no wire jobs in any can (prison) he runs."

Wire-man. See **Wire**, def. 1 & 2.

Wire-tapper. A swindler who pretends to intercept secret inside information on crooked horse races, stock deals, etc., to mulct victims.

Wise up. 1. To familiarize oneself or another with the ways of the underworld. "Them first-time loser (imprisoned for a first felony) punks (youngsters) wise up early in a bit (while serving a prison term) now." **2.** To become aware of, or cause another to become aware of, as of any furtive action; to warn. "Wise them gees (fellows) up to cop a mope (get away) before the fireworks pop (shooting starts)." **3.** (Imperative) Take care! Listen! Use your wits! "Wise up, you, and take a powder (go away). You know you draw heat (attract police attention)."

Wobbler. A **wing-ding** beggar, that is, one who throws wing-dings or fits to engage sympathy.

Wolf. 1. (P) An active and aggressive pederast. **2.** A seducer of women; an aggressive lesbian.

Wood. 1. Money. "That shylock made his bundle (fortune). He's got plenty of wood stashed (hidden away)." **2.** (Used chiefly in the negative) Anything trivial or worthy of contempt; something to sneer at. "That hanging (harsh) judge in Supreme Court hit him with (sentenced him to) twelve boffos (years) and that ain't wood."

Wooden biscuit. A hand-carved imitation pistol, frequently made in prison to bluff one's way out.

Woodpecker. A typist.

Woody. 1. (Rare) Crazy; insane. **2.** Prison crazy, i.e., mentally softened by monotonous prison routine for a long period.

Wop. (P) Any fractional portion of any calendar unit of time. "Three (years, or months, or weeks, or days) and a wop (a fraction of a year, or a month, or a week, or a day) and I hit the pavement (will be released)."

Work, n. Criminal activity.

Work, v. To operate as a criminal or racketeer. "I worked the short-con (as a confidence swindler) for years till I got this drop (charge)."

Work a short. 1. To pick pockets on a crosstown trolley or bus line, or any other line of short-distance public transportation. "The cannon-squad (pickpocket squad) loused up (spoiled our chances) the get-ons (for picking pockets at train stations); we'll work the shorts a while." 2. To try picking pockets on one's own without accomplices. [Note: This is seldom done and only by an expert.]

Work a spill. To pick pockets at railway, subway, or elevated stations.

Work a tip. To pick pockets in a crowd deliberately assembled.

Work blind. To commit a crime without plan or previous information. "Working blind gets you a swag (long period) of time (prison term). Get hip (become wise) and get yourself a tipster (some one to plan the crimes for you)."

Work (the) blinds. To burglarize apartments when occupants are absent, without foreknowledge of loot, conditions, etc.

Work flats. 1. To burglarize flats and apartments, usually unarmed, while the occupants are absent. 2. (P) To work as a porter on **flats** (the ground floor of a cell-block).

Work for the State. 1. To work as a defense attorney, against the interests of one's client and, hence, to aid the State in securing his conviction; to neglect the interest of a client, especially one in poor circumstances. "Skid (get rid of) that shyster (lawyer). He works for the State unless you got plenty of wood (money)." 2. (P) To refuse to steal easily obtained prison stores at the request of one's fellow convict. "That fleabag (good-for-nothing) works for the State. He wouldn't give you a match outa the office. What a muzzler (traitor to the code of the underworld)!"

Workhouse-bit. (P) A very short state prison sentence, or the rump end of a term nearly completed. "Gettin' short (near the end of one's sentence)? You bum, you never had but a workhouse-bit."

Workhouse-bum. See **Workhouse-stiff.**

Workhouse-stiff. 1. One who has served a term in a city or county penitentiary, jail, or workhouse. 2. (State prison) A petty thief, usually an inmate of a workhouse or jail; a convict with a very short sentence; a convict who has already served all but a few months or days of his terms. "What are you beefing (complaining) about, you workhouse-stiff? You can pull that bit (serve that prison sentence) on one ear (just as if you were taking a nap)!"

Working-stiff. Any person who works for a living. ["Working-stiff ideas"— the mode of thought of honest working people.]

Work one's points. To calculate one's moves well; to establish a position of confidence with the intention of betraying it ultimately; to swindle.

Workout, n. 1. A third degree beating by the police. 2. (P) A beating with or without weapons by guards or fellow convicts. "They're tryin' to bug (commit to an insane asylum) that dude (fellow) the screws (guards) gave a workout to." [Note: Committing inmates to insane asylums has been too common a means of avoiding responsibility for abuse and persecution by prison guards.]

Workout, v. To give a **workout.**

Works. 1. A violent beating; murder. 2. (P) A severe prison sentence. 3. All; the whole of everything. "That's all the works, Trig, I ain't h.o.-ing (withholding) a pretzel (any of it)." 4. The complete details, as of a crime; a full confession. "You better lam (get out of town), Moe. I hear your broad (girl) got picked up (was arrested) and spilled the works (confessed everything)." 5. A pistol, knife, or other weapon. 6. A woman of loose morals; a passive degenerate. 7. The climax of a confidence swindler's operations.

Work the breaks. To pick pockets in

crowds pouring out of subways, railroad depots, baseball games, etc.

Work the hole. To pick pockets in the subways.

Worm. Silk cloth.

Worm-worker. A thief who specializes in stealing silk. [Compare **Loftman.**]

Wrap a joint up. 1. To close a shady establishment; to close one's living quarters; to quit a place; to cease patronizing an establishment. 2. (P) To secure a transfer from a shop or office assignment, or from one prison to another. "I'm angling (scheming) to wrap this joint up. The hacks (guards) are handing me buckwheats (persecuting me)."

Wrapper. (P) Cigarette paper.

Wrap up. 1. To give up; to resign from, as from a criminal enterprise; to quit. "I'm wrapping up, Lou. They're hitting guys with (sentencing thieves to) too much time (prison terms)." 2. (P) To refuse to carry out one's work assignment. "Wrap up and hit (have yourself sent to) idle (idle company, inmates with no assignments, who are permitted to remain completely idle). What do you get breakin' your hump (back) for the state for nothin'?" 3. To accomplish easily; to complete without great effort. "A treyer (three-year term) is a sleeper (very short sentence). I'll wrap this bit (sentence) up without taking my shoes off (without any trouble at all)." 4. To win domination over; to control. 5. To commit suicide.

Wrap up a ghee. To sever one's association with a person. "I'm wrapping this ghee up. I don't like to mark any one lousy (slander anyone) without I'm sure, but I think he's h. o.-ing (cheating us of part of the loot)."

Wrap-up rap. (P) A formal charge of refusal to work. "I'm all loused up with (not liked by) this p. k. (Principal

Keeper). He's bugged up (has been angry) since I got that wrap-up rap when the weave-shop hack (guard) was hitting me with the buckwheats (was persecuting me)."

Writ-bug. (P) A convict who makes a practice of petitioning for writs of habeas corpus and other legal writs without sufficient cause.

Write one's own ticket. 1. To name one's own prison sentence in a bargain with the judge and district attorney [not necessarily a matter of bribery]. 2. To name one's work assignment or prison to which one is to be transferred. [Note: The practice of writing one's ticket, once common, is now becoming obsolete.]

Write-up, n. (P) A formal report lodged against an inmate for rule violation.

Write up, v. (P) To report a convict for violation of rules.

Wrong. In violation of the underworld code.

Wrong beef. See **Wrong rap.**

Wrong bit. A prison sentence for a charge of which one is innocent; an illegal sentence.

Wrong dice. See **Fading dice.**

Wrong drop. 1. A false arrest. 2. (P) A lock up for a rule violation of which one is innocent.

Wrong fall. 1. An arrest on a charge of which one is innocent. 2. (P) A lockup for a rule violation of which one is innocent.

Wrong ghee. 1. An informer; anyone who is known to have deviated, however slightly, from the once rigid underworld code. 2. Any non-member of the underworld who is not to be trusted by the underworld; one who may be relied upon to seek police aid on the slightest provocation; a thoroughly law-abiding citizen.

Wrong joint. Any establishment or

prison where underworld standards are disregarded; any place frequented by persons looked upon with contempt by members of the underworld.

Wrongo. See **Wrong ghee.**

Wrong pinch. See **Wrong fall,** def. 1 & 2.

Wrong rap. A false charge; an unjustified conviction, or sentence of imprisonment.

Y

Yaffle. (West, mid-West, Central and Southwest area) 1. To assault, especially by placing an arm-lock about the head, as a prelude to robbery. 2. To grab; to seize.

Yam. (Chiefly in South) To talk excessively; to jeopardize oneself and one's associates by boasting of one's criminal exploits.

Yam-yam. (Negro term; rare among whites) An opium-gum pill, especially for chewing or dissolving in the mouth.

Yank a sticker. To withdraw a warrant pending against a convict currently serving a term in prison. "If the D. A. (District Attorney) yanks that sticker, I got three (days) and a get-up (morning to serve before being released)."

Yap. A stupid person of no consequence; a seemingly gullible prospective victim of thieves, especially swindlers.

Yard. 1. One hundred dollars. 2. (P) Outdoor recreation area. ("On the yard!" [Imperative]—It's recreation time.)

Yard and a half. 1. One hundred and fifty dollars. 2. (P; loosely) A dollar and fifty cents; a year and six months. 3. A pinochle meld of 150 points in trumps.

Yegg. (Obs.) An old-time safecracker who specialized in post-office robberies and travelled hobo-fashion.

Yell, n. The act of yelling.

Yell, v. 1. To confess one's guilt to police; to confess and implicate one's accomplices; to give testimony against an accomplice or any underworld associate. "That rat (informer) yelled to the bulls (police) on his partners, and got himself loused up (a bad reputa-

tion). His partners beefed (confessed) too." 2. (P) To betray one's fellow-convicts or lodge any complaint against them with the authorities.

Yell murder. Emphatic form of yell, v.

Yellow tin. A gold badge carried by headquarters detectives of upper grades, as precinct sergeants and lieutenants; a counterfeit gold badge used by extortionists. [Compare **White tin.**]

Yelp. See **Yell,** n. & v.

Yelper. An informer.

Yen. 1. The craving of an addict for drugs, especially of an habitual opium smoker. 2. Any craving.

Yen-gow. A cleaner for opium pipes.

Yen hok. A long thin needle-like instrument which is dipped into a tin of opium gum. [Note: The gum is twisted about the yen hok as spaghetti is twisted around a fork, then held over the lamp until well roasted like beef on a spit. The gun assumes the appearance of a sponge about half the size of a fingernail when ready. Two or three puffs dissolve the pill. An occasional smoker uses five or six pills; an addict requires twelve or more for satisfaction. A subsequent craving for water is partially alleviated by chewing hard candy. Water or alcohol generally causes a violent stomach reaction in smokers.]

Yen-pock. An opium pill prepared for smoking. [Note: Yen-pocks are sometimes dissolved in coffee and swallowed.]

Yen-pop. Marijuana.

Yen-shee. The residue, or ash, in the bowl of an opium pipe, sometimes drunk by addicts after it has been strained and dissolved.

Yen-shee bowl. The small bowl of the opium pipe into which the residue drips.

Yen-shee gow. A cleaner for the inside of opium pipes.

Yen-shee rag. A cloth for cleaning, cooling, and holding opium pipes.

Yentz. 1. To cheat. "The rags (newspapers) called it a two-G (two-thousand dollar) touch (robbery). If that's the McCoy (true), I got yentzed for five yards (hundred dollars)." 2. To be carnally intimate with a passive partner.

Yentzer. A cheat; one who defrauds his associates of their full share of loot, or turns state's evidence when arrested, or in any other way violates the ethics of the underworld; a policeman, or any other official, or buyer of stolen goods, who does business with the members of the underworld and fails to fulfill his side of the bargain. "There's a yentzer shoving down (pocketing a portion of loot) in this troupe (group). The next score (theft) everyone's gotta turn out (turn his pockets inside out)."

Yentzing. Any unfair treatment, as an excessively severe sentence, a frame-up, or a betrayal. "That swaggie (receiver of stolen goods) will give you a yentzing; he's murder (rotten). Give him the h. o. on this stuff (hide this portion of loot) and fence it blind (sell it to someone as legitimate goods). It ain't too hot (it hasn't excited too much police attention)."

Yen-yen. The recurring desire for additional doses of a drug.

Yip, n. A small dog.

Yip, v. To complain.

Yuk. (Rare) A pal; a criminal partner.

Yuld. (Jewish-American) A fool; a sucker; an easy mark.

Z

Zex. 1. (Jewish-American, variant of "secks," abbr. of **six-to-five**) The exclamation of warning of danger, or equivalent gesture or sound. 2. (Imperative) Look out! Danger! Police! Stop!

Zex-man. A lookout.

Zib. (Leavenworth Federal Prison) A brainless dolt; a fool.

Zigaboo. (Southern variant) A Negro. [See **Jig.**]

Zingers, or **zinger.** 1. Any powerful influence capable of decisively affecting the legal disposition of a criminal case whether favorably or adversely. (a) "The zingers are in for a spring (acquittal) on this rap (charge)." (b) "The D. A. (District Attorney) is puttin' the zingers in with the Board (Parole Board). It's full max (maximum term) for me." 2. Scandal or slander deliberately disseminated. "That ghee (fellow) is an undercover fink (informer). Put the zingers on him." 3. Any deliberately disparaging personal remark.

Zipper. To shut up; keep quiet.

Zook. An old decrepit prostitute.

Zool. 1. An Italian, especially of the Old World, nonassimilated type. 2. A stupid, inept person.

Zulu. A Negro.

ENGLISH-
UNDERWORLD
SECTION

For a detailed description of these underworld terms, see the Underworld - English Section of this work. Cross references are indicated by bold-face type. The bold-face references are only to terms within this section.

A

Abandon. See Cease; Leave.

Abandon criminal associates. Crawl out; ditch; dump; heel; leave; take a powder on; welch. "So you crawled out and let that Jake's mob kick my lemon (head) in, you fink."

Abortion, perform an. Pull a rabbit.

Abuse, n. Buckwheats; honey; hosing; humping; kicking around; kifing; lousing around; pushing around; quinine; screwing; screwing around. "Give that crumb plenty of honey; he's wrong (a squealer)."

Abuse, v. Buckwheat; break one's balls; hit with buckwheats; hose; hump; knock up; louse around; play the dozens; push around; ride; screw; screw around; shag; take one over the hurdles, yentz. "Listen, punk, you ain't screwing me around. Hip up (get wise)."

Abuse, take vigorous stand to resist. Declare oneself; kick over; kick up; straighten out; talk turkey; tell off. "Kick over if you don't wanta stand a shake (pay blackmail). Declare yourself."

Accident insurance racket. See Insurance racket, accident.

Accomplish. Pull off.

Accost. Approach; buzz; flag; to give one a flop; to give one a play; to give one a promote; to give one a rumble; thumb; to give one a toss; tumble. "Don't tumble, that stiff (pauper) ain't got a meg (cent)."

Accosting, act of. Approach; buzz; 'eeler; flop; play; promote; rumble; toss; tumble. "Put the feeler on Rocky for a touch (loan)."

Accusation, serious. Stiff beef; tough rap.

Accusation, unjust. Bum beef; bum finger; bum rap; frame-up; hummer; phony rap; plant; wrong beef; wrong rap. "I didn't clip (rob) you, Rubber Lip. That's a bum rap."

Acquire. Promote. "Nice rod (gun) I promoted, huh?"

Act decisively. Spring. "There's the damper (cash register) open and the ghee at the stick (cashier) busy. Spring."

Act impulsively. Take a brodie; take a flier.

Act of decision. Spring. "Make the spring as the cop rounds (turns)."

Admission, gain. Ace in; mooch in; work one's points.

Adulterate, as liquor or drugs, for purposes of fraud. Cut; doctor; needle; phony up; spike. "Someone phonied up this lush (whiskey)."

Adulterator of alcoholic liquor. Needleman.

Advantage. Al-joe; alzo; edge; fix; gaff; gimmick; in; nuts; spot; zinger. "I got the gimmick on this muzzler 'cause I'm heeled (armed)."

Advantage, concede an. Spot. "I'll spot that flea a chiv (knife) and win!"

Advantage, take. Break one's balls; break one's hump; burn up; hump; knock up; knock up a stir; knock up with contracts; louse around; phutz; pratt; pull a fast one; push around; put the blocks to; put the boots to; screw; screw around; work one's points. "Ring in (introduce) them tops (crooked dice) and I'll put the blocks to him."

Advertising fraud. Limb; tap; tap game. "Put the tap on this scorf-joint (restaurant) for an ad. Make it a good bite (sum of money)."

Advertising fraud, engage in. Bite; limb; limb a joint; limb it; put the tap on; tap. "Bite these joints for a half a C (fifty dollars)."

Advertising fraud, engaged in or by means of. On the bite; on the limb; on the tap. "Got a creed (credentials), or are you hustling (stealing) on the limb with the Workers' Journal?"

Advertising fraud, publication used in. Joint; limb-joint.

Advertising fraud, solicitation in. Bite; tap.

Advertising fraud, solicitor in. Adman; tap-man.

Affect airs. Put the hat on. "Don't put the hat on with me, bum."

Affectation. Grandstand play; putting the hat on.

Afraid. See **Fear.**

Agent for crooked establishments. Capper; conny; shill; steer; steerer; steer-man; tout. "Mike's a tout for that rigged joint (crooked gambling establishment) off Bughouse Square."

Agitate. Adjy; bug up; burn up; get one's pratt; needle; put the needles in; put the zingers in; ride; steam up; throw wood on the fire. "Keep bugging me up and I'll flip you on your keister (rump)."

Agitation. Needles; zingers. "Giving me zingers, eh, adjy (agitator)?"

Agitator. Adjy; fireman; hatchetman; needle-man; steam-up ghee.

Aid another to the limit. Front for; go down the line for; go the route for; go to bat for; hold one's end up; take care of one for. "Declare yourself to them dogs (cowards). I'll go to bat for you."

Alarm, sound any mechanical. Toot the tooter.

Alcohol. Alky; mule; white; white line.

Alcoholic liquor. Gage; hardware; hootch; moonshine; potato water; scat. (See also **Gin; Jamaica Ginger; Whiskey.**)

Alcoholic liquor, illicit. Coffin-varnish; king kong; magic; moonshine; re-run; smoke; third-rail; two-and-over.

Alcoholic liquor, plant to distil illicit. Barrel house; boiler; plant; sneaker. "The Feds just knocked off (raided) that sneaker on the hill."

Alert to, become. Blow wise; spot the gaff; get hep; get hip; get hep to the gimmick; hep up; hip up; get hip to the lay; peg a set-up; rumble; get smart to the score; snap out of one's hop; take a flop; take a toss to oneself; take a tumble; tumble; wise up. "Take a tumble, sucker, them broads (cards) got ears (bent corners for cheating)."

Alias, n. See **Name, real** or **assumed.**

All, n. Business; jackpot; works. "That's the works. I'm clean (broke)."

Alley, dark. Arch.

Alter checks. Kite checks; kite stiffs.

Alter for purposes of fraud. Doctor; phony up.

Alter stocks, bonds, etc. Kite stiffs.

Ambitious. Out for a rep; looking to glom the stepping dough. "Watch them punks out for a rep; they're dynamite (dangerous)."

Anger a person. Bug up; burn up; get one's pratt; mess with; sizzle; steam up. "You get my pratt. Dummy up (shut up)." (See also **Rage.**)

Angry. Bouncing; bugged up; burning up; geed up; hopped up; hot in the biscuit; sizzling; steamed up. "What's got you hot in the biscuit, Needles?" (See also **Belligerent.**)

Anus. Brown; rip; round-eye; snatch. (See also **Buttocks.**)

Apartment. Barnacle; camp; crib; dump; joint; kip; pad; varnished joint. "I'm hitting the kip. Shape up (come up) later."

Apartment, as burglary site. Crib; cold slough; hot slough; shack; slough. (See also **Burglary.**)

Aphrodisiac, n. Wampole.

Apologize. Cop all kinds of pleas; cop a plea; cop out; crawl; square oneself. "That mouse (informer) copped all kinds of pleas when Charley Crabs hit him in the cruller (shot him to death)."

Appearance, deceptive. Blind; cover; front; screen.

Appease. Con-along; schmear; square. "You ain't squaring me with that short-con (smooth talk). Get it on the line (pay off)."

Appeasement. Schmear. "Fix the fuzz (cops) with a little schmear."

Application, make. Put in for. "I'm putting in for a commute (commutation of sentence) when I got ten boffos (years) in (in prison)."

Appointment. Meet. "I gotta meet to hit the turf (steal)."

Appointment, fail to keep an. Miss a meet; stand one on a corner.

Appointment, keep an. Keep a meet; make a meet; shape; show.

Appointment, make an. Make a meet. "Make a meet with them Brooklyn biscuits (girls) for Sunday."

Armed. Heeled; loaded; lugging iron for; mitted; packing a rod for; rodded up. "Get rodded up, Lefty's mob is out gunning for (seeking to kill) us." (See also **Knife, carry a; Knife, carrying a; Pistol, carry a.**)

Arm oneself. Heel up; load up; lug iron for; pack a rod for; rod up. "When you're loaded up, hit the scatter (meeting place)."

Arranged, advantageously. All sewed up.

Arrangements, make. Make a connection; promote; pull a wire; put the fix in. "Pull a wire to square this beef (charge) quick."

Arrest, n. Booby-pinch; brodie; collar; crimp; drop; fall; flop; glom; grab; hook; jackpot; jam; knock-off; pinch; run-in; slough-up; snare; snatch; trip; tumble. "This drop is a joke, a mopery rap (a trivial charge)."

Arrest, v. Bag; belt out; whip down to the booby; toss in the calaboose; throw in the clink; collar; crimp; drop; gaff; get; glom; glom onto; grab; hook; jackie up; knock down; knock off; knock out; make a pinch; nail; nick; nip; pinch; slap in the piss can; put the bite on; put

the glom on; put the grab on; put the slough on; put the snatch on; run in; slough; slough up; snag; snare; snatch; sneeze; tab. "Joe Beans was just sloughed on a heist (holdup)." (See also **Prison, discipline for rule violation in.**)

Arrest, accept stoically. Stand a pinch; stand for; stand for a pinch; take the knock. "Okay, copper, I'll take the knock but this rap won't stick (discharge is certain.)"

Arrest, and convict. Break one's license.

Arrest, escape. Duck a pinch; miss a collar. "I mooched out (left) and just missed a collar when the bulls (police) crashed the joint."

Arrest, lose member of gang by. Lose a man.

Arrest, on charge held in underworld contempt. Square-John pinch. "Two bills (two hundred dollars) to beat a lousy square-John pinch—driving without a license. What a yuld (sucker)I am."

Arrest, on suspicion. Forty-eight; forty-eighter; highway mopery; mopery; mopery collar; mopery in the first degree; mopery pinch; mopery rap; pickup. "What a workout (beating) I got from the dicks (police) on that forty-eighter, three busted ribs and a few teeth."

Arrest, on trumped-up charge. Bum beef; bum rap; frame; frame-up; hummer; phony collar; phony drop; phony fall; phony grab; phony knock; phony pinch; phony snatch; plant; stiff; wrong drop; wrong fall; wrong pinch. "I don't mind a wrong fall but the fuzz (police) might peg (recognize) me on a right rap (charge of which one is guilty)." (See also **Criminal charge, unjust.**)

Arrest, red-handed. Dead-bang; dead-bang rap; right fall; right rap. "A dead-bang fall and the rapper (complainant) won't pull off (withdraw his complaint)."

Arrest, resist. Bang it out; bang out; stick and slug.

Arrest, result of incaution. Phony collar; phony drop; phony fall; phony grab; phony knock; phony pinch; phony snatch.

Arrest as suspicious character. Give a ghee a toss; pickup.

Arrested, be. Drop; fall; flop; jammed up; jugged; take a brodie; take a collar; take a drop; take a fall; take a flop; take a pinch; take a snare; take a tumble; take the knock; walk into a collar.

Arrested, be (in or at). Fall from.

Arrested as suspicious character, p.p. Get a forty-eighter.

Arrested red-handed. In the barrel; banged to rights; buried; caught flat-footed; snared dead bang; caught dead bang to rights; caught with jeans at half mast; snared flat-footed; washed up.

Arrested red-handed, one who is. Dead pigeon.

Arson, act of. Touch-off. "Richard (any detective) just grabbed a firebug (arsonist) right on a touch-off on Elm Street."

Arsonist. Fiero; firebug; match; spark; torch; touch-off man.

Artistic. Long-haired. "Pipe the long-haired ghee (fellow). What's his grift (racket), the abbey (defrauding the pious)?"

Asiatic native. Skibo. "See the skibo about that poppy (opium)."

Asleep. On the kip; on the nod; out. (See also **Sleep.**)

Aspirin-tablet addict. Aspirin-hound.

Assault, n. The business; a chill; deal; dust-off; fat lip; five-and-fifty-five; going over; kicking around; lumping; lumps; once-over; shellacking; slugging; whacks; workout; the works. "You get lumps if you single-o (hold out) on me." (See also **Murder; Shooting.**)

Assault, v. Belt out; blind; boff; boot; boot around; chill; chop down; clip; cold-cock; cop; cop a heel; cop a sneak; cop a Sunday; double-bank; drop; dump; dust off; flatten; flip; gang up; get; give a deal to; give one the blanket; give one the works; go to town; guzzle; hand it to one; heel; kick one's cruller in; kick one's lemon in; kick one's sconce in; knock dead; lace; lump; lump-up; measure; poke; put the boots to; put the slough on; put the slug on; shellack; slap down; slough; slough around; slug; stretch; take a whack at; take one over the hurdles; timber up; whack; work out. (See also **Bludgeon; Knife-wound, inflict a; Shoot.**)

Assault and rob, without weapon. Arm; bushwhack; mugg; put the arm on; put the mugg on; put the muscle on; put the slug on. (See also **Assault; Robbery by unarmed physical force; Strong-arm man.**)

Assaulted, be. Get a fat lip.

Associate with. Ace in; double with; fill; hook up with; mess with; mob up; play ball; ring in; tie up with.

Attempt, v. Look to; take a brodie; take a stab at; take a whack at; whack. "Let's take a brodie at clipping (robbing) this guy."

Attendance, to be in. Shape up.

Attorney, assigned by court to defense. State lawyer; state mouthpiece. "I ain't going to bat (trial) with no state mouthpiece."

Attorney, canvasser of prison writ petitioners. Stir-agent.

Attorney, criminal defense. Front; lip; mouthpiece; mugger; spieler; spouter; tangle-jaw; tongue; warbler.

Attorney, district. Cutter; the D. A.

Attorney, fee of. Fall dough; knock-off; nut.

Attorney, friendly to underworld. Right mouthpiece. "I gotta get a right mouthpiece to do business with (bribe) the bulls (police)."

Attorney, in defense of capital cases. Death-House . . . (coupled with surname); Ropes . . . (coupled with surname). "That shyster (low-grade lawyer), Death House Murphy, loses every knock-off (murder) case he handles."

Attorney, prison inmate. See **Prison, inmate amateur lawyer in.**

Attorney, regarded contemptuously. Cop-a-plea mouthpiece; mouthpiece who works for the state; two-bit-mouthpiece; two-bit shyster.

Attorney, unscrupulous. Fixer; springer; two-for-one shyster.

Attorney, writer of defense briefs. Ghost.

Attorney-general, U.S. or State's. The A.G.

Automobile. Boat; boiler; breezer; buggy; crate; golfer; gondola; heap; load; rig; rubber; shed; slicker; stranger.

—**Buick,** B.I.; **Cadillac,** Caddy, golfer; **Dodge,** Ducker; **Essex,** Hudson-pup; **Ford,** Spider; **Lincoln,** pap; **Studebaker,** Studie.

Automobile, depository for stolen. Doghouse; drop-off; dump; hole; hot boiler farm; hot car farm; plant; stash.

Automobile, dismantle an. Strip a crate. "Strip that crate we used on the heist (robbery) and stash (hide) the markers (license plates)."

Automobile, dispose of a stolen. Move a job; push hot boilers; push hot ones.

Automobile, engaged in, or by theft from. On the schlepp.

Automobile, insurance fraud theft of. Consent job; owner's job. "I got a couple more consent jobs for us. The owners won't beef (complain) till we got the crates (cars) stripped (altered)."

Automobile accelerator. Gun.

Automobile horn, sound an. Toot the tooter.

Automobile license plates. Markers; pads; plates; tags.

Automobile license plates, change. Switch plates.

Automobile, painter of stolen. Dauber.

Automobile, properly registered. Clean one.

Automobile, steal an. Clout a heap.

Automobile, steal articles left in. Schlepp. "Poke Nose just schlepped a turkey (bag) with a nice swag (loot) in it."

Automobile, stolen. Bent one; bent rubber; hot boiler; hot crate; hot heap; hot load; hot one; hot rig; hot short; hot trap; kinky; overnighter; overnight job; stranger.

Automobile, theft of articles left in. The schlepp.

Automobile, thief who steals contents of. Schlepper.

Automobile theft, professional. Hot boiler racket, hot crate grift.

Automobile thief, amateur. Joy-rider.

Automobile thief, professional. Buggy-bandit; crate hustler; hot boiler hustler; hot rig grifter; kink.

Automobile tire. Baloney; doughnut.

Automobile tires, etc., remove and steal. Strip a crate.

Automobile tires, stolen or in illegal traffic. Bent rubber.

Automobile used in commission of crime. Cover car; drop car; getaway boiler; getaway car; getaway load; lam car; pickup car.

Avenue. See **Road.**

Avoid a person. Chill; cold-duke; duck; pass up; put the chill on.

Avoid a sentence to prison or redhanded arrest. Miss a bit. "I hear Joe the Lug just missed a bit on a bum rap (baseless charge)."

Awful. Eighteen-carat; murder; nuts; poison; rough; sad.

B

Backer, financial. Stakeman. "Who's the stakeman behind that gaff-joint (crooked gambling house) on the stem (main street)?"

Backing, financial. Stake.

Bad. Bum; eighteen-carat; murder; nuts; poison; rough; sad.

Badge. Tin.

Bag. See Baggage.

Baggage. Keister; meter; peter; slough; swag-bag; turkey.

Baggage car. Blind baggage.

Baggage thief. Keisterman.

Baggage thief's victim. Keister mark.

Bail, free on. Half in stir. "I ain't hustling (stealing) with that bug (halfwit). He's half in stir already."

Bail, jump. Buy new shoes; hop bail; lam. (See also Escape.)

Bail bondsman. Springer. "Get fall dough (lawyer's and bondsman's fees) ready in case the springer makes bail for Joe."

Bail out. Get one out of hock; spring.

Ballyhoo, v. Bally.

Bank, n. Damper; jay; jug.

Bank, deposit in a. Sock away.

Bankbook. Damper-pad. "That scratch-mob (forgery gang) must have beat (robbed) me for my damper-pad. I'll phone the jug (bank)."

Bank-robber (s). Damper-mob; jugheavy; jugman; jug-mob.

Bank-robbery, armed. Jug-heist; jugrap. "We gotta get a good wheelman (driver) for that jug-heist; it's a tough score (job)."

Barber. Axeman; butcher.

Bar from admission. Bar out; bar out of a joint.

Bartender. Apron.

Bed. Barnacle; camp; crummy; doss; flop; joint; kip; pad.

Bedding, bundle of. Bindle.

Bedroom. See Bed.

Beer, container for. Growler.

Beer, set up a fresh barrel of. Put a stiff on the buck.

Beg. Batter; bite; bum; chisel; ding; flag down; free load; give one a hustle; give one a promote; grub; hit the stem; hit the turf; make a riffle; mooch; needle; nick; pivot; pling; put the bite on; put the handle on; put the hustle on; put the promote on; put the sleeve on; stem.

Beg from missions. Take a dive. "All the bums in town are taking a dive up at Father Mike's mission to score for (get) a handout."

Beggar. Bit-borrower; bum; chiseler; dingbat; ding-dong; ding-donger; dinger; grubber; moocher; plinger; professor; promoter; ragbag; rubber bum; rustler; slum-bum; stemmer; twister; wing-ding; wobbler.

Beggar, contemptibly inept. Cipher; geezo; stiff.

Beggar from missions and clergy. Fluker; mission stiff; psalm-singing muzzler.

Beggar who subsists on family's income. Family pimp.

Beggar of food. Free loader.

Beggar who subsists on wife's income. Legal pimp.

Beggar who subsists on income from a working girl. P.I. "Why, you lousy dancehall P.I., step out and hustle (steal) a buck if you won't work."

Beggary. Bite; bum; ding-dong; grub; handle; hustle; make; mooch; needle; nick; pling; promote; riffle; stem; story.

Beggary, engaged in. On the bite; on the bum; on the ding-dong; on the grub; on the hustle; on the make; on the mooch; on the needle; on the nick;

on the pling; on the riffle; on the stem; on the turf.

Beggary, proceeds of. Bite; make; score; touch; two-bit score.

Beggary, trickery in. Throwout. (See also **Illness, feigned.**)

Bell. Dinger.

Bell, ring a. Hit the dinger; toot the tooter.

Belligerent. On the arm; balky; flip; limber; on the muscle; out for a rep; snorky. (See also **Angry.**)

Belligerent person. Arm-man; a balky; flip geezer; guerilla; muscle-man; prison tough guy.

Belligerent person, check a. Straighten out; tell off.

Bet. See **Chance; Gamble; Gambler,** etc.

Bet. See **Double-cross; Inform upon self** and/or **Accomplices** or **Others.**

Betrayal. Deal; fast one; hosing; quickie; quick-one; screwing; screwing around; sell out; split; squawk; turn-in yell. "Listen, crumb, if you give me a hosing and rat (inform) on me, I'll leave a chiv (knife) in your ribs." (See also **Double-cross.**)

Betrayer. See **Cheat; Person, contemptible; Informer.**

Betting commissioner. Banker; book; bookie.

Betting commissioner, accept bets as a. Make book.

Betting commissioner, total bets of a. Play.

Betting commissioner, total income of a. Take.

Beware, interj. See **Danger, warning expressions of.**

Bewildered, a. In a fog; on the merry-go-round.

Big shot. Apple; big apple; big ghee; biggie; big number; big shot; big spud; connection; connection ghee; connection man; k.i.; number; polly; prison hustler; ring ghee; shot; winey; wire; wire-man.

Big shot, pretended. Phony.

Blackmail, n. See **Extortion.**

Blackmail, v. See **Extort.**

Blackmailer. See **Extortionist.**

Blacksmith shop. Pig-joint. "Buster Brown's running a pig joint where all the pete-men (safe-crackers) get their tools made."

Bloodhounds. Catsup-hounds; ketchup-dogs; ketchup-hounds.

Bloodhounds, evade pursuit of. Beat the pups. "This stir (prison) ain't tough to crash out of (escape from) if you can beat the pups."

Blow on bicep. Arm-cramper.

Bludgeon, n. Blackjack; business; conk-crusher; convincer; duffy-silencer; guinea-wrench; knucks; mace; nickel-bat; persuader; sap; sap-stick; stick; works.

Bludgeon, v. Bend a bar over; blackjack; conk; conk on the cruller; jack; pistol-whip; sap; sap up. (See also **Assault, v.**)

Bludgeon, carry a. See **Armed; Arm oneself.**

Blunder, n. Bloomer; blow-card; screw-up.

Blunder, v. Jim a deal; piss up; pull a bloomer; pull a pisser; rank a play; screw up.

Bluntly. Cold-turkey.

Boast, v. Crack one's jaw; noise off; sling; sling the crap; sound off; talk; three-sheet; yam. (See also **Talk; Talk excessively** or **belligerently.**)

Bomb, n. Football; guinea football; pineapple; ticker.

Bomb-maker. Can-maker.

Book, n. Hard-covered book.

Bookmaker. The book; bookie.

Bootlegger. Dynamiter.

Bore, rescue one from a. Bail out; give one a break; get one out of hock; spring.

Bore with garrulity. Bend one's ear.

Boston. Fagtown.

Bother, v. Mess with.

Bouncer. See **Strong-arm man.**

Brain. See **Head, brain,** or **mind.**

Brass knuckles. Knucks. "Get knucks and sap-sticks (bludgeons) and we'll go down and work that mob out (beat them)."

Bread. Double-o; dummy; punk.

Bread, a toasted slice of. Shingle.

Bread and water. Angel cake and wine; cake and wine; dry; piss and punk; punk-and-plaster.

Bribe, v. Fix the alzo; put in the bag; buzz; crack business; do business; fix; fix the fuzz with some soft; gaff; get it on the line; gimmick; kick in; make a deal; pay off; reach; put in the sack; schmear; see; spike; square; square oneself; stake; straighten out; take care of; talk business; write one's own ticket; pull a wire; put in the zingers.

Bribe, above a. Untouchable.

Bribe, accept a. Do business; play ball; take.

Bribe, amenable to offer of a. Can be bought; can be bought but won't stay bought; hungry; in the sack; in the satchel; out for a buck. "Crack (talk) business to these coppers; they're out for a buck."

Bribery, immunity purchased by. See **Criminal activity, bribed immunity in.**

Bribery, sums of money used as. Chop; fall dough; freight; grease; knock off; nut; pay-off; rake-off; schmear; take. "The nut is gonna be heavy to square (fix) this rap (charge) but we gotta pay."

Bribe-taker. Ballplayer; business-copper; businessman; connection; connection ghee; connection man; fixer; polly; right copper.

Brokerage establishment, illegal. Clearing house; stiff-joint. "Get them hot (stolen) bonds down to the stiff-joint and smash (cash) them."

Brood, v. Eat one's heart out.

Brothel. Cab-joint; call-joint; camp; cat-house; creep-joint; crib; hook-joint; hookshop; house; house of all nations; nautchery; nautch-joint; panel-joint; rib-joint; shebang; walk-up.

Brothel, patron's visit to. Short time.

Brothel, proprietor of a. Head pimp; sporting girl's manager; stable-boss.

Brothel, proprietress of a. Auntie; housemother; madam.

Brothels, chain of. Line; stable. "Hit every joint on the line and pick up our cut (share of the proceeds)."

Buick automobile. B.I.

Buffalo. Polack Town.

Bullet. Pill; slug; stumer.

Bullet-proof vest. Corset. "The wheelman (driver) wears this corset on the touch (robber.) It'll stop a few slugs if they come."

Bulky. Balky.

Bundle. Bindle.

Bungle. See **Criminal activity, bungle a venture in.**

Burglar, armed extra hand. Gun. "Get a good gun to fill on this caper (robbery) in case there's heat (police trouble)."

Burglar of banks. Gopher; one of a gopher-mob; heavy; jug-heavy; one of a jug-mob.

Burglar of house and apartment. Cold slough worker; crasher; flat-worker; fly; hot slough worker; midnight; midnighter; moonlighter; owl; porch-climber; prowler; screwman; second-story worker; shacker; slough-worker; spider.

Burglar of safe and vault. See **Safe or vault burglar.**

Burglar, specialist in fur and silk lofts. Loft-man; one of a loft-mob; loft-worker; worm-worker.

Burglariously, enter. Bash in; crash; crash in; jimmy; kick in; make an entry; make an in; push; push in.

Burglarize. Clip a joint; crack a crib; knock off a joint; knock over a joint; prowl; push a joint; take a joint.

Burglar's tools. Bar; bar-spreader; blade; briars; chopper; double; hardware; james; jimmy; jumper; nippers; outsiders; pig; screw; shamus; spreader; stem; stick; wire-gun.

Burglary. Cold slough prowl; a piece of loft work; owl job; prowl; shack; shacking touch.

Burglary, engaged in. Bashing in joints; crashing in joints; kicking in joints; knocking off joints; on the prowl; prowling; pushing flats; pushing joints; pushing stores; on the shack; shacking; working flats.

Burglary of safes and vaults. See **Safe** or **vault burglary.**

Burglary alarm. Bug; dinger. "Zex (look out)! There goes the bug! Hit the lam-car (getaway car)."

Burglary alarm, divert a. Slap on a jumper; kill a bug. "We gotta kill the bug before we make the in to this worm-joint (silk loft)."

Burglary alarm, install or **set a.** Bug; put a bug on.

Burglary protection, keep a dog as. Mutt up.

Buttocks. Biscuit; bucket; can; canetta; getaway; keister; pratt; spread. (See also **Anus.**)

Buttoned securely. Nailed. "No cannon (pickpocket) likes a score (theft attempt) in an insider (inside pocket) that's nailed."

By means of. On the —.

C

Cache, n. Drop; drop-joint; drop-off; hide-out; plant; shade; stash.

Cache, v. Ditch; duck; plant; stash. "Stash them patsies (pistols) quick, there's law (police) in the joint."

Cadillac automobile. Caddy; golfer.

Call vile names. Play the dozens. "None of them cracks (remarks) about my family. Save that playin' the dozens stuff for bastards and dudes with whores in the family."

Capable. There. "Mickey's there with a rod (gun) all right."

Capital punishment, condemned cell. The C.C.'s.

Capital punishment, condemned chamber. Up back; dance hall; in the back; in the backroom; schweiner.

Capital punishment, death-chair switch operator. Baker; juice ghee.

Capital punishment, escape. Get an anchor; beat the chair; get bugged; get clemo; get a commute; get a life-boat; make the bughouse; beat the rope.

Capital punishment, execute by electrocution. Burn; fry.

Capital punishment, be executed by electrocution. Burn; hit the chair; electric cure; fry; go; ride old smoky; squat; be topped.

Capital punishment, execute by hanging. Crook; jerk; stretch; string up; swing; top.

Capital punishment, be executed by hanging. Catch rope; be crooked; dance; go through the trap; stretch; stretch hemp; swing; be topped.

Capital punishment, execution by electrocution. See Electrocution.

Capital punishment, execution by firing squad. Old man cole.

Capital punishment, execution by hanging. Rope.

Capital punishment, the walk to death in. Last mile; last waltz; trip up back.

Caro. See Automobile.

Cards. See Playing cards.

Carnival. Carny; gilly-show; rag-bag.

Carnival barker's speech. Bally; spiel.

Carnival, collector and guard with. Plum-picker.

Carnival, concession operator with. Agent; gunner; man behind the gun; man behind the stick; stick-man; thief.

Carnival, dishonestly operated booth in. Clip-joint; clip-stand. "We just fixed the fuzz (police) with some soft (money); the gimmick (crooked device) is on in all the clip-stands." (See also Swindle establishment.)

Carnival, distress call in. Hey, rube!

Carnival, employee or follower of. Carny; hedgehopper; hop-scotcher; talent. "We just picked up a couple of hop-scotchers from McGuirk's outfit. Ghees (fellows) with real grift sense (crooked talent)."

Carnival, of or pertaining to. Carny.

Carnival, laborer with. Ruffy.

Carnival, larcenously useful around. Talented.

Carnival, lawyer for. The L.A.; patch. "Send the patch to square (bribe) the sheriff so we can spring with the gaff (operate crookedly)."

Carnival, main thoroughfare through. Midway.

Carnival, money holding of customer in. How thick? line; strength. "See what the mark's (victim's) line is before we beat (rob) him."

Carnival, move often from one to another. Hop-scotch.

Carnival, newcomer among followers of. A J.C.L.

Carnival, skill at larcenous phases

256

of. Talent. "This J.C.L. (Johnny-come lately) has plenty of talent working the tip (spectators)."

Carnival, thief who follows. Carnygrifter; conducer; grifter; lumber; talent. (See also **Swindler; Shell game; Thief.**)

Carnival, visitor to. Degenerate; knocker; lice; stunkey. "Them lousy stunkeys don't go for a meg (spend a cent) and they beef murder (complain about everything)."

Carnival games. See **Swindle, n.**

Cash, n. See **Dollar; Money.**

Cash, v. Smash. "Smash this stiff (check) down at the jug (bank)."

Cashier. Broad on the damper; ghee on the damper; ghee on the gun; man behind the gun; man behind the stick; stick; stick-man.

Cash register. Chip; damper; dinger; stick.

Cash register, on duty at the. On the damper; on the gun.

Cash register, steal from. Tap; weed. "I weed about a fin (five dollars) from the damper (till) a day."

Castrate. Nut. "They ought to nut those short-arm bandits (rapists) instead of giving them bits (prison sentences)."

Catch, v. See **Arrest.**

Cease. Chop; fold; fold up; kick over; knock off; pack in; wrap up.

Cemetery. Bone-orchard.

Cent. Meg; red.

Cents, ten. Demier; thin one.

Cents, twenty-five. Cutor; quetor.

Chain-gang, escape from. Beat the pups. (See also **Prison, escape or attempt to escape from.**)

Chain-gang, guard over. Chain-gang Charley; the johnny; johnny creep; 'ong-chain Charley; long-line skinner.

Chain-gang, leg chains of. Bull chain; rattler.

Chain-gang, leash supporting legchain in. The G-string.

Chance, n. Brodie; flier; stab; wack; whack. "I'd take a whack at heisting (holding up) that joint if I had my rod (gun)."

Chance, take a. See **Attempt, v.**

Chauffeur. Wheelman. "Have the wheelman run down the roads (drive along the escape route) in case of a blow (pursuit)."

Cheap. Two-bit. "Them two-bit touches (thefts) ain't worth the bit (prison sentence) you get if you fall (are arrested)."

Cheat, n. Double-banker; h. o. ghee; skunker; yentzer. (See also **Person, contemptible.**)

Cheat, v. Gaff; go South; hipe; h. o.; hose; hump; louse around; play the nine of hearts; pratt; pull a fast one; pull a quickie; pull a sneak; put the blocks to; put the boots to; put the cross on; put the horns on; put the prongs to; screw; screw around; shag; single-o; take one over the hurdles; yentz. (See also **Cuckoldry, practice.**)

Check. Ducat; kite; paper; scratch; stiff; stiffo.

Check, forged. Bouncer; funny paper; hot paper; kite; rubber; script; short story; sour paper; stumer.

Check, overdraw account by. Kite.

Checkbook. Damper-pad. "Grab his damper-pad and we'll scratch (forge) a couple of stiffs (fraudulent checks) on him."

Chicken, mud-baked. Gump.

Chicken-thief. Gump-glommer.

Chocolate pudding. Ant-paste.

Chump. See **Fool.**

Cigarette. Pill; tailor-made.

Cigarette, extinguish a. Clinch a butt; clip a butt; dinch a butt.

Cigarettes, fresh. Slow burners.

Cigarette, hand or machine-made. Pill.

Cigarette, make a hand-rolled. Fill a blanket; roll a pill; twist one.

Cigarette, materials for making. Makin's; rollin's.

Cigarette, partly smoked butt of. Clincher; clipper; dincher; lip-burner; snipe.

Cigarette, retrieve a. Glom; snag; snare; snipe; spear; put the glom on; put the snare on.

Cigarette, retriever of. Sniper.

Cigarette, smoke a. Blow one up; cop a drag.

Cigarette, paper. Blanket; wrapper.

Cigarettes, stale. Fast burners.

Cigarettes, tobacco for making. Bull; Duke's; dust; fillin's; jack; weed.

Cities: Boston, Fagtown; **Las Vegas,** Vegas; **Los Angeles,** L.A.; **Pittsburgh,** Smoky City; **San Bernardino,** San Berdoo; **San Pedro,** Pedro.

City, prosperous. Boomer. "I'm stepping out to them boomers with a cannon mob (pickpocket gang) with the alzo (police protection)."

City, small. Jerk town; jerkwater; tank.

City or **Town attractive to underworld.** Big town; wide-open joint; right tank; two-stemmer.

City unattractive to underworld. Hot joint; stiff joint; tough town; tough town to do business; wrong tank.

Classify. Make; peg. "I pegged that bull (policeman) a mile with them flat feet."

Clemency, executive. Clemo; commute; lifesaver; spring. "I got a connection-ghee (fixer) trying to get Blubberhead a commute out of stir (prison)."

Clergyman. Buck; devil-dodger; gospel ghee; holy Joe; long-haired boy; sin hound; sky pilot.

Clergyman friendly to underground. Right buck.

Clergyman, impersonation of a. The abbey.

Clergyman, impersonator of a. Abbey; fireproofer.

Climax, n. See **Consummation, as of a crime.**

Climax, v. See **Consummate, as a crime.**

Close an establishment. Fold a joint; fold up; slough a joint; wrap a joint up. "The nut (expense) is too big so we're wrapping this joint up."

Clothesline. Berry.

Cocaine. See **Narcotic, powdered.**

Codfish, creamed. Hollywood stew.

Coerce. Gueril; louse around; muscle in; muscle out; push around; put the arm on; put the chill on; put the gorill on; put the heat on; put the mugg on; put the nuts on; put the shake on; put the squeeze on; on the shake; on the squash; take care of; throw one's weight around; turn on the heat. (See also **Assault; Extort.**)

Coercion. Arm; chill; gaff; gueril; heat; mugg; nuts; shake; squeeze.

Coffee. Flit; jamoka; mouthwash; mud; spow; smoke.

Complain. Get out the crying towel; make a bum beef; put up a beef; put up a holler; put up a sucker's holler; put up a squawk; sing; sing 'em; sing the weeps; sound off.

Complainant. Rapper.

Complain to authorities. See **Inform upon self.**

Complaint. Beef; beef department; blast; holler; roar; rumble; squawk; sucker's holler; yell. "All the suckers we been taking on the shake (extortion) are on the beef department to the law (police)."

Complaint, delay criminal victim's. Stall a beef. "When we lam (flee) out of the joint after the heist (robbery), stall any beef till we make the getaway load (car)."

Conceal a fugitive from justice. Bury; hide out; hole up; plant; stash. "I got Gimpy stashed in Mamie's nautch-joint (brothel) till the heat (police activity) dies down."

Conceal anything illegal, contraband, etc. Bury; duck; plant; put up; stash; unload.

Conceal kidnap victim. Put in the hole; stick in the hole.

Conceal one's activities, past, facial features, etc. Cover up.

Conceal oneself, especially as a fugitive. Do a crouch; duck; flatten out; hide out; hole up; plant; stash oneself away.

Concentrate upon. Give a play; play.

Concentration upon. Play. "This mark (victim) is worth a good play. The score (proceeds) will be plenty if he goes."

Confess guilt. See **Inform upon self; Third degree, break under and inform.**

Confide in. Buzz; crack to; lay the gaff; spring with the score. "Don't crack to that bezark (girl) of yours about touches (robberies)."

Confidence game. See **Swindle, n.**

Confidence man. See **Swindler.**

Confront with an officer's badge. Flash the button; flash the tin.

Confront with a weapon, badge, etc. Hit one with; smack with; spring with. "Don't spring with the piece (pistol) till I crack (say so)."

Consummate, as a crime. Blow off; spring; spring the gaff. "The mark (victim) is all readied up. Spring the gaff and blow (flee)."

Consummation, as of a crime. Blowcard; blow-off; pay-off. "The blow-off was the dicks (police) mooched in right in the middle of the score (robbery) and we had to lam (flee)."

Contaminate with underworld undesirable persons or practices. Crumb up; knock up; louse up; mark lousy; mark wrong; rank a joint.

Contemptible in value. Lousy; two-bit.

Contemptible thing to do. Fink caper; lousy caper; rat caper.

Contingent upon. ("If things turn out well") If money. "When the trick (robbery) is over, we cop a heel (flee) out of town—if money."

Contraceptive device. Rubber.

Contraceptive salesman. Rubber hustler.

Contribute money. Come through; get it up; kick in with a buck; see; send one a buck; stake; straighten out.

Control, position of. In the saddle.

Convict, n. See **Prison, inmate of.**

Convict improperly. Clean up the calendar; to give one a deal; frame; frame up; put the chuck on. (See also **Frame up.**)

Convict of criminal charge. See **Trial by jury, find guilty in.**

Convince. Con; con along; duke in; promote; rope in; give one a short-con; swindle in.

Cop-fighter. Bull-buster; bull-fighter. (See also **Fighter.**)

Copy, n. Dead ringer; ringer. (See also **Duplicate key.**)

Cornered. See **Predicament, in a.**

Corpse. Stiff.

Corrupt. Racket up. "Them two-bit (cheap) mouthpieces (lawyers) got the courts all racketed up."

Counterfeiter. Queer hustler; raiser.

Counterfeit metal money. Cluck; stiff; stumer.

Counterfeit money. Backs; boodle; fronts; funny paper; green goods; hot dough; queer; shuffle; stiff.

Counterfeit money, pass. Hit one with; push queer; shove; shove queer; smack with. (See also **Forged checks, pass.**) "We'll push this queer in crap games and nautcheries (brothels) only."

Counterfeit money, passer of. Pusher; queer pusher; shover.

Courage. Balls; clock; guts; heart; moxie; stomach; ticker.

Cowardice. Ague; bum clock; chill.

"You got the chill. I can see it in your kisser (face). No heists (holdups) with you for me."

Cowardice, exhibit. Cop a plea; cop all kinds of pleas; cop out; crawl out; dog it; turn copper-hearted. (See also **Abandon criminal associates; Inform upon self.**)

Craving, n. Yen; yen-yen. "When the old yen-yen gets them junkies (narcotic addicts) they'd bury their mothers for a bang (shot)."

Credentials, forged. Button; creed; flash; paper; tin. "On the shake (extortion) don't spring (exhibit) your creed too quick."

Credit, force extension of. Put on the arm; put on the cuff; hang up; put on the muscle.

Credit, on. On the arm; on the cuff; on the muscle.

Crime, petty or mean. Fink caper; lousy caper; rat caper; spitting on the sidewalk; stabbing a horse and stealing his blanket.

Crime instructor. Fagin.

Crime of profit. Beat; boost; caper; clout; make; score; take; touch; trick. (See also entries for specific crimes.)

Criminal. Arm-man; blotto; broad a ghee hustles with; gorilla; guerilla; hep broad; hep ghee; hip ghee; hipster; hood; hooligan; knock-around broad; knock-around ghee; moll; racket broad; racket dude; racketeer; racket ghee; tumuler. (See also **Gangster; Thief.**)

Criminal, aide or sycophant of. Airedale; bum; buzzard; gapper; gummio; gummy; lob; pratt-boy; punk; wallflower. (See also **Lookout.**)

Criminal, habitual. Bitch-of-a-criminal; habitual; fourth-offender; fourtime loser; repeater; three-time loser; two-time loser.

Criminal, having the legal status of a habitual. All caught up; all washed up. "I done three bits (prison terms)

so I'm washed up. It's the book (life) if I fall again."

Criminal, reckless. Blind hustler; blind steer ghee; cowboy; mad hatter.

Criminal, shield covering operations of a. Cover man; front; gapper; shill; stall; stick. (See also **Pickpocket, aide to.**)

Criminal, tools of. Hardware; books; pig; stuff. (See also **Burglar's tools; Pickpocket's tools; Prison-escape implements; Safe or vault burglary tools.**)

Criminal, trial by jury of. See **Trial by jury, undergo.**

Criminal activity. Action; musclework; work. (See also **Criminal activity, venture in.**)

Criminal activity, accomplish by timely blow in. Cop a sneak; hit and run; rank and lam. "The wheelman (driver) moves easy till we grab the keister (bag) with the dough, then rank and lam."

Criminal activity, accustomed territory in. Beat.

Criminal activity, area of bribed immunity in. Al-joe; alzo; licensed spot; set-in. "Rougho Ralph's got this alzo. If we crash in (invade), it's fireworks (shooting) with him and the cops."

Criminal activity, attractive object of. Good for a lay; ready.

Criminal activity, beat rivals to. Cop a sneak on. "Mike and Al are set to clip (rob) this joint. We'll cop a sneak on them tonight."

Criminal activity, bribed immunity in. Al-joe; alzo; fix; gaff; gimmick; in; license; licensed grift; licensed gunning; murder grift; set-in.

Criminal activity, bungle a venture in. Blow; bollix; boot; boot around; crab; crab a play; crimp; crumb a deal; jim; jim a deal; louse up; mess up; miss up; murder; piss up; piss in a snowbank; play a bloomer; pull a bloomer; queer; rank; rank a joint;

rank a mark; rank and lam; rank a play; screw up.

Criminal activity, bungled. See Criminal activity, profitless venture in.

Criminal activity, carry out a profitable venture in. Do handy; hit the jackpot; make; make a riffle; make a score; make a touch; ring the bell; score. (See also Steal.)

Criminal activity, carry out a venture in. Beat a mark; clip a mark; make a score; make a touch; to do a piece of work; pull a job; pull a caper; pull a trick; score.

Criminal activity, carry out ventures cautiously in. Pick one's spots.

Criminal activity, cease participation in. Count me out; count out; declare out; push out. (See also Cease.) "I'm pushing out of the heavy (safe-cracking) racket. It's crumbed up (spoiled)."

Criminal activity, engage in every type of. Play the field. "I owe the fence (buyer of loot) a G-note (thousand dollars) so I'm playing the field for a quick buck."

Criminal activity, execute task swiftly in. Pull a one-two play, pull a fast one; pull a quickie; pull a sneak; rank and lam; stick, cop, and blow.

Criminal activity, exhaust area or victim in. Burn up; hump to death; knock up; louse up; rank; screw up. "We gotta fold up (close activities) in this tank (town); we got it burned up."

Criminal activity, exhausted as area or victim of. All caught up; all washed up; crumbed up; loused up; poison; ranked; wrapped up.

Criminal activity, explain plans for. Spill the lay; lay the gaff; hip up on the score; spring the gaff.

Criminal activity, informed in plans for, p.p. Hip to the lay; hipped up; in.

Criminal activity, inspect site for. Case; case out; clock; lay out; peg a joint; put the pike on; run the roads down; smoke a joint; spot.

Criminal activity, inspector of site for. Caser. "Get a good caser to peg that joint (inspect robbery site) before we take (rob) it."

Criminal activity, interruption of. See Interruption of a crime.

Criminal activity, leave meeting place for scene of. Break out; charge out; go on a trick; go out on a touch; mooch out on the grift; get out on the hustle; go out on a piece of work; plunge out on a score; shape up; cut out on the stem; step out on a caper; hit the turf.

Criminal activity, move into large scale. Step; step out; go after stepping dough.

Criminal activity, nervous in. On the gog; having the leaps.

Criminal activity, non-remunerative. Grubbing grift. (See also Criminal activity, profitless venture in.)

Criminal activity, non-violent. Making a clean buck; grift; light time; turning a smart buck.

Criminal activity, occupied in petty. To be lousy and attempt to scratch. "That creepo (weasel) never got glommed (arrested) for nothing but being lousy and attempting to scratch."

Criminal activity, period of successful operation in. Run.

Criminal activity, plan for. Dope; gaff; lay; layout; play; score; set-up; works.

Criminal activity, post assignment in. Spot. "Hold that spot and hit anyone in the head (shoot anyone) who tries to crash (leave)."

Criminal activity, police protected. Alzo; license; licensed grift; licensed gunning; murder grift.

Criminal activity, proceeds of. Score; take; touch. (See also Stolen, counterfeited, or other money sought by police; stolen goods.)

Criminal activity, profitable venture in. Candy; a sweet make; nice thing;

nick; red one; a nice score; a good touch.

Criminal activity, profitless venture in. Blank; bloomer; fritzer; lemon; piss-up; rank; skunk; stiff; stiffo; a t.b.; turkey. (See also **Thing, relatively, or wholly worthless.**) "There's a mark (victim) I figured would make a nice touch (profitable theft) and he turns out a stiffo."

Criminal activity, regularly engaged in. In action; on the hustle; nustling; on the make; on the move; out for a buck; on the promote; racketeering; on the sail; stepping out; tumuling; on the turf.

Criminal activity, repeat against same victim. Go back for seconds; play a matinee; rehash; reload.

Criminal activity, return from. Come off a trick. "Everybody hit the scatter (hangout) when we come off this trick and hole up (hide)."

Criminal activity, share with another in. Cut in for a gapper's bit; cut in on a touch; declare in; fix it for one to fill; put a buck one's way; ring in; shove a buck one's way.

Criminal activity, site for. Lay, layout; spread. "I eased out (studied) the layout and it's all set for the heist (robbery)."

Criminal activity, spotter of victims of. Caser; feeler; finger; fingerman; marker; mob-marker; prowler; spotter; steerer; ten percenter; tipster.

Criminal activity, supply with faulty leads in. Blind steer; bum steer; steer wrong; wrong steer.

Criminal activity, supply with leads in. Duke in; give one a steer; give one a send in; tip; tip off; tout.

Criminal activity, swiftly executed. Fast one; hit-and-run play; rank-and-lam play; sneak play; quickie; sleeper.

Criminal activity, talent in. Griftsense; talent. "Look at that shill (tout for crooked gaming concessions) work

a tip (crowd)! He's got grift-sense."

Criminal activity, tip leading up to. Blind steer; blow up; bum steer; dope; gaff; goulash; hot wire; info; lay; layout; phony steer; press; send-in; set-up; steer; tip; tip-off; wire.

Criminal activity, undertake without leads. To go on a blind steer; cowboy; hustle; hustle blind; pull a Jesse James; step out blind; take a brodie; take a flier; work blind.

Criminal activity, venture in. Beat; caper; clout; job; make; piece of work; racket; riffle; score; touch; trick.

Criminal activity, victim of. Blank; come-on; degenerate; giver-up; hoosier; jay; keister mark; lemon; lush; mark; mooch; pay-off ghee; sailor; scissorbill; springfield; square-John; stiff; sucker; touch; tough giver-up; turkey; yuld.

Criminal activity, docile victim of. Good giver-up; lush; sweet mark; soft giver-up; soft touch; sweetheart. (See also **Person, easily deceived** or **robbed; Person, slow-witted** or **inept.**)

Criminal activity, victim who resists. Lush who won't go; sucker who kicks over; mark who kicks up; sleeper; tough giver-up. "Someone must have put the horns (jinx) on me. Every touch (robbery) I hit up against tough givers-up."

Criminal activity, violently engage in. Hit the heavy time; tumul.

Criminal activity, violent method of. Hard way; heavy; heavy time; tumuling.

Criminal activity, watch for interference during. See **Lookout, serve criminally as a.**

Criminal aide to inside job. In; inman; inside-man. "The in-man will leave the back window unlatched in this slough (house)."

Criminal assault. See **Rape.**

Criminal charge. Fall; knock; rap. (See also **Arrest, Complaint.**)

Criminal charge, euphemism for. Attempt to gog; picking a berry; highway mopery; lousy and attempt to scratch; mopery; spitting on the sidewalk; stabbing a horse and stealing his blanket; waiting for a streetcar. "I told them social workers I was in for attempt to gog and they was too jaggie (stupid) to know it meant none of their business."

Criminal charge, find record of long pending. Dig up on.

Criminal charge, petty or supported by little evidence. Mopery; mopery collar; mopery in the first degree; mopery pinch; mopery rap; stiff rap; walk-out rap; wrap-up rap.

Criminal charge, serious and supported by ample evidence. Right beef; right fall; right rap; stiff beef; tough rap.

Criminal charge, unjust. Bum beef; bum finger; bum rap; frame-up; hummer; phony rap; plant; wrong beef; wrong rap. (See also **Accusation, unjust; Arrest, on trumped-up charge; Frame-up.**)

Criminal code, disloyal to. All muzzler; crumby; crummy; hundred per cent wrong; lousy; mangey; out of turn; pea soup; phony; phony - baloney; wrong. "There's a fink (informer) who's all muzzler. We'll double bank (gang up on) him and chiv (cut) him." (See also **Untrustworthy.**)

Criminal code, loyal to the. Aces; d.d.; forty; from Chicago; good people; jake; keen; keeno; kosher; McCoy; pat; patsy; right; right people; soiid; up-and-up. "He's the fall guy (protector of guilty associates) for a heist (hold-up) mob; yeah, he's right people."

Criminal code, person disloyal to the. See **Informer; Person, contemptible.**

Criminal code, person loyal to the. Ace; ghee from the West; good head; good people; one of the Johnson family; one-way ghee; right ghee; right guy; righto; right people; square egg; square skirt; sticker.

Criminal code, prove loyal to the. Ace it; ace through; come through; keep one's nose clean; shape up right; stack up okay; stand up; stick; stand the gaff. (See also **Aid another to the limit; Third degree, refuse to talk under.**)

Criminal code, prove disloyal to the. See **Abandon criminal associates; Inform upon self** and/or **Accomplices or others; Third-degree, break under and inform.**

Criminal complainant. Knock-man; lemon; main ghee; rapper; sucker.

Criminal complainant, effect withdrawal of charges by. Chill; fix; jerk off a rapper; spike; square a rapper.

Criminal complaint, effect withdrawal of. Chill a beef; chill a rap; fix a rap; squash a holler; square a beef; square a collar; square a pinch; square a rap. (See also **Warrant, effect withdrawal of pending.**)

Criminal complaint, quash. Chill a beef; chill a rap; fix; get off a hooker; kill a rap; play the deuce of clubs; get the rapper to pull off; squash a rap; square; square a rap; square a pinch; yank a sticker. "See if you can get to the rapper (complainant) and chill this rap or I'll get hit with the book (maximum sentence)." (See also **Warrant, effect withdrawal of pending.**)

Criminal complaint, refuse to press. Chill; jerk; pull; pull a beef; pull off; pull a pinch; pull a rap; yank a beef.

Criminal court, grand jury section of. Downtown. "We tried to kill the rap (quash the charge) in Magistrate's Court but they held me for down town."

Criminal court, on calendar for trial or sentence .n. Going to bat; up. "The shyster (lawyer) says I'm up to get my bundle (sentence) tomorrow."

Criminal court malpractice. Bargain day; cleaning up the calendar; throwing the book away; two-for-one.

Criminal court prisoners' pen. Bull pen; tank.

Criminal exploits, relate. Chop up jackpots; cut up touches.

Criminal exploits, tales of. Jackies; jackpots; touches; old touches.

Criminally active. On the grift; on the hustle; on the make; playing the field; on the promote; in the racket; on the turf. "Mugger Mike just hit the bricks (left prison) last month, and he's back on the turf already."

Criminal novice. See **Underworld newcomer.**

Criminal record. Pedigree; record.

Criminal record, having no. Cherry. "The kid was cherry when he stepped out on this score (robbery) and they hit him with the book (gave him the maximum sentence)."

Criminal record, investigate thoroughly a. Dig up on. "I gotta get bail quick before they print (fingerprint) me and dig up on me."

Criminals, gang of. See **Gang, n.**

Criminal scapegoat, make one a. Charge with picking a berry; clean up the calendar; give one a deal; make one a fall guy; frame up; make one a lob; make one a pack horse; make one a victim of the two-for-one. (See also **Abuse.**)

Criminal suspect, exhibit before victim. Line up; stand up.

Criminal suspect, exhibition before victim. Line-up; phony line-up; show-up; stand-up. "They gave me a phony line-

up with half a dozen fresh-shaved bulls (policemen) and the sucker (victim) had to peg (identify) me."

Criminal suspect, find fingerprints of, at scene of crime. Make one's prints. "If they make my prints on that lam-car (getaway car), I'm a dead pigeon (as good as arrested)."

Criminal suspect, identification of. Blow; flop; rumble; toss; tumble.

Criminal suspect, identified as. Get a blow; get fingered; made; pegged.

Criminal suspect, identify. Give one a blow; call the turn; finger; make; make one's kisser; make one's mugg; make one's prints; peg; put the finger on; rumble; shag; toss; tumble.

Criminal suspect, identify fingerprints of. Make one on his prints.

Criminal veteran. Old-timer.

Cripple, n. Crip.

Croupier. Bank; book; cutter; house; man behind the gun; man behind the stick; stick-man.

Crowbar. Bar; James; Jimmy; shamus; stick.

Crowd of people. Push; tip.

Crowd of people, select victim of theft from. Weed a tip.

Crusade against crime. Beef; squawk. (See also **Complaint.**) "What a beef in the morning rag (newspaper) about heists (holdups). Flatten out (lay low) till the pollies (politicians) cool the thing out."

Cuckoldry, practice. Put the horns on; stretch the rubber; two-time.

Cuckoldry, the symbol of. Horns.

Curse, v. To call the bitch's curse down upon one; put the horns on. (See also **Call vile names.**)

D

Danger, one who warns of. See **Lookout.**

Dangerous. Dynamite.

Danger, warning expressions of, interj. Amscray; awlay; bleaso; butso; cheese it; chicky; duck; freeze; hep up; on the hip; hip up; ixnay; jiggers; knock off; lay off; leeasaw; mope; nix; oblay; ooscray; screasew; six-to-five; smarten up; snap out of your hop; wise up; zex.

Danger, warning of. Crack; highball; lunger; office; wire.

Danger, warn of. Crack; flag; highball; hep up; hip up; smarten up; tip; tip off.

Dead by violence. On a slab.

Death, marked for. All caught up.

Death by violence. The hard way. (See also **Murder.**)

Death chamber. Back up.

Debt, in. In hock; in the barrel; in the hole; on the nut. (See also **Penniless.**)

Debt, out of. Off the nut; out of hock.

Defeat, n. Shellacking.

Defeat, v. Shellack. "I'm getting the right connection-ghee (fixer) and I'll shellack that D.A. dizzy on this rap (criminal charge)."

Degeneracy. See **Pederasty; Sodomy.**

Delay, v. Stall.

Delay, purposeful. Stall; pull a stall. "I'll hipe the cashier (rob his till) while the drawer is open."

Delay outcry of criminal victim. Stall a beef. "If we get a blow (interference) on this pete-job (safe-cracking job), stall the beef while we blow (flee)."

Demand for money, meet a. Come through; get it on the line; get it up; kick back; kick in; pay off; see; send one a buck.

Dentist. Butcher.

Desert, v. See **Abandon criminal associates; Leave.**

Deserter. Dumper; heeler: "Don't use him as zex-man (lookout) on no more touches (robberies); the lousy dumper left me without a crack (warning) when I got my last pinch (arrest)."

Details, explain. Lay the gaff. "Come on down to the scatter (hangout) and I'll lay the gaff on this take (robbery)."

Detain. Stall.

Detective, department store. Floor dick.

Detective, hotel. House dick.

Detective, police. Big-eyes; policeman. (See also **Policeman.**)

Detective, private. April fool copper; pink; correspondence school dick; soft heel; spotter.

Detective, railroad. Railroad bull; railroad dick; shack.

Dice. Bones; perfects.

Dice, draw operator's percentage in game of. Cut.

Dice, paraphernalia and terms in game of. Backboard; bird-cage; fade; gate; gunner; hard way; miss out; money; out; snake-eyes; throw boxcars; throw snake-eyes.

Dice, prepared crooked. Bottoms; busters; coolers; edgework; fading dice; flats; miss-outs; platinum loaders; right dice; shapes; tappers; tops; t's; wrong dice.

Dice, professional in game of. Cutter; gaffer; dice hustler; pad-roller.

Dice, roll and spin in cheating. Gaff; pad-roll; put the spin on; take on a blanket.

Dice, the cheating element in. The gaff; the gimmick.

Die, v. To get a back-gate commute; chalk out; check out; croak; go; kick in; kick off; shove over; slam off.

Die by suicide. To take a back-gate

commute; hang up; hit oneself in the bonnet; hit oneself out; pack in; save one for oneself; string up; swing; take a rope; wrap up.

Difficulty. Tough gaff. (See also **Trouble.**)

Direct, v. Steer. "This ghee (fellow) just hit the street (left prison). Steer him to the right people (underworld loyal people)."

Direction. Steer.

Direction, faulty. Blind steer; bum steer; wrong steer.

Dirty. Crumby; crummy; lousy.

Disappointment, a bitter. Ball-breaker.

Discharge from custody. Put on the bricks; floater; get a floater; get hours; put on the pavement; put on the sidewalk; put on the street; spring; turn out; get a twenty-four. (See also **Trial by jury, acquit of charges in.**)

Discharge from custody, a. Floater; forty-eight; forty-eighter; spring; turnout; twenty-four; walk-out.

Discharge on one's own recognizance. A D.O.R.

Disciplinarian. Ball breaker.

Disclose one's plan, purpose, character, etc. Spring; spring one's duke; spring with a crack; tip one's duke. "I think this creep (informer) is out to beat (rob) me. Wait'll he springs his duke."

Discourage. Chill; chill off; chill up on; cold duke; put the chill on.

Disguise, n. Get-up; make-up.

Disguise. Cover up. "You gotta cover up on this trick (robbery). If they peg (recognize) our kissers (faces) I'll get hit in the noggin (shot dead)."

Disguise, steal wearing no. Give up one's kisser; give up one's mugg. "No capers (robberies) where you gotta give up your mugg for me; too easy to get made (recognized in the Rogue's Gallery)."

Disgust, expression of. Balls!

Dishonest, inherently. To have grift sense; to have larceny in one's heart; on the promote.

Disloyal. See **Criminal code, disloyal to; Untrustworthy.**

Dismissal, curt order of. Blow; cop a breeze; cop a figary; cop a heel; cop a mope; screw; take a brodie; take it on the duff; take it on the lam.

Display, v. See **Exhibit, as money, weapons, etc.**

Dissuade. Chill; chill off; put the hooks in; put the needles in; put the zingers in.

Distil, as illicit alcohol. Cook.

District attorney. See **Attorney, district.**

District attorney's office, malpractice in. Bargain; bargain day; cleaning up the calendar; deal; two-for-one.

Do, ably or easily. Go; mess with; pull; wrap up. "With a good mouthpiece (lawyer) I can wrap up a turn out (release) on this rap (charge)."

Doctor, n. Butcher; croaker; pill roller. (See also **Abortionist.**)

Doctor, friendly to underworld. Right croaker.

Doctor, venereal specialist. Stick croaker.

Dodge automobile. Ducker.

Dog. Pootch; yip.

Dollar. Ace; bean; boffo; buck; cabbage; case note; caser; clam; ducat; frogskin; lamb's tongue; plaster; rag; simoleon; skin; slug; smacker; toadskin.

—**Half a.** Half a case; half a slug.

Dollars, one and a half. Yard and a half.

—**Two.** deuce; **Three.** dreece, treyer; **Five.** fin, finif, five spot, five spotter, half a saw, lamb's tongue, nickel note, pound, a V; **Ten.** saw, sawbuck, sawski, tenner, ten spot; **Twenty.** double-saw, double-sawbuck; **Fifty.** half a C, half a yard; **One hundred.** a C-bill, C-note, yard; **One thousand.** a G, G-note, grand.

Domestic servant. Deckhand; kitchen mechanic.

Door. Out; sneak-gate. "You heist (hold up) the guard at the sneak-gate of the vault; Joe get the dude at the bug (alarm button) and the jug (bank) is ours."

Double-cross, n. Cross; cross-up; double-bank; screw-up. (See also **Betrayal.**)

Double-cross, v. Cop a heel; cop a sneak; cross; cross up; double bank; screw up; two time. (See also **Betray.**)

Doubtful. Jury's out; on ice. "Maybe we hit (shoot) this fink (rat). The jury's out till we shape (gather) at the meet (hang-out)."

Drink alcoholics. Hit the pot; lush; lush up; slop up.

Drunkard. Barrel-house bum; bimmy; lush; rubadub bum; rum-dumb; smoke-bum; stew-bum; white-liner. "Hitting that lousy lush again? You, rubadub bum, that rubbing 'alky will knock you off (kill you)."

Drunkards, robbery of. See **Robbery of drunkards.**

Drunken orgy. Bender.

Duplicate, n. Dead ringer; dead spit; ringer.

Duplicate key. Double. "Get a double made of that screw (key) and we'll prowl (burglarize) the shack (house) tonight."

Dwelling. Crib; shack; shanty; slough. (See also **Apartment; Hotel or Rooming house; House.**)

E

Earring. Dangler.

Eat. Chuck; graze; scorf.

Educate in underworld lore. Hep up; hip up; tell one the score; smarten up; wise up.

Effeminate. Faggoty. "I never figured this faggoty talking guy was a dick (detective) till he flashed the button (shield)."

Effrontery. Balls; moxie. (See also Courage.)

Electric chair. Baker; chair; flame-chair; hot seat; hot spot; hot squat; old monkey; schweiner. (See also Capital punishment.)

Electric light. Dimmer; glim. "Butso (look out)! Douse (put out) that glim."

Electrocution, sentence of death by. The chair. (See also Electric chair.)

Elmira reformatory. The Beach.

Emasculate. Nut.

Emphatically. In spades.

Encounter, v. Go up against. "That was the toughest mark (victim) to beat (rob) I ever went up against on the gun (picking pockets)."

Enrage. Bug up; burn up; get one's pratt; steam up.

Enraged, p.p. Bugged up; having a bug on; hot; hot in the biscuit; sporting a bug; steamed up.

Ensnare. Duke in; rope in; swindle in; swindle up.

Enter. Mooch in.

Enterprise, illegal. See Profession or Business, one's.

Entree. Connection; contact; in. "Get an in with the legit stiffs (workers) in this joint and line up (get the information on) the peter (safe)."

Equal, everything being. Horse-to-horse. "Get rodded up (armed). Horse-

to-horse we can muscle (force) that mob out of the grift (racket)."

Escape, n. Beat; fadeout; figary; mooch; mope; out; powder; push; run-out powder; spring; tear-away. (See also Prison, escape.)

Escape, v. Amscray; beat; beat the pups (South); blow; breeze; burn up the pavement; cross the road; take it on the Dan O'Leary; dust; fade out; do a fade-out; heel; hop; mooch; mooch out; mope; rabbit; scram; screw; shag; skip; smoke; snake; take a powder; take it on the duff. (See also Prison, escape or attempt to escape from; Fugitive from justice, become a.)

Escape, means of. Out. "Louie's got a double-sawbuck (twenty years) in State's (State prison) and he's got to find an out."

Escape, shoot way to. Bang out; crash out; stick and slug.

Essex automobile. Hudson-pup.

Established. Set.

Establishment. Joint; lay; layout; plant; spot.

Establishment, catering to overworld. Hot joint; legit joint; square-John spot; up-and-up joint; wrong spot.

Establishment, low grade. Dump. (See also Brothel; Narcotics establishment; Rendezvous of perverts; Rendezvous of pickpockets; Rendezvous of thieves; Rendezvous of vagabonds.)

Establishment using decoys to lure and rob patrons. Cab-joint; creep-joint; mugg-joint; rigged joint; steer-joint; take-joint. (See also Swindle establishment.)

Establishment with underworld approval. Right joint; wide-open joint.

Establishment with underworld disapproval. Creep-joint; crimp-joint; crumb-joint; hot joint; joint stiff with wrong people; joint lousy with wrong people; joint swagged up with wrong people; stiff-joint; wrong joint. "Don't play that crumb-joint no more. It's lousy with stoolies (informers) and junkies (drug addicts)."

Esteemed by. Aces with.

Event. Happening.

Evidence, innocent of incriminating. Clean.

Exactly. On the lemon; on the noggin. "Don't take no less than a G (thousand dollars) from the fence (loot buyer). That'll meet the nut (expense) on the lemon."

Examination. Case; double-o; gander; gun; gunning over; pike.

Examine. See **Surveillance, keep under.**

Excluded. Out.

Ex-convict. Ex-con; ex-vic; ghee one knew up above; grad; dude one knew in lag; schoolmate; state-grad.

Excuse, face-saving. Out.

Execution, stay of. Anchor.

Executioner. The baker.

Exhaustion, be overcome by. Piss up; shoot one's load; shoot one's lump.

Exhibit, as money, weapons, etc. Break out; flash; hit one with; smack with; spring with. "When you spring with a tin (policeman's badge) them junk (drug) peddlers kick in (pay extortion) quick."

Exhibit officer's badge. Flash the button; flash the tin.

Exit, n. Out.

Exonerate an accomplice. To be a fall guy; to be a pack horse; spring; take the knock; take the rap; turn out. "I can turn out my partner on this rap (charge) but I gotta wind up with my joint in my hand (in prison serving time)."

Expenses. Case dough; the nut.

Expenses, clear. Get off the gun; get off the nut; make the nut.

Expenses, meet one's share of. Hold

one's end up; kick in with one's end of the nut.

Expert, n. Ringer; shark; sharp; whip. (See also **Go-getter.**)

Explosives. Combo-shot; dinah; grease; mulligan; noise; oil; peter; picric; puff; seam-shot; shot; soup; stemshot; stew; string.

Explosives, detonation of. Shot.

Extinguish. Choke; douse.

Extort. Bite; bite to death; bleed; lineup; make citizens; pull one's leg; push around; put on the arm; put on the cuff; put on the muscle; put the B on; put the bite on; put the gorril on; put the handle on; put the shake on; rattle; shake; shake a joint; shake down.

Extortioners, paying sums to. In line. "Throw a few pineapples (bombs) in them joints and keep the suckers (victims) in line."

Extortion. Arm; badger; bite; legpulling; muscle; pressure; shake; shakedown; squeeze; squeeze rates. (See also **Loan shark racket.**)

Extortion, engaged in or **by means of.** On the arm; on the bite; on the muscle; on the shake.

Extortion, submit to. See **Face, pay extortion in fear of extortioner's.**

Extortionist. Badger; horseman; legpuller; shake-man; shakester. (See also **Loan shark.**)

Eyeglasses. Cheaters; glims; googs; make-up.

Eyes. Glimmers; glims; lamps; peepers.

Eyes, artificial. Gravel-eyes.

Eyes, discolored. Shiners.

Eye suspiciously. Burn up; pike off; rumble. "Who's the ghee (fellow) burning us up? Law (a detective)?" (See also **Surveillance, keep under.**)

F

Face, n. Kisser; moosh; mugg; squash.

Face, disguise or **conceal in robbery.** Wear cheaters; cover up; slap on some glims; flash the googs; throw on a make-up; phony up one's get-up.

Face, pay extortion in fear of extortioner's. Pay off on the moosh; kick in on the squash. "This rabbit-snatcher (abortionist) don't need no creed (credentials) flashed on him; he's set to pay off on the moosh."

Face, show one's in robbery, etc. Give up one's kisser; give up one's mugg.

Face a victim while picking his pocket. Kiss the dog.

Fail. See **Criminal activity, bungle a venture in.**

Failure. Blank; bloomer; miss-up; piss-up; stiff. (See also **Criminal activity, profitless venture in.**) "I'm looking to dig up a few scores (robberies) to make the nut (expenses) but it's a miss-up so far."

Farmer. Alvin; apple-knocker; hill billy; plow-jockey; swamp angel.

Fastened. Anchored; nailed. "I put the duke down (put my hand in the victim's pocket) but his poke (wallet) won't go; must be nailed."

Fate, in the hands of. See **Doubtful.**

Fated. In the cards.

Favor, n. Contract. "I gotta contract I want you to handle for me to connect me with a good swaggie (buyer of stolen goods)."

Fear, n. Ague; no balls; bum clock; chill; no guts; no moxie; no ticker.

Fear, accomplish by inspiring. Put on the arm; cuff; put on the cuff; chill; chill off; put on the muscle; put the

chill on. (See also **Coerce; Threaten with.**)

Fear, be overcome by. Blow one's roof; blow one's top; chill; chill up on; chill off; cop all kinds of pleas; cop a plea; dog it.

Feel for valuables in fear of pickpockets. Fan. "Jostle the mark (victim) so he'll fan; then I'll beat (rob) him for the okus (wallet)."

Feet. Barkers; boots. "Give him the boots when I flip him."

Fellow, remarkable. See **Person, wonderful** or **remarkable.**

Female impersonator. A drag. (See also **Pederast, passive; Sodomist, oral.**)

Fight, verbal or fistic. Jackpot; jam; run-in; swindle. "You're getting too flip belligerent) with that kisser (mouth). I ain't going to bail you out (rescue you) from no more swindles. See also **Gunfight; Knife-fight; Shooting.**)

Fighter. Dukester; tumuler. (See also **Strong-arm man.**)

Fighter of policeman. Bull-buster; bull-fighter.

Fighter of prison guards. Screw-fighter; screw-hater.

Fight with. Put up one's dukes; to give one a fat lip; go up against; hook up with; tangle ass with; tumul with. (See also **Assault; Knife-wound, inflict a; Shoot.**)

Filled with. Crumbed up with; crummy with; lousy with; stiff with; swagged up with. "This joint is stiff with dicks (detectives) and fleepers (informers)."

Fingerprint, v. Print.

Fingerprints, n. Calling-card; prints. "Mitt up (wear gloves) prowling (burglarizing) this slough (house). Don't leave no prints."

Fingerprints, find at scene of crime. Make one's prints.

Fingerprints, identify criminal by means of. Make one on one's prints.

Fingerprints, take one's. Print.

Fingerprints, wear gloves to avoid leaving. Mitt up.

Fingers. See **Hands** or **fists.**

Firearms. Artillery; business; hardware; heat; iron; works. (See also **Machine-gun; Pistol; Pistol, equipped with silencer; Rifle; Shotgun; Shotgun, sawed-off.**)

First offender, criminal. First-time loser; jay. (See also **Prison, inmate newly arrived in.**)

Flashlight. Bull's-eye; dimmer; flash; glim; shiner.

Flat, n. See **Apartment.**

Flatter, v. Build up; give one a line of crap; con; con along; promote; put the promote on; schmear; short-con.

Flattery. Build-up; con; crap; promote; schmear; short-con. "Don't try to give me that short-con. I been conned by experts and they scored for (got) peanuts (nothing)."

Flee. See **Escape, v.**

Follow. Dog; freeze onto; put a spot on; put a tail on; put the clown to bed; on one's quiff; shag; tail; tail down. "The town clown (constable) knocks off (quits) at midnight. We put the clown to bed before we take (rob) the mark (establishment)."

Followed, p.p. Get a tail; pick up a tail. "Look out you don't pick up a tail on your way to the meet (appointment)."

Follower. Tail.

Follower, elude a. Duck a tail; shake a tail.

Following, the act of. Tail.

Following, the act of, in jewel-theft. Stone tail. "We got a caser (surveyor of robbery prospects) working on a stone tail that ought to make a sweet score (haul)."

Following closely. On one's biscuit; on one's can; on one's canetta; hot on one's pratt; hot on one's tail; on one's keister; on one's pratt; on one's quiff; on one's tail.

Fool, n. Airedale; as'ole; apsay; dingbat; fall guy; load; lob; mark; pack horse; popcorn; sapadilla; sausage; slob; sucker; yuld. (See also: **Person, easily deceived or robbed; Person, slow-witted or inept.**)

Fool, play the. Fart around; screw around. "You ain't gonna get nowhere in a racket farting around with legit stiffs (working people)."

Force or threat of force. The arm.

Force way in. Bash in; crash; crash in; make an in; kick in; push in. (See also **Enter; Burglariously, enter.**)

Ford automobile. Spider.

Forge checks or negotiable instruments. Scratch; scratch paper. (See also **Alter for purpose of fraud.**)

Forged check depository. Clearing house; stiff-joint.

Forged check or Negotiable instrument. See **Check, forged.**

Forged checks, pass. Bounce; bounce bum paper; bounce sour paper; fly kites; hang paper; hit one with; lay; lay paper; lay sour paper; push a stiff; push kites; push paper; smack with; smash a stiff; stiff. (See also **Counterfeit money, pass.**)

Forged checks, passer of. Bill-poster; butterfly man; kiteman; paper-hanger; paper layer; paper pusher; pusher; sheet-passer; shover.

Forger. Penman; raiser; scratcher; scratch-man; one of a scratch-mob; script writer; short story writer. (See also **Forged checks, passer of; Forger, crude.**)

Forger, crude. Penciler; tracer.

Forgers, gang of. Scratch-mob.

Forgers, headquarters of. Plant. "Blow town (flee). The coppers just crashed (raided) the plant."

Forgers, victimizing banks. Jug-mob.

Forgery, act or profession of. The scratch.

Forgery, criminal charge of. Paper-hanging fall; scratch rap.

Forgery, engaged in or by means of. On the scratch.

Forgery, humorous euphemism for. Being lousy and attempting to scratch. "You oughta see that social worker dame look at me when I told her I was was in for being lousy and attempting to scratch. She took a powder (fled) quick."

Forgery, signature to be duplicated in. Scratch. "I'm gonna get this mooch's (victim's) scratch on a petition so the tracer (forger) can get it on a stiff (forged check)."

Fornicate. Bang; cop a bean (with a virgin); get off the gun; get off the nut; give one a stab; give one the business; give one the works; hose; hump; lay; lay the leg; plow; put; put the blocks to; put the boots to; screw; stab; throw one a hump; yentz.

Fornication, an act of active. Bang; cut; daub of the brush; hose; hump; hymie; lay; put; screw; stab; yentz.

Fornication, practice promiscuous. Chippy around; put out; put the horns on; stretch the rubber; two-time.

Fornicator. Gash hound; turk; wolf.

Fourth-offender, criminal. Four-time loser. (See also **Criminal, habitual.**)

Frame up. Give a deal to; kangaroo; louse around; pin a rap on; put the chuck on; put the frame on; railroad; ride; screw; screw around; sell out; throw the book away; give one a wrong rap; yentz.

Frame-up, n. Deal; fast one; frame; frame-up; hurdy; lousing around; plant; quickie; ride; screwing around; sell-out; yentzing. (See also **Accusation, unjust; Criminal charge, unjust.**)

Freed from imprisonment. On the bricks; back in circulation; out; on the pavement; on the sidewalk; on the street; on the turf. "Bill Beans is back on the street. He was sprung (released) on some kind of teck (technicality)." (See also **Discharge from custody.**)

Free of cost, anything. Freebie.

Free of cost, obtained. On the arm; on the cuff; on the ice; on the muscle. "I'm getting a couple of nice patsies (pistols) from the tipster (informant on criminal leads). Strictly on the muscle."

Free world, specifically part of the underworld. The blot; the turf. (See also **Underworld.**)

Free world, outside prison. The bricks; the outside; the sidewalk; the street. "Mickey's broad is back on the turf (street-walking). She's only on the bricks a couple of weeks."

Freight-cars. Crawlers; danglers; deadheads; drags; gondolas; John O'Briens; rats; rattlers.

Freight-cars, rob. Rattle. "Come on down and rattle a few. We ain't been on a scoring (paying) trick (robbery) in a month."

Freight-cars, robber of. Eight-wheeler; rat-crasher; seal-buster.

Freight-cars, roof of. Deck.

Freight-cars, understructure of. The rods.

Freight-cars, working at robbery of. On the rats.

Frequent, v. Give a play; hit; play. "What do you say we give a play to the prowl (burglary) section, them sloughs (houses) on the West side?"

Friendly with. Aces with; jake with; right with.

Fugitive from justice. Corner-turner; duster; hotfoot; ghee on the lam; lamester; lammie; red hot.

Fugitive from justice, become a. Do a crouch; flatten out; hide out; hole up; hop; hop a parole; hop bail; hop town; kick a parole; lam; take it on the lam; pull a Greeley; scram; screw; screw town; hit the shade. (See also **Escape.**)

Fugitive from justice, sought as a. Half in stir; hot; hot as a forty-five; in Mexico; on the lam; having one's mug on the board; red hot; sizzling. "They got my mugg on the board down at whisker's joint (the post office). I gotta screw (flee)."

Furs. Skins. "I cut in on a nice score (robbery) in skins with a mob of loftmen (loft thieves)."

Fur loft or store. Skin-joint.

Furnished room. See **Apartment.**

Fur theft. The skin.

Fur theft, engaged in or by means of. On the skin.

Fur thief. Skin-worker.

G

Gamble, n. See Chance.

Gamble, take a. See Attempt; Criminal activity, undertake without leads.

Gambler. Hustler. See also Betting commissioner; Playing cards, cheat at.)

Gamble without means to pay losses. Bet on the muscle; go over one's head.

Gambling, accept losses stoically in. Take the knock.

Gambling, operated honestly. Play with the gaff; play without the gimmick; level the play; show for one's money; strictly on the legit; go with the tripod off; up-and-up.

Gambling, win heavily in. Break the book; kill a (the) Chinaman.

Gambling come-on. Bait; double-willie; grease. "This carny (carnival) grift (racket) is getting tough. Feed them mooches (customers) some double-willie and heat the tip up (warm the crowd's enthusiasm)."

Gambling fraud. See Swindle, n.

Gambling house, dishonestly operated. Gaff-joint; rigged joint; take-joint.

Gambling house, steal chips in. Chip cop.

Gambling house proprietorship. Bank; book; cutter; house.

Gambling losses, refuse to pay. See Payment, refuse to make.

Gambling paraphernalia. See Dice; Playing cards; Carnival, dishonestly operated booth in.

Gang, n. Combination; combo; finger-mob; mob; outfit; tribe; troupe.

Gang, get together members of. Rustle out. "Rustle out the mob and tell 'em to heel up (arm themselves). There's a swindle (trouble)."

Gang, join a. Double with; fill; hook up with; mob up; play ball; ring in; tie up with.

Gang, number of. —handed; —string; —strong. "We gotta step out four-handed on this caper (robbery) account of the kip (watchman)."

Gang, obtain membership in. Ace in.

Gangfight. See Gunfight; Knife-fight.

Gang-leader. Big apple; big ghee; biggie; big number; big shot; ghee who runs the mob; ghee with the brass nuts; lion tamer; main ghee; pusher.

Gang-leader, figurehead. Front; front ghee; front man. "Mike Muscles is only the front for that combo (combination). Gunboat's the big ghee (real leader)."

Gangster. Goniff; hood; hoodlum; hooligan; mob ghee; mobster. (See also Criminal; Gunman; Murderer, professional; Thief.)

Garage for stolen automobiles. See Automobile, depository for stolen.

Gem. See Jewelry, n.

Get together, as money, food, etc. Rustle up.

Gin. Jump-steady; white. (See also Alcoholic liquor.)

Girl. See Woman, n.

Girl, young. Jail-bait. (See also Woman.)

Girl-crazy. Cow-simple.

Give. Come through; get it on the line; get it up; give up; go; kick in; put out; put a buck one's way; shove a buck one's way; stake. "Charley the Chink staked me to a front (outfit) when I come out of stir (prison) and steered (directed) me right." (See also Victim of crime, yield as a.)

Glance, n. Flash; gander; once-over; the o.o.; pike; squint.

Glance, v. Gander; get a load of; pike; put the squint on; take a gander at. "Take a gander at that slum-joint (jewelry store). Gotta case that out (study it) for a heist (robbery)." (See also Look at.)

Glare, n. The bad-eye. "Can (stop)

American Underworld Lingo

that bad-eye crap; I don't go for (feel intimidated by) that."

Glare, v. Bad-eye; burn; burn up; to act the lion-tamer; make a kisser.

Glib-tongued. Thick-slung.

Gloves, wear. Mitt up. "Can't leave no prints (fingerprints) in this shack (house). Mitt up."

Glutton. Mean scorfer.

Go-between. Connection; connection ghee; fixer; the l. a.; mister fix; patch; shifter; wire; wire-ghee; wire-man.

Go-getter. Hustler; live-wire; promoter; rustler. (See also **Expert.**)

Going on. Moving. "What's moving on the turf (in the underworld)?"

Gold, melted-down scrap. Break-up.

Gold coin. Ridge.

Gonorrhea. See **Venereal disease.**

Good fellow. See **Criminal code, person loyal to; Person, likeable; Underworld, person cooperative with.**

Gossip, n. See **Agitation; Agitator; Person, talkative; Rumor; Slander.**

Gossip, v. See **Agitate; Slander; Talk.**

Gossip, channels of. See **Grapevine,** n.

Go straight. Die; fold up; hang up; hit the legit; level it; pack in; play the level; go strictly on the legit; go up-and-up; wash up; wrap up.

Go to. Hit; play. "Think I'll hit a tea-pad (marijuana establishment) and boot the gong around (smoke) a bit." (See also **Prison, go to one's cell in.**)

Go to bed or **one's quarters.** Hit the kip.

Grab, v. Glom; glom onto; glaum onto; put the glom on; put the snare on; snatch; snag. (See also **Arrest; Purse, snatch a.**)

Grapevine, n. Two-one; wire. (See also **Rumor.**)

Graveyard. Bone-orchard.

Gravy. Skilly.

Greet. Flag; flop; give one a flop; give one a toss; highball; rumble; tumble. "Don't give that crumb (low fellow) a toss. He's plenty wrong (traitorous)."

Greet, fail to. Chill; chill up on; flag; not give one a flop; pass up; put the chill on; not give one a rumble; not give one a toss; not give one a tumble.

Greeting. Flop; hello; highball; rumble; tumble. "What're you giving me them fancy hellos for? A bite (loan) or something?"

Greeting, cordial or **ostentatious.** Big hello; big rumble.

Greeting, hostile or **contemptuous.** Chill; cold-duke; kiss-off.

Grimace, n. A kisser; A moosh; "What's the kisser for, you figure you rate a bigger cut (share) of the swag (loot)?"

Grimace, v. Make a kisser.

Grudge against. Hard-on for. "Them screws (guards) in stir (prison) all had a hard-on for me and they sure gave me honey (abuse)."

Guard. See **Prison, guard in.**

Guarded by watchman or **residents.** Kipped. "This prowl (burglary) is gonna be candy (easy). The joint ain't kipped or mutted up (guarded by a dog)."

Gun. See **Pistol,** n.

Gunfight. Fireworks; fourth of July; war.

Gunman. Rod; rodman; stick-man; torpedo. (See also **Criminal; Gangster; Murderer, professional; Thief.**)

H

Hacksaw blades. Briars.

Haircut. Bandhouse clip; double-o.

Hand, v. Duke; weed. "Duke me the okus (wallet) as soon as you make (rob) the mark (victim)."

Hand in game of playing cards. Duke; mitt.

Handcuff, v. Cuff.

Handcuffs. Bracelets; cuffs; irons; nippers; slave-bracelets.

Handkerchief. Duster; snot-rag; tear-duster.

Hands or **fists.** Duke; dukes; fin; flipper; hook; meat-hooks; mitt.

Handshake. Mitt-glom. "You're a-round mitt-glomming like you were running for office. Who're you looking to beat (rob) out of what?"

Handshaker. Duker; fin-flipper; glad-hander; mitt-glommer.

Hanger-on. Beachcomber. (See also **Criminal, aide** or **sycophant of.**)

Happening. Come-off. "What a come-off! I'm mooching out (leaving) a joint I just clipped (robbed), loaded with swag (loot) when this copper wants to frisk (search) me. I lammed (fled)."

Happening, remarkable. See **Thing, wonderful** or **remarkable.**

Happy. Blowing one's roof; blowing one's top; high; high as a kite; hopped up; popping one's nuts; tea'd up.

Hardware store. Pig-joint.

Harlot. See **Prostitute** or **Loose woman.**

Hat. Dicer; skimmer.

Head, brain, or **mind.** Biscuit; bonnet; conk; cruller; idea-pot; knob; lemon; noggin; pumpkin; sconce; squash; think-pot.

Headlock. The arm.

Hearse. Glass wagon

Heart. Clock; pump; ticker.

Heart, weak. Bum clock; bum ticker; bad pump.

Hemorrhoids. Grapes.

Heroin. See **Narcotic, powdered.**

Hide, v. Do a crouch; flatten out; hide out; hole up; hit the shade. (See also **Conceal oneself.**)

Hiding place. Cover; hideout; hole; plant; shade; sneezer; stash.

Highway robber. Snaffler. (See also **Holdup man.**)

Hobo. Bindle-boy; bindle-bum; bindle-stiff; blanket-stiff; drifter; floater; gay cat; Jesus stiff; jungle-buzzard; mission stiff; necktie bum; ragbag; road agent; scenery bum; scratch-house bum; shield; stiff; stiffo; stumble bum. (See also **Vagrant.**)

Hobo, disability certificate used in panhandling by. Ducat.

Hobo, food solicited by. Dry lump; handout; lump; set-down.

Hobo, money solicited by. Handout.

Hobo, personal property bundle of. Bindle; crum; crumb; crummy; turkey.

Hobo, solicit as a. See **Solicit.**

Hobo rendezvous. See **Rendezvous of vagabonds.**

Hold, force, and effect, as a criminal charge. Stick; take. "If this knock-off (murder) beef (complaint) sticks, I'm buried (sure to die or get a long prison term)."

Holdup, n. Get-up; heavy; heavy-time; heist; lift; push-up; stick-up; throw; throw-up; toss.

Holdup, v. Get up; heist; to break one's cherry on a heist; lift; put up; scuffle; stick up; throw; throw a joint in the air; throw up; toss; tumul. (See also **Rob.**)

Holdup, bank. Jug-heist.

Holdup, crude. Hijacking; scuffle; tumuling. (See also **Robbery by unarmed physical force.**)

Holdup, truck. Hijack; truck-lift.

Holdup command. Belly the wall;

belly up; dance; elevate; get 'em up; hang your nose on the wall; reach.

Holdup from park ambush. Bushwhack.

Holdup gang, bank specialists. Damper-mob; jug-mob.

Holdup man. Footpad; gun; heavy; heavyman; heister; heist-man; hijacker; jigger; push-up ghee; stick-up ghee; throw-up ghee. (See also **Highway robber.**)

Holdup men, gang of. Mob, heist; mob of hijackers; stick-up mob.

Holdup profession. Bushwhack; getup; heavy; heist; the heist racket; hijack; lift; scuffle; stick-up; the stickup racket; throw.

Hold up railroad trains. Pull a Jesse James.

Homeless. On the bum; carrying the banner; carrying the stick. (See also **Penniless.**)

Home town neighbor. Homey.

Homosexuality. See **Fornication, an act of active; Pederasty (passive).**

Hope, v. Pull the nut. "I'm sure pulling the nut that this trick (robbery) goes okay. I'm in the barrel (in debt) for plenty."

Horse race, fraudulent. Boat race.

Hospital. Bone-factory.

Hotel or rooming house. Dump; dosshouse; fleabag; flop; flophouse; flopjoint; kip. (See also **Apartment; Apartment, as burglary site; Lodging house.**)

Hotel, act of evading payment of bill in. Heel. "I just took it on the duff from (left) that fleabag (rooming house) on the heel."

Hotel, evade bill payment in. Heel.

Hotel dead-beat. Heeler.

House, n. Shack; shanty; slough. (See also **Apartment; Apartment, as burglary site.**)

Hurry, v. Bounce; dust.

Hurry, in a. On the button; on the duff; on the hot; on the lam; one-two; tearaway. "Mickey just passed me on the tearaway with two dicks (detectives) hot on his pratt (following him closely)."

Hymen. Bean; cherry.

Hypochondriac, n. Hypo.

Hypocrite. Phony; two-way ghee. (See also **Person, contemptible.**)

Hypocrite, pious. Fluker; mission stiff; psalm-singing muzzler. "There's a psalm-singing muzzler sent me to the can (prison) on a hummer (false charge) and he almost lives in the church." (See also **Swindler, pseudoclergyman.**)

Hypodermic narcotic, addiction to. On the hype; on the hype-stick; on the hypo; on the light artillery; on the needle; shooting the pin. (See also **Narcotic, addicted to.**)

Hypodermic narcotic addict. Banger; bangster; hypo; jabber; jaboff; needle knight; needle man.

Hypodermic narcotic addict's equipment. Artillery; banger; hype-stick; light artillery; needle; pin.

Hypodermic narcotic injection. Bang; main-line bang; shot; shot in the arm.

Hypodermic narcotic injection, take a. Bang; hit the main line; shoot the pin; take a shot; take a shot in the arm.

I

Idle. On one's biscuit; on one's can; on one's canetta; on one's keister; on one's pratt; on one's quiff.

Ignore. Chill; flag; pass up; play the iggy; put the chill on. "Chill them finks (informers) when they give you a rumble (greeting). You'll only louse yourself up (ruin your reputation) with good people."

Ignoring, act of. Chill; iggy.

Illegal. Knock-around; racket; shady. "That's a racket joint he's running, but I ain't sure what the grift (game) is."

Illness, feign. Chuck a dummy; put on an act; stall; take a brodie; throw a wing-ding.

Illness, feigned. Brodie; dinger; twister; wing-ding.

Imitation. Larry; ringer.

Immediately. At the kick-off; off the pop; at the pop-off.

Impairing the morals of a minor. I.M.M.

Imprison. Lag; settle. (See also **Sentence.**)

Imprison after long criminal career. Break's one's license. "So you took a drop (were arrested) at last. Well, they figured to break your license after that nice run."

Imprisoned, p.p. See **Prison, in.**

Imprisonment, freed from. On the bricks; back in circulation; out; on the pavement; on the sidewalk; on the street; on the turf.

Incident. Come-off. "Did you see the come-off down at the stash (hang-out) when the shamus (policeman) tried to frisk (search) us?"

Include as an extra or **specialist in crime.** Cut in; declare in; ring in.

Included. Fill; in. "Yeah, I'm set to fill on the caper (robbery) as long as I score for (get) a full end (share)."

Incoherent. Screwy.

Income of a crime or **racket,** etc. See **Criminal activity, proceeds of.**

Indulge in. Give a play; hit; knock off; play. "What do you say we knock off a little lush (alcoholic liquor)?"

Infant, newborn female. Split-tail.

Infant, newborn male. Reg'lar feller.

Inferior, a. Lousy; phony; phony-baloney; two-bit. "That two-bit meatball (fool) couldn't hustle with me (steal with me). He's on the mahoska (using drugs)."

Influence, n. Alzo; connection; fix; hooks; in; license; nuts; set-in; wire; zingers. "We got the alzo on this beat (territory) and them other cannonmobs (pickpockets) better keep out."

Information. See **Criminal activity, tip leading to.**

Information, false. Blind steer; bum steer; phony steer; wrong steer.

Information, supply with. See **Criminal activity, supply with leads in.**

Inform upon self and/or **accomplices** or **others.** Beef; beef murder; belch; blow the gaff; blow the whistle; bury; clean up the calendar; come clean; come through; crimp; cross up; do a solo; do business; dog it; double bank; drop a kite on; drop a tab on; drop the chuck on; dump; eat cheese; finger; finger cold turkey; fink; give one a bit; go wrong; hang; holler; holler copper; holler murder; hose; hump; knock; knock out; loud talk a ghee; louse around; make a deal; mouse; peach; peep; puke on; put the blocks to; put the boots to; put the chuck on; put the cross on; put the finger on; put the prongs to; put up a beef; put up a holler; put up a squawk; put up a sucker's holler; rank; rap; rat; roar; screw; screw around; sell out; send up; shag; shoot one's bazoo off; shoot one's kisser off; shoot one's mouth off; shoot one's yap off; sing;

snitch; spill; spill the works; spill one's guts; squawk; squawk murder; stool; switch; take the stand against; talk; tip; tip off; turn; turn copper; turn in; welch; whistle; to blow the whistle; yell; yell murder; yelp; yentz; yip. (See also **Third degree, break under and inform.**)

Informer. One who is all copper; badge man; bad man; ballplayer; bat-carrier; buzz-man; beefer; belcher; canary; cheese-eater; con P.K.; copper; one who is copper-hearted; creep; crimp; crump; Dep's man; dumper; finger; fingerman; fink; flea; fleabag; fleeper; one who is frail; geepo; g-man; gum-foot Gus; gunzel; heel; one who is hundred per cent wrong; knock-man; leech; ghee who has a license; one who louses himself up; mouse; muzzler; nose; note-dropper; penman; P.K.'s man; plant; rat; shit-heel; shit-heeler; snake; snitch; snitch; snitcher; stool; stoolie; stoolo; stool-pigeon tanker; twenty-two-fifty man; two-way ghee; warden's man; wrong ghee; wrongo; yelper; yentzer. (See also **Person, contemptible.**)

Injustice. Deal. "I'm getting a deal if I get hit with a bit (prison sentence) on this mopery rap (foolish charge)." (See also **Accusation, unjust; Criminal charge, unjust.**)

Inquisitive, a. On the earie; on the gun; on the i.c.; on the lake; on the mooch; on the pike; playing the bird with the long neck; on the prowl; on the squint.

Insane, become. Blow one's roof; blow one's top; break up; play with the squirrels.

Insane, mentally defective or **criminally.** Batty; bugs; clink-cuckoo; ding-aling; easy; kinky; playing with the squirrels; screwy; stir-buggy; stir-bugs; stir-crazy; stir-nuts; stirry; stir-simple; stir-wacky; woody.

Insane, hospital for the mentally de-fective or **for the criminally.** Booby-hatch; bug-house; cackle-factory; fit house; funny factory; giggle academy; nut house; nuttery.

Insane, interne in hospital for the mentally defective or **for the criminally.** Man in the white coat; net; ghee with the net. "You'd better look out for the ghee with the net, Mike; you're one dingaling (madman)."

Insane person, mentally defective or **criminally.** Bug; dingaling; screwball; stir-bug; stir-wack; wack; wacko; whack; wheel.

Insane, psychiatrist in hospital for the mentally defective or **for the criminally.** Bug doctor; man in the white coat; ghee with the net.

Insane, send to hospital for the mentally defective or **for the criminally.** Bug; drop the net on.

Insane, sent to hospital for the mentally defective or **for the criminally.** Make the bughouse; get the straw hat and the red tie.

Insult, n. Bird; chirp; crack; crap; five-and-fifty-five; lunger. (See also **Abuse.**)

Insult, v. Chirp; crack; needle; play the dozens; slap in the kisser with; smack in the kisser with. "Can you imagine that muzzler (low fellow) smacking me in the kisser with that crack (nasty remark)." (See also **Abuse.**)

Insurance racket, accident. The oil business.

Insurance racket, principal in accident. Flopper; repeater; twister.

Insurance racket, tricks of accident. See **Beggary, trickery in.**

Insurance racket, victimization of underwriter in accident. Set-up.

Intercept. Knock off. "Joe sent me a kite (uncensored letter) out of stir (prison) but a wrong screw (guard who couldn't be bribed) knocked it off."

Intercept a written message. Knock off a kite; knock off a tab.

Intercourse, sexual. See **Fornication.**

Interest in, lose. Chill; chill off; chill up on.

Interrupt. Bust in; lip in; push in. "If you keep lipping in when people are chopping up jackies (telling stories) you'll get a fat lip (punch in the mouth)."

Interruption of a crime. Blow; blow card; blow off; flop; rank; rumble; toss; tumble. "We got the rumble when the score (robbery) was in the bag (near successful conclusion)."

Intoxicated. Charged up; having one's edge; gaged; geezed up; get one's load on; have a load on; heeled; high; high as a kite; lushed up; on the nod; paralyzed; primed; having a skinful; slopped up; stinko.

Introduce. Duke in; to provide with an in; straighten out.

Introduction. Duke-in; in; send-in.

Intrude brazenly. Bust in; crash; crash in; push in.

Invade rival gang territory. Buck a combination; buck a combo; cut in; declare in; push in.

Iron out. Square. "Sam's good people (a good fellow), and I don't want no swindle (trouble) with him. We gotta square this thing."

Italian, n. Chestnut-stabber; guin; guinea; guinzo; guinzola; greaseball; jibboney; meat ball; pineapple; zool.

J

Jail, v. See **Imprison**.

Jail, accommodating penniless transients. Flop-joint.

Jail, approved by habitues. Right joint. "If you gotta pull a bit (serve a term) in the jug (jail), hit the county (county jail); it's a right joint."

Jail, county. Bandbox; bandhouse; bing; booby; booby-hatch; bridewell; calaboose; can; canister; clink; clinkeroo; county; damper; doss-house hatch; jug; piss-can; pogey; pokey; tank. (See also **Police station house; Prison**.)

Jail, dirty, ill-administered and/or filled with lowest characters. Creep-joint; crumb-joint; crummy; dump; fleabag; louse-trap.

Jail, easy to escape from. Crackerbox.

Jail, in hot climate. Frying pan.

Jail, prisoner awaiting transfer to prison from. Dipsy.

Jail, rife with homosexuality. Peg-house.

Jail, town or city. See **Jail, county**.

Jail, United States Federal. G-joint; Fed joint.

Jail, venally administered. Connection can; connection joint.

Jamaica ginger. Jake; jakey.

Jam or jelly. Red lead.

Jewelry, n. Flash; gullion; ice; rocks; slum; slum-gullion.

Jewelry, act of following victim to rob. Stone tail.

Jewelry, circular piece of. Hoop.

Jewelry, diamond, set pieces of. Ice; rocks; simple simon.

Jewelry, emerald, piece of. Green ice.

Jewelry, imitation or cheap piece of. Piece of crap; gullion; junk; larry; Mexican diamond; paste; slum; slum-gullion.

Jewelry, pendant piece of. Dangler.

Jewelry, precious metal settings of. Break-up. "We got four G's (four thousand dollars) for the stones (gems) and the two bills (two hundred dollars) for the break-up."

Jewelry, salesman of. Slum-peddler.

Jewelry salesman's wallet. Gullion-poke; slum-poke.

Jewelry establishment. Gullion-joint; ice-house; slum-joint; stone-joint.

Jewel thief. See **Thief, jewelry specialist**.

Join forces with. Ace in; double with; fill; hook up with; mob up; play ball; ring in; tie up with.

Joke, at another's expense. Needles; rib; zingers. "I got a bug on (bad mood). Don't give me no zingers or none of that crap (nonsense) today."

Joker, practical. Ghee who farts around; kibitzer.

Joke with. Fart around; give one a kibitz; give one needles; rib; take for a ride; take for a sleigh-ride.

Judge, n. Beak; bench-nibs; Blackstone; Father Time; monk; Pontius Pilate; wig.

Judge, severe. Hanging judge; hard rapper; a judge with plenty of numbers; a tough geezer with time.

Justifiable. Legit. "Give me every meg (cent) I got coming. I got a legit beef when you beat (rob) me of my full end (share)."

Justifiable complaint. Legit beef; legit holler; legit squawk.

K

Keep it. (Imp.) Sit on it; whip it.

Key, n. Screw.

Key, duplicate. Double.

Kick, n. Boost; heist; root.

Kick, v. Boost; heist; root. "Boost that fleeper (low fellow) in the biscuit (buttocks) and chase him."

Kick in the backside. Heist in the pratt; root in the keister.

Kidnap. Glom; put in the hole; put the glom on; put the grab on; put the snatch on; snare; snatch; sneeze; stick in the hole. (See also Arrest; Grab.)

Kidnapper. Snatch-man; sneezer.

Kidnapping. Body snatch; snatch.

Kidnapping, faked. Phony snatch.

Kidnapping, ransomer in. Pay-off ghee.

Kidnapping, successful consummation of. Pay-off.

Kidnapping, unsuccessful consummation of. Blow-off. "The blow-off came when the bulls (police) found the dude (man) we had stuck in the hole (kidnapped)."

Kidnapping go-between. Contact; contact ghee.

Kidnapping of a dog for sale or ransom. Pooch-snatch; yip snatch.

Kill. See Murder; Shoot.

Kiss, n. Slobber.

Kiss, v. Slobber; swap spits.

Knife, n. Axe; blade; business; canojerod; chiv; chopper; convincer; dirk; hardware; hook; mahoska; piece; prod; shiv; steel; sticker; toad-sticker; works.

Knife, carry a. Heel up; lug; lug a chiv; pack; pack a chiv; pack heat.

Knife, carrying a. Heeled; loaded; packed up. (See also Armed.)

Knife, carrying with intent to kill. See Murder, seek with intent to.

Knife, remove from person and conceal. Stash a chiv; duck a chiv; ditch a prod; unload.

Knife, threaten with a. Pull a chiv; put a chiv on; put it on one; put the heat on.

Knife-fight. Chivving match; cutting match; shivving match.

Knife-fighter. Axeman; chiv-man; ghee who packs a chiv.

Knife-wound. Brand; chop; jig-cut; mark; rat mark; stool mark.

Knife-wound, inflict a. Brand; carve initials in one; chiv; chop; chop down; clip; cut; cut a new kisser for; dig; mark; mark one's kisser; open up; shiv; slice; stick.

Knock down. Knock on one's biscuit; knock on one's can; flatten; flip; knock on one's keister; knock on one's pratt; knock on one's quiff. (See also Knock unconscious.)

Knocked down, be. Hit the deck.

Knock unconscious. Cold-cock; flatten; put the chill on. (See also Knock down.)

L

Labor union organizer, delegate, etc. Labor-skate.

Ladies' man. Lover.

Landlord, cheat one's. Heel a joint.

Large, numerically. Boxcar numbers; telephone numbers.

Last dollar. Case buck; case dollar. "Go easy on the nut (expenses). That's our case dough."

Last money remaining. Case dough.

Las Vegas. Vegas.

Law, disregard processes of. Throw the book away. "That creep (low fellow) on the bench threw the book away and buried me (railroaded me) when I was going to beat the rap (win acquittal)." (See also **Criminal court malpractice.**)

Law-enforcement body. Big department; the law.

Lawyer. See **Attorney.**

Leave, v. Blow; breeze; check out; cop a mope; cut out; duck; dust; fade; do a fadeout; fade out; heel; heel out; hit the road; kick out; kick out of; lam; mooch; pull a Crater; push out; screw out; skip; snake out; turf it; walk out. (See also **Escape.**)

Leg-irons. Anklets; boot; bull-chain; clinker; clinkers; lam-bean; Oregon-boot; rat-shackle; rattler; tracer-chain.

Leg-irons, device to lift and carry chain of. G-string.

Legs, n. Gams; pins; shafts; sticks.

Lesbian. See **Sodomist, active female.**

Letter, smuggled. Cannonball; kite; stiff.

Liar, n. Con-man; con-merchant; conner; crap merchant; oil merchant; phony; promoter; spieler. (See also **Swindler.**)

Lie, n. Bull; build-up; con-line; crap; gurdy; hurdy; line of crap; promote; schmear; short-con; sleigh-ride; spiel.

Lie, v. Build up; con; con along; promote; schmear. (See also **Swindle.**)

Life imprisonment. See **Sentence, lifetime prison.**

Lincoln automobile. Papa.

Liquor, illegally distil. Cook; re-run, turn over.

Liquor, smuggle into country. Run rum; whip over.

Liquor dealer, illicit. Dynamiter; white-liner.

Liquor establishment. Barrel house; beer flat; inkpot; jinney; alky joint; lush joint; juice-joint; juke-joint; lush-dive; skee-joint; smoke-joint. (See also **Alcoholic liquor, plant to distil illicit.**)

Liquor orgy. Bender.

Liquor ships, smuggler's. Rum row.

Liquor smuggler. Rum-runner.

Liquor-smuggling motorboat. Rum-runner; sneaker.

Listen. Bag onto; get on the earie; get a load of; ride the earie; tune in.

Listener. Elephant ears; earie; erie; tin-ear.

Listening, a. On the earie; on the lake; sails are flapping. "Dummy up (shut up)! That guy on the earie looks like the law."

Loaf, v. Bum around; fart around.

Loafer. Coffee-and pimp; dance hall pimp; family pimp.

Loafing. On one's biscuit; on one's can; on one's canetta; on one's keister; on one's pratt; on one's quiff. "Get out on the turf (stealing) if you won't work, bum. You can't live on your canetta." (See also **Penniless.**)

Loan. Bite; score; touch. (See also **Beggary.**)

Loan, secure a. Bite; score; take; touch. (See also **Beg.**)

Loan shark. Shark; shylock.

Loan shark, agent of a. Shadow. "That shylock's (loan shark's) shadow has me hooked for two C's (two hundred dollars), and I can't get even with that vigerage-and (multiple interest) racket."

Loan shark, defaulting borrower from. Weasel.

Loan shark, victim of a. Rabbit.

Loan shark racket. Shylocking.

Loan shark racket, mulct victim in. Make a grab.

Loan shark racket, usurious interest rates in. Vigerage; vigerage-and.

Lock, v. Button.

Lock up. See **Arrest.**

Lodging house. Creep-joint; crummy; doss house; dump; fleabag; flop; flophouse; flop-joint; kip; louse trap. (See also **Hotel** or **rooming house.**)

Look, n. See **Glance, n.**

Look at. Burn up; case; cop; cop a gander; gander at; gap; get a load of; glom; gun; get on the i.c.; lamp; pike off; pipe; play the bird with the long neck; put the squint on; round; rumble; smoke; give a toss; tumble. "Don't even give that joint a toss 'cause it ain't worth clipping (robbing)."

Look at in fear, awe, etc. Big-eye.

Look at threateningly. See **Glare.**

Lookout. Gapper; hawk; jigger; jigger-man; lookout; outside man; spotter; tip; zex-man.

Lookout, serve criminally as a. Anchor; case; gap; lay butzo; lay jiggers; lay zex; spot.

Lookout, station one as a. Plant. "Just plant the moll (girl) outside the joint to lay zex (watch for interference), and I'll make the score (theft)."

Look searchingly through a place. Smoke a joint.

Loose woman. See **Prostitute.**

Loot, n. See **Stolen goods.**

Los Angeles. L.A.

Lose. Blow; boot; drop. (See also Criminal activity, bungle a venture in.)

Lost, a. In the crapper; in the donicker; in the sack; in the satchel; in the sewer.

Lot of. Slew of; swag of. "I hear Buttonnose Bill hit stir (went to prison) with a swag of boffos (years to serve)."

Luck, the symbol of bad. Bitch; bitch of a set-up; bitch's curse; bad break; hoodoo; horns; jinx; snake-eyes.

Luck, wish one bad. To put the bitch's curse on one; jinx; put the horns on. "I ain't made a good score (theft) in months. Some flea (low fellow) must have put the horns on me."

Lucky. Having a big keister; what a canetta; what a keister; to be a load; what a rip; what a spread; wide open. "You had a two-year run (period of crime without arrest) now. What a rip!"

Lure, n. See **Criminal, shield covering operations of a; Gambling come-on.**

Lure, v. Bait.

Lure to crooked establishments. Shill; steer; tout. "Step out and tout some suckers (victims) to the joint or we'll never get off the nut (meet expenses)."

M

Macaroni. Makko.

Machine gun. Brownie; chatterbox; chatterer; chopper; coffee-grinder; grind organ; hand organ; sho-sho; spray; sub; ta-ta; tommy; typewriter.

Machine-gun case. Violin case.

Machine-gunner. Organ-grinder; tommy-ghee.

Magazine, periodical, etc. Joint; limb-joint; sheet.

Make a bad selection. Draw a bloomer.

Manacle, n. Boot.

Many, n. Boxcar numbers; slew; swag; telephone number.

Marijuana. Gage; gonga; goof; griffo; mota; muggles; stink-weed; tea; weed; yen-pop.

Marijuana, addicted to. Hooked on the gage.

Marijuana, smoke cigarettes containing. Bang a reefer; blast; blast the roach; blow one's roof or top; boot the gong around; get one's gage up; hit the gage; hit the goof; hit the tea; kick the gong around.

Marijuana, trafficker in. Gage hustler; muggles pusher; tea-man.

Marijuana addict. Goof; snake; tea-man; viper.

Marijuana cigarette. Goof butt; muggles; reefer; roach.

Marijuana establishment. Tea-pad.

Marijuana establishment, cost of visit to. Pad-dough.

Marijuana establishment, visit a. Hit a tea-pad.

Marked for death. All caught up; all washed up; caught up; got to go; washed up. "That fink (informer) is all caught up. He's gotta catch lead (be shot to death)."

Marry, legally or by common law. Double with; hook up with; tie up with.

Mask one's features. Cover up.

Mask one's features, neglect to. Give up one's kisser; give up one's mugg. "I gotta cover up (wear a mask) on this heist (hold-up) 'cause I know too many guys around here to give up my kisser."

Masturbate. Beat the bishop; beat the dummy; beat the pup; cabaret; diddle; flog the pork; go cabareting; go to town; jerk off; kick the gong around; night club; go night clubbing; pull off; snap the rubber; snap the whip.

Masturbation, chronically addicted to. Married to Mary Fist.

Masturbator. Diddler; jerk; jerk-off.

Matchbox or Sulphurated portion of. Striker.

Matches, n. Splits; sticks.

Materialize. Shape up. "This score (robbery) will shape up after we case (study) the joint for a week or two."

Meal, free. Dukes; freebie; handout; set-down; sit-down.

Meal, light. Coffee-and.

Meal, one who seeks a free. Free loader.

Mean act. Fink caper; rat caper.

Meat. Bull; mountain goat. (See also Steak.)

Miser. Single-o; tough giver-up.

Mislead, v. Bum steer; to give one a bum steer; to give one a gurdy; to give one a hurdy; sleigh-ride; wrong-steer. "You wrong-steered me on that wheelman (driver). He's a dog (lacking in courage)."

Money. Boodle; buck; bundle; buttons; cabbage; chips; chunk; color; cush; dough; geedus; gelt; grease; iron; jack; kale; line; lump; oday; rocks; roll; scratch; silk; sock; spinach; wad. (See also Cent; Dollar.)

Money, attractive inflow of. Good buck; nice buck; nice dollar.

Money, bare expense. Nut dough; short dough.

Money, be in possession of a sum of. Holding.

Money, bill of large denomination. Course note.

Money, counterfeit. See Counterfeit money.

Money, earned by approved means. Clean buck.

Money, easy. Candy; clean buck; nice buck; smart buck; smart dollar.

Money, for legal fee, bail, bribery, etc. Fall dough.

Money, gift, loan, or bribery sum of. Stake.

Money, hard earned or of contemptible origin. Blood dough.

Money, having no. See Penniless.

Money, lodging. Flop-dough; pad-dough.

Money, looking for easy. Out for a buck; playing the field.

Money, metal. Chicken feed; chink; hard; hard stuff.

Money, newly acquired sum of. Fresh.

Money, obtain. Get off the nut. (See also Beg; Criminal activity, carry out a profitable venture in; Solicit; Steal.)

Money, paper currency. Course note; frog-backs; rag; silk; soft. (See also Dollar; Money.)

Money, shrewdly acquired sum of. Smart buck; smart dollar; smart dough.

Money, theft of all the victim's. Pocket touch.

Money, unimportant sums of. Boy scout dough; chicken feed; crabs; eppis; Mexican bankroll; Michigan bankroll; peanuts; pretzels; tin; wampum; washers; wood.

Money, withheld by cheating associates. H.o. dough; oats; rake-off; tips. "There'll be no h.o. dough going south (into concealment) out of this touch

(robbery). Everybody turns out (turns pockets inside out)."

Money belt. Boodle-belt; skin-plaster.

Months, imprisonment for six. A sixer.

Morals of minors, impairer of. Diddler. (See also Pederast, active; Pederast, passive; Rapist; Sodomist, oral.)

Morphine. See Narcotic, powdered.

Morgue. Icebox; slab.

Motorboat. Rum-runner; sneaker.

Mouth. Bazoo; belcher; clam; gash; gob; hash trap; moosh; north-and-south.

Move about stealthily. Case; get around; mooch; mooch around; mooch in; mooch out; mosey; prowl. "Who's that geepo (suspicious looking fellow) mooching around? Shapes up like a dick (detective) to me."

Move close to a table, stand, etc. Belly up.

Murder, n. Bang-job; bump-off; chill; knock-off; ride; works. (See also Assault; Knife-fight.)

Murder, v. Bang in the head; bang in the noggin; bang out; blot out; bump; bump off; burn down; chill; clip; croak; drill; toss in the drink; drop; dump; get; give one the business; give one the works; hit in the bonnet; hit in the cruller; hit in the head; hit in the noggin; hit in the sconce; hit in the squash; hit out; hit with a lily; knock off; plant; put the chill on; put the cross on; rub out; put in the sack; shove over; put on a slab; stretch; take care of; take for a ride; take one out to the country. (See also Assault; Knife-wound, inflict a; Shoot.)

Murder, find corpse of victim of. Find in a hallway; find in the drink; find in the river; find in the sack.

Murder, marked for. See Marked for death.

Murder, site for disposal of victim of.

Country; drink; dump; plant. "You gotta hit that crumb in the sconce (shoot that informer in the head) and drop him out in the country."

Murder, seek with intent to. Gun for; lug a chiv for; lug iron for; pack a chiv for; pack a rod for. ·

Murderer, professional. Bang-man; butcher; dropper; hatchet-man; knock-off ghee; red hot; torpedo; trigger.

"The Dutchman's got a couple of his triggers gunning for the dudes that knocked his kid brother down." (See also **Gangster.**)

Murderer, spotter of victim of. Finger; fingerman. "I know Danny Knuckles knocked my partner off (killed him) but I want the fingerman that pegged (identified) him for the torpedo (killer)."

N

Nag, v. Be on one's biscuit; be on one's can; be on one's canetta; be on one's keister; be on one's pratt; be on one's quill; be on one's tail. "I'm gonna blow my parole (flee the jurisdiction) 'cause the parole dude (agent) is on my tail day and night." (See also Abuse.)

Nagging, n. See Abuse, n.

Name, real or assumed. Flag; handle; label; monicker; phony handle; phony monicker; phony tag; stage name; tag.

Narcotic. Dope; junk; mahoska; mooch; stuff. (See also Aphrodisiac; Marijuana; Narcotic, powdered; Opium.)

Narcotic, addicted to. On the habit; hooked; on the junk; on the mahoska; on the schmeck; on the stuff; up against it. (See also Marijuana, addicted to; Opium, addicted to.)

Narcotic, adulterate. Cut; doctor; phony up.

Narcotic, adulterated measure of. Phony bingle; cut-deck.

Narcotic, feigned illness to procure. See Illness, feign.

Narcotic, make occasional use of. Chippy; chippy around; fart around with junk.

Narcotic, measure or dose of. Bindle; bing; bingle cadillac; can; charge; deck; load; o.z.; piece; shot; skinful; speedball. (See also Hypodermic narcotic injection; Opium, measure or dose of.)

Narcotic, obtain, by feigning illness. See Illness, feign.

Narcotic, occasional user of. Joyrider.

Narcotic, person familiar with but not addicted to. Square; square Willie.

Narcotic, powdered. Bingle; burnese; C; C and M; candy; cecil; coke; cubes; dust; dynamite; foolish powder; gee; H; happy dust; M; majonda; mojo; morph; noise; reindeer dust; schmeck; snow; white stuff; whizz-bang.

Narcotic, traffic in. Peddle; push gage; push junk; push muggles; push reefers; push schmeck; push the mooch; shove mahoska. "I got a chance to make a nice buck with a license (guaranteed police immunity) but I can't see pushing junk."

Narcotic, traffic in. Junk pushing; mahoska peddling; shoving the stuff.

Narcotic, trafficker in. Bingle; C-pusher; H-pusher; junker; junk-peddler; junk-pusher; mooch-pusher; M-pusher; peddler; shover; tea-man. (See also Marijuana, trafficker in.)

Narcotic, unadulterated. See O.K.

Narcotic, under influence of. Caught in a snowstorm; charged up; coked up; having an edge; gaged up; geed up; geezed up; have a load on; heeled; high; high as a kite; hitting the ceiling; hopped up; junked up; spending a night on the rainbow; on the nod; primed; riding a wave; taking a sleigh-ride; stinko; tea-ed up.

Narcotic, use. Blow coke; blow snow; cork the air; hit; hitch up the reindeer and we'll go for a sleigh-ride; hit the needle; kick the mooch around; shoot the pin. (See also Marijuana, smoke cigarettes containing; Opium, smoke.)

Narcotic addict. Cokey; C-user; d.a.; dynamiter; H-user; junker; junkey; kokomo; moocher; M-user; schmecker; sniffer; snowbird; user. (See also Hypodermic narcotic addict; Marijuana addict; Opium addict.)

Narcotic addiction, free oneself of. Boot a habit cold turkey; kick a habit; kill a chinaman.

Narcotic addiction, recurrence of. Kick-back; yen-yen.

Narcotic establishment. C-joint; H-joint; camp; junkey; M-joint; mooch crib; mooch-joint; snowbank. (See also **Marijuana establishment; Opium establishment.**)

Necklace. Rope.

Neighbor. Homey.

Nerve. See **Courage.**

Nervous indigestion, prison induced. Stir belly.

Newcomer. Blow-in.

Newspaper. Joint; rag; sheet; snitch-sheet; stiff; stiffo.

Nitroglycerine. See **Explosives.**

Nitroglycerine, prepare. See **Safe** or **Vault, perpare for explosion in burglary of.**

No good. See **Bad; Worthless, relatively** or **wholly.**

Northerner. Snow-digger.

Nose or **long-nosed person.** Hook; hooko; nozzo; schnozzo.

Note, n. Cannonball; kite; scratch; stiff; stiffo; tab; tag. "I just got a kite from The Beetle's joint down in Miami. He's got a big nautchery (brothel) making a nice buck (good income)."

Notice, n. Blow; flop; rumble; tumble. "Them suckers passing by didn't give us a blow when we were kicking in (burglarizing) that skin-joint (fur-store)."

Notice, v. Give a ghee a toss; give a joint a play; give a joint a toss; give a thing a flop; give a thing a toss; rap; rumble; take a tumble; tumble. "I didn't even tumble the copper until he put the rod (pointed his gun) on me."

Nymphomaniac. Gash-hound; horneo; hot tomato.

O

Occupied by sleeping residents. Kipped. "We crashed (burglarized) the joint and didn't even know it was kipped till the rumble (alarm)."

Occurrence. Come-off.

Ocean. Drink.

O.K., a. Aces; al-joe; alzo; twenty-two carat; forty; goods; jake; keen; keeno; kosher; McCoy; nuts; pat; patsy; right; solid.

Onlooker. Gapper; kibitzer. "We'd have never got a toss (been noticed) beating (robbing) the mark (victim) if it wasn't for that gapper."

Open (limited to the eyes). Peeled.

Operator of wheel or game. Agent.

Opium. Dream gum; dreams; dream wax; hop; pop; poppy; pox; yam-yam. (See also **Narcotic.**)

Opium, addicted to. On the gonger; hitting the pipe; laying on the hip; on the three-taps. (See also **Narcotic, addicted to.**)

Opium, measure or **dose of.** Pill; toy; yam-yam; yen-pock.

Opium, occasional user of. Joy-rider; pleasure smoker.

Opium addict. Bowler; gonger; gong-kicker; habit-smoker; hophead; pipey; three-tapper.

Opium addict, accessories of. Engine; glim; g-rag; granny; suey pow; yen-gow; yen-hock; yen-shee; yen-shee bowl; yen-shee gow; yen-shee rag.

Opium establishment. Den; joss-house; layout; pop-joint; three-tap joint. (See also **Narcotic establishment.**)

Opium pipe. Bamboo; gonger; poppy pipe; stick.

Opium, prepare. Chef; chef left and right; cook; roll a pill.

Opium, smoke. Burn the midnight oil; hit the pipe; kick the engine around; lay on the hip; lay up. (See also **Marijuana, smoke cigarettes containing.**)

Opium tender. Chef; cook.

Oriental, n. Skibo.

Outcome. Blow-off; come-off; pay-off. "Let's see what the pay-off is when he comes to bat (goes to trial). He oughta beat the rap (be acquitted)."

Outcry. See **Complaint.**

Outcry, delay criminal victim's. Stall a beef. (See also **Swindle.**)

Outwit. Con; cop a heel on; cop a sneak on; give one a hustle; give one a promote; hump to death; phenagle; promote; pull a fast one; pull a quickie on; put the hustle on; put the promote on; short-con; work one's points. (See also **Swindle.**)

Overcoat. Benny; flogger.

Overcoat of professional shoplifter. Boosting ben; swag benny; swag flogger.

Overlook. Pass up (See also **Greet, fail to.**)

P

Padlock, n. Paddy.

Palm-reader's establishment. Mitt-joint.

Panhandle. See **Beg.**

Parasite. See **Beggar.**

Pardon a convict. Hand out clemo; commute; spring.

Pardon of a convict. Clemo; commute; life-boat; lifesaver; spring.

Parole. See **Discharge from custody.**

Parole, denied. Do it all; get all of it; get the book; get the bookful; get buried; finish up; flop; get hit with; get hit with the book; go down; get the max; get max less compo; get a turn-down; be washed up.

Parole, deny application for. Boff with an ace; boff with a deuce; bury; crimp; hit with boffos; hit with the book; hold back; nix; smack with one specker; smack with two speckers; toss the book at; turn down.

Parole, eligible for release on. Due out.

Parole, forfeit eligibility for. Blow a parole. "Mickey just blew his parole chivving (cutting with a knife) the guy that ratted (informed) on him."

Parole, get preliminary hearing for. Make the rounds. "I meet the board (of parole) next month. Yeah, I made the rounds—hospital, chaplain's office, bug-doctor (psychiatrist) and all."

Parole, granted. Broke from stir; make parole; make the board; make the boast; draw a rain-check; spring; score for a turn-out.

Parole, granted by mandate of law. Got to go. "I got to go on this flat (determinate) bit (sentence). No way for the board (of parole) to louse me around (detain me arbitrarily)."

Parole, reduction of sentence by. Brass; copper; good time; parole time; short time. "Four months a year good time is something I earned. The board oughta have to kick in (credit me) with that."

Parole, term served during denials of. Life on the installment plan; hold-back time.

Parole, under restrictions of. Broke from stir; owe short time; owe time.

Parole, violation of terms of. Violation.

Parole, violator of terms of. Violator. "Twenty violators came in on that draft (inter-prison transfer of men). Jeez, they bring ghees back for mopery (trivial irregularities)."

Parole board. Board.

Parole board, appear before the. Meet the board; go up. "I go up tomorrow for my bundle (term of years imposed by parole board)."

Parole board, flee supervision of. Blow parole; hop parole; jump a parole; kick a parole; kick over on a parole; make the arrival and screw; shake a parole.

Parole board, nervously awaiting hearing by. Dancing.

Parole board, nervousness prior to hearing by. Leaps; parolitis; shortitis.

Parole board, receive notice of decision of. Get the ducat; get the slip; get the ticket.

Parole board, unfavorably regarded by. Hooks are in; needles are in; zingers are in. "I got no way to make that board. They get tabs (letters) that louse you up (recommend your further imprisonment) and the zingers are in against you."

Partner. Broad one hustles with; ghee one hustles with; partner on the rap; sidekick; yuk.

Partnership, accept. Count me in; declare oneself in; fill.

Partnership, extend. Cut in; declare in; ring in.

Partnership, request or demand. Count me in; declare oneself in; cut oneself in.

Pass anything to a confederate. Duke; weed. "Weed me the soft (currency) and stick the mark's (victim's) poke (wallet) back in his pratt-kick (back pocket)."

Passerby. Gapper.

Pass test of legitimacy, as credentials, etc. Stand up. "That tin (badge) will stand up on a shake (extortion) anywhere."

Pass test of police interrogation. See **Third degree, refuse to talk under.**

Patronage, give an establishment one's. Give a joint a play; hit; play.

Patronage of an establishment, discontinue. Wrap a joint up.

Pawn, in. In hock, in soak.

Pawnbroker. Uncle.

Pay, v. Come through; get it on the line; give up; go; kick in; pay off; see; slap down.

Payment, refuse to make. See in the alley; meet under the arch; give one the arm; bet on the muscle; put on the cuff; free load; get oneself locked up; give a run; give one a cuff; hang up; kick over; kick up; pay off in the alley; pay off under the arch; put the sleeve on; stiff; welch.

Pearls. Teardrops; tears.

Peddler, novelty. Pitchman.

Pederast, active. Daddy; joker; keister-bandit; papa; prussian; short-arm bandit; short-arm heister; turk; uncle; wheelman; wolf.

Pederast (active), formerly passive. Reformed punk; wolf out to get even.

Pederast, passive. Apple pie; aunt; bender; bindle boy; boy; brat; Mr. Brown; business; candy; charity stuff; chicken; coozey; drag; double-barreled ghee; flap; floosie; fruit; fruit for the monkeys; fruit under the old system; gal-boy; gash; gazooney; ginch; girl; gonzel; gunzel; hat; hide; hump; hump for the monkeys; hump under the old system; hunk of hat; hunk of quiff; hunk of skin; hunk of snatch; kid; kife; lay; morph; morphodite; nephew; nola; one of the Brown family; piece of pratt; piece of snatch; pink pants; poger; pogie; pratt-boy; punk; quiff; receiver; ringtail; round-eye; round-heels; skin; slavey; snatch-peddler; stern-wheeler; tail; taker; one who has been tampered with; trade; twidget; two-bit hustler; two-way ghee; whiskers; Willie; works.

Pederast (passive), brothel featuring. Camp; fag-joint; peg-house. (See also **Rendezvous of perverts.**)

Pederast (passive), in female attire. Drag.

Pederast (passive), perverted by force, etc. Made fag; made gunzel; made punk.

Pederasty (active), an act of. See **Fornication, an act of active.**

Pederasty (active), commit an act of. Brown; corn-hole; go to town; peg; plow; pratt; pull a trick; ride the deck; turn a trick. (See also **Fornicate.**)

Pederasty (passive), discovered in act of. Jeans at half mast.

Pederasty (passive), engage in. Bend over; take it in the biscuit; take it in the brown; take it in the can; take it in the canetta; go; take it in the keister; take it in the pratt; put out; to be put; receive; take it in the round-eye; take.

Pederasty (passive) force into act of. Give one the blanket; give one the business; give one the works; put a chiv to and hump; put the arm on and stab.

Pendant, jeweled. Dangler.

Penis. Dick; dummy; gun; joint; pup; tool.

Penitentiary, city or county. Bandhouse; Bridewell; the pen.

Penitentiary, state or federal. See **Prison.**

Penniless. On one's biscuit; on the bum; on one's can; on one's canetta; carrying the banner; carrying the stick; caught flat-footed; clean; taken to the cleaners; taken to the driers; dry; in hock; in the barrel; on one's keister; on the nut; panic is on; on one's pratt; on one's quiff; scrubbed; having the shorts; skunked; stiffed; tapped out.

Penny. See **Cent.**

Peril, expose one to. Set one up. "Look, crumb, if I thought you set me up giving me a wrong steer (misinformation) on that score (robbery) I'd carve my initials in your kisser." (See also **Abandon criminal associates.**)

Persecute. See **Frame-up; Nag.**

Persecution. See **Abuse; Frame-up.**

Person. Bird; bum; dude; geezer; ghee; head; joker; mick; mickey; stiff.

Person, alert and crime-conscious. Fly-horse; gapper; hep-ghee; hip-ghee; live-wire.

Person, boorish. Tough man. "You're a tough man with that big bazoo (mouth). You're lousing yourself up (ruining your reputation) here."

Person, contemptible. All muzzler; creep; crum; crumb; dog; eel; false alarm; flea; fleabag; fleeper; gummio; heel; h.o. ghee; iceman; jig-lover; mutt; muzzler; one who is pea soup; phony; poison; punk; pup; scratch-house bum; shit-heel; shit-heeler; snake; stiff; stiffo; weasel. (See also **Cheat; Informer; Pederast, passive; Pimp; Rapist; Sodomist, oral; Stolen goods, cheat in fixing share of.**)

Person, criminally insane or mentally defective. See **Insane person, mentally defective or criminally.**

Person, disloyal. See **Cheat; Informer; Stolen goods, cheat in fixing share of.**

Person, easily deceived or robbed. Duck soup; one who is easy; easy giver-up; hoosier; imbeciles; john; live one; load; lush; mark; red one; one who is round-heeled; ghee with round heels; sailor; sure thing; sucker; sucker for a left; one who is sweet; sweetheart; dude who is wide open; yap; yuld. (See also **Person, slow-witted** or inept; **Sure thing.**)

Person, friendly to underworld. See **Underworld, person cooperative with.**

Person, generous. Mark; sweetheart; touch. "My rapper (complaining witness) was a real touch. I gave him a short-con (sob story), and he pulled off (refused to press the charge)."

Person, handsome or trim. Sharp stuff.

Person, important. Apple; big shot.

Person, influential. See **Go-between.**

Person, inquisitive. Dude on the earie; flyhorse; gapper; ghee on the gun; geezer on the i.c.; joker on the lake; bird on the mooch.

Person, interesting. Character.

Person, large-nosed. Hook; hooko; nozzo; schnozzo.

Person, lazy. Blanket-presser. (See also **Beggar; Loafer.**)

Person, likeable. Ace; dude, swell; geezer, right; good head; one-way ghee; stiff, o.k. (See also **Criminal code, person loyal to the.**)

Person, loyal. See **Criminal code, person loyal to the.**

Person, penurious. Iceman; single-o; tough giver-up.

Person, poor sport in give-and-take. One who lays it but can't handle it.

Person, scapegoat for big shots. Fall guy; lob; pack horse.

Person, selfish. See **Person, penurious.**

Person, sexually abnormal. See **Masturbator; Nymphomaniac; Pederast, active; Pederast, passive; Sodomist, oral.**

Person, shrewd or capable. Ringer; shark; sharp; sharp stuff; smart money; whip.

Person, slow-witted or inept. Apsay; as'ole; blank; blown-in-the-glass-stiff;

butcher; chump; cluck; clunk; deadhead; dope; fall guy; free hole; gazabo;
geepo; geezo; glom; goniff; jag; jaggy;
jerk; lemon; lob; lobby; lug; master
mind; meatball; poison; popcorn; rum-
dumb; saperoo; scrub; one with a six
hat and fifty shirt; slob; stiff; stiffo;
stumble-bum; t.b.; whip; yap; yuld; zib.
(See also **Person, easily deceived or
robbed.**)

Person, suspicious-looking. Bird; geepo; strange weed. "Who's the geepo
burning us up (watching us inquisiti-
tively)?"

Person, talkative. Beefer; gabo;
spieler; waxer. (See also **Liar.**)

Person, unlucky. Ghee with the
bitch's curse; hoodo; jinx; ghee with
the horns on.

Person, wonderful or **remarkable.**
Dilley; dobey; duzey; honey; pisscut-
ter; pisser; pisseroo; sweetheart; whip.

Persons, teeming with undesirable.
Crumbed up with; crumby with; lousy
with; stiff with; swagged up with.

Persuade. Con; duke in; hook; promote; rope in; short-con; swindle;
tout. "You ain't touting me into copping
a plea (admitting) that I'm making a
play for your broad (girl), Buster. Bum
rap (unjust charge)."

Persuade, fail to. Piss in a snowbank.

Pest. Ball-breaker; kibitzer; tough
man.

Pester. Break one's balls; break one's
hump; fart around; knock up; mess
with.

Petty. See **Worthless, relatively** or
wholly.

Photograph, n. Kisser; mugg; mugg
on the board.

Photograph, v. Mugg.

Photograph gallery. Mugg-joint.

Physician. See **Doctor.**

**Picking pockets, empty and discard
wallet in.** Skin a skin; weed a poke.
"Skin the skin and ditch (get rid of)
it."

Pickpocket. Booster; cannon; carnygrifter; chain-man; claw; dig; digger;
dip; grifter; gun; gunsmith; hijacker;
hook; hooker; jostler; lift; moll-whiz;
pratt-digger; prattman; short hustler;
shot; supertwister; third-rail; tool;
whiz; wire; wire-man.

Pickpocket, aide to. Cover; cover-
man; shade; stall.

Pickpocket, aid in escape of. Split
out; stall a beef. "When I make (rob)
the yuld (sucker), everybody split out
and, Jake, you stall the beef even if
you have to drop (knock down) the
sucker."

Pickpocket, alert to tricks of the.
Pratt-wise. "This sucker ain't there (his
wallet is not in the pocket indicated).
A pratt-wise guy, eh?"

Pickpocket, immune area to work as.
See **Criminal activity, area of bribed
immunity in.**

Pickpocket, immunity to work as.
See **Criminal activity, bribed immunity
in.**

Pickpocket, jostle victim as aide to.
Give one a raust; hijack; load; put a
mark on; put one's back up; put off;
put up; raus; raust; set one up; shade;
shill; split out; stall; stick; stick a
mark; stick up; throw one a hump;
weave a mark.

**Pickpocket, jostling victim as aide
of.** Hijack; raus; raust.

Pickpocket, pass loot to aide as. Duke
the poke; weed the poke; unload; weed.
"Weed the poke as soon as you make
(steal) it and lam."

Pickpocket, plan itinerary as. Route
the grift.

Pickpocket, shield operations of a.
Cover; cover the duke; do the Mary
Ellen. "Step close and cover the duke
while I kiss the dog (face the victim
while robbing him)."

Pickpocket gang. Cannon-mob; grift-
mob; gun-mob; jug-mob; whiz-mob.

Pickpocket profession. Cannon; dip;

grift; gun; lift; the Mary Ann; the Mary Ellen; whiz.

Pickpocket profession, fagin in the. Gunmaker.

Pickpocket profession, revive skill in, after prison term. Get a grindstone and sharpen it.

Pickpocket profession, signals used in. Chirp; lunger. (See also **Danger, warning expressions of.**)

Pick pockets. Beat; boost; dig; dive; drop the duke; kiss the dog; lift; make; make a mark; make a poke; put the duke down; reef; riffle; whiz.

Pick pockets in crowd. Work the get-ons; out on the shorts; work the put-offs; work a short; work a spill; work a tip; work the breaks.

Pickpocket squad of police. See **Police pickpocket squad.**

Pickpocket's tools. Nippers.

Pimp, n. Cadet; coffee-and pimp; dance hall pimp; Mac; mackerel; p.i.; pineapple; sporting-girl's manager; steerer; tout.

Pimp, v. Run a stable of hustlers; have a sister-in-law; steer; have a string of hustlers; tout.

Pin-ball machine. One-arm bandit.

Pinned securely, as a pocket, paper money, etc. Nailed.

Pinochle, meld of one hundred fifty in. Yard and a half.

Pistol. Artillery; barker; biscuit; blow; business; canister; canojerod; convincer; difference; equalizer; flash; gat; hardware; heat; heater; jerry; lug; mahoska; oscar; patsy; pea-shooter; persuader; pickle; piece; potato; prod; rod; roscoe; slim; smoke-pole; smoke-wagon; snub-noser; spud; stick; tool; toy; works.

Pistol, armed with a. See **Armed.**

Pistol, carry a. Carry iron; heel up; lug; lug a rod; pack a heater; pack a rod; pack heat.

Pistol, carry as bodyguard or tool of big shot. Lug iron for; pack a rod

for. "I ain't packing no rod for the biggie (big shot) for a lousy six-bits (seventy-five dollars) a week and maybe have to hit people in the lemon (kill people)."

Pistol, criminal charge of having a. Gun rap.

Pistol, equipped with silencer. Dumbgat; gagged-gat; hush-hush; sissy-rod.

Pistol, imitation. Wooden biscuit.

Pistol, point a. Lay a barker on; lay a rod on; put it on one; put the heat on; stick the heater on.

Pistol, reach for a. Reach.

Pistol, remove, from one's person and conceal. Ditch a rod; stash a biscuit; unload.

Pistol-holster. Smoke-poke.

Pistol-pocket. Smoke-poke.

Pitcher. Growler.

Pittsburgh. Smoky City.

Plainclothesman. See **Detective; Policeman.**

Plan, n. See **Criminal activity, plan for.**

Plan, v. Line up; ready up. "Ready up that score (robbery) for next week. The nut (expense) is getting heavy." (See also **Criminal activity, inspect site for.**)

Playing cards. Broads.

Playing cards, arrangement of a pair in stud poker. Wired. "I had aces wired when the bulls (police) busted in and took the joint apart (wrecked the establishment)."

Playing cards, cheat at. Broadsman; mechanic; tub-worker; whip.

Playing cards, cheat in dealing of. Bottom deal; cold-deck; crimp; second-deal.

Playing cards, devices used in fraud with. Case; daub; gaper; glasswork; hog box; holdout box; shoe.

Playing cards, fraudulent dealing of. Crimp; gaffed deal; Greek bottom; haymaker's shuffle; mechanic's grip; second deal. (See also **Swindle (shell**

game), with playing cards.)

Playing cards, fraudulently marked. B-backs; broads with ears; coolers; edgework; fish-backs; greasy aces; hot paper; humps; lacework; paper; pin-work; readers; slick-backs; strippers; ups-and-downs; wedges.

Playing cards, fraudulently stacked. Cold deck.

Playing cards, interpret fraudulent marks upon. Read.

Playing cards, the card dealt which spoils hand of. Blow-card.

Plead abjectly. See Cowardice, ex-hibit.

Plead guilty to gain leniency. Cop a plea; cop out.

Plead guilty to gain leniency, offer to. Bargain; do business; make a deal; talk business. "I gotta do business with the D.A. This rap (criminal charge) can't be beat."

Plea of guilty to gain leniency. Plea.

Plot, n. Caper; score; swindle; trick. "Nigger Dan is cooking up some kind of caper and I'd sure like to find out what the score is."

Plot, v. Angle; phenagle; promote. "I gotta phenagle an out from this swindle (trouble) I'm in with Big Frenchy's combo (gang)."

Pocket, n. Kick; poke.

Pocket, inside breast. Upstairs.

Pocket, inside coat. Insider; pit.

Pocket, inside vest. Double-insider.

Pocket, left rear trousers. Left pratt; port pratt; pratt-kick.

Pocket, left side. Port.

Pocket, left side trousers. Port britch.

Pocket, rear trousers. Pratt-kick.

Pocket, right rear trousers. Right pratt.

Pocket, side coat. Sidekick.

Pocket, side trousers. Britch; britch-kick.

Pocket, theft from rear trousers. Pratt-score.

Pocket, theft from side trousers. Britch-score.

Pocket, trousers watch. Fib; mouse-kick.

Pocket, theft from trousers watch-. Fib-score; fib-touch.

Pocket, vest. Pit.

Pocket, theft from vest. Pit-score; pit-touch.

Pockets, empty, in view of fellow thieves. Dig deep; come through; get it on the line; get it up; turn out.

Point out as victim of theft, murder, or betrayal. Finger; mark; put on the spot; put the cross on; put the finger on.

Police, United States government. Big department; Fed; gazers; G-man; monkey; prohy; whiskers.

Policeman. April fool copper; big eyes; bull; clown; C.O. dick; cop; cop-per; crapper dick; dick; Dolly sisters; door-shaker; elbows; elephant ears; finger; flatfoot; flatty; fuzz; fuzzy; Gallagher and Sheehan; geepo; Ger-man; ghee from downtown; gold badge man; gumfoot; harness-cop; John Law; keystone cop; knock-man; law; lizzie-lousy; mama bull; Mike and Ike; mo-ther bull; peeler; plant; Richard; right copper; reach; roller; shamus; shine; skipper; slapman; slewfoot; sneezer; square bull; town clown; yentzer.

Policeman, alert. All copper; fuzey; hep-ghee; hip-ghee; live wire; savage.

Policeman, assaulter of. See Cop-fighter.

Policeman, badge of. Button; flash; tin; white tin; yellow tin.

Policeman, dishonest. See Bribe-taker.

Policeman, exhibit badge of a. See Exhibit officer's badge.

Policeman, trail homegoing town. Put the clown to bed.

Policeman, uniform of a. Harness.

Police attention. Blow; dragnet; flop; G-heat; heat. "That snatch (kidnap-ping) drew a lot of G-heat and the

F.B.I. has got the town knocked up (shut up tight)."

Police attention, attract undesirable. Bring heat; draw heat; raise heat.

Police attention, intensify. Put the heat on; rumble; turn on the heat.

Police attention, no longer intensified. Cold; cool; heat's off.

Police attention, to moderate. Cool off.

Police attention, receiving intensified. Hooks are out; hot; hot as a forty-five; hot as a pistol; red hot; sizzling.

Police examination, methods of. Deal; dust-off; gaff; hose; kick; once-over; pump; rubdown; work-out. "The bulls (police) picked me up on a forty-eight (forty-eight hours' investigation) again and handed me a dust-off." (See also **Assault.**)

Police examination (methods of), subject to. Dust off; hose; knock up with forty-eights; sweat; take over the hurdles; third-degree; turn on the heat; turn the hose on; work out. (See also **Question.**)

Police examination (methods of), subjected to. Go through the mill. (See also **Police examination [methods of], subject to.**)

Police malpractice. To ride one around the horn; clean up the calendar; hit with a swag of forty-eights; give one a phony line-up. (See also **Frame-up.**)

Police patrol van. Black Maria; clatter; paddy-wagon; the wagon.

Police pickpocket squad. Cannon-squad; elbows; whiz-bulls.

Police raid. Knock-off; slough-up; tip-over.

Police raid, execute a. Knock off; knock over; pull a joint; slough; slough up; tip over.

Police raid, put out of business by a. Slough a joint. (See also **Close an establishment.**)

Police riot squad. Strong-arm squad.

Police squad-cars. Prowl-car; squad car; whistler.

Police station house. Bing; booby; booby-hatch; brig; can; clink; cooler; coop; damper; downtown; hatch; hook; hoosegow; jug; pisscan; roller; sneezer.

Police station house, examination room of. Blue room; Coney Island; griddle; pump.

Police trap. Set-up.

Police trap, lure into. Put the chuck on; set up.

Police trap, step unwarily into. Walk into a collar.

Policy numbers lottery. Numbers; policy game.

Policy numbers lottery, boss of. Bank; banker; number baron; number man; pay-off ghee.

Policy numbers lottery, make a bet in. Play the numbers.

Policy numbers lottery, make a winning in. Hit; hit the numbers.

Policy numbers lottery, subordinates in. Comptroller; runner.

Policy numbers lottery, winning bet in. A hit.

Politician. Heeler; polly; right-polly; springer; stowaway.

Poolroom. Pill-joint.

Poor house. Pogey.

Pornography. Hot stuff.

Possessing as assets. Holding. "We ain't got enough to meet the nut (expenses). What are you holding?"

Postage stamp. Sticker.

Postage stamp, stolen or counterfeited. Hot sticker.

Pot, coffee or tea. Growler.

Prearrange. Bag; fix; gaff; gimmick; gimmick up; put the fix in; put the gaff in; put the hooks in; put the zingers in; sack; spike; square. "We gotta put the zingers in before I go to bat (trial), or I hit the can (be convicted and go to prison)."

Precisely. See **Exactly.**

Predicament. Jackie; jack-pot; swindle; squeeze.

Predicament, find oneself in a. Get swindled into a bitch of a jackpot; throw boxcars; throw snake-eyes; wind up with your joint in your hand.

Predicament, in a. In the barrel; buried; have a case; look like curtains; on the griddle; holding the bag; holding the sack; in the center; in the middle; in the sack; in the satchel; be a dead pigeon; up salt creek; on the spot; swamped; under the gun.

Predicament, put in a. Duke in; jackie up; jam up; louse up; put in the middle; put on the spot; queer; rank; rope in; screw up; swindle up. "Just when I'm going to make a nice score (theft), you had to come along and rumble (speak to me). You ranked me right."

Predict. Call the turn.

Pretender. Actor.

Price. Freight; knock-off; nut.

Prison, n. Bastille, big house; brig; can; canister; college; greystone college; hook; hospital; jug; lag; limbo; mill; nick; prod; slough; soak; State's; stir; sugar house. (See also **Jail, county; Police station house; Reformatory.**)

Prison, administrative offices of. Front.

Prison, approved by habitues. Right joint.

Prison, bars in a. Slats.

Prison, bath taken in a. Carbolic dip; whore's bath.

Prison, be discharged from. Check out; cut out; go; go home; hit the bricks; hit the pavement; hit the sidewalk; hit the street; kick out; leave one the bucket; spring.

Prison, cell-door barrier in. Brake.

Prison, cell in. Cave; coffin; den; drum; hatch; hole; hut; kip; pad; shebang.

Prison, get one out of cell for recreation, etc. Bail one out; get one out of hock; spring. "Hey, Buddy, the screw (guard) forgot to pull the brake on this tier. Get me out of hock so I can hit the yard."

Prison, go to one's cell in. Hit the kip; lock in.

Prison, occupy cell in. Cell; lock. "Where do you lock, Joe?"

Prison, return to cell in. n. Lock-in; lock-up; slough-in. "What time is afternoon slough-in in this can (prison)?"

Prison, return to cell in. v. Lock in; hit the kip; slough in. "Big Ben (escape siren) is going to blow. There's a beat (escape) so we gotta lock in."

Prison, cell-block in. Big top; C.C.'s; idle; menagerie; reception.

Prison, cell tiers of. C.C.'s; flats; range. "Flip your chiv (knife) out on the flats. They're frisking (searching)."

Prison, chaplain of. Buck; gospel ghee; holy Joe; long-haired boy; right buck; sin hound; sky pilot.

Prison, commit to. See **Sentence, impose a prison.**

Prison, contraband cooking stove in. Boiler; hot boiler; hot one; hot stove.

Prison, contraband home brew in. Batch; gumdrop cocktail; penitentiary highball; potato water; pruno. "Yeah, Butso, a little shellac poured through the center of a loaf of bread and you got enough gumdrop cocktails to gage up (get intoxicated)."

Prison, contraband or stolen stores in. See **Stolen goods.**

Prison, contraband metal detector in. Snitcher. "Wrap that chiv (knife) in this rubber cloth and you'll beat the snitcher at the door."

Prison, contraband money in. See **Money.**

Prison, contraband newspaper in. Hot one; hot paper; hot stiff; stiff. "Duck (hide) that hot stiff. This screw (guard) is a muzzler (mean fellow)."

Prison, contraband postage stamps in. Hot stickers; sticker. "I got a kite (uncensored letter) to fly (send out). Got a sticker?"

Prison, contraband or **stolen stores, induce one to carry in.** Hit with a swag. "You got some moxie (nerve) hitting me with a swag when you know I'm up for parole and can't stand a drop (report)."

Prison, contraband or **stolen stores, refuse to traffic in.** Work for the state. "That crumb works in the kitchen and you can't score him for nothing. Ah, the flea is working for the state!"

Prison, contraband or **stolen stores, traffic in.** Peddle; push hot boilers; push hot ones; push swag; score; take.

Prison, contraband or **stolen stores, trafficker in.** Angel; connection; connection ghee; connection man; peddler; scoring ghee; stir-hustler; swagger; swagman; wire; wire-ghee; wire-man. "I gotta get me a new commissary connection. I ain't scoring for (getting free) nothing."

Prison (contraband in), discard during search. Hit the flats with: unload; whip. "Hit the flats with that hot boiler (contraband cooking stove) if they fan (search). It's a cooler (bread-and-water cell) beef (charge)."

Prison (contraband in), having on one's person. Heeled; loaded; padded. "I'm loaded with swag (stolen stores). I hope there's no frisk (search)."

Prison, cook of a. Belly robber; gut robber.

Prison, crazy or **mentally defective from long confinement in.** See **Insane, mentally defective** or **criminally.**

Prison, deliver articles from cell to cell in. Make a pass; pass; whip over.

Prison, delivery devices from cell to cell of. Pass-can; pass ghee; pass-line; trolley. "Throw that pass-line down when the hack (guard) makes his rounds, and I'll pass you some hot stuff (pornography)."

Prison, deputy warden of. See **Prison, principal keeper of.**

Prison, die in. Get a back-gate commute; cheat them. (See also **Die by suicide.**)

Prison, disciplinary cells or **wings of.** Back; back room; beach; bing; blue room; box; brig; calaboose; clink; clinkeroo; cooler; coop; dark cell; hatch; hole; hoosegow; icebox; ironhouse; izo; isolation; keister; kitty; limbo; plant; slough; sneezer; sol; solly.

Prison (disciplinary cells or **wings of), released from.** Back in circulation; back in the population.

Prison, disciplinary court of. Porch; Warden's court.

Prison, disciplinary diet in. See **Bread and water.**

Prison, disciplinary officer of. Ghee with the brass nuts; man with the brass nuts.

Prison, disciplinary report amply sustained in. See **Arrest, redhanded; Criminal charge, serious and supported by ample evidence.**

Prison, disciplinary report of minor character in. Booby; mopery; mopery in the first degree; square-John pinch; stiff; stiffo; wrap-up rap. "The screw (guard) just chalked me in (reported me) for talking in line—a wrap-up rap."

Prison, disciplinary report or **action in.** Bag; banner; chalk-in; deadlock; keep-locked; knock-off; look-in; shingle; shot; sign; snare; snatch; stinger; ticket; turn-in; write-up. (See also **Arrest; Complaint.**)

Prison, disciplinary report unmerited. Mopery collar; mopery pinch; mopery rap. (See also **Arrest, on trumped-up charge; Criminal charge, unjust.**)

Prison, disciplinary report, withdraw or **effect withdrawal of.** Pull a beef; pull a pinch; pull a rap; pull off; square a beef; square a collar; square a pinch; square a rap; squash. (See also **Bribe.**)

Prison, disciplinary tag on cell-door in. Banner; keep-locked; keep-locked banner; keep-locked shingle; shingle; sign.

Prison, discipline by confinement in segregation wing of. Bury; plant; put in the hole; salt; slap in the box; throw the key away.

Prison, discipline by time loss penalty in. Smack in the kisser with; slap in the kisser with. "Blackie got slapped in the kisser with sixty days and thirty more in the bing (punishment cell) for that kite (smuggled letter)."

Prison, disciplined by confinement in segregation wing of. Hit the box; do penance; hit isolation; hit izo; hit the beach; hit the icebox; hit the plant.

Prison, discipline for rule violation in. Bury; chalk in; deadlock; double-lock; get one right; hang a rap on; hang a shingle on; hit with a tin; jam up; keep locked; lock in; lock up; pencil; put in a beef; put in a pinch; put in a rap; put the pencil on; shoot with square chalk; give one a sign; slough up; sting; take one's number; turn in; write up. "Some hack (guard) put in a beef on me, and I don't even know what the rap (charge) is." (See also **Arrest.**)

Prison, disciplines of harsh character in. Barrel; boat; spot; standup; sweatbox; walking the line.

Prison, discipline rule-violation severely in. Have plenty of numbers; throw the book away.

Prison, doctor in. See **Doctor.**

Prison, dormitory in. Bull pen; dommo.

Prison, escape. Beat; crush; blow; break; bush-parole; cornfield clemo; a Dillinger; getaway; hideout; hole; lam; mope. (See also **Escape.**)

Prison, escape or attempt to escape from. Beat; beat a joint; beat a stir; beat the pups; blow stir; breeze; chop a bar; cop a breeze; cop a figary; cop a heel; cop a mope; cop a sneak; crack out; crush out; dig a hole; dust out; go; go over the hill; hide out; hit the hump; hit the wall; lam; make a break; make a beat; make a joint; make a stir; go over the hill; push a can; spread the eagle; take clemo; take it on the lam. (See also **Escape.**)

Prison, escape implements. Barspreader; blade; briars; chopper; John Sperl.

Prison, escape-proof bars of. Spinners.

Prison, escape siren of. Big Ben; beat whistle; lam whistle.

Prison, escape siren of, sound. Blow the whistle; toot the tooter.

Prison, planning an escape from. To have go-go in one's eyes; looking for an out; have rabbit blood.

Prison, expression acknowledging thanks in. Thank the judge that sent you here.

Prison, expression of cynicism in. Better him than me. "I hear Flippy Leo got hit in the head (killed) on a heist (hold-up). Well, better him than me."

Prison, expressions of greeting or leave-taking in. Hold it up; Hold your head; How's you and me?; Howzit?; Take it easy.

Prison, expressions of humor and ridicule in. Bag your head; Blow your nose; Come out swinging; Find a home; Get under the bed; Hang up; Oh, sing it; Spit; Strike a home; Take a rope.

Prison, factory in. Jute-mill; shop.

Prison, farm of. Farm; outside. "I'm getting short (nearly eligible for release), and I'd like to get a job outside but I can't get this hooker (pending warrant) off."

Prison, find contentment in. Find a home; strike a home. "Yeah, bum, you sure found a home. You do a soft bit (easy term)."

Prison, food served in. Chuck; gooby; gullion; skilly; slum; slumgullion.

Prison, forfeits in games in. Arm-cramper; cramper; ears; leg-cramper; macaluccis; noses.

Prison, graveyard of. Bone-orchard; thirty-three gallery. "If you keep lousing me around (bothering me), you're going to finish this bit (sentence) on thirty-three gallery."

Prison, group detention cell in. Bull pen; tank.

Prison, guard force of trouble-shooters in. Strong-arm squad.

Prison, guard in. Boss; bull; bum; creep; crimp; fink; hack; law; man; mulligan; muzzler; roach; screw; shamus; soaker; spindle; turnkey; turret-man. (See also **Chain-gang, guard over.**)

Prison, guard's cane or club in. Bat.

Prison, guard newly employed in. New fish; new ghee; new hack; new screw.

Prison, guard popular among inmates of. Con's man; right screw.

Prison, guard unpopular among inmates of. All copper; all screw; ball-breaker; dog; hundred per cent screw; muzzler; screw's man.

Prison, guard-turret on wall of. Tower.

Prison, guard's assignment as punishment in. Hit a tower. "Our shop hack (guard) ain't gonna like to hit the wall, but he got in a jackpot (trouble) with the warden and he's gotta hit a tower."

Prison, hard labor in. Jook.

Prison, harsh. Tough can; jook-joint; lousy joint to pull a bit; fleabit stir.

Prison, honestly administered. Tough can to do business.

Prison, hospital in. Bone-factory; pogey.

Prison, ill-administered, etc. type of. Creep-joint; crumb-joint; crummy; dump; flea-bag; louse-trap.

Prison, in hot climate. Frying pan.

Prison, in. Away; in the big house; buried; doing a bit; doing penance; doing time; on ice; in; inside; in the can; doing a jolt; in the jug; laying in state; pulling time; salted; in stir; in slough; making spaces; doing a stretch; stored away; stowed away; up the river; washed up.

Prison, inmate of. Canary; con; lag; mick; mickey; vic.

Prison, docile and peace-loving inmate of. Lover. "I ain't no tough guy in stir (prison), wise guy, I'm strictly a lover."

Prison, inmate amateur lawyer in. Hapas capas; writ bug.

Prison, inmate benefactor of associates in. Angel; connection; front; momma. "Momma Murphy is sure taking care of me since he hit the mess hall. When he hits the bricks (goes home), I'll starve."

Prison, inmate check-up in. The count.

Prison, inmate column with portable toilets in. Bucket brigade.

Prison, inmate-conducted court in. Kangaroo court.

Prison, inmate's consecutive number in. Big number; low number; old number; number. "Oh, an old number, eh? That don't give you no license to screw me around (abuse me)."

Prison, inmate 1st, 2nd, 3rd, etc., offender in. Habitual; first-time loser; second-time loser; two-time loser; three-time loser; repeater.

Prison, inmate haircut in. Band-house clip; chop; double-o; stir-chop.

Prison, inmate hater of guards in. Screw-baiter; screw-fighter; screw-hater.

Prison, inmate insubordination in. Silent insolence.

Prison, inmates' masturbation in. Night-clubbing. "You better knock off (stop) that night-clubbing, jerk, or you'll wind up in the funny factory (insane asylum)." (See also **Masturbate**.)

Prison, indulge in inmates' masturbation in. Cabaret; go cabareting; kick the gong around; night club. (See also **Masturbate**.)

Prison, inmate naive in ways of life in. Depression bum; legit stiff; necktie bum; square-John. (See also **Underworld newcomer**.)

Prison, inmate nervous indigestion in. Stir belly.

Prison, inmate newly arrived in. Fish; fresh fish; ghee fresh off the street; new fish; new jice; new mick; new mickey; relief.

Prison, inmate packages from home in. Boodle; bundle; home relief; score; swag; touch.

Prison, inmate privileges in. Count out; license; ring job; scoring job. "Now that my partner got a bit (prison term) I get no more home relief (food packages). I gotta get a scoring job in the kitchen."

Prison, inmate sycophant of clergy in. Jesus stiff; psalm-singing muzzler.

Prison, inmate newly arrived in tradition regarding. One's fish; kangaroo court; one's relief. "My number is 12104 and that new dude's is 13104. Hey, that makes him my relief! I gotta send him a pack of butts."

Prison, inmate trusty in. Big ghee; biggie; big number; big shot; con turnkey; dep; Dep's man; number; outside man; P.K.'s man; ring ghee; state man; trusty; stockholder; Warden's man. "This bum scores for (gets) all ring (big shot) jobs around here. These stockholders sure bug me up (get me mad)."

Prison, inmate uniform in. Tent.

Prison, inmate with long term in. Lifer; long-timer; low number dude; one who has an old number; old-timer.

Prison, inmate with short term in. Short-timer; workhouse bum; workhouse stiff.

Prison, inmate working assignment in. Ring job; scoring job; spot; wire job; work the flats. "I gotta get me a spot, not too tough a job. Then this workhouse bit (short term) will be a pushover."

Prison, insecure. Cracker box.

Prison, issued items to inmates of. State; state-o; state stuff. "Sit on that state. I wouldn't smoke that crap if I had to knock off (stop smoking)."

Prison, legendary rumor source in. Two-one. "That phony story must have come from two cell, one gallery—which is the doniker (toilet) if you're a new mick (newcomer)."

Prison, letter or note in. Cannonball; kite; tab; tag.

Prison, letter smuggled from. Cannonball; crooked kite; hot one; kite; stiff.

Prison, intercept letter smuggled from. Glom a cannonball; knock off a kite.

Prison, smuggle letter from. Fly; fly a kite; push a kite; tab a kite.

Prison, write a letter or note in. Scratch a tab; tab a kite.

Prison, letter-boxes of officials of. Box; Dep's box; P.K.'s box; Warden's box.

Prison, liberally administered. Playhouse.

Prison, lock inmates in cells of. Slough; slough in; slough up.

Prison, lock-up of inmates in emergency. Slough-up.

Prison, lock oneself in protective custody in. Get oneself a banner; get oneself a shingle; get oneself locked up; get oneself sloughed up; hit isolation; hit izo; lock oneself up.

Prison, mess hall fare in. Main line. "What's on the main line today? More lousy gullion (tasteless food)?"

Prison, money earnings of inmates in. Blood-dough.

Prison, name one's own assignment in. Write one's own ticket. "This P.K. (principal keeper) goes for young punks. They write their own ticket with him."

Prison, officers of the guard in. Braid; brass; brass hat; ghee with the brass nuts; man with the brass nuts.

Prison, out of. See **Freed from imprisonment.**

Prison, overcome the restraints of life in a. Knock up a stir; become stirwise. "You do handy, Knuckles. You got this stir knocked up."

Prison, playing card substitutes in. Rocks.

Prison, principal keeper of. Dep.; P.K.

Prison, psychiatric or psychological tests in. Blocks; bug test.

Prison, be subjected to psychiatric or psychological tests in. Get hit with the blocks; play with the blocks.

Prison, psychopathic observation cells in. Dark cell; observation; obso; screen-cell. (See also **Prison, disciplinary cells or wings of.**)

Prison, subject to psychopathic observation in. Bag; drop the net on; put the glom on; put the grab on; put the snatch on; slough in the dark cell; snare. "The man in the white coat (psychiatrist) is gonna wind up sloughing you in the dark cell if you mooch (walk) around here with that jerky look on your kisser (face)."

Prison, record folio of inmate of. Jacket.

Prison, recreation center of. Reck; yard.

Prison, return with new sentence to. Go back for seconds.

Prison, rife with homosexuality. Peghouse.

Prison, riot or refusal to work in. Kick-over; kick-up. "Half the joint is gonna hit the bing (punishment cells) and blow (lose) a year for that kickover in the mess hall."

Prison, riot or refuse to work in. Break up; buck; fold; fold up; kick over; kick up; pack in; slam; wrap up.

Prison, abide by rules and regulations in. Play the legit; level it; hit the up-and-up.

Prison, abide by rules and regulations to extreme degree in. Work for the state.

Prison, short-term. Flop-joint.

Prison, short-circuit of radio line in. Anchor.

Prison, toilet facilities of. Bucket; tin throne. (See also **Toilet.**)

Prison, transfer inmates from one to another. Boat; draft; ride; ship.

Prison, transfer of inmates from one to another. Boat; draft; ride; shipment; show-boat; trip.

Prison, transfer to another, to seek. Break up a bit; check out; fold; make a boat; make a joint; make a stir; wrap a joint up. "I gotta break up this bit. Maybe if I drop a tab (letter) putting the bite on the warden I can make a boat to a connection can (prison where favors can be bought)."

Prison, United States Federal. G-joint.

Prison, venally administered. Connection can; connection joint.

Prison, visiting day in. Big day.

Prison, visitors to. Hoosiers; outsiders. "Them hoosiers gun us over (stare at us) like we were monkeys in the zoo."

Prison, warden of. Belly robber; big noise; big shot; big spud; gut robber; king; main ghee; man; skipper.

Prison, wind up in. Wind up with your joint in your hand.

Prison wise. Joint wise; stir wise. (See also **Sophisticated.**)

Prizefighter. Dukester; tanker.

Problem, difficult. Tough gaff.

Proceeds of crime. See **Criminal activity, proceeds of.**

Profession or **business, one's.** Dodge; grift; play; racket.

Profit, show a. Get off the nut; hit the jackpot; make a bite; make a score; make a touch; score; touch.

Profitable. Red; sweet. "That tip (crowd) was sure red today. We made a sweet bundle."

Profitable undertaking. See **Criminal activity, profitable venture in.**

Prohibition act, enforcement agent of. See **Police, United States Government.**

Proprietorship in. Cut; end; piece; piece of a joint; slice.

Proprietorship in, acquire by coercion. Make a grab; muscle in; push in; take over.

Prosperous. In the bucks; have one's bundle; in the chips; doing handy; flush; flushed; got a buck; have a buck; heavy; heavy heeled; heeled; holding heavy; in; in the red; in the stepping dough; be a live one; loaded; made; have a nice buck; have a nice dollar; have a nice thing; off the nut; have it socked away; have it stashed; strong.

Prostitute or **loose woman.** Bat; beast; bimmy; biscuit; bitch; blister; blouser; bum; call-girl; charity stuff; chippie; coffee-and hustler; coozey; creep; dog; douche-bag; flap; flossie; floosie; gash; ginch; hat; hide; hooker; hump; hunk of hat; hunk of quiff; hunk of skin; hunk of snatch; hustler; kife; kite; knock-around broad; lay; Mary Magdalene; mat; merchandise; muff; nautch-broad; peddler; piece of pratt; piece of snatch; pig; quiff; round-heels; sister-in-law; skin; snatch-peddler; twidget; two-bit hustler; works; zook.

Prostitutes, organized group of. Stable of hustlers.

Prostitution, commit an act of. Turn a trick.

Prostitution, practice. Hit the turf; hustle; on the hustle, step out; on the turf, get out; go out for a buck.

Prostitution, restricted area for. The line.

Protect interests of. Go down the line for; go to bat for; hold one's end up; take care of.

Protect with burglary alarm. Bug; put a bug on.

Protect with dog. Mutt up.

Prove oneself. Shape up; stack up. "Let Eddie the Earbender fill as zexman (lookout) on this trick (robbery) and see how he stacks up."

Proxy. Front.

Prunes. Nigger-heads.

Psychiatrist or **psychologist.** Bug doctor; ghee in the white coat; man in the white coat; ghee with the net.

Punishments. Consult the following terms in the Underworld-English section of the Dictionary: **angel cake and wine; balls; the barrel; the Beach; dark-cell; dry (n.); Oregon boot; rat-shackle; spot (5); walk the line; sweat-box; tracer-chain; turn the hose on; warden's court.**

Purse. See **Wallet.**

Purse, rid self of stolen. Ditch a leather.

Purse, snatch a. Bushwhack; buzz; glom a leather; make a poke; moll-buzz.

Purse-snatcher. Bushwhacker; buzzer; leather-glommer; moll-buzzer.

Purse-snatcher, engaged as or operating as a. On the moll-buzz; on the snatch.

Pursue. See **Follow.**

Pursuer, elude a. See **Follower, elude a.**

Pursuit. See **Following, act of.**

Put away. Bury; ditch; duck; plant; sock away; stash.

Pyromaniac. See **Arsonist.**

Q

Quality, anything of. Sharp stuff. (See also **Thing, wonderful or remarkable.**)

Question, v. Buzz; give a ghee a toss; griddle; pump; put the B on; snake out; spring with a crack. "The bulls (police) buzzed me all night and one of them sprung with a crack about that Jersey knock-off (murder)." (See also **Police examination, [methods of], subject to.**)

Quickly. See **Hurry, in a.**

Quiet, v. See **Shut up.**

Quit. See **Cease; Leave.**

R

Raconteur. Character.

Racehorse. Beetle. (See also **Horse race, fraudulent.**)

Racehorse, abuse of, used to handicap. Night ride.

Racehorse, inferior. Cooler; stumer.

Racehorse, narcotics administered to handicap a. Soup.

Racehorse, prearranged to win fraudulently. Dead cert.

Rage, v. Blow one's roof; blow one's top; bounce; to have a bug on; bug up; burn up; declare oneself; pop off; sizzle; sound off; sport a bug on; stem up. (See also **Anger a person.**)

Rage, overcome by. See **Angry.**

Railroad, brakeman on a. Fiddlesticks; shack.

Railroad station. Rat stand. (See also **Station, any transit system; Subway station.**)

Railroad train, baggage car of. Blind-baggage.

Railroad train, rob a. See **Hold up railroad trains; freight-cars, rob.**

Railroad train, robber of. See **Holdup man; Freight-cars, robber of.**

Railroad train, robbery of. See **Holdup, n.**

Raise a sum of money. Get it up; rustle. "I ain't got no fall dough (bail and legal fees, etc.) so you gotta step out (steal) and get it up."

Rape, n. Line-up; short-arm heist; short-heist; skin-heist.

Rape, v. Line up; short-arm heist; short heist. (See also **Pederasty [passive], force into act of.**)

Rape or seduce near relative of associate. Play the dozens. "If I snare (catch) that creep playing the dozens

with my sister, I'll stick a chiv (knife) in him."

Rapist, n. Arm-man; diddler; keister-bandit; short-arm bandit; short-arm heister; skin-heister.

Raw deal. Deal; gurdy; hurdy; kicking around; sell-out. (See also **Abuse; Accusation, unjust; Double-cross.**)

React. Kick back. "We muscled into Irish's alzo (protected area) so we gotta figure him to kick back. Heel up (arm yourself)."

Reaction. Come-back; kick-back.

Recidivism, n. Life on the installment plan.

Recidivist, n. Bitch-of-a-criminal; habitual; four-time loser; repeater; three-time loser; two-time loser. (See also **Criminal, habitual.**)

Recognize a person. Make a ghee; peg a ghee.

Recognize character of a person. Peg a ghee. "I pegged that ghee for a rat (informer) when I found out he was hanging around that lush-joint (drinking establishment) with a lot of bulls (policemen)."

Recognize character of a place. Make a joint; peg a joint. "The drop (hiding place) for the hot crates (stolen cars) was in a nice neighborhood, and the fuzz (police) couldn't make the joint."

Recognize character of. Peg.

Recognize, fail to. Not give one a flop; pass up; not give one a rumble; not give one a tumble.

Recommend. Duke in; give one a steer; steer; tout.

Recommendation. Duke-in; send-in; steer. "Get me a send-in to that polly (politician). Maybe he can spring (get out of prison) my partner."

Recover lost advantage. Pull out of the bag.

Red light district. The line.

Reformatory. Crime school; the El; kindergarten; nursery.

Reformatory term. Nursery stretch.

"That kid's no racket-ghee (thief). He went to the El (Elmira reformatory) on a bum rap (unjust charge) and he's been bouncing in and out of the can (prison) since."

Reformatory, United States Federal. G-joint.

Refusal. Turn-down.

Refuse, v. Turn down.

Release from custody. See **Discharge from custody.**

Reliable. There. "You're always there when I need a ghee (fellow) to front (appear and speak) for me, Brownie. You're aces (swell)."

Religious. Long-haired.

Religious pretender. See **Hypocrite, pious.**

Remark, v. Crack; spring with a crack.

Remark, pointed. Crack.

Remark, sarcastic or **disparaging.** Crack; crimpers; hooks; needles; zingers. "Did you hear that fleabag (low fellow) sticking the zingers in about me, laughing like he wasn't leveling (serious)."

Remove money from wallet or **purse.** Skin; skin a skin; weed; weed a poke. "Skin the skin, whip it (throw it away), and let's lam (flee)."

Rendezvous of perverts. Camp; fag-joint; fruit market; market.

Rendezvous of pickpockets. Gun-joint.

Rendezvous of thieves. Big store; dinghe; hideout; hole; jungle; meet; plant; scatter; shebang; spot; stash. "We got a meet (appointment) down at the stash. Let's bounce (hurry) down."

Rendezvous of vagabonds. Bug-house Square; jungle; the scratch park; skid row.

Rendezvous of vagabonds, retire to, between travels. Jungle up.

Renegade. Fence-jumper; hedge-hopper.

Rent, evade payment of. Heel a joint.

Repay. Kick back; pay off.

Repercussion. Come-back; kick-back.

Report to headquarters by telephone. Buzz; ring in.

Reprieve. Anchor.

Reputation, underworld. Rep.

Reputation (underworld), seeking a. Out for a rep.

Reputation (underworld), shrewdly building a. Pick one's spots. "You ain't kidding nobody, you scratchhouse bum, picking your spots. Them dudes (fellows) you're pushing around (abusing) ain't nobody."

Resist. Bang it out; kick back; kick over; stick and slug.

Resistance. Come-back; kick-back; kick-over; kick-up.

Restaurant. Coffee-and joint; mulligan joint; scorf-joint.

Restitution, make. Kick back. "The bench nibs (judge) cracked to my lip (lawyer) that he'd give me an s.s. (suspended sentence) if I kicked back part of the dough I snared (stole)."

Restore stolen property. Kick back. "I know the punks that heisted (held up) your joint. They'll kick back or make a slab (end in the morgue)."

Retaliate. Get hunk; kick back; stick it in and break it off.

Retaliation. Come-back; kick-back.

Revolver. See **Pistol.**

Reward for arrest of "wanted" person. Reader with a tail; tail. "I just saw your mugg (photograph) in the whiskers joint (post office). There's a reader with a five G (five thousand dollar) tail for you."

Ribs. Slats.

Ridding self of person. Chill; dust-off; kiss-off; lug; raus; raust. "Give that muzzler (low fellow) the dust-off. He draws heat (police attention)."

Ride freight-cars by bribing brakeman. Ride on the green; ride on the red. "The red (I.W.W. card) ain't no good in the East. Gotta ride on the green."

Ride freight-car top. Grab scenery; ride the deck; ride as a scenery bum.

Ride freight-car understructure. Ride the rods.

Rid self of undesirable persons. Air; boat; chase; chill; ditch; duke out; dump; dust off; gate; kiss off; lug; muscle out; put the chill on; put the skids to; shake; skid. (See also **Victim of criminal activity, rid self of.**)

Rid self of undesirable person, help one to. Bail out; give one a break; get one out of hock; spring. "When you see that ear-bender (talkative fellow) putting lumps on my ear, smarten up and bail me out."

Rifle. Blunderbuss; long rod; smoke-pole; smoke-wagon.

Riot, v. Kick over.

River. Drink.

Road. Drag; midway; stem.

Road, principal. Main drag; main stem.

Roam. Drift; float; hop-scotch.

Rob. Beat; clean; clip; dry; go up against; heel; kife; make; phutz; reef; riffle; take; yentz. (See also **Alter checks; Alter for purposes of fraud; Burglarize; Cheat; Criminal activity, carry out a profitable venture in; Criminal activity, carry out a venture in; Counterfeit money, pass; Dice, roll and spin in cheating; Extort; Forged checks, pass; Freight-cars, rob; Hold up; Hold up railroad trains; Loan shark racket, mulct victim in; Pick pockets; Playing cards, cheat in dealing of; Rob drunkards; Rob by unarmed physical force; Safe or vault, burglariously open a; Stolen goods, cheat associates of share of; Swindle.**)

Rob, attempt to. Give a play; give a joint a play; make a play for. "Look at the boodle (bankroll) that ghee (fellow) is flashing. I'm going to make a play for him."

Rob and leave penniless. Beat one for his socks; take to the cleaners; take to the driers; scrub; clip for the works.

Rob a person. Beat a mark; clip a mark; make a mark; take a mark.

Rob a place. Beat a joint; heel a joint; make a joint; make a mark; take a mark; throw a spot in the air; tip over; turn off.

Robber. See **Thief.**

Robber, highway. Snaffler. (See also **Holdup man.**)

Robber, user of unarmed physical force. See **Strong-arm man.**

Robber of display windows by smashing. Window-crasher.

Robber of drunkards. Diver; flop; lush-diver; lusher; lush-roller; lush-worker.

Robbery. See **Holdup profession.**

Robbery, by unarmed physical force. Arm; bushwhack; mugg; muscle. "You don't need no piece (gun). That mark (victim) will go on the muscle."

Robbery, difficult. Tough gaff.

Robbery, disguise self in. See **Face, disguise or conceal in robbery; Gloves, wear.**

Robbery, disguise worn in. See **Disguise; Eyeglasses.**

Robbery, execute a. Knock off; knock over; pull; take; turn. "We can knock over this joint three-handed (with three men) and score for (get) a nice end (share)."

Robbery, of display windows by smashing. Window-crash.

Robbery, of drunkards. Lush-dive; lush-roll; lush-working; rolling lushes.

Robbery, searcher of victims in. Frisker.

Robbery, search victims of. See **Search.**

Robbery, watch an assigned post in. Hold down.

Rob by unarmed physical force. See **Assault and rob.**

Rob display windows by smashing. Crash; kick in; pull a window-crash.

Rob drunkards. Lush-dive; lush-roll; roll.

Rob homosexuals. Cruise; pick fruit; play the fruit market.

Room. See **Apartment.**

Rough-and-tumble, n. Rowdy-dowdy; tumuling.

Round up associates. Rustle out.

Ruinous development. Blow card.

Rumor, n. Blow-up; hot wire. (See also **Grapevine.**)

Rump. See **Buttocks.**

Run-around, n. Gurdy; hurdy; sleigh-ride.

Rustic. Hoosier.

S

Safe or vault. Biscuit; box; can; canister; cannonball; coffin; crib; keister; pete; peter; a V.

Safe or vault, alarm system of. Bug; harness. "Don't touch that harness on the peter (safe) till I put a jumper (diverter) on the bug (alarm) wires."

Safe or vault burglar. Box-man; box-worker; can-opener; can-shooter; cribman; heavy; heavyman; ironworker; Johnny Yegg; mechanic; pete-man; valentine; yegg.

Safe or vault burglar, bank specialist. Jug-heavy.

Safe or vault burglar, user of crude force as. Puncher; ripper; stick-man. "Any ripper with a good can-opener (ripping instrument) can take that keister (safe) like candy."

Safe or vault burglar, user of explosives as. Bang-man; blower; shooter; soup-man.

Safe or vault burglar, user of oxy-acetylene as. Burner; torch-man.

Safe or vault burglar, user of tunneling method. Gopher; gopher-mob.

Safe or vault burglary. Cracking cribs; heavy; heavy time; box work; busting petes; knocking off peters; pete job; peter racket; pete work; the rip; taking boxes.

Safe or vault burglary, a leisurely act of. Week-ender.

Safe or vault burglary, apply drill in. Stem in.

Safe or vault burglary, bungle mechanical details in. Jam a pete

Safe or vault burglary, crude. Punch-job; rip-job.

Safe or vault burglary, explosives used in. See Explosives.

Safe or vault burglary, oxy-acetylene type of. Burn-job.

Safe or vault burglary, soak and boil dynamite for. Cook soup.

Safe or vault burglary, soap enclosure for explosives in. Mud fence.

Safe or vault burglary, touch off explosives in. Blow; shoot a jug.

Safe or vault burglary, tools used in. Can-opener; come-along; pry; puller; stem; a V. (See also Burglar's tools.)

Safe or vault burglary, use crude force in. Punch; punch guts out; rip. "Knock that combo (combination dial) off with the hammer and I'll punch the guts out of this old-time V (vault)."

Safe or vault burglary, use explosives in. Blow.

Safe or vault burglary, use oxy-acetylene in. Burn.

Safe or vault, combination mechanism of. Combination; combo; guts.

Safe or vault, difficult to burglarize. Cannonball; cycle.

Safe or vault, easily broken open. Cracker box; fireproof peter; gingerbread pete; shell; shell-V.

Safe or vault, inner compartment door of. Duster; flunk.

Safe or vault, open burglariously a. Crack; crack a crib; unbutton a box.

Safe or vault, painted facsimile as used by burglars to cover work. Screen.

Safe or vault, prepare for explosion in burglary of. Lather up; ready up; soup up; soup on; torch a squib. "Get the soap and lather up that keister (safe) while I get the shot ready (explosive)."

Safe or vault, time-lock protected. Gopher; timer.

Saloon. Barrel house.

Salt cellar. Lighthouse.

San Bernardino. San Berdoo.

Sandwich. Ball lump; dukee.

Sane. Conked up okay.

San Pedro. Pedro.

Satchel. See Baggage.

Sauerkraut. Shrubbery.

Sausages. Beagles.

Save. See **Put away.**

Scapegoat. Fall guy; lob; pack horse.

Scheme, n. Swindle. (See also **Criminal activity, plan for.**)

Scheme. v. See **Outwit.**

School, n. Knowledge box.

Search, n. Frisk; a general; once-over; pat; prowl; rubdown; shake-down; stand-up; strip-frisk; toss.

Search, v. Fan; frisk; give a ghee a toss; give a joint a toss; go through; pat; prowl; shake down; sound; strip-frisk; take a joint apart; toss; turn upside down and shake.

Search, submit to a. Stand a fan; stand a frisk. (See also **Pockets, to empty in view of fellow thieves.**)

Second-story man. See **Burglar.**

Seedy-looking. Beat up.

Segregation block. Bing; box.

Seize, v. See **Arrest; Grab; Kipnap; Purse, snatch a.**

Selfish. Single-o. "You single-o muzzler (weasel), why don't you cut me in for an end (share) of that grift (racket) of yours?"

Sentence, prison. Bit; bundle; boffos, bundle of; chunk; crimp; G-bit; hitch; jolt; knock; new bit; old bit; package; penance; piece; rap; ride; screwy bit; stretch; time; trick.

Sentence, adjust badly and serve a harsh prison. Bring time the hard way; do tough time; pull a tough bit.

Sentence, begin serving the last year of a prison. Break a year. "Next week I break the year and this bit (term) will be a pushover."

Sentence, commit on a prison. Belt out; break one's license; bury; hang; lag; nick; slough; tronk. "Well, Rattler, you had a nice run on the cannon (picking pockets). You figured to have your license broke."

Sentence, determinate prison. Flat bit.

Sentence, effect reduction of prison. Get a bit chopped.

Sentence, embezzling banker's usual prison. Banker's bit. "That five to ten year banker's bit is a pretty soft touch for them creeps."

Sentence, exercise clemency in reducing prison. See **Pardon a convict.**

Sentence, exercise of clemency in reduction of prison. See **Pardon of a convict.**

Sentence, five-year prison. Five boffos; fin; finif; fiver; five spot; five spotter; handful; pound; five smackers; five spaces; five-specker; five spotter.

Sentence, good behavior reduction of prison. Brass; copper; good-time; jawbone time; short time. "With six months good-time off my deuce (two-year term), this bit can be done on one ear (very easily)."

Sentence, good conduct allowance denied in serving a prison. Do it all; rot in stir. "Them muzzlers on the board (parole board) are making me do it all, and I never got a pinch (report) in the can (prison)."

Sentence, illegal prison. Phony-baloney bit; screwy bit.

Sentence, impose a prison. Belt out; boff; bury; crimp; dish out; drill; give one a bit; give one the business; give one the works; hit; hit one with; hit with a bit; knock; send up; settle; slap in; slap in the kisser with; slap with; smack in the kisser with; smack with; soak; toss the book at; wack; whack.

Sentence, impose a severe prison. Hit with the book; smack with the works; toss the book at.

Sentence, indeterminate prison. Banker's bit; garter; split bit.

Sentence, justified prison. Right bit. (See also **Criminal charge, serious and supported by ample evidence.**)

Sentence, last day of a prison. Flop; get-up; roll-over; sleeper; wake-up. "After tomorrow I got a roll-over, then I push out of this crumb-joint (dirty and mismanaged prison)."

Sentence, last year of a prison. Break a year.

Sentence, length of prison. (One, two, three, etc.) boffos; smackers; spaces; -specker; -spotter. "Mad Mike just got hit with (sentenced to) a seven-specker in State's (state prison)."

Sentence, lifetime prison. All of it; book; bookful; business; cat-life; double-life; from now on; life; life bit; phony-baloney life; rosary; triple life; washout. "Them judges must be nuts handing out them cat-life bits (terms). You can't do no more than one life."

Sentence (lifetime prison), allowance of earlier parole in a. Phony-baloney life. "He ain't got no natural life bit; it's one of them phony-baloney life stretches (terms) with ten-year parole."

Sentence, maximum prison. All of it; book; business; from now on; jackpot; max; plenty of numbers; telephone number bit; works.

Sentence, narrowly escape prison. Beat a rap; beat a stretch; miss a bit; spring; get a turn-out; wiggle out.

Sentence, nervously nearing end of prison. Dancing; have the leaps; have parolitis; have shortitis.

Sentence, obtain court permission to name prison in which one will serve. Write one's own ticket.

Sentence, obtain one or more transfers serving a prison. Break up a bit. "I'm gonna break up this bit even if I have to make the bughouse (hospital for the criminally insane)."

Sentence, one-day jail. Set-up.

Sentence, one-year prison. Ace; one boffo; one smacker; one space; one-specker; one-spotter.

Sentence, one-year-and-six-months prison. Yard and a half.

Sentence, receive a prison. Draw; get hit with; get settled for; take a bit; take a jolt; take a knock; take a rap; take a stretch.

Sentence, receive a lenient prison. Get a break; score for a break; get a valentine.

Sentence, receive a severe prison. Get hit with the book; get the book; hit the jackpot.

Sentence, reduce length of prison. Chop a bit. "I got the fix in with a couple of pollies (politicians), and the judge is gonna chop my bit."

Sentence, serve an easy or short prison. Sleep off a bit; do a bit on one leg; do a bit with one's shoes on; do sleeping time; do soft time; do a bit on one ear; knock up a stir; pull a soft bit; do a bit without taking one's shoes off.

Sentence, serve a prison. Bring; do a bit; do a chunk; do a hitch; do a jolt; do a piece; do a stretch; do penance; do time; go through the mill; pack away; pack in; pack time away; pull; pull a bit; pull time; serve time, stand the gaff.

Sentence, serve life on a prison. Do it all; do the rosary; rot in stir.

Sentence, serve (number of) years of a prison. Bring —; do—; pack away—; pull—; pull—boffos.

Sentence, serving the last of a prison. Coming down hill; over the hump; getting short.

Sentence, severe prison. Big bit; long bit; box-car numbers; bundle; chunk; haul; heavy bit; heavy time; load; stagger bit; stiff rap; long stretch; telephone number bit; tough bit; tough gaff; tough rap. (See also **Raw deal**.)

Sentence, short or easy prison. Few; hanger; light time; pushover; set-up; sleep; sleeper; sleeping time; soft bit; workhouse bit.

Sentence, six-month jail. Sixer.

Sentence, six-year prison. Six boffos; sixer; six smackers; six spaces; six-spotter; six-specker.

Sentence, small remaining portion of prison. Butt; sleeper; wop. "One year and a wop and this bit (term) is licked."

Sentence, suspension of prison. Draw; an s.s.

Sentence, ten-year prison. Ten boffos; saw; sawski; sawbuck; ten smackers; ten spaces; ten-specker; ten-spotter; tenner.

Sentence, three-year prison. Three boffos; dreece; three smackers; three spaces; three-specker; three-spotter; trey; treyer.

Sentence, time credited in jail awaiting a prison. Jail time.

Sentence, twenty-year prison. Twenty boffos; double-saw; double-sawbuck; twenty smackers; twenty spaces; twenty-specker; twenty-spotter.

Sentence, two-year prison. Two boffos; deuce; two smackers; two spaces; two-specker; two-spotter.

Sentence, unjustified prison. See **Criminal charge, unjust.**

Sentence, voluntarily accept a prison, as part of a bargain. Settle for; spring the other ghees on the rap; stand for; take a bit; take a bum beef; take a bum rap; take a rap; take the knock; talk business; turn out one's partner.

Sentenced to city or county penitentiary. Get the pen; get hit with the pen.

Sentenced to prison rightfully. Settled right.

Sentenced to prison wrongfully. Settled wrong.

Sentences, several consecutive prison. Life on the installment plan.

Sever relations. See **Cease.**

Sever relations with a person. Wrap up a ghee.

Sexual excess. See **Fornication, an act of active.**

Sexual gratification, act of. See **Fornication.**

Sexual gratification, find. See **Fornicate.**

Sexually erratic person. See **Masturbator; Nymphomaniac; Pederast, active; Pederast, passive; Rapist; Sodomist, oral.**

Sexually promiscuous manner, act in a. See **Fornication, practice promiscuous.**

Sexually stimulated. Horny; hot; hot in the biscuit; steamed up.

Sexual relationship, engage in a meretricious. See **Sodomous union, joined in.**

Share, v. Brass up; put out; stake; wack; whack. "Hip up (get wise) and whack that score (proceeds of theft) so I get a gapper's (onlooker's) bit (share) anyhow."

Shave face or **head.** Scalp.

Shell game. See **Swindle, shell game.**

Short-change racket. See **Swindle, short-change type of.**

Shirker of work. Actor; gold bricker; staller.

Shirk work. Gold brick; tool. (See also **Illness, feign.**)

Shirt, durable. Thousand-mile shirt.

Shoe, n. Barker; kick.

Shoot. Bang; blast; chop down; drill; drop; fan; fog; get; hit in the biscuit; hit in the bonnet; hit in the cruller; hit in the head; hit in the noggin; hit in the squash; knock down; peg slugs; plug; poop; pour it on; slip one the heat; throw lead; throw slugs; toss lead; turn it loose; turn on the heat; wing.

Shooting. Bang-job. (See also **Assault; Murder.**)

Shooting, lose gang member by. Lose a man.

Shooting, threaten with. See **Pistol, point a; Pistol, reach for a.**

Shoplift. Boost; clout; lift.

Shoplifter. Booster; derrick; lift.

Shoplifter's concealment device. Hooks. "Doris the Derrick beat (robbed) that joint of five G's (five thousand dollars) in swag (loot) hanging it on the inside armpit hooks of that boosting ben (shoplifter's coat)."

Shoplifter's concealment trick. Underneath. "Mae got a mink coat and two silver foxes in that bag underneath. Them balloon skirts do it."

Shoplifter's overcoat. Boosting-ben; swag-benny; swag-flogger.

Shoplifting profession. Boost; boosting grift; clout; derrick; lift.

Shot, p.p. Catch slugs.

Shotgun. Blunderbuss; flatback; smoke-pole; smoke-wagon.

Shotgun, sawed-off. Long cut short; sawed-off.

Shovel, n. Muckstick.

Show one's mettle. Shape up; stand the gaff; stand up.

Shut up. Bag your head; bag your lip; blow your nose; can; chop; clam up; d.d.; dummy up; fold up; get hep; get hip; get under the bed; hang up; stick your head; knock off; lay down; lay off; spit; zipper.

Sickly appearance. Rough; sad; tough.

Sight, in. On the deck; in the center; in the middle; on the line. "Get that dough on the line. It ain't no good in your kick (pocket)."

Signature. Scratch.

Silk, n. Worm.

Silk thief. Worm-worker. (See also **Burglar, specialist in fur and silk lofts.**)

Silver, melted-down scrap. Break-up.

Simplify. Cut to the breaks.

Single out. Weed.

Siren, sound a. Toot the tooter; blow the whistle.

Sit down. Park the biscuit; stash the frame.

Skilful. Bang-up; red hot; be a ringer; be a shark; be a sharp; have plenty of stuff; have talent; there; be a whip.

Slander, n. Crack; crimpers; hooks; needles; zingers. "Some flea (low fellow) is putting the old crimpers in and lousing me up (ruining my reputation) around here."

Slander, v. Crack; knock; louse up; mark lousy; mark wrong; put the crimpers in; put the hooks in on; put the needles in on; put the zingers in on; sizzle.

Sleep, n. Doss; flop; kip.

Sleep, v. Flop; hit the flop; plough the kip; pound the bell; pound the ear.

Slot-machine. One-arm bandit.

Slut. See **Prostitute** or **loose woman.**

Smoke a cigarette. See **Cigarette, smoke a.**

Smoke a marijuana cigarette. See **Marijuana, smoke cigarettes containing.**

Smoke opium. See **Opium, smoke.**

Smuggle past immigration or **customs barriers.** Move the laundry; run rum; whip over. "Moving the laundry used to be a nice racket. The Chinks (Chinese) paid a few bills (hundreds) a head to get in."

Smuggler. Monkey-runner; rum-runner.

Smugglers' motorboat. See **Motorboat.**

Snub, n. Iggy. "What are you giving me the old iggy for? Someone putting the crimpers in (slandering) on me with you?" (See also **Greeting, hostile** or **contemptuous.**)

Snub, v. See **Greet, fail to.**

Snuff, n. Snoose.

Social affair. Racket.

Sodomist, active female. Bull-dyker; dyke; lady lover; les; wolf.

Sodomist, oral. Cruise; fag; faggot; fairy; flinch-bird; fluter; gobbler; guzzler; madam; muzzler; nance; nibbler; snake-charmer. See also **Pederast, passive.**)

Sodomist (oral), perverted by force. Made fag. (See **Pederast [passive], perverted by force,** etc.)

Sodomists (oral), sailors as viewed by. Sea food.

Sodomist (oral), with woman subjects. Bumper; muff-diver.

Sodomist, reformed. Reformed.

Sodomists, brothel featuring. See **Pederast (passive), brothel featuring.**

Sodomists, dance or **party of.** Drag.

Sodomists, rendezvous of. See **Pede-**

rast (passive), brothel featuring; Rendezvous of perverts.

Sodomists, seek out to rob or patronize. Pick up a cruise; play the fags; go to market; play the fruit market.

Sodomous exhibition. Circus; daisy-chain; sixty-nine; trip around the world.

Sodomous gestures, overtures, etc. Blubber; goose; play; pogie bait; promote. "You ain't bumming all my candy for them punks. Go buy your pogie bait."

Sodomous overtures, make. Make a play for; play; promote; run the tier; try to get even.

Sodomist (passive), femininely attired. Drag.

Sodomous practices, quasi-. Dry rub; hand job.

Sodomous taint, one free of. Canned goods; cherry; truck driver.

Sodomous union, joined in. Married, to be; shot-for-shot, to go; sixty-nine, to play; stew for beans, to swap; swap spits.

Sodomous woman. Double-barreled broad.

Sodomy, an act of active. See **Fornication, an act of active.**

Sodomy, commit an act of oral. Cop a doodle; cop a joint; grab a hot one; nibble; play a schweinet; snare one; turn a trick.

Sodomy, sheep employed passively in. Sheep-herder's wife.

Solicit. Brace; buzz; feel out; flag down; hit up; How's you and me?; put the gorill on; put the shake on; put the snare on; reach. (See also **Beg.**)

Solicit as a prostitute. See **Prostitution, practice.**

Solitary confinement chamber. Blue Room.

Sophisticate, n. Hep-ghee; hip-ghee; hipster.

Sophisticated, a. Hep; hip; hip to the lay; knockaround; smartened up.

Sophisticated, become or **contribute**

toward another's becoming. Hep up; hip up; smarten up.

Sore, self-inflicted. Bug. "You can't kick over (refuse to work) in this can (prison) so I raised a bug on my hand to check in the hospital."

Southerner. Rebel.

Spaghetti. Lead pipe.

Spaniard or **Spanish-American.** Greaseball; spig; spik.

Spokesman. Front; front-ghee; frontman; mouthpiece.

Start. Pop-off.

State trooper. Statey.

Station, any transit system. Breaks; dump; get-on; put-off; spill. "I see that cannon-mob (pickpocket gang) working the spill when I got off." (See also **Railroad station; Subway station.**)

Stay of execution. Anchor.

Steak. Rubber. (See also **Meat.**)

Steal. Bag onto; beat; bend; boost; clean; clip; clout; cop; glaum onto; glom; glom onto; glu; grab; grab off; grift; grub; hijack; hit the turf; hustle; make a riffle; make one for; nick; pick a berry; play; put the glom on; put the grab on; put the snatch on; put the snare on; racketeer; riffle; screw around; scrub; snaffle; snag; snare; snatch; sting; swipe; turn; turn a trick; weed; work.

Steal by "sneak-thief" technique. Cop a sneak; heel; mooch; prowl.

Steal recklessly. See **Criminal activity, undertake without leads.**

Stew. Mulligan.

Stigma. Brand; rap; "Finko Farley's got the rap of being wrong (an informer) but I don't know no one he ever buried (betrayed)."

Stigmatize. Brand; louse up; mark; mark lousy; mark wrong; pin; rap.

Still. Boiler.

Stocks and other negotiable paper, exchange dealing in. Clearing house; hot-stiff joint; stiff-joint. "I'm gonna fence (sell as loot) these bonds in that hot-stiff joint down in William Street."

Stocks and other negotiable paper, hypothecation of. Blue sky racket; kiting stocks.

Stocks and other negotiable paper, sell fraudulently. Reload; stiff.

Stocks and other negotiable paper, swindler in. Dynamiter.

Stolen, counterfeited or altered negotiable paper. Hot paper; stiff. (See also **Check; Check, forged.**)

Stolen, counterfeited or other money sought by police. Marked dough; kinky; mazuma; hot scratch.

Stolen and the object of police search. Bent; dynamite; hot; hot as a forty-five; hot as a pistol; kinky; red hot; sizzling.

Stolen goods. Haul; hot stuff; junk; load; mahoska; merchandise; nick; stuff; swag. (See also **Criminal activity, proceeds of.**)

Stolen goods, bag for concealment of. Swag-bag.

Stolen goods, burden innocent person with. Hit with a swag.

Stolen goods, carry. Lug swag.

Stolen goods, cash. Bundle; cush.

Stolen goods, (large) cash sum in. Heavy paper.

Stolen goods, (small) cash sum in. Short dough. "We scored for (got) plenty of collat (negotiable loot) on that trick (robbery) but short dough."

Stolen goods, criminally receiving. Receiving.

Stolen goods, dealer in. Buyer; fence; receiver; stop; swag-buyer; swagger; swaggie; swagman; taker; uncle; yentzer.

Stolen goods, deal in. Handle swag; receive.

Stolen goods, divide. Brass up; cut up a touch; divvy; split; stake; wack; whack.

Stolen goods, establishment of dealer in. Drop; drop-joint; dump.

Stolen goods, gem specialist dealing in. Iceman.

Stolen goods, innocent dealer in. Blind fence.

Stolen goods, having on one's person. Loaded; padded; swagged-up.

Stolen goods, jewelry. See **Jewelry.**

Stolen goods, pocket for concealing. Swag-pocket.

Stolen goods, precious metal settings of. Break-up. "The rocks (diamonds) ought to bring us a nice chunk and a little extra score (profit) from the break-up."

Stolen goods, readily negotiable. Collat.

Stolen goods, return. Kick back.

Stolen goods, return of. Kick-back.

Stolen goods, sell. Fence; push; push swag; shove; unload.

Stolen goods, sell to innocent receiver. Fence blind; hit with a swag.

Stolen goods, share of. Aigey; bit; butts; chop; cut; divvy; end; piece; rake-off; slice; split; split-up; ways; wack; whack.

Stolen goods, (share of) cheat associates of. Burn; dump; go south; hold out; h.o.; screw with the works; shove down; go single-o; go sixty-forty; weed. (See also **Cheat.**)

Stolen goods, (share of) cheat in fixing. Burner; dumper; h.o.; h.o. ghee; single-o; two-way ghee. (See also **Person, contemptible.**)

Stolen goods, (share of) large. Big bit; big corner; big end; big piece. "I gotta get a big end on this pete-job (safe-cracking job), or I don't step out. You dudes (fellows) need me 'cause I know the racket."

Stolen goods, (share of) minor aide's. Gapper's bit; gapper's end. "You got nothing to do but stand around and lay zex (serve as lookout) so you get a gapper's bit, ten percent. If you don't like it, screw (get out of here)."

Stolen goods, (share of) satisfy associates regarding fair. See **Pockets, empty in view of fellow thieves.**

Stolen goods, share due informant. Finger's end; tipster's bit.

Stolen goods, (share of) small. Short end. "You ain't giving me no short end. Turn out (empty your pockets), and we'll see who's holding out."

Stolen goods, valueless. See **Thing, relatively or wholly worthless.**

Stool pigeon. Bat-carrier.

Stop, v. See **Cease.**

Store, general. Seven-up.

Story, humorous. Gag; hot one; hot stuff. (See also **Thing, wonderful or remarkable.**)

Story-teller. Character; hot bum.

Stove, contraband electric. Boiler; hot boiler; hot one.

Straighten out oneself. Square oneself.

Strait-jacket. Camisole; jacket.

Stranger. Blow-in; bum; floater; geepo; strange weed; weed. (See also **Prison, inmate newly arrived in.**)

Street. See **Road.**

Street, the main. See **Road, principal.**

Strikebreaker, n. Fink; goon; noble.

Strike, break a labor. Fink.

Strong-arm man. Arm-man; conk-crusher; duster; forty strong; front; front ghee; front man; gorilla; guerilla; guzzler; heeler; mugg artist; mugger; muscle; muscle-man; ruffy; shadow; tumuler.

Studebaker automobile. Studie.

Stupid. Sad; having stones in the head.

Stupid person. See **Person, slow-witted or inept.**

Substitute, n. Ringer. (See also **Expert.**)

Substitute, v. Put the hipe on; put the switch on; ring in; switch.

Subway station. Breaks; hole; chutes. (See also **Station, any transit system; Railroad station.**)

Suffer. Eat one's heart out.

Suffix, superlative. -Eroo; -ola. "Jake, old Jakeroo, where did you score for

(get) that gat (pistol)! What a pistola!"

Sugar. Sand; white gold.

Suicide, commit. See **Die by suicide.**

Suit of clothing. Flash; frock; front; get-up; rig.

Sure thing. Candy; cold lay; gravy; handout; hanger; pipe; pushover; score; set-up; soft touch; wrap-up. "This score (robbery) is a wrap-up. Don't need a biscuit (gun)." (See also **Person, easily deceived or robbed.**)

Sure thing, so easy as to be a. Cold; in the bag; in the sack; in the satchel; sweet; wrapped up.

Surgeon. See **Doctor.**

Surly. See **Belligerent.**

Surrender to police. Turn oneself in.

Surveillance, keep under. Burn up; case; gun; peg a joint; pike off; rumble; smoke; spot.

Surveillance, rigidly exercising. On one's biscuit; on one's can; on one's canetta; on one's keister; on one's pratt; on one's quiff; on one's tail. "Them parole ghees (parole agents) are sure on my keister since I hit the bricks (was discharged from prison)."

Surveillance, under. Under the gun.

Swear, to. Bible.

Swindle. Bunco; bundle-hipe; con; con-game; con racket; faro bank; flop game; gaff; Georgia scuffle; gimmick; glim-racket; green goods game; grift; hipe; lemon game; match game; money machine; over-issue; pay-off; peekaboo; Roumanian box; the seal; short-con; spud; story; switch. (See also **Insurance racket, accident; Lie.**)

Swindle, v. Build up; bundle hipe; cap; con; con along; cross-fire; cuff; duke in; gaff; gimmick; give one a hustle; give one a play; grift; hipe; hook; hustle; make citizens; play; pluck; put the hipe on; ready-up; rib; rope in; sandwich; set up; pull a sleeper; sling; spiel; spring; spring the gaff on; spring with a crack; stiff; take for a sleigh-ride; take to the cleaners; take to the driers; thimble-rig; tout; whipsaw. (See also Cheat; Dice, roll and spin in cheating; Out-wit; Rob; Rob and leave penniless.)

Swindle, feign salvation in mission. Grab salvation; take a dive. "All the bums are taking a dive for coffee-and down at that mission on the corner. They got a hot devil-dodger (preacher) spieling there."

Swindle, fraudulent advertising. Bite; limb; tap; tap game; ad racket; "Gimme that phony joint (magazine), and I'll pull the tap on a few of the shops on the stem (avenue). A C-note (hundred dollars) a page."

Swindle, operate in the fraudulent advertising. Bite; limb it; work on the limb; put the bite on; put the tap on; tap. "The Bugle won't renew my creed (credentials), so I'll limb it on my own and give them nothing. The clearing house (check discounting agency) will smash (cash) the stiffs (checks) for a cut (discount)."

Swindle establishment. Flat-joint; fold-up; front; layout. (See also **Establishment using decoys to lure and rob patrons.**)

Swindle (gambling or carnival), cheap prize to lure on victims of. Hoop; larry; prop; slum; slum-gullion.

Swindle (gambling or carnival), crooked elements used in. Gaff; gaff-board; gimmick; pinch; tripod. "With the gimmick on that wheel, I can stop it on a hair and beat (rob) the marks (victims) so they love it."

Swindle (gambling or carnival), crowd spectators forward to be enticed into. Belly up; give one the push. "Get down in the tip (crowd) and give the marks the push. We got the alzo (bribed immunity from police interference) in this tank (town)."

Swindle (gambling or carnival),

defraud victim crudely and flee in. Georgia scuffle; stick, cop and blow.

Swindle (gambling or carnival), device to lead victims on in. Come-on; double-Willie; grease. "Give 'em plenty of double-Willie. Two chances for the price of one is the grease this tip (crowd) needs."

Swindle (gambling or carnival), fake roll of money used in. Backs; flash-dough; fronts; Mexican bankroll; Michigan bankroll.

Swindle (gambling or carnival), increase stakes in. Hipe; press the bank-roll; put the hipe on; sweeten. "The hoosiers are playing for peanuts (practically nothing). Put the hipe on and we stick, cop and blow (rob them and slip away quietly)."

Swindle (gambling or carnival), risky for small returns in. Georgia scuffle; grind. "What a Georgia scuffle taking (robbing) these jaspers (farmers). You almost got to slug (assault) them."

Swindle (gambling or carnival), talk spectators into participation in. Bally; heat up a tip; spiel.

Swindle, glimpse money held by intended victim. Gage the line; put the squint on.

Swindle, glimpse taken of money held by intended victim. Squint.

Swindle, progressive stages of confidence talk in. Blast; build-up; convincer; crack; cross-fire; fog; gig; hipe; line; lingo; make; oil; one-two play; play; pressure; promote; promotion; rib; riffle; spiel; work one's points; works. "I'll give this mark the build-up, then Charley will spring with the crack about a little game. After we let him win a few skins (dollars); that will be the convincer and we got him."

Swindle, pseudo-clergyman's victimizing of the devout in. The abbey. "Some creep put the bite on my mother with the old abbey wrinkle, a kick-in (contribution) to save the heathen Hottentot or something."

Swindle, removal of victim after robbing him from scene of. See **Rid self of person, help one to.**

Swindle, remove victim after robbing him, from scene of. See **Rid self of undesirable persons.**

Swindle, shell game. Hicks; hucks; nicks; nuts; shell-game.

Swindle (shell game), matchbox variation of. Match.

Swindle (shell game), operate in the match-box variation of. Play the match.

Swindle (shell game), with playing cards. Three-card monte; tossing the broads.

Swindle (shell game), steps used in playing card variation of. Bend; put the bend on; take the bend off; toss the broads. "Jeff put the bend on so the sucker figured they were in league to clip me, but when we hiped the play (increased the bets) I took the bend off the key card and he was snared (trapped)."

Swindle, short-change type of. Cutting cake; fold; hipe; laying the note; the push and slide; second-count.

Swindle (short-change type of) divide proceeds of. Cut cake; slice shortcake.

Swindle (short-change type of) engage in. Give one the fold; hipe; lay paper; lay the note; push the note; put the hipe on; shove the note.

Swindle (short-change type of) proceeds of. Shortcake.

Swindle, sow gold dust in mining. Salt.

Swindle, total sum on hand taken from victim of. Pocket-touch. "If I had to take the dude (fellow) to the jug (bank), I could figure a score (proceeds) like this, but a pocket-touch of eight G's (eight thousand dollars)!"

Swindle, victimize same person for second time in. Re-hash; reload.

Swindler, n. Bunco-steerer; buzzer; capper; come-on ghee; con-broad; conducer; con-ghee; con-man; con-merchant; conner; conny; do-little; duker; faker; glim-hustler; gunner; hedgehopper; hiper; hustler; jug-mob; lemon-mob; mush-faker; oil-merchant; phenagler; pitchman; promoter; ring-man; shark; sharp; sharpie; sharp-shooter; sheet-writer; shill; shillaber; shiller; slum-worker; spieler; spiel-worker; steerer; stripper; sure-thing ghee; t.b.; thimble-rigger; tout; wire-tapper. (See also **Dice, professional in game of; Insurance racket, principal in accident; Liar; Playing cards, cheat at.**)

Swindler, fraudulent advertising. Ad-man; tap-ghee; tap man; tapster.

Swindler, pseudo-clergyman. Abbey; fire-proofer.

Swindler, shell game. Nut-squealers; thimble-rigger.

Swindler using playing card variation of shell game. One of a broad-mob; broadsman; broad-tosser.

Sycophant. Beachcomber. (See also **Criminal, aide or sycophant of.**)

Syphilis. See **Venereal disease.**

T

Table, surface of. Deck.

Take, v. Cop.

Take one at a disadvantage. Cop a heel; cop a sneak; double-bank. (See also Advantage, take.)

Talk, n. See Underworld argot.

Talk, v. Beef; chop it up; chop up jackpots; crack; cut it up; cut up jackies; cut up touches; kick the gong around; punch the gun; shoot the lemon; sling; sling the crap; sling the lingo; spiel; spring; spring with a crack.

Talk, refuse to. See Shut up.

Talkative. Gassy; thick-slung; loose with the stinger.

Talkative person. See Person, talkative.

Talk excessively or belligerently. Bend one's ear; noise off; pop off; shoot one's bazoo off; shoot one's kisser off; shoot one's mouth off; shoot one's jay off; sound off; yam.

Task, difficult. Tough gaff.

Tea. Nux.

Tear gas. Bug-juice; eye-wash.

Technicality, legal. Teck.

Telephone, communicate with one by. Buzz.

Telephone line, tap a. Put a bug on.

Tense, a. Hot; red hot; sizzling. "Since somebody put the finger on (betrayed) the main ghee (leader) of this outfit, the joint has been red hot."

Tent. Black top.

Terrorist. See Gangster; Strong-arm man.

Terrorize. See Assault, threaten with; Coerce; Criminal activity, violently engage in; Extort.

Testicles. Balls; knockers; nuts.

Testimony, betray no underworld secrets in giving. Stand up.

Testimony, betray self or another by giving. See Inform upon self and/or accomplices or others.

Theft. See Criminal activity, venture in.

Thief, n. Grifter; hustler. (See also Automobile thief, amateur; Automobile thief, professional; Baggage-thief; Burglar of house and apartment; Burglar of safe and vault; Carnival, thief who follows; Cheat; Chicken thief; Criminal; Criminal, aide or sycophant of; Criminal aide to inside job; Dice, professional in game of; Extortionist; Forged checks, passer of; Forger; Forger, crude; Freight-cars, robber of; Fur thief; Gangster; Highway robber; Holdup gang, bank specialists; Holdup man; Insurance racket, principal in accident; Kidnapper; Loan shark; Lookout; Pickpocket, aide to; Playing cards, cheat at; Purse-snatcher; Robber of display windows by smashing; Robber of drunkards; Robber, user of unarmed physical force; Safe or vault burglar; Shoplifter; Silk thief; Stolen goods, dealer in; Swindler.)

Thief, amateur. Depression bum; dinner-pailer; joy-rider; legit-stiff; square; square-John; working stiff. "This racket's getting all crumbed up (spoiled) with them dinner-pailers taking a day off work to make a touch (theft)."

Thief, church poorbox. Church-rat.

Thief, international swindler. A K. I. (Literally, a knight of immunity.)

Thief, jewelry specialist. Iceman; pennyweighter.

Thief, overcautious. Baseman; center fielder; distance ghee; first baseman; outfielder; second baseman; sure-thing ghee; third baseman.

Thief, overcoat. Flogger-stiff.

Thief, petty. Alley rat; boy scout; buzzard; coffee-and hustler; creep; crib; ding-donger; do-little; door-matter; duster; fluker; gandy-dancer; gum-shoe-worker; jungle-buzzard; keister-man; mooch; punk; rustler; scratch-house bum; skip; slum-bum; slum-hustler; two-bit hustler; workhouse bum; workhouse stiff. (See also **Person, slow-witted** or **inept.**)

Thief, sneak. Clouter; heeler; mooch-er; prowler. "Some heeler just fished a pack of ten G's (ten thousand dollars) from the teller's window in the Grand Street jug (bank)." (See also **Shop-lifter; Thief, petty.**)

Thief who operates alone. Eagle; lone wolf; single-o.

Thief who cheats associates. See **Stolen goods, (share of) cheat in fixing.**

Thing, wonderful or **remarkable.** Dil-ly; dobey; duzey; honey; piss-cutter; pisser; pisseroo; sweetheart; whip.

Thing, relatively or **wholly worthless.** Buttons; crabs; crap; doodly; eppis; gullion; ice; junk; lemon; peanuts; pretzels; stiff; stiffo; tin; wampum; wood. "I wound up with crabs for my end of that caper (robbery) after cas-ing the joint (surveying the scene) for two weeks." (See also **Criminal activity, profitless venture in.**)

Third degree, break under and inform. Break; crack up; open up. (See also **Inform upon self** and/or **accomplices** or **others.**)

Third degree, police chamber of in-quisition in. See **Police station house, examination room of.**

Third degree, refuse to talk under. Ace it; clam up; dummy up; hold out; stand pat; stand the gaff; stand up; suck in one's guts.

Third degree, rigors of the. See **As-sault; Raw deal.**

Third degree, subject prisoner to rigors of the. See **Assault.**

Thought, n. Flop; rumble. "I never gave it a rumble that we might fence (sell) that swag (loot) blind (to an in-nocent buyer)."

Threat, n. Accident; glass wagon.

Threaten with. See **Exhibit, as money, weapons,** etc.; **Pistol, point a; Pistol, reach for a.**

Threaten with arrest. See **Exhibit** officer's badge.

Three-card monte. See **Swindle (shell game), with playing cards.**

Thrill, n. Bang; boot; kick.

Ticket. Ducat.

Tiepin. Prop.

Tiepin, safety catch of a. Anchor.

Tires. See **Automobile tires.**

Tobacco. See entries under **Cigarette.**

Toilet. Altar; crapper; donicker. (See also **Prison, toilet facilities of.**)

Tongue, n. Stinger.

Town. See **Cities; City.**

Trail, v. See **Follow.**

Trail, throw pursuer off one's. See **Follower, elude a.**

Train robbery, engage in. Pull a Jesse James.

Traitor. See **Informer; Person, con-temptible.**

Traitor, expose a. See **Stigmatize; Slander,** v.

Traitor, turn. See **Abandon criminal associates; Inform upon self** and/or **ac-complices** or **others; Third-degree, break under and inform.**

Tramp. See **Hobo; Vagrant.**

Trapped, a. Stiffed in; swamped.

Treasurer, n. Ghee with the boodle; pay-off ghee.

Trial by jury, acquit of charges in. Flag; nix; spring on a teck. (See also **Discharge from custody.**)

Trial by jury, be acquitted of charges in. Beat; beat a rap; hit the bricks; hit the pavement; hit the sidewalk; hit the street; spring; walk out.

Trial by jury, find guilty in. Belt out; bury. (See also **Convict improperly; Plead guilty to gain leniency.**)

Trial by jury, plead guilty and leave accomplices to face. See **Abandon crim-inal associates.**

Trial by jury, undergo. Go to bat; go up.

Trial by jury, undergo after accomplices' desertion. Hold the bag; hold the sack; go to bat single-o.

Trick, n. Fast one; gaff; gag; gimmick; quickie; quick one. (See also **Swindle.**)

Trick, v. See **Outwit.**

Tricks of the criminal trades, use the. Work the angles; do handy; get around; grift; knock up the grift; mooch around.

Trouble, n. Jackpot; jam; screw-up; swindle; tumul.

Trouble, in. Jackied up; in a jackpot; jammed up; messed up; panic is on; screwed up; squeezed; swindled up; in a swindle.

Trouble-maker. See **Agitator.**

Trouble-making. See **Agitation.**

Trousers. Droppers; strides; tailor-mades.

Truck-robber. See **Holdup man.**

Truck-robbery. See **Holdup, truck.**

Truth. Lowdown; McCoy; up-and-up; works.

Truth, tell the. Spring with the legit; level; give it to one on the up-and-up; spill the works.

Tuberculosis victim. Lunger.

Turn around. Round.

Typewriter. Chatterbox.

Typist. Woodpecker.

U

Umbrella. Mush.

Umbrella-thief. Mush-faker.

Unbutton. Unslough.

Uncertain. Jury's out; on ice. "Woody Willie says the jury's out on that score (robbery) he's casing (surveying). Have to wait."

Unconscious. Cold; cold-cocked; flattened; out.

Underworld, n. Blaht; bricks; outside; pavement; sidewalk; street; turf. "Mike's back on the street hustling (stealing)."

Underworld, loyal to the. See Criminal code, loyal to.

Underworld, person cooperative with. Ace; blaht; good guy; one of the Johnson family; knock-around guy; racket guy; right broad; right buck; right croaker; right ghee; right guy; right mouthpiece; righto; right people. (See also Bribe-taker.)

Underworld, returned to from imprisonment. See Freed from imprisonment.

Underworld, teach one the ropes in. Hep up; hip up; wise up.

Underworld argot. Double-talk; lingo; grifters' lingo.

Underworld argot, talk in the. Spiel in double-talk; crack in the lingo; lingo; spiel in the lingo; spring in the lingo. (See also Talk.)

Underworld disrepute, bring into. Crumb up; knock up; louse up; mark lousy; mark wrong; rank a joint.

Underworld newcomer. Depression bum; dinner-pailer; jay; John; legit-stiff; mick; new mick; square-John; working stiff.

Underworld sophisticate. Ghee who's been around; dude who knows the score; sharp stuff; slicker; smart money. (See also Criminal.)

Unfasten. Unslough.

United States government jurisdiction. Fed; G. "That G heat (Federal agents' attention) is bad. Knock off (stop) pushing them queer (counterfeited) stamps."

United States Government Law Enforcement Agency. Big Department.

Unprofitable. Blue. (See also Worthless, wholly or relatively.)

Untrustworthy. Copper-hearted; no bargain; not so hot. (See also Criminal code, disloyal to the.)

Urge, v. See Persuade.

Usurer. See Loan shark.

Usury. See Loan shark racket.

V

Vagrancy, a charge of. Vag.

Vagrancy, arrest or jail for. Vag.

Vagrant. Drifter; floater; stiff; tomato-can vag; vag. (See also **Hobo**.)

Valise. See **Baggage**.

Vanish. Pull a Crater. (See also **Fugitive from justice, become a.**)

Vanishing, act of. A Crater. (See also **Escape.**)

Venereal disease. Clap; dog; dose; head cold; package; the rahl.

Venereal disease, combination of. Full house.

Venereal disease, examination of males for. Short-arm inspection.

Venereal disease, freshly contracted. Lulu.

Venereal disease, infect with a. Burn; dose up; rahl up; set one up.

Venereal disease, neglected. Old clap, ten-year-old dog; old dose.

Venereal disease, specialist in treatment of. Stick-croaker.

Vermin, n. Crabs; crum; crumb; greyback; seam-squirrel; shimmy-lizard.

Vermin, afflicted with. Crumby; crummy; lousy.

Vermin, rid self of. Crumb up; read a shirt.

Victim of crime. See Criminal activity, victim of.

Victim of crime, prepared listings of. Sucker list.

Victim of crime, yield as a. Give up; go; figure to go; get in line; kick in; kick loose; pay off; pay off on the moosh; pay off on the squash; pay off on the tin; see; spring; stand for; stand for a heist; stand for a shake.

Victim of criminal activity, rid self of. Give one a raust; lug a mark; play the deuce of clubs; put the lug on; raus; raust; unload. (See also **Rid self of undesirable person.**)

Violence. Muscle; muscle-work; tumul.

Violence, by means of. On the arm; on the muscle.

Violent criminal. See **Strong-arm man; Robber, user of unarmed physical force.**

Virgin, n. Canned goods; cherry.

Virginal. Never tampered with.

Visiting day. Big day.

Vulnerable. Ready; sucker for a left; wide open.

W

Wager. See Chance; Gamble; Gambler; etc.

Wait, v. & n. Stall.

Waive. Flag; pass up.

Walk, n. Dan O'Leary; duff; mooch; powder. (See also **Escape.**)

Walk, v. Ankle; go by hand; mooch. (See also **Escape.**)

Walk the railroad tracks. Count ties.

Wallet. Leather; okus; poke.

Wanted by the police. See **Fugitive from justice, sought as a.**

"Wanted" circular. Dodger; general; mugg on the board; reader; reader with a tail.

Warden. See **Prison, warden of.**

Warn of danger. See **Danger, warn of.**

Warning of danger. See **Danger, warning expressions of; Danger, warning of.**

Warrant for arrest. Ducat; general; hooker; reader; reader with a tail; sticker; ticket.

Warrant, effect withdrawal of pending. Squash a ducat; kick a hooker; jerk off a sticker; yank a sticker; pull off a ticket.

Warrant, procure prison discharge to face pending. Go down on a hooker; step out in bracelets; step out in cuffs; step out in irons.

Waste, v. Blow; piss away; splurge on the line. (See also **Lose.**)

Waste time or opportunity. Fart around; screw around.

Watch, n. Black gold souper; block; kettle; phony super; super; thimble; turnip.

Watch, v. See **Eye suspiciously; Look at; Surveillance, keep under.**

Watch and chain. Layout.

Watchdog, protect by. Mutt up.

Watchman. Bugster; clocker; doorshaker; hack; kip; sleeper.

Watchman, guarded by a. Kipped.

Water, any body of. The drink.

Weapon. See **Bludgeon; Brass knuckles; Knife; Machine gun; Pistol; Pistol, imitation; Pistol, equipped with silencer; Rifle; Shotgun; Shotgun, sawed-off; Tear gas.**

Whine, v. See **Complain.**

Whiner. Beefer.

White race, member of. Pink.

Whiskey. Brown; skee. (See also **Alcoholic liquor.**)

Whore. See **Prostitute or loose woman.**

Wince. Make a kisser.

Wish, v. See **Hope.**

Witness, defense. Alibi ghee.

Woman. Bag; baloney; band; barlow; barnacle; bat; beast; beetle; bezark; bim; bimbo; bimmy; blister; broad; dame; doll; frill; head; jane; moll; muff. (See also **Prostitute or loose woman.**)

Woman, entertaining or unconventional. Hot tomato.

Woman, carnival troupe member. Bree.

Woman, respectable. Good-head; legit-broad; square-skirt.

Woman awaiting release of prisoner. Square skirt who is waiting for a ghee; broad who is waiting for a dude.

Woman who engages in professional crime. Broad a ghee hustles with; knock-around broad; gun-moll; moll-whiz; racket broad.

Working man. Chump; dinner-pailer; drifter; jay; John; legit-ghee; legit-stiff; peasant; scissorbill; slob; square; square-John; square plug; up-and-up ghee; working-stiff.

Worthless, relatively or wholly. Coffee-and; crumby; crummy; lousy; no bargain; no spinach; not so hot; not so kosher; pea-soup; phony-baloney; two-bit.

Wreck, v. Axe; take a joint apart.

Writ, legal. Paper.

Writ of habeas corpus. Hapas capas.

Writ of mandamus. Goddamus.

Write. Bang out; buzz; knock out; scratch; slap out.

Write a note, letter, etc. Drop a kite; drop a tab; knock out a kite; knock out a tab; tab a kite.

Y

Yield. Go. "The sucker is gotta go on a shake (extortion) when you spring (exhibit) a creed (credential) like that on him. You look like law (a policeman) anyhow."

Yield, likely to. Figure to go.